Property of Park Place

LIONS

of the

WEST

Also by Robert Morgan

LIONS

— _of the_ —

WEST

Heroes and Villains
of the Westward Expansion

ROBERT MORGAN

A Shannon Ravenel Book
Algonquin Books of Chapel Hill
2011

ℝ

A Shannon Ravenel Book

Published by
Algonquin Books of Chapel Hill
Post Office Box 2225
Chapel Hill, North Carolina 27515-2225

a division of
Workman Publishing
225 Varick Street
New York, New York 10014

Library of Congress
Cataloging-in-Publication Data
Morgan, Robert, [date]
Lions of the West : heroes and villains of the westward expansion /
Robert Morgan.—1st ed.
p. cm.
"A Shannon Ravenel Book."
Includes bibliographical references and index.
ISBN-13: 978-1-56512-626-8
1. United States—Territorial expansion. 2. West (U.S.)—History—To 1848.
3. Pioneers—United States—Biography. 4. Pioneers—West (U.S.)—Biography.
5. Presidents—United States—Biography. I. Title.
E179.5M67 2011
978'.02—dc23   *2011023832*

10 9 8 7 6 5 4 3 2 1
First Edition

To Mrs. Elizabeth Rogers,
Who taught me American History

THE WEST IN THEIR EYES

THERE is more of the material of poetry than we imagine diffused through all the classes of the community. And upon this part of the character it is, that the disposition to emigration operates, and brings in aid the influence of its imperceptible but magic power . . . The notion of new and more beautiful woods and streams, of a milder climate, deer, fish, fowl, game, and all those delightful images of enjoyment, that so readily associate with the idea of the wild and boundless license of new regions; all that restless hope of finding in a new country, and in new views and combinations of things, something we crave but have not. I am ready to believe, from my own experience and from what I have seen in the case of others, that this influence of imagination has no inconsiderable agency in producing emigration.

> — *Timothy Flint,*
> *popular nineteenth century writer*
> *about the frontier*

THE proud Anglo-Saxon race . . . possessed of that roving spirit that moved the barbarous hordes of a former age in a far remote north, had swept away whatever stood in the way of its aggrandizement.

> —*José María Tornel,*
> *Mexican secretary of war, 1836*

THERE is properly no history; only biography.

> —*Ralph Waldo Emerson*

— CONTENTS —

LIST OF MAPS

BRIEF CHRONOLOGY OF THE WESTWARD EXPANSION ERA

—

1743 Thomas Jefferson born April 13 in Albemarle County, Virginia.

1749 Peter Jefferson, father of Thomas, and Joshua Fry survey boundary line between Virginia and North Carolina.

1760 Thomas Jefferson studies at College of William and Mary.

1762 Thomas Jefferson reads law with George Wythe.

1767 Andrew Jackson born March 15 at Waxhaw on North Carolina–South Carolina border.
John Quincy Adams born July 11 in Braintree, Massachusetts.

1769 Thomas Jefferson elected to Virginia House of Burgesses.

1774 John Chapman born September 26 in Leominster, Massachusetts.
Jefferson publishes *A Summary View of the Rights of British America*.

1775 American Revolution begins April 19 with battles at Lexington and Concord, Massachusetts.
Jefferson serves as delegate to Second Continental Congress in Philadelphia.
Daniel Boone cuts trace through Cumberland Gap into Kentucky.

1776 Jefferson writes Declaration of Independence.

1777 Battles of Saratoga in New York: Freeman's Farm, September 19; Bemis Heights, October 7. Washington moves his army into winter quarters at Valley Forge.

1779 Joel Roberts Poinsett born March 2 in Charleston, South Carolina.

1780 Battle of Kings Mountain, South Carolina, October 7.

1781 John Quincy Adams serves with legation in St. Petersburg, Russia.

Jefferson writes to George Rogers Clark in Kentucky asking for large fossil bones.

Jefferson begins *Notes on the State of Virginia*. Battles of Cowpens, South Carolina, January 17. British surrender at Yorktown, October 17.

1782 Martha Randolph Jefferson dies September 6.

1783 Treaty of Paris, September 3.

Jefferson returns to Continental Congress where he helps draft Ordinance for Government of Northwest Territories.

1784 Alexander McGillivray concludes Creek treaty with Spain. Zachary Taylor born November 24 in Virginia.

1785 Jefferson succeeds Franklin as minister to France, meets Buffon and other French scientists. Publishes *Notes on the State of Virginia*.

1786 Winfield Scott born June 13 near Petersburg, Virginia. David Crockett born August 17 in State of Franklin.

1787 Andrew Jackson admitted to bar in North Carolina. John Ledyard sets out to walk across Russia and then North America.

1788 Andrew Jackson moves west to Nashville, meets Rachel Robards whom he will later marry.

1790 Jefferson becomes Secretary of State in Washington's cabinet, begins quarreling with Alexander Hamilton and the Federalists.

1793 Sam Houston born March 2 near Lexington, Virginia. Jefferson commissions André Michaux to explore the West and resigns from Cabinet.

1794 Jay's Treaty bitterly opposed by Jefferson and others. Battle of Fallen Timbers, August 20, near Toledo. Antonio López de Santa Anna born in Mexico.

1795 James Knox Polk born November 2 in Pineville, North Carolina.

1796 Jefferson elected vice president, John Adams president.

1797 John Chapman moves to western Pennsylvania wilderness.

1798 Andrew Jackson serves as judge of Tennessee Superior Court. Jefferson writes the Kentucky Resolutions.

1800 Jefferson elected president. Nicholas P. Trist born June 2 in Charlottesville, Virginia.

1802 Andrew Jackson elected major general of Tennessee militia.

1803 Louisiana Purchase. Jefferson commissions Meriwether Lewis to explore the West to the Pacific, June 20. John Quincy Adams elected to Senate.

1804 John Chapman plants apple trees in Ohio wilderness.

1806 Lewis and Clark return from the Pacific. Nonimportation Act passed by Congress. Zebulon Pike explores headwaters of Arkansas River.
Houston family moves to Tennessee.

1807 Embargo Act passed by Congress. John Quincy Adams breaks with Federalists.

1808 James Madison elected president. Winfield Scott commissioned captain in U.S. Army.

1809 Jefferson returns to Monticello. Kit Carson born December 24 in Madison County, Kentucky.

1810 Mexican revolt against Spain begins.

1811 Tecumseh tours the South. Battle of Tippecanoe River, November 7.

1812 United States declares war on Britain, June 18.

1813 Fort Mims Massacre triggers Creek War, August 30.
Perry's victory over the British on Lake Erie, September 10.

1814 Jackson defeats Red Stick Creeks at Horseshoe Bend, Alabama, March 27.
Scott's victory over the British at Chippewa, July 5.
British burn Washington City, August 24. Treaty of Ghent signed December 24.

1815 Jackson defeats British at New Orleans, January 8.

1816 James Monroe elected president.

1817 John Quincy Adams becomes secretary of state.

1818 Treaty with Britain on U.S.-Canada boundary at forty-ninth parallel to Rocky Mountains.

1819 Adams-Onís Treaty with Spain.

1820 Missouri Compromise excluding slavery in new states north of 36°30'.

1821 Mexican independence from Spain. Treaty of Cordoba, August 23.

1823 Sam Houston elected to Congress from Tennessee.

1824 John Quincy Adams elected president. Mexican constitution adopted.
Treaty with Russia on boundary of Alaska.

1825 Erie Canal opens. James K. Polk elected to Congress from Tennessee.
Joel R. Poinsett becomes ambassador to Mexico.

1826 Deaths of Jefferson and John Adams, July 4.

1827 David Crockett elected to Congress from Tennessee. Nicholas Trist becomes clerk in State Department. Houston elected governor of Tennessee.

1828 Andrew Jackson elected president.

1829 Houston resigns as governor of Tennessee. Kit Carson explores the Gila River country.

1830 John Quincy Adams elected to Congress from Massachusetts.

1831 Play *Lion of the West* by James K. Paulding acted in New York by James Hackett.

1832 Houston tried in Congress for attacking legislator. Goes to Texas December 1.

1833 Santa Anna elected president of Mexico.
Nicholas Trist appointed consul in Havana.

1834 *A Narrative of the Life of David Crockett of the State of Tennessee* published.

1835 R. H. Dana arrives in California. Crockett loses election for Congress, leaves for Texas.

1836 Crockett dies at Alamo, March 6. "Gag law" passed by Congress. Houston elected commander of Texas army, defeats Santa Anna at San Jacinto, April 21.

1837 Smallpox wipes out many Indian villages in the West.

1838 Cherokee Removal to Arkansas Territory. Mexico fights "Pastry War" with France in which Santa Anna loses a leg.

1839 James K. Polk elected governor of Tennessee.

1840 William Henry Harrison elected president. *Two Years Before the Mast* by R. H. Dana published.

1841 Harrison dies and John Tyler becomes president. Winfield Scott becomes General in chief of the army July 5.

1842 Frémont's First Expedition along Oregon Trail, with Kit Carson as scout.

1843 Frémont's Second Expedition to the Far West.

1844 Polk elected president. "Gag law" repealed December 3.

1845 Texas annexed by United States. Frémont's Third Expedition to the Far West.
John Chapman dies in March at Fort Wayne, Indiana.
Andrew Jackson dies at Hermitage, June 8. Polk begins diary, August 26.
Trist becomes chief clerk of the State Department. "Manifest Destiny" becomes slogan.

1846 United States declares war on Mexico May 13. Bear Flaggers declare independence from Mexico June 14. Battles of Palo Alto, May 8; Resaca de la Palma, May 9; Monterrey, September 20–24. Frémont and Stockton take San Diego, Los Angeles, Santa Barbara in August. Kearny claims Santa Fe, August 18, fights at San Pasqual, December 6–11.

1847 Los Angeles retaken January 8–9. Battles of Buena Vista, February 22–23; Veracruz, March 22–26; Cerro Gordo, April 17–18. Trist arrives in Mexico, May 6. Battles of Contreras, August 19–20; Churubusco, August 20; Molino del Rey, September 8; Chapultepec, September 12–13.
Scott enters Mexico City, September 14.

1848 Taylor elected president. Gold discovered in California January 24. Treaty of Guadalupe Hidalgo signed February 2.
John Quincy Adams dies February 23. Trist arrested in Mexico in April.

1849 Polk dies. Gold rush in California.

1853 Gadsden Purchase establishes the boundary between Mexico and New Mexico and Arizona.

PRESIDENTS AND VICE PRESIDENTS
BEFORE THE CIVIL WAR

———

Term	President	Vice President
1789–1793	George Washington	John Adams
1793–1797	George Washington	John Adams
1797–1801	John Adams	Thomas Jefferson
1801–1805	Thomas Jefferson	Aaron Burr
1805–1809	Thomas Jefferson	George Clinton
1809–1813	James Madison	George Clinton (d. 1812)
1813–1817	James Madison	Elbridge Gerry (d. 1814)
1817–1821	James Monroe	Daniel D. Tompkins
1821–1825	James Monroe	Daniel D. Tompkins
1825–1829	John Quincy Adams	John C. Calhoun
1829–1833	Andrew Jackson	John C. Calhoun (resigned 1832)
1833–1837	Andrew Jackson	Martin Van Buren
1837–1841	Martin Van Buren	Richard M. Johnson
1841	William H. Harrison (d. 1841)	John Tyler
1841–1845	John Tyler	
1845–1849	James K. Polk	George M. Dallas
1849–1850	Zachary Taylor (d. 1850)	Millard Fillmore
1850–1853	Millard Fillmore	
1853–1857	Franklin Pierce	William R. D. King (d. 1853)
1857–1861	James Buchanan	John C. Breckinridge

PROLOGUE

THE EMPIRE FOR LIBERTY

---

*I*N 1831 the actor-producer James H. Hackett presented in New York a play by James Kirke Paulding called *Lion of the West,* based loosely on the legends of David Crockett and other frontier figures. The play was an instant and runaway success and was later presented to acclaim in other American cities and in Britain. In Colonel Nimrod Wildfire, Paulding created the type of the backwoods humorist and teller of tall tales. Claiming to be half alligator and half horse, the colonel bragged, "I can jump higher—squat lower—dive deeper—stay longer under and come out drier!" than anyone foolish enough to challenge him. The play thrilled city audiences who felt superior to the frontiersman but also dreamed of aggressively expanding the United States into the promised land of the West. The president at that time, who personified the passion for westward expansion, was Old Hickory, Andrew Jackson of Tennessee. Congressman David Crockett, in the audience for the play in Washington, D.C., was called out and saluted by Hackett, and rather than being offended, he seemed to enjoy the burlesque of his public image.

It could be argued that the caricature of *Lion of the West* allowed audiences to laugh at traits and attitudes in themselves they might otherwise have been ashamed of: the overweening arrogance, the claims of being chosen, the brash air of destiny. In the hyperbolic braggadocio of the backwoodsman such attitudes were good for laughter, and the viewers could indulge themselves in the satire while remaining a safe distance from attitudes and actions in which they were all complicit, such as the belief they were justified in killing Indians and taking their land.

Thomas Jefferson, the quintessential American dreamer, whose vision of the future republic had from the beginning stretched over the mountains to the Mississippi Valley, perhaps over the farther mountains to the great harbors on the Pacific, had called his envisioned nation "the Empire for Liberty." In retrospect we can see the contradiction that Jefferson and most of his contemporaries could not: the oxymoron of imperial power promoting the spread of "liberty." It is a contradiction Jefferson passed on to the new nation that has come down to us in the present day, the fixed idea that imperial might can be exercised in fostering democracy on foreign soil.

"There is properly no history," Ralph Waldo Emerson wrote, "only biography." It is natural and perhaps necessary for historians and storytellers to view the dramatic shifts of history through the actions of a few famous figures, whether heroes or villains. Certainly the story of the westward expansion of the United States has many examples of each, and sometimes it seems the villains outnumber the heroes. But often the same figure can be seen as both. Andrew Jackson probably did more to extend democratic power to a greater number of citizens of the nation in that era than anyone except Jefferson. Yet he is blamed for displacing and destroying much of the native population in the Southeast. Jackson's protégé, James K. Polk, often called Young Hickory, is one of the least attractive men to ever serve as president of the United States, yet even his severest critics concede that Polk accomplished, uniquely, almost miraculously, all he had promised when elected.

The poet Walt Whitman believed that written accounts always miss the reality, the specifics and multiplicity of history. Commenting at the end of the Civil War, he said, "The real war will never get in the books." For Whitman a true account would be a great catalog of the many different soldiers and their actions. The war was "that many-threaded drama, with its sudden and strange surprises, its confounding of prophecies, its moments of despair, the dread of foreign interference, the interminable campaigns, the bloody battles, the mighty and cumbrous and green armies." The real story of the time was "the untold and unwritten history of the war—infinitely greater (like life's) than the few scraps and distortions that are ever told or written."

A true story of the westward expansion would be the account of the

actions, thoughts, emotions, words, and persons of the unnamed thousands, the people on the ground, who are the living flesh and blood of history. Historians may concentrate on the famous, but most of what happens is the composite deeds of common folk. There is no better example of this paradox than in the narrative of the westward expansion. We must consider the "lions" of the West, but it was the unnoticed thousands on foot and on horseback, in wagons and ox carts, who made the story a fact, who wrote history with their hands and feet, their need and greed, their sweat, and often their blood.

The historian John Buchanan has called the westward expansion, or Manifest Destiny, "the greatest folk movement of modern times, in which, for the most part, the people led and government followed." It would be hard to overstate the importance of this insight. While it is understandable that we see history mostly in terms of the deeds of a few, our grasp of what actually happened will be flawed and limited if we do not consider the story of the almost invisible many who made the notable deeds possible, even inevitable. In the words of the Mexican historian Josefina Zoraida Vázquez, "The North Americans kept up this continuous expansion, and the United States government followed their footsteps."

Take, for example, Andrew Jackson's victory over the Red Stick Creeks at Horseshoe Bend on the Tallapoosa River in March of 1814. His success in that campaign and the subsequent treaty negotiations led to the opening of much of Georgia and Alabama for white settlement. But a precipitating factor of the Creek War was the incursion of thousands of white squatters into Creek territory in Georgia and southern Alabama. The Red Stick rebellion was inspired not only by the eloquence of Tecumseh but also by the skirmishes and killings between whites and Creeks as whites cleared land and hunted game on traditional Creek territory. Andrew Jackson's victory at Horseshoe Bend was a result of this ongoing activity, not its initiation. After the massacre at Fort Mims in August 1813, the Creeks were doomed to lose their vast holdings. The thousands who risked their lives to possess Creek lands are mostly forgotten. It is Jackson's victory that we remember.

Behind the overwhelming force of American expansion was the phenomenon called "the American Multiplication Table." Birthrates in North America were much higher than in Europe. Large families begat

large families, doubling the population every twenty years. With swelling immigration, this exploding population needed space to put down roots, and the space available was to the west, always following the sun. Lord Castlereagh, British foreign minister, is supposed to have quipped in 1814 that Americans won victories not on the battlefield but "in the bedchamber." In 1800 there were only sixteen states in the Union; by 1824 there would be twenty-four.

"What is history," Napoleon is supposed to have said, "but a fable agreed upon?" All written history is distortion through selection. As Whitman suggests, a true history would be infinitely detailed, infinitely long. In that sense all written history must be what Bernard DeVoto called "history by synecdoche," where a part, a feature, is made to imply the whole. By its very nature narrative can represent only by implication, explicit about some parts, suggesting the many. Each detail should be significant, suggesting the unrecounted others. In this book I try to create a living sense of the westward expansion of the United States through brief biographies of some of the men involved. But it can be, at best, only a partial story.

Those who study history often come to feel that it as a living organism, with a will and energy, a whim and persistence, all its own, beyond explanation, beyond logic. The turns and surprises, the lulls and lunges, remain mysterious, following rules we can only speculate about, codes we try to decipher. The historian and diplomat George F. Kennan liked to recount a Russian fable to satirize individuals or governments who claim that they have decisively influenced history. A fly rides on the nose of an ox all day while it plows, and when the ox returns to the village at the end of the day the fly proudly proclaims, "We've been plowing." The ox of history goes its way, unaware of the hitchhiking, braggart fly. What we cannot deny is the fact of the westward expansion, and while conceding that much of the story is tragic, a narrative of ruthlessness and greed on a cataclysmic scale, we cannot deny the poetry of the westward vision either, the lust to explore and know, to *see* the splendor of the mountains and rivers and deserts, to learn as well as to possess.

The novelist Leo Tolstoy viewed history as a kind of mysterious force following predetermined paths the human mind is slow to grasp. For him the historical process was inexorable, exhibiting little freedom. "The ac-

tions of so-called makers of history and leaders of war depend on the actions of countless other people . . . natural law determined the lives of human beings no less than the processes of nature itself." In *War and Peace* Tolstoy writes, "The force that decides the fate of peoples does not lie in military leaders, not even in armies and battles, but in something else." The novelist urged the student of history to "look into the movements of those hundred thousand men who took direct immediate part in the events; and all the questions that seemed insoluble before can be readily and certainly explained." Tolstoy's favorite metaphor for history was weather, hard to predict with accuracy, impossible to control, yet a palpable fact.

One of Tolstoy's most important heirs in Russian literature is Boris Pasternak, poet and author of the novel *Doctor Zhivago*. The poet-doctor of the title, Yuri Zhivago, near the end of the narrative, in the collapsing world following the Russian Civil War, writes a series of poems and meditations on love, the individual in society, and history. "The forest does not change its place, we cannot lie in wait for it and catch it in the act of change . . . And such also is the immobility to our eyes of the eternally growing, ceaselessly changing history, the life of society moving invisibly in its incessant transformations."

In isolation in the countryside, in the midst of catastrophic events of his life and the life of Russia, having lost his muse and lover, Zhivago contemplates the mystery of historic change. "No single man makes history. History cannot be seen, just as one cannot see grass growing. Wars and revolutions, kings and Robespierres, are history's organic agents, its yeast." For Zhivago the individual life is paramount, even, or especially, in the midst of the most confusing dramas of history. The romantic Emerson may proclaim, "Every revolution was first a thought in one man's mind." But the closer we look the more we understand that revolutions actually occur because of ideas in many minds at once.

One of America's most distinguished historians, Henry Adams, near the end of his life, conceded that he understood little of the process of history. He recognized it was a matter of dynamics, forces, mysterious yet inexorable as the laws of physics and chemistry. "A dynamic law requires that two masses—nature and man—must go on, reacting upon each other, without stop, as the sun and a comet react on each other, and that any appearance of stoppage is illusive."

Following Adams's suggestion, I would appeal to a chemical metaphor for the story of the westward expansion. The tens of thousands of settlers, hungry for land, adventure, opportunity, are like the molecules of an element compelled to combine with another, the territory of the North American West. No law, no government, no leader, could stop that accelerating chemical process until the combining was complete. The celebrated or reviled leaders are partly figureheads that help us give shape to the messy narrative of this history. The real history is the unstoppable reactions of countless entities combining to create new compounds. Romantics might describe the course of events as alchemy, critics as destructive breakdown of natural substances.

With the exception of Nicholas P. Trist, the lives of all these men—Jefferson, Jackson, Chapman, Crockett, Houston, Polk, Scott, Carson, and John Quincy Adams—have been chronicled many times, often by outstanding historians and biographers. My hope is that recounting them briefly and in sequence here may create an integrated narrative where the separate lives link up and illuminate each other, making complex, extended events more accessible to readers in the twenty-first century. The discovery and exploration of the West is a large part of the story of who we are. And it is important that we know something of the Mexican side of that story as well. Where possible, I quote from Mexican historians to remind us that their versions of events are often, though not always, different from the accounts we are familiar with. We will not understand the story of the westward expansion if we do not recognize that the Mexican side of the narrative is an essential part of *our* story as well. Millions from south of the border cross into the United States every year looking for opportunity and security. This movement is as unstoppable as the rush into Missouri and California of a previous century. Where people want to go, they will go. Politicians or generals may take credit or blame for the events, but they are more responders than creators of the large shifts and migrations.

Those who had explored the wonders and dangers of the West, and survived to return and tell of their experiences, were said to have "seen the elephant." As students of history we try to see the elephant, too. But, to extend the metaphor, it is our duty to try to see not just part of the animal but the whole beast, in so far as that is possible, in all its beauty, terror, ugliness and complexity. The story is by turns tragedy and romance, horror and thrilling struggle; a wrestling with the elements, deserts and deep snows, distances and disorientation, starvation and eating of boot leather, lizards, tree bark, and human flesh. It is a story we recount with shame, commitment to fact, and sometimes pride, sometimes exuberance. While some deeds were done on an epic scale, more often events unfolded in the harsh close-up of ambush at a turn in the trail, the warrior dying of smallpox, the scout drinking mule blood to survive, the raw recruit's first sight of the Sonoran desert at sunset. The brutality often overwhelms the poetry of the land, but the land is still there, its poetry a fact, threatened now not by weather or predators but by progress.

The diplomat and historian George F. Kennan, while mostly concerned with foreign policy, had trenchant and profound things to say about the way we Americans tend to view ourselves. He saw as a special weakness "a certain moralistic and legalistic posturing on our part—a desire to appear, particularly to ourselves, as more wise and more noble than we really were." Throughout his long career Kennan was eloquent and often merciless in his critique of American character in the conduct of diplomacy. When he looked at our history he found "a curious but deeply-rooted sentimentality on our part . . . arising evidently from the pleasure it gave us to view ourselves as high-minded patrons, benefactors, and teachers of . . . people seen as less fortunate." It was Reinhold Niebuhr who warned against the habit of always seeing ourselves as the innocent party in any dispute, whether private or national. George F. Kennan, near the end of his distinguished career, would offer his fellow Americans "a plea for . . . a greater humility in our national outlook, for a more realistic recognition of our limitations."

As we begin to examine the vexed story of the westward expansion and the lives of some of those involved in it, let us keep Kennan's hard words in mind. Our greatest hope for the study of history, and of representative lives, is that we may learn from both the successes and the mistakes and begin to understand which is which. It has been said that America's aggressive expansionism is evidence of a preoccupation with the future, not the present. With luck we might learn to direct that energy and passion toward effective, essential, and better goals.

LIONS

of the

WEST

United States, 1854

Ceded by
Britain,
1818

NEW
HAMPSHIRE

VERMONT

MAINE

MINNESOTA

WISCONSIN

MICHIGAN

NEW YORK

MASSACHUSETTS

RHODE
ISLAND

CONNECTICUT

IOWA

PENNSYLVANIA

NEW JERSEY

The Louisiana
Purchase
from France, 1803

ILLINOIS

INDIANA

OHIO

DELAWARE

MARYLAND

KANSAS

MISSOURI

KENTUCKY

WEST
VIRGINIA

VIRGINIA

DISTRICT OF
COLUMBIA

The United States,
1783

NORTH
CAROLINA

OKLAHOMA

ARKANSAS

TENNESSEE

SOUTH
CAROLINA

MISSISSIPPI

ALABAMA

GEORGIA

TEXAS

LOUISIANA

FLORIDA

Annexed from
Spain, 1813

Ceded by
Spain, 1819

Ceded by
Spain, 1819

Annexed from
Spain, 1810

— One —

THOMAS JEFFERSON

SEEING THE ELEPHANT

THOMAS JEFFERSON's attention seems always to have been turned toward the West. The West was the place of unexplored riches, the promise of adventure, commerce, the future. The possibilities and hope offered by the waterways and lands over the mountains were never far from Jefferson's mind, even as events forced him to turn his attention to the political conflicts unfolding in Virginia and the other colonies. Jefferson loathed the crowding of cities and came to believe that the best hope for his society was the movement into the land beyond the Appalachians, even beyond the Mississippi. It was in the West where yeoman farmers could "avoid the miseries of the concentrated urban working classes."

From the time of his youth the author of the Declaration of Independence had dreamed of exploring and claiming the West—to the Mississippi and maybe all the way to the Pacific. On February 2, 1848, almost twenty-two years after Jefferson's death, his grandson-in-law, Nicholas P. Trist, special peace commissioner from the United States, signed the Treaty of Guadalupe Hidalgo near the shrine of the Virgin of Guadalupe outside Mexico City, ending the Mexican-American War. Both countries pledged to cease hostilities, and for fifteen million dollars the Republic of Mexico agreed to cede to the United States Texas and all of the territory that would become New Mexico, Arizona, California, Nevada, Utah, half of Colorado and a chunk of Wyoming. With ports on the Pacific, the American Republic could become a world power, promoting prosperity, democracy, and the pursuit of happiness across North America and beyond. The continental and hemispheric vision Jefferson had contemplated from the height of Monticello was now realized but at a terrific cost.

———

As a boy growing up in colonial Virginia, Thomas Jefferson was sent to a school conducted by the Reverend James Maury at Fredericksburg. Reverend Maury gave the inquisitive boy a solid grounding in classical languages as well as the basic arts and sciences. According to Edward L. Bond, Maury "had a passion for science and corresponded with friends about discoveries he made in the Blue Ridge Mountains." In his sermons Maury preached that man was put on earth to pursue happiness, "to possess & enjoy every Thing, that can render us easy & quiet & contented here, & blessed & happy hereafter." Maury taught that the Creator made man "to communicate Part of his own Happiness to us." The reverend believed in "natural Religion" and quoted Bolingbroke, "That no Religion ever appeared in the World, whose natural Tendency was so much directed to promote the Peace & Happiness of Mankind as Christianity."

Maury had a collection of fossils, rocks, and seashells that fascinated young Jefferson. The parson also had a special interest in the wilderness lands farther west and the exploration of the North American continent. On January 10, 1756, Maury wrote to an uncle back in England that whatever country becomes "master of [the] Ohio and the [Great] Lakes at the end of [the present war] must in the course of a few years . . . become sole and absolute lord of North America." The reverend added that in a few years either the Potomac or the Hudson River would become "the grand emporium of all East India commodities."

The man who educated the young Jefferson was thrilled at the prospect of finding a water passage to the West and the Pacific and therefore access to the promising China trade and the Indies. And the Reverend Maury was not alone. He was merely echoing the talk and the passion of many around him. As the Seven Years' War, called the French and Indian War in America, came to an end, it remained to be determined who would ultimately control the Mississippi Valley and the route to the Pacific.

Jefferson had been born in 1743 to an interest in western lands and western waters. His father, Peter Jefferson, landowner and surveyor, had with his neighbor Joshua Fry published a "map of the middle British colonies in America." In 1746 Peter Jefferson had helped survey "the Fairfax line" for seventy-six miles across the wilderness of the Blue Ridge Mountains to determine the extent of the grant to Lord Fairfax. In 1749 Peter Jefferson and Joshua Fry were commissioned to survey the boundary between North Carolina and Virginia for ninety miles beyond the line marked by William Byrd more than twenty years earlier. According to Lee Alan Dugatkin, Peter Jefferson "instilled in his son a passion for exploring unknown regions."

When Peter Jefferson died in 1757, his friend Dr. Thomas Walker became one of young Thomas's guardians. Walker was not only a medical doctor and man of science. He had also been commissary to General Edward Braddock's army on its way to defeat on the Monongahela in 1755. Before that he had explored the western lands of Virginia, and in 1750, commissioned by the Loyal Land Company, he had gone farther west and found the gap called by the Indians Ouasciota, which he renamed for the Duke of Cumberland. Hoping to find the Blue Grass region and the Ohio River, Walker and his men wandered in the mountains of eastern Kentucky for several weeks and eventually found their way back to Virginia through what became known later as Pound Gap. Among the militia on the way to Braddock's defeat was twenty-year-old Daniel Boone of North Carolina, who may well have heard of Cumberland Gap for the first time from Dr. Walker.

Even as a boy Jefferson loved travel literature, geography, and history. He read John Ogilvy's *America,* about the exploration and settlement of Virginia. Maury had taught him the importance of storytelling and memorization, along with a knowledge of classical languages and literature. But Jefferson also loved the outdoors, and he walked or rode for miles in the countryside around his home at Shadwell day after day. Later he took long walks with William Small, his instructor at the College of William and Mary, "walks in which Small would point out all the wonders around them." He already had an interest in gardening and landscaping. Because he was so active in the foothills of the Blue Ridge Mountains, Jefferson acquired what Reverend Maury called a "mountain constitution." He spent much time "tracking, trailing and hunting."

From his earliest memory, Thomas Jefferson was fascinated by the natural world around him. His curiosity seemed limitless, and he made lists of everything: birds and animals, minerals and fossils, rivers and mountain ranges. In the words of historian Silvio Bedini, he had "a compulsion to collect and record in pocket memorandum books random bits of information." He studied maps and Indian tribes, Indian languages. He studied farming and chemistry, natural history, weather, soils, and the bones of extinct animals. He loved geology and was thrilled by the way bones and sediments and stones and tree rings were documents for reading the past. As a boy he collected fossils along streams and in the hills. He studied agriculture and cultivation and became a lifelong gatherer and distributor of seeds to others. As Lee Alan Dugatkin tells us, "Jefferson possessed a 'canine appetite' to learn more about everything."

But young Jefferson was not just a romantic and visionary. While he delighted in the natural world and knowledge for its own sake, he also believed that science should be practical and useful. No matter what he studied, he always considered the ways knowledge could be put to the service of the developing society around him. Among the properties that Jefferson inherited was a tract in the mountains of Virginia that included Natural Bridge. As a boy, he liked to go there and study that wilderness wonder, which he called "the most sublime of nature's works." He measured its height and width with great care and speculated on its creation by forces of water and time. He described crawling on his knees to the edge and looking down 270 feet to the stream, an experience so intense it gave him a headache. But standing beneath the grand arch was the reason to come there. "It is impossible for the emotions arising from the sublime, to be felt beyond what they are here; so beautiful an arch, so elevated, so light: and springing as it were up to heaven, the rapture of the spectator is really indescribable!"

Like Thoreau after him, Jefferson often described the beauties of the American wilderness the way Europeans described cathedrals, temples, and other works of art. It is interesting that Jefferson was not only a student and lover of the natural world but a builder and architect as well, along with Benjamin Latrobe, the leading American architect of his time. There are few examples in our history of such a range of excellence and achievement in one human being. Added to that, Jefferson had a passion for invention and history. And of course he had a great aptitude for politics and political thought also.

As a student at the College of William and Mary, Jefferson,
tioned, became a member of the circle around William Small, th
and philosopher, and he studied with the Welshman Goronwy
poet and linguist and educator. Day after day he was exposed to b
conversation among these men of the Enlightenment at Willian
He studied calculus and James Gibbs's *Rules for Drawing the Severa
of Architecture,* which emphasized intuition in design. He became
nated by American Indian oratory, as well as classical oratory, thou
himself would never be an orator.

Jefferson was fortunate to read law with the outstanding Ge
Wythe. Though self-educated, Wythe was a polymath and class
scholar. It was while Jefferson was studying for the bar that the cont
versial Stamp Act was passed by the British parliament. From Wythe a
others he inherited the discussion of natural law and natural right ve
sus positive law. He read Pufendorf's *Of the Law of Nature and Nation
among many other such treatises, and began drafting and revising th
ideas and the phrases that would later be incorporated in the Declaration
of Independence.

As a law student, Jefferson experimented with condensing texts. He
found he could catch the essence of a page of prose in a careful sentence
or two. All his life he would be fascinated by economy and precision
in language. He seemed to never tire of revising a text for clarity, force
and depth. One of his first tutors, the Reverend William Douglas, had
stressed the importance of strict record keeping. It was a lesson not lost
on Jefferson, who kept meticulous accounts of his businesses, thoughts,
reading. After a fire destroyed his ancestral home at Shadwell, along with
many of his books and papers, he dedicated himself to making copies of
all his letters, documents, and essays. Later he would exhort the explorers
André Michaux and Meriwether Lewis to make multiple copies of their
journals and observations for safekeeping, copying some on birch bark
as well as paper.

All his life Jefferson liked to collect curiosities and specimens. He
accumulated arrowheads, Indian pottery, axes, calumets. He collected
specimens of plants, seeds, birds, animals. Wherever he lived, his home
resembled a museum. He filled Monticello later with mammoth bones
and kept a prairie dog Lewis and Clark had sent back from the West at

the White House. He kept a pet mockingbird, which sat on his shoulder and took seeds from his lips as members of his cabinet watched. As the anthropologist David Hunt Thomas points out, Jefferson, "through his involvement with Peale's Museum, the American Philosophical Society, and the Corps of Discovery . . . spearheaded the development of natural history museums in America."

As a student of geography and former governor of Virginia, Jefferson knew in 1781 about the many bones found at the salt licks in Kentucky, especially at the place called Big Bone Lick in northern Kentucky near the Ohio River. Indians had told early explorers about the place of giant bones. A French explorer claimed to have seen the skeletons of "seven elephants" there. Daniel Boone had seen the site of the large bones when he first explored Kentucky in 1769–70.

Jefferson had a special interest in extinct animals and sought information about giant prehistoric mammals all his life. He collected a number of tusks and bones and had a good sense of the size of the megatheres. We don't know if Jefferson discussed the bones of giant prehistoric animals found in Kentucky with Daniel Boone, but it is likely that he did. Boone was serving as a representative from Fayette County, Kentucky, in the Virginia legislature in December of 1781, when Jefferson wrote to George Rogers Clark, the commanding general of the Virginia militia in Kentucky, and William Clark's older brother, "Having an opportunity by Colo. Boon I take the liberty of calling to your mind your kindness in undertaking to procure for me some teeth of the great animal whose remains are found on the Ohio. Were it possible to get a tooth of each kind, that is to say a foretooth, grinder &c. it would particularly oblige me."

We assume Boone carried the letter back to Kentucky when the legislative session ended, for on February 26, 1782, General Clark wrote back to Jefferson, "I Received your favor [letter] by Colo. Boon. I am unhappy that it hath been out of my power to procure you those Curiosities you want except a large thigh Bone that dont please me being broke. I expect to get the whole this spring." What Jefferson would refer to as "the big buffalo" was likely the bones of the woolly mammoth at Big Bone Lick and other places in Kentucky.

Equal to his passion to study the bones of what would become known as the woolly mammoth, was Jefferson's zeal to learn the geography of the

American West. On March 18, 1782, his close friend James Madison wrote from Philadelphia that he had been attempting to procure a 1650 map of North America. "It represents the South sea at about 10 days travel from the head or falls I forget which of James River . . . There is just ground to suspect that this representation was an artifice . . . to entice emigrants from England by a flattering picture of the advantages of this Country . . . and the facility it afforded of a trade with the Eastern World."

While everyone knew that the South Sea (the Pacific) was far more than ten days travel from the headwaters of the James River in Virginia, the fact remained that even a scholar of geography such as Jefferson knew little about what lay beyond the Mississippi. That ignorance fired both his imagination and his determination to explore and perhaps to possess those unknown lands. He collected every map and every travel report he could find and pored over their details and inconsistencies, attempting to resolve the contradictions. But the Spanish in New Spain, or Mexico, who controlled the Southwest from the Mississippi to the Pacific, guarded all knowledge they acquired of the region. In the words of the historian Alan Taylor, "The Spanish concealed what they did know about the Pacific, lest the information only benefit the piracy of their English and French rivals."

On November 7, 1782, Colonel Arthur Campbell, far to the west on the Holston River, wrote to Jefferson, "Permit me to present to you a large Jaw tooth of an unknown Animal lately found at the Salina in Washington County . . . The Salina lyes near that branch of the Cherokee River (the Tennessee) called North Holstein." Campbell was a politician eager to ingratiate himself with ex-governor Jefferson. His letter shows that word had gotten around that the author of the Declaration of Independence was keen to study prehistoric animal bones as he was preparing his *Notes on the State of Virginia.*

On November 26, 1782, Jefferson wrote again to General George Rogers Clark in Louisville. "I should be unfaithful to my own feelings were I not to express to you how much I am obliged by your attention to the request I made you on that subject. A specimen of each of the several species of bones now to be found is to me the most desirable object in Natural history, and there is no expense of package or of safe transportation which I will not gladly reimburse to procure them safely . . . Any observation of your own on the subject of the big bones or their history, or on any thing else in the Western country, will come acceptably to me, because I know you see the works of nature in the great, and not merely in detail . . . Descriptions of animals, vegetables, minerals, or other curious things, notes as to the Indians, information of the country between the Missisipi and the waters of the South sea &c."

Reading Jefferson's letters to Clark and others, we feel the intensity of his curiosity. There is something luminous about his passion and exuberance to learn, to put down his questions and record his findings. Even after the death of his wife, Martha, on September 6, 1782, when Jefferson was deeply grieved, he never stopped writing. He was never bored.

On January 6, 1783, Jefferson wrote to Clark once again. Though he seems not to have received the mammoth bones yet, he had not given up. "You were so kind in a former letter as to inform me you had procured for me some teeth and bones of the big buffalo. In the letter above mentioned I took the liberty of asking you to endeavor if possible to procure me one of every species of the bones now remaining, that is of every member or part. This request I again repeat and that I shall chearfully incur the necessary expences of good package and carriage."

One of the marks of a good scientist is patience, tenacity, a willingness to try again and again. In his persistence to learn about the extinct animals by studying their bones, Jefferson was tireless, always courteous, always willing to try again to obtain specimens. At the time he wrote that letter, he was planning to sail to France as the new minister from the United States, but the prehistoric animals of the Ohio Valley were still much on his mind.

On December 4, 1783, Jefferson wrote yet again to Clark, this time from the temporary national capital in Annapolis, Maryland. As one of the outstanding legal thinkers of his time he had been helping to draft notes for a future Constitution, but the mammoth bones still occupied a place in his thinking. "I received here about a week ago your obliging letter of Oct. 12. 1783. with the shells and seeds for which I return you many thanks. You are also so kind as to keep alive the hope of getting for me as many of the different species of bones, teeth and tusks of the *Mammoth* as can now be found. This will be most acceptable."

Jefferson then went on to address an equally great concern of his, that the British might establish a claim on the West by exploration and study there. "I find they have subscribed a very large sum of money in England for exploring the country from the Missisipi to California. They pretend it is only to promote knoledge. I am afraid they have thoughts of colonising into that quarter. Some of us have been talking here in a feeble way of making the attempt to search that country. But I doubt whether we have enough of that kind of spirit to raise the money. How would you like to lead such a party?"

A nightmare for Jefferson was the thought that the British, because of their greater resources and imperial ambitions, might preempt the exploration and then the claiming of the West. He wanted desperately to find out what was out there. From the first, scientific exploration and American growth and prosperity were linked in Jefferson's thinking. But in 1783, as the republic fumbled its way toward a constitution and effective government, with no money in the treasury, such an ambition seemed to most little more than a fond dream. Jefferson understood that with a quickly growing population Americans could, and would, spread into the western territories. He wrote, "Our rapid multiplication will expand itself . . . and cover the whole northern, if not the southern continent."

While Jefferson had always worried about British or French control of the West, he showed less concern for the Spanish presence in North America. As Joseph J. Ellis phrases it, "Jefferson regarded Spanish ownership of the vast western region of North America as essentially a temporary occupation that conveniently bided time for the inevitable American sweep across the continent." Jefferson believed it was only a matter of time until the weak Spanish empire broke apart, and "the various pieces of that empire . . . maybe even Cuba" would fall into American hands. One of the ways Jefferson was especially prescient about the westward expansion was that he understood that the zealous settlers themselves would accomplish what no government or army on its own could do. The United States could avoid going to war over Spanish territory "till we have planted such a population on the Mississippi as will be able to do their own business, without the necessity of marching men from the shores of the Atlantic 1500 or 2000 miles thither."

Unlike many of his contemporaries, especially in New England, Jefferson would favor emmigration from other lands, because he knew the western territories would be populated by emigrants. In 1790 Jefferson as secretary of state would organize the first national census. In the words of the scholar Kenneth Prewitt, "The territory would spread to the Pacific and would be added peacefully through treaty and purchase."

———

THE CONNECTION between the revolutionary spirit in science and the revolutionary spirit in politics has often been observed. The leading scientific minds in America, Franklin and Jefferson, were also among the leaders of the American Revolution. The new spirit of inquiry, experiment, boldness, escape from the dogmas of the past, seemed to inspire their work in both spheres. A fresh atmosphere of questioning and a willingness to consider radically different approaches to government and the investigation of the natural world seemed to spread through Europe, Britain, and North America.

It is fitting that the founder who served as architect of the Declaration of Independence, and to a large extent designer of the new republic lurching into being, was also the architect of Monticello, Poplar Forest, and the University of Virginia. From Paris, Jefferson would urge his colleagues in Richmond to build a capitol modeled on a Roman temple in Nîmes. The result would have an impact on American public architecture down to the present day. In the design of the Virginia capitol in Richmond, Jefferson influenced "the classical style of public buildings in America." In addition, Jefferson worked with Latrobe to plan the capital city of Washington, and he had a hand in the design of the executive mansion, the future White House, called at the time "the president's house." The architect of his nation had long been interested in building. When Jefferson was twenty-five years old he began leveling ground on top of the little mountain outside Charlottesville, which he called Monticello. No Virginia planter before him had chosen to place his house on a mountaintop. His choice revealed Jefferson's love of height and view and echoed the elevation of his thought and ambition and ideals. In placing his estate on the hilltop Jefferson followed the example of his Italian master of classicism, Andrea Palladio, whose *Four Books of Architecture* were among Jefferson's bibles and whose famed Villa Rotunda sat atop an eminence near Vicenza, Italy.

On the slopes of Monticello, Jefferson planted fruit trees — apples, peaches, pears, plums, pomegranates, figs, and walnuts — creating a delightful world of fertility, vitality, symmetry, vision, dignity, and repose. Jefferson's classicism reflected his love of the firm and exact and his respect for the ancient past. He valued simplicity and reserve, poise, confidence. In his designs he hoped to blend both the mathematical and natural into a perfect unity. He studied the proportions and lines of classical buildings, and he collected seeds and rootstocks of a vast variety of useful and ornamental plants for his grounds and gardens.

Jefferson's love of the classical expressed not only his taste for a style of building and landscaping but also the political ideals of liberty that he associated with ancient Greece and the Roman republic. He wanted to turn away from the architecture he associated with monarchy and feudalism and reinforce republican ideals through buildings. Classical art was rational, derived from "the discovery and imitation of Nature or those permanent and universal principles that transcended time, locality, and particularity." Jefferson's originality lay in his ability to adapt those ideas and ideals to the needs and possibilities of North America.

"His eye, like his mind, sought an extended view," the biographer Dumas Malone tells us. Emerson would later write, "We are never tired, so long as we can see far enough." Jefferson wanted to live where he could see farthest, to the distant chain of mountains, to the future, and the Far West where that future would be realized. Through elevation, he hoped to achieve in his personal life both privacy and vision. Because of its height, the wells of Monticello would often go dry in a drought. But that was an irritation and liability he was willing to live with.

At about six feet three, Jefferson was physically taller than the other founders, including Washington, and in several senses he tried always to stand tall on high ground, politically, intellectually, morally. At least one historian has also pointed out that he often "had his head in the clouds." But while Jefferson might be disastrously impractical in his personal life, going deeper and deeper into debt, he tried to be very practical when planning and acting for the good of his country. One of the best illustrations of that practicality is his purchase of Louisiana in 1803, which violated his own strict interpretation of constitutional authority. For the future good of his nation, Jefferson was willing to override his personal opinions and contradict himself. Like Whitman, he contained multitudes. And he never let his passion for science and curiosity about exploration push aside his concern with commerce and economic expansion, though he would always mistrust urbanization.

Jefferson's closest friend, and perhaps the man who understood him best, was James Madison. Though younger and always deferential to Jefferson, Madison would sometimes surpass his mentor in the originality and depth of his thought, especially about government. It was Madison, for example, who pointed out that success in foreign policy depended on the character and accomplishment of domestic affairs. One secret of their long friendship was that Madison understood the contradictions in the older man's personality. In the words of Gordon S. Wood, "Madison knew his friend and knew that Jefferson's fanciful and exaggerated opinions were usually offset by his very practical and cautious behavior." John Quincy Adams, who admired both men, would later demonstrate his own insight and eloquence in summing up the relationship between Jefferson and Madison. "The mutual influence of these two mighty minds upon each other is a phenomenon, like the invisible and mysterious movements of the magnet in the physical world, and in which the sagacity of the future historian may discover the solution of much of our national history not otherwise easily accountable."

Howard Hugh tells us that Jefferson "delighted in the notion that there were natural laws and a universal order which human reason could comprehend and employ in resolving social, political and economic issues." From the height of Monticello, he contemplated not only the future and nature of the new country but also the vast interior of the continent symbolized by the blue mountains to the west, and he drew up an ordinance for that territory before he left for Paris in 1785.

All his life Jefferson delighted in music, and he played the violin. While he inspected his grounds and fields on horseback, he would sing, and while he rode in a carriage with his children and later grandchildren, he led the group in song. A relative would later recall, "Mr. Jefferson [was] always singing when ridin' or walkin'; hardly see him anywhar outdoors but what he was a-singin'. Had a fine clear voice." Jefferson's delight in music seems to fit with his taste for classical architecture, natural law, the harmony and order inherent in all things. Though he was never a "great dog fancier," everything else around him seemed to claim his alert attention. And his granddaughter Ellen Randolph Coolidge would later recall that he seemed to take as much pleasure in conversing with children as with "older and wiser people."

It was Jefferson's loyalty to his native land that had provoked him to write his major work on natural history. Retiring from the fray of the governorship of Virginia in the closing days of the Revolution, he returned to Monticello and wrote *Notes on the State of Virginia*. The ostensible occasion was to answer the scientists in Europe who had belittled both the wildlife and the natural resources of the North American continent. While others were bringing the war to a close and negotiating with the British an end to hostilities and a division of territory, Jefferson in his mountain retreat, surrounded by family and servants, wrote a description of the land he loved. One might have expected him to write an account of the momentous political events in which he had been involved. Instead, he wrote of rivers and mountains, trees and mammoth bones, American Indians and agriculture, the evils of slavery, and the navigation of rivers.

While *Notes on the State of Virginia* includes many descriptive passages that could almost be considered poetry, it is also a scientific document, full of exact measurements, statistics, calculations, tables, lists, dry facts. Like William Byrd's *History of the Dividing Line* before it, and William Bartram's *Travels* of 1791, after it, *Notes* was inspired by the peculiarly American combination of scientific exactness and romantic poetry, informed by a love of the useful and pragmatic and a sense of unfolding destiny. It is a combination that would later be raised to further literary heights by Emerson, Thoreau, and Whitman.

Jefferson began *Notes* as an answer to a questionnaire circulated by François de Barbé-Marbois, secretary to the French legation in Philadelphia in 1780. Jefferson was governor of Virginia at the time, but he somehow found the leisure to begin setting down his answers to the disparaging remarks about North America made by Buffon in his esteemed *Histoire naturelle* and a Dutchman named Corneille de Pauw, who had never seen the New World but in 1738 published *Recherches philosophiques sur les Américains,* in which he declared the land in North America was either desert or swamp, woods or mountains. The water was foul, the fog unhealthy, and the climate so cold seeds froze in the ground. Lizards, snakes, and other reptiles dominated the landscape, and all animals except insects were stunted compared with European varieties. Dogs there were too listless to bark and too lazy to breed. Animals there had syphilis and men lacked virility. Oddly enough, the intellectuals in Europe seemed to believe de Pauw, ignoring the many specimens of American wildlife sent to Europe by scientists such as Swedish Peter Kalm and Pennsylvania's own John Bartram.

When Jefferson set out to answer these skeptics of American vitality, he chose to rebut them in their own terms. "The opinion advanced by the Count de Buffon is (1) That the animals common both to the old and new world, are smaller in the latter, (2) That those peculiar to the new are on a smaller scale, (3) That those which have been domesticated in both, have degenerated in America : and (4) That on the whole it [America] exhibits fewer species."

Going into great detail and using precise figures, Jefferson refutes Buffon's contentions one by one. Presenting a table with the relative weights of European and North American animals, including elk, bison, otter, beaver, he shows that American animals are usually bigger than their old-world counterparts. Some, such as the American moose, are indeed much larger than any similar beast in Europe. His second table lists dozens of animals such as mink and fox squirrels not known in Europe at all. And then he compares the recorded weights of domesticated animals, cows, horses, hogs, and sheep, and notes that those on the western side of the Atlantic surpass those on the eastern side.

It is in his description of the animals in North America that Jefferson went furthest in refuting the slights of Buffon and de Pauw. He is especially eloquent in describing the bones of the mammoth found in the northern part of the region. "(1) The skeleton of the mammoth (for so the incognitum has been called) bespeaks an animal of five or six times the cubic volume of the elephant, as Mons de Buffon has admitted. (2) The grinders are five times as large, are square, and the grinding surface studded with four or five rows of blunt points: whereas those of the elephant are broad and thin, and their grinding surface flat. (3) I have never heard an instance, and suppose there has been none, of the grinder of an elephant being found in America. (4) From the known temperature and constitution of the elephant he could never have existed in those regions where the remains of the mammoth have been found."

Jefferson pointed out that no bones of the mammoth had ever been found farther south than the salt licks of the Holston River in far western Virginia. Therefore the animal was a creature of the north and not of the tropics. "The truth is, that a Pygmy and a Patagonian, a Mouse and a Mammoth, derive their dimensions from the same nutritive juices . . . But all the manna of heaven would never raise the mouse to the bulk of the mammoth."

With rigor, facts, and logic, Jefferson refuted Buffon step by careful step. Buffon blamed the cold and excessive moisture of North America for making animals there weaker and smaller than their European counterparts. Buffon, who never did fieldwork himself and never traveled to North America, believed that North America had been under water for ages and had never completely dried out. He saw America as "covered by immense swamps, which render the air extremely unwholesome." Jefferson wrote, "It is by the assistance of *heat* and *moisture* that vegetables are elaborated from the elements of earth, air, water, and fire. We accordingly see the more humid climates produce the greater quantity of vegetables. Vegetables are mediately or immediately the food of every animal: and in proportion to the quantity of food, we see animals not only multiplied in their numbers, but improved in their bulk, as far as the laws of nature will admit."

Jefferson is leading up to an extended list of animals of Europe and of North America, to demonstrate again and again that animals on his continent are equal if not superior to those across the Atlantic in size. And he adds that no naturalist such as Peter Kalm, who actually traveled and studied the specimens of North America, has argued they were inferior to those of Europe. And besides the wildlife, Jefferson defends the livestock of America, arguing that horses in the United States are just as large and vigorous and strong as they are in the Old World.

But while the defense of American wildlife and agriculture and life in general provides the occasion for *Notes,* the glory of the work is the loving detail, the passion for the natural world of his native land, that shines

United States, 1781

through the lists and tables, statistics and comparisons. Jefferson had an eye for the significant detail and evocative phrase. His book is, among other things, a celebration and homage to his birth country.

Luckily for us, Jefferson thought of Virginia as extending across the Appalachians into the Ohio Valley and beyond, to the Mississippi Valley. In fact, when the English had begun to explore the continent, Virginia was all of eastern North America. When he was writing, Virginia included Kentucky, but it also seemed to encompass much of the interior of the continent. And writing of the rivers, Jefferson was always thinking of future navigation, commerce and communication. In speaking of the "Great Kanhaway" he says, "In some future state of population, I think it possible, that its navigation may also be made to interlock with that of the Patowmac, and through that to communicate by a short portage with the Ohio."

For most of his life Jefferson believed that the great rivers of the West must "interlock," by which he meant their headstreams came very close to each other. Therefore, it would be only a short portage from the headwaters of one river to another. Jefferson was better informed about the geography of North America than almost anyone else. He had studied all available maps made by explorers. The idea that one river system led easily to the next, making water travel possible across the continent from one ocean to another, was deeply fixed in his mind, as it was in others', and would only be erased when Lewis and Clark returned from the Pacific with exact measurements of the Rockies and the distances of the difficult terrain between the sources of the Missouri and the tributaries of the Columbia.

Though Americans did not have access to the mouth of the Mississippi, controlled in 1782 by the Spanish, who claimed also the whole Louisiana Territory, Jefferson believed the Father of Waters would become the main highway of commerce in the future of the region west of the Alleghenies. "From the mouth of this river to where it receives the Ohio, is 1000 miles by water, but only 500 by land, passing through the Chickasaw country. From the mouth of the Ohio to that of the Missouri is 230 miles by water, and 140 by land. From thence to the mouth of the Illinois river, is about 25 miles. The Missisipi, below the mouth of the Missouri, is always muddy, and abounding with sand bars, which frequently change their places."

Jefferson already knew that the Missouri River carried more water than the Mississippi and drained a larger land mass. He described it as "remarkably cold, muddy and rapid" and states that its period of flooding is June and July. Echoing the French of a hundred years before him, Jefferson described the Ohio River as "the most beautiful river on earth.

Its current gentle, waters clear, and bosom smooth and unbroken by rocks and rapids, a single instance only excepted." The exception he was referring to was the falls of the Ohio at Louisville.

But in his catalog of western rivers, commerce and travel were never far from the thoughts of the visionary. Because the Hudson River was often frozen in winter, he foresaw a route from the Chesapeake as more promising for the future of travel, as "vessels may pass through the whole winter, subject only to accidental and short delays."

Before Jefferson's *Notes* was printed in Paris in 1785, the Spanish had closed the Mississippi to American traders on June 24, 1784. Even as Jefferson described the glories and potential of the West, he worried about the vulnerability of the nation on its western border. In the words of the historian Jenry Morsman, "If the United States could not control New Orleans, then the unity of the entire nation would be at risk."

In his lyrical description of the mountains of Virginia, Jefferson evokes the beauty of the highlands, the rivers that have carved their blue shapes and contours, the cliffs, and splendor of Natural Bridge, the remote valleys with inhabitants who have never traveled more than a few miles from their cabins. But always the scientist, Jefferson laments that the height of the mountains has never been established with any accuracy, either by barometer or by leveling. He estimates the highest peaks are about 4,000 feet. Later measurements in the Black Mountains and Smokies would prove him off by about half a mile. Mount Mitchell in North Carolina reaches 6,684 feet above sea level.

Some of the memorable prose in *Notes on the State of Virginia* is to be found in the chapter titled "Productions Mineral, Vegetable and Animal." It includes more of Jefferson's beloved lists. Of the lead mines in Montgomery County he wrote: "The veins are at sometimes most flattering; at others they disappear suddenly and totally. They enter the side of the hill, and proceed horizontally." But Jefferson surpasses himself in describing the springs of the region, the hot springs, the sweet springs, the medicinal springs, both sulfur and chalybeate, and burning springs where natural gas escaping from the ground could be lit by candles or by lightning. Most memorable is his description of "syphon fountains," meaning the springs commonly called ebbing and flowing springs. These springs gushed out of the ground for a period and then slackened until they were almost empty. Jefferson is apparently the first writer to understand what caused the cycle of ebbing and flowing. For many years such springs were considered a mystery by settlers and the Indians before them. Jefferson surmised that reservoirs inside rock filled to overflowing and were drained by channels or crevices that acted as siphons, emptying the basins inside the hill, which then had to refill to the brim as the cycle began again.

Jefferson gives a sentimental catalog of vegetables or plants in the region. In most cases he presents the Latin names for each species or variety, as in "Cherokee plumb. Prunus sylvestris fructus magori" and "Wild plumb. Prunus sylvestris fructus minori." He mentioned that he called the laurel, *Kalmia augustifolia,* plain ivy, as residents of the Blue Ridge region do to this day. Jefferson was fascinated by both international science and the local culture around him.

———

JEFFERSON ALSO defends the Native Americans, the Indians, against the calumnies of Buffon, who had asserted that "the savage is feeble, and has small organs of generation; he has neither hair nor beard, and no ardor whatever for his female; although swifter than the European because he is better accustomed to running, he is, on the other hand, less strong in body; he is also less sensitive, and yet more timid and cowardly; he has no vivacity, no activity of mind."

One by one Jefferson refutes most of these errors. It was especially irritating to him to see the great French naturalist make assertions he could not possibly support with evidence. Having never been in North America, how could Buffon claim to know that the Indians lack "the most precious spark of the fire of nature . . . They lack ardor for their females, and consequently have no love for their fellow men: not knowing this strongest and most tender of all affections, their other feelings are also cold and languid; they love their parents and children but little; the most intimate of all ties, the family connection, binds them therefore but loosely together . . .They have only few children, and they take little care of them. Everywhere the original defect appears: they are indifferent because they have little sexual capacity."

Jefferson's comment on this passage is, "These I believe to be just as true as the fables of Aesop." Jefferson knew, as a student of Indian life on the frontier from boyhood, that Indian families were as closely knit and as affectionate as white families. In fact, Indians were extremely indulgent with their children compared with white parents, rarely reprimanding or punishing them. Other things being equal, Native American men were as ardent in love as their white counterparts. One source of Buffon's errors was a misunderstanding of the statistics about birthrates. Because most Indians were seminomadic people, living each year through cycles of plenty and famine, rarely storing enough reserves to last through a long winter or an extreme drought, their fertility rates were lower than those of whites. But given a more consistent diet and protection from the elements, and a similar lifestyle, the birthrate of the two races was about the same. When Indian women married white men and lived as white women did, their fertility was very much the same as that of white women. Indians "are known, under these circumstances, of their rearing a dozen children," Jefferson writes.

Buffon had said that Indian men are less virile because they have less hair, but Jefferson points out that Indians pluck out their body hair, and traders who had married Indian women had attested that they grew pubic hair and body hair same as white women. Jefferson also notes that when bravery is called for, Indians have proved to be particularly brave, and when they fight they prefer to die rather than surrender. "[H]e meets death with more deliberation, and endures tortures with a firmness unknown almost to religious enthusiasm with us."

One of the mistakes Jefferson does make, however, is in his generalizations about Indian women. It is a mistake whites have made for hundreds of years. Jefferson states, "The women are submitted to unjust drudgery. This I believe is the case with every barbarous people." He adds that Indian women are stronger than white women, but only because of the heavy labors they have to perform. And white men are stronger than Indian men because they work harder. To Europeans in general, it seemed Indian men lazed about while their women did all the work in the village. Men did nothing but hunt and go to war.

The fact is that in almost every Indian nation men did the heavy work when it was required, such as clearing fields, removing rocks, and building weirs in rivers for trapping fish. But their division of labor was such

concerned about opening Indian lands in the West for white settlement. His hope was that land could be bought from the Indians, and he considered the ways the Indians might be coerced into selling their territories. Writing to Governor William Henry Harrison of the Indiana Territory in 1803, he suggested, "To promote this disposition to exchange lands, which they have to spare and we want, we shall push our trading uses, and be glad to see them run in debt, because we observe that when these debts get beyond what the individuals can pay, they become willing to lop them off by a cession of lands."

———

THE PARTICULAR embarrassment of *Notes on the State of Virginia* for future students of Jefferson's thought derives less from his comments about Native Americans than from his meditations on African Americans and slavery. While Jefferson was quite explicit in his condemnation of the evils of slavery, he had no practical recommendations about how that institution might be ended, except for the mass deportation of black people, believing the sad history of slavery in North America made peaceful and productive coexistence of the races impossible once the slaves were freed. In *Notes* he writes, "Deep rooted prejudices entertained by the whites; ten thousand recollections, by the blacks, of the injuries they have sustained; new provocations; the real distinctions that nature has made; and many other circumstances, will divide us into parties, and produce convulsions which will probably never end but in the extermination of the one or the other race." It would be hard to think of a bleaker view of the consequences of emancipation. Even worse, Jefferson seemed to believe in the inherent inferiority of blacks to whites: "It appears to me, that in memory, they [African Americans] are equal to the whites; in reason much inferior, as I think one could scarcely be found capable of tracing and comprehending the investigations of Euclid; and that in imagination they are dull, tasteless, and anomalous."

Describing the physical characteristics of black people, Jefferson writes, "They secrete less by the kidnies, and more by the glands of the skin, which gives them a very strong and disagreeable odour." And then he refers to the sexual traits of African Americans: "They are more ardent after their female: but love seems with them to be more an eager desire,

than a tender delicate mixture of sentiment and sensation. Their griefs
are transient." While some contemporaries condemned *Notes* for Jefferson's critical view of slavery, future generations would condemn the book
for its biased view of African Americans. In his apocalyptic vision of the
result of emancipation, Jefferson revealed the worst of his prejudices and
the weakest aspect of his thought about the American future. Like many
who would follow him, since he could not see a workable solution to the
painful reality of slavery, Jefferson turned his attention elsewhere, especially to the West. For a half century the West would provide the most
effective diversion from confronting the apparently insoluble dilemma
of slavery.

One of the many paradoxes of Jefferson's career is the fact that he was
a slave-owning aristocrat, yet perhaps "the most important apostle for
liberty and democracy in American history." In fact, Jefferson became
the second-largest slaveholder in his part of Virginia, even while having
written that "the abolition of domestic slavery is the great object of desire
in those colonies where it was unhappily introduced in their infant state."
Jefferson had no doubt that slavery morally degraded owners even as it
kept its subjects in misery. Richard Hofstadter reminds us that Jefferson
"tried to get slavery banned from the Northwest Territories in his Ordinance of 1784." The paradox of Jefferson the gentle, cultured, consci-
entious thinker being a slave owner has troubled his admirers for more
than a century. In the words of Bernard Bailyn, "An accommodation
was somehow made between brutality and progressive refinement." It has
been pointed out that Virginia in general became less and less concerned
with revolutionary and democratic ideals as slavery took a deeper hold on
the region in the late eighteenth and early nineteenth centuries.

Surprising as it may seem to modern readers, it was Jefferson's criticisms of slavery in *Notes* that his contemporary political opponents used
against him. In the words of Lee Alan Dugatkin, "Throughout his political career, Jefferson's opponents pointed to his slavery comments in
Notes to paint Jefferson as a danger to the economy of the South and the
nation." The sins of one age are sometimes viewed as virtues in a later
time, and vice versa.

One possible solution to the dilemma of slavery that was considered
was expansion of the nation into the West. Jefferson speculated that if

slavery were diffused over a greater area the pernicious institution might die a natural death. Sadly, by the time of the Missouri Compromise of 1820, the Sage of Monticello saw that far from dying out, as a result of expansion to the West, slavery threatened more than ever to wreck the Union. "I regret that I am now to die in the belief," Jefferson wrote, "that the useless sacrifice of themselves by the generation of 1776 . . . is to be thrown away by the unwise and unworthy passions of their sons."

To protest Buffon's assertions about the lack of cultural achievement in North America, Jefferson argues that the inhabitants of northern Europe were without learning or letters when the Romans crossed the Alps almost two thousand years before: "It was sixteen centuries after this before a Newton could be formed." Buffon argues that "America has not yet produced one great poet," but Jefferson asks, how long did it take the European countries to produce one great poet? Almost a thousand years in the case of each European language and culture. And while America may not have produced a great poet in her first 170 years, she has produced a great leader in George Washington, a great scientist in Benjamin Franklin, a great astronomer in David Rittenhouse.

And Jefferson adds that while Americans were just beginning to realize their potential, after the Revolutionary War, older, richer cultures such as Britain seemed to be waning. "The sun of her glory is fast descending to the horizon. Her philosophy has crossed the channel, her freedom the Atlantic, and herself seems passing to that awful dissolution, whose issue is not given human foresight to scan."

Jefferson had never planned to publish *Notes on the State of Virginia*. Begun as a set of answers to questions by the diplomat Barbé-Marbois, the work kept growing in depth and comprehensiveness as one revision followed another. He circulated manuscript copies to friends but realized that was too expensive and time consuming. In Paris he had a hundred or so copies printed, and those were passed from hand to hand as the work took on a life of its own. Its fame spread in Europe and Britain as well as in North America. The historian Kevin J. Hayes has pointed out that *Notes* "stands at the crossroads of manuscript culture and print culture." But Jefferson's treatise is also "a transitional work connecting the Augustan Age to the Romantic era. A masterpiece of the Enlightenment, it presents an articulate and rational delineation of its subject spoken by a Man of Reason. Occasionally, however, the Man of Feeling takes over from the man of Reason and imbues the narrative with passion." Hayes adds that it was Jefferson the dreamer who made *Notes* "one of the classics of early American literature."

After he wrote *Notes on the State of Virginia,* Jefferson served in the Continental Congress in 1783–84 and was sent to Paris in 1785 as minister to France. He decided that the most effective way to refute Buffon's aspersions on North American wildlife was to procure a giant moose and have it stuffed and shipped to the great scientist in France. After endless delays, such a specimen was collected by General John Sullivan and, after a comic opera of mishaps, finally reached France with its hair falling out. Jefferson planned to give the moose to the scientist in person. Buffon graciously received the mounted moose and promised to revise chapter 14 of his *Histoire naturelle* to reflect his changed opinion about North American wildlife. But within a few months he was dead. Jefferson's respect and affection for the French deepened whereas in his negotiations with the British he became convinced that the English were decidedly selfish. This coolness toward the British and affinity for the French would influence many of his actions and policy decisions later.

One reason so many European intellectuals believed, and were encouraged to believe, in the degeneracy of North American climate, soil, and wildlife, was the fear of losing population through immigration to the New World. Frederick the Great encouraged the expression of such opinions. Immanuel Kant wrote that Americans were degenerate and weak. Hegel spoke of "American impotence." The poet John Keats, having read William Robertson's biased *History of America,* wrote that America was a place where "great unerring Nature once seems wrong." The fact that Keats's brother George had lost much of the family fortune in a venture with John James Audubon in North America may have colored the poet's view point. The drain of population to North America was scary to leaders and thinkers alike. Stating that the continent across the Atlantic was a place of syphilis and blight seemed a way to stem the desertion from Europe. But as time passed, Jefferson seemed to win the argument as writers such as Alexander von Humbolt expressed enthusiasm for Jefferson's *Notes* and the backlash against Buffon was carried on by authors such as Emerson and Thoreau. Emerson would celebrate forward-looking vision:

"The eyes of man are set in his forehead, not in his hindhead." In his exuberance, he would go even farther: "Can we never extract this tapeworm of Europe from the brain of our countrymen?"

———

WHILE HE was in Paris in 1787, Jefferson made another attempt to persuade someone to explore the western half of the North American continent. He met an adventurer named John Ledyard, born in Groton, Connecticut, in 1751, who had sailed with James Cook on his second voyage to the Pacific. Ledyard had published a colorful account of his travels in 1783, *A Journal of Captain Cook's Last Voyage to the Pacific.* There he recalled that when he reached the West Coast of North America he had felt he was touching home, even though Connecticut was thirty-five hundred miles from the Pacific Northwest.

It seems that it was Ledyard who initiated contact with Jefferson in Paris and proposed that he, Ledyard, journey across all of Russia to the Pacific coast and somehow cross from Kamchatka to North America. Once ashore he would make his way inland, following the rivers, crossing the mountains, studying the native tribes he encountered and keeping an exact account of the plants and animals, the soil and the climate, the rivers and minerals.

Jefferson was skeptical about the likely success of the venture, but he couldn't say no to the proposal and so offered his support. "He is a person of ingenuity & information," Jefferson wrote of Ledyard. "Unfortunately he has too much imagination." But added that if Ledyard survived, "he will give us new, curious, & useful information."

Bernard DeVoto has described Ledyard as the first American to grasp the opportunities of the Northwest fur trade. He could see the lucrative commerce that would spring up in the Pacific Northwest. In the period just after the Revolutionary War, Ledyard had tried to find backers for his scheme but failed. In Paris he had formed a partnership with the famous John Paul Jones, but that came to nothing.

Ledyard proposed to Jefferson that he would cross the American continent, once he had reached it, on foot, with no horses and no white companions. He would catch a ship in the Aleutian trade at Kamchatka, and after he set foot on the American coast he would just keep walking until he reached the Mississippi and then the United States. Ledyard charmed Jefferson and they spent hours discussing the plan. Since Ledyard could carry no scientific instruments with him on his proposed dash across Russia and North America, Jefferson suggested that he tattoo on his arm the measure of an English foot, and showed Ledyard "how he could determine latitude with nothing more than this measurement, two sticks, and a circle drawn in the dirt." Jefferson also described to him a way of measuring the breadth of a river and suggested that once he had made these calculations, Ledyard could record the result on his own skin with tattoos made from berry juice.

Jefferson gave Ledyard some money for his explorations, but Ledyard wrote Jefferson from St. Petersburg that he possessed "only two shirts and yet more shirts than shillings." Though Ledyard crossed European Russia and reached Irkutsk, his progress had been monitored by Catherine the Great's police. He had to spend a long winter in Irkutsk, and in February 1788 he was arrested as a spy to prevent him from reaching Kamchatka. The Russians wanted no one interfering with their own fur trade and colonial plans for the Pacific coast of North America. Ledyard was hurried all the way back to Europe, and he died in 1789 in Cairo, on yet another unlikely expedition.

———

AMONG THE many distinguished French scientists of the time was the botanist André Michaux. Born in 1746, three years after Jefferson, he had collected specimens in Europe and Asia. In 1785 he was commissioned by the French government to establish nurseries in North America and send plants back to France. For seven years he developed very successful nurseries in Charleston, South Carolina, then in 1792 botanized in eastern Canada. In 1801 he would publish one of the most important books on the trees of North America, and later his work would be continued by his son, François André Michaux.

In 1792 Michaux proposed to the American Philosophical Society that if it could raise the funds to support him he would make a scientific exploration of the American West, to the Mississippi and beyond. The proposal could not have been more welcome to Jefferson, now secretary of state in Washington's first cabinet, who set about to raise the necessary funds on behalf of the society. There was so much interest in such an expedition that more money was raised than the botanist had asked for. Frugal President Washington himself contributed $100. Altogether Jefferson raised $1,569.

On January 22, 1793, Jefferson wrote a letter to Michaux, in the form of a contract, requesting him "on his return to communicate to the said society the information he shall have acquired of the geography of the said country it's inhabitants, soil, climate, animals, vegetables, minerals and other circumstances of note." And then on April 30 of that year Jefferson wrote out his instructions for Michaux in a list that sounds much like the one he composed ten years later for Meriwether Lewis. He told Michaux he must reach the Pacific Ocean by first exploring the Mississippi and Missouri Rivers, beginning at Kaskaskia on the Mississippi.

> *When, pursuing these streams, you shall find yourself at the point from whence you may get by the shortest and most convenient route to some principal river of the Pacific ocean, you are to proceed to such river, and pursue it's course to the ocean. It would seem by the latest maps as if a river called Oregon interlocked with the Missouri for a considerable distance, and entered the Pacific ocean, not far Southward of the Nootka sound . . .*
>
> *You will, in the course of your journey, take notice of the country you pass through, it's general face, soil, rivers, mountains, it's productions animal, vegetable, mineral so far as they may be new to us and may also be useful or very curious; the latitude of places or materials for calculating it by such simple methods as your situation may admit you to practice, the names, numbers, and dwellings of the inhabitants, and such particularities as you can learn of their history, connection with each other, languages, manners, state of society and of the arts and commerce among them.*
>
> *Under the head of Animal history, that of the Mammoth is particularly recommended to your enquiries.*

While Jefferson could be described as a great dreamer, his dream was driven by practicality and political genius. After warning Michaux to expose himself to no unnecessary danger, and to protect his health, both for his own sake and the sake and interests of the Society, he added:

*Consider this not merely your personal concern, but as the injunction of
Science in general which expects it's enlargement from your enquiries, and
of the inhabitants of the U.S. in particular, to whom your Report will open
new feilds and subjects of Commerce, Intercourse, and Observation . . .*

*They will expect you to return to the city of Philadelphia to give in to
them a full narrative of your journey and observations, and to answer
the enquiries they shall make of you, still reserving to yourself the bene-
fits arising from the publication of them.*

Jefferson knew the proposed expedition was dangerous and did
not even consider sending the explorer toward the Southwest and the
Spanish-controlled territories of New Mexico and California. Jefferson
assumed the headwaters of the Missouri touched or "interlocked with"
the headwaters of the Oregon or Columbia River. That was the common
belief at the time, and the hope was a small portage would take an expedition from one watershed into another. For centuries geographers had
believed there was a Great River of the West, if only it could be found.

But once again Jefferson was to be disappointed. In the meantime
the French ambassador to the United States, who called himself "Citizen Genet," had begun to promote a scheme in which Americans would
aid France in attacking Britain and Spain and seizing the port of New
Orleans as the Napoleanic wars were getting underway. No sooner had
Genet arrived in the United States than he began "fitting out French
privateers in U.S. ports to seize British ships." George Rogers Clark of
Louisville had been brought into the plan and commissioned a major
general in the French army. After the American Revolution Clark had not
prospered. Deeply in debt and still trying to collect reimbursement for
equipping and supplying his own militia in the Western Campaign, he
had tried a number of enterprises, including running a gristmill. Drinking heavily, Clark, the hero of Vincennes in 1779, may have seen the
establishment of a French colony in the Mississippi Valley as a possible
solution to his many disappointments. The Citizen Genet scheme must
have seemed a surprising opportunity. Genet also brought Benjamin
Logan, former general of the Kentucky militia, into his plan.

Edmond Charles Eduard Genet (1763–1834) had been sent by the Revolutionary French government as minister to the United States in 1793.

As already mentioned, he made clear his hope for American support of the attack on the Spanish in Florida and Louisiana and on British ships in the Atlantic. But President Washington refused to get involved in the foreign wars, and powerful men in the government such as Vice President John Adams and Secretary of the Treasury Alexander Hamilton were suspicious of the French in any case. While Jefferson was more sympathetic to the French nation, there was little he was willing to do to aid the scheme Genet proposed. The project Jefferson cared about was Michaux's proposed exploration. It was hoped that Spanish officials in Louisiana would hardly notice a lone French botanist crossing their territory.

Jefferson later recorded that he met with Genet in Philadelphia in the summer of 1793, when Genet let it be known that France would approve the addition of Spanish territory to the United States. "I told him," Jefferson wrote later, "that his enticing officers & souldiers from Kentucky to go against Spain was really putting a halter about their necks, for that they would assuredly be hung, if they commd. hostilities agt. a nation at peace with the U.S. That leaving out that article, I did not care what insurrections should be excited in Louisiana."

But among those Genet persuaded, or perhaps ordered, to join his plot was André Michaux. Michaux signed on as a secret agent for the Genet mission and in effect destroyed the prospect for his scientific expedition to the West. Michaux left Philadelphia on July 15, 1793. He carried with him the official commission for George Rogers Clark in the French army. But Genet's plans had been made public, and everyone who saw the French botanist along the way seemed to suspect he was an agent for the French government. Some hoped to join him in conquering Louisiana. Michaux reached Lexington, Kentucky, then Kaskaskia, Illinois, on the Mississippi, but by then he had come to see the hopelessness of his political mission. Michaux never bothered to cross the Mississippi to St. Louis to join the other secret agents of the French who were supposed to be waiting there. The unlucky George Rogers Clark never really got started raising the militia in Kentucky to march to New Orleans.

In the meantime, President Washington had demanded that Genet be recalled by his government. But before the visionary Frenchman could be hurried out of the country his government in Paris fell and it was not safe for him to return to France. If he set foot on French soil he would be guillotined, so he requested and was given asylum in America, where he married and settled down for a long life of peaceful obscurity. In 1794 Genet's successor officially called off the project.

But Michaux's work in North America was not over. Though he would be recalled to France after the debacle of the Genet affair, he would return with his son François André Michaux to study the forests of the continent, and after Andre's death in 1802 François André would publish a classic work on trees of North America, *North American Sylva,* in 1817.

———

THOUGH JEFFERSON was out of the country while the Constitution of the United States was completed, he wrote letters of advice and support for the work done by close friends such as Madison, later called Master Builder of the Constitution, and when he was made secretary of state in 1790 he returned to serve in Philadelphia. Within a year he was quarreling with Secretary of the Treasury Alexander Hamilton not only over different ideas about the financial institutions and systems of the new country but also over fundamental issues about the very nature of the republic. Hamilton believed in a strong central government to direct and guide the country. Jefferson's vision was of a looser confederation of states, each master of its own destiny. Jefferson believed in strict construction of the Constitution wherein only the powers explicitly specified were given to the federal government. It has been said that the seeds of the American Civil War were already sown in the quarrel between the two most brilliant members of Washington's first cabinet. Hamilton's arrogance also irritated his fellow Federalists. John Adams referred to Hamilton as "the bastard brat of a Scots peddler." Hamilton, in secret communication with the British minister, worked to undercut the efforts of the other cabinet members.

In 1794 Jefferson's distrust of the British caused him to reject the treaty John Jay had negotiated with Britain, which he saw as submission to British interests and policies. Disillusioned by the treaty, by the ongoing quarrel with Hamilton, and perhaps by the controversy over the Genet affair, Jefferson resigned from the cabinet and returned to Monticello. One has the impression he was always looking for an opportunity to return to his mountain retreat, his Thoroughbred horses, and his study, leaving public affairs behind.

It is interesting that Jefferson, for all his eloquence with a pen, never seems to have been an effective public speaker. There is no evidence that he ever spoke at all in the 1775–76 Continental Congress where he became famous for writing the Declaration of Independence and in effect became the voice of the American Revolution for posterity. To his contemporaries, he appeared shy and retiring, especially in comparison with Virginia orators such as Patrick Henry and Edmund Pendleton. Sometimes his shyness made him seem both arrogant and evasive to those around him. When elected president in 1800 and duty-bound to give his first inaugural address, according to Joseph J. Ellis, "His delivery was so subdued that very few members of the audience could hear what he said." As chief executive Jefferson communicated mostly in writing, practicing what Ellis calls a "textual presidency." Jefferson may have spoken in public only twice in the eight years of his administration, delivering the two inaugural addresses.

Jefferson's reluctance to speak in public is another of the many paradoxes about his nature. However much he avoided oratory, his ideas and words "left such a deep impression on the future of his country that, despite persistent attempts to discredit his reputation," he is still the primary spokesman for American democratic ideals.

The Sage of Monticello could not stay out of politics for long. Put forward by friends and admirers in the presidential election of 1796, Jefferson came in second to John Adams and was made vice president. It was while serving in that anomalous office in 1798 that Jefferson wrote the Kentucky Resolutions opposing the Federalists' Alien and Sedition Acts and supporting limited states' rights. The document caused a furor among the Federalists and their allies, even after James Madison revised it into a milder version as the Virginia Resolutions. The division that would lead to the nullification controversy in the Jackson administration, and eventually to civil war, had already been opened and begun widening.

When Jefferson was elected president in 1800, he found overwhelming problems on almost every front. In 1801 he discovered that Spain, after the Treaty of San Ildefonso of 1800, was in the process of transferring

Louisiana to France as part of the settlement of their long-standing conflict. With the aggressive Napoleon already controlling New Orleans and the mouth of the Mississippi, the United States would be more vulnerable than ever. Napoleon's imperial ambitions were well known. Jefferson, a realist about territory in spite of his constitutional opinions, wrote to the ambassador to France, Robert R. Livingston, "The day that France takes possession of New Orleans . . . we must marry ourselves to the British fleet and nation." Secretly Madison sent aid to François-Dominique Toussaint-Louverture who led the rebellion against the French in Haiti. Jefferson planned, if necessary, to send an army to occupy the Lower Mississippi. It is thought that reading Alexander Mackenzie's account of his expedition across the continent, published in 1801, also spurred Jefferson to move toward acquiring Louisiana. With Mackenzie's exploration the British were strengthening their claim and hold on the Northwest.

He then instructed Livingston to offer to purchase New Orleans from France, along with western Florida, and appointed James Monroe "minister extraordinary and plenipotentiary" to aid Livingston in Paris. Congress voted two million dollars for the offer. Luckily for the United States, the French were becoming disillusioned with their prospects in North America. A revolt in Haiti had forced Napoleon to rethink his plan of an American empire.

On April 11, 1803, the French foreign minister, Charles-Maurice de Talleyrand-Périgord, told Livingston that France was ready to negotiate the sale of the whole Louisiana Territory, and a treaty was signed August 30, 1803. The United States agreed to pay fifteen million dollars for the vast region of the Mississippi and Missouri valleys and to assume responsibility for the claims against the French government by U.S. citizens. After months of agonizing, Jefferson was finally willing to brush aside any doubts about the constitutionality of the purchase. The treaty was ratified by the U.S. Senate in October 1803, and the American flag was raised in New Orleans on December 20 of the same year. It would be years before the exact western boundaries of the purchase were established. With the Louisiana Purchase, Jefferson demonstrated what his enemies called the inconsistency of his policies. Others prefer to see the purchase as evidence of flexibility in his thinking and in his methods. It is also an example of the ambivalence in

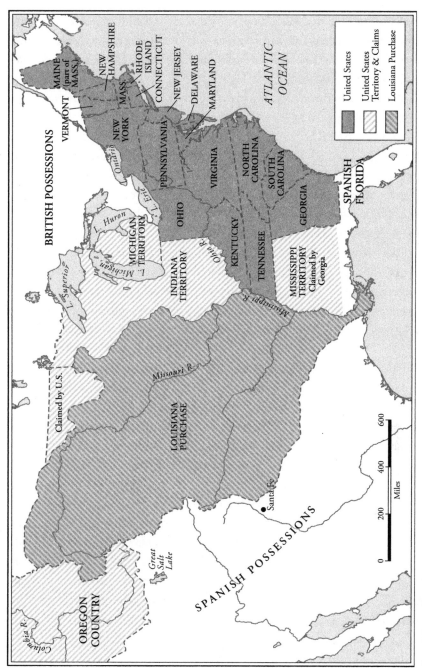

Louisiana Purchase, 1803

his thinking and the complexity of his many-faceted mind and career. Jefferson understood that lands could only be claimed effectively by people settling there. He had " a firm belief in what might be called demographic imperialism."

In anticipation of the acquisition of Louisiana, Jefferson had already been making new plans to explore the West. The year before, when reading Alexander Mackenzie's *Voyages from Montreal,* he had found a glorious description of the potential of the Columbia River and its basin. On June 20, 1803, he wrote to Meriwether Lewis, his private secretary and friend, a final draft of a document he had been revising for months, "Your situation as Secretary of the President of the U.S. has made you acquainted with the objects of my confidential message of Jan. 18, 1803 to the legislature." Not only had Jefferson asked Congress to authorize negotiations for the Louisiana Purchase, he had asked for funds for an exploratory expedition to the West well before the purchase was certain to be made. In preparation, he had instructed Lewis to study botany and zoology as well as navigation and navigational instruments. He had sent Lewis to Philadelphia to study drawing with the Peales and plants with William Bartram. Lewis had learned surveying methods, and he was acquainted with existing maps of the Missouri River, the Pacific coast, and Spanish territory in the Southwest. What was mostly unknown was the great area between the Missouri watershed and the Pacific. Jefferson's message to Lewis "embraces years of study and wonder, the collected wisdom of his government colleagues and his Philadelphia friends . . . his excitement at realizing that at last he would have the facts, not vague guesses, about the Stony [Rocky] Mountains . . ."

Jefferson wrote to Lewis, "Instruments for ascertaining, by celestial observations, the geography of the country through which you will pass, have been already provided." Articles for trading with the Indians had to be purchased, along with arms for at least a dozen men, and "boats, tents, & other traveling apparatus, with ammunition, medicine, surgical instruments, and provisions."

Lewis was also authorized to gather volunteers from the army to serve under his command. He would have the military authority of a captain in the U.S. Army. The governments of Spain, France, and Great Britain had already been informed of the upcoming mission, and Lewis would have a passport from their ministers to protect him in the territories claimed by those countries. This would turn out not to be the case with Spain, which would unsuccessfully send soldiers to try to intercept Lewis and William Clark, younger brother of George Rogers Clark, and turn them back. A letter from the minister of England "will entitle you to the friendly aid of any traders of that allegiance with whom you may happen to meet."

The historians Peter Onuf, Douglas Seefeldt, and Jeffrey Hantman have pointed out that "Jefferson's design for the expedition epitomized the Enlightenment quest for order and control." Though he had already had many conversations with his private secretary about the planned exploration, Jefferson spelled out explicitly the goals of the project: "The object of your mission is to explore the Missouri river, & such principal streams of it, as, by it's course and communication with the waters of the Pacific ocean, whether the Columbia, Oregon, Colorado or any other river may offer the most direct & practicable water communication across this continent for the purposes of commerce."

As late as 1803, indeed until Lewis and Clark returned from their expedition, Jefferson believed there must be a viable water route to the Pacific from the Missouri River. Strange as that may seem to us, this assumption of a passage to the "South Sea" had been common among geographers and scholars of geography for three hundred years. It was the residue of Columbus's dream of reaching the Indies across the Atlantic. A rough estimate of the size of the planet had been known since antiquity, but for a number of reasons the scale and width of the North American continent remained something of a mystery. Perhaps one factor was the difficulty of calculating longitude. It was only when the chronometer was developed around 1705 that reasonably accurate calculations of longitude could be made.

The great blank on the map that needed to be filled in was the area from the eastern edge of the Rockies to the coastal waters near the mouth of the Columbia River. No one but Indians had crossed that land or knew its heights or extent. Jefferson had a precise and detailed sense of geography. Had he not been so busy with all his other interests and obligations, one might imagine him as an important mapmaker, with his passion for accurate representation, his draftsmanship and devotion to the study of land.

"Beginning at the mouth of the Missouri," he wrote to Lewis, "you will take observations of latitude & longitude, at all remarkable points on the river, & especially at the mouths of rivers, at rapids, at islands, & other places . . . that . . . may . . . be recognized hereafter." Jefferson, long fascinated by tools and instruments, gave his explorer instructions in the use of compass and logging of distance and told him to note the variations in the magnetic compass readings as he moved up the river to the west.

Neither Jefferson nor anyone else was prepared to learn of the hundreds of miles of forbidding terrain that separated the head of navigation of one river from the head of navigation on the other. Certainly some of the Indian tribes in the region could have told the president differently, but they were out of communication for reasons of language, distance, and war. Besides, the Native Americans had many horses for travel and it might not have occurred to them that it was even desirable to haul boats and tons of baggage from the Missouri watershed, through weeks of travel, to the Pacific watershed.

"The interesting points of the portage between the heads of the Missouri, & of the water offering the best communication with the Pacific ocean," Jefferson wrote, "should also be fixed by observation . . . Your observations are to be taken with great pains, & accuracy, to be entered distinctly and intelligibly for others as well as yourself." To ensure survival of the documents, several copies should be made and carried by different members of the party.

And then Jefferson added one of the most unexpected and often quoted sentences in the letter. "A further guard would be that one of these copies be on paper of the birch, as less liable to injury from damp than common paper." Knowing that the records of the expedition would be carried in canoes and mackinaw boats, on horseback and human backs, through rain storms and snow storms, Jefferson was concerned about the vulnerability of paper. Where Meriwether Lewis was to acquire such pages of bark along the Missouri is not clear. Perhaps Jefferson meant for him to procure a supply of the bark in the East before setting out. Or maybe Jefferson thought Lewis's party could pause to chop down birch trees and peel their bark on the way up the river.

One of the best known passages in Jefferson's directions to Lewis is the list of things to be noted about native people along the way. Since commercial interest in the West "renders a knoledge of those people important," a special effort must be made to learn the names of populations of each nation encountered, as well as

> the extent & limits of their possessions;
> their relations with other tribes of nations;
> their language, traditions, monuments;
> their ordinary occupations in agriculture, fishing, hunting,
>   war, arts, & the implements for these;
> their food, clothing, & domestic accommodations;
> the diseases prevalent among them, & the remedies they use;
> moral & physical circumstances which distinguish them from
>   the tribes we know;
> peculiarities in their laws, customs & dispositions;
> and articles of commerce they may need or furnish, & to what extent.

Jefferson also wanted Lewis to gather information about "the state of morality, religion, & information among" the natives. Like most enlightened men of his time, Jefferson believed that those who went among the Indians should seek to "civilize & instruct them," but he also realized that to do so Europeans must "adapt their measures to the existing notions & practices of those on whom they are to operate." The last clause of the sentence shows something of Jefferson's sophistication. English missionaries and administrators usually failed with the native people because they wanted to teach Indians to behave like Europeans. French and sometimes Spanish missionaries were often more successful because they understood that they themselves had to adapt to Indian customs before they could have any effective impact. Had all Americans been as sensitive to this particular issue as Jefferson and Meriwether Lewis, our history might have been very different. To negotiate with others, trade with others, live beside others, we must first know something about who they are and how they view us and their own world. It is a simple principle to state but hard to practice in strange places and on dangerous occasions.

Significantly, Jefferson places study of the indigenous population ahead of his other lists of scientific objects of study. Only after he has described some of the things he wanted to know about the natives did he catalog his other scientific interests. For Jefferson the West was not just the land but also the people who had lived there for thousands of years. The priority of his scientific interest was the study of the people.

One of the most memorable passages in Jefferson's letter to Lewis is his instructions about the treatment of native people. In no place does Jefferson's idealism show through more than in this section. "Treat them in the most friendly and conciliatory manner," he urged, and "allay all jealousies as to the object of your journey, satisfy them of it's innocence, make them acquainted with the position, extent, character, peaceable & commercial dispositions of the U.S., . . . & of our wish to be neighborly, friendly & useful to them." He authorized Lewis to arrange visits of the chiefs to Washington at public expense, if they desired it, and to offer to educate their young. He also told Lewis to carry with him on the expedition "some of the matter of the kine-pox" to inoculate against small pox, which had already killed so many Indians. The inoculation might be especially important in the village where they would pass the winter.

Since it could not be known beforehand whether a given Indian tribe or nation would be welcoming or hostile, it was important for the expedition to have enough men to defend itself. But if a large group of Indians adamantly stood in the way of the expedition, "you must decline it's farther pursuit, and return." Not only must the lives of the Corps of Discovery be saved, but the information they have accumulated must be protected.

Jefferson recommended that Lewis commission friendly Indians to carry back letters and copies "of your journal, notes & observations of every kind," to the settlements at Cahokia and Kaskaskia on the east bank of the Mississippi. That way he could be informed at every stage of the progress of the expedition up the river and to the West Coast. Sensitive messages should be put in code.

And then he gave Lewis a list of his interests in the physical landscape that reads like a passage from a poem by Walt Whitman or a paragraph by Henry David Thoreau.

> the soil & face of the country, it's growth & vegetable
>   productions, especially those not of the U.S.
> the animals of the country generally, & especially those
>   not known in the U.S.

the remains or accounts of any which may be deemed rare
   or extinct;
the mineral productions of every kind; but more particularly
   metals, limestone, pit coal, & saltpetre; salines &
   mineral waters, noting the temperature of the last,
   & such circumstances as may indicate their character;
volcanic appearances;
climate, as characterized by the thermometer, by the proportion
   of rainy, cloudy, & clear days, by lightning, hail,
   snow, ice, by access & recess of frost, by the
   winds prevailing at different seasons, the dates at
   which particular plants put forth or lose their
   flower, or leaf, times of appearance of particular birds,
   reptiles or insects.

Jefferson added that he thought it especially important to know the land between the headwaters of the Rio Brava, meaning the Rio Grande, and the headwaters of the Rio Colorado. He was not sure whether the country between these rivers and the Missouri was mountainous or flat land. Few people had studied the existing maps of the west as thoroughly as Jefferson had, yet he thought that by going up the Missouri Lewis might be able to learn "anything certain of the most Northern source of the Missisipi & of it's position relatively to the lake of the woods," which English and French traders had described. And Jefferson wanted to know the distance from the mouth of the "Ouisconsing" (Wisconsin) River to the mouth of the Missouri. But it is not clear how Lewis was expected to acquire that information while going up the Missouri, unless he happened to meet someone who knew the exact distance.

Furthermore, if the Pacific coast was reached, the prospects for the fur trade there should be studied. The present center of the fur trade was farther north, at Nootka Sound on Vancouver Island, where British and Russian companies were already dominant. Most important, Lewis should find out if the United States could conduct business in the far northwest by going up the Missouri instead of sailing all the way around Cape Horn, as was the present practice.

When Lewis arrived at the Pacific coast he was to look for a port and if possible send two of his crew back to the United States by sea with copies of the journals and notes made crossing the continent. And if Lewis determined that it was too dangerous to return overland, Jefferson urged him to return with all his men by sea, either around the tip of South America or Africa. Since he would be without money, he must use letters of credit to pay for his passage.

If Lewis decided to return by land, Jefferson asked him to again make such observations "as may serve to supply, correct or confirm those made on your outward journey." Each member of the expedition would not only be paid in full when they returned to the United States but would also be given a grant of land, as other soldiers were. Last he tells Lewis, "Repair yourself with your papers to the seat of government" once other duties were discharged.

And then Jefferson thought of one more contingency. In case Lewis should suffer death on the journey west, he should leave a signed document written in his own hand "to name the person among them who shall succeed to the command on your decease." But as the voyage continued he should feel free to change the designated successor as he learns more about the character and competence of his men. And such a successor should be given authority to name his successor in case of his own demise. It does seem that Jefferson thought of everything on that day, June 20, 1803. Reading certain passages of the letter to Meriwether Lewis we are reminded that among his many other accomplishments, Jefferson was a gifted if reluctant lawyer.

THE COMPREHENSIVENESS, specificity, and prescience of Jefferson's commission to Lewis certainly reveal the range and depth of his intellect, his learning, his enthusiasm and curiosity. Presumably written in one day, the instrument contains an astonishing amount of detail, erudition, and vision. No one, not even Thomas Jefferson, could have written such a letter without having spent years studying and contemplating the subject and purpose of such a project. In fact, we know that the letter of June 20, 1803, was the culmination of many drafts. He was still keen to study the "elephant" bones, the fossils, the prehistory of the West. The letters he had written to George Rogers Clark, John Ledyard, and especially André Michaux were earlier drafts of this letter to Lewis. The instructions are precise and thorough because he was revising a document he had spent much of his life composing. It has been said that the most important secret of good writing is rewriting. We know that the Declaration of Independence was a reworking of ideas and phrases Jefferson had already used in the pamphlet *A Summary View of the Rights of British America* of 1774, and in an earlier draft for the Congress called *Declaration of the Causes and Necessity of Taking Up Arms.* Jefferson's letter to Lewis was at the very least a fourth draft of a request he had started writing to George Rogers Clark twenty-two years before.

Another secret of good writing is the selection of the right subject. In the pages written on June 20, 1803, Jefferson included much of his lifelong thought and experience, his aspirations and hopes for himself and his country. The letter was the articulation of his vision of the future. However violent and tragic much of the settlement of the West might turn out to be, and however tainted with greed the later policy of Manifest Destiny, Jefferson's intentions and ambitions were of a different order. Though that vision was to be compromised, perverted, distorted, and abandoned by later leaders, we should not forget what it was and what it was intended to be in the beginning. If Jefferson was mistaken, he was mistaken in his optimism, his hope, his aspiration for what his new country might become as it explored the continent and promoted trade and "intercourse" with the Indians and other natives. It is hard to think of a better alternative dream for the future of the republic, unless it was a republic without slavery.

More than any other leader or thinker of his time, Jefferson understood that the future of the United States lay in the westward movement, because the new country found its best inspiration and energy in that expansion. As Joseph J. Ellis puts it, "Securing a huge swatch of [the West] for posterity meant prolonging for several generations the systemic release of national energy that accompanied explosive movement of settlements across unsettled spaces . . . It was America's fountain of youth."

But there is another dimension to Jefferson's vision of the westward expansion of the republic, one he may have only partly understood himself. While he certainly felt a hunger, a need, even a greed, to acquire the new territories, the rival Federalists feared incorporating the western territories and western peoples would degrade the quality of the nation. But Jefferson rejoiced at the prospect of the changes that would ensue from the expansion. "Those of the western confederacy will be as much our children and descendants as those of the eastern, and I feel myself as much identified with that country, in future time, as with this." Jefferson did not know how to solve the dilemma of slavery, but the westward expansion was not only a possibility, it was a thrilling transformation, already under way, to be embraced with open arms.

Jefferson was not worried about the size and diversity of the expanding nation. In fact he celebrated the prospective complexity from the high plain of his idealism and vision of American potential.

— *Two* —

ANDREW JACKSON

Old Hickory at the Bend

*I*T IS probably impossible for us in the twenty-first century to understand what land meant to poor white people in the eighteenth and early
nineteenth centuries. Newly released indentured servants, called redemp-
tionists, who had never owned a square foot of property of their own
looked west at regions where for a few cents an acre they might acquire
tracts of rich farmland along streams and running back to picturesque
hills. People of ambition who already had land in the East dreamed of
gaining even more land and greater riches and prominence in the West.

For those in debt, or in trouble with the law, the frontier offered an
opportunity for salvation, to start over, with a clean slate, in a place
where no one knew them. Beginning with nothing but two hands, a few
tools, and determination, they might clear land and work it and rise to
prosperity. Or failing again, they could move on farther into the new territory and try once more. There seemed no end to the wild lands to the
west—if only Indians could be cleared away—and no limits to hope.
All you needed were an ax, a rifle, and a wife, and maybe a horse or ox.
But even if you had no wife, one could be found among the Indians.
In fact, for settling down at the edge of the wilderness, an Indian wife
might be the best of all. She already knew the land there and the ways of
extracting necessities and even luxuries from the forest. And she could
do much of the farmwork and make clothes from buckskin with fancy
beadwork or colorful clothes from cloth bought from traders. An Indian
wife might make it safer also. After all, married to an Indian woman, you
were halfway a member of the nation yourself.

To the Scots Irish, such as Andrew Jackson's ancestors, free or cheap land must have seemed a dream too wonderful almost to believe. Born in Scotland, they had been sent to Northern Ireland to drive away the Catholics and make Ireland Protestant. Later, when that land was needed by the wealthy English for grazing sheep, they were displaced again, and those who could came to the New World in the years before the Revolution. But eastern land was already claimed and expensive by the time they arrived. That left the Appalachian foothills and the farther frontier claimed by Cherokees and other Indian nations, and most attractive of all, the land beyond the mountains, Kentucky and Tennessee, and the vast expanse of land to the southwest, all the way to the Mississippi and New Orleans, much of it controlled by the Creek, or Muscogee, Indian confederacy.

———

THE GREATEST battle ever fought between white Americans and American Indians began as a civil war among factions of the Creek Nation and ended with Andrew Jackson and his Cherokee allies and friendly Creeks destroying the forces of the militant Red Stick Creeks on March 27, 1814, at a loop in the Tallapoosa River in Alabama called Horseshoe Bend. As with almost all major battles between whites and Indians, there were Indians fighting with deadly force against other Indians.

The Creeks of Andrew Jackson's era were a part of a Muskogean confederacy that had stretched over much of Florida, Georgia, Alabama, and Mississippi. Related nations included Choctaws, Apalachees, Alabamas, Chickasaws, Yamasees, and Seminoles. They spoke a language of the Hokan-Siouan family. The group the whites called Creeks, because their villages were situated on streams, sometimes called themselves Muscogee but more often identified themselves by clan name: Yuchis, Coosas, Cowetas. Their towns were divided between white (peace) villages and red (war) villages. War leaders were drawn from the red villages; leaders in peacetime, from the white. Their spirited ball games were played as a substitute for intraconfederacy warfare.

As with most nations of the region, the Creek economy was based on corn, beans, and squash agriculture and trade in tanned deer hides. They also made and traded nut oil and bear fat. Hickory nut oil was made by boiling the nuts in their shells and skimming off the oil, called milk. A delicacy they served to visitors was sweet potatoes bathed in nut milk. Divided into matrilineal clans, they were traditionally led by hereditary chiefs who sat on thrones or in elaborate arbors. But after the devastation of European diseases in the seventeenth century, the survivors formed themselves into "coalescent societies," drawn from different clans and tribes. By the late eighteenth century, many Creeks lived and dressed much like their white neighbors. In war, the Creeks took scalps and often tortured captives at a post in the town square. The Spanish had given the Creeks a reputation for artistry in torture, saying they were expert at skinning prisoners alive and setting fire to splinters stuck all over prisoners' bodies. Since these tortures were common among many nations, there is little reason to think the Creeks were more dedicated to cruelty than other tribes. But such practices were part of their legend in colonial times and after.

Their houses were made of upright poles, wattled and chinked with mud, with thatched or bark roofs. After they acquired metal tools they built dwellings of logs. Palisades or log forts were also common. They made cloth from buffalo hair or plant fiber, and men wore breech clouts while women wore apron skirts. "Purification by emetics was a common religious observance," one historian has said. For council meetings, they smoked pipes and drank a powerful caffeine beverage called *acee,* the "black drink," made from the yaupon plant, *Ilex vomitoria.* Sometimes the black drink had a purifying emetic effect. More often, the emetic they used for purification was *possau,* made from button snakeroot, especially for the important Turkey Dance.

In the late eighteenth century Creek Country included the land between the Oconee River in Georgia and the Tombigbee River in Alabama. According to the anthropologist Robbie Ethridge, "Upper Creeks lived on the Tallapoosa, Coosa, and Alabama Rivers in present-day Alabama, and the Lower Creeks lived on the lower Chattahoochee and Flint Rivers in present-day Georgia." With forty-eight Upper Creek towns and twenty-five Lower Creek towns, their population was between fifteen thousand and twenty thousand. Besides deerskins, they sold both Indian and black slaves to the whites. Individuals who were part African and part Indian were called "mustees."

The Indian agent for the Creeks was Benjamin Hawkins (1754–1816). A man of science and humanistic learning, a friend of Jefferson's, and a former senator from North Carolina, Hawkins was sent by President Washington in 1796 to Georgia as "principal agent for Indian affairs south of the Ohio." Hawkins was so successful as agent he became *isti atcagagi*, "beloved man," among the Creeks, a title "denoting wisdom, accomplishment, and trust." His *Sketches of the Creek Country in the Years 1798 and 1799* is a major source of our knowledge about the Creek confederacy, their language and culture and land.

No land in North America was more desirable to the whites than Creek country. A world of rivers and smaller streams, hardwood forests alternating with pine woods, rich bottomlands and rolling hills perfect for pastures, the botanist and explorer William Bartram had sung its praises in his *Travels* of 1790. In fact, he said the forests of longleaf pine sang "a solemn symphony of the steady Western breezes, playing incessantly, rising and falling through the thick and wavy foliage." There were great canebrakes along the streams, sometimes rising thirty feet high.

Though traditionally known for their gracious hospitality, the Creeks, as the deerskin trade declined, ran up large debts at the Creek Factory, the government-owned trading post. The debts were paid by annuities given for tracts of Creek land. To the Creeks, these cessions were rituals of gift giving, but as the practice continued, the Creeks saw their vast territories eaten away. At best, the boundary lines were vague, as whites and blacks and Indians encroached on one another's claims, killed or stole each other's livestock. Creek belief was based on a principle of balance and purity, war and peace, man and woman, day and night. The white invasion created an ever greater imbalance, and prophets told them the main deity, "Master of Breath," Hisagita misi, was displeased.

One of the most famous leaders of the Upper Creeks was Alexander McGillivray (ca. 1759–93), son of a Scottish trader in Georgia, Lachlan McGillivray, and a half-French, half-Creek mother named Sehoy Marchand. McGillivray was classically educated in Savannah and Charleston, but when his Loyalist father lost his estate in Georgia during the American Revolution, he chose to live with his mother's people, who had always sided with the British, first against the Spanish and then against the Americans. McGillivray would become known as the

Great Beloved Man among the Creek nation. Abigail Adams would later write of McGillivray, "He is grave and solid, intelligent and much of a Gentleman."

McGillivray rose to be a main chief of the Upper Creeks, negotiating a treaty with Spain in 1784 and with the United States in 1790. The treaty ceremony was accompanied by much hoopla, and the new American government made him a brigadier general and he promoted a rich trade with the Americans and drew traders and speculators into Creek territory. For himself he built a large plantation worked by African slaves, and he encouraged other Creek leaders to do the same. Near the end of his short life, he led attacks on American settlements encroaching on Creek lands.

The Creeks had impressed Hernando de Soto by their height, their proud bearing, and their love of ornament. Their greatest annual celebration was the Green Corn Dance, welcoming fertile crops. While they did not have private ownership of land, the crops produced on the land could be owned privately. Among the seventy or so scattered towns, there was no central government. As more and more white settlers crowded onto their lands, the Creeks, in their widely separated towns, were sharply divided among themselves about how to deal with the incursion and about the future of their people.

The Lower Creeks, especially those living along the Chattahoochee River, led by a chief named William McIntosh, had assimilated much of the lifestyle of the whites and did not feel as threatened by the white settlements. In any case, they did not think a policy of hostility toward whites and the United States was the wisest course. Most had adapted to the new ways and many had intermarried with whites and lived much like other frontier people, taking white names, building cabins, and wearing European-style clothes.

It has often been pointed out that a common source of misunderstanding between native people and white settlers was their different concepts of "ownership" of land. Indians tended to see ownership as tribal, whites as individual. Also, native peoples thought of ownership more in terms of the fruits of the land, the crops, the game, the herbs, the wood, not the dirt itself. Often whites who purchased land from Indians later felt they had been tricked, as native people returned to hunt there.

Few whites understood that under tribal law, landownership was usually passed through the women of a family or village. There is evidence that some whites were taken in by Creek males who pretended to sell land they in fact did not own, aggravating the tension between the races.

The Upper Creeks, living in central and southern Alabama on the Coosa and Tallapoosa rivers, tended to resist white ways. They resented the encroaching Americans from Tennessee in the north and Georgia and the Carolinas in the east. Young warriors among the Upper Creeks were especially angered by the growing presence of whites in their extended territories, and they were encouraged by British agents to resist the Americans.

In the early nineteenth century a militant band of young warriors began to grow among the Upper Creeks, calling themselves Red Sticks because their war clubs were painted red. They were led by a chief named Red Eagle. Ironically, Red Eagle's father had been Scottish, and his mother had both Scottish and French blood. His uncle was Alexander McGillivray. Red Eagle was at most one-eighth Muscogee by blood, but he had been raised among the Muscogees and he identified completely with the most militant of the Upper Creeks. A man of great charisma, eloquence, and courage, he rose to become the main leader of the nationalist and nativist faction. There were many prophets, chiefs, and holy men among the Red Sticks, but Red Eagle was the undisputed leader. The whites called him William Weatherford.

———

THE ANGER that had been growing among many Indian nations since the Europeans arrived in North America was fanned in the early nineteenth century by the Shawnee leader, Tecumseh, and by his brother, known as the Prophet. Since a resounding defeat of the Shawnees and Miamis at Fallen Timbers near Toledo on August 20, 1794, Tecumseh and his brother had been preaching a pan-Indian rebellion against white Americans. Tecumseh was probably one of the most powerful orators in world history. He could mesmerize an audience and stir his listeners to fury. Over the years he had gathered a considerable following in the Great Lakes region and beyond. When the U.S. government offered to buy Shawnee lands, Tecumseh replied, "Sell a country! Why not sell the air, the clouds and the great sea, as well as the earth? Did not the Great Spirit make them all for the use of his children?"

Tecumseh's message was simple: if all the Indian nations would unite into a great confederacy they could drive the whites back to the Atlantic ocean and force the ones who survived the Indian onslaught to return to Europe. Tecumseh preached that this final expulsion would happen only if all native people returned to their old ways, resisted the corruption and seductions of white society, and united from the Great Lakes to the Gulf of Mexico. He was especially angered that so many native women had been corrupted by giving themselves to white men. His brother, the Prophet, said he could foresee this great cleansing war to expel the white evil and leave the continent free for Indians again. But to accomplish this goal the Indians would have to purify themselves and eschew white ways in order to please the Great Spirit and win this ultimate victory. The white race and its diseases had been sent to punish Indians for their failures of character and piety.

In 1811 Tecumseh, whose mother was Creek, made a tour of the South and preached his vision of a vast Indian alliance that would kill all whites or cleanse them from North America. Even Indians who were not inclined to believe him were spellbound by his eloquence and passion. He persuaded the Red Stick warriors to join his mighty cause, promising they would be rid forever of the hated whites with their diseases, whiskey, ignorance, and arrogance.

It is interesting that Tecumseh's sermons were similar to those of the white evangelists of that era in the movement called the Second Great Awakening that was sweeping through Kentucky and Tennessee—another of the many instances where white and Indian cultures imitated and even mirrored each other. The call for an apocalyptic revival seemed to be in the air, however different its stated goals. The white evangelists promised salvation through piety and the blood of Jesus. The Indian prophets and preachers promised a millennium through renewed piety and the blood of whites.

When Tecumseh roused his listeners to the highest pitch of frenzy, as a white evangelist might, they sometimes went into an ecstatic dance called the Dance of the Lakes, which had been learned from the Shawnees. In the euphoria, they felt all-powerful and invulnerable. Tecumseh was especially intent on converting to his cause a leader of the Creeks called Big Warrior, Menawa. But Big Warrior was skeptical of Tecumseh's claims of divine power, foresight, and destiny. Enraged that his authority was questioned, Tecumseh shouted, "Let the white race perish. They seize your land; they corrupt your women; they trample on the bones of your dead! Back whence they came, upon a trail of blood, they must be driven . . . Burn their dwellings—destroy their stock—slay their wives and children, that the very breed may perish."

When Big Warrior remained unconvinced, Tecumseh jabbed his finger into the chief's face and cried, "Your blood is white . . . You do not believe the Great Spirit sent me. You shall believe it. I will leave directly and go straight to Detroit. When I get there I will stamp my foot upon the ground and shake down every house in Tookabatcha."

As it turned out 1811–12 was the year of the great earthquakes in the central United States. After Tecumseh left, the earth began rocking and rumbling and the houses in the village of Tookabatchee began to shake and collapse. Even those who had not believed Tecumseh before became convinced of his divine powers and vision. More warriors, including Menawa, began to join the Red Stick faction.

Another event that appeared to the Creeks to be a portent of divine will was the outbreak of war between Britain and the United States in 1812. Tecumseh had been working with the British in the years leading up to the War of 1812. Britain had been arming Indians all along and encouraging them to attack Americans. The British had never evacuated many of their forts in the Great Lakes area, even though they had promised to do so in the peace treaty of 1783 ending the Revolution. Now events seemed to be falling into place for a great coordinated attack on the American settlements from Canada to the Gulf of Mexico. Tecumseh, Red Eagle, Big Warrior, and other Indian leaders believed the time had come for an all-out campaign against the hated United States.

As small raids were made against the white settlements in the border areas of Georgia and Tennessee, the settlers built blockhouses and forts and armed themselves. The war with Britain stirred fear and patriotic fervor among the Americans on the frontier. The alliance between the Spanish in Florida and the militant Indians, and the British in Canada and on the high seas, sent a chill through all the settlements. "To mock the Americans' hunger for their land" the Indians would sometimes stuff dirt in the mouths of whites they had killed.

The civil war that broke out between the Upper and Lower Creeks in 1813 sealed the fate of the confederation. The trigger of the civil war was a chief named Little Warrior, who, returning from a visit with the Shawnees, was told by some Chickasaws that hostilities had broken out between the Upper Creeks and the United States. Thrilled by the news, Little Warrior and his band killed seven white families on the frontier. The Indian agent Benjamin Hawkins demanded the murderers be punished, and the tribal council agreed. But the warriors sent out to do the execution had to fight a battle to accomplish their task. Red Sticks killed nine of the executioners, burned several villages friendly to the whites, and slaughtered a lot of livestock.

A bigger battle began with an attack by whites and half bloods against the hostile Creeks at Burnt Corn, a village about a hundred miles north of Pensacola. The party of settlers raided a group of Red Sticks led by Chief Peter McQueen, who was also part white. The Red Sticks escaped, leaving behind most of their ammunition. The whites sought safety in a nearby fort built by Samuel Mims, who was himself part Creek.

Mims was a prosperous merchant who had built his store and trading post about forty miles northeast of Mobile. His stronghold was an acre of land enclosed by log pickets, with two gates and five hundred gun ports about forty-two inches from the ground. A militia of 120 men, led by Major Daniel Beasley, a lawyer with little military training or experience, had been stationed at the fort because of the threat from the Red Sticks. On August 30, 1813, there were nearly three hundred friendly Indians, mostly Lower Creeks, mixed bloods, and whites taking refuge at the fort, along with three hundred slaves.

On August 30 Major Beasley sent out no patrols, posted no sentries. Apparently he felt there was no real threat from the Red Sticks. The day was very hot and humid, and the heat made everyone reluctant to move. Children played their games on the ground inside the fort, and soldiers slouched on benches in precious shade. Since no hostile Indians had been seen in several days, at least one of the gates was left open. Everyone waited for the drum roll that signaled the noon meal was ready inside the fort.

The day before, two slaves who had wandered a few miles into the woods away from the fort, ran back and claimed, all out of breath, that they had seen Indians in war paint. Major Beasley, who had sighted no hostile Indians himself, assumed the slaves were trying to create excitement and stir up trouble. Instead of directing a patrol to investigate the report, he ordered the two slaves whipped for lying, and did not even bother to close the gate of the fort.

During the night, the painted Indians the slaves had spotted, plus about a thousand more, approached the fort and lay down in the brush and trees, just out of sight. Their leader, Red Eagle, had told them to remain still for hours after the sun rose, waiting for the drum signal that called those in the fort to dinner at noon. They watched the soldiers saunter about in the heat and listened to the children laugh and call out in their play. According to some reports, Major Beasley was drunk.

The instant the drum sounded the children quit their games and ran to eat, followed by the soldiers. The Red Sticks rose from their cover and charged the stockade, screaming their awful war cries. Beasley ran to close the front gate, but the gate was stuck. As he strained to shove the gate closed, the Red Sticks rushed in and clubbed him to death. Trampling the major's body, the attackers flooded into the fort.

Each of the Red Sticks carried a rifle or musket, a war club, and a bow and arrows. The arrows were tipped with steel spikes. A survivor named Thomas Holmes later said, "With few exceptions they were naked . . . It is impossible to imagine people so horribly painted. Some were painted half red and half black . . . Their faces were painted so as to show their terrible contortions."

Soldiers and settlers ran for their rifles, grabbed butcher knives, shovels, anything that could be used for defense. A few of the Red Sticks were killed, including five prophets who had promised that the Great Spirit would make white men's bullets split and curve harmlessly around Red Stick bodies. The deaths of their prophets gave momentary pause to their followers but only for a few seconds. Returning to the attack with renewed fury to avenge the killing of their spiritual leaders, the warriors butchered every white person in sight. A number of settlers took refuge in the main building inside the fort, and the Red Sticks set the building on fire, then shot or stabbed or clubbed the survivors who ran coughing out of the smoke and flames.

William Weatherford (Red Eagle) later said he was blackmailed into attacking the whites. The Red Sticks had threatened to kill his wife and children if he did not join their war. He claimed that he tried to stop the killing once it was clear the fort had been overrun, but the warriors were so consumed with passion for killing they threatened to murder their own leader if he stood in their way. Women and children were clubbed to death and hacked to pieces. Scalps and ears, noses and private parts, were cut away from bodies while some were still alive. The friendly Indians and many of the slaves were killed also, though a number of slaves were taken prisoner to serve the Red Sticks.

A dozen soldiers cut a hole through the stockade wall and escaped into the woods. They were the only other survivors. Reports of the number present and slaughtered at Fort Mims vary. According to Thomas Holmes, 553 were killed, including 453 women and children. Women who were pregnant had babies cut from their wombs. All corpses were stripped of their clothes and scalped. Finally, the bodies were left to swell and decay in the relentless sun.

A Major Kennedy, who led a group of soldiers to the site a few days later, found a nightmare of decaying, mutilated bodies, partly eaten by animals and pecked by vultures. A mirage of flies hovered in the stench over the burned and plundered fort. Kennedy later wrote, "Indians, negroes, white men, women and children lay in one promiscuous ruin. All were scalped, and the females of every age were butchered in a manner which neither decency nor language will permit me to describe. The main building was burned to ashes, which were filled with bones. The plains and woods around were covered with dead bodies."

———

NEWS OF the Fort Mims atrocity spread quickly all along the frontier and across the United States. Because so many white settlers, slaves, and militiamen were killed, the conflict among the Creeks was no longer a civil war but an attack on the United States, its citizens, and soldiers. And because the Red Sticks were encouraged and in some cases supplied by the British, their fight became part of the War of 1812. Without knowing it, the Red Sticks, with that killing in August of 1813, doomed not only their movement but the future of the extended Creek Nation. Free to hunt and roam over a vast territory before, the Red Sticks triggered a course of events that had been waiting to happen. In retrospect, history often takes on a character of inevitability. What happened was going to happen. The Creeks were going to lose their large tract of land that stood in the way of white settlement of the West. But the massacre at Fort Mims accelerated the process by focusing the attention of the bordering states, the federal government, and men who were hungry for expansion on the millions of acres of choice Muscogee land. The massacre sent ripples of terror across the American frontier. A nation threatened by the British from the Atlantic and Canada, and unofficially by the Spanish in Florida, found itself threatened in the interior and the Southwest by the fanatical followers of Tecumseh and the other pan-Indian nationalist prophets. The killings at Fort Mims sounded an alarm that could not be ignored, especially in the Tennessee country, where a number of settlers had already been killed by Red Stick raiders.

THE COMMANDER of the Tennessee militia was Major General Andrew Jackson of Nashville. A man of fierce temper and inexorable will, Jackson had been wounded in a feud with Thomas Hart Benton and his brothers in Nashville in September 1813. Jackson had fought a number of duels in his life and was known never to back away from a threat or ignore a slight or possible slight. The historian Daniel Walker Howe tells us, "Even by frontier standards Jackson possessed a particularly touchy sense of honor." As a lawyer, judge, former senator, entrepreneur, militia commander, and wealthy landowner, he was well known in Nashville and all over Tennessee as a leader who inspired and demanded unswerving loyalty. Though he had little military training or experience, he had won the position of commander of the state militia through his political connections and his undoubted gifts for leadership. In the fight with the Bentons, Jackson had been shot in the shoulder, and for a few days it appeared he might not recover. But to everyone's surprise he did not die and was mending slowly at his estate outside Nashville called the Hermitage, nursed by his beloved wife, Rachel Donelson Robards Jackson, when he learned of the massacre at Fort Mims.

However weak from unhealed wounds and pain, he recognized this was the opportunity he had been waiting for all his life. Since his boyhood in the Carolinas, when he had been wounded and imprisoned by the British in the Revolution, he had dreamed of military glory and of revenge on the British. The Red Sticks of the Creek Nation were not Red Coats, but they *were* encouraged by the British and supplied with arms and ammunition by the enemies of the United States, including the Spanish in Florida. Jackson craved military glory and suddenly the opportunity was at hand.

But it was not just military fame that Jackson craved. From the time of his youth when as a young man he had migrated to Nashville, then in the far western part of North Carolina, he had nursed a passion for the expansion of the American union into the West. A man of unlimited ambition, vanity, and determination, he was also committed to the new democratic experiment called the United States of America. It was in the west of the new country that this son of a Scots Irish weaver and a poor farmer had risen so quickly. He had married Rachel, the woman of his dreams, after her first husband abandoned her. He had acquired much land, many slaves, and numerous friends and followers. And while he demanded and secured positions of power and leadership, he was committed to the ideal of a society where ordinary people could prosper and rise, free to go about their lives as they chose. Andrew Jackson was, first to last, a seriously flawed man, but his dedication to democratic ideals was deep and lasting. What he sought most of all was more territory in the West, into which that ideal could spread, take root, and flower. Standing in the way were the despised British, the Spanish in Florida, and their Indian allies. On a personal level Jackson was fond of Indians. He had many Indian friends, and he and Rachel adopted two Indian boys to raise as their own sons. But Jackson also viewed the Indians, and especially the Muscogees, with their wide land claims, as obstacles in the way of the vision he shared with Jefferson—of a continental United States populated by whites.

———

ANDREW JACKSON, later called Old Hickory by the whites, and Sharp Knife and Old Mad Jackson by the Creeks, was born March 13, 1767, near Waxhaw on the North Carolina–South Carolina border. His father died before he was born, and Jackson's mother, Elizabeth Hutchinson Jackson, served as housekeeper for a prosperous relative while she raised her three sons. Throughout his boyhood he was always aware that he was a "poor relation." His mother inspired him to be independent, but careful to cultivate friends, and to think of himself as a leader. From the beginning he had a terrible temper and never turned away from a fight. His character showed a relentless will, a sometime brutality that alternated with great loyalty and tenderness toward his friends, women and children, and the weak and dependent.

Studying the life of Jackson, one cannot help but feel there is an inevitability about him. Jackson seemed always driven by forces much larger than himself. He was the personification and genius of the spirit of the frontier. He was the essence of the pioneer will raised to the second power. He seems at once a creation of history possessed by its demons and the creator of much of the history of his era and region. The perfect expression of the will and passion and aspiration of the people of his times, he became one of the most popular presidents in the history of the United States. Americans have been described as both bullies and saints, and the label fits nobody better than Andrew Jackson.

Jackson's mother had thought he would become a Presbyterian minister because of his way with words, the force with which he could speak and persuade. At an early age Jackson read the Bible cover to cover. His favorite work of fiction, Oliver Goldsmith's *Vicar of Wakefield,* concerned a clergyman. But the wildness and fury in Jackson made it unlikely he would devote his life to the pulpit. When at age thirteen he was ordered to clean a British officer's boots, he refused, was beaten, cut across the wrist and cheek with a saber, and thrown in prison. His mother somehow raised the money to ransom him, then died of cholera while trying to help her nephews, who were prisoners of war in Charleston. After the deaths of his mother and brothers, who also died of wounds and disease in the Revolution, Jackson developed a dislike and distrust of the British that stayed with him for the rest of his life.

At the age of fourteen Andrew Jackson was on his own. Later he would say, "The memory of my mother and her teachings were after all the only capital I had to start in life, and on that capital I have made my way."

His mother had advised him to avoid quarrels, but it took him many years to learn to follow her admonition, and those who knew Jackson later in life discovered that he could fake temper tantrums to get his way with people.

While Jackson was tall and lean and tough—about six feet one—he also suffered from various ailments and infections. All his life he seemed vulnerable to attacks of dysentery and other abdominal complaints, and the wounds he received in duels did not help to strengthen his constitution. At the same time he had a relentless and unbending will power and greater strength than any around him.

Not long after his mother's death Jackson inherited "three hundred or four hundred pounds sterling" from the estate of his grandfather in Scotland. Journeying to Charleston to claim this small fortune, Jackson got caught up in the festive spirit of the port city, celebrating the end of British occupation, and ended up gambling away all of his inheritance. With only his fine horse left, he returned to Waxhaw and briefly attended a country school. Soon after that he spent a term teaching at a similar school. From his parents he inherited two hundred acres but discovered that the hard farmwork that had killed his father was not to his liking.

The way for an ambitious young man on the frontier to rise in the 1780s was to study and practice law. According to H. W. Brands, "In the 1780s the law was almost as much a frontier as the western reaches of the national domain." Formerly the most successful lawyers had been Tories, and now that they were gone, newcomers with much or little training rushed in to fill the vacuum. Anyone who could talk his way past a board of examiners could be licensed to hang out his shingle.

Jackson apprenticed himself to study law in Salisbury, North Carolina, with one Spruce Macay. While studying law books in Macay's library, Jackson and the other law students lived in the village tavern. By day the young men learned to search titles, file court papers, trace precedents, and do the legwork for Macay. By night they caroused, played practical jokes, consorted with the local prostitutes. Jackson in particular acquired a reputation for recklessness.

He continued his legal education with a Revolutionary War veteran named Colonel John Stokes. Jackson was a quick learner and Stokes a man of influence, and within six months the North Carolina Superior Court of Law and Equity examined the twenty-year-old Andrew and pronounced him fit to practice law.

Just as he began his career as a traveling attorney in the back country, Jackson was sued for disorderly conduct. This did not help him attract clients and he found it hard to pay his debts. Local legend says that during this time he once slipped away from an inn owned by one John Lister without paying his bill. Lister was unable to collect but kept the bill, and years later when Jackson became a hero for his victory at New Orleans in January 1815, Lister wrote across the yellowed bill "Paid at the battle of New Orleans."

In those days Jackson was often seen at parties, receptions, balls, and other social occasions. His tall, lean looks and his fine clothes were noticed. However poor he might be he always seemed dressed in the latest fashions and mounted on a spirited horse. Years later one Annie Jarret Rutherford would recall: "He always dressed neat and tidy and carried himself as if he was a rich man's son . . . He was full six feet tall and very slender, but yet of such straightness of form and such proud and graceful carriage as to make him look well-proportioned . . . when he talked to you he always looked straight into your own eyes . . . there was always something about him I cannot describe except to say that it was a *presence*, or a kind of majesty I never saw in any other young man."

BENJAMIN FRANKLIN had said that the West held the key to the American future. By the time Jackson was practicing law in North Carolina in the 1780s, the valleys of the Tennessee and Cumberland rivers across the mountains were being settled. Many made the journey from Virginia down the Holston and then the Tennessee River all the way to the Ohio, then up the Ohio fifteen miles to the mouth of the Cumberland, and up the Cumberland several hundred miles to French Lick, which soon became known as Nashville, founded by James Robertson, one of the great men of the American frontier. He had known Daniel Boone at Watauga, and he had joined Richard Henderson to settle in the Transylvania land on the Cumberland. According to the historian John Buchanan, he "could . . . travel thousands of miles alone through perilous wilderness, establish a settlement deep in hostile country, treat with or fight Indians as the occasion demanded, and a myriad of things necessary for survival on a frontier." Robertson would prove an important mentor to Andrew Jackson.

While the area that became Tennessee was at that time claimed by North Carolina, the Spanish governor in New Orleans, Esteban Miró, colluded with the traitorous American general James Wilkinson to make the Mississippi Valley a territory allied with Spain. Wilkinson encouraged the new settlers on the Cumberland to refer to their region as the Mero [Miro] District.

In pursuit of his own fortune and future, Jackson accepted an appointment as solicitor for the western region of North Carolina in the new village of Nashville. He and his friend John McNairy set out westward through the wilderness, first to the town of Jonesborough and then to the Cumberland. On the way Jackson got into an argument with the distinguished lawyer Waightstill Avery over some legal point and ended up fighting a duel with the celebrated veteran of the Revolution. Duels at the time could be sparked by relatively trivial events on the frontier. Luckily the savvy Avery delayed the confrontation until Jackson's temper had cooled. Both men agreed to fire and miss, and the affair ended with a handshake.

At Nashville, the new settlement on the Cumberland, Jackson fell in love with the married Rachel Robards. She was described as having a "beautifully molded form, lustrous black eyes, dark glossy hair, full red lips, brunette complexion, though of brilliant coloring, a sweet oval face rippling with smiles and dimples." Separated from her unfaithful husband, Rachel met Jackson when he stayed at her mother's boardinghouse. Robards returned from Kentucky to patch things up with his estranged wife and became jealous of Rachel's friendship with the young lawyer from North Carolina. When Jackson learned of Robards's suspicions, he protested his and Rachel's innocence and, of course, challenged the husband to a duel. Robards refused, and Jackson moved out of the Donelson house to Kasper Mansker's Station nearby. But innocent or not, Jackson was already deeply attached to Rachel Robards, who all agreed had been badly treated by her husband. Around 1789 Jackson determined to marry Rachel himself and she decided to trust her future to the tall, passionate lawyer.

It is not clear when Rachel and Andrew became lovers, but when Robards once again threatened to return from Kentucky and claim his wife, the lovers decided Rachel should go to Natchez on the Mississippi, beyond the husband's reach. Mrs. Donelson accompanied her daughter on the trip, and when Jackson saw mother and daughter safely established in Natchez, he returned to Nashville.

At some point between 1790 and 1791, Rachel and Jackson returned to Nashville as man and wife. Hearing that Robards had sued for divorce on the grounds of adultery, they claimed to have been married in Natchez and by the spring of 1791 had begun their married life in Nashville. However irregular their courtship and marriage had been, they were so deeply in love they assumed any questions or rumors would fade over time. What they did not know was that Robards's proceedings for divorce had been held up. The Virginia legislature granted Robards the right to sue for divorce on December 20, 1790, but the proceedings were delayed. The divorce was not actually granted until September 27, 1793, after Kentucky had become a separate state.

On a visit to Jonesborough in 1793, Jackson discovered that the divorce from Robards had only then been granted and that for at least two years he and Rachel had been living together illegally. Hoping to put the issue behind them once and for all, the couple had a quiet ceremony before a justice of the peace January 18, 1794. Later, when he was running for office, Jackson's political opponents would dig up the story and use it to smear him.

But as H. W. Brands writes, "The union, however irregularly accomplished, provided Jackson an emotional security he had never experienced. Fatherless since birth, motherless since his early teens . . . Jackson made Rachel the emotional center of his universe."

With his business partner, John Overton, Jackson bought and sold large tracts of land in the region. With little American money in circulation, land became the medium of exchange on the frontier. Six hundred forty acres, or a square mile, was the most common unit of trade. Jackson hoped to prosper as a merchant or supplier for the Nashville region but found himself so deeply in debt, in part because cash was hard to come by, that he had to abandon the business.

Already a public figure around Nashville, Jackson became close friends with a powerful political figure named William Blount. When Blount was expelled from the U.S. Senate, for secretly plotting to take Louisiana and Florida from the Spanish, he helped Jackson win the appointment to replace him. Jackson had already proven to be a memorable public speaker. Avoiding the manner of an orator, he spoke to his listeners in precise, calm, persuasive sentences. But when angered, he spoke in a rush of profanity and denunciation, attempting to demolish any opponent, and then would halt, as though confused by his own intensity.

One of Jackson's greatest rivals was John Sevier, a Revolutionary War hero, the first governor of Tennessee. Before he became governor of the new state, Sevier had held the cherished post of general of the regional militia. When Governor Sevier tried to give the position to a political ally, it triggered a long feud between Jackson and the hero of the Battle of Kings Mountain.

While Jackson served in the U.S. Senate in Philadelphia, he came to despise the Federalists with their pro-British sympathies. Jefferson, who presided over the Senate as vice president, agreed with Jackson's sentiments. But the Sage of Monticello was not impressed with Jackson's manner and temper. Later he would question Jackson's fitness for high office. Jefferson, with his courteous, even courtly, manner, his patrician birth and intellectual preoccupations, would say to Daniel Webster of Old Hickory, "He is one of the most unfit men I know of for such a place [the presidency]. He has very little respect for law or constitutions . . . he is a dangerous man." At least that is what Webster, an enemy of Jackson, would later claim. But in a letter to Jackson on December 18, 1823, Jefferson wrote, "I recall with pleasure the remembrance of our joint labors while in the Senate together in times of great trial and of hard battling. Battles indeed of words, not of blood, as those you have since fought so much for your own glory and that of your country. With the assurance that my attamts [attachments] continue undiminished, accept that of my great respect and consdn." It is likely that over the years Jefferson had come to view Jackson in a different light; the man from Tennessee proved an important agent for realizing Jefferson's dream of a more democratic country reaching far into the West.

But Jackson had no taste for serving in the legislature. The endless delays and wrangling frustrated and infuriated him. He was a man of action, not of committees and negotiation. Years later Jefferson would supposedly tell Daniel Webster that in the Senate Jackson could hardly speak he was so choked with rage. Jackson would always prove more effective as an executive than as a legislator.

In 1798 Jackson resigned from the Senate and returned to Rachel and his business interests in Nashville. He believed in his destiny but could see that his route to glory did not lead through the legislature. Year by year Jackson's stature in Nashville and in the region grew. He had become a Royal Arch Mason. He seemed to know everyone, and his friends were as devoted as his enemies were determined to oppose him. Perhaps hoping to silence Jackson as a political rival, John Sevier appointed him to the Tennessee Superior Court of Law and Equity, which convened in different towns cross the state. It was a position of dignity and authority, both of which Jackson craved.

Once when a notorious bully defied the court, Jackson left the bench, had himself sworn in as a deputy, grabbed a pistol, shed his judicial robe, and stalked the villain into the street. The culprit, Russell Bean, had cut off the ears of his infant stepchild in a drunken rage. Everyone was afraid of him. A crowd gathered to observe the defiant criminal, but Jackson pushed them aside, held out the pistol and shouted, "Surrender, you infernal villain, this very instant, or I'll blow you through." To everyone's astonishment the bully handed over his weapons and submitted to arrest. When asked later why he had given in so meekly to Judge Jackson, the miscreant Bean answered, "Why, when he came up, I looked him in the eye, and I saw shoot. There wasn't shoot in nary other eye in the crowd. So I says to myself, says I: Hoss, it's about time to sing small, and so I did." The anecdote is only one of many where Jackson demonstrated his unusual presence and authority at dramatic moments, over an individual or over a crowd.

Serving as a judge on the superior court circuit, Jackson was often away from Rachel and his home in Nashville and some of her letters to him about his absence seem virtually hysterical. He was her main source of security, and he was away as much as he was home. The pay for his position was not great, and he was too preoccupied on the bench to look after his other interests properly. Jackson believed it was his duty to serve the public and to lead. But the judgeship, he came to realize, was not a stepping-stone to greater glory.

Luckily, in 1802 the command of the Tennessee militia became a possibility. Jackson had long believed that the commander of the militia had the most important position in a time of crisis. Washington, for instance, had risen to fame and greatness first as the commander of the Virginia militia in the Indian wars. Though he was trained as a lawyer and served as a judge, Jackson had always dreamed of military honors and saw himself in the company of Washington, of his rival John Sevier, and of Julius Caesar. Jackson also had special admiration for Napoleon, not only for his brilliant success on the battlefield but for his leadership as well, which had brought order and purpose to his country ravaged by the excesses of the French Revolution.

At that time the major general of the Tennessee militia was elected by the military officers. Jackson believed he could keep his judgeship while serving as militia commander. The problem was that John Sevier had completed his third term as governor and was required by law to step down. It made perfect sense that Sevier, known to the Indians as Noli-chucky Jack, should again assume command of the state militia.

When the votes for the position were counted, Sevier had won most of the votes in the eastern part of the state and Jackson most of the votes cast in the Cumberland region to the west. To everyone's surprise the result was a tie. Sevier suggested they vote again, but Jackson declared such a second ballot unconstitutional. The tie must be broken by the governor.

The new governor, Archibald Roan, had been Jackson's friend since they both studied for the bar in North Carolina and were licensed to practice on the same day. Roan did not forget his old friend and cast his vote for Jackson. On April 1, 1802, Jackson was commissioned major general of the Tennessee militia. In an objective sense Jackson had little qualification for such a command. Except for his work as a courier in the Revolution, he had no experience as a soldier. He had not served in the ranks or as a junior officer. He had no training in strategy or tactics. Most of his experience was in court or in business. Instead, Jackson had a relentless ambition, an unusual air of authority and audacity, and extraordinary intelligence, a flair for language, and a belief in his destiny and the future of his country. He also had an uncanny ability to inspire loyalty in other men. His sense of himself was intimately connected to the course of the Republic. He fit the pattern of other self-made generals in American history such as Daniel Morgan and Nathan Bedford Forrest. If there is such a person as a "natural soldier," Jackson was it, as he was to prove at a bend in the Tallapoosa River in 1814.

In the decade following his election as major general of the militia Jackson became increasingly prominent in the affairs of the region. In 1803 he quarreled bitterly and publicly with John Sevier, and the following year he resigned as judge of the superior court. In 1805 he got drawn into the scandal known as the Burr Conspiracy.

Aaron Burr was a man of great charm, vice president of the United States from 1801 to 1805, who, it is thought, had planned, in cahoots with General James Wilkinson, to create an independent state in the Old Southwest with close ties to Spain. Burr tried to persuade Jackson to support him but was trapped in his own scheme and denounced by Wilkinson, an even greater scoundrel. It was discovered years after his death in 1825 that Wilkinson had been in the pay of the Spanish. He had sworn allegiance to the Spanish and for fifteen years had collected two thousand dollars annually as "Agent 13 of the Spanish government." The affair may have strengthened Jackson's belief in the importance of the Union and his permanent distrust of the issue of states' rights. To Jackson, then and later, the unity of the nation was more important than any single region. He believed the states could realize their destiny only as a united entity and that as separate sovereign powers they would only create war and chaos. For him, the struggle for popular rights, and for the prominence of the United States among other nations, was part of the struggle for North America, all of North America.

In 1806 Jackson became involved in a quarrel that had to do with betting on his famous racehorse, Truxton. He ended up killing one Charles Dickinson in a duel and was himself wounded in the duel but recovered. The duel and the death of Dickinson provided fuel for Jackson's rivals and enemies, and though he carried Dickinson's bullet the rest of his life, rumors that Jackson had cheated in the duel floated around Nashville for years.

One of the contradictions in Jackson's character was that while he could be harsh, even cruel, when challenged or angered, he was always gentle, even tender, to his wife, Rachel, to children and horses, and to slaves. He went out of his way to protect and help those in his care. He never neglected the welfare of his wards. Nicholas Trist, who would later serve as Jackson's private secretary, would tell James Parton, Jackson's early biographer, "There was more of the woman in his nature than in that of any man I ever knew—more of a woman's tenderness toward children, and sympathy with them."

———

ALMOST EVERYTHING about the War of 1812 is a paradox. It has been called the Second War of Independence, yet the United States lost more battles than it won against the British. Not one of the issues for which war was declared in 1812 was resolved when the peace treaty was signed in Ghent, Belgium, on December 24, 1814. Overall American military performance was poor, and the British would invade Maryland, rout the Americans at Bladensburg August 24, 1814, and burn the Capitol and White House in Washington. But some of the major military heroes in American history would emerge from the war. And after the war, thanks to Jackson, most Americans felt they had won a great victory against the British Empire.

There were at least four leading causes of the War of 1812: (1) the British interference with American trade with Europe; (2) the British impressment of American sailors to serve on British warships; (3) the arming of Indians in the West by the British to attack American settlements; and (4) the bitter division in American politics between the Federalists of New England and the Democrats of the southern and middle Atlantic states.

Throughout the 1790s and early nineteenth century, Federalists in the Northeast had favored closer ties with England, while Democrats such as Jefferson often sought closer relations with the French. During the long continental war with Napoleon, the British tried to prevent the profitable American trade with France, and France sought to prevent American ships from supplying Britain with needed goods. Because of the British impressment of sailors, their practice of supplying Indians in the West with arms and encouraging native attacks on Americans, the Jefferson (1801–9) and then Madison (1809–17) administrations looked more favorably on the French. To prevent American trade with the French, the

British with their powerful navy blockaded both American and European ports. Jefferson's "peaceful coercion," the Embargo Act of 1807, which closed all American ports, was a failure, and subsequent policies of the Democrats, favoring the French, made war almost inevitable. In the words of the historian Walter LaFeber, "Americans were more dependent on British textiles, iron, and steel than the British were on American goods" such as tobacco and cotton. At that time the British sold Americans twice as much as they bought from the United States while the French purchased seven times as much from the Americans as they sold them.

During the long campaign against Napoleon that culminated with victory at Waterloo in 1815, the British needed more sailors than were available for their vast navy. Since many of their former sailors had left the navy to join the American merchant fleet and sometimes the American navy, British warships began stopping American vessels and impressing their former sailors, or those they accused of being former sailors, back into service. Sometimes American citizens were seized in the practice John Quincy Adams called "this authorized system of kidnapping upon the ocean." Most Americans were outraged as the practice continued. John Quincy Adams also observed that "the British look upon us as a *foreign nation,* and we must look upon them in the same light."

Though the U.S. Congress declared war on Britain on June 18, 1812, the nation was embarrassingly unprepared to fight against the greatest army and navy on earth. American privateers attacked British ships, but the British navy retaliated with a vengeance. By 1813 what warships the Americans had were bottled up in harbors by the blockade. The United States had few regular soldiers, and in any case the Democrats preferred to rely on state and local militias.

The contention between the Federalists of the North and the Democrats of the middle Atlantic and southern states was almost as bitter as the conflict between the United States and Britain. New England merchants, who made considerable profits from the war in Europe, objected to the disruption of their trade. Federalists adamantly opposed "Mr. Madison's War." The resentment against the Democrats and the war was so great in New England that in 1814 representatives from those states would meet in Hartford to discuss, among other issues, seceding from the Union.

Powerful politicians in Washington, collectively referred to as the War Hawks, including Henry Clay of Kentucky, Peter B. Porter of New York, Felix Grundy of Tennessee, and John C. Calhoun and Langdon Cheves of South Carolina, hoped the war with Great Britain would enable the United States to claim Florida from Britain's ally, Spain. "War hawks wore black armbands" to show their mood. But Napoleon's promises to the United States of support against Britain proved empty, as the emperor struggled for his own survival on the continent.

Though ill prepared for any extended conflict, the United States was fortunate that Britain had to concentrate most of her forces on the fight with France. In the words of Walter LaFeber, "The British . . . had three fighting *ships* for every U.S. *cannon*" in 1812. Americans suffered humiliating defeats when they attempted to invade Canada, and General William Hull surrendered Detroit without firing a shot on August 16, 1812. It began to seem that Americans could do nothing right.

And then on September 16, 1813, Lieutenant Oliver Hazard Perry (1785–1819), commanding the ship *Niagara* on Lake Erie, won a significant battle over the British Great Lakes navy. "We have met the enemy and they are ours," he reported to General William Henry Harrison. On October 5, 1813, General William Henry Harrison defeated the British and their Indian allies, including the leader Tecumseh, at the Battle of the Thames in Ontario. When the other Indians there realized their great leader had been killed, a member of the Kentucky militia recalled, they "gave the loudest yells I ever heard from human beings and that ended the fight." The next year American forces led by General Jacob Jennings Brown (1775–1828) and General Winfield Scott (1786–1866) gave a good account of themselves on the Niagara frontier at the Battles of Chippawa and Lundy's Lane, on July 5 and July 25, 1814, respectively. Those battles helped shore up American confidence, even as British forces landed in Maryland and burned Washington on August 24, 1814. Flames from the conflagration could be seen almost thirty miles away.

Oddly enough a sudden hurricane hit the British forces marching out of Washington and wreaked more damage on His Majesty's army than the Americans had. When the British mounted an attack on Fort McHenry and Baltimore a few weeks later, they were repulsed by a vigorous defense. The lawyer Francis Scott Key (1779–1843), on board a

British warship to negotiate the release of prisoners, witnessed the prolonged bombardment of Fort McHenry on September 13–14 and wrote "The Star Spangled Banner" to commemorate the American victory.

Another significant naval battle won by the Americans, but often forgotten, was fought by Captain Thomas Macdonough (1784–1825) near Plattsburgh, New York, on Lake Champlain on September 11, 1814. A major British force, led by Sir George Prevost, governor general of Canada, was sailing down the lake to attack forts in New York. Commanding the ship *Saratoga,* with its twenty-six guns, Macdonough defeated the British *Confiance* with its thirty-seven guns. Prevost and the British were forced to turn back to Canada. Macdonough has been called "the best American naval officer" in the war by Donald R. Hickey. And Andrew Jackson's defeat of the Red Stick Creeks, allies of the Spanish and British, at Horseshoe Bend in Alabama on March 27, 1814, went a long way toward strengthening the American presence on the Gulf Coast.

While there is a good bit of truth to J. W. Pratt's assertion that "popular mythology soon converted defeat into victory," it should be remembered that given the attacks on American ships by the superior British navy, and the attacks on American western settlements by the British army and their Indian allies, just maintaining the status quo could be seen as an important victory. Improbable as it may seem to some, the War of 1812 went a long way toward restoring American confidence in its independence. The United States had fought another war with the British Empire and survived intact. The war may have seemed insignificant to the British, many of whose citizens were hardly aware they were fighting the United States, but to Americans maintaining the status quo antebellum was victory enough. The calm confidence and leadership of Madison throughout the war should not be underrated. The elderly John Adams would comment, "Notwithstand[ing] a thousand Faults and Blunders, [Madison's administration] acquired more glory and established more Union than all the three Predecessors, Washington, Adams, Jefferson, put together."

American negotiators at Ghent, Belgium, in the summer and fall of 1814 successfully opposed all British demands for additional territory on the North American continent. John Quincy Adams impressed the British negotiators at Ghent with his eloquence, his erudition, and his firmness. The American team, which included Henry Clay and Albert Gallatin, made few concessions to British demands. In a literal sense America ended the war just where it had begun, but in a significant way the young nation came out of the conflict with a new national pride and sense of purpose, as though it had proven itself anew. The treaty was signed December 24, 1814, but before the news traveled across the Atlantic Andrew Jackson delivered a resounding defeat to the British army led by General Sir Edward Packenham at New Orleans on January 8, 1815. Though Americans got no concessions from the British about impressment of sailors on the high seas, the issue was moot anyway with the end of the Napoleonic Wars. And though there would continue to be conflicts with British-armed Indians on the Northwest frontier, Tecumseh and his pan-Indian confederation had been destroyed. The United States was about to enter, it was said, an "era of good feeling," inspired by an ever greater preoccupation with expansion into the West.

WHEN WAR broke out between the United States and Britain in 1812, Andrew Jackson was left on the sidelines, far out west in Tennessee. For years Jackson had felt it was his destiny to achieve military fame, but until that point the opportunity had eluded him. In the meantime he ordered musters and rallies of the state militia and waited. A new governor of Tennessee was elected, Jackson's friend and ally, Willie Blount, half brother of William Blount.

Jackson had great faith in the Tennessee militia, even though it remained untested in war. He had noticed during the Revolution that ordinary men, poor men, made better soldiers than the rich. "In the day of danger the wealthy enjoy too much ease to court danger." He trusted the plain farmers and laborers who made up his forces to do as he asked when called upon.

Before the War of 1812 broke out, the "defeat" (there were twice as many white casualties as Indian) of the Shawnees by William Henry Harrison at the Tippecanoe River in 1811 had forced Tecumseh, who was not present at that battle, to form an even closer alliance with the British. As the war began, the Indians with British aid won a number of victories against Americans in the Northwest, at Prophetstown, Mackinaw, and

Detroit. And in the South both the Spanish in Florida and the British encouraged Red Stick Creeks to attack American settlements. News that a large group of whites had been murdered near the mouth of the Chicago River reached Jackson in Tennessee.

"The disaster of the northwestern army should rouse from his apathy every man," Jackson told his militia recruits. "These are the times that distinguish the real friend of his country from the town-meeting bawler and the sunshine patriot." About three thousand men volunteered for the militia, giving Tennessee its Volunteer State nickname. Jackson was ordered to take his troops to New Orleans to defend that important port city. But when they reached Natchez, Jackson was directed to halt by none other than General James Wilkinson, commander of the army of the West, who had been found not guilty in a 1811 court-martial. Little as he trusted Wilkinson, Jackson had no choice but to follow his orders. While waiting in Natchez, Jackson received another letter, from Secretary of War John Armstrong, ordering him to disband his troops and return home. His weapons and supplies were to be forwarded on to Wilkinson. Jackson wrote to Armstrong, protesting, among other things, the surrender of the militia arms to Wilkinson. Surely his men were not intended to return unarmed through the dangerous Mississippi territory. But the orders stood, and Jackson transferred his weapons and supplies to Wilkinson, whom he hated because of the 1805 Burr conspiracy.

Jackson ordered his officers to give up their horses to the wounded, and he walked with them. "It is my duty," he wrote to Rachel, "to act as a father to the sick and to the well and stay with them untill I march them into Nashville." Against his orders and at his own expense, Jackson made sure that all the sick in his army were brought back with his other men to Nashville. It was at this time that he came to be called Old Hickory for his strength and determination as he marched with his men back to Tennessee. And he began to be revered by his troops, and also by the public, even as he chafed at being sidelined far from the battles with the British and their allies.

It was in the aftermath of the abortive campaign to Natchez that the quarrel between Jackson and Thomas Hart Benton broke out. The affair started as an argument between Benton's brother Jesse and William

Carroll, a friend who had served in the militia under Jackson. Jackson agreed to be a second in the duel between Carroll and Jesse Benton, and when Benton received an embarrassing wound in the buttocks, Thomas Hart Benton blamed Jackson and accused him of behaving "in a savage, unequal, unfair, and base manner." Never one to back down from an insult or challenge, Jackson marched into the City Hotel in Nashville to confront Benton, and a shootout occurred. Jackson took a bullet in the shoulder that shattered a bone and cut an artery. Several more shots were fired and then daggers were brought out when the pistols were empty. Jackson's brother-in-law Alexander Donelson and his friend John Coffee were also involved in the shooting and stabbing.

Among the witnesses to the fight were Charles Frémon, his wife, Anne, and their son John Charles, who after he changed his name to John C. Frémont would later marry Thomas Hart Benton's daughter Jessie. It would be John C. Frémont who would carry Jackson's dream of westward expansion all the way to California in 1846, with the help of Kit Carson and Thomas Fitzpatrick.

Bleeding dangerously and hardly conscious, Jackson was carried to a hotel room. Amputation of his arm seemed in order, but Jackson refused. His wound was treated with slippery elm and poultices made of Indian remedies. When the bleeding stopped, there was serious threat of gangrene. But miraculously, as mentioned before, Jackson did not die, but his recovery was slow, and he was still quite weak when news of the Fort Mims massacre reached Nashville.

Some in Nashville were inclined to blame Jackson for the fight. It was no longer the frontier town it had been in the 1790s, and now such fights were looked upon as signs of backward culture and crude, uncivilized behavior. But suddenly the news from Fort Mims took everyone's mind off the fight between Jackson and the Bentons. A much bigger battle was looming, and far more bloodshed. Daniel Walker Howe, one of Jackson's most severe critics among modern historians, views Jackson as the personification of many of the worst features of American culture of his time. In his Pulitzer Prize–winning volume *What Hath God Wrought*, Howe tells us, "Old Hickory's own image and record, as a hero who stood outside and above the law, typified a strain in American frontier culture that encouraged violence." The historian Amy Greenberg has argued that the expansionist ruthlessness of the Jacksonian Democrats can be explained by the ideal of "martial manhood" in the violent frontier world in which they were nurtured. The Fort Mims massacre elicited both Jackson's extreme determination and his brutality.

Jackson understood that the Fort Mims killings signaled a new stage in the tense relations between the large Creek Nation and the whites. Tecumseh had inspired the pan-Indian rebellion he had been hoping for and preaching for years. But Tecumseh himself would be killed at the Battle of the Thames in Ontario, just after the war he had triggered in the South got under way. The number of Creeks led by Red Eagle was large and growing. Many Creeks who had remained neutral before, encouraged by the Spanish in Pensacola and the "victory" at Fort Mims, decided to join the militant Red Sticks. It was the threat Jackson had been fearing and the chance he had been waiting for.

The Fort Mims massacre seemed to raise Jackson from his sickbed. "Brave Tennesseans!" he proclaimed. "Your frontier is threatened with invasion by the savage foe. Already they advance towards your frontier with their scalping knives unsheathed, to butcher your wives, your children, and your helpless babes. Time is not to be lost."

From Fayetteville, Tennessee, where he had gone to muster his troops, Jackson wrote to Rachel, "My health is good and my arm mending fast." In fact, he was still wearing his arm in a sling and he remained weak. But there is no doubt that the excitement of gathering an army took his mind off his ailments and wounds. Finally he was getting into the war, and he knew that war with the Creeks was the best way of obtaining their extensive lands for white settlement.

Jackson told his officers, including John Coffee, commander of the cavalry, to carefully cultivate the friendly Creeks. Much would depend on the help from those who had not joined the Red Sticks. Jackson ordered that all friendly Indians "wear white plumes in their hair, or deer's tails," so they could be easily recognized.

Marching south in three columns, for safety, at the rate of thirty miles a day, Jackson heard rumors that the Red Sticks had gathered at a place called Ten Islands on the Coosa River. Spies who saw Indians there suggested there might be as many as a thousand. But the first enemy the Tennessee militia encountered was hunger. Expecting contractors to deliver the needed rations to them as they marched, they had not brought enough wagons of supplies for such a large force. Indian villages along the way were attacked and robbed, their stores of grain confiscated. In at least one case the raiders seized a supply of corn at a village called Littefutchee but had no wagons to transport the grain back to the main body of Jackson's forces.

When John Coffee's cavalry attacked the town of Tallushatchee they killed 176 warriors and took 80 prisoners. "He has executed this order in elegant style," Jackson wrote of his friend Coffee. Among the prisoners taken was an infant boy, named Lyncoya, whom Jackson sent back home to Rachel to be raised as a son and companion to their already adopted son Andrew Jackson Jr. and their adopted Indian boy, Theodore.

Jackson's plan was to hew a road, like the Federal Road built in 1811 from Milledgeville, Georgia, to Mobile, straight through Creek territory, not only as a military road but also as a way for Tennesseans to reach Mobile and the Gulf. Such a road would give access to whites and also have the effect of weakening Creek power. Conquerors since the Romans and before have known that one of the most effective ways of subduing and claiming a region is to build roads into it. A road leads both actually and symbolically to possession.

Jackson had long had it in mind to encroach into the region the Spanish influenced from their stronghold at Pensacola, Florida. It is clear from what he said and what he did that this was an important purpose of the campaign. Subduing the Red Sticks was essential, but it was only a stage in the larger enterprise of securing the Gulf and Florida and the western lands for the United States. For Jackson that was the most holy cause, the Grail, as it were. As a boy he had fought the British in the Revolution in South Carolina; as a man he would fight them and their proxies in Alabama and Florida and Louisiana, and later from his desk at the White House he would continue the campaign against the British Empire.

But in the meantime Jackson had to deal with the hostile Creeks. Major General Thomas Pinkney of Charleston, commander of the seventh military district, and nominal head of all the forces, was supposed to help him in the campaign, as was Brigadier General Thomas Flannoy of the sixth from New Orleans. The army of East Tennessee under General John Cocke was directed to join Jackson in northern Alabama.

In addition, an army from Georgia commanded by General John Floyd, and another from the Mississippi Territory under Brigadier General Ferdinand L. Claiborne were to aid in the attack on the Red Sticks. As it turned out, because of poor communications, weak organization, and the considerable distances involved, there was little coordination among the several forces. The most significant actions were taken by Jackson and the Tennesseans, aided by the Cherokees and friendly Creeks.

Though short of supplies and still weak from his wounds, Jackson told his quartermaster William B. Lewis, "I am determined to push forward if I have to live upon acorns." Because of the victory at Tallushatchee, more Creek villages that had planned to stay neutral committed themselves to Jackson's cause. Jackson established his temporary headquarters at Fort Strother, on the Coosa River. About thirty miles to the south lay the village of Talladega, inhabited by Creeks who opposed the Red Sticks. When Red Eagle surrounded the village with a thousand warriors and threatened to destroy it, a chief who disguised himself in a hog skin escaped and warned Jackson of the siege.

Though he was waiting for a force from East Tennessee to arrive with reinforcements and supplies, Jackson decided not to hesitate but to attack at once. On November 9, 1813, his army of twelve hundred infantry and eight hundred cavalry came within half a mile of the Red Sticks surrounding Talladega just at dawn. Jackson organized his forces in a crescent, with cavalry at either end.

Jackson's plan was similar to that of General Daniel Morgan at Cowpens in the Revolution on January 17, 1781. An advance unit was to engage the Red Sticks, then pull back to the main line. As the enemy followed the retreat, the cavalry would attack from the sides and rear. The plan went like clockwork—at first. The Red Sticks charged after the retreating advance line, screaming and slashing with tomahawks, firing muskets, and the mounted troops closed in behind them.

But for some unexplained reason, a unit of infantry on the right began to withdraw and many Indians plunged through the gap in the crescent and escaped into the woods. Reserves were called in to close the break in the line, but as many as seven hundred Red Sticks had already gotten away, more than two-thirds of the enemy. The three hundred left were shot to death. What could have been a total victory that might have ended the Creek War was only a partial triumph and Jackson lost fifteen dead and eighty-five wounded in the encounter.

When Jackson returned to Fort Strother he hoped to find the East Tennessee army there with new troops and fresh supplies. But they had not arrived. A starving soldier is supposed to have approached Jackson and asked for something to eat. "I will most cheerfully divide with you what I have," the general answered. He reached into his pocket and pulled out a few acorns, which he offered to the hungry militiaman.

Besides a shortage of supplies, Jackson faced another seemingly insurmountable challenge. Many of his men believed their enlistments would expire in December 1813, one year after the aborted campaign to Natchez. When their twelve months were up, they would go home. That they were near starvation and without winter clothes added to their determination to return home before Christmas. A great many were barefoot and without coats, and a cold rain had set in and continued day after day. Colonel William Martin, commander of the most restless of the regiments, argued that his men should be allowed to return home at the very least to get heavy winter clothes and supplies. But Jackson knew that once his army was disbanded, it would be extremely difficult to gather it again. The most important leaders of the hostile Creeks, Red Eagle (William Weatherford) and Big Warrior (Menawa) remained at large.

To buy time, Jackson told Colonel Martin and the threatening mutineers that he would forward their requests to leave before Christmas to Governor Blount. Jackson knew it would take several days for the letter to reach the governor, and he assumed Blount would refuse to let the enlistments expire only two months after the beginning of the Creek campaign.

Among the soldiers in Jackson's army, serving as a scout in John Coffee's brigade, was one David Crockett of western Tennessee. At twenty-seven Crockett was not yet known as a politician and yarn-spinning humorist. He had worked primarily as a farmer and teamster and hunter to support his family on the frontier. It was the killings at Fort Mims that inspired him to join the militia in the late summer of 1813. As an expert woodsman his job was to spy out the country as they advanced into Creek territory. When he could, Crockett killed game to help feed the hungry men in his unit. Without winter clothes, and knowing that his wife had bitterly opposed his joining the militia, Crockett was among those anxious to depart for home.

Many of the volunteers said that December 10, 1813, was the day their enlistment ended. On November 17 Jackson had faced down an entire brigade, threatening to shoot anyone who deserted. After a dangerous standoff that seemed to last an eternity, the rebelling soldiers one by one returned to their posts. When desperately needed supplies finally arrived, Jackson hoped the crisis had passed.

But as the dreaded December 10 approached, Jackson argued that if the men would stay together and not disband, they could vanquish the Red Sticks in a few weeks and then go home with honor. On December 9 Jackson placed his artillery both in front of and behind his troops. Loyal militiamen were positioned along the road leading to Tennessee. Jackson rode along the line of the mutinous brigade praising their previous bravery and warning that if they left now they would disgrace not only themselves but their families as well. He said that if they tried to leave they would have to kill him first. Jackson then ordered the artillery men to light their matches and be ready to fire into the mutineers. Suddenly the rebelling officers stepped forward and pledged to stay until reinforcements arrived.

On December 12, 1813, General Cocke arrived from East Tennessee with fifteen hundred men. Reluctantly Jackson let his soldiers leave. Then, to his astonishment, he was informed that Cocke's men would also be released in a few days, their enlistments having expired. Jackson had no choice but to tell them to go on home. But he begged the volunteers to reenlist and return to see the Creek War to its conclusion. Not even Washington at Valley Forge had faced such a mass desertion by his army. And if that wasn't enough, General Coffee told Jackson that because the infantry was retiring from the field, most of the cavalry had gone home also.

Jackson was left with just the Second Brigade, which had enlisted for only three months. They expected their service to end January 14, 1814. As it turned out, Governor Blount sided with the militia against Jackson, and just before Christmas, he told the general to retreat north to Tennessee. No more troops could be provided for him.

At that point most men would have given up and gone home. Jackson seemed beaten on every side. Just as he had been close to defeating the Red Sticks, his army had been taken away from him. But like Washington before him, Jackson seemed inspired by calamity. As Robert Remini says, "Jackson seemed to gain interior strength by his many misfortunes. He was one of those extraordinary men who flourish with adversity . . . A strong, obstinate streak surged within him whenever his situation seemed hopeless."

Jackson wrote Blount an angry letter reminding him of his duty to the security of Tennessee, and to the country now at war with Britain. Tennessee was expected to provide five thousand men to protect the frontier. If the Red Sticks were not defeated, the Cherokees, Choctaws, Chickasaws, and friendly Creeks might decide to join the rebellion. "I have long since determined when I die I will leave my reputation untarnished," Jackson wrote to the governor. "You have only to act with a little energy for which you will be applauded by your Government. Give me a force for 6 months . . . and all may be safe. Withhold it, and all is lost and the reputation of the state and yrs. with it." Jackson seemed to be almost alone in the war against the Red Sticks. He wrote to General Thomas Pinkney, overall commander for the district, that he had only a hundred and thirty men left at Fort Strother.

Everything changed with the new year. Responding to Jackson's spirited, provocative letter, Governor Blount ordered a new enlistment of twenty-five hundred troops, and to his surprise found there was a renewed popular support for the war against the hostile Creeks. Blount also learned that the War Department in Washington wanted the attack against the Red Sticks to proceed. Officers and men who had left Jackson in December began to return. Jackson, isolated at Fort Strother deep in the Creek country, was the last to hear the news and was taken by surprise when eight hundred new recruits suddenly appeared at the forest fort.

Jackson immediately marched his new untrained troops deeper into the Creek country. He knew now that a large force of Red Sticks were camped at the place called Tohopki by the Creeks, named Horseshoe Bend by the whites, on the Tallapoosa River. In a hundred-acre enclave in a loop of the river, with a large barricade across the neck of land, the Red Sticks felt invulnerable. Jackson and his men camped at Emuckfaw

Creek, only three miles away from the fortress at the Bend. A war dance was in progress at Tohopki and Jackson knew he had been spotted and would be attacked.

Prepared, Jackson was able to repulse the attacking force. After the Red Sticks retreated, Jackson sent John Coffee with four hundred men, including some friendly Creeks, to burn the camp at Horseshoe Bend. But they found the enclave heavily defended. No sooner had Coffee and his men retreated to Jackson's camp at Emuckfaw than the Red Sticks attacked again, this time from the right of Jackson's line. Jackson's brother-in-law Major Alexander Donelson was killed. Hiding behind logs and trees, the Red Sticks kept up a deadly fire until a charge led by Billy Carroll dislodged them. But hitting Jackson's force at three points, the Red Sticks proved their tactical expertise. Jackson ordered his men to pull back and march to Fort Strother.

As the little army moved north, the Red Sticks followed and attacked at Enotachopco Creek. Jackson ordered the rear of his column to fire on the Indians and planned for his forward forces to divide and flank the hostile Creeks on either side, as they had done at Talladega. But the raw recruits gave way before the maneuver could be completed.

Jackson's voice was always high pitched, and when he was excited it rose even higher. Screaming at his men to hold their ground, he ordered them to regroup and confront the enemy. "In the midst of a shower of balls, of which he seemed unmindful, he was seen . . . rallying the alarmed, halting them in their flight, forming his columns, and inspiriting them by his example."

When the firing was over twenty of Jackson's men were dead and seventy-five wounded. But there were about two hundred dead Creeks lying on the ground. It had been a close call, but Jackson had saved his untrained army to fight another day.

When news of the victories at Emuckfaw and Enotachopco reached Washington in the depths of the War of 1812, Jackson's name began to be connected to heroism. There had been so many American defeats, one after another, that the exploits in Alabama sounded like triumphs. Jackson was understandably thrilled to know he was being praised in the capital and that hundreds of additional men were on the way to join him. Though he received a frantic letter from Rachel asking him to return home — she was saddened and shaken by the death of her brother, frightened that her husband would also be killed — Jackson knew that he was finally closing in on both the Creek enemy and the military glory he longed for and believed was his destiny.

As units of men kept arriving at Fort Strother, Jackson's army seemed to grow by the day. On February 5, 1814, Colonel John Williams and the Thirty-ninth Infantry Regiment joined the militia already there. Jackson now had regular, trained troops under his command. By the first of March he had almost five thousand men to organize and prepare as a force to destroy the remaining Red Sticks. He required strict obedience and sent Generals Cocke and Roberts home when they questioned his tough new measures. There would be no more mutiny or talk of desertion in his army. Some muttered that if American generals in the North had behaved like Jackson the whole sorry war might have gone differently.

A young militiaman named John Woods, who deserted his post one cold morning, was executed on March 14, 1814. Jackson's enemies would later make use of the incident to portray Old Hickory as savage, ruthless, ignorant, and cruel. But it was observed that from that moment defiance and insubordination in Jackson's army ceased. John Reid later reported that the action was painful to Jackson himself but had been "essential to the preservation of good order . . . and a strict obedience afterwards characterized the army."

On the same day Woods was executed, Jackson marched his men out of Fort Strother and established a base at Fort Williams, thirty miles to the south on the Coosa River. Hearing from General Pinkney that supplies would be sent from Mobile to a place called the Hickory Ground where the Tallapoosa and Coosa rivers converged, he began marching again toward the Red Stick stronghold at Horseshoe Bend.

Among Jackson's four thousand men were many Creek allies. There seems to be no record of exactly how many Creeks fought with his forces, but between four and five hundred Cherokees would join him also. At Tohopki about a thousand Red Stick warriors and three hundred women and children waited for Jackson and his men. They had built the breastworks at the neck of the peninsula in a crescent so that attackers, especially those in the middle, would be exposed to fire from both sides.

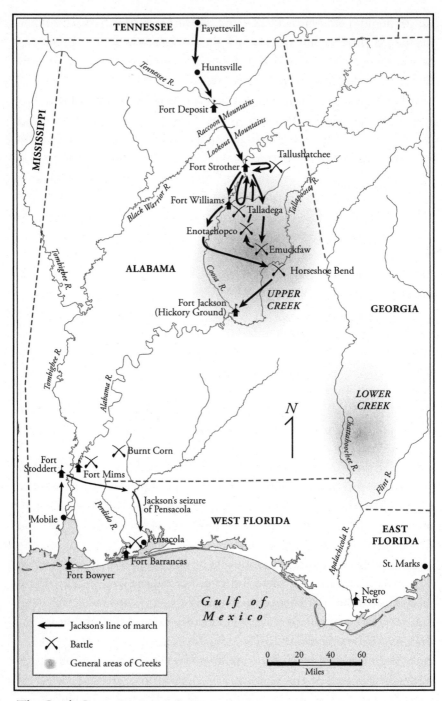

The Creek Campaign, 1813–1814

With care and deliberation, Jackson moved his men to Emuckfaw and on March 27, 1814, arrived within sight of the Bend. "It is impossible to conceive a situation more eligible for defense than the one they (the Red Sticks) had chosen," he later wrote to General Pinkney, "and the skill which they manifested in their breast work, was really astonishing."

As they approached the Bend, Jackson directed Coffee and his cavalry and as many as five hundred Cherokees and one hundred friendly Creeks to take positions across the river opposite the village, to prevent any Red Sticks from escaping across the river. Jackson had two artillery pieces, a three-pounder and a six-pounder, which he set up on a small hill facing the barricade. Around 10:30 a.m., the cannon began firing, but the balls bounced off the heavy logs of the barrier. The shooting continued about two hours with no results. The defenders shouted insults and curses over the barricade. Medicine men danced the Dance of the Lakes in colorful costumes and chanted spells to destroy the attackers.

On the other side of the river, as they listened to the firing, several Cherokees swam across the stream to steal canoes the Red Sticks had left there. With the canoes a larger party, led by Captain Gideon Morgan and Captain William Russell, began crossing to attack the village. Many Creeks were killed, as more and more Cherokees and friendly Creeks paddled across the river. Morgan's forces overcame the warriors in the rear and set fire to the village and all its storehouses.

When Jackson saw the smoke from the burning cabins he ordered an assault on the barricade. Colonel Williams and the Thirty-ninth Infantry charged through air filled with bullets and arrows from the ramparts. Major Lemuel P. Montgomery of the Thirty-ninth was the first to climb over the wall, yelling to his men to follow him. A bullet hit his head and he fell dead.

Among those rushing the wall was twenty-one-year-old Third Lieutenant Sam Houston. An arrow plunged into his thigh, but Houston jumped over the barricade and later took two bullets in the chest and shoulder. His wounds that day would make him a hero, and he would become a close friend of Andrew Jackson.

As more and more soldiers poured over the barricade, the Red Sticks began to pull back. The regular soldiers were armed with bayonets, and some carried swords. Militiamen used rifles and muskets as clubs. The

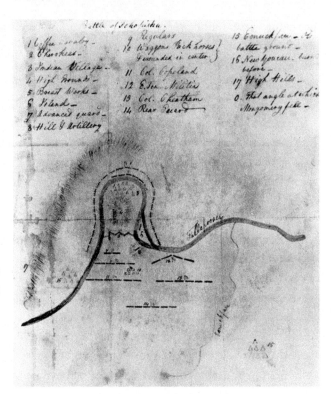

Andrew Jackson's Map of the Battle of Horseshoe Bend, March 27, 1814. *Courtesy of Tennessee Historical Society*

Red Sticks had vowed never to surrender, and they kept their word. When it was clear they were overwhelmed by superior numbers, many backed away, hoping to conceal themselves in brush or ditches.

Captain Morgan and the Cherokees and friendly Creeks, having set the village afire, took most of the women and children prisoner. Some warriors dashed toward the river to flee in the sycamore wood canoes they'd left there and, finding no canoes, tried to swim across to safety. Many who made it to or across the stream were shot by Coffee's men stationed on the opposite bank.

According to Jackson's later report the battle lasted five hours, from 10:30 a.m. to 3:30 p.m., but the killing continued until dark and even to the next morning. Jackson had expected Red Eagle to be among the warriors at Horseshoe Bend, but the notorious chief happened to be away when the battle occurred. The leader at Tohopki was Big Warrior, Menawa. Around sunset Menawa, seriously wounded by seven bullets, lay unconscious among a pile of dead bodies. When he came to after dark, he crawled to the river, miraculously found a canoe left there by Morgan's men, and made his escape downstream.

The leading prophet of the Red Sticks, named Monahee, was found dead, shot in the mouth. Jackson is reported to have said, "Heaven designed to chastize his impostures by an appropriate punishment." The bodies of two other prophets were also found. Jackson believed these were the last of the holy men who had promised a mystical victory over the whites and the rival faction of the Creeks.

Jackson ordered a careful count of the bodies on the peninsula. Five hundred fifty-seven dead were found, and Coffee's men thought as many as three hundred had been killed in the river. Most historians put the loss at Horseshoe Bend at around eight hundred. Their figures suggest that as many as two hundred Red Sticks did escape the carnage. It is the greatest number of Indians killed in any recorded battle in American history. When the prisoners were counted there were found to be three hundred forty-seven women and children and three warriors. Jackson ordered that the prisoners be humanely treated.

The Cherokee forces had lost eighteen killed and thirty-six wounded. The friendly Creeks had lost five killed, eleven wounded. Among Jackson's white soldiers there were twenty-six killed and one hundred seven wounded. The Thirty-ninth Infantry Regiment, which had led the attack on the breastworks, had lost seventeen killed and fifty-five wounded. The relatively high loss among the Cherokees probably reflects the initiative they had taken to swim across the river and seize the canoes and then attack the village from the rear at the beginning of the battle. One of the ironies of American history is that Jackson's Cherokee allies in the Creek War would later by his orders be stripped of their lands in the east and removed to Indian Territory in the west. Jackson would argue that removal to the West was the only way to save the eastern nations from extermination by white settlers. Though some Cherokees would agree with Jackson's policy, many never forgave him for his betrayal of his former allies. Chief Junaluska, who fought at Horseshoe Bend, later said that had he known Jackson would drive the Cherokees from their beloved Smoky Mountains, he would have killed the general himself at the Bend.

When Jackson wrote to Governor Blount the next day of the total victory at Horseshoe Bend, he could not be certain that the war with the hostile Creeks was over. Spies reported that remaining Red Sticks from the so-called war towns had gathered at Hothewalee at the Hickory Ground and planned to make another stand against the Americans.

Around the middle of April, Jackson moved his army away from Fort Williams down the left bank of the Coosa River, planning to deliver a final blow to the Red Sticks gathered at the Hickory Ground. As Jackson's force approached, many Red Sticks fled toward the Spanish at Pensacola. Jackson expected the remaining warriors to fight him and camped not far away at a site that had been the French Fort Toulouse and was to become Fort Jackson. Instead of offering battle, the remaining Red Sticks, individually and in small groups, began presenting themselves at Jackson's camp, offering unconditional surrender.

The African Americans who had been captured at Fort Mims the summer before and one white woman named Polly Jones and her child were turned over to Jackson. A few of the leading Red Stick chiefs were arrested and held. But when the leader of the hostile Creeks, Red Eagle himself, walked into the camp and surrendered, Jackson was so surprised he told the great warrior he was not sure how to treat him.

"I am in your power," Red Eagle, who spoke English, answered. "Do with me as you please. I am a soldier. I have done the white people all the harm I could. I have fought them, and fought them bravely: if I had an army, I would yet fight, and contend to the last: but I have none; my people are all gone. I can now do no more than weep over the misfortunes of my nation."

Jackson was much impressed by the dignity, courage, and eloquence of his defeated enemy. Red Eagle was the leader of the attack at Fort Mims, but stripped of his power the man seemed admirable in his brave appearance. But whatever emotion Jackson felt, he knew his purpose was to destroy the Red Stick rebellion, and his overall goal was the acquisition of the Creek territory for white settlers. If the West was to be American, the Creeks had to be pushed out of the way.

Jackson told Red Eagle that the only way the Creek nation could be saved was total surrender to the United States forces. Otherwise the fight would go on. "I have not surrendered myself thoughtlessly," Red Eagle replied. "Whilst there were chances of success, I never left my post, nor supplicated peace. But my people are gone, and I now ask it for my nation, and for myself." Red Eagle promised to persuade the other Red Sticks to accept Jackson's terms, and a few days later Jackson let him leave with a group of his followers to begin that mission. Harsh as he could be in battle, or when threatened by mutiny, Jackson knew when to be a diplomat. Red Eagle now became William Weatherford again. Robert Remini tells us, "When the War of 1812 ended he retired to a large farm in Monroe County, Alabama, and became a respected planter. Occasionally he visited Old Hickory at the Hermitage." It is said Weatherford trained race horses for Jackson.

Jackson never lost sight of his main ambition, which was the claiming of Creek lands. The Creek domain stretched from central Georgia to Chickasaw and Choctaw land near Mississippi. With settlers crowding in from Tennessee in the north and Georgia and the Carolinas in the east, there was a desperate need for new territory. Jackson understood that hunger for Creek land because he knew it in himself. He had been one of those people, and he was still one of those people, now risen to power and prominence. But his hunger for land was only part of a larger hunger for the unity and power of the United States. He dreamed of a United States that would cover the continent and not be encumbered by foreign powers such as Britain and Spain. He believed in the Union the way Lincoln would later, and Sam Houston. The nation of Creeks stood in the way of that Union the way the nullifiers of South Carolina would in 1830, and the seceding states would later still. Even more than his own glory—and he had infinite ambition—Jackson cared about the future of the Union and was willing to do whatever was necessary to break anything that stood in the way of that Union and its destiny. He was a man possessed by forces even he may not have fully understood.

On April 20, 1814, General Pinkney and Benjamin Hawkins, trusted Indian agent to the Creeks, arrived at Fort Jackson to negotiate a treaty with the Creek Nation. Jackson marched his men north to Fort Williams and addressed them one last time as their commander. He was skilled at both writing and delivering such speeches. "Your general is pleased with you," he said. "He salutes you and compliments you . . . Within a few days you have annihilated the power of a nation, that, for twenty years, has been the disturber of your peace . . . The bravery you have displayed . . . will long be cherished in the memory of your general, and will not be forgotten by the country you have so materially benefitted."

At Fayetteville, Tennessee, where the army had mustered the autumn before, the men were discharged. Jackson rode on to Nashville where enthusiastic crowds waited to cheer him. Speeches were made, and at a banquet at the Bell Tavern Jackson was presented a ceremonial sword. Old Hickory gave another speech, one of the best of his career. His words left no doubt of the central purpose of his campaign. "We have conquered. We have added a country to ours, which, by connecting the settlements of Georgia with those of the Mississippi Territory . . . will become a secure barrier against foreign invasion."

On May 28 Jackson was offered the rank of major general in the U.S. Army, to replace William Henry Harrison who was retiring, and he accepted. In his capacity as a major general of national forces Jackson returned to Fort Jackson and called all the Creek leaders to a conference. Many Red Sticks had joined the Spanish in Florida, and the British were known to have landed three hundred men at Pensacola to aid an attack on the Americans. It was not a moment to be lenient, and Jackson believed the Creeks must submit completely to the United States or be destroyed if they got in the way of the struggle with Britain and Spain.

As the chiefs assembled, both the friendly and the formerly hostile, Jackson told them they must pay for the expenses incurred by the United States in fighting the war with the Red Sticks. By his reckoning, the Creek Nation owed the United States twenty-three million acres of territory, about three-fifths of Alabama and one-fifth of Georgia.

The Creeks were astonished by Jackson's pronouncement. Those who had sided with the Americans had expected to be rewarded for their loyalty. Instead, they were to be stripped of most of their lands, same as the Red Sticks. Jackson spoke as much for the western settlers as for the U.S. government at the conference when he made his demands. But he was the official commander and the designated negotiator on the spot. It was at this point that the Creeks began to call him Sharp Knife, or Pointed Arrow, and Old Mad Jackson. He showed no willingness to negotiate or listen to protests or arguments. Allies such as Chief Shelocta were flabbergasted, but their protests washed off Jackson like gentle spring rain.

With the Spanish and British just a few miles away in Pensacola, and some Creeks joining them, hoping to attack the Americans, Jackson was adamant. The Creeks must give up their land for their own nation's security. "Until this is done, your nation cannot expect happiness, nor mine security . . . Your rejecting the treaty will show you to be enemies of the United States—enemies even to yourself."

The chiefs responded that General Pinkney had promised them rewards for their alliance with the United States, not penalties and annihilation. Jackson shot back that Pinkney had spoken without authorization from Washington. He, Jackson, was now the official in charge. The Creeks had no choice but to sign the treaty, unless they wanted to go to war with their ally, the United States. The once proud nation of Creeks was humiliated and would never rise again in such force against the American settlers or army. On August 9, 1814, Jackson added a kingdom of choice land to that available to white settlers. It was what he had planned and fought for all along. The treaty at Fort Jackson demonstrated Jackson's ruthless brilliance even more than had the battle at Horseshoe Bend.

"What Jackson had done had the touch of genius," Robert Remini would write. "He had ended the war by signing a treaty of peace with his allies! Most of the Red Stick chiefs had by this time fled to Florida and planned to continue their warfare. Thus Jackson converted the Creek civil war into an enormous land grab that insured the ultimate destruction of the entire Creek Nation."

Jackson's cruelty to the Creeks set a pattern that would continue through the removal of the Cherokees and other nations to the west in the 1830s. But as a result, few Indians sided with the British in the remainder of the War of 1812, and a number of Choctaws fought with Jackson at New Orleans in January 1815, in the victory over the British that would propel Old Hickory to unprecedented hero worship in his country and to the White House in 1829. Even his enemies conceded that Jackson knew what he was about as he aided the Republic and its land-intoxicated settlers pushing farther and farther into the glorious West. Jackson had created a precedent that would, sadly, define much of the westward expansion.

Three

JOHN CHAPMAN

APPLES AND ANGELS

THOMAS JEFFERSON once wrote, "The greatest service which can be rendered to any country is to add an useful plant to its culture." He could have been thinking of John Chapman, the Johnny Appleseed of American legend.

The modern apple is related to the rose, a member of the Rosaceae family. Historical botanists believe the apple originated in the region south of the Caucasus Mountains. They were cultivated in ancient times, before recorded history. The Romans recognized seven varieties in the third century BC. Apples were growing in Britain by the time the Romans arrived there. From ancient times "the Apples of Knowledge" was an important figure of speech for human culture and intelligence.

Early settlers in North America brought both apple seeds and "propagating wood," meaning grafting shoots and root stocks, into the new colonies. In 1649 Governor John Endicott of Plymouth, Massachusetts, gave William Trask five hundred three-year-old apple trees in exchange for two hundred acres of land. It was not long after their settlement before both Virginia and New England were exporting apples back to Britain and Europe.

The growing of apples seems always to have been a part of culture in general. Wherever cultured people went they took their orchards with them. And the cultivation of fruit trees was acquired early on by the American Indians from the invaders. Larger native nations in the east such as the Iroquois and Cherokee soon had extensive orchards of apples and peaches of their own. The apple was a thing of beauty, both literally and figuratively. That which was most desired, most loved, was "the apple of the eye."

Apples thrive in the zone between 30 degrees and 60 degrees latitude in both the northern and southern hemispheres. They need winters with at least fifty days below 45 degrees Fahrenheit but cannot stand temperatures below −40 degrees Fahrenheit. At least one hundred days free of killing frost are required from blossom time to fruit. They do best where there is plenty of water, and plenty of sunshine late in the summer.

Orchardists will tell you that topography is more important than the quality of the soil, because drainage is essential. Therefore rolling hilltops or sloping hillsides are preferred, both for water drainage and for "air drainage," where the coldest air can sink away into the valley below on frosty spring nights. Orchards located south and east of mountains have the best protection from cold fronts. Large bodies of water nearby tend to moderate winter conditions and delay spring blossoming until nights are frost free.

Because apples require cross pollination, it is important to have several varieties growing near each other. Trees take six to eight years to begin producing fruit and should be pruned when young. When apples are picked, care must be taken not to damage the spur buds for next year's blossoming. Apples keep best when stored at around 32 degrees Fahrenheit.

From the earliest times apples were primarily eaten as fresh fruit. If stored properly in a cool place they will keep for months. But from the beginning, apples were also crushed to make cider. When left to age and ferment the sweet cider becomes hard cider, often the favorite beverage on the frontier. Left to ferment even longer the hard cider becomes vinegar, used to flavor and preserve food, as pickling was a common method of keeping many fruits and vegetables. For some the perfect way of preserving apples was to distill the hard cider into applejack or apple brandy. In many early households on the frontier applejack was more common than corn liquor, or moonshine.

Housewives sliced fresh apples and dried the pieces in the sun or by the fire to keep throughout the winter for pies. They also made spicy apple butter, and golden, amber, and rosy jellies from different apple varieties, as well as plain applesauce.

A peculiar trait of the apple is that when grown from seed the new tree may or may not produce apples like the one the seed was taken from. There is only about a one in six chance that apples grown from seeds will duplicate the parent. Apples grown from seedlings may be small, of different colors and flavors, but still good enough for cider making and pie fillings, jams, jellies, and vinegar. To ensure consistency, an apple must be grafted, that is, a branch of the desired variety inserted and fixed in a living young tree. Expertise at grafting seems as old as apple culture itself. And modern scientists, while improving the techniques, have not essentially changed this ancient art.

Apple trees grown from seeds, while not preferred by most orchardists, were, however, still valuable on the frontier, producing useful trees of varying quality and size, and fruit welcome to the early settlers, whatever its color and flavor. Some would even say fruit grown from seedlings has a richer, tangier taste, preferable to the blander, more predictable flavors of fruit from grafted trees. Seedling fruit seemed to have a place out in the forest, on land just claimed from primeval wilderness.

Along with livestock, an orchard was among the most valuable assets a settler could acquire. With a cow, an ox, a few acres of corn, perhaps a few chickens, and a grove of apple trees, a family could survive and thrive. Fields along streams, orchards on hillsides, were a sign of prosperity, growth, promise for the future. An orchard was a mark of confidence in the future, a mark of well-being and culture.

———

THOUGH HE was by no means the first, or even the best, the most famous orchardist of North America was one John Chapman, who became known in his own lifetime as Johnny Appleseed. Like Daniel Boone, he became such a character of legend and folklore that people forgot he was a real person. He was very real and known among the settlers and Indians of western Pennsylvania, Ohio, and Indiana as a planter of fruit trees, a roving missionary who slept in the woods and preached Swedenborgian mysticism, which few understood. He respected all living things, including mosquitoes and rattlesnakes, conversed with animals large and small, as well as with angels, created orchards for those who would follow him, barter apple trees, and cleared little patches in the wilderness fenced with brush for all to use. While he planted tens of thousands of apple trees in the newly cleared soil, his greatest husbandry by far was the seeding of myths about himself. His story would influence the way Americans of the region viewed and remembered themselves. Americans have been described as either bullies or saints, and John Chapman inspired a sense of saintliness in the developing culture. However brutal and relentless the westward surge may have been, there was a romantic, visionary side to it in the minds of the people, and nobody represented the peaceable, spiritual side of the quest for land and settlement in the West better than the person — and legend — known as Johnny Appleseed.

———

JOHN CHAPMAN was born in Leominster, Massachusetts, on September 26, 1774, according to the records of the First Congregational Church there, on the eve of the American Revolution. One might almost say he was born with the Revolution. He also came into the world in the season of apple picking and cider making, in the valley of the Nashua River where the New England coastal plain gives way to the rolling foothills of the Appalachians.

John's father, Nathaniel Chapman, a farmer and carpenter, could trace his lineage back five generations in Massachusetts to Edward Chapman, from Shropshire, England, who reached Boston in 1639. When Edward died in Ipswich, Massachusetts in 1678, he willed to his second wife "ten good bearing fruit trees near the end of the house." The Chapmans had been orchardists for generations.

John was the second child of Nathaniel and his wife, Elizabeth Simon Chapman. Nathaniel was a member of the local militia, reorganized as the Minutemen when the quarrel with Great Britain gathered momentum. Nathaniel is believed to have fought at the Battle of Bunker Hill in June 1775 and to have been part of Washington's army in New York the next year.

As the Revolution got under way, John's mother became ill, and among the documents Chapman's biographer quotes is a letter she wrote to her husband on June 3, 1775, while he was away in the Continental army. "Remember, I beseech you, that you are a mortall and that you must submit to death sooner or later and consider that we are always in danger of our spiritual enemy. Be, therefore, on your guard continually, and live in a daily preparation for death — and so I must bid you farewell and if it should be so ordered that I should not see you again, I hope we shall both be as happy as to spend an eternity of happiness together in the coming world which is my desire and prayer."

A year later, on June 26, 1776, his mother gave birth to her third child, a son, and in July, a few weeks later, she died. After his mother's death, John and his siblings lived with the Simon family in Leominster. In 1777 Captain Chapman married eighteen-year-old Lucy Cooley of Long-meadow, south of Springfield, Massachusetts, on the Connecticut River. When he was released from the Continental army in 1780, it is believed he moved his family to Longmeadow.

In the early 1780s the Connecticut Valley was near the edge of the wil-derness that stretched across the Berkshires, the Hudson Valley, and into the wide western region around and beyond the Great Lakes. Besides going to school, where he was taught a handsome handwriting, young John worked on the family farm and, we assume, swam, canoed, and fished in the Connecticut River. To become such a skilled woodsman and husbandman he must have had a long apprenticeship.

There are many legends about how John Chapman reached the fron-tier of western Pennsylvania by 1797, when he was twenty-three years old. Some say he wandered as far south as Philadelphia, and then to the Po-tomac and Virginia, before settling on the Allegheny River north of Pitts-burgh. There is no firm evidence of his whereabouts until he appeared, with his younger brother, Nathaniel, in the deep forests of red, black, and white oak near the New York State boundary on the Allegheny. The land was cheap and safe for settlers, after General "Mad Anthony" Wayne's victory over the Indians at Fallen Timbers in Ohio on August 20, 1794, and the Treaty of Greenville signed the following year.

John Chapman's name appears in the records of a trading post run by Edward Hale at Franklin on the Allegheny River in the winter of 1797–98. Looking for a spot to start a nursery, he chose an acre on Brokenstraw Creek, called Cushanadauga by the Iroquois. The name came from the tall grass and cane that grew there on the rich bottomlands.

Though Chapman tried to claim several tracts of land in the wilder-ness around Franklin, he found in every case that someone had beaten him to it, or "jumped" his claim. Such land grabbing and cheating were common on the frontier and bribing of surveyors and land office clerks was as common as changing the dates on surveys and deeds.

Chapman's name appears on the federal census of 1801, which reports he was living alone several miles above the trading post on French Creek. Senecas and Munsee Indians were common in the area. Though Chapman was already planting trees in the region, perhaps working as a laborer, and learning to survive in the woods and on the edges of society with very little, he seems never to have actually owned land in the Allegheny Valley. At least no one has found a deed in his name. But he was already sowing the seeds of his legend. He seems always to have had a knack for making people remember him. Almost sixty years later one R. I. Curtis would recall, "He was a singular character. I knew him in Venango county, Pennsylvania, nearly sixty years ago, when a child of eight or nine years . . . He was very fond of children and would talk to me a great deal, telling me of hardships he had endured, of his adventures, and hair-breadth escapes by flood and field."

One story Chapman liked to tell about himself was about being chased by Indians. Slipping into the shallows of a lake, he hid himself in reeds and cattails and actually took a nap while the Indians searched for him. Other local people remembered that he could walk many miles on ice in winter, on bare feet. "He seemed to be as much at home with the red men of the forest as with his own race," a man named Newton would recall. It is a theme that will appear again and again in the stories about Chapman, his bare feet on ice, and his ease in the forest and rapport with the native people.

Other early legends stressed his skill with an ax. "He could chop as much wood or girdle as many trees in one day as most men could in two," the story ran. Most of the early stories feature Chapman's physical prowess, his toughness, his endurance. He is reported to have lived one whole winter on "butternuts." He is also said to have floated many miles down French Creek "on a cake of ice." Paddling his canoe down the Allegheny River when there was much ice on the stream, he pulled his craft onto a block of ice, so the story goes, lay down inside the canoe, and went to sleep. When he woke up, he was a hundred miles below his intended destination. The image of him sleeping in the canoe on the floating ice suggests both his confidence and his lack of hurry or concern about reaching his destination. He was at home and at ease with his wandering, dreamy and certain of his destiny.

One legend has it that Johnny Appleseed arrived in Pittsburgh around 1798 and started a nursery business. He shared whatever he had with those passing through bound for the lands farther west. When asked why he gave away what he worked for, he answered, "The bees work without wages. Why should I not do the same?" Even while he was still alive such stories were planted in the rich soil of the public imagination and have continued to grow to this day. In fact, there is no evidence that Chapman ever lived in Pittsburgh. He sought out the wilder country farther west, where there were no roads and few paths except those made by animals and Indians.

The earliest stories have Johnny Appleseed arriving in the new territory lugging a leather bag of apple seeds. When asked why he did not settle down and start a permanent nursery, he explained that settlers' cattle would destroy his young trees before they matured. His planting must be farther west, always ahead of the settlers, giving his groves time to mature before cattle arrived. His plan was to sell young apple trees to the settlers when they reached the western lands. Chapman began his planting in the Muskingum Valley of eastern Ohio, in the region called the Seven Ranges. Hunters, scouts, the earliest settlers, never forgot seeing him roving and working there.

There is no record of Chapman actually growing apple trees until February 1, 1804, when he signed a promissary note to his older sister, Elizabeth, her husband, and their children, and on February 3, 1804, he signed another to Nathaniel Chapman. The latter reads:

> *Franklin. February 4, 1804, for value received I promise to pay Nathaniel Chapman or order the sum of one hundred dollars in land or apple trees with interest till paid as witness my hand.*
>
> *John Chapman.*

The notes suggest that the whole Chapman family had moved to western Pennsylvania by 1804, part of the general migration to the West. Chapman's brother, Nathaniel, had already settled in the area of future Marietta, Ohio, near the mouth of the Muskingum River. Neighbors in

Pennsylvania would later remember that John was at that time clearing patches in the forest, fencing them with brush, and planting apple trees in the newly cleared soil. He would "wash out of the pomace at cider mills a bushel or two of seeds, and return with them on his shoulder, plant them at the proper time, enclose the spot with a brush fence, and pay some attention to the cultivation . . . He never grafted any."

Chapman from first to last disapproved of grafting apple trees as a means of propagation. It seems he thought the process unnatural and therefore to be avoided. It has also been reported that he did not want to "hurt" plants by cutting them, inserting shoots and binding them. But his preference for seeding rather than grafting may have more to do with practicality than anything else. Crossing a large expanse of wilderness, going deeper and deeper into the western lands, Chapman could carry bags of seeds where he could hardly have transported many shoots and living root stocks. A bushel could contain three hundred thousand apple seeds. Given Chapman's ambition and the range of his activities, seed planting must have been his best option.

Chapman was not the first or the only person bringing fruit trees to the wilderness. The French had long ago given some of the Indian tribes of the region apple trees. At Marietta, farther down the Ohio, one Rufus Putnam by the year 1796 had started an apple orchard with grafted stock. What was unusual about Chapman's enterprise was his plan and method of moving his nurseries with or just ahead of the settlement of the frontier. Other tree merchants made permanent nurseries, primarily along the routes of travel. Only Chapman lived in such an itinerant manner that he could keep going farther and farther into the wilderness; the settlers followed in his tracks. Simon Kenton had killed game in Kentucky and left it along the trails for arriving settlers to use. The vegetarian Chapman anticipated the future white settlement of the Ohio valleys by having fruit trees there waiting for the new arrivals.

Those who claimed land in Kentucky, and later in Ohio, were expected to clear at least an acre and build some sort of dwelling within a year. Some of their "dwellings" were little more than piles of sticks in an opening in the woods. In 1792 the Ohio Company stipulated that for their claims to be valid, settlers on hundred-acre tracts must plant at least fifty apple trees and twenty peach trees within three years. As Chapman biographer Robert Price writes, "When orchards had been established, the land had been mastered."

———

ONE REASON people who encountered Chapman never forgot him was his eccentric attire. Known to trade apple seedlings for cast-off clothes, he might be seen wearing odds and ends from many wardrobes. Usually barefoot, he was sometimes given old shoes and boots, wearing one kind of shoe on one foot and another on the other. In any case, he usually passed his footwear on to someone who needed it more than he and went barefoot again. For ease of travel through the forest he wore pants cut off around the knees or just below. Some reported his coat was made from a coffee sack with holes cut for neck and arms. Most notorious was his headgear. Many stories say he wore as a hat the pot in which he cooked his mush. The metal functioned as a helmet, protecting his head from limbs as well as sun and rain.

It is certainly possible that Chapman wore his cooking pot on his head at times. But more plausible are the stories about the kind of cap he fashioned to protect his face from the rain and glaring sun. According to an article by W. D. Haley published in *Harper's Monthly Magazine* November 1871 (only twenty-six years after Chapman's death) he made his preferred cap from "pasteboard with an immense peak in front, and having thus secured an article that combined usefulness with economy, it became his permanent fashion." The crown of the cap was shaped like the French army kepi, and the long bill made of cardboard was not unlike those worn by deep-sea fishermen today.

In all the stories that have come down to us, Chapman, in spite of his strange costume and his odd manner, was treated with courtesy by the settlers, even by the children. He seems to have had a presence that encouraged them to respect him. Perhaps his behavior was so selfless and odd most people held him in awe. He was known to show great affection for little girls, giving them bits of colorful ribbon and calico cloth. And he was a gifted storyteller who could keep his listeners, both old and young, enthralled for hours.

Among the Indians still living in that part of Ohio, Chapman was recognized as "a great medicine man" because of his unusual appearance and habits, and his knowledge of herbs. He was said to thrust pins and needles into his flesh to demonstrate his immunity to pain. Certainly he showed a fortitude against the elements, sleeping outside in all weather, that even the Indians could envy and respect. He respected the Indians in turn. Most likely many native people saw him as a kind of holy fool, carrying his bag of seeds and hoard of stories, to be honored and deferred to, at once inspired and afflicted in his mind.

——

DURING THE War of 1812 legends of John Chapman's related activities grew. Since he traveled most of the time visiting his various nurseries in the woods, it is quite possible he did serve as a messenger to the settlements, warning of the approach of the British or hostile Indians. When the war between Britain and the United States broke out, the threat to the settlements in Indiana in the Tippecanoe River region was renewed. Or so the settlers feared. There were still Indian villages in northwest Ohio, especially in the area around the Mohican River. Over the years since the 1794 Battle of Fallen Timbers, the Indians had been bullied and harassed by white settlers.

John Chapman knew that countryside intimately. He had camped and planted trees and herbs there, and he knew both the white settlers and the Indians. One of his largest nurseries was on the banks of the Mohican. By 1812 he had gone farther north, planting apple trees by streams that flowed toward Lake Erie. One stream, the Huron River, drained land that had been reserved for residents of Connecticut who had their homes burned during the Revolution. The district was called Fire Lands.

One of the first settlers in the Fire Lands was Caleb Palmer, and in 1812 Chapman was living some of the time at Palmer's house there. The Ohio frontier had become especially dangerous after General William Hull had surrendered—without resistance—Fort Detroit to the British on August 16, 1812. When the American army protecting the border with Canada left, the British and their Indian allies were free to attack the settlements as they pleased. On July 17 the American garrison at Mackinac had also surrendered to the British without firing a shot. On August 6, 1812, the riflemen of the Ohio Volunteers were ambushed near Detroit and many were killed.

In the Northwest it looked as though the American settlers would have to fight off an invasion from Canada. Thus they commissioned John Chapman to travel down the Huron River once a week, to Lake Erie, and report back any Indian or British activity. If Indians were sighted, a signal gun was to be fired. On August 21, 1812, the alarm was for real. A settler named Hanson Reed heard Chapman calling from the woods late in the afternoon, "Flee for your lives—the Canadians and Indians are landing at Huron." The local settlers gathered their cattle and a few belongings and marched through mud and thick underbrush to Caleb Palmer's house at New Haven. News arrived that Fort Detroit had fallen and that the settlements to the northwest on the Maumee River had been overrun. There was no one to protect the towns in the region. All those at New Haven agreed to go on to Mansfield, a larger town. Traveling at night, carrying what they could, they reached Mansfield on Sunday morning. But finding little protection in the cabins and one blockhouse at Mansfield, they moved on to Fredericktown, twenty miles away.

A rider overtook the party with news that three hundred British soldiers and six hundred Indians had landed and driven all the settlers away from the mouth of the Huron River on Lake Erie. Luckily this information turned out to be false. Those who had landed proved to be prisoners from Detroit released by the British. Scared and exhausted by their journey from New Haven to Mansfield, the settlers had to decide what to do.

Tension was so high and fears so great that confusion caused a local Indian settlement to be burned, an elderly Wyandotte Indian to be shot and tomahawked to death, and a white trader to be killed and scalped in return. It was John Chapman who volunteered to make the dangerous journey to Mount Vernon to warn settlers and request assistance for Mansfield.

According to an early historian named A. Banning Norton, Chapman made his journey on horseback. But since Chapman usually traveled on foot, it is more likely he ran the thirty miles through woods he was familiar with. "Flee for your lives," he shouted at each cabin along the way. "The British and Indians are coming upon you, and destruction followeth in their footsteps."

But another settler recalled that he shouted to all along the route, "The spirit of the Lord is upon me, and he hath anointed me to blow the trumpet in the wilderness, and sound an alarm in the forest; for, behold, the tribes of the heathen are round about your doors, and a devouring flame followeth after them."

Though Mansfield survived otherwise unharmed, just eight miles east there was a raid on the Black Fork of the Mohican River on September 15, 1812, when a Reverend James Copus of Mansfield and a party of soldiers were attacked and the minister and three soldiers were killed. Many settlers' cabins in the area were burned and soon white families abandoned the whole region. Finally General Reasin Beall, commander of regional forces, got his supplies and directed the building of small fortifications up and down the rivers of that part of Ohio, but most settlers left the area. Even though the British never invaded there, fear in the region was so great few of them returned to their homes until after Perry's victory over the British navy on Lake Erie on September 10, 1813. By then all the Indian towns were gone.

According to some reports, Chapman made other dangerous journeys to warn settlers and carry messages between the towns. It is likely that most of his service was as a courier. Some stories describe him as a wound dresser and nurse to the injured. But those accounts are later additions to the folklore of the saintly Johnny Appleseed.

———

IT WAS not known until recently just when Chapman became a follower of the Swedish scientist, theologian, and mystic Emanuel Swedenborg (1688–1772). Swedenborg, who lived in London in his later years, had many devotees in Britain, including the poet and artist William Blake. While Swedenborg had not intended to found a new church or denomination of Christianity, he sought to influence Christians and modern thinkers of all varieties of belief. After his death in 1772, however, some of his followers in London founded the Church of the New Jerusalem to espouse his ideas and aspirations and to publish his extensive writings. Members of the church brought his teachings to the New World and in the late eighteenth century were printing selections of Swedenborg's visionary, mystical writings and distributing them as best they could in the new republic. The first congregation in the United States was founded in Baltimore in 1792. Swedenborg deeply influenced some romantic poets, both in Britain and Europe, and in North America. In 1817 the General Convention of the New Jerusalem met in Philadelphia. One of the stated missions of the convention was the dissemination of Swedenborg's writings to the western frontier. In 1995 Professor Joe Besecker of Urbana University discovered that Chapman almost certainly encountered the teachings of Swedenborg in his wanderings in the Ohio wilderness. Researching the Bailey and Barclay families in frontier Ohio and their connection to the founding of a school that became Urbana University near Springfield, Ohio, he found it was Maria Barclay's husband, Judge John Young from Pennsylvania, who influenced Johnny Appleseed's conversion to the Swedenborgian religion from the Congregational church.

While Swedenborg began his career as a distinguished scientist and served on the Swedish Board of Mines much of his life, he was also something of a visionary, predicting nebular theory, magnetic theory, the machine gun, the airplane, and other later inventions. And in middle age he became increasingly set on showing that the physical world coincided with the spiritual universe. Around 1743–45 he began to believe he was in contact with angels, not only in dreams and supernatural visions but in everyday working life as well. He felt he had been given a particular commission to bring his new understanding and insight to humanity at large. He was destined to found the New Church, not as a literal building or organization but as a fraternity of the enlightened of whatever denomination or country.

In 1747 Swedenborg resigned from the Swedish Board of Mines and spent the rest of his life studying and writing, publishing both his mystical works and his more conventional scientific studies. At the core of Swedenborg's teaching was the "doctrine of correspondences" between the material and the spiritual worlds. Swedenborg believed the souls of the dead merge into one great soul or human being. He believed Christ was the greatest example of humanity, but he rejected the doctrine of original sin and atonement. He encouraged his followers to believe in coincident and coextensive physical and spiritual worlds, both of which the enlightened could communicate with. The heaven, the New Jerusalem seen in Revelation 21:2, is present for all who will accept and perceive it. Nature is the physical sign, the manifestation, of the spiritual world which is our home and our legacy.

The name Chapman means "cheap man," or peddler of cheap broadsides or books in the towns and countryside of England. The name is particularly appropriate because John Chapman was also a businessman, an important trader, peddler, and promoter not only of apple trees and medicinal herbs such as catnip, dog fennel, pennyroyal, hoarhound, rattleroot, and remedies for everything from rheumatism to malaria but of Swedenborg's tracts and gospel as well. He was the colporteur of the New Jerusalem in the green wilderness of the West.

A settler named E. Vandorn would later recall camping with Chapman in the forest and listening to him talk about his encounters with rattlesnakes, bears, and wolves. And then "he changed the conversation and introduced the subject of Swedenborg; at the same time he began to fumble in his bosom and brought forth three or four old half-worn-out books. As we were fond of reading, we soon grabbed them, which pleased Johnny."

Others who camped outdoors with Chapman described his contentment in living in the woods. Amos Harding, an ancestor of President Warren Harding, quoted the tree peddler, who lay on his back by the fire and said, "I could not enjoy myself better anywhere—I can lay on my back, look up at the stars and it seems almost as though I can see the angels praising God, for he has made all things for good."

Johnny was always happy to share what he had with fellow campers, and to partake of their provisions, such as bread and butter, but not meat. He was even known to take a dram of applejack or other libation when offered. He liked to tell stories about his affinity with Indians, and his respect for rattlesnakes. When he was younger, he had killed a rattlesnake that bit him, and he had been sorry ever since. Indians did not kill rattlers.

But all conversations with Chapman eventually turned to spiritual things, and to the teachings of Swedenborg. By 1817 his work for Church of the New Jerusalem had become so well known it was reported in a letter written from Philadelphia to the Manchester Society for Printing, Publishing and Circulating the Writing of Emanuel Swedenborg in England:

There is in the western country a very extraordinary missionary of the New Jerusalem. A man has appeared who seems to be almost independent of corporal wants and sufferings. He goes barefooted, can sleep anywhere, in house or out of house, and live upon the coarsest and most scanty fare. He has actually thawed the ice with his bare feet.

He procures what books he can of the New Church; travels into the remote settlements, and lends them wherever he can find readers, and sometimes divides a book into two or three parts for more extensive distribution and usefulness.

This man for years past has been in the employment of bringing into cultivation, in numberless places in the wilderness, small patches (two or three acres) of ground, and then sowing apple seeds and rearing nurseries.

These become valuable as the settlements approximate, and the profits of the whole are intended for the purpose of enabling him to print all the writings of Emmanuel Swedenborg, and distribute them through the western settlements of the United States.

———

WILLIAM SCHLATTER of Philadelphia would later write that he had been in correspondence with Chapman since 1815. Francis Bailey, a minister there, had become the first "receiver" of the "New Heavenly Doctrine" in the New World. Among the subscribers to Bailey's edition of the work of Swedenborg was Benjamin Franklin near the end of his life. The Bailey family would be instrumental in spreading the teachings of Swedenborg west into the Ohio country. It was William Schlatter, importer and wholesaler of dry goods in Philadelphia, who became the primary supplier of Swedenborgian literature to John Chapman.

On May 4, 1817, Schlatter wrote to a fellow Swedenborgian in Wheeling, "I have sent some books to Mr. Chapman, do you know him and has he received the Books, he travels about in Ohio and has much to do with appletrees; I am told he is a singular man but greatly in love with the New Church doctrines and takes great pains in deseminating them."

The Reverend Jonathan W. Condy of Philadelphia, traveling in Ohio at the time, reported meeting Chapman and "finding him to be intelligent, with an absorbing desire to promote the doctrines of his church." Chapman had become the chief contact, for a while, between the base of the Swedenborgian church in Philadelphia and its mission in the western

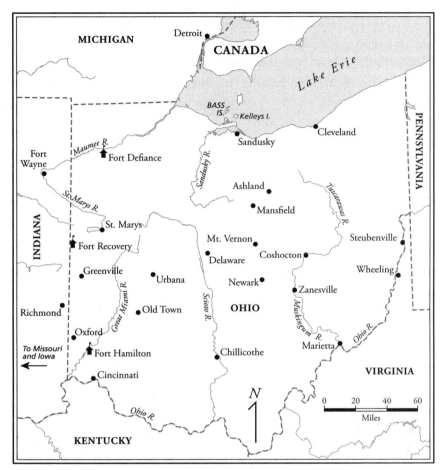

Johnny Appleseed Country, 1840

territory. Because he had little cash and primarily traded by barter, young apple trees, and herbs for clothes and supplies, Chapman wrote to Schlatter offering to trade one of his parcels of land for more printed Swedenborgian literature. Schlatter and other leaders of the New Church understood how valuable a tract of Ohio land would be, but it seems they had exhausted their supply of the books by Swedenborg at that time: "The land that he offers is valuable and if your society had the books we would send them and receive the land and appropriate it for the use of a new Church and School." Schlatter wrote. But there is no record of a deed for such a transfer of land.

It was probably William Schlatter who penned a tribute to John Chapman for the June 1822 Fifth General Convention of the New Churchmen in Philadelphia. "One very extraordinary missionary continued to exert, for the spread of divine truth his modest and humble efforts, which would put the most zealous members to blush. We now allude to Mr. John Chapman, from whom we are in the habit of hearing frequently. His temporal employment consists in preceding the settlements, and sowing nurseries of fruit trees, which he avows to be pursued for the chief purpose of giving him an opportunity of spreading the doctrines throughout the western country.

"In his progress, which neither heat not cold, swamps nor mountains, are permitted to arrest, he carries on his back all the New Church publications he can procure, and distributes them wherever opportunity is afforded. So great is his zeal, that he does not hesitate to divide his volumes into parts, by repeated calls, [to] enable the readers to peruse the whole in succession."

Chapman not only loved to leave Swedenborg's writing with those he encountered, but he enjoyed discussing the content of the books with all who would listen. He was in no hurry. He could spend hours describing his adventures in the wilderness, his beliefs, and the insights of the New Church doctrine. One settler, quoted in *Harper's Monthly* in 1871, remembered his visits in detail.

> *It was his custom, when he had been welcomed to some hospitable log-house after a weary day of journeying, to lie down on the puncheon floor, and, after inquiring if his auditors would hear "some news right fresh from heaven," produce a few tattered books, among which would be a New Testament, and read and expound until his uncultivated hearers would catch the spirit and glow of his enthusiasm, while they scarcely comprehended his language. A lady who knew him in his later years writes in the following terms of one of those domiciliary readings of poor, self-sacrificing Johnny Appleseed: "We can hear him read now, just as he did that summer day, when we were busy quilting up stairs, and he lay near the door, his voice rising denunciatory and thrilling — strong and loud as the roar of wind and waves, then soft and soothing as the balmy airs that quivered the morning-glory leaves about his gray*

beard. His was a strange eloquence at times, and he was undoubtedly a man of genius."

Several settlers described Chapman lying on the floor of a cabin with his feet propped up on a log near the fireplace while he exhorted and explicated the subtle thought of Swedenborg. He claimed to have frequent conversations with angels. Judge Stanbery of Newark, Ohio, would later write of Chapman, "His main bump seemed to be to leave the books of Swedenborg whenever he could get anybody to read them, and leave them until he called again . . . His books were very old. He got them somehow from Philadelphia. He had great thirst for making converts."

Some settlers thought Chapman insane, others that he was possessed by demons. None seemed to think him dangerous. He was an oddity. Indians, who were used to tolerating prophets, holy men, and those possessed by unseen spirits, apparently accepted him more easily than whites, and never harmed him. He returned the favor by arguing that most troubles on the frontier were started by whites, not Indians.

It is interesting that much of Chapman's Swedenborgian message parallels and is contemporary with the strain of the Second Great Awakening called Millennialism. Jonathan Edwards of the First Great Awakening had introduced the idea that the thousand years of the millennial reign of peace and bliss on earth, foretold in Revelation 20:4–6, might precede, not follow, the Second Coming of Christ. It seemed appropriate that the New Jerusalem would be created in the new nation in the New World. The most forceful expression of this vision was put forth by Samuel Hopkins in 1793 in *Treatise on the Millennium.* That work would influence a generation of American preachers who promised their congregations that the kingdom of heaven was about to unfold right here on American soil in their lifetimes. Hopkins's vision of the future included much that was practical as well as spiritual. Families would be reunited in love, legal disputes be settled. There would be new tools and inventions for paving roads, moving mountains, making clothing, and building buildings. The new republic would become a place of unprecedented progress, more wonderful even than words could describe.

Chapman, as far as we know, won few converts to the Church of the New Jerusalem. The teachings of Swedenborg were intellectual, too subtle, and too calm to appeal to most settlers. They preferred the more emotional, demonstrative religion of the revivals sweeping through the region in the spillover from the Second Great Awakening that had been ignited in Kentucky. Sect after sect, camp meeting after camp meeting, came into the region. Chapman's happy talk of correspondences between the physical and spiritual worlds, of conversations with angels and the dead, caused little excitement among those looking for emotional release from their harsh lives through shouting, jerking, speaking in tongues, through holy laughing and holy cursing.

Swedenborg believed the scriptures were not to be taken literally but as an account of spiritual meaning, corresponding to higher truth. Indeed, the natural world was to be read as a text, even a hieroglyph, communicating truths from the Divine Being. Resurrection was merely a continuation of the spiritual life beyond the physical.

According to the known accounts, Chapman lived a life of confidence and happiness. Many who knew him envied his good cheer and dedication to his work. He is said to have attended an outdoor revival meeting in Mansfield, Ohio, later in his life, where the preacher on the stump shouted, "Where now is there a man who, like the primitive Christians, is traveling to heaven barefooted and clad in coarse raiment?" The preacher asked the question several times, and finally Chapman rose and walked closer to the preacher, placed one of his bare feet upon the stump that served a pulpit, pointed to his coffee-sack coat, and said, "Here's your primitive Christian!" The richly clad preacher was so taken aback he stopped the service and dismissed the crowd.

The real Johnny Appleseed was not without a family in his middle and later years. His half sister, Persis, who was nineteen years younger than John, was only a girl of nine when the Chapman family had moved to southeast Ohio. Persis had married a man named William Broom, and around 1817 they had moved west to Perryville and then to Mansfield, Ohio. Chapman employed Broom as his assistant for the rest of his life. Johnny had so many nurseries by then he needed help to manage and cultivate them.

When Chapman moved west of the Maumee into Indiana around 1834, the Brooms followed him. Much of the last decade of his life would be spent in Indiana as he moved his business westward one county and township at a time. For the rest of his life Chapman roved back and forth between his holdings in Ohio and the new orchards in Indiana, wandering from one clearing to another, cleaning weeds and brush away from his trees, trading trees for whatever the settlers wanted to give him.

Chapman died near Fort Wayne, Indiana, in March of 1845, in a cabin that belonged to his friends Mr. & Mrs. William Worth. He had stayed there before. It was reported he was stricken by the "winter plague," likely pneumonia, and lived for about two days. Samuel C. Fletter made a coffin for the old orchardist and later said that at death Chapman wore "a coarse coffee-sack, with a hole cut in the centre through which he passed his head. He had on the waists of four pairs of pants." The body was buried in the David Archer graveyard two and a half miles north of Fort Wayne.

————

WHILE JOHN Chapman did not write himself, the life he lived seemed like a poem, and he has inspired many American poets, including Vachel Lindsay, Carl Sandburg, Edgar Lee Masters, Mary Oliver, and the novelist Louis Bromfield, among others. When Henry David Thoreau wrote his essay "Wild Apples" around 1860 near the end of his life, he may or may not have heard of Johnny Appleseed, but passages in the essay suggest that he had. By then the legend of Johnny Appleseed had spread back over the Alleghenies to his native state of Massachusetts and taken root in that rocky soil.

"It is remarkable how closely the history of the Apple-tree is connected with that of man," Thoreau begins his meditation, stressing the kinship of apples to the rose, true grasses, and the mint family. He traces evidence of apple culture back to the Romans and Greeks and beyond, and quotes the Song of Solomon: "As the apple-tree among the trees of the wood, so is my beloved among the sons . . . Stay me with flagons, comfort me with apples."

Thoreau points out that the apple goes wherever man migrates, along with the horse, cow, and dog. And then he observes:

Our Western emigrant is still marching steadily toward the setting sun with the seeds of the apple in his pocket, or perhaps a few young trees strapped to his load. At least a million apple-trees are thus set farther westward this year than any cultivated ones grew last year . . .

The flowers of the apple are perhaps the most beautiful of any tree's, so copious and so delicious to both sight and scent. The walker is frequently tempted to turn and linger near some more than usually handsome one.

Like John Chapman before him, Thoreau preferred apples grown from seeds. "I love better to go through the old orchards of ungrafted apple-trees, at whatever season of the year, — so irregularly planted: sometimes two trees standing close together; and the rows so devious that you would think that they not only had grown while the owner was sleeping, but had been set out by him in a somnambulic state." Thoreau as the heir of the Romantics knew that the source of the poetic imagination itself was supposed to be located in the reverie, in the hypnagogic state between sleeping and waking where the mind is most receptive to the breeze of inspiration from the cave of dreams or the unconscious.

The apple trees Thoreau prefers are those that have returned to the wild or sprung up from seeds on their own. It is that blend of culture and the wild that thrills him. Wild fruit has a much stronger, spicier tang than domesticated apples. Its flavor is more memorable. Thoreau quotes an old farmer who says wild apples "have a kind of bow-arrow tang." But he concedes that wild fruit is best eaten in the field where it grows. The most "spirited and racy when eaten in the fields or woods, being brought into the house, has frequently a harsh, and crabbed taste."

Thoreau laments the passing of the old orchards planted at the edge of the wilderness, "when the pomace-heap was the only nursery, and trees cost nothing but the trouble of setting them out. Men could afford then to stick a tree by every wall-side and let it take its chance. I see nobody planting trees today in such out-of-the-way places . . . Now that they have grafted trees, and pay a price for them, they collect them into a plat by their houses, and fence them in."

Thoreau, like John Chapman, wanted to live between the original wilderness and the tidy plots of modern civilization, taking the best from both worlds, preaching a gospel of beauty and spiritual independence combining wildness with culture for all who would listen. That beauty and that spirituality were to be found in the West, in the interior of the continent, and deep in the interior of the human mind, and the human imagination.

Though legend has portrayed John Chapman as humble as St. Francis, wearing rags and living on cornmeal mush, he was in fact no pauper. Chapman had owned no land in the Allegheny Valley of Pennsylvania in his youth, but records in Ohio show that he owned a number of tracts of land there, and leased or rented others. Over the years he acquired so many parcels and planted so many trees in them for settlers to buy or barter for, that he became a substantial business man, though he continued to dress and live much as he always had. As he grew to middle age and beyond, it's thought he slept indoors more, especially in winter, boarding with friends in the areas around north central Ohio where most of his orchards grew.

It is something of a mystery why certain people become figures of myth and folklore. Many people do eccentric things, or generous things, seem odd to those around them, yet are forgotten. What is it that makes virtually everyone who knew them remember and talk about a Daniel Boone or a John Chapman? Once the stories start people seem to never tire of passing them on and embellishing the anecdotes, the quotes, the tall tales that grow taller with each telling.

In each instance it is because the figure answers a need in the culture in which they live. In the case of Daniel Boone it was a figure who represented the exceptional courage, curiosity, strength, and vision so many aspired to. The members of a culture seize on such a figure because they want to see themselves reflected in that person. The stories reveal how they like to see themselves, the potential, the ideal of an age. The stories make them believe they are almost like the heroes. If given the chance they too could go into the uncharted wilderness of the West and live for months, even years, not only surviving but thriving, amid the dangers and pristine beauty.

In the case of Chapman the projected ideal is at once more simple and more complex. At the most basic level the Chapman stories concern a pioneer who goes out into the west to plant trees to trade to settlers who will follow him. He is not an explorer or trader, a hunter, trapper, or scout like Boone. But he is out there in the zone between the whites and the Indians, in the beautiful valleys of Ohio, seeding culture, the sweet-est and prettiest and most useful products of culture, in little patches in the woods for those who will come later. As such he is a patriot and patron saint of the frontier, like Boone, or even Washington, who as a youth surveyed Natural Bridge.

The complexity of the figure of Chapman has to do with his mys-terious eccentricities. Though he serves the advancing frontier society, he hardly fits into it. Though he plants the trees and sells them or just gives them away for ragged clothes or a comb of honey, he lives out in the woods like an Indian, like a Merlin. He is the presiding spirit of the forest, elusive, mysterious. He appears with a bit of ribbon for the girls, a few apple trees, a story about being bitten by a rattlesnake, and talks about angels and signs of the spiritual world around us, and then he is gone again, fading back into the forest.

The appeal of the Johnny Appleseed stories is complex because, in one sense, they are about the westward expansion, the acquiring and settling of land, the expulsion of the Indians, the clearing and improvement of land, the accumulation of property, the relentless ambition of the indi-vidual and society as a whole. But the Chapman story is also about the opposite of all those things. In the legend the Johnny Appleseed figure is selfless, generous. What he accumulates he shares with others, often giv-ing it away. He goes barefoot, with a mush pot on his head. He sleeps on leaves in the forest. His ambition is to be independent and to preach the new gospel and to serve others. He might be a figure of fun to some, but for most he answered a deep sense of purpose, discipline, and selflessness they recognized in themselves but mostly suppressed.

For not only was Johnny Appleseed happy in serving others, he was also happier than most people they knew. He was the master of life on his own terms. No doubt the real John Chapman suffered doubts and depression and regrets as all the rest of us do, but the Johnny Appleseed everyone remembered and talked about knew exactly what he was up to. He lived as he wanted, for the purposes he had chosen; and how many of us can claim as much? From that perspective he was a spectacular suc-cess. Under the greed and ambition in ourselves there is another yearn-ing, for the freedom to go our own way, to meet life on our own terms, to be left to our own desires, passions, and chances. It is the romantic strain in us that would produce a Thoreau, an Emily Dickinson.

Johnny Appleseed may have been preaching Swedenborg to the isolated settlers, but he was implicitly preaching something else, an ultimate freedom to just be yourself, unconcerned with status, fashion, excess possessions or comforts. His saintliness and selflessness may have inspired some of the stories, but many more were told that glorified his independence, his life in the country of wonder and the wonderful. The stories of Johnny Appleseed appeal to the side of us that wants to believe we too could step out of the routines and boundaries and timidity of our lives and go wherever and whenever we like. We want to believe that somewhere inside of us we have that reckless courage to move, to survive in the elements. It is one of our favorite fantasies, called by Walt Whitman the "open road," and Johnny Appleseed is its personification, its genius.

It is a fantasy not just about freedom, but freedom in a special place, the West, where the forests are touching the prairie and the view opens out farther and farther under a soaring, infinite sky. Johnny Appleseed plants Edens, and spreads his Eden, with fruit that is unforbidden, and the land he steps across is the promised land of the true West.

— Four —

DAVID CROCKETT

COMEDIAN AND MARTYR,

HIS LIFE AND DEATH

$\mathcal{I}$T IS something of a mystery to modern readers why the figure of the backwoods humorist and comedian became so popular in the midnineteenth century. Writers filled the pages of magazines and newspapers and the stage with stories of Mike Fink, the Keelboatman, and the Big Bear of Arkansas, the backwoods wits who outwit the city slickers. Magazines such as the *Spirit of the Times* carried feature after feature about the doings and sayings of these characters on the rivers and trails of the western country. Another popular entertainment was the minstrel show in which white actors performed in blackface. Pretending to be African Americans, the performers could say things that would have been offensive coming from a white. As one historian puts it, "Performance in blackface provided a convenient license for satire, since assaults on respectability could be attributed to ignorant blacks and still get laughs." The backwoods comedians were popular for similar reasons. It was easy for audiences to look down on backwoods settlers, or "Butternuts," so called because of the gray homespun they wore. Sometimes they were also called Hoojers, meaning "ill-mannered rustics" (possibly from the Dutch *hoog:* tall man, big lout), source of the name Hoosiers.

It is quite possible that laughing at and with the rough figures from the Old Southwest was an effective way of ignoring the actual world of the West where Indians died from diseases and bullets and where slaves were brought, one human being at a time, into the newly cleared paradise. Laughter somehow gave legitimacy to what was after all a very unfunny struggle to possess and dispossess. Laughter smoothed over the rough edges of the national determination to expand and annex and soothed the troubled conscience.

But the original of the type, the man who more than anyone else inspired the fashion for backwoods humor and became one of the most famous Americans in our history, was far more complex than a mere frontier buffoon. While David Crockett was indeed one who played pranks on political rivals and could bring an audience to its feet, or knees, beating its thighs in laughter, his failures and disasters were what won him his greatest success and fame. And it was his death at the hands of Mexican soldiers at the Alamo March 6, 1836, that enshrined him among the immortals of American history and legend. While many figures of the time were able to play the buffoon effectively, or let others portray them as such, only Crockett was primarily remembered for what he had suffered and lost. If Johnny Appleseed is the saint of the western frontier folklore, Crockett is its martyr.

———

DAVID CROCKETT was born on August 17, 1786, on the Nolichucky River in what would become Tennessee but was then the short-lived state of Franklin. As a youngster he worked hard grubbing roots in new ground and clearing land for others, to pay his father's debts. He left home early to work as a teamster and to wander. Even as a child he showed independence and resourcefulness and a tendency to find failure, however much effort he expended. His education was minimal, but he had an excellent memory and the ability to make people laugh. He could entertain with colorful stories and was willing to make himself the butt of his own jokes.

Crockett's ancestors had been as restless as he was. His great-great-great-grandfather, Antoine de Crocketagne, had been converted to Protestantism in the seventeenth century in the south of France. When Huguenots were ordered to leave France, he fled with his family to England and then Ireland. Antoine's third son, Joseph Louis, married Sarah Stewart and in 1708 became part of the Irish migration to America.

Settling first in New Rochelle, New York, they moved on to Pennsylvania. Their son William was born in 1709, and by 1718 the family was living in Virginia. Crockett's mother, Rebecca Hawkins, came from English stock that had arrived in Virginia in 1658. Her grandfather, Joseph Hawkins, was married in 1739 to Anneke Jane Edwards, of a Quaker family. Crockett's aunt Sarah Hawkins had married John Sevier, hero of the Battle of Kings Mountain.

It was David's grandfather, also named David, who had moved his family across the mountains in 1775, from Lincoln County, North Carolina, and was killed by Cherokees in an attack in 1777 near future Rogersville, Tennessee. It has been recorded that the grandfather brought with him into the overmountain wilderness "a parsel of books" weighing fifteen pounds. David's father, John Crockett, survived the violence of the Revolutionary period on the frontier and married Rebecca Hawkins around 1780, settling in what was then Washington County, but later Greene County, North Carolina. John Crockett seemed unlucky in his business ventures. A gristmill he built with Thomas Galbreath was swept away by a flood. He tried speculating in land but did not prosper in that enterprise either. In 1794 he moved his family to a property on Mossy Creek in Jefferson County but lost the land because of debt. It was on a portion of that property that John set up a tavern, but he never seemed to get out of debt.

Unlike many on the frontier, John Crockett was literate enough to sign his name. He would live until September 15, 1834, never succeeding at any of his businesses. His story is not unusual among the early settlers of Tennessee and Kentucky. His famous son would record in his autobiography that he himself was born "at the mouth of Lime Stone, on the Nola-chucky river." Crockett would give few details of his first twelve years, but it is easy to imagine the boy's life on the river made famous as the home of John Sevier.

The fertile soil along the Nolichucky grew great maple trees and giant sycamores lined the banks of the stream. The land was still marked by buffalo trails, though the bison themselves were gone. Deer gathered at the salt licks. In Constance Rourke's words, "Panthers crouched in tall sycamores. Wildcats were at home there. Black bears crept into hollow trees. Settlers in the new country were buried in corners of the river valleys with cabins far apart, each with a small tract chopped out of the wilderness."

It is said that David's father trained him as a hunter by giving him a rifle each day with only one load of lead and powder. With no shots to spare the boy became an expert marksman. He learned to call turkeys and other game, and he paddled on the river in a dugout canoe. In his autobiography Crockett would begin his life story by describing how his father, deep in debt around 1798, sold his son's services to one Jacob Siler to help drive a herd of cattle to Rockbridge County, Virginia. David helped drive the cattle to Virginia, but when they reached their destination Siler would not release him to return home. On a snowy night the homesick twelve-year-old slipped away and joined a group of travelers on their way back to Tennessee. Worn out and disillusioned, David finally reached home in the winter or spring of 1799.

Crockett next attended for a few months a school taught by one Benjamin Kitchen, but finding study and the birch rod of the teacher not much to his liking, he played hooky from the classroom. David so much feared the paternal wrath that he ran away from home when his father discovered his delinquency, hiring himself out to a Jesse Cheek to drive cattle to Front Royal, Virginia. One of his older brothers joined him on the drive. After reaching Front Royal, David decided he would return to Tennessee, hoping his father's fury had waned. With his pay of four dollars, he set out. But on the way he met Adam Myers, a teamster from Greeneville, Tennessee, who urged him to join his party on its way to Gerardstown, near Winchester, Virginia. From there they would return directly to Tennessee. Though he met his brother on the road, David refused to return with him and instead continued on to Gerardstown. When Myers was not able to find cargo to carry back to the West, David was forced to work as a farm laborer in the area to support himself. His pay was twenty-five cents a day.

In the spring of 1800 Myers and David journeyed on to Baltimore. A wagon was damaged when a horse bolted, and while repairs were being made David visited the harbor and was offered a berth on a ship bound for London. Myers, however, angrily refused to release David, threatening to whip him, and thus blocked his possible career as a sailor. The boy escaped from Myers, who had also refused him his pay, and on the road back to the West encountered a man named Henry Myers who agreed to confront Adam Myers and demand the withheld pay. When it turned out Adam Myers was broke, the penniless Crockett set out toward home with Henry. Before they parted, Henry took up a collection from fellow travelers and gave Crockett three dollars.

The three bucks were spent by the time David reached Montgomery County, Virginia. There he was forced to work as a laborer for James Caldwell and then Elijah Griffith. Griffith himself got into debt and disappeared without paying David. It was not until February or March of 1802 that Crockett crossed the wide New River in a borrowed canoe and set out for home once again. On the way, he stopped for a few weeks with his uncle Joseph Crockett in Sullivan County, Virginia, then met up with his brother and continued on his way to Tennessee.

Crockett was by then sixteen, and when he reached his father's tavern he did not introduce himself. It was only when he sat down for supper that his older sister "recollected" him and rushed to embrace the prodigal son. The whole family gave him a warm welcome. It was time for David to finally get some schooling, but his father, in debt for thirty-six dollars to man named Abraham Wilson, asked David to work out the debt. When that note was paid, he worked off a second for forty dollars owed to John Kennedy, a Quaker from North Carolina. After that debt was paid, he continued to work for Kennedy, hoping to earn enough money for new clothes. One of Kennedy's sons taught school, and Crockett agreed to work for him in exchange for six months of instruction in reading and writing and learning "to cypher some in the three first rules in figures." Those months were all the formal education Crockett would ever have.

It was at about the age of seventeen that the romantic Crockett began to fall in love with the girls around the region. He was stuck on a niece of Kennedy's who came for a visit, but she was already engaged. He then began to court a young woman "whose name is nobody's business." She was in fact Margaret Elder, and though they became engaged, David's partying and frolicking made her decide to marry another. Unaware of that, Crockett went to visit Margaret in Dandridge, Tennessee, carrying a marriage licence dated October 21, 1805. When he stopped at a house on the way, he was told Margaret was to marry another man the following day. Surprised and hurt, he turned around and went home. "I continued in this down-spirited situation for a good long time," he later wrote.

But in less than a year Crockett had found another sweetheart and wed. His bride, won through determined courting, was an Irish girl named Mary Finley, called Polly. They were married August 14, 1806, three days before his twentieth birthday. As was the custom, when Crockett approached the Finley cabin on his wedding day, he sent friends ahead to ask for a drink. When they returned with a full jug as a sign of welcome, David and his friends proceeded. To Crockett's surprise, he was stopped outside the cabin by Polly's father, who explained that Mrs. Finley was now opposed to the match. She first spoke harsh words to David, and then apologized, saying she only hated to lose her daughter, and the union was solemnized. The couple rode to the Crockett home for the infare party. All his life Crockett loved dancing and it is certain they had a long and lively wedding party, with many horns of spirits consumed. A neighbor would later say, "Nobody can dance longer or sing longer or get into more scrapes than that lad of Crockett's." It was said that he "footed it gayly" with the ladies.

In his autobiography Crockett would describe his satisfaction after the marriage. "I thought I was completely made up, and needed nothing more in the whole world. But I soon found this was all a mistake—for now having a wife, I wanted every thing else; and, worse than all, I had nothing to give for it." Though happily married, Crockett was broke, and not for the last time.

In the years following his marriage, Crockett would struggle to support his family, as children arrived at regular intervals, first John Wesley, then William, then Margaret. As Crockett put it, "I found I was better at increasing my family than my fortune." Determined to improve their circumstances, in 1811 Crockett decided to move south and west to the Duck and Elk river country. With the help of his father-in-law he journeyed into that wilderness and claimed and cleared a place on the Mulberry Fork of Elk River in Lincoln County. Game was plentiful there, and "It was here that I began to distinguish myself as a hunter, and to lay the foundation for all my future greatness . . . Of deer and smaller game I killed abundance; but the bear had been much hunted in those parts before."

This was the first leg of his long journey to the frontier West. The settlement of central Tennessee was well under way by then, and the Crocketts joined the tide spreading into that country of rolling hills and rivers, encroaching closer and closer to Creek and Chickasaw territory.

As he said, it was on Mulberry Creek that Crockett began to acquire the reputation for hunting that was central to his fame. He had a pack of coon hunting dogs and neighbors liked to say, "Crockett can outsmart most any coon or possum." It was also said that he knew how "to throw his voice so it would follow his dogs along the ground between ridges of the hills, and that his hunting call could travel even round the shoulder of a steep bluff."

In early 1813 Crockett moved his family again, from Lincoln County to Rattlesnake Spring Branch of Bean's Creek in Franklin County, near the Alabama line. They were living on Rattlesnake Spring Branch when the Fort Mims massacre occurred on August 30, 1813. A messenger to Andrew Jackson in Nashville passed through Franklin County with the news and even before the general was informed of events at Fort Mims the local militia, including Crockett, began to muster in Winchester, Tennessee. Since Crockett already had a reputation as an expert hunter, he was chosen to serve as scout and to supply meat for his unit.

Crockett's memories of his service in the Creek War were especially vivid, and years later he would recall the night patrols in hostile territory. "The moon was about the full, and the night was clear; we therefore had the benefit of her light from night to morning, and I knew if we were placed in such danger as to make a retreat necessary, we could travel by night as well as in the day time." He was present at the battle of Tallushatchee and participated in the killing of most of the inhabitants. "We now shot them like dogs," he would later write. He even remembered eating potatoes from the cellar of a burned dwelling cooked in "the oil of the Indians we had burned up on the day before [which] had run down on them."

On November 7, 1813 Jackson's army marched to the relief of the friendly Creek village of Talladega. It was supposedly on the return to Fort Strother after Talladega that the independent Crockett was taken before Jackson for some infraction of the rules when he heard the general say, "Be always sure you're right—then go ahead," which later became Crockett's much repeated motto.

Crockett was one of the rebellious militiamen who demanded to go home in December of 1813 when supplies ran out and they had no winter coats. Though he would later claim the men had faced down the general, we know it was actually the other way around, with Jackson threatening to shoot the first man who stepped forward. But Crockett did return to his family when his three-month enlistment expired on December 24, 1813. And he did not rejoin the militia service until September 14, 1814, thus missing the major battle at Horseshoe Bend. By the time he was mustered out on March 27, 1815, he had risen from private to the rank of third sergeant. While serving his second enlistment he participated in Jackson's campaign to Pensacola, and his unit stayed in Florida to keep an eye on the local Indians while Jackson and the main army marched on to New Orleans to meet the British. On his return journey to Franklin County, Crockett recalled passing the site of the battle of Talladega and seeing Indian skulls scattered about like gourds in "a great gourd patch." Though Crockett would later alter and embroider some details of his account of the Creek War in his autobiography, the gist of his narrative is clear-eyed and shows a remarkable candor.

Before Crockett returned from the militia, his wife Mary gave birth to their third child, Margaret (also called Polly). Mary would die the following summer, possibly from complications after the birth. In his autobiography Crockett says, "Death, that cruel leveller . . . entered my humble cottage, and tore from my children an affectionate good mother, and from me a tender and loving wife."

With three children to look after, one an infant, Crockett soon began courting a widow, Elizabeth Patton, whose husband had been killed in the Creek War. She had two children of her own and a prosperous farm of about two hundred acres. She also had savings of about eight hundred dollars. According to James Shackford, Elizabeth Patton "was a large woman, a sensible woman, and she evidently had greater managerial ability and more regular habits than David." And so in 1816 Crockett "married up" and his career began to take off. At the wedding party, as all the guests were gathered in the Patton home, a pig wandered into the room as though an invited guest. With great ceremony Crockett ushered the hog out the door, commenting, "Old hook, from now on, *I'll* do the grunting around here."

Always restless, Crockett made an exploring trip into Alabama, looking for land in recently surrendered Creek territory. Thousands of settlers were pouring into the new states of Mississippi and Alabama, admitted to the union in 1817 and 1819, respectively. While away from home he was attacked by an illness, probably malaria, and barely survived. When he returned to his family he found that his traveling companions had returned and told Elizabeth he was dead. Anticipating Mark Twain's comment about his own reported death, Crockett later drawled, "I know'd this was a whapper of a lie, as soon as I heard it."

Instead of moving to Alabama, he took his family farther west to Lawrence County, Tennessee in 1817. Though stricken again with "ague and fever," he chose a spot on Shoal Creek far from any settlement or "law." It was here that Crockett was appointed a magistrate and began his career in public life. He was popular, both as an official and as a neighbor and leading citizen. Crockett had been elected a lieutenant of the local militia, and he was soon elected colonel of the Tennessee militia. His gift for humor, self-deprecation, and common sense charmed people. With the capable Elizabeth running his household, he was free to attend the meetings where the political life of the region was conducted. Crockett was the right man at the right time in the new "squatter democracy" of the western frontier. His dry wit struck just the right note for people struggling to establish their community and their lives at the edge of the wilderness. In 1818 he was elected town commissioner for Lawrenceburg. One of the positions he filled was as a member of "Juries of View," which oversaw the building of roads in the new territory. As a hunter and scout, Crockett was in his element in the building and maintaining of roads around hills and across swampy bottom land and across streams.

The land in that part of Tennessee was flat and miry, especially along creeks and rivers. Roads made of logs laid on the wet ground were called rail roads. Because he had helped build so many of these corduroy roads, Crockett was able to later brag that he had constructed many "rail roads at little or no expense other than honest labor." His eastern listeners may have assumed he was talking about iron rails, but some newspapers reported Crockett was so ignorant he didn't know what a railroad was.

On January 1, 1821, Crockett resigned as commissioner of Lawrenceburg and ran as representative for the Tennessee legislature. Though he claimed to be ignorant of politics, he proved to be adept at making his opponents appear foolish or pretentious, and he himself modest and likable. Humor was his main tool in campaigning, but he also knew that most voters were fond of applejack or corn liquor, and there always seemed to be something to drink around his campaign stops.

Crockett and James K. Polk began their careers in Tennessee politics at about the same time. It would be hard to imagine two more different politicians than the humorless, formal Polk and the folksy, wise-cracking Crockett. Polk is supposed to have said to Crockett at a rally, "Well, colonel, I suppose we shall have a radical change of the judiciary at the next session of the Legislature." Crockett later claimed he had backed away from the discussion because he didn't know what "judiciary" meant. The people loved his modesty, which was almost certainly false in this case since he had served as commissioner, magistrate, justice of the peace, and juror for years. But such pretended ignorance was part of a pose that won him votes then and later.

The area of Tennessee to which Crockett had moved, in the far western part of the state, was called the Shakes because of all the earthquakes that had struck the region since the cataclysmic temblors of 1811–12 that created Reelfoot Lake and made the Mississippi and Ohio rivers run backward briefly. The force of the quakes had broken big trees off at the stumps and made deep crevices in the earth. The regions of broken down trees were called hurricanes. It was a world of swamps and thickets, and canebrakes sometimes thirty feet high.

Crockett's new place was just southeast of Reelfoot Lake, described by the folklorist Constance Rourke: "It was wild and strange, with cypresses showing their black-green tops in lines above the water. The earthquake had shaken them many feet below the hillsides where they had grown. Soon the lake was covered by great yellow lilies, so that to come upon it suddenly was to find a yellow light glowing in the midst of the shadowed water . . . Here too were the great snapping turtles with great heads and armored scales that became famous in Tennessee legend." Crockett would sometimes brag that as a baby he had been rocked in a snapping turtle's shell for a cradle.

In this western region, even as he became more and more involved with political life, Crockett hunted bears more often than ever before. The thickets sheltered hundreds of bears and he concentrated on hunting them for their skins, for their delicious flesh, and for the oil that could be rendered from their fat. Crockett seemed to have a special affinity for bears and bear hunting, which he found challenging and exciting. Bears were evasive and resourceful. He once remarked, "Bears is witty." He hunted with his favorite rifle, which he called Betsey or Old Betsey, the name of his second wife. Of the rifle he is supposed to have bragged, "She's a mighty rough old piece but I love her, for she and I have seen hard times together. If I hold her right she always sends the ball where I tell her. She mighty seldom tells me a lie. My dogs and I have had many a high time of it, with old Betsey." It was said on the frontier that a man should choose a rifle as carefully as a wife. Crockett's comments sound indeed like they refer as much to a lover as to a firearm.

One of the sayings about Crockett that got passed around as a joke was that he could grin at a coon or possum and make it fall out of a tree. Hunters said he "could grin most any varmint right out of countenance." It was a legend Crockett encouraged with his own stories. Once he treed a particularly large coon and tried to grin him down. "So I grinned and grinned, and there he sat looking more like an old coon every minute with his stripes and rings . . . I got into a pretty savage humor when he didn't fall, so at last I clomb the oak, but — it was nothing but a knot-hole, 'thout any bark on it."

Known in this period as "the great bear hunter of the West," Crockett was making advances on other fronts as well. He began to teach himself to read better. In his autobiography Crockett wrote, "I improved my handwriting in such manner as to be able to prepare my warrants, and keep my record book, without much difficulty." He read everything he could find, newspapers, almanacs, the few books available. As noted, he had an excellent memory, and though he had perfected the public pose of the ignorant backwoodsman, his vocabulary and range of allusion show that he was much more than that. His anecdotes and jokes, accent and manner, were something he put on and exaggerated, along with the buckskin jacket and coonskin cap. He created a persona that had its roots in fact but was mostly artifice. The result was ever greater popularity and recognition. He made people remember him. His fame grew and many people remembered him as over six feet tall, though he was really only a little over five feet ten inches.

Crockett's first term as a Tennessee state legislator began September 17, 1821, at Murfreesborough, then the state capital. He was placed on the standing committee of propositions and grievances. From the beginning to the end of his political career he was most concerned with protecting the rights of the poor claiming land in the western regions. He voted to free settlers in the western district from paying double taxes as a penalty for late payment. And he submitted a proposal to prevent several grants of land made on the same military warrant. He introduced bills to protect the inhabitants of the West from powerful speculators and excessive taxation.

As James Shackford puts it, "This matter of west Tennessee Lands was to be Crockett's major concern for the rest of his political life—and [was] finally to prove his undoing." When the state of North Carolina granted the land that would become the state of Tennessee in 1796, it stipulated that all warrants issued by North Carolina to veterans would be honored by the new state. A congressional line was drawn north to south, just west of central Tennessee, and those with old miliary warrants could claim land only east of that line. When there proved to be not enough land east of the demarcation to satisfy all the warrant claims, the issue became controversial as claims were made in the western part of the state where land should have been open to all for purchase and settlement. The controversy was aggravated by the common practice whereby warrant holders divided their allotment into smaller parcels to secure only the best lands "fit for cultivation." The poor were helpless against this practice of the big warrant holders who tended to preempt all the choice property. From the first, Crockett focused on this thorny issue and never gave it up. He would also fight for more adequate representation of the western population in the legislature. The people of the new territories were taxed heavily yet had little to say in the legislature. It was one of the issues that had brought on the American Revolution and it was an issue on which Crockett never conceded defeat.

It was in this first stint in the state legislature that Crockett was called derisively "the gentleman from the cane." Crockett seized on the phrase and used it himself, and the distinction gave him even greater popularity.

He also brought down laughter on his detractor by pinning a cambric ruffle, like the ruffle his detractor wore, to his own rough shirt when he rose to speak. The anecdote is one of dozens that show how "the gentleman from the cane" could use an insult directed at him to win favor with the voters and fellow politicians.

The tragedy of Crockett's political career had its sources in his dislike of Andrew Jackson. On the surface this is surprising since both men were from the backwoods, had fought their way up from poverty, and were passionately committed to the settlement of western lands. Both worked vigorously to defend the rights of the poor and to extend power beyond the privileged few to those in the former Indian territories of the old Southwest. You might think that Jackson and Crockett would have been fast allies. And for a time they were, sort of.

But besides the many traits and concerns they had in common, these two men had deep, indelible differences. Remember, Crockett was a private among the rebelling militiamen who demanded to go home in December 1813 and were faced down by the indomitable Jackson. Crockett never liked military officers, thinking them arrogant and aristocratic, but from the first, Jackson had seen himself as a leader, a man of destiny, a hero like Washington, like Caesar, like Napoleon. From his youth he had worn the most expensive clothes he could acquire, ridden the finest horses he could buy, and perfected the manners of a gentleman. And while Jackson might walk with his men as Old Hickory when the need arose, he did so in the finest uniform that could be had. Jackson lived like a man of wealth, in a great house with white columns, with many acres, many slaves, blooded race horses in his stables. Crockett lived all his life in cabins and boarding houses.

But there was a deeper difference between the two men. Jackson was known as a killer, not only of Indians in the Creek War and of the British at New Orleans in 1815 but also of men in duels. Jackson had blood on his hands. In contrast, Crockett was a humble, joking man who fought with humor and self-deprecation. Crockett fought no duels and usually portrayed himself as a loser in everything but bear hunting. His ordinariness, his failures, endeared him to people as much as his humor. His life story was made up of one debacle after another, leading to the ultimate debacle at the Alamo.

Crockett and Jackson also viewed themselves and their country in very different ways. While he worked for the rights of the people of the West, Jackson lived like the richest of the southern planters. The fact is, he intended for the world he created to be ruled by men like himself, heroes, owners of vast lands, patriarchs who treated common people and slaves as though they were children. Jackson saw himself in almost a feudal light. As Jon Meacham points out, Jackson thought of himself as a father to the nation. There is a paternalistic air to almost everything he ever said or wrote. But Crockett was one of the common people, in his speech, in his dress, in his vision of the future, and Jackson's personality and the vested power Old Hickory and his cronies held in Tennessee and Washington were repugnant to him. And because he despised Jackson he blindly—but willingly—let himself be used as a tool by Jackson's political enemies, the Whigs.

———

THERE IS much that we don't know about Crockett's second wife, Elizabeth Patton Crockett, born May 22, 1788. But everything we do know suggests she was an unusually capable, strong, and loyal wife. The biographer Mark Derr uses the words "frugal" and "industrious" to describe Elizabeth. Born to one of the leading families of western North Carolina, near Asheville, she was willing to go to the Tennessee frontier with her first husband and first cousin, James Patton, and then move even farther into the western wilderness with Crockett. In addition to two children she had when she married Crockett, she gave birth to four more. Given Crockett's fame, it is surprising just how little information we have about this helpmeet who survived him and later moved to Texas to take up the land grant the new republic and then state gave to the widow of its hero.

Though Crockett's biographers have tended to ignore or skirt over the issue, there has always been some confusion about the actual date of Elizabeth's marriage to Crockett. Many sources give the date of the ceremony as May 1816. But their first child was born September 16, 1816, which suggests they had become lovers months before the wedding.

We know that Elizabeth was a careful and concerned wife from several anecdotes recounted in Crockett's autobiography. As Christmas approached in late 1823, he had spent so much time hunting for a winter supply of meat he ran low on gunpowder. A brother-in-law not far away had secured an extra keg for him, but there had been heavy rains and the swollen rivers had begun to freeze. Elizabeth begged her husband not to go for the powder, fearing he would either freeze to death or drown in the flooded streams now icing over. Taking his rifle "Betsey," he made his way through deep snow, and with great difficulty he reached his brother-in-law's house, exhausted, wet, and nearly frozen. There he recuperated and waited two days, hoping the weather would improve or the streams freeze over solid. While there he shot two deer for the relatives.

After three days he figured he might as well set out for home, guessing the streams were frozen thick enough for him to walk across. But carrying the keg of powder on his shoulder he crashed through the ice and had to break a way through the frozen stream. Once across he saw fresh tracks in the ice and decided to follow them, thinking it must be a bear. Luckily the tracks led right to his own cabin. Elizabeth had sent out a young man to look for Crockett. "When I got home," Crockett later wrote, "I wasn't quite dead, but mighty nigh it; but I had my powder, and that was what I went for."

It was Elizabeth who hired a man to go to Alabama in 1817, when it was reported that Crockett had died there, to find out what had happened and if possible recover his money and personal effects. Though it turned out Crockett himself arrived home, pale and weak, before the man sent to search for him returned, the incident shows how Elizabeth was able to take charge, even when she thought her second husband had died.

Like many women of the frontier, Elizabeth had to look after the household while her husband was away on hunts and then for longer periods while he was campaigning or serving in Congress in faraway Washington. With wild animals, snakes, alligators in the cane, and Indians sometimes prowling around, it was a daily struggle against heat or cold, floods or drought, blizzards or hail storms, that destroyed garden crops. Cows had to be milked, horses fed, eggs gathered, fires made, water carried, clothes washed, sick children nursed, thread spun, and cloth woven. Only with such a wife could Crockett have pursued the life of a hunter and then politician as he did. One measure of the respect and affection between Crockett and Elizabeth's father, Robert Patton, is the fact that when Robert died November 11, 1832, Crockett was made co-executor of his will. Though the will would be contested in court by Elizabeth's siblings, and Elizabeth's brother George refused to distribute his father's money as directed in the will, Crockett's appointment says a good deal about his status in the family and in the world by that time.

According to their youngest daughter, Matilda, Crockett called Elizabeth "Bet." When he lost the election of 1835 he is supposed to have told his wife, "Well, Bet, I am beat, and I'm off for Texas."

Elizabeth's thrift and good management were all the more important because Crockett himself tended to let money slip through his fingers. Both his heavy drinking and his gambling worried his wife. As the biographer Mark Derr says, "Crockett himself could be profligate — buying drinks at every opportunity, gambling and helping out people in need — and frequently stretched his resources beyond their limit." It had been Elizabeth's eight hundred dollars that paid for building the gristmill, the distillery, the gunpowder factory they had owned by 1820. With thirteen tracts of land between them, amounting to about 614 acres, they had seemed well on their way to prosperity on Shoal Creek when Crockett was first elected to the Tennessee legislature. But the flash flood that destroyed the mill and gunpowder factory in September 1821 set them back so drastically they had to sell their land to pay debts and move on farther west. It was a story that would be repeated throughout Crockett's career. Just when it looked as though he was going to make his fortune something always intervened, and he was broke again. Though Crockett expected Elizabeth to blame him for investing all her money in the mill and distillery and gunpowder factory lost in the flash flood, she only advised him to pay off all his debts as he was able. As Crockett explained, it was "better to keep a good conscience with an empty purse, than to get a bad opinion of myself, with a full one."

David and Elizabeth's four children were Robert Patton Crockett born in 1816, Elizabeth Jane born in 1818, Rebekah Elvira (called Sissy) born in 1819, and Matilda born in 1821. In all Elizabeth would oversee a family of nine children, as well as managing the family businesses, buying, selling and leasing of land, running several farms, and supporting Crockett's speculations, hunting, and political efforts. To repay her, Crockett always promised to make a great fortune with his next enterprise. If other men could, why couldn't he? On his last trip, to Texas, he promised to make a fortune there.

As with many women of the time, Elizabeth was barely literate. But she was no less capable for it. According to Buddy Levy, "She had grown accustomed to fiscal irresponsibility and disaster in nearly every one of his schemes," but she begged Crockett to give up drinking and in 1829 he agreed. During his campaigns and while serving in Washington he may have fallen off the wagon from time to time, but it seems he sustained long periods of sobriety in his later years. "I . . . have not tasted one drop of Arden Spirits sense I arrived here nor never expect to while I live nothing stronger than cider," he wrote in a letter to his brother-in-law George Patton from Washington.

Several biographers have assumed that after Crockett lost the election of 1831 Elizabeth gave up on him because of his long absences and waste of money on campaigns and moved to another house to live separately. This confusion apparently comes from the fact that the Crocketts owned several properties and farms in the Gibson County area, and when she leased or sold one property Elizabeth would move to another, so at times Crockett would be farming and hunting in one place while his family lived at another. There is no real evidence of an estrangement between the couple. While the marriage may not have been romantic, Elizabeth seemed able to tolerate his long absences, and when Crockett left for Texas in 1835, he promised to return and bring her and their family to the new territory.

———

IN HIS political campaigns Crockett was, like Johnny Appleseed, the first creator of his legend. As with most legends, there was a substantial body of fact behind Crockett's reputation. He *was* a superb bear hunter, and he *did* fight with the Tennessee militia in the 1813–14 Creek War. But as a soldier he served primarily as a scout and provider of game for his company. As noted, he was home on leave when the great battle of Horseshoe Bend occurred March 27, 1814, though he rarely troubled to mention his absence on that fateful day in his campaign speeches and writings.

What Crockett did mention repeatedly was how often he was cheated, taken advantage of, overtaken by bad luck, became a victim of bad weather, acts of God. Crockett had a gift for making himself remembered as a victim of disasters. While Crockett's claims of ignorance charmed his listeners, it was his stories of how he encountered disasters that won him the most admirers.

Though he had already served in the Tennessee legislature, Crockett was defeated when he ran for the U.S. Congress in 1825. He found himself unable to overcome the accusations and fabrications leveled against him in the rowdy political campaign of his rival. Smarting from the failure, he turned to other enterprises. To recover from his humiliation in the polls, Crockett undertook a new line of business. Farmers and traders on the frontier in Kentucky and western Tennessee had been taking loads of produce and goods down the river to New Orleans for decades. Everything from deer hides to whiskey, ginseng to wild honey, could be floated down the Ohio and its tributaries to the Mississippi on flatboats and on down to the Crescent City for a profit, and the settlers returned home with their pockets full of money.

Hiring a crew of men, Crockett took them to a lake on the Obion River west of his home and put them to work making staves for barrels from cypress wood. Since almost everything on the frontier was moved in barrels, whether gunpowder, flour, whiskey, ginseng, or tobacco, there was a great demand for coopers, and for the materials they used. Crockett's plan was to make thirty thousand staves, load them on two flatboats made there on Obion Lake, and float the cargo down to New Orleans for a substantial profit. That he had little or no experience in river navigation did not seem an obstacle to him.

At the site south of Reelfoot Lake, Crockett and his men began felling trees and carving staves. Staves had to be strong and limber and tapered at both ends so when bent in a cooper's tool they fit tightly in the bulging shape common to barrels. In theory, it was a promising venture. The cypress wood was there for the taking, and his men soon learned how to cut the staves. An experienced worker could cut and shape scores of staves in a day.

To increase his profit, Crockett left his men to carve staves and build two flatboats to float the cargo, and went bear hunting himself. Bear meat was preferred by most to venison, and fat from all the acorns and other mast eaten meant the sweet flesh could be smoked and seasoned as bear bacon. There was also a market for the skins, and bear fat could be rendered down to oil, which sold for more than the meat itself. It is also likely Crockett preferred the excitement of bear hunting with his dogs to the drudgery of cutting and shaping wooden staves day after day.

The woods of western Tennessee at that time were teeming with bears. He soon killed, butchered, and salted down enough meat to last for months. But no sooner had he laid in the supply of bear meat than a neighbor invited him to go on another hunt. Never one to disappoint a neighbor, Crockett agreed, and soon had killed fifteen more bears. Afterward he returned to his work crew on Obion Lake and worked for a few days there. But soon he found an excuse to take his young son hunting, perhaps to instruct him in the fundamentals of pursuing bears. The first afternoon they killed three bears in the vicinity of Big and Little Clover Lick creeks.

Crockett invited a poor man who was grubbing new ground for a pittance to join the hunt and gather more meat than he could possibly earn by his labor. At the end of the hunt he gave the man a thousand pounds of bear meat. This hunt occurred during the last week of 1825.

Early one morning they started out through a "hurricane," a stretch of forest where a storm or earthquake had knocked down thousands of trees. Crockett knew that bears liked to hide among such fallen timbers. They killed three bears quickly but were slowed down not only by the fallen trees, but by huge cracks in the earth caused by the many earthquakes in the area. The crevices were traps for both bears and men. When the dogs set off on a new bear trail late in the day, Crockett followed in the gathering dusk.

It was a dangerous gambit. Crockett plunged through freezing swamp water, thick brush, fallen logs, and the fissures. When he came to a poplar tree with a shadow in the limbs, he fired at the shadow and a bear fell to the ground. While the animal fought with the dogs, Crockett unsheathed his long knife, but he could see nothing. The bear fell into a crevice about four feet deep and he shot it again. Only wounded, the bear scrambled out of the crack and attacked the dogs. Then the bear retreated to the crevice and both dogs and hunter followed. Taking a long pole Crockett prodded the beast. "So I got down, and my dogs got in before him and kept his head towards them . . . I made a lounge with my long knife, and fortunately stuck him right through the heart; at which he just sank down, and I crawled out in a hurry. In a little time my dogs all come out too, and seemed satisfied, which was the way they always had of telling me that they had finished him."

And then Crockett relates in his autobiography one of the episodes that became an essential part of his legend. In the bitter cold he tried to start a fire to warm himself, but all the wood within reach was wet. Knowing he was in danger of freezing in the dark, he jumped and shouted to get his blood circulating. When that did not work he started climbing a tree about two feet in diameter and straight up for thirty feet to the first limbs. All night he shinnied up the tree and then slid down. When daylight came he hung the bear killed the night before out of reach of varmints and found his way back to camp.

Colorful as the story is, it probably contains only a grain of truth. Shinnying up a tree thirty feet is such taxing work he would probably have collapsed with numbness and exhaustion and frozen to death long before the night was over. Probably he did climb such a tree a time or two, looking for a glimpse of the fire at his camp. More likely he wrapped himself in the bear skin and waited for the day.

Crockett returned to the stave making crew on Obion Lake in January of 1826 and helped finish thirty thousand staves as well as two flatboats. The boats were big clumsy things with an oar on either side and a rudder in the rear, and they depended on the current to propel them. With luck the oars and rudder would help turn the craft away from sandbars and deadly logjams. Neither Crockett nor his crew knew much about river travel.

The plan was to float downstream all day, then tie up on shore to camp at night. But the first day on the mighty river Crockett found it impossible to guide the flatboats to shore. The swift Mississippi current was more powerful than he had anticipated. He found he had little or no control over the flatboats. Rivermen in passing craft shouted advice to them, but it did little good. There seemed no way to steer the heavy flatboats. Other boatmen advised them to forget pulling to the bank and continue on down the river. Word of their plight must have spread, for people gathered at landings along the banks with lanterns, waving and shouting directions.

To keep them from being separated in the dark, Crockett lashed the two boats together, making the craft even clumsier to handle. Finally they got through the treacherous bend called the Devil's Elbow and Crockett decided not to try again to reach the shore.

Exhausted by his futile efforts to land the ungainly craft, Crockett thought the worst was over and went into the cabin below the deck to rest. He wished he was back hunting bears, where he at least had some control over events. He was far beyond his competence on the river.

Suddenly he heard a great crash and men running back and forth on the timbers above him. The boats had hit a cluster of "sawyers," or floating trees. The boat he was on began to tilt and slide under the forward boat in the powerful current. Water poured into the hatchway with such force he could not get through it. In the dark, amid crashing logs and churning water, Crockett tried to find an opening made for dipping up river water. He found the hole, but it was too small to crawl through. He yelled and screamed for help as water rose to his shoulders and his neck. His men found him and tried to pull him through the opening.

Crockett yelled for them to jerk him out of the sinking boat even if his arms tore off. Pulling with all their strength, they got him through, tearing off his clothes and scraping away flesh. Crockett later claimed he was "literally skin'd like a rabbit." The boat he had been trapped in sank. He and his men clung to the other boat, now lodged on the logjam. They sat all night, barefoot and freezing, Crockett completely naked and painfully wounded. But having come so close to drowning, Crockett was exhilarated just to be alive. Around sunrise a boat drew near and took them all to Memphis just down the river.

It was a major turning point in Crockett's life, for the man who rescued him and his crew turned out to be an enthusiastic encourager and supporter of his political career. The rescue after he had come so close to dying, and lost all he had worked for, is an essential part of the Crockett story. Not only was he saved from death in the cold river, he was reborn as a politician and candidate for Congress, and as a legend on the national scene. He recounts, "Here I met with a friend, that I never can forget as long as I am able to go ahead at anything; it was a Major Winchester, a merchant of that place: he let us all have hats, and shoes, and some little money to go upon, and so we all parted."

As Buddy Levy tells us, once he was rescued, "Crockett and his men hit the town, partying all night long, sharing horn after horn and telling tales of their travels and near-death adventures . . . Small crowds gathered at each tavern they visited, and Crockett held forth, cheers and laughter going round with each unbelievable tale. Marcus Winchester took keen note of the attention Crockett received, impressed with the way people gravitated toward him and responded to him."

Levy points out that once he had recovered, Crockett seemed stronger than ever, after washing up naked and bloody on the shore at Memphis. His tall tales and good humor, his adventures and cheer, won him many listeners. Winchester saw that Crockett was a spokesman for a whole constituency and culture just emerging as a force on the political scene in what was to be called the Age of Jackson. Winchester would later lend Crockett money for his campaign to run once more for Congress and would prove a friend again and again in Crockett's political career, speaking for him, lobbying for his candidacy. Thanks to Winchester and to his own humble charm, Crockett was elevated to the U.S. Congress in 1827 and began to make his reputation on the national stage.

It was common practice in those days to go into taverns while on the stump and buy drinks for voters. Everybody seemed to do it. Here Winchester was again in support. "As he thought I needed, he would occasionally hand me a little more cash; so I was able to buy a little of '*the creature*,' to put my friends in a good humour, as well as the other gentlemen, for they all treat in that country; not to get elected, of course — for that would be against the law; but just, as I before said, to make themselves and their friends feel their keeping a little."

As a congressman, Crockett was neither a great failure nor a great success. The surprise to many was his independence from Jackson, the popular president from Tennessee, and from the Jackson Democrats such as James K. Polk. In fact, it was his independence from his fellow Tennesseans in Washington that gave Crockett both his fame and his notoriety. Whigs were always looking for ways to embarrass the Democrats and block their legislation. Early on they began to cultivate Crockett as a weapon in their arsenal. Crockett gave so many speeches in his homespun manner he was viewed as an entertainer, a kind of stand-up comic in the House of Representatives. Though he had encouraged writers to portray him as a character and wise-cracking backwoods philosopher, the lies and exaggerations about him grew so outrageous that he decided to write his own autobiography, called *A Narrative Life of David Crockett of the State of Tennessee,* to correct the errors and further his political career, perhaps even propel him to the White House. "Most authors seek fame, but I seek for justice—a holier impulse than ever entered into the ambitious struggles of the votaries of that *fickle, flirting* goddess," is the way he began his memoir.

In his narrative Crockett says, "I have endeavoured to give the reader a plain, honest, homespun account of my state in life, and some few of the difficulties which have attended me along its journey." In fact, his *Narrative,* published in 1834, concentrates most on the cruel obstacles Crockett had to overcome. He knew it was his extraordinary struggle over insurmountable odds that created his strongest hold on public attention and affection.

He portrayed himself as the victim of one misfortune after another, as well as the slander of his enemies. He sought to reinforce in the public mind the image of himself as humble, humorous, and hounded by bad luck, almost as though he were rehearsing for his ultimate role in history as martyr in the cause of liberty at the Alamo.

At the beginning of his memoir he concedes that he does not understand his own notoriety. "I can't tell why it is, nor in what it is to end. Go where I will, everybody seems anxious to get a peep at me." He then describes the poverty of his background and his bad luck to be only a fifth son, not the blessed seventh. Crockett says that the narrative of his life is an account of his troubles. He describes how his father's gristmill washed away in a flood, foreshadowing the loss of his own mill years later.

After the story of his engagement to the lovely Margaret Elder being broken off, Crockett claims, "My heart was bruised, and my spirits were broken down . . . I was only born for hardships, misery and disappointment." It is a note Crockett will strike again and again. He tells how later in the Creek War colonel Coffee ignores Crockett's warning about the location of hostile Indians, because he is only a private, then responds to the same information delivered by an officer. "When I made the report, it wasn't believed, because I was no officer; I was no great man, but just a poor soldier."

In the *Narrative* Crockett goes into detail about his service in the militia during the Creek War and repeatedly refers to himself as a "rough sort of a backwoodsman." The death of his first wife Polly is remembered in moving terms. "It was the doing of the Almighty . . . and as painful as is even yet the remembrance of her sufferings, and the loss sustained by my little children and myself, yet I have no wish to lift up the voice of complaint."

Crockett describes himself as ignorant and clumsy at public speaking, at least at first. "The thought of having to make a speech made my knees feel mighty weak, and set my heart to fluttering." But of course he wins the audience when he does address them and allows as how he becomes known as an especially effective speaker.

Crockett dramatizes at length his suffering in cold water and ice to bring the keg of gunpowder home on Shoal Creek in 1822. And he reminds the reader again and again of his humble origins and his struggle to rise from poverty. "I want the world to understand my true history, and how I worked along to rise from a cane-brake to my present station in life."

Because Crockett opposed Jackson's policies, including the removal of Indians to the West, he was slandered and attacked without mercy. "This was considered the unpardonable sin. I was hunted down like a wild varment, and in this hunt every little newspaper in the district, and every little pin-hook lawyer was engaged . . . and every one of these little papers kept up a constant war on me, fighting with every scurrilous report they could catch."

Hoping to maybe win the presidency, Crockett portrays himself as the victim of political storms as well as natural floods, blizzards, and hurricanes. He will not ever be Jackson's "dog," he pledges. "What is more agreeable to my feelings as a freeman, I am at liberty to vote as my conscience and judgment dictates to be right, without the yoke of any party on me." And then he promises to the citizens of the United States, "You will find me standing up to my rack, as the people's faithful representative, and the public's most obedient, very humble servant."

IN ALL, Crockett would be elected to Congress three times, in 1827, 1829, and 1833. And while he made a vivid impression on all who knew him and became something of a national figure in contemporary political life, he never succeeded in getting through the legislature the bill that meant most to him, guaranteeing cheap land for the poor who needed it most. Throughout his political career Crockett fought for the right of the poor to acquire their own holdings, and again and again he was defeated.

The Whigs, who opposed the Jacksonian forces, grew increasingly interested in exploiting Crockett as an ally. Who better to oppose the Tennessee backwoodsman from Nashville than another Tennessee backwoodsman from the canebrakes? There began to be talk of running Crockett for president at some point in the future. It was probably all a ruse to confuse and divert their opponents and the electorate, but nobody could be sure, and Crockett seemed delighted to receive the attention, forgetting that his political base was in Tennessee where the people adored Old Hickory.

To promote him as a figure on the national scene it was suggested that Crockett make a tour of the Northeast, entertaining crowds and winning friends. The journey lasted three weeks, from April 25 to May 13 or 14, 1834. He referred to the travel as a "towar for his health." Crockett was wined and dined and fussed over in Baltimore, Philadelphia, Jersey City, New York, Newport, Boston, Lowell, Providence, and Camden. He spoke at rallies, banquets, and private clubs. A book titled *Tour* was printed under his name.

Crockett was willing to be exploited by the Whigs, both for his personal ambitions and his hopes for a land bill to make cheap land available for the poor in the West. For all his foolish posturing, Crockett was serious about the issue of helping the poor acquire the land they desired and needed in the western regions. Crockett did not write *Tour,* but he was willing to fix his name to the folksy, "backwoodsie" exaggerations.

Everywhere he stopped on the tour, Crockett attacked Jackson and his policies, calling him a would-be monarch. In Philadelphia he spoke at the stock exchange and visited the waterworks, the mint, and the asylum. He was presented with a fine shotgun. In New York and Newport he was received by cheering crowds, who turned out for the spectacle of "the Gentleman from the Cane." In Lowell, Massachusetts, Crockett seemed to become a supporter and fan of industry and manufacturing and gave high praise to the textile mills there. Everywhere, he blasted Jackson and his party, ignoring the fact that it was Jackson's reforms and popularity that had made his own candidacy possible. His speeches became strident and extreme in their hatred of Jackson. He forgot he had far more in common with Jackson than with the New England and northeastern Whigs. The words he spoke and wrote were less his own and more the opinions of his handlers and managers. His attacks on Jackson came to sound so emotional they began to undermine the image of good sense and humility, as well as humor, he had created.

Whatever the people of Tennessee thought of the issues and Jackson's policies, they revered Old Hickory as their particular hero. The victor of Horseshoe Bend and New Orleans was sacred to the memory of the country. Crockett had begun to alienate his constituents, serving the Whig party and not the voters who had sent him to Washington three times. He was blamed for being absent from Congress during his tour. As his popularity in Tennessee waned Crockett became even more bitter toward Jackson and the Democrats. In July of 1834 he wrote that if Martin Van Buren, Jackson's favored choice, were elected the next president he would "leave the united States, for I never will live under his Kingdom before I will Submit to his government I will go to the wildes of Texas I will Consider that government a Paradice to what this will be." Little did Crockett know how prophetic his threat would prove to be. In the following election of 1835 the excesses of his attacks on Jackson and the Jacksonian Democrats cost Crockett his seat in Congress.

Ironically, one of the issues on which he opposed Jackson was the removal of eastern Indian nations, such as the Cherokees and Choctaws, from their tribal lands to Indian Territory in the West. In an 1830 speech Crockett, or someone who wrote the speech for him, vigorously opposed the removal of Indians from their treaty-guaranteed lands in the eastern states. By defeating Crockett in his fifth campaign for Congress, the Jacksonians would, in effect, remove *him* to the West as well.

After Crockett lost the election of 1835 to Adam Huntsman, who had a wooden leg, he is reported to have told a group in Memphis, "Since you have chosen to elect a man with a timber toe to succeed me, you may all go to hell and I will go to Texas." He was partying at the time and saying farewell to friends and supporters. According to one eyewitness he was dressed in his campaign costume of buckskin and coonskin cap, and carried his rifle with shot pouch and powder horn slung over his shoulder.

Crockett had been thinking of going to Texas for some time. Thirty-six years before, his hero, Daniel Boone, had left Kentucky for Spanish-controlled Missouri to make a new start. Crockett was drawn to Texas in the same spirit, disgusted with Tennessee and the United States, hoping for a new life in the province of Mexico that was proclaiming its independence. Thousands of others were heading that way also. According to Walter LaFeber, "By 1834, a widely used geography primer already showed Texas . . . as part . . . of the United States." Once he had accepted his defeat by the Jacksonians, Crockett began to feel an elation about his journey to explore the opportunities in the West.

Accompanied by several friends, Crockett traveled down the Mississippi to the mouth of the Arkansas River and ascended that stream to Little Rock. Setting out overland, they reached the Red River and explored its valley for several days before crossing into Texas. While some of the party turned back to the United States, Crockett and his nephew William Patton signed an oath of loyalty to the new Republic of Texas and continued by way of Washington-on-the-Brazos toward San Antonio. At the time hundreds of emigrants from the United States were arriving in Texas every month, hoping to claim land in the newly independent territory.

At Lost Prairie on the Red River, Crockett traded his fine watch to one Isaac N. Jones for thirty dollars and a cheaper timepiece, saying he was running low on cash. After Crockett's death, Jones wrote a letter of condolence to Elizabeth. "With his open frankness, his natural honesty of expression, his perfect want of concealment, I could not but be very much pleased. And with a hope that it might be an accommodation to him, I was gratified at the exchange, as it gave me a *keepsake* which would often remind me of an honest man, a good citizen and a pioneer in the cause of liberty, amongst his suffering brethren in Texas."

On January 9, 1836, Crockett wrote from San Augustine: "I have taken the oath of government and enrolled my name as a volunteer." Mexico required that all citizens become Roman Catholics and own no slaves, but historians have pointed out most Americans simply ignored those laws.

From the letter to his oldest daughter, Margaret, and her husband, Wiley Flowers, it is clear he intended to move his family to Texas. He assured them he was pleased with the way things had turned out. "I am rejoiced at my fate. I had rather be in my present situation than to be elected to a seat in Congress for life. I am in hopes of making a fortune yet for myself and family, bad as my prospect has been."

Crockett had to sign the oath of allegiance to the new Republic of Texas in order to vote or be elected to office. But the awkward fact was that there were two governments claiming to represent the new republic. The bitter political rivalry in the United States between the Jacksonian and the anti-Jacksonian factions had preceded Crockett's move west. As would be expected, he sided with the anti-Jacksonians. Because he assumed Sam Houston was loyal to the Jacksonians, Crockett chose to cast his lot with the opposite side once again. Carrying his grudge against Andrew Jackson and his supporters from Tennessee to Texas turned out to be a fatal mistake for Crockett. His hatred for Jackson had destroyed his political career in the United States and would cost him his life in Texas.

Crockett and Houston had been friends earlier, but the political struggles in Tennessee and Congress had drawn them into opposing camps. Houston never faltered in his loyalty to Jackson and Jacksonian ideals. As Crockett studied the political landscape in Texas he found that the forces at San Antonio opposed the newly appointed commander of the Texas militia, Sam Houston. That fact almost certainly influenced Crockett's decision to proceed to the Alamo and join William Travis and the other anti-Houston forces there. As James Shackford puts it, "If Houston represented Jackson and the Jackson concept of 'liberty' there was no question on which side David would take his stand." Apparently Crockett would not sign the oath of loyalty to Texas until the word *republican* had been inserted, which, to him, meant anti-Jackson. Crockett arrived at the Alamo in San Antonio in early February 1836.

Since all who fought at the Alamo were killed, there has been much disagreement about what actually happened there. Two women who survived the massacre, Susanna Dickerson and Señora Candelaria, gave different accounts. Even the Mexicans who participated in the destruction left contradictory stories. The large Mexican army under General Antonio

López de Santa Anna, surrounded the old mission called the Alamo and killed all the men fighting there on March 6, 1836, but many aspects of the siege and final battle remain controversial. What is certain is that on January 17, 1836, Sam Houston, commander in chief of Texas military forces, sent James Bowie to San Antonio to order Colonel James C. Neill to blow up the Alamo, the fortified mission there, and retreat to the northeast to join the main army. But William Travis, who had replaced Neill before the orders arrived in San Antonio, refused to recognize the authority of Houston and determined to remain at the Alamo.

Colonel James W. Fannin, who was not at the Alamo but at Goliad, later made the same decision and refused to retreat from that isolated position far to the south of the Alamo and Houston's forces. In the meantime Houston had asked for and gotten his commission to command from both parties at the new convention of the Texas government.

Houston set off with his little army for Gonzales, Texas, east of San Antonio, and ordered Colonel Fannin to destroy La Bahia, the fort at Goliad, and retreat. By then he already had word of the fall of the Alamo. "I am induced to believe from all the facts communicated to me that the Alamo, has fallen, and all our men are *murdered*!. We must not depend upon Forts. The woods and ravines suit us best." Like all men Houston had weaknesses and made many mistakes, but when the stakes were highest he seems to have thought clearly and taken the long view. It is not illogical to compare him to Washington in his coolness in emergencies and his ability to think objectively. Both Travis at the Alamo and Fannin at Goliad were insubordinate to their commander, with lethal results. When Fannin at the last minute decided to abandon Goliad, his army was apprehended by a large Mexican force, returned to Goliad, lined up against the wall, and executed. Only a few men who jumped over the wall escaped to tell of the massacre.

Few doubt that Crockett believed he was doing the right thing, staying with Travis to defend Texas independence against the cruel dictator General Antonio López de Santa Anna. It was, of course, because of his passionate opposition to everything Jacksonian that he sided with the mutinous Travis, perhaps unaware at first of the size of the approaching Mexican army. It is unlikely Crockett thought the crumbling Alamo could withstand a long siege and assault by superior forces. He probably

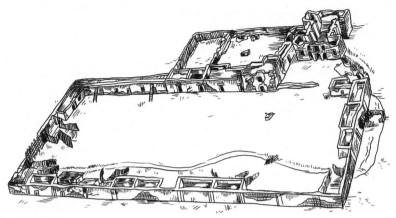

The Alamo, 1836

assumed that the men at Goliad, as well as Houston's forces, would come to their aid before it was too late.

In a speech in 1859 explaining why he was not able to save those defending the Alamo, Houston listed Crockett as among those who opposed his authority. "Travis, Fannin, Crockett, Bowie, were all brave and gallant spirits; they never, while living employed falsehood and slander to carry a point or injure a character; their acts were open and bold; their policy of warfare was to divide, advance, and conquer. My policy was to concentrate, retreat and conquer." Careful to protect the reputations of the martyrs of the Alamo and Goliad, Houston gently explained their strategic mistakes, only implying their treasonous insubordination.

The biographer James Shackford states flatly that it was Crockett's hatred for Andrew Jackson that destroyed him. But we should not ignore the factor of the bad leadership of William Travis. Regardless of his attitude toward Sam Houston as commander in chief, an officer holding a position such as the Alamo should have sent out scouts who could have informed him, before it was too late, of the approaching Mexican army and taken appropriate action. Ramón Martinez Caro later reported that of the 5,000 soldiers Santa Anna had in his army, 1,542 of them were killed by the defenders of the Alamo. Travis had under his command about 150 able men, so the heroes of the Alamo killed about 10 Mexican soldiers each before they were overcome.

The events at the Alamo in February and March of 1836 have a messiness and complexity that have only compounded the ambiguity of the "real story." It is not even known for certain exactly when Crockett arrived there. The date was somewhere between February 5 and 10. In one account Crockett camped along San Pedro Creek near the old cemetery, and James Bowie rode out to escort him into town. On the night of February 11 a large party was given in Crockett's honor. During the party William Travis, who had replaced Neill as commander of the fort, was warned by Bowie that a large Mexican army was headed toward San Antonio. Travis was courting a beauty on the dance floor, and after assuring Bowie the enemy could not arrive in San Antonio for two weeks, returned to the dance.

Though Travis had been given command by Neill before he left, the men of the garrison asked to elect their own leader. Some preferred Crockett, but he refused, saying he only wanted to be a "high private." The volunteers chose James Bowie as their commander, and he celebrated by getting drunk and releasing all prisoners from the town's jails. Travis wrote to Texas president Henry Smith asking for more soldiers for the fort, or a transfer to another command. He warned of the approaching Mexican army. Travis did not know that Henry Smith had already been replaced as president by James Robinson.

Many defenders of San Antonio had been called away earlier for a futile expedition to Matamoros. To consolidate his army to confront the larger Mexican force, Houston had sent Bowie to order Neill to destroy the Alamo and join him farther to the east and north. It is thought that Travis and many of his men assumed that the Texas militia would come to their aid in the defense of San Antonio, which they saw as a crucial position to hold in the overall struggle. Houston did not believe it was possible to hold the Alamo against the larger Mexican army. Colonel James Fannin, who commanded the fort at Goliad, was both inexperienced and timid, and he offered little hope for rescuing the men at San Antonio.

On February 23 the Mexican cavalry entered San Antonio unopposed as the defenders retreated to the Alamo. Crockett and twelve men were assigned to defend a picket wall on the south side between the barracks and the church. The Mexicans hoisted a red flag on the tower of the old San Fernando Church, signaling that no prisoners would be taken.

Both Travis and Bowie assumed command of the situation, sending out separate orders. Then Bowie fell ill with either pneumonia or typhoid, and had to take to his bed. Travis was now in sole command. For several days the Mexican artillery bombarded the fortress. When a company approached the south wall, Crockett and his men drove them back with a hail of bullets. It was said that Crockett killed a Mexican as far away as two hundred yards.

On February 25 the Mexicans mounted two attacks but were repulsed. In his account Travis wrote, "The Hon. David Crockett was seen at all points, animating the men to do their duty." Enrique Esparza who was only a child at the time would later recall, "Señor Crockett seemed everywhere. He would shout from the wall or through the portholes. Then he would run back and say something funny. He tried to speak Spanish sometimes. Now and then he would run to the fire we had in the courtyard where we were to make us laugh."

As a leader Crockett felt it was his duty to cheer and revive the spirits of those under siege. Some reports say he even played a fiddle to entertain the soldiers and citizens under attack. Crockett and other men slipped outside the fort in the dark to burn some *jacales,* wooden sheds near the walls that could provide cover for the Mexicans. They began to dig a well inside the walls, since water for the Alamo was provided by an irrigation ditch, an *acequia,* from the San Antonio River, which the Mexicans could have cut off at any time.

On February 26 Colonel Fannin at Goliad was ordered to take 320 men to San Antonio to aid the defenders there. Though he set out on the mission, his confusion and cowardice caused him to turn back. On February 27 men slipped out of the Alamo and returned with corn and cattle to feed the garrison. Most believed that if they held out long enough, either Houston or Fannin would come to their aid. On March 1 a group of reinforcements did ride into the Alamo—around thirty members of the Gonzales Mounted Rangers. Apparently the Mexicans were not keeping a close watch on the fort that day.

According to some reports, Crockett and other officers rode out to Cibola Creek Crossing in late February to escort more volunteers back to the Alamo. They all waited for Fannin's troops to arrive from Goliad only to be disappointed day after day. On March 3 Travis wrote his final message. "I am determined to perish in the defense of this place, and may my bones reproach my country for her neglect."

The next day Santa Anna's artillery moved in for the final attack. Travis asked all the men who were willing to stay and fight to step across a line he made in the sand. Only one volunteer refused to take the step. Before daylight on March 6, 1836, Santa Anna ordered almost two thousand men with ladders, crowbars, and axes to climb the walls and destroy gates and pickets. The garrison was still asleep, resting from their labors the night before. When Travis woke and ran to the wall, he was struck by a bullet and died as the battle began. The Alamo was without a leader.

The Mexicans attacked the north wall twice and were driven back. On the third try they placed ladders against the wall and the Alamo's artillery was useless in repelling them. The cannons were seized by the Mexicans and turned on the defenders inside the fort.

Crockett and his men defended the south wall. As the Mexicans poured over the walls, some defenders ran outside and were cut down by Mexican cavalry. Mexicans found Bowie in his bed and killed him. The church where the women were hiding was taken. The last defenders retreated to the Long Barracks and, one by one, were killed.

A SLAVE named Joe, who had belonged to William Travis, stated on March 20 that "Crockett and a few of his friends were found together, with twenty-four of the enemy dead around them." Only a few days later the people of Nacogdoches issued a proclamation: "David Crockett (now rendered immortal in Glory) had fortified himself with sixteen guns well charged, and a monument of slain foes encompasses his lifeless body."

Many newspapers across the United States carried accounts of Crockett fighting to the death with his rifle in one hand and his knife in the other. Whatever the actual circumstance of his death, Crockett is likely to remain a hero in American history. As Randell Jones says, "His presence at the Alamo alone has warranted his celebration even today as a hero of the common man. His death there, regardless of the circumstances, greatly inspired the Texas armies, which decisively prevailed in the revolution that ended just seven weeks later at San Jacinto in an attack prosecuted by Crockett's fellow Tennessean, Sam Houston."

———

EVERY VERSION of the events at the Alamo describes Crockett's death there in a different way. Señora Candelaria, who lived to be 105, contradicted herself in the many interviews she later gave. As a very old woman, she settled on a version describing Crockett as one of the first to die in the attack. "He advanced from the Church building towards the wall or rampart running from the end of the stockade, slowly and with great deliberation, without arms, when suddenly a volley was fired by the Mexicans causing him to fall forward on his face, dead."

According to Señora Candelaria's report, there was nothing heroic about Crockett's death, except for his presence at the Alamo. He was not even carrying a rifle when he was struck down by Mexican bullets. He fell flat on his face in the dirt, dead by the time he hit the ground. To fall "forward on his face," as Señora Candelaria recalled, suggests weakness and failure.

The legend that grew up immediately after the fall of the Alamo, however, had Crockett bravely fighting to the last moment. When his ammunition ran out, he swung his rifle as a club, killing Mexican soldiers pouring into the fort. When his body was found later, it was surrounded by the corpses of the Mexicans he had killed. One of the greatest stories of martyrdom in American history was born and would continue to grow for the next century and beyond. Whatever the truth of his political career, and the tall tales and wisecracks attributed to him, no one could deny the fact of his death at the hands of Santa Anna's troops, even though there was a vague rumor later that Crockett had been taken prisoner and forced to work in the mines in Mexico. The deaths at the Alamo electrified both Texas and the United States and gave unprecedented determination and support to the cause of Texas independence. Few in Texas or elsewhere doubted that the new government and territory would eventually join the United States. Sam Houston and the other founders of the Republic of Texas could not have asked for a more effective event to inspire support for their cause than the deaths at the Alamo and Goliad. And by far the most famous death was that of Crockett, who had come to Texas in the cause of liberty.

In his own account of the aftermath of the fall of the Alamo, Santa Anna recorded that he commanded the officials of San Antonio to identify the bodies of Travis, Bowie, and Crockett, and then he ordered that all bodies be burned on a great funeral pyre. It took a day to burn all the remains of the fallen.

More than a century after the events, a translated diary of one José Enrique de la Peña appeared, giving an account of the fall of the Alamo from the Mexican perspective. Crockett was described as a "naturalist . . . very well known in North America for his strange adventures." He was listed as one of seven prisoners taken by soldiers serving under General Manuel Fernández Castrillón. When ordered by Santa Anna to execute the prisoners Castrillón resisted and the seven were killed with swords by members of Santa Anna's personal guard. "The Mexican officers ran the prisoners through. None begged for mercy; all died with dignity."

Peña's account burst like a bombshell on the field of Alamo scholarship, and American TV legend. The great Crockett had been executed, not fighting to his last breath. The publication of Peña's diary or memoir caused revisionist historians to begin rewriting the story of the Alamo. It was as though they had suspected all along that Crockett's role in the siege had been exaggerated and his heroism was more a matter of folktale and Hollywood than of fact.

But soon other historians began questioning Peña's account of Crockett's death also. Writers such as Dan Kilgore in *How Davy Died* pointed out that many passages in the diary were inserted later. And in fact the authenticity of the text that had been translated was far from certain. As a result of study of the handwriting, it was even suggested that the "diary" was a forgery by one John A. Laflin. Once the first surprise aroused by the document died down, most scholars realized that they were no more sure about how Crockett actually died than they had been before. Since all accounts by eyewitnesses differ, historians were forced (and free) to draw their own conclusions.

Whatever the manner of his death, two things remain certain about Crockett's role at the Alamo. First, he had the courage to stay at the fort and help the defenders after he knew a large Mexican army was approaching. In no account did he attempt to abandon his friends there. Second, after the event, his death, along with the deaths of the others, inspired Texans to fight vigorously and win independence from Mexico and inspired the citizens of the United States to support the Republic of Texas and to think of annexing Texas as a new state. In his death, Crockett served the cause of Texas independence and the westward expansion of the United States more effectively than he ever could have while alive.

As a number of historians, including James Shackford, have pointed out, Crockett in his death achieved a fame he could not have dreamed of in his life. Throughout his career in Congress, he had fought for the rights of the poor to acquire land of their own. Though his land bill had been defeated by the political machinations of the time, a version of it was later proposed by Crockett's son John Wesley Crockett after he became a U.S. congressman. The bill became law, and the poor in the West were given the opportunity to acquire land for twelve and a half cents an acre. It is likely Crockett's fame from the Alamo helped his son get this legislation approved by Congress in February 1841, almost five years after Crockett's death. Along with his old nemesis Andrew Jackson, Crockett became the most important hero of the poor, the common citizens.

In an eloquent eulogy near the conclusion of his biography of Crockett, Shackford wrote, "His life was one of wholehearted dedication to his own concepts of liberty. He died staking his life against what he regarded as intolerable tyranny. A poor man who had long known the devastating consequences of poverty and all his life had fought a dedicated fight for the right of the dispossessed to a new opportunity, he died defending a poor and insecure people . . . The simplicities of backwoods life had not prepared him to comprehend all of the intricacies of political machinations. In the death of this pioneer of geographical boundaries was born the hardy pioneer fighter for the rights of all men to liberty and opportunity."

More than any other hero in American history, Crockett made his greatest contribution through his apparent failures and catastrophes. The man who barely escaped drowning in the Mississippi in January 1826 and was stripped of his barrel staves as well as his shirt and pants and much of his skin, who was voted out of Congress in 1835, and who died at the Alamo in 1836 proved one of the most influential and inspirational figures of his era, gaining most by what he was not able to keep. It is an old story with many echoes, that of gaining a life through losing it.

— Five —

SAM HOUSTON

THE PRESIDENT WHO LOVED TO DANCE

$\mathcal{M}$OST OF Sam Houston's life was a kind of dance between calamity and triumph. Probably no major leader in American history ever veered more dramatically between extremes of failure and humiliation and victory and glory. Certainly none that we know loved to party and celebrate and dress up in colorful and dramatic clothes more than Sam Houston. It was said that he would dance all night as long as there was fiddle music and a lovely lady present. Ironically, he came from a community and church that disapproved of all partying and dancing.

The Houstons were strict Presbyterians, Scots Irish who crossed the Atlantic from Ulster in 1735 and landed, as most of their kind did, in Philadelphia: Sam Houston's great-grandfather John Houston; his widowed mother; his wife, Margaret; and six of their seven children. After struggling seven years in Pennsylvania, where the Quakers hardly welcomed Presbyterians, the Houstons followed the popular migration route west to the Susquehanna and south across the Potomac, then up the Shenandoah River into the heart of Virginia. Traveling the old Warrior's Path of the Indians, by then called the Great Wagon Road, John Houston bought 228 acres near future Brownsburg in the Blue Ridge Mountains.

The Houstons first attended the Old Providence Church and then broke away to found the New Providence Church. Sunday services lasted from ten in the morning until dark, with a one-hour dinner break. Sermons were grim and the congregation dour. But strict and austere as it might be, church was almost the only social life in the community. The rest of the week was taken up with the hard work of clearing land, cutting timber, planting and cultivating the soil between stumps and deadened trees, milking cows, butchering hogs, and weaving flax and wool for clothes.

John Houston's son Robert built a substantial house near his father's and married Mary Davidson, also of a prosperous Scots Irish family. Their home had two stories, white columns in front, and a commanding view of the valley and his extensive property. When Robert died in 1760 at the age of forty-one, he left the fine house on Timber Ridge to his son Samuel. Samuel was the most dashing of Robert Houston's sons. When the Revolution came to Virginia, Samuel served as an officer and paymaster of Daniel Morgan's Virginia Rifles at the battles of Saratoga, Cowpens, and Guilford Courthouse. He married a wealthy Scots Irish beauty named Elizabeth Paxton and ended his service in the Continental army as a major. After the war he served in the Virginia militia.

Elizabeth Houston has been described as a "Roman matron." She taught her children a love of education and culture, as well as respect for discipline and moral strength. She gave birth to six sons and three daughters. Her fifth child, Sam, was born March 2, 1793, in the fine house on Timber Ridge, the same year Jefferson wrote to André Michaux to commission the botanist to explore the Mississippi Valley. Later writers liked to portray Sam Houston as having started life in a log cabin on the frontier, but in fact he was born to a family of substance and standing in the Virginia Valley, ten years after the Revolution ended in 1783.

According to all reports, young Sam was his mother's favorite. Though he attended school briefly, he was mostly educated at home in his father's library where he read Brown's *Gazetteer,* Jedidiah Morse's *Geography Made Easy,* and Charles Rollins's *Ancient History.* Every Sunday the family attended the nearby Timber Ridge Church. Sam hated the long services, though the tedium was sometimes broken by demonstrations of ecstatic fervor known as "the jerks." Major Houston disapproved of such displays of emotion and once aroused the fury of the participants by escorting a woman in the throes of enthusiasm outside the sanctuary.

The old Warrior's Path ran close to the Houston house and every day Sam could watch the hunters, traders, speculators, and settlers passing on their way to the western regions, to Kentucky and Tennessee. A few miles away, the wonder of the Natural Bridge drew visitors to view its splendor, on land once owned by Thomas Jefferson. The great leaders of the new republic, Washington, Jefferson, Madison, Monroe, and Patrick Henry, inspired him as examples of leadership. And in his boyhood Sam knew many veterans of the French and Indian War and the Revolution.

As a major in the Virginia militia, Sam's father, Samuel Houston, had to pay his own expenses and was away from home much of the time. That meant Elizabeth Houston and the children had to look after the plantation. When Samuel Houston died suddenly in 1806 or 1807, he left so many debts that the Timber Ridge property had to be sold. "One sword, $15 . . . One Riding Chair and harness, $55 . . . one pistol 50 . . ." appraisers wrote of his estate. Elizabeth chose to move her family to the wilder country of east Tennessee, near Maryville, where she had relatives. Young Sam's journey to the West had begun.

The trek to Tennessee was long and exhausting. Roads were little more than trails or ruts through the forest, crossing creeks at fords, blocked by fallen trees, washed away in hard rains. During storms a road became a dashing torrent. Elizabeth, who had been born to affluence, drove one of the teams herself. But other Houstons had already moved to Tennessee, which had become a state in 1796, and Elizabeth and her family would not be among total strangers there.

Elizabeth Houston built a house on Baker's Creek, on property near Cherokee land. The small one-story house would eventually grow into a substantial two-story dwelling, but at first it was little more than a cabin. On this new farm Sam had to work in the fields much as he had back in Virginia. Slaves were too expensive for the Houstons, as they were for most families in the area. Sam never cared for farmwork and, like his father, preferred other occupations, such as serving in the military. Even so, he would always view his mother as a heroic figure. She was educated, intelligent, and ambitious for her family. He remembered her as "gifted with intellectual and moral qualities . . . Her life shown with purity and benevolence, and yet she was nerved with a stern fortitude."

Though he had little formal schooling, Sam acquired a love of reading, and his favorite book was Alexander Pope's translation of *The Iliad*. He fell in love with the heroic couplets of that version, the stories of heroes, the sweep of history and destiny told with soaring eloquence.

The accounts of Hector and the great Achilles, Odysseus and Priam, inspired Sam to dream of his own destiny and potential glory. He carried the book with him the rest of his life and hoped to model himself on Homer's heroes and their actions.

Sam quit school around the age of sixteen and was put to work briefly in a dry goods store. When his older brothers tried to force him to continue to serve as a store clerk, an occupation that bored him, he ran away and sought refuge with the Cherokee Indians at Hiwasee Island, with the family of Chief Ooleteka. The Overhill Cherokees had come from the high mountains to the east, and they viewed themselves as Yunwiya, "the principal people." It was the whites who gave them the name Cherokee, probably a version of the Creek word *tciloki,* meaning "people of a different speech." They had already intermarried with white people and adopted many white ways. In his 1791 *Travels,* William Bartram described the Cherokees as having "divine simplicity and truth, friendship without fallacy or guile, hospitality disinterested, native, undefiled, unmodified by artificial refinements." While Bartram may have romanticized the Cherokees a little, there is no doubt of their hospitality and generosity to those they saw as friends. Like most Indian nations, they often chose to accept people of other tribes or races into their families and villages. Living among the Cherokees, as a member of Chief Ooleteka's family, Houston acquired many Indian habits and tastes that would stay with him for the rest of his life. The history of Texas and the United States would be deeply influenced by things Houston learned at Hiwasee Island. The Cherokees had a special relish for dancing, long dances that might last all night, with both men and women participating. He took part in the festivities that marked the procession of the seasons, the milestones of a year and a life, the Corn Dance and the Harvest Dance. Some dances were celebrations, some religious rites, some fertility rituals, and some all of these things combined. The freedom, euphoria, togetherness, and sensuality of the dancing gave Houston a whole new way of looking at human life and potential, and human relationships, lessons he never forgot.

Ooleteka was a descendant of the great chief Attakullakulla and was described by the renowned botanist and explorer Thomas Nuttall as "a Franklin amongst his countrymen." With his own father dead, Sam sought a replacement, and the Hiwasee chief became a mentor and protector. When his white brothers tracked him down to Hiwasee Island, Sam told them he preferred "measuring deer tracks, to tape—that he liked the wild liberty of the Red men better than the tyranny of his own brothers, and if he could not study Latin in the Academy, he could, at least, read a translation from the Greek in the woods, and read it in peace. So they could go home as soon as they liked."

During his three years with the Cherokees, Sam seems to have acquired another habit—a taste for colorful and exotic and sometimes outlandish dress. Throughout the rest of his life he appeared in bright vests, unusual hats or turbans, togas, Indian garments, sashes, decorated boots or moccasins. Later, Secretary of War John C. Calhoun would give him a furious dressing down for visiting President Monroe in such garb.

Ooleteka gave Houston the name Kalanu, "the Raven," and adopted him into his family. For the rest of his life Sam would be the Raven of that clan of the Cherokees as well as Sam Houston of the Scots Irish. In his own mind he compared himself with the heroes of *The Iliad* and contemplated his future. Many of the Scots Irish traders who did business with the Cherokees had native wives. It is has been said that Cherokee women had a special preference for red-headed men. Many of the offspring of these marriages became leaders of the Cherokee nation. Ooleteka's sister was married to John Rogers, and their sons, John, William, and Charles, became Sam's close friends. The boys hunted, trapped, fished, and explored together, and from them Sam learned much about tribal culture and the Great Smoky Mountains. He also loved to whittle and carve wood. He carried pieces of wood and a knife in his pockets at all times and was known to whittle wherever he was, in taverns or on the floor of the U.S. Senate. Since many Cherokees were skilled carvers, it is possible this habit was also acquired while living at Hiwasee.

Cherokee tradition maintains that Sam and Tiana Rogers, sister of his friends and niece of Ooleteka, became lovers. Whether this is true or not, it is likely he found Indian ways far less restricting than those of the culture in which he was raised. Houston was always a great favorite with women, to the end of his life, and there is no reason to think he was not popular even then with the Cherokee girls, and especially Tiana Rogers, whom he would marry many years later, in the Indian Territory of the

West. Other things about Indian culture also influenced him, including the Indian love of oratory. The eloquence and dignity of Ooleteka would be a model for leadership he never forgot. It was the custom of Cherokees, especially chiefs, to refer to themselves in the third person. For the rest of his life Houston would surprise friends and opponents alike by referring to himself as "he" and by using colorful and unusual figures of speech.

At age nineteen Houston left his Cherokee family and taught school for a term at Baker's Creek, not far from his mother's house. He charged eight dollars a term for tuition, one third of which could be paid in colorful calico cloth, one third in corn, and one third in cash. At the museum on the schoolhouse site a set of lead knuckles he owned is on display. There is no report he ever used the knuckles, but he may have kept them handy to intimidate would-be troublemakers. He loved history and geography and was already an eloquent speaker. But he knew little mathematics, and though his school teaching was a modest success, he gave it up after six months. The War of 1812 had broken out, and in March 1813 he joined the army. His mother gave him a gold ring before he left home inscribed with the one word: HONOR.

Though Sam enlisted in the army as a private, he was commissioned ensign in the Thirty-ninth Infantry Regiment on September 13, 1813. The Creek War had begun on August 30 when the Red Stick warriors killed nearly five hundred people at Fort Mims in Alabama. Andrew Jackson and the Tennessee militia invaded the Creek Country that fall, and on February 13, 1814, the Thirty-ninth Infantry arrived at Fort Strother to join Jackson's forces. Houston had by then become a third lieutenant.

At Fort Strother, Houston met many men who would figure prominently in his later life. Most important was Andrew Jackson, who became Houston's mentor and lifelong friend. With Jackson that winter and spring were Thomas Hart Benton, John Eaton, James Gadsden, William Carroll, and William Lewis. David Crockett had served with Jackson in the fall but had gone home in December of 1813.

On March 14, the Thirty-ninth Infantry descended the Coosa River on flatboats to Fort Williams, forty-five miles from Horseshoe Bend on the Tallapoosa. After the Cherokees crossed the river behind the village of Tohopki, at Horseshoe Bend, on March 27, stole the many escape canoes the Red Sticks had left there, and set fire to the buildings, Jackson ordered an assault on the barricade that protected the peninsula. The Thirty-ninth Infantry led the attack. When their commander, Major Lemuel P. Montgomery, was killed climbing over the wall, Houston was just behind him. An arrow entered Houston's thigh as he dropped to the ground inside the fort. Houston ordered a subaltern to jerk the arrow out. When the projectile was finally extracted, it tore so much flesh the wound bled profusely. Houston had to climb back across the barricade to have the wound dressed. He was so severely injured Jackson ordered him not to return to the battle.

Attacked by the Cherokees and friendly Creeks from behind, by the militia and United States Infantry from the front, some Red Sticks sought the protection of fallen logs and brush near the river. The general called for volunteers to flush them out. Ignoring his wound, Houston grabbed a rifle and led an attack on a hideout. Only a few yards from the brush he was hit by two bullets in his right shoulder. He fell and lost consciousness and was carried away while other men set fire to the leaves and brush, driving the Red Stick warriors from their hiding place.

An army surgeon removed one of the bullets from Houston's shoulder but could not reach the other. With the severe wound in his thigh, Houston had lost so much blood it was unlikely he would live anyway. The doctor moved on to other wounded men more likely to survive and Houston was left lying on the cold ground all night, while the killing continued. The pain of his three wounds brought him in and out of consciousness while the last of the Red Sticks were being finished off and the women and children taken prisoner. As the sun came up, other soldiers saw Houston was still alive and, though in great pain, he seemed to have regained a little strength. He was carried away from the battlefield on a rough litter. It was unusual for someone with three such serious wounds to live. And even if he did survive the trauma, he was likely to die of infection, peritonitis, or gangrene. It is not likely that Houston himself expected to live. But he did. His constitution was so strong, or his will to live so strong, that he survived one day and a night, and then another, lying by the campfire, carried on litters, floating in boats, bumping on rough roads in wagons. He was taken back to Fort Williams, then to Fort Strother, and within two months all the way back to his mother's house on Baker's Creek. Elizabeth Houston did not recognize her son at first because he had lost so much weight.

Houston had participated heroically in one of the most significant battles in the War of 1812 and in American history. Along with the victory at New Orleans on January 8, 1815, Horseshoe Bend would, as we have seen, make Andrew Jackson the greatest American hero of his era. And in the wake of his glory, Jackson would draw many others to prominence and fame and perhaps greatness, including Third Lieutenant Sam Houston, whom everyone expected to die of his wounds at Horseshoe Bend.

BUT THE War of 1812 was far from over. On August 14, 1814, the British landed on the banks of the Chesapeake and marched toward Washington City almost unopposed. On August 24–25 they burned both the White House and the Capitol, in retaliation for the American attack on York, Ontario, a year earlier. It had taken Houston several months to recover enough to get back on a horse. By late summer he was at least strong enough to ride to the nation's capital to seek further medical help. When Houston arrived in Washington, the city was in ruins. It is not known whether he found further treatment for his wounds before returning to Tennessee. He had also hoped to lobby for a permanent commission in the army, but with the capital in charred ruins there was no point in remaining. After he returned to Tennessee he obtained the commission and reported for duty in Nashville the following July 4. He was posted to New Orleans where, in spite of his wounds, he became a popular man about town. He missed few receptions, dances, parties, and banquets.

Later Houston served in Nashville, where his association with Old Hickory became even closer. Around this time he was initiated into the Masonic Order, as almost all the leaders of the day were. Washington, Madison, Monroe, and Andrew Jackson were all brother Masons. Initiated April 19, 1817, at Cumberland Lodge No. 8 in Nashville, Houston found his connection to Freemasonry useful, then and later. He, and most Americans of the time, were familiar with the many paintings depicting Washington in his Masonic apron and sash laying the cornerstone of the new Capitol in the planned Federal City on September 18,

1793. And the connection between Masonic brotherhood and leadership had grown since the Revolution.

In the autumn of 1817 Jackson, commander of the army of the Southeast, asked Houston to persuade his adoptive father Ooleteka and other Cherokee chiefs to remove their people to the western Arkansas Territory. Like Jackson, Houston came to believe the eastern Indians' only hope for survival was to move their nations to the West. If they tried to stay on their traditional lands, they would eventually be exterminated. Because of his long experience with the Cherokees, Houston knew that American Indians usually adhered to treaties, or "paper talk," more faithfully than did whites. But the Cherokees were reluctant to go west because in their culture the West was considered an evil place, "the Darkening Land, abode of the Black Man, the god of evil . . . The Cherokees had no wish to turn their backs on the East, the Sun Land . . . In all the legends the Cherokee people knew, the West symbolized darkness, death and defeat." But Ooleteka and the Hiwasee band of Cherokee were persuaded by their kinsman Houston to go West in exchange for new lands there as well as gifts of blankets, tools, horses, and other livestock and goods. Houston journeyed to Washington with several chiefs to plead for better conditions for the Indians who made the distant move.

Perhaps to give himself greater freedom as a negotiator, Houston resigned his commission in the army at Washington and arrived with the Indian delegation at the office of Secretary of War John C. Calhoun, in full Indian costume. This was when Calhoun gave Houston the tongue lashing for his sartorial impertinence. Houston never forgot the insult and despised Calhoun for the rest of his life. He would always view Calhoun as a small, spiteful, mean-spirited, and arrogant man, with traitorous ideas about states' rights.

Like other ambitious men of the time, like Jackson himself, Houston decided to study law. Once done with his mission to the Cherokees, he became an apprentice to Judge James Trimble in Nashville. After a few months, Houston, with his excellent memory and gift for argument, was admitted to the Tennessee bar. It was at this time in Nashville that Houston attempted another profession as well. He began acting with the Dramatic Club of Nashville. In a sense, Sam Houston was always, first to last, an actor. He had a powerful voice and a commanding presence.

He had a superb memory and a gift for eloquence. He played a villain in John Home's *Douglas,* a nobleman in Louis-Sebastien Merrier's *Point of Honor,* and a drunken porter in a play called *We Fly by Night.* Apparently he was at his best in comedy. The director of the Dramatic Club, Noah M. Ludlow, later said Houston as an actor was "the *largest,* if not the most gifted with dramatic ability." Some reports say Houston was at least six feet five inches tall. He may have seemed that tall to many, but actually he was about six feet two inches.

The challenge was to find the role for which he was best suited, at which he could excel. As many ambitious and gifted people do, he spent years auditioning and studying for possible parts—schoolteacher, soldier, Indian agent, lawyer. After practicing law for only a few months in Lebanon, Tennessee, Houston was elected district attorney of Davidson County. Soon his popularity and political connections won him the commission of major general of the Tennessee militia, the same post Andrew Jackson had held years earlier. His law practice, by then in Nashville, was growing. Often he talked to friends about buying land in Texas and moving to that reputed paradise in the West. The seed had been planted.

There was beginning to be a lot of talk about Andrew Jackson running for president in 1824. Friends of Old Hickory needed to be positioned in high places to aid in the campaign. Houston was selected to run for Congress from the Ninth Congressional District of Tennessee in 1823. As Jackson's favorite, he was sure to win. Houston was only thirty years old, but he had his high rank in the Tennessee militia and was a popular and successful lawyer in Nashville.

Thomas Jefferson had referred to the Tennessee Constitution, partly drafted by Andrew Jackson in 1796, as the "least imperfect and most republican" of any known constitution. Jackson and his friends believed the West was more democratic than the eastern states, and they planned to bring that "least imperfect and most republican" spirit to the country as a whole. As a step toward the White House, Jackson took a seat in the U.S. Senate.

When Houston headed to Washington to take his place in Congress in October 1823, he stopped at Monticello with a letter of introduction to Jefferson. Now age eighty, Jefferson was still active and curious about events in the West. He had reservations about Jackson but recognized Old Hickory might well be a leader of the future. After all, it was the Sage of Monticello who had worked to acquire the West for Americans and to give more power to the common people. However different their personalities, Jackson was undoubtedly Jefferson's successor, taking up the torch of republican ideals and westward expansion. In his old age Jefferson met face-to-face with Sam Houston, the man whose victory at San Jacinto in April of 1836 would make possible Jefferson's dream of expanding the United States west to the Pacific.

———

HOUSTON SERVED in Congress in the reflected brilliance of Andrew Jackson. The victor of New Orleans was treated as if he were already a president or head of state. Few doubted that he would become president in fact. The only question was when. As the most gifted orator in the Jackson camp, Houston was called upon to present Old Hickory's views to Congress. His eloquence gave him visibility and prominence in that chamber and in the capital. When Lafayette visited Washington in 1824, Houston was one of the dignitaries selected to escort the old Revolutionary War hero around.

After Henry Clay helped John Quincy Adams defeat Jackson for president in 1824, Jackson and his friends were more determined than ever to win the White House in 1828. And though many considered him a rowdy, unpredictable ruffian, Houston was called on again and again to be Jackson's spokesman. In 1826 Houston fought a duel and was wounded by his opponent, a General White, but Jackson remained loyal and Houston's political career continued on track. Jackson urged Houston to become the governor of Tennessee, to look after affairs back home. From Jackson, Houston learned to take the long view, to plan far ahead. "Jacksonianism was for the ages not just two terms," as Marshall De Bruhl puts it.

With Old Hickory's backing, Houston easily won the governorship of Tennessee and was inaugurated October 1, 1827. As governor, he continued Jackson's policies and supported the hero of New Orleans in the election of 1828. In a bitter campaign against John Quincy Adams and Henry Clay, Jackson was astonished when the old scandal of his elopement to Natchez with Rachel Robards thirty-nine years before was dredged up. Rachel was called a scarlet woman, an adulteress, and a whore by Jackson's political opponents. The now elderly and pious Rachel was devastated by the accusations about events she had assumed were long forgotten.

Though Jackson won the election by a considerable margin, his exuberance was dashed when Rachel died suddenly on December 22, 1828, the day before a great victory celebration was planned for Nashville. Both Jackson and Houston blamed their political enemies for the beloved woman's death. To some historians it has seemed that Rachel chose to get out of his way just as her husband assumed the presidency.

Houston was thirty-six years old and he had never married. Despite his reputation for carousing and womanizing, he knew that marriage would be an asset to his political career. He began to court Eliza Allen, a very pretty twenty-year-old girl from a rich and distinguished family. Houston had known her and her parents for several years. Eliza had been in love with William Tyree, a young lawyer who had recently died of consumption, and her family encouraged her to respond to Governor Houston's attentions. When Houston proposed, Eliza, again at the urging of her parents, accepted.

Instead of traveling to Washington to be present at his mentor's inauguration as president, Houston stayed in Nashville and married Eliza Allen on January 22, 1829. The couple was mismatched and miserable from the start. Besides the great age difference, historians have speculated that Houston's scars and still unhealed war wounds may have shocked the young girl. And it is thought she was still in love with William Tyree, had never loved Houston, and was forced into the match. Everything Houston did and said seemed distasteful to Eliza.

Whatever the reason, Eliza seemed both disappointed and dismayed by her marriage. Some have suggested the marriage was never consummated. On the second night after the wedding, she and Houston stayed with the Martin family at Locust Grove on their way to Nashville. A heavy snow had fallen, and when Eliza came down to the parlor in the morning she watched through the window as her husband threw snowballs at the Martin girls in the yard. When the girls bombarded the governor in turn, the new bride said to her hostess, "I wish they would kill him." Mrs. Martin was taken aback by her comment and thought she might have misunderstood, but Eliza said again, "Yes, I wish from the bottom of my heart that they would kill him."

Some historians have suggested that Houston offended his young bride by attempting to introduce her to sexual practices of the Cherokees or the sporting houses of New Orleans. We will never know exactly what it was about Houston that repelled her so. But relations between Sam and his bride did not improve. In fact, they just got worse. He seemed able to please every woman he encountered, except the one he had married.

Staying in two miserable rooms at the Nashville Inn with her husband, Eliza missed the warmth and comfort of her family's country mansion called Allenwood. A visit home in March, after the death of a young brother, made her even more unhappy when she had to return to Nashville. There is reason to believe that Eliza was immature even for her twenty years. She came to hate Sam, and nothing he could do lessened her animosity. In his frustration and confusion he drank more than ever.

On the night of April 8, 1829, Sam accused her of being unfaithful to him, of being in love with someone else, of deceiving him by marrying him. We will never know all the things he accused her of or whether his attack was physical as well as verbal. He was a large, eloquent man with an ugly temper. Whatever he did frightened and hurt the young woman deeply. She protested that she was innocent of all he charged her with.

Leaving his wife alone in the inn, Houston sought the counsel of a friend, then returned to their rooms and apologized and assured Eliza he did not believe her to be unfaithful. But she could not be comforted. Her unhappiness over the previous two and a half months, and the shock of Houston's accusations, could not be reversed by apologies and it's likely that in his brutal accusations Eliza saw her means of escape from the man she loathed. She now had a plausible excuse for leaving the governor. He had deeply offended her and impugned her morals and behaved as no gentleman would. Both her family and the world at large would see it was so. She would never have to be reconciled to the beast she abhorred. Houston might be the governor of Tennessee, a general of the militia, and friend of Andrew Jackson, but to her he was a ruffian, a bully, a drunk, and a degenerate. The next day she left for Allenwood and the arms of her family.

Houston wrote a drunken and at times incoherent letter to Eliza's father, apologizing for his behavior. He begged that the whole family put the matter behind them. Houston was all too aware of the effect of such a scandal on his political career. "She was cold to me," Houston wrote, "& I thought did not love me. She owns that such was one cause of my unhappiness. You can judge how unhappy I was to think I was united to a woman that did not love me. This time is now past, & my future happiness can only exist in the assurance that Eliza & myself can be happy & that Mrs. Allen and you can forget the past, — forgive all & find your lost peace & you may rest assured that nothing on my part shall be wanting to restore it. Let me know what is to be done."

Though historians have rarely noted it, it seems clear that Houston's offense included more than harsh words. His abject apologies suggest the guilt of a man who has committed violence against someone defenseless. Everything in his letter implies that he knew his father-in-law held the stronger hand in this poker game. What was at stake was not just his marriage to Eliza Allen, however much or little he cared for her, but his political future. At the age of thirty-six he had risen from poverty and obscurity to prominence in the world. If Old Hickory had made it to the White House by a similar route, maybe he could too. At this moment everything seemed to depend on the whim of a frightened and spoiled young girl. Houston could hardly believe he had made himself so vulnerable. The Allens never answered his letter.

Hoping to keep the collapse of his marriage a private matter, Houston soon heard that he had been burned in effigy in nearby Gallatin, Tennessee. The Allen family seemed to have made the whole affair public. Trying to salvage his political career as well as his marriage, Houston rode to Allenwood and begged Eliza, on his knees, with tears streaming down his cheeks, to return to Nashville with him. Eliza was unmoved by his dramatic entreaties. Returning to Nashville, the humiliated governor spent a week drinking and stumbling in his efforts to survive the scandal, as he was again burned in effigy and denounced by angry crowds, this time in the capital. His political enemies rejoiced and fed the flames. One report said Houston roamed the streets of Nashville at this time dressed in a calfskin, perhaps imitating the shame of Nebuchadnezzar in the Bible, who crawled on all fours in his degradation and ate grass with the kine. And then Houston, drunk, asked to be baptized by a prominent minister but was refused the comforts of the church.

Going sleepless night after night, drinking heavily, wandering Nashville, and studying his options, Houston decided he had no choice but to resign as governor of Tennessee. On April 18, 1829, he concluded his letter of resignation with these words: "In reviewing the past, I can only regret that my capacity for being useful was so unequal to the devotion of my heart." As Houston brooded in his rooms at the Nashville Inn, he recalled he had heard a raven crying along the road to his wedding. Because Ooleteka had named him the Raven, Houston had thought it was a favorable talismanic sign. Now he saw it had been a warning, an evil omen.

Among the friends who tried to comfort Houston at this time of hopeless despair must have been David Crockett. Misery is said to love company and the two politicians had much to lament. Crockett was always good company, as was Houston. Both men were already thinking of the West as a place to start over, recover reputations, make fortunes. They must have discussed the attraction of Texas and the western territories, though it's unlikely either could have guessed how closely their destinies would be connected there as they rose to enduring fame.

On April 23, 1829, Houston left Nashville in disgrace, traveling west on borrowed money. At Clarksville, Tennessee, two men representing the Allen family accosted him and demanded that he sign a statement clearing Eliza of the charge of unfaithfulness. Refusing to sign anything, Houston said he would kill anyone who impugned his wife's honor. His humiliation total, Houston considered throwing himself in the river to drown as the steamboat continued down the Cumberland to the Ohio and then down the Mississippi. But an eagle swooped out over the water before him and soared away toward the setting sun. He took that as an omen that he too would rise again. "I knew then," he said later, "that a great destiny waited for me in the West."

———

HOUSTON'S RECOVERY was neither quick nor uncomplicated, but on the journey west he seemed to find again some of his energy and charm. He made friends with an Irishman named Haralson, and the two traveled by steamboat and flatboat to the Arkansas Territory. Houston had recovered his spirits enough to play cards and drink and thrill his listeners with his yarns.

At the landing on the Arkansas River, Chief Ooleteka greeted his adopted son, Kalanu, and welcomed him back into the family. Ooleteka had moved west and built a great house and prospered. He had many slaves and more than five hundred cattle. The old chief had adopted the name John Jolly for his dealings with government officials. But most Cherokees had not done so well in the new territory. Unscrupulous government agents cheated them of their federal cash allotments, and Indians native to the region, such as the Osages, resented the incursions into their territory. Government officials were happy to let the Indians fight among themselves, perhaps hoping they would exterminate each other.

Attempting to both rebuild his fortunes and help the Cherokees, Houston became a trader and a spokesman for the people. He lobbied both the Indian agents and the government in Washington. In December 1829 Ooleteka sent him to Washington as ambassador for the Cherokees. Because he was friends with Andrew Jackson, Houston spent much time at the White House.

One of the ironies of Houston's career, as mentioned, is the fact that he sided with Jackson's policy of removing the eastern Indian nations to the West. As a defender of Indian rights, especially Cherokees', he would be expected to resist their loss of traditional lands and relocation to a strange place. Instead, he had come to see the future of the eastern-dwelling Cherokees as bleak at best. In Marshall De Bruhl's words, "Like Jackson he also believed that removal was their only option and that a protective national government would watch over them forever."

While his friend David Crockett voted against the bill for Indian removal in 1830, possibly to please the anti-Jackson forces, Houston never wavered in his support for Old Hickory's policies. The renowned Houston biographer Marquis James speculated that Houston supported the removal of Indians to the West in part because he dreamed of creating an Indian state or empire west of the Mississippi where he could be the leader. In such a state he could rebuild his political fortunes. Houston was in Washington on April 30, 1830, when at a celebration of Jefferson's birthday Jackson gave his famous toast, "Our Federal Union. It *must* be preserved," and in effect announced that he would squash John C. Calhoun and the nullifiers of South Carolina.

Later, speaking to a congressman from South Carolina, Old Hickory said, "Give my compliments to my friends in your State and say to them, that if a single drop of blood shall be shed there in opposition to the laws of the United States, I will hang the first man I can lay my hands on engaged in such treasonable conduct, upon the first tree I can reach." Houston would never forget the lesson from his mentor about the sanctity and preservation of the Union. He never doubted the danger and fatal consequences of the states rights' issue. In the tendency toward disunion lay the seeds of chaos, violence, and ultimate failure of the American republic.

At that point Houston became a trader in Arkansas, using all his government and Cherokee contacts. He settled in completely. He married his old sweetheart, the widowed Tiana Rogers Gentry, who, as the niece of Ooleteka, was Cherokee royalty, with extensive property, horses, cattle, and a number of slaves. (The famous Will Rogers was descended from one of her brothers.) When he fell desperately ill of fevers, Houston was treated by Cherokee medicine men. Even so, Houston continued his heavy drinking, and he took up writing. In a series of five articles for the *Arkansas Gazette* published between June and December of 1830, under the pen name Tah-Lohn-Tus-Ky, he attacked corrupt Indian agents, the bungling of the removal policy and its execution, and defended his own actions as a trader. But Houston's attacks were somewhat duplicitous, for even while lashing out at corrupt agents he was arranging lucrative deals for himself in trading with the Indians. Perhaps he felt his case was different, since he was a member of the nation and enjoyed privileged status.

One of the bitterest setbacks of Houston's career occurred in May of 1831 when he ran for a seat on the Cherokee Tribal Council. To his astonishment he was defeated. He had never lost an election before, from major general of the militia, to congressman, to governor of Tennessee. He was a member of the Cherokee Nation and married to the niece of Chief Ooleteka. He had lobbied for the Cherokees and negotiated treaties between the Cherokees and the other nations in the territory, including the Osages.

It appears the Cherokees rejected Kalanu, the Raven, for a position on the tribal council not because he was born white or because he had left Tennessee under a cloud of scandal but because of his heavy drinking and unpredictable behavior. He had, as well, taken part in yet another duel that made him look ridiculous. Some Cherokees dubbed him "Big Drunk." In his anger and disappointment over the defeat, Houston confronted Ooleteka. When his adopted father told him he must curb his drunkenness, Houston was so furious he struck the venerable chief who had stood by him since he was a teenager. Young men present restrained him from seriously injuring the leader of the western Cherokees, but Kalanu's disgrace was total. His attack on Ooleteka was the lowest point of his life.

We can only guess at Tiana's response to Houston's bad conduct. In complete ignominy, Houston packed his belongings in a buffalo-skin sack and, wearing his colorful calico shirt and buckskin leggings, left for Nashville. On the steamboat going up the Mississippi, be bragged about setting up an independent colony in the Pacific Northwest. Still drinking excessively, he defended himself in the newspapers when reports of his bad behavior in the West followed him eastward and were published. Oddly enough, around this time he learned that Eliza was disposed to a reconciliation with him. But too much had happened for him to go back to her. Marquis James suggests that in the very fierceness of Houston's defense of Eliza's honor and his refusal to blame the Allen family there is something strange, as though he were protecting some secret guilt either of himself or his former bride.

In disgrace both in the East and the West, he again left Nashville, presumably for Arkansas Territory, but was called back to east Tennessee with the news that his mother was dying. Hurrying to Baker's Creek, he wept by the bedside of his strong Presbyterian mother, whose greatest disappointment had been the shame of her favorite son. At her deathbed Houston had to confront the scale of his failure. He had risen to great heights, and fallen to utter degradation. Bad luck and political enemies had contributed to his fall, but he himself was the main author of his tragic story of shame, silly bragging, drunkenness. He had crushed all his mother's hopes for him, for the future of the family. Before she died,

Elizabeth gave him her final blessing. After helping to carry her coffin to the graveyard behind the little church, he headed once again for Indian Territory in the West.

HOUSTON IS one of those people who seem to have been everywhere and to have encountered everyone of their era. Traveling to Washington in December 1831 with a group of Choctaw leaders to lobby the federal government to honor its promises to that nation, he plunged once again into political affairs. On his way west, Houston had boarded a steamboat at Memphis and met a French nobleman, Alexis de Tocqueville, who was touring the United States to study its penal system. Houston was dressed in his colorful manner and riding a fine horse when he came aboard. Tocqueville was not impressed and described Houston as an example of the "unpleasant consequences of popular sovereignty."

Tocqueville may have had romantic expectations about the new republic when he arrived, but the miserable conditions of the Indians, the degradations of the slave system, and the crushing of the Nat Turner rebellion in 1831 soon disillusioned him. He could see Americans as they could not see themselves. Tocqueville could not have known that he had met one of the country's future leaders, dressed in his calico shirt and beaded leggings and too handy with the bottle and brag. And certainly Houston had no idea he had met one of the most important thinkers of his time, an unparalleled student of American culture.

Since gold had been found in north Georgia, Houston plunged headlong into land speculation in that region. He had somehow acquired title to ten thousand acres of land in Tennessee, but no gold was found on the tract. He formed a connection with James Prentiss and the Galveston Bay and Texas Land Company. But just as Houston was hoping to restart his career as a land speculator, briefly back in Washington, D.C., he got into a quarrel with Congressman William Stanbery of Cincinnati. It had been reported in the anti-Jackson *National Intelligencer* that Stanbery accused Houston of fraud in his dealings with funds for Indian rations. When Houston wrote to the congressman demanding to know if he had in fact made the accusation, Stanbery retorted, "I cannot recognize the right of Mr. Houston to make this request." Knowing Houston's reputation, Stanbery began to carry two pistols and a dagger. Ten days later Houston confronted the legislator on Pennsylvania Avenue.

Houston carried a walking stick made from hickory grown on the grounds of the Hermitage. As Houston began to beat the congressman with the stick, Stanbery drew a pistol and pulled the trigger, but the charge did not go off. Houston later claimed he was only defending himself. He beat Stanbery so forcefully he broke the man's arm and left a concussion on his skull. It was Friday, April 13.

On April 17 Houston was arrested for attacking a member of the legislature and brought before the House of Representatives. It was an election year and everyone understood the trial was a contest between Jackson and the anti-Jackson forces. Newspapers all over the country took up the fight. Not even his resignation as governor of Tennessee and the scandal of his marriage had brought Houston so much notoriety. Jackson invited Houston to stay at the White House during his trial and Old Hickory pulled every string to help his rash protégé. None other than Francis Scott Key, author of "The Star Spangled Banner," was chosen to defend Houston. Key's main argument was that Houston was attacking Stanbery, not Congress. It was a personal matter and a defense of personal honor. Old Hickory bought his friend a fine suit to wear at the trial, in place of his flashy Indian costume. Houston socialized with leading Democrats such as James K. Polk, Judge Felix Grundy, and Speaker of the House Andrew Stevenson in the evenings and on weekends. Houston described the dour, abstemious Polk as a "victim of the use of water as a beverage."

On May 7, 1832, Houston appeared in the House to defend himself. His speech was a masterpiece, perhaps the most brilliant of his career. He began by saying that he had never been charged with violence before, forgetting his previous brawls and duels. He knew he was addressing not just Congress but the nation and his future. Following Key's line of argument, he asserted that the House had no right to try him. No such right was provided in the Constitution. Houston argued that the right to defend himself and his honor *was* guaranteed by the Constitution. A corrupt and entrenched legislature was a threat to democracy. He pointed to the flag that hung in the chamber, subject of Key's poem, and said,

"But sir, so long as that flag shall bear aloft its glittering stars—bearing them amidst the din of battle, and waving them triumphantly above the storms of the ocean, so long, I trust, shall the rights of American citizens be preserved safe and unimpaired, and transmitted as a sacred legacy from one generation to another, till discord shall wreck the spheres—the grand march of time shall cease—and not one fragment of all creation be left to chafe on the bosom of eternity's waves."

As Houston pointed at the Stars and Stripes and the portrait of Lafayette, the audience went wild with cheers and applause. A young woman tossed a bouquet at Houston, who took a gallant bow. The famous actor Junius Brutus Booth rushed forward to salute the speaker. "Houston, take my laurels!" the player exclaimed.

To the public, Houston had been exonerated. But after four days of wrangling debate the House found him guilty, 106 votes to 89. He was to be given a reprimand by the Speaker, his drinking companion Stevenson. On May 14, 1832, Houston was ordered to return to the chamber to receive his rebuke, which turned out to sound more like praise than censure. He was allowed to file a pro forma protest, and the case was over.

Stanbery angrily pursued fraud charges against Houston and sued him in civil court, but again Houston was let off with a fine of five hundred dollars, which he never paid. The controversy seemed to restore his confidence in himself, and to improve his reputation with the public. He was a national figure once again. Pleased by the way events had turned out, Jackson appointed Houston ambassador to the Indians of the Southwest. No assignment could have been more agreeable to the Raven. Like Daniel Boone before him, Houston all his life seemed to have a special affinity with Indians and a destiny connected to them. In the words of Marquis James, "He had found the Caucasian's capacity for 'coldness' and 'treachery' superior to that of an Indian. Near the close of his stormy life, Sam Houston said he had yet to be wronged or deceived by an Indian, but every wound he had known was the work of those of his own blood."

———

LIKE DAVID Crockett after him, Houston first went to Texas to explore the opportunities there, in the place sometimes described as "the New

Estremadura," after the noted region of Spain and Portugal. No doubt he had heard that the Texans were rebelling against their Mexican rulers and knew of the skirmishes between Anglos and Mexican soldiers. But officially Texas was still Tejas, a province of Mexico. Houston went there with Jackson's blessings as a land speculator and to set himself up as a lawyer at the capital, Nacogdoches. It has been said that as Houston crossed the Red River on December 1, 1832, into Mexican territory an eagle circled overhead, as he "splashed into the muddier Rubicon." He bought enough land for himself, a headright, to qualify as a citizen of Mexico. He even converted, nominally, to the Roman Catholic Church, a condition of citizenship, becoming "a Muldoon Catholic," as such converts were called, after Padre Miguel Muldoon, who received many Anglos into the church for a certain donation. And he negotiated with the Comanches on behalf of President Jackson.

Many historians believe that Jackson had suggested to Houston that he do everything in his power to further Texas independence and bring it into the Union as a new state. There is no documentary evidence for such a conversation, but subsequent events show that it almost certainly took place before Houston left Washington after his trial. Houston knew that whatever he did to further the cause of Texas independence had the approval and backing of the president of the United States. Houston knew quite well that it had long been Old Hickory's hope to add Texas to the Union. Jackson had sent his ambassador, Anthony Butler, to Mexico City to persuade the Mexicans to sell Texas to the United States. But Butler failed in his assignment and was eventually recalled. Jackson was pleased when Houston informed him that nineteen out of twenty Texans preferred annexation to the United States and were ready to declare independence. On February 13, 1833, he wrote to the president that Texas "has already beaten and repelled all the troops of Mexico from her soil . . . She can defend herself against the whole power of Mexico, for really Mexico is powerless and penniless."

Neither Jackson nor Houston understood how determined the Mexicans were not to yield territory to the greedy neighbor to the north. The Mexicans felt vulnerable, not least because of the rapid turnover of their governments after the revolution of 1810–21. They had won independence at the Treaty of Cordoba August 23, 1821, but had failed to establish a stable national government. Between 1821 and 1857 there would be at least fifty changes in the presidency. On July 16, 1821, Stephen Austin and Erasmo Seguín had "crossed the international boundary at the Sabine River and entered Texas," planning to bring a colony of Anglo settlers into the region. Stephen Austin became Esteban Austin. Since then Americans had poured into Texas by the hundreds. By the mid-1830s Anglos in Texas outnumbered the Mexicans about ten to one. As the team of Mexican historians led by Ramón Alcaraz would write in *The Other Side* in 1848, "The disadvantage of her [Mexico's] position could not be concealed from the keen sight of the United States, who watched for the favorable moment for their project." The Mexicans feared the neighboring republic that showed every sign of intending to spread its dominion over the whole continent. Alcaraz and his team stated, "The first settlers of the United States pursued the same ends, and . . . the descendants of Washington do no more than imitate the conduct of their forefathers." As more and more Americans streamed into Texas, a revolt against Mexico City seemed more likely. The Americans could see the weakness of Mexico, and worst of all, the Americans were not afraid to fight for what they wanted. "In their choice of expedients they preferred those which had the charm of violence," the Mexican historians would explain. There were already more than twenty thousand English-speaking immigrants in the province. Fearing rebellion, the Mexican government had stopped legal immigration into Texas. This served only to keep the most desirable immigrants away. Outlaws, con men, deadbeats, and adventurers continued to arrive from the east and slip across the border. Stephen Austin journeyed to Mexico City to negotiate an end to the ban on immigration and better terms for Texas but ended up being thrown in jail as Antonio López de Santa Anna consolidated his grip on power and became dictator of Mexico.

The historian T. R. Fehrenbach, in *Fire and Blood: A History of Mexico*, stresses the long-standing hostility between Hispanic and Anglo cultures. "Mexican leadership, liberal or conservative, had inherited an historic hatred of Anglo-Saxon marauders that went back to Drake." But at its deepest level the cultural, spiritual, and political differences between Mexico and the United States went even further back into history, with sources in mutual distrust and disdain. Fehrenbach goes on to say, "The Hispanic contempt was rooted in cultural outlooks that went back to Rome, and which saw Northerners as cold, rude, insensible barbarians . . . The Mexican attitude toward the United States, therefore, was a dangerous combination of arrogance and fear." Many would not agree with Fehrenbach's sweeping summary of relations between Mexico and the United States, but his comments provide a springboard for discussion of that troubled history. "The resolving of the question [of dominance in North America] need not have been more painful or dishonorable for Mexico than for the Canadians . . . But the Mexican leadership could not accept reality, and in continuous failure heaped lasting humiliation upon all Mexican heads, for it could not make adjustments gracefully or peacefully."

Few Americans understood much about Mexican history and Mexican culture. The new republic was led by *criollos* of pure Spanish blood, some of whom looked back to a royalist past, while others dreamed of a more democratic Mexico. As the modern Mexican historian Enrique Krauze tells us, "Mexico — or more precisely its elite leadership — essentially became a being with two faces, one assuming that a return to the past was possible, the other yearning to wipe it all out and begin anew." Krauze also points out that Mexicans had a preference for absolute power, derived from both the deity of the Roman Catholic Church and the terrifying gods of the Aztecs. The patron saint, the Virgin of Guadalupe, had been brought by Hernán Cortés from his native region of the Estramadura, but many saw her with dark skin, Indian features. In their leaders, Mexicans looked for charisma and a sense of sacred mission more than practical policies and abilities. Both conservatives and liberals tended to see themselves as "the Children of Cuauhtemoc," the last emperor of the Aztecs, who had resisted and been killed by Cortés. Few bothered to point out that the Aztecs themselves had been "latecomers, invading and conquering and spilling more blood than Cortés ever did." It has been suggested that Mexico in the nineteenth century was still a medieval society without a class to lead it as a modern state. The leader Lucas Alamán once stated that Mexico was neither an empire nor a nation but rather "a theatrical performance, or a dream."

In 1803 the explorer Alexander von Humbolt had described Mexico as "the country of inequality. Nowhere does there exist such a fearful difference in the distribution of fortune, civilization, cultivation of the soil and population." After achieving independence from Spain in 1821 and adopting a constitution in 1824, Mexico referred to itself as a republic. But the description had little connection to the reality. As the historian Robert W. Merry tells us, "Mexico, despite its pretense to constitutional government, was a dysfunctional country."

Mexican historian Francisco Bulnes (1847–1924) places much of the blame for the Texas rebellion on the Mexican government. "The constitution of 1824 deprived the Texans of the good position which they had acquired when they were considered to belong only provisionally to Coahuila," he wrote. But as a part of the state of Coahuila, with the capital hundreds of miles away across deserts and Indian lands, Texans found it almost impossible to get a hearing in the courts or in the government. The policy seemed to be to ignore Texas altogether. Bulnes continues, "The state of Coahuila fulfilled its mission as proven by its provincialism, its misery, and the almost impossibility of its communicating with Texas across immense deserts ruled by savage hordes . . . the state . . . had not laid out or opened a single road . . . The Texas colonists were left to take care of their own defense or to perish." The immigrants, who had become Mexican citizens, were discriminated against in the courts. "This law peremptorily forbade the colonists, who were *naturalized Mexicans,* to engage in retail commerce because this activity could only be exercised, according to this illegal decree, by those who were native-born Coahuilans."

As with the American Revolution before it, the Texas Revolution was chaotic and brutal, unfolding as a series of stumbles, rivalries, and atrocities, culminating in sacrifice, significant courage, leadership, and glory. Sam Houston had been prepared for his role in the fight for Texas independence by both his former failures and successes. His previous success gave him confidence, boldness, eloquence, and fame, all essential for a leader. His many failures enabled him to take the long view, with unusual tenacity, and also a touch of humility he had not demonstrated before. The Houston of the Texas Revolution was not the man of his previous two decades. Events in Texas changed him for the better. By studying his actions we watch him grow as a leader once he reached Texas. He became cautious, objective, cunning in new ways. He was a moderate, hoping independence could be achieved one careful step at a time. His behavior showed a new patience and practicality. The unfolding events seemed to make him as much as he made the events.

Leaving his Cherokee wife and his former life behind him, Houston plunged into the growing political ferment of Texas. He involved himself in both land speculation and the political conventions in San Antonio de Bexar and San Felipe, and a new energy and momentum seemed to gather in him. He appeared to be everywhere and involved in everything. He became friends with James Bowie and rode with him to both San Antonio de Bexar and San Felipe. He began to court a well-connected beauty in Nacogdoches named Anna Raguet. He became a close friend of Adolphus Sterne and his wife, Eva, in Nacogdoches. And like many others he was probably associated with those who smuggled goods from the United States across the Texas border. In his law practice he defended the poor and became known as an advocate for the disadvantaged.

The sentiment for independence gained strength when Texans learned their ambassador, Stephen Austin, had been arrested by Mexican authorities on January 3, 1834, and was being held in Mexico City. In the past Austin had proven savvy in dealing with Mexican authorities. Fluent in Spanish, he had pledged loyalty to the constitution of 1824. In the words of T. R. Fehrenbach, "Austin . . . knew that the Hispanic mind would accept many defeats and compromises but only if appearances were observed." But under Santa Anna's dictatorship things had changed in Mexico. The quiet, diplomatic Austin had many detractors in Texas, but his detention turned him into something of a hero and changed Austin himself from a quiet negotiator to a determined revolutionary. He decided Texas must sever itself from the corruption and brutality of Santa Anna and Mexico.

Back in Nacogdoches, Houston practiced law, courted the coy seventeen-year-old Anna Raguet and waited for events to evolve. When Houston traveled to New York in 1834 to confer with the Galveston Bay and Texas Land Company and James Prentiss, he told many he encountered, including the actor Junius Brutus Booth, that he was working for Texas independence. To the tragedian he bragged, "I am made to revel in the Halls of the Montezumas." When he attended the theater in Cincinnati, on his way back to the West, the crowd in Congressman Stanbury's hometown hissed at him until Houston was forced to leave the theater.

No doubt that experience showed him more clearly than ever that his destiny lay far to the southwest. Back in Texas he bided his time, waiting calmly for events to mature in an inevitable and irreversible process. His law practice in Nacogdoches thrived. What he would not do was talk about his marriage to Eliza Allen. There had been no divorce. When a close friend asked him to comment on his first wife, he angrily stormed out of the house.

Stephen Austin was released from prison in Mexico in December 1834, and he returned to Texas determined to fight for independence. Affairs in Mexico were unstable, its policies inconsistent, chaotic. Mexican political history of the time has been described as "kaleidoscopic." When William B. Travis and a group of rebels attacked the fort at Anahuac, the Mexican army abandoned the garrison on June 30, 1835. The Texas Revolution proper had begun. When Santa Anna sent an army of five hundred commanded by his brother-in-law General Martín Perfecto de Cós to Bexar, Stephen Austin sounded a call for Texans to organize both politically and militarily. "WAR is our only recourse. There is no other remedy," the former diplomat asserted.

On October 2, 1835, an event occurred at Gonzales that is often called the Lexington of Texas. A unit of the local militia refused to return a cannon lent them by the Mexican army for defense against Indian raids. A small battle took place, and the army withdrew. By some accounts, this is considered the actual beginning of the Texas Revolution. The rebels hoped that moderates in other Mexican states would join their cause but found few allies south of the Rio Grande.

Houston was made commander of the militia at Nacogdoches, and he issued a proclamation on October 8, 1835: "The morning of glory is dawning upon us. The work of liberty has begun . . . Let your valor proclaim to the world that liberty is your birthright. We cannot be conquered by all the arts of anarchy and despotism combined."

His words show a new eloquence and maturity in Houston. Before he had been the master of flowery speech. Now he inspired with a deeper, more philosophical note. Houston sold four thousand acres of land to raise quick cash and ordered a handsome uniform with general's stars and a sword sash from New Orleans.

The Texas forces converged at Gonzales that October, but James

Bowie and James Fannin argued about who was in command. Stephen Austin stepped in to be the general himself to calm things down. A convention was held in San Felipe, home of the only newspaper in Texas, the *Telegraph and Texas Register*. The convention issued a declaration on November 7, 1835, at once proclaiming independence *and* loyalty to the Mexican constitution of 1824, which had been pushed aside by Santa Anna's dictatorship. A provisional government was established under the authority of "organic law." Henry Smith was elected president and Sam Houston was made commander of all Texas military forces.

The revolution was under way, but with little coordination among the different forces. Travis and the men who had seized San Antonio de Bexar were outside Houston's command. James Fannin wanted to be his own commander and followed no orders from Houston. Stephen Austin was now away lobbying in Washington for recognition of Texas independence. The General Council stumbled and fumbled its way forward, trying to establish order and a government. There had been fights at Goliad, Gonzales, and Conception. Houston tried to assemble and train an army. He planned to fight a defensive, Fabian-style war against the larger Mexican forces. Many of the other officers wanted to take the fight to the enemy and invade Mexico. Houston knew it was important to buy time until a larger Texas force could be assembled and equipped and trained. He may have hoped that at some point the United States would aid in the struggle, as George Washington had waited for the French to enter the American War of Independence. President Jackson would indeed order General Edmund Pendleton Gaines with an American army to take a position in Louisiana near the border of Texas and to keep an eye on events there. In June of 1836 Gaines and his army would enter Texas territory and occupy Nacogdoches, though the United States remained officially neutral.

One of the ironies of the Texas Revolution is that few of the earlier residents of Texas took part in the fighting. The Mexican claim that the rebellion was the act of citizens of the United States has a certain basis in fact. Many of the soldiers at the Alamo, at Goliad, and with Houston at the end in the battle of San Jacinto were recent arrivals in Texas. Many came, like Houston and Crockett, seeking a new start. Others came to take part in the struggle for independence. Some joined simply for adventure, perhaps hoping to achieve glory. But it should not be forgotten that a number of the Hispanic citizens of Texas did take part in the fight for independence. Most prominent was Lorenzo de Zavala, who had served as governor, senator, cabinet officer, and minister to France for former Mexican governments. He was also a hero of the 1820–21 Mexican Revolution. Opposing the dictator Santa Anna, Zavala had fled to Texas and now threw in his lot with Austin and Houston. In the coming struggle he would prove an important leader.

Houston's strategy was not to the taste of many of the volunteers. They wanted to plunge into battle right away and get it over with. He had little control over what groups to the west and south chose to do. Houston planned to wait until March of 1836 to attack the Mexican forces at San Antonio, when his own army would be ready for such a campaign. But Ben Milam organized a group of three hundred volunteers and took back the town on December 10, 1835, against Houston's orders. Milam was killed by a sniper, but his men held San Antonio. President Henry Smith referred to the group there as a "mob nicknamed an army." Their hurried taking of San Antonio made Houston look weak and indecisive to many who wanted immediate action and did not consider the Mexican army a serious threat.

The fact was that most of those in the Texas forces were young and inexperienced, looking for excitement, idealistic about the cause of liberty. One of the most idealistic was James Butler Bonham, a friend of William Travis's from South Carolina. He wrote to Houston, "Permit me through you to volunteer my services in the present struggle of Texas without conditions." Bonham, at least, had experience serving in an Alabama militia, the Mobile Greys.

Houston did his best to set up recruiting offices, supply depots, and training stations, and he asked friends back in Tennessee to send books on military courtesy and procedure, illustrations of uniforms. As mentioned before, he had ordered a fine general's uniform for himself from a tailor in New Orleans. He also ordered that his collection of books, as well as his extensive wardrobe, be packed in trunks to accompany him on the campaign. He wanted to be equipped for his role in history.

Few in Texas seemed to understand Houston's deliberate and slow-paced strategy. Sentiment was so strong for an attack that Houston could do little to stop a force that set out to cross the Rio Grande to Matamoros. That venture was a blunder and waste of valuable manpower and resources just as he was trying to build an effective army.

Dealing with insubordination, lack of supplies, slow communications, rivalries, and inflated egos, Houston came close to despair. This is the time when his experience of previous failures probably served him best. He had hit bottom before, and he knew his only hope was to continue the struggle. Persistence was everything. His strategy might not win in the end, but it was his (and Texas's) only hope. A convention planned for March to organize a permanent government may have encouraged him to think some order could be salvaged from of the shambles.

Houston sent Bowie to San Antonio on January 17, 1836, to order that the Alamo be blown up and the men and artillery there join forces at Gonzales to the east. Houston rode to meet with Dr. James Grant and the forces marching toward the Rio Grande and Matamoros. But on January 20 a messenger arrived with the news that Henry Smith had been replaced as president by David G. Burnet and Colonel James Fannin had been put in charge of Texan forces marching toward Matamoros. The hotheads had taken over the General Council in San Felipe and Houston was relieved of command. He left the army and headed for Washington-on-the-Brazos. What he found there was a government split into factions and in complete disarray. In effect, there was no government of Texas. But James Fannin had managed to usurp Houston's command, and both Bowie and Travis at the Alamo refused to obey the order to blow up the fort and evacuate their men and ordnance to consolidate forces at Gonzales.

Houston returned to his home in Nacogdoches and resumed negotiations for a treaty with the Cherokees and other Indian nations. It was important that the tribes not take the side of Mexico in the conflict. Using the advantage of his connection with the Cherokees, Houston secured a treaty that was signed February 23, 1836, by the Cherokees and twelve other nations, agreeing that they would live in peace with each other and with the new government of Texas. Probably no one but Houston could have succeeded in getting such an agreement at that unstable time. The treaty was crucial to the future of Texas and represented one of the most important achievements of Houston's career.

Things started to move rapidly in the late winter of 1836. The Republic of Texas began in the village of San Felipe, where representatives gathered on February 29, 1836, and set about organizing a government the next day. Houston's gift for leadership was recognized by a majority of the delegates. A declaration of independence was produced and ratified on March 2, 1836, in honor of Houston's forty-third birthday. Houston, who was clearly the most able leader present, was again offered command of the armies, and he stated the conditions under which he would accept the command. He had learned his lesson from the chaos of the winter before. Houston would be "endowed with all the rights, privileges and powers due to a Commander in Chief in the United States of America." In the United States the commander in chief was also the president, as Houston well knew.

With his authority guaranteed by the convention, Houston left immediately to take charge of the army. On the way he is said to have dismounted from his horse and put his ear to the ground, listening for the sound of cannon fire from the Alamo. It was a trick he had learned from the Cherokees. But the ground was silent. He arrived in Gonzales, about sixty miles east of San Antonio, on March 11, 1836, to a euphoric and tumultuous reception by the troops. But two Mexicans coming from San Antonio told him the Alamo had fallen and all the defenders had been killed. Houston wrote to Fannin at Goliad, ordering him to blow up the fort there and retreat to the east. "You will, as soon as practicable after receipt of this order, fall back upon Guadalupe Victoria, with your command, and such artillery as can be brought with expedition."

The widow of Lieutenant Almaron Dickerson arrived from San Antonio with her baby daughter and a slave named Ben. They carried a message from Santa Anna ordering all Texans to submit to Mexican authority. They told of the slaughter at the Alamo and the burning of the bodies in the square. The generalissimo had refused to set up a field hospital for his own wounded, and more than a hundred Mexican soldiers died after the battle "from injuries that could have been successfully treated." Santa Anna's cruelty had the opposite effect from what he had intended. Instead of submitting to his forces, the inhabitants of Texas began to flee to the east in a flight called the Runaway Scrape. Houston ordered Gonzales burned to the ground and began to move his army toward the east also. His decision to retreat infuriated many Texans who did not understand his strategy. They expected him to make a stand and fight immediately.

One of the true heroes of the Texas Revolution was the old plainsman and scout called Erastus "Deaf" Smith. Houston relied on him as a messenger and spy. It was he who brought the three survivors of the Alamo into Houston's camp. Though handicapped by deafness, Smith was able to compensate through resourcefulness and experience, courage and dedication. (Later a county in Texas would be named Deaf Smith County.)

In March 1836 Houston not only had the example of the Alamo, and then Goliad, to teach him the danger of being trapped in a fortress and surrounded by a larger army. He carried with him the memory of Horseshoe Bend, where the determined warriors of the Red Stick Creeks had dug in behind a supposedly impregnable fortification and were then destroyed by the Cherokees from behind and by Jackson's forces assaulting the barricade. The only hope for a smaller army, neither well trained nor equipped, was to be evasive and avoid major engagements until an opportune moment arrived and then to attack with all-out effort.

Houston had fewer than 375 men when he pulled out of Gonzales; he had few horses and fewer supplies. His men had little or no training and were short of weapons and ammunition. As he contemplated his plans at night in camp, Houston whittled on a stick. The casual whittling masked the uncertainty and alarm he felt. Luckily the Mexican army was slowed down by lack of grass for its many fine horses. The Texans set fire to the grasslands as they retreated, until heavy rains made burning the prairie impossible. But the rain helped Houston's forces also, by turning the roads into mud and swelling rivers and smaller streams. Santa Anna's wagon trains bogged down, and his large army had to search for forage and means of crossing flooded streams.

Settlers, fearing more Mexican atrocities, threw themselves on the mercy of Houston's little army. Most had nothing but what they could carry in their arms or pockets. In steady rain, with few rations or other supplies, with a large crowd of civilians following him, Houston worked his soldiers toward the Brazos. As more men joined him Houston had as many as fourteen hundred people depending on him. The ever-active Deaf Smith kept him informed of the progress and whereabouts of the

Mexican army. Houston provided the music for his men himself, playing reveille and tattoo on a drum, as he had learned as a young soldier in Tennessee.

Instead of obeying Houston's orders, Fannin had stayed with his forces at Goliad, hoping to win glory for himself in a fight with the Mexicans. Then he thought better of his decision to remain and marched his men out of the fort, only to be captured by General José de Urrea's army and returned to Goliad. Santa Anna ordered all the Goliad soldiers executed, and only a few who ran away from the murder squads escaped. Some bodies were burned in a great pile while others were left to rot on the plain and be picked bare by vultures. The atrocities at Goliad inspired still more men to join Houston's army. The dictator had already killed many Mexicans, but it was the executions at Goliad that blackened Santa Anna's name in the eyes of the world. The people of Texas saw they could expect no mercy from Santa Anna. The choice was to fight or be killed. As T. R. Fehrenbach tells us, "The slaughter of some four hundred North American adventurers at Goliad destroyed Santa Anna's international reputation as no execution of Mexicans could have."

Even so, the Texas army never had more than eight hundred fighting men, from a population of about thirty-five thousand. Though it is not a well-known fact, there were a good number of African Americans with Houston's force. Some were free volunteers, and more were slaves accompanying their masters.

By March 17 Houston had reached the Colorado River. As news of the deaths at the Alamo and Goliad spread, more men began to arrive and join the Texas army. By the time he got to the Colorado Houston had at least six hundred fighting men.

The countryside they moved through was a scene of eerie emptiness. Farms were abandoned and livestock were left in pens or foraging on their own. A ranger named Noah Smithwick sent to protect the inhabitants later recalled, "Houses were standing open, the beds unmade, the breakfast things still on the tables, pans of milk moulding in the dairies. There were cribs full of corn, smoke houses full of bacon, yards full of chickens than ran after us for food, nests of eggs in every fence corner, young corn and garden truck rejoicing in the rain, cattle cropping the luxuriant grass, hogs, fat and lazy, wallowing in the mud, all abandoned."

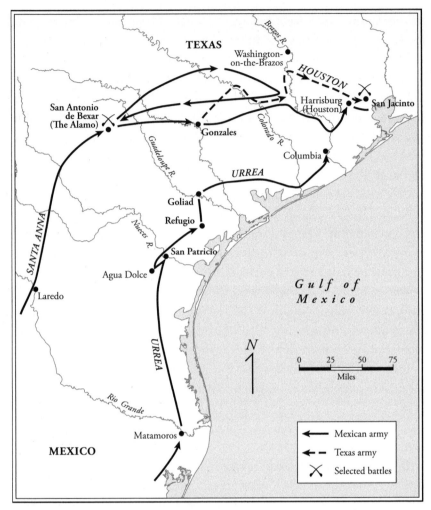

Mexican Invasion of Texas, 1836

President Burnet and his government, fearing the approach of the Mexican army, moved from San Felipe de Austin east to Harrisburg. Instead of following them, Houston decided to move his army up the west bank of the Brazos River toward Washington, along the stream called by the Spanish the Rio de los Brazos de Dios, the River of the Arms of God. No doubt the Texans prayed they would be protected by the arms of God. It was a risky and controversial decision. Houston was angry that the government had fled the capital, for its flight inspired even more panic throughout the population of Texas.

Burnet and his government have been much criticized by historians for their retreat to Harrisburg and then on to Galveston, as the Mexicans drew closer. Their withdrawal has been described as "craven" by Marshall De Bruhl, cowardly and hysterical by others. Houston wrote to the new secretary of war, Thomas J. Rusk, on March 29, 1836, "For Heaven's sake, do not drop back again with the seat of government! Your removal to Harrisburg has done more to increase the panic in the country than anything else that has occurred in Texas."

Rusk's response was to leave the rest of the cabinet in Harrisburg (future Houston) and join Houston's army at Mill Creek. He stayed with the army until its final battle. Some have said Rusk was sent by the governor to report on Houston's drinking. But at this time Houston seemed to be treating the pain from his old wounds with opium, not alcohol. Houston explained little of his strategy to his men, frustrating both civilians and soldiers. His silence has been compared to the reticence of Indian leaders, reluctant to explain their plans. Like Lincoln, his "policy was to have no policy." But it is also likely his plans were mostly up in the air, taking shape as events unfolded.

———

JOSÉ ENRIQUE de la Peña and other Mexican officers might be disturbed by the brutal murders at the Alamo, Goliad, and Refugio (where thirty-four wounded were executed by the Mexicans on March 16, 1836), but they did not publicly oppose Santa Anna. To have done so might well have cost their own lives. Even so, a Colonel Garay and a Señora Alvarez were able to save a few of Fannin's men at Goliad on their own initiative. They are among the heroes of Texas history.

Santa Anna has been described by the noted Mexican historian and statesman, Lucas Alamán, as "a conjunction of good and bad qualities; a natural and sprightly talent, without moral or literary cultivation; an enterprising spirit, but lacking in fixed purpose or determined objectives . . . [He had] clarity of perception in forming general plans for a revolution or a campaign, yet great ineptitude in the directing of a battle." Of Santa Anna, T. R. Fehrenbach has written, "He had once been a good soldier, and could still conduct an energetic campaign. But with his fantastic uniforms, callous cruelty, crates of fighting cocks and hordes of passing whores, and his incredible blindness to anything but the superficial, he was a disastrous ruler."

Santa Anna is one of the most complex figures in Mexican history. In all, he would serve as president of the republic eleven times. He was six feet tall, with dark complexion, and military bearing. In the words of Robert W. Merry, the general had "a showman's flair, a gambler's temperament, and a military man's resolve—but without any discernable conviction." He had a seemingly miraculous ability to reinvent himself. Enrique Krauze describes him as "a creole caricature of Bonaparte." Krauze explains that Santa Anna's strange career was possible because with all his contradictions and pomp, he mirrored the Mexico of those times. The historian Alamán had called Santa Anna "the barometer of national upheavals, the specter of the society, of its romanticism and megalomania." Throughout his life he conducted himself like an actor "always playing a role, striking a pose."

As both armies labored eastward the heavy rains continued. Creeks spread out of banks over the fields and prairie. The army might as well be marching through lakes and swamps. News of the massacre at Goliad made the men even more fearful for their families. Houston raged at his officers to maintain discipline and keep the troops together. The Mexican army struggled against the same unceasing rain and deepening mud, and Santa Anna had more artillery and baggage than the Texans to move along the bottomless roads and trails. It was a stroke of luck that Captain John E. Ross of the steamboat *Yellow Stone* agreed to take the Texas army across the Brazos when Houston chose to move. He knew Santa Anna would have great difficulty in crossing the river with his larger army. The *Yellow Stone* had a distinguished history on the Mississippi and Missouri. It would prove invaluable in the Texas Revolution.

On April 12 it was reported that Santa Anna had crossed the Brazos with six hundred of his men and was marching toward Harrisburg. President Burnet had ordered Houston to fight Santa Anna and if possible stop the Mexican army at the Brazos. "Sir, The enemy are laughing you to scorn . . . You must *retreat* no farther. The country expects you to fight: The salvation of the country expects you to do so."

Houston was furious at the rebuke and moved his army across the Brazos farther north. In retrospect, it is clear that Houston was waiting for an opportune time to attack the Mexicans while he built up his forces, but to many at the time it seemed he was just avoiding a confrontation with Santa Anna. At times he may have doubted his own strategy, as the Mexican army came closer and closer to reconquering all of Texas.

As April rains continued, Houston knew he must reach the ferry at Lynchburg on the San Jacinto River before Santa Anna got there and blocked him from further retreat and from protecting northeastern Texas. As the Texans slogged through mud and standing water, Houston walked with his men and helped wrestle wagons out of the mire. As Jackson had done on the march from Natchez to Nashville in 1813, Houston won the undying love and loyalty of his men by struggling in the mud with them. But fleeing settlers tended to blame Houston for their plight. One Mrs. Pamela Mann refused to let him have her yoke of oxen. Houston gave in and didn't requisition her team. It was rumored that Houston was retreating all the way to the Sabine River, the border with Louisiana, and Houston was happy for the Mexicans to think that. He agreed to let Wily Martin and four hundred men separate from the main force and march toward the Sabine, perhaps to confuse Santa Anna. But the men marching with Houston now were resolute and dedicated. They were less than a thousand out of the whole population of Texas, but as they marched they began to shout, "Victory or Death" and "Remember the Alamo." Houston sensed that they were almost ready to meet Santa Anna.

On April 18, the anniversary of Paul Revere's ride, Houston reached Buffalo Bayou, opposite the burned village of Harrisburg. Texans had intercepted a Mexican courier and found in his saddlebags Santa Anna's plan to divide his army. According to Daniel Walker Howe, "Houston saw that his moment had arrived." Santa Anna and his six hundred men were about fifteen miles to the southeast, marching toward Lynch's Ferry. Another thousand Mexican soldiers were on the Brazos forty miles to the west. Santa Anna was in pursuit of Burnet and the Texas government, and on April 17 he had come close to capturing them before they sailed away to Galveston.

On April 19 Houston wrote to his friend Henry Raguet in Nacogdoches that he was preparing to meet Santa Anna at last, though he had only seven hundred men. "It is wisdom growing out of necessity to meet the enemy now." Houston had waited for the right moment to strike and endured the criticisms of both civilians and fellow officers. Now suddenly, instead of retreating further, he was pursuing Santa Anna. In a proclamation to the people of Texas on April 19 Houston said, "It is vain to look for present aid: none is at hand. We must now act or abandon all hope! . . . Be men, be freemen, that your children may bless their fathers' names!"

He had to beat Santa Anna coming from the south before he seized the ferry at Lynchburg and crossed the San Jacinto River and before the large force from the Brazos rejoined *el presidente.* Houston marched his army all day, and, after a short rest, all night. At daybreak they could see the level ground on the point of land between Buffalo Bayou and the San Jacinto River. Mexican scouts were sighted monitoring their progress.

Houston camped within half a mile of the ferry landing. Santa Anna was three hours away from the ferry when the Texans reached it. Houston's men slaughtered several cows and began to roast them for breakfast. They were camped among oak trees hung with swaying Spanish moss. Suddenly, as they were starting to eat, the Mexican army appeared and assembled into battle formation. The Texans ran for their arms and lined up to confront the enemy. A brief skirmish followed, and then the Mexicans retreated into a small grove of trees. The ground there has been called the Plain of St. Hyacinth (San Jacinto, in Spanish). Santa Anna ordered that camp be made without much consideration for the location. Clearly *el presidente* felt he had Houston trapped, with the river and bayou behind the Texans. General Cós with another five hundred to eight hundred men would arrive the next day. There was no need to rush a battle that was certain to be another victory for the Mexicans.

Making camp under an oak tree that he called Camp Safety, Houston wrote to President Burnet that he was confident that his men would win a victory if they would "march to their duty and not fly like recreants from danger." Then he lay down to sleep under the tree, resting his head, some say, on his saddle. But according to Marquis James, he used a coil of rope as a pillow.

Houston slept late the next morning, or maybe just pretended to sleep. And when he woke he saw an eagle in the bright April sky. "The sun of Austerlitz has risen again," he exclaimed. Deaf Smith arrived to tell Houston reinforcements were approaching to join Santa Anna's army. Houston asked the veteran scout to leave camp and then return, announcing that he had been mistaken. Around nine in the morning there was sudden movement in the Mexican camp as General Cós arrived with additional soldiers. Knowing they were now outnumbered almost two to one, the Texans became alarmed. But Houston assured his men that no additional troops had joined Santa Anna. The Mexican general was marching his men in a circle to give the impression of greater numbers. Houston later told Santa Anna that he had waited until Cós had arrived to attack, to avoid making "two bites of one cherry." That is, he thought it more effective to fight one larger battle rather than two smaller ones.

While his junior officers urged Houston to attack the Mexicans, and the senior officers voted only to defend themselves, Houston kept his own counsel. He seemed to be waiting for some signal, a sign that his men were ready for an all-out attack. At three in the afternoon he decided the moment had come.

Because of the grove of oaks, Houston's preparations for battle went unnoticed by the Mexicans taking their siesta, confident they could destroy the Texans any time they chose. It never occurred to Santa Anna that Houston would attack *him,* much less attack at siesta time. Most historians agree that Santa Anna now had about 1,350 men, while Houston had about 800. *El presidente* himself was said to be in his fine tent with his mulatto mistress, later called "the Yellow Rose of Texas." (Santa Anna would later write, "I never thought that a moment of rest . . . could be so disastrous.") He had not even placed lookouts in advance of his front line.

It was about four in the afternoon when Houston swung up on the fine stallion that he had named Saracen and rode out in front of his men. He drew his saber and pointed it at Santa Anna's forces beyond the stand of oak trees and shouted "Remember the Alamo!" in his orator's voice.

On the left Houston placed Sidney Sherman leading the Second Infantry Regiment and Edward Burleson leading the First Infantry Regiment. On the right he arranged the two pieces of artillery, the Twin Sisters, and on the far right four companies of infantry led by Lieutenant Colonel Henry Millard. Mirabeau Buonaparte Lamar's cavalry was divided into two companies to flank the Mexicans from the right.

Moving quickly through the oak trees and onto the open ground, Houston led his men toward the unsuspecting Mexicans. Recently acquired fifes and drums began to play "Will You Come to the Bower," and the rhythm seemed to spread through the whole corps. Houston rode back and forth among the companies yelling, "Hold your fire. God damn it, hold your fire!" When they were within two hundred yards of the Mexican front line, the two cannon opened up and sprayed the surprised Mexicans with grapeshot and scraps of horseshoes. Suddenly "orange dots" of rifle fire greeted the Texans.

The Texans shouted from one side of their line to the other, "Remember the Alamo! Remember Goliad!" advancing toward the Mexicans faster, firing and reloading as they moved, as the two cannon blasted shot after shot at the scurrying Mexicans. Soon the field was completely covered with smoke from the black powder. The Mexicans ran back and forth trying to find weapons, trying to form and reform their lines.

Houston's stallion Saracen fell under him, and he grabbed another horse, but it too was shot out from under him. At this time the general himself was hit and his right ankle shattered by a musket ball. As his boot filled with blood, he found another horse and rode again into battle.

The Texans climbed over a nominal breastwork of baggage and seized the brass cannon. Within eighteen minutes the Texans found themselves in control of the ground. But Houston's soldiers seemed determined to kill as many of the enemy as possible. The momentum of the killing seemed to build, not wane. They shot or sabered Mexicans attempting to surrender. Houston was no longer in control of his men. Mexicans attempted to surrender, shouting "Me no Álamo! Me no Álamo!"

Still mounted on his third horse, ignoring his shattered ankle, Houston shouted for his men to stop the killing and reform their lines. But Mexican soldiers, surrendering, wounded, or running away continued to be shot, stabbed, or clubbed to death. General Manuel Fernandez Castrillón was shot even as he tried to surrender. As Houston rode back and forth, weak from loss of blood, his men cheered him. He later said two ravens appeared above the captured brass cannon.

Barely able to keep himself in the saddle, Houston returned to the oak tree under which he had slept the night before and, too weak to dismount, fell to the ground. He was laid on a blanket and attended

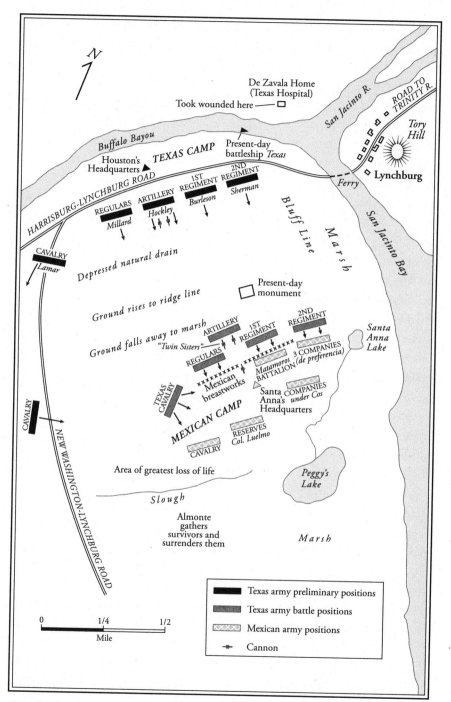

Battle of San Jacinto, April 21, 1836

by a surgeon named Dr. Alexander W. Ewing. Only half conscious, the general mistook Colonel Juan Nepomuceno Almonte's four hundred surrendering Mexicans for fresh reinforcements and exclaimed, "My God, all is lost."

More than 650 Mexican soldiers had been killed or lay dying. Ramón Martínez Caro, secretary to Santa Anna, later described the scene: "To the right and to the left, as far as the eye could see, a double file of corpses . . . There was a small creek, at the edge of the woods, where the bodies were so thickly piled upon each other that they formed a bridge across it."

While seven hundred prisoners were taken, Santa Anna himself had escaped minutes after the battle began, riding to the west to join the forces of General Vicente Filisola. On April 22 Captain James Austin Sylvester and six men were searching the area. Around eleven in the morning they caught up with a Mexican running out on the open prairie. Having no idea who the man was, they took him prisoner and marched him back to the battlefield. When the prisoner grew too tired to walk further he was allowed to mount behind Private Joel Robison. In gratitude, Santa Anna gave Robison a gold braided vest he still wore beneath his civilian disguise. It was a trophy that would be loaned out to be worn at weddings in the region for years afterward.

Only after they brought their prisoner to join the other captives did Sylvester and his men discover who they had captured. The Mexican prisoners, officers and men alike, when they saw the new arrival, stood up and shouted, *"El presidente, El presidente!"* His cover blown, the prisoner asked to be taken to General Houston.

Houston still lay on his blanket under the oak tree, two days after the battle. His wound had been dressed but he was still in great pain. Colonel Almonte was brought to him as an interpreter. Santa Anna was too agitated to speak, and begged to be given some opium. When he had taken the drug he calmed down. According to some, the Mexican general greeted Houston with a Masonic handshake. Santa Anna asked Houston to be generous in victory and explained that he had only been following orders at the Alamo. And he denied he had ordered the killings at Goliad: that had been General Urrea's decision. The dictator said that if Houston would spare his life, he would order all the Mexican army to withdraw south of the Rio Grande.

A Mexican army larger than Houston's was only a day's march away from San Jacinto when Santa Anna was defeated and captured. Instead of coming to the generalissimo's relief, General Filisola turned his army to the south and marched toward the Rio Grande. As T. R. Fehrenbach tells us, "A unified nation under a powerful leadership could have avenged San Jacinto within months." No such unity or leadership existed.

Almost all the soldiers in Houston's army wanted to execute Santa Anna for the atrocities at the Alamo, Goliad, and Refugio, but Houston had the dictator protected. Some have suggested it was the Masonic connection that saved Santa Anna's life. But Houston knew Santa Anna was worth more alive than dead. Houston hoped to negotiate with Santa Anna for Mexican recognition of the independence of Texas. But even more important was a show of statesmanship and dignity to the world, now that the battle was over. At the moment of his greatest victory, Houston also demonstrated his new maturity and political wisdom.

As Houston lay in the grass weak from his wound and loss of blood, he munched on an ear of raw corn. To the men gathered around him he gave kernels of the corn, calling it "San Jacinto corn." They were directed to take the seeds and plant crops that would feed the new Republic of Texas. Texas farmers in the future would brag that their fields were ripening with San Jacinto corn.

When a Lieutenant Hitchcock brought news of the victory at San Jacinto to President Andrew Jackson a week later, Old Hickory was ecstatic. "I never saw a man more delighted," Hitchcock later wrote. "He read the dispatch . . . exclaiming over and over as though talking to himself, 'Yes, that is his writing. I know it well. That is Sam Houston's writing' . . . The old man ordered a map . . . and tried to locate San Jacinto."

By protecting Santa Anna and returning him to his own country, Houston would show the world that the new Republic of Texas was a civilized, law-abiding nation, ruled by discretion, reason, and diplomacy. General Antonio López de Santa Anna slept in his own tent that night, with his opium pipe beside him, on his fine camp bed. Houston and the Texas government would protect him and eventually send him to Washington to confer with President Andrew Jackson before he was returned to Mexico on an American ship.

While he was in the United States, Santa Anna was interviewed by

Joel Roberts Poinsett, the former ambassador to Mexico. The dictator told the diplomat "that he thought a hundred years would go by before his people would be fit for liberty. He felt that all they could understand was despotism but there was no reason that despotism could not embody wisdom and virtue."

Some soldiers who fought with Houston were rewarded only with a sack of corn and a jug of whiskey for their services. But many were given tracts of land in the new republic. A square mile, or 640 acres, was the standard bounty for privates. Erastus "Deaf" Smith, the renowned scout who had been the eyes if not the ears of his general, was awarded any property he chose, other than a fort, church, or government building, in San Antonio. His portrait was painted and hung in the Texas Hall of Fame.

Within a few months Houston would be elected president of the Republic of Texas, and the United States, undecided about annexing Texas as a state, partly because of the issue of slavery, would recognize the Lone Star Republic as an independent nation. When Texas was annexed by the United States in 1845 and Houston elected governor, he became the only man in American history to be governor of two states as well as president of another country. After his divorce from Eliza and the death of Tiana Rogers, Houston would marry a southern beauty from Alabama, Margaret Lea, and give up drinking. He would build a house for his lovely bride in Huntsville, Texas, that resembled a steamboat, steamboats being associated with romance in his experience. He would help raise a son and four daughters, and serve as a U.S. senator from the new state of Texas. And loyal to Jackson's beloved Union to the end, he would be expelled from the governorship when he adamantly opposed secession in 1861. Whatever office he held, he never seemed to tire of celebrations, dances, and colorful costumes that reminded him of his heroes in history, among the Indians, and in *The Iliad*.

— *Six* —

JAMES K. POLK
YOUNG HICKORY KEEPS A DIARY

April 16, 1847. Mr. Trist set out on his mission to the
Head Quarters of the army this morning with full powers to
Treat with the authorities of Mexico for peace.
—from the diary of James K. Polk

*B*ECAUSE OF HIS close connections to Andrew Jackson, who lobbied long and hard to make his protégé, James K. Polk, president, many
called the politician from Columbia, Tennessee, Young Hickory. Along
with Sam Houston, Polk was one of Old Hickory's favorite keepers of the
Democratic Party flame. The old warrior at the Hermitage had entrusted
both his leading followers with the sacred duty of assuring the annexation of Texas and expansion of the republic to the west. While Jackson
and Houston shared many characteristics of manner as distinguished
soldiers, backwoods militia leaders, hard drinking camaraderie, along
with graciousness and charm with women, and a love of fine clothes,
Polk was more austere.

Devout all his life, Polk dressed and behaved much as an ordained minister might. Married to a great beauty named Sarah Childress, he never
had children. It is thought by many biographers that he may have been
sterile as a result of a crude operation for kidney stones in his youth. Polk
was solemn and serious, sober and industrious, and apparently without
a sense of humor. For all of that, he was a master politician, sometimes
described as the most successful president in American history. Assuming
office in 1845, he began to keep a diary on Tuesday, August 26, 1845, as negotiations over the boundary of Oregon got under way with Great Britain.
Recording almost every night the events of the day, he sometimes aired his
anger and frustrations; at other times he merely made note of facts. The

diary is never confessional or apologetic. Polk was always certain he was right, and the diary served as a forum for drafting later letters and speeches and searing accusations of his rivals and enemies. In the words of the historian Robert W. Merry, Polk was "small of stature and drab of temperament . . . He didn't much like people. What he liked was politics." Merry refers to Polk as "in many ways a smaller-than-life figure, but he harbored larger-than-life ambitions." The politician Gideon Welles would sum up Polk this way: "He possessed a trait of sly cunning which he thought shrewdness, but which was really disingenuousness and duplicity."

When Polk ran for the office of president in 1844, he promised that if elected he would not run for a second term and that he would accomplish four main goals: (1) ending the excessive tariff that hurt farmers and small businesses, (2) establishing a stable national financial system, (3) resolving the question of the boundary of Oregon, and (4) acquiring California with its important harbors. By the time he left office in 1849, he would have accomplished all he had promised. His extraordinary labors and anxieties probably shortened his life, for he died within a few months of leaving office. Polk was the last major president to share Jefferson's ideal of a largely agrarian republic with limited federal interference in the affairs of the states. According to Walter LaFeber, Polk would be rated by most historians "as one of the half-dozen 'great' presidents."

JAMES KNOX POLK was born in a log cabin near Pineville, North Carolina, November 2, 1795. His ancestor Robert Polk, a soldier who had married the daughter of an Irish nobleman, brought his family to Maryland in search of cheaper land and opportunity. The next generation settled in the Cumberland Valley of Pennsylvania, then moved again in the 1750s to the North Carolina frontier at Sugar Creek, near Charlotte. In many ways the Polks were typical Scots Irish settlers, except they were more prosperous than most. The future president's mother, Jane Knox Polk, was descended from a brother of the Scottish Reformation leader John Knox. The young Polk seemed to have inherited much of the zeal, dedication, toughness, and brilliance of the churchman. Like many families in the hill country of North Carolina at that time, the Polks following James's grandfather Ezekiel and father, Samuel, across the mountains to the valleys of middle Tennessee in 1806, settled in the new town of Columbia on the Duck River, a tributary of the Tennessee, where Samuel Polk had acquired preemptive rights to thousands of acres of choice land.

While the Polks had long been staunch Presbyterians, both James's father and grandfather had quietly become Deists, skeptical of the Calvinistic doctrines of the Presbyterians. Their behavior was something of an embarrassment to his mother, and to young James, who all his life would be a devoted attender of church services. On the occasion when the infant James was to be baptized, his father quarreled with the Presbyterian minister and stormed out of the church with his family, leaving his son without benefit of the sacrament. James K. Polk would not be baptized until just before his death fifty-four years later, and then at the hands of a Methodist minister.

Samuel Polk thrived in Columbia, becoming a judge, community leader, and in time a wealthy man, speculating in land. Young James suffered from delicate health and had chronic pain from urinary stones. In 1812 he was placed in a covered wagon for an eight-hundred-mile journey to Philadelphia for surgery. By the time they reached Kentucky, the seventeen-year-old was seized by such cruel pain that surgery was performed in Danville by Dr. Ephraim McDowell. With only brandy as an anesthetic, the country doctor "made an incision behind the young man's scrotum and forced a sharp, pointed instrument called a gorget through his prostate and into the bladder. The urinary stone, or stones, were then removed with forceps." However gruesome the operation, James recovered quickly and went on with his education.

Almost certainly the greatest influence on young Polk was his mother, Jane Knox Polk. A strong-willed, deeply religious woman, she instilled in her son a piety and discipline that stayed with him all his life. She encouraged in him an austere, stoic outlook, ignoring infirmities, overriding obstacles. As the biographer Sam W. Haynes says, "As James matured he turned inward, giving no hint of the frustration which his inability to participate in strenuous outdoor activities with other boys his age must have caused him. Serious and self-contained, he learned at an early age to be the master of his emotions."

While not an athletic or combative youth, as Jackson and Houston were, James was an exceptional scholar, outshining other students, first at an academy in Murfreesboro, Tennessee, then at the University of North Carolina at Chapel Hill, which he entered as a second-semester sophomore in January of 1816. An outstanding debater, Polk was elected president of the prestigious Dialectic Society and graduated first in his class in May 1818. Perhaps suffering from overwork at the university, Polk was so frail he was not able to make the long journey back over the mountains to Tennessee until October of that year. When he returned to Chapel Hill in June of 1847, it would be as president of the United States.

Polk returned to a Tennessee that was enjoying rapid growth and prosperity. His father and brother-in-law were founding a bank, building a Masonic temple, and starting a steamboat company on the nearby river. Polk headed to Nashville to study law, probably with an eye toward entering politics. The renowned lawyer and politician Felix Grundy became Polk's first mentor. When Grundy was elected to the state legislature, Polk agreed to apply for the position of clerk of the state senate in Murfreesboro. With Grundy's help, Polk won the post and performed his duties with the thoroughness and accuracy that distinguished his whole career. He was paid a handsome six dollars a day. When the legislature was not in session, Polk completed his legal studies and was admitted to the bar in June 1820. He had also acquired a full knowledge of parliamentary procedure and legislative customs.

Following the Panic of 1819, voters were more demanding than ever for a voice in the affairs of the nation. So far the nation had been run by the old guard on the East Coast. As the economy began to recover and growth accelerated, especially in the West, a new determination and aspiration began to take hold of the population. Leaders who represented the people, not the elite, began to be heard. As Sam W. Haynes tells us, "A new era of increased participatory democracy had arrived." In Andrew Jackson and Felix Grundy, Tennessee was blessed with just such leaders.

As a lawyer Polk became known as a stickler for strict detail and precise procedure. His love of precision in legal language made him the butt of jokes by the likes of David Crockett for using terms like *radical change* and *judiciary*. Nevertheless, Polk thrived at the law, and he became a friend and protégé of Andrew Jackson and a favorite of Rachel Jackson. And he began to court the beauty Sarah Childress, whose family was close to the Jacksons.

Sarah Childress came from an affluent background and was educated in private academies in Tennessee and at the Moravian Female Academy in Salem, North Carolina. It is thought she was introduced to James K. Polk while he served as clerk of the state senate in Murfreesboro. Polk was almost twenty-four and Sarah was sixteen. She "had large brown eyes, long dark hair, and a rich olive complexion. By all accounts, she was vivacious and outgoing, and her formal education was far above the norm for women of her generation." Besides beauty, Sarah had keen intelligence and quick wit, and her charm was such that she could speak her mind without seeming forward or ill mannered. She would serve as her husband's most important political adviser. In 1822, as he began the practice of law and the courtship of Sarah Childress, Polk decided to run for the state legislature. He won both a seat in the House of Representatives and the hand of Sarah. They wed on New Year's Day 1824, when he was twenty-eight and she twenty.

When Andrew Jackson won and then lost the presidential election of 1824 to John Quincy Adams, thanks possibly to the machinations of Henry Clay, Polk was among the many Jacksonians who dedicated themselves to guaranteeing that their hero would make it to the executive mansion in the next election. To aid in this enterprise, as well as to further his own political ambitions, Polk chose to run for the U.S. Congress in 1825. The relatively frail Polk spent six months on horseback, riding from one end of his district to the other, making speeches and asking for the votes of farmers, blacksmiths, storekeepers, hunters, preachers, and deacons. He even memorized jokes and humorous anecdotes to enliven his speeches. When the votes were counted in August of 1825, he had won.

To understand much of Polk's actions during his political career, it is important to remember he was committed to Jefferson's ideal of an agrarian America, ever expanding westward, offering new opportunity, growth, prosperity through new lands. As Sam W. Haynes tells us, he "viewed the young republic as a new arcadia, free from the vice and corruption of Europe. The pastoral world he sought to preserve required no special legislative action in order to flourish, its self-reliant citizens asking little of their government but a simple guarantee of liberty." But it should be remembered that Polk also, like Jefferson, was deeply committed to a national commercial prosperity, hopefully on a continental or even hemispheric scale. Polk and other Jacksonian Democrats of the era tended to brush aside the issue of slavery. In the words of Robert W. Merry, they "considered slavery a side issue . . . that just got in the way of the important political objectives."

Always an eloquent speaker, Polk became known as the "Napoleon of the stump." He used his seat in Congress as a forum in which to defend Andrew Jackson against the slander from the Adams-Clay faction, who referred to Old Hickory as "a military chieftain." It was a tempestuous era in Washington, with accusations and insults flying through the air from both sides and a duel between Secretary of State Clay and Senator John Randolph of Virginia. The capital city was still under construction at that time, and it was sometimes described, perhaps derisively, as the "city of magnificent distances," as the boulevards and avenues were laid out with the completed buildings few and far between. For the first session in 1826 Sarah Polk stayed home in Columbia, but in the fall she accompanied her husband to the nation's capital where she helped with Polk's correspondence and began to charm the society of the district. Few American politicians have been as lucky in their spouses as James K. Polk.

Polk would never be a man of the people, but he worked tirelessly to communicate with fellow legislators and with the public. John Quincy Adams would say Polk "has no wit . . . no gracefulness of delivery, no elegance of language," but through infinite hard work Polk overcame his limitations and won elections. "In the end, he had manufactured a believable public persona for himself, a creation of his own indomitable will."

In 1827 Polk was reelected to Congress and worked hard to ensure that Old Hickory would be elected the next year to the presidency by a landslide. The two men kept up a lengthy correspondence. When Jackson won and took office in 1829 he had to confront two pressing economic issues: the Bank of the United States, which Jackson felt bullied and exploited southern and western interests, and the high tariff that proved damaging to southern agricultural interests. Jackson distrusted paper money and believed it was a means of cheating ordinary people. Only gold and silver could be trusted. These issues would concern Polk also until the end of his political career.

It was while he was campaigning in support of Jackson that Polk had the most profound religious experience of his life. Since hundreds of potential voters gathered at revivals held as camp meetings, Polk and other politicians found those services excellent venues for political appearances. At a camp meeting outside Columbia, he heard the Reverend John B. McFerrin, a Methodist circuit rider, address a large gathering. The sermon had a deep effect on Polk, who was used to dry, reasoned Presbyterian preaching. It was not just the eloquence and fervor of McFerrin's words that stirred him but the democratic inclusiveness of the message as well. The Methodist preached a hopeful gospel intended for all who would listen, appealing not just to an elect or an elite but to all of humanity. Polk was stirred in ways that probably surprised him. He would continue attending Presbyterian services with Sarah, but when she was not around he would choose a Methodist place of worship. Methodism inspired him with a vision of warmth, openness, and hope, different from the more visible aspects of his personality. And the controversy over slavery was looming larger and larger. Both Jackson and Polk were slave owners known as benign masters. The issue of spreading slavery into the new territories of the Southwest became more and more the overriding issue, influencing almost every other subject before Congress and the administration.

In the Adams-Onís Treaty of 1819, Spain ceded Florida to the United States. In exchange for Florida, Spain sought a guarantee that U.S. claims for the Louisiana Territory would not extend beyond the Mississippi watershed or beyond the Sabine and Red rivers into Texas. In return, Spain agreed to recognize U.S. rights in the Northwest above the forty-second parallel. As a congressman Polk "carried the water for Old Hickory" on important issues before the House, including the Indian Removal Act of 1830, which authorized the administration to buy southeastern tribal lands and move the resident natives to territories west of the Mississippi. Polk also supported Jackson in the nullification crisis of 1832. With backing from the White House, Polk was elected Speaker of the House on December 7, 1835.

At this time of heated debates and bitter controversies over Jackson's policies, Polk conducted himself in Congress with notable aplomb. While opponents shouted and denounced and insulted Polk personally, he seemed to keep himself above the fray. One congressman from New Hampshire would say of Polk that he "sustained himself as well as any man could have done, through the last long, laborious, fatiguing and stormy session. And notwithstanding the furious attacks upon him . . . embarrassing him with question after question of order, his equanimity was never disturbed."

In 1839 Polk was elected governor of Tennessee and already had his sights on higher national office. But Young Hickory suffered a humiliating defeat in his bid for reelection as governor in 1841. Hoping to be chosen as vice presidential candidate when Van Buren ran for the presidency in 1844, Polk played a delicate game of promoting himself without seeming to be ambitious. In his private life, he and Sarah were disappointed year after year by their failure to produce offspring. Frustrated, Polk drove himself harder and harder to make his mark on the national political stage. But he was no match for the folksy, charismatic James "Lean Jimmy" Jones. In what became known as the "Log Cabin and Hard Cider" campaign of 1841, the Whigs won the gubernatorial race in Tennessee.

Hoping to keep his name before the public eye, Polk ran for governor of Tennessee again in 1843 and was once more defeated. Many assumed his political career was over. Only Polk himself, and Old Hickory in retirement at the Hermitage, seemed to believe he had a future in elected office. By 1844 the most controversial issue facing candidates for national office, besides the national bank, was the annexation of Texas. Many if not most northerners opposed annexation because, lying south of the 36°30' latitude of the Missouri Compromise of 1820, Texas would be admitted as a slave state and increase the power of the slaveholding South in national government. Even some who very much wanted Texas added to the Union feared that annexation would provoke a war with Mexico, especially if the boundary of Texas was claimed to be the Rio Grande instead of the Nueces River.

Complicating the controversy over Texas was the unresolved question of the boundary, indeed the claim itself, of Oregon. Since war with Great Britain over Oregon was not out of the question, a war with Mexico, where Britain or some other foreign power might take the side of Mexico, was to be avoided if at all possible. Sam Houston, president of the Republic of Texas, let it be known that he was considering talks with Britain about a possible alliance of the Lone Star Republic with John Bull. English mills needed the cotton being grown on Texas plantations. As the historian Joel Silbey tells us, "The British Empire had never made a secret of its intention to contain the United States and prevent it from expanding its influence beyond its present territorial limits."

As it turned out, President Tyler put before Congress a bill to annex Texas April 27, 1844. John C. Calhoun came close to sabotaging passage when he wrote a letter not merely defending slavery but praising it. Richard Hofstadter would later sum up Calhoun's brilliant but frustrated career: "The essence of Calhoun's mistake as a practical statesman was that he tried to achieve a static solution for a dynamic situation." And Martin Van Buren effectively put himself out of contention for the presidency by declaring his opposition to annexation. Old Hickory and most of the country would never support someone who opposed westward expansion. "You might as well . . . attempt to turn the current of the Mississippi as to turn the democracy from the annexation of Texas," Jackson is reported to have said. The hunger to extend into the West ran deeply and subtly through most aspects of American life. Tyler's bill was defeated, but before he left office he brought it up again. On December 29, 1845, by a vote of 27 to 25, Texas would be added to the Union.

Old Hickory summoned Polk to the Hermitage and told him he was to be the next Democratic candidate for president. "Texas must be ours!" Old Hickory exclaimed. And the country had a sacred duty for "extending our laws over Oregon." Jackson must have sensed that he was about to see the fulfillment of his long held dream, and the dream of Jefferson as well.

At the Democratic Convention in Baltimore in May of 1844 Van Buren won a plurality of 146 votes on the first ballot but not the two-thirds required for the nomination. He would have needed 177 to win. On subsequent ballots support for Van Buren declined. After five ballots with no winner, the convention descended into chaos.

It was Polk's friend Gideon Pillow, and the famed historian George Bancroft from Massachusetts, who began to turn things around. Bancroft admired Polk and suddenly saw Polk as the only solution to the deadlock. Among the seeming chaos on May 29, the tide began to turn in favor of Polk, and when Benjamin Butler of New York changed his support from Van Buren to Polk, the convention unanimously nominated James K. Polk of Tennessee as its candidate.

On May 24 a telegraph wire had been successfully tested between Baltimore and Washington, D.C. When news of Polk's nomination was flashed over the thirty-six-mile distance, Democrats in the capital roared their approval. Polk was seen as the savior of the Democrats at this troubled time. Polk's nomination seemed something of a miracle, both to those who supported him, and to those who opposed him. The Whig slogan became "Who is James K. Polk?" Only those who understood the influence Old Hickory still carried in his declining months at the Hermitage were not surprised.

If the nomination of Polk seemed to many little more than an accident, it was an accident Polk had spent his life preparing for. He was ready for the struggle he'd sought for so many years. But Polk's opponents kept repeating the phrase, "Who is James K. Polk?" The question was asked in many newspaper articles and speeches. He had always done his work with method and efficiency, and he lived his political life in the shadow of the nation's great hero, Andrew Jackson. Throughout his career the abstemious Polk had associated with hard-drinking, larger-than-life individuals such as Jackson, Houston, and Cave Johnson. But when Polk won the election for president in 1844 by a very slim margin (49.5 percent to Clay's 48.1 percent), he quickly let it be known that *he* would be president, not a mouthpiece or lieutenant for anyone else. "I intend to be *myself* President of the United States," Polk wrote to his friend Cave Johnson on December 21, 1844. He was ready to move into "the house that Jackson built," but once there he meant to be sole lord and master.

Polk and the Democrats won the election of 1844 because they favored annexation of Texas, westward expansion, limited federal government, and confidence in the people to choose their own destiny. They also supported increased immigration, welcoming those from Ireland and other countries into the rapidly growing republic, and many historians believe it was the new immigrant vote that tipped the close election to Polk. John Quincy Adams and other Whigs saw Polk's election as the death knell for civilization in North America. They believed Young Hickory was nothing more than a puppet for that "ruffian" Old Hickory. With the annexation of Texas and maybe other territories in the Southwest, the power of the slaveholding South would be unchecked. Polk's election and the annexation of Texas aggravated the bitter polarization within the Democratic Party and the country that would lead to the Civil War.

Echoing Luke 2:29, Old Hickory wrote to Andrew Jackson Donelson when he heard Polk had been elected, "The glorious result of the presidential election has rejoiced every democratic bosom in the United States . . . And as to myself I can say in the language of Simeon of old 'Let thy servant depart in peace' as I have seen the solution of the liberty of my country and the perpetuity of our glorious Union."

Sadly, Jackson's populism (and Polk's) was a vision of liberty that did not extend to African Americans. While defending and extending the rights of common people, it apparently did not occur to them that the common man included all races and ethnic groups, not to mention women of the common people. But added to that irony is the fact that abolitionists, suffragists, and civil rights leaders would later build on the democratic work of Jackson and Polk to extend those rights to citizens of different races and gender.

However the future might view Polk's policies, he was confident of both the practicality and rightness of his vision. "Foreign governments do not seem to appreciate the true character of our Government," he wrote in his inaugural address. The goal of the United States was "to enlarge its limits . . . to extend the dominion of peace over additional territories and increasing millions." He went on to say that "Our title to the country of Oregon is 'clear and unquestionable,' and already are our people preparing to perfect that title by occupying it with their wives and children."

In his allusion to settlers and immigrants in the territories of Texas and Oregon and other lands of the West, Polk touched on the greatest truth in his address and implicit in his policy. The real reason Texas could be, would be, and was annexed was that so many Americans had already gone there, and more were on the way. With their *tejano* neighbors, the Americans in Texas had already defeated Santa Anna's Mexican army at San Jacinto in 1836. And with seven thousand American settlers already in the Northwest, the British Hudson's Bay Company was pulling out of the territory, after stripping it of beaver and other fur-bearing animals. There were about ten times as many American settlers as British in the area. In a very important sense, government actions and government policies only *followed* and made official what the vast movements of the rapidly growing population to the west had already made a fact. It was not the American government that had claimed and settled the Willamette Valley. It was the thousands of settlers who had already made the trek across the continent and claimed land there and opened stores, built churches, started schools. Thousands of Americans had settled in California also. It was a continuation of the story that had started in Kentucky in 1775, in Tennessee in 1772. Government treaties were often official recognition of vast changes made by the people themselves, one individual, one family, one small group at a time. Government could only acknowledge the facts and acts, the sacrifices and recklessness, the ruthlessness, of thousands of ordinary people creating history on the ground. In the words of Walter LaFeber, "Expand or die became the shadowy underside of American thinking."

At the beginning the settling of Oregon and Texas was not so much a government policy as a common enterprise of thousands of private citizens. A population speaks with its feet and hands and willpower, in numbers that cannot be stopped.

———

THE PEOPLE OF the United States have traditionally known little about their sister republic to the south. This lack of interest and lack of knowledge about Mexico has contributed to almost two centuries of misunderstandings, confrontations, resentments. Though sharing a border of more than a thousand miles, the two countries have been divided by deep differences of language, religion, culture, and history. In the early nineteenth century Mexicans were just as ignorant about the United States. In the words of the historian Gene M. Brack, most Mexicans knew "only that they had neighbors to the north who had risen against a legitimate sovereign, and that these neighbors were mostly heretics." Better informed liberals in Mexico resented the United States for remaining neutral in the struggle of Mexico to throw off the colonial yoke of Spain that led to independence in 1821. Brack suggests that envy of American prosperity bred malice in many Mexicans also. Ramón Alcaraz and the committee of Mexican historians who would write *The Other Side* in 1848 asserted, "[The United States] desired from the beginning to extend their dominion in such manner as to become the absolute owners of almost all this continent."

When the Spanish created New Spain (Mexico) after Cortés's conquest of the Aztecs and Tenochtitlán in 1519–21, they established a feudal system where almost all the real power was in the hands of the *peninsulares,* also called *gachupines,* officials born in Spain, and with the clergy of the Roman Catholic Church. After the revolution of 1821, three centuries later, the *gachupines* were expelled and replaced by the *criollos,* men of pure Spanish blood who were born in New Spain. Amid civil unrest, where one regime after another was toppled by coups, they attempted to rule a nation where most of the population was mestizo (mixed blood), Indian, mulatto, or black.

The Mexican distrust of the North Americans seems to have been there from the beginning. As Alan Taylor tells us, "In late 1788 the viceroy of New Spain warned his superiors in Madrid: 'We should not be surprised if the English colonies of America, republican and independent, put into practice the design of discovering a safe port on the South Sea, and try to sustain it by crossing the immense land of this continent above our possessions of Texas, New Mexico, and the Californias . . . I truly believe that as of now we ought to try to elude its effects, all the more when we see that we are now threatened by the probes of Russia, and those that can be made by the English." As early as 1768 the Spanish had sent a military expedition up the Pacific coast "to occupy the best harbors with a system of forts, known as presidios, supported by missions run by Franciscan priests."

A significant episode of Mexican-American history that few in the United States know anything about involves the story of Joel R. Poinsett (1779–1851), the first American ambassador to Mexico. A member of a Huguenot family in the low country of South Carolina, Poinsett was educated in both England and the United States. His father was a renowned and prosperous medical doctor who owned several houses and plantations around Charleston. All his life Joel Roberts Poinsett suffered from delicate health, which may have prevented him from pursuing the military career he aspired to. As a youth, he was educated by Timothy Dwight in Connecticut; studied medicine at Edinburgh; military science at Woolwich, England; and read law with H. W. DeSaussure in Charleston but completed none of these courses of study. His real education came through the study of languages and history and from travel in Europe, Russia, Asia, and the Near East. He also toured extensively in the northeastern United States and preferred his own country to any other. While in Russia he made such an impression on Tsar Alexander I and the court that "John Quincy Adams, who was never profuse with compliments, reported in 1809 that both the Empress and the Empress Dowager had inquired about the American traveler and expressed high esteem for him." Described as "one of the most versatile and cosmopolitan Americans of his time," Poinsett was fluent in both French and Spanish. Interested in the fine arts, the sciences, botany, and history, Poinsett was sent by the Madison administration on a special commission to South America in 1810. In Argentina he encouraged independence, and in Chile he helped create a constitution for the newly formed government. In Santiago he established close ties to the liberal insurgents and even took part in some military actions. His involvement in the affairs in Chile would be remembered favorably by many Latin Americans but not by conservatives in Mexico. As a diplomat, Poinsett was considered in Washington a notable success, and he served as a representative from South Carolina in Congress from 1821 to 1825.

Though Poinsett was born into the South Carolina aristocracy, his sympathies were always with the people, the Union, and republican ideals. As a member of the South Carolina legislature he proposed limiting the number of African slaves in the state, hoping white immigrants would in time replace slave labor and that slavery would wither away naturally. He enthusiastically supported "internal improvements," cutting canals, dredging rivers, building turnpikes. The Buncombe Turnpike across South Carolina into the mountains of North Carolina and on to Tennessee was one result of his policies. The famed Poinsett Bridge across the North Fork of the Saluda River in Greenville County, a handsome work of masonry, still stands. The turnpike "was designed not only to serve local traffic but to draw products of eastern Tennessee and western North Carolina to Charleston . . . [Poinsett] gave special attention to the upper end [of the turnpike], which, when completed, was said to be one of the best mountain roads in the United States."

Sent by the Monroe administration as a special envoy to the newly independent Mexico in 1822, Poinsett witnessed the failure of Emperor Iturbide's reign. But the diplomat felt great affection for the Mexican people and their country. Writing a diary as a series of letters to a friend, he published *Notes on Mexico* in 1824, a book that was well received. The *North American Review* described the volume as "the best account which can be found of the present state of Mexico, both in regard to the character of the people and their prospects as an independent nation."

From Mexico he brought a plant with leaves that turned bright red at Christmastime, called by the Mexicans *flor de nochebuena;* it came to be called poinsettia by Americans. He was an obvious choice when John Quincy Adams picked a minister to send to Mexico in 1825. But Poinsett's reputation for his actions in Chile preceded him to Mexico. As a result the conservatives and monarchists distrusted him, and the British ambassador, Henry George Ward, used that distrust to undercut Poinsett's efforts. To counter the powerful British influence exercised through the Scottish-rite Masonic lodges, Poinsett encouraged the formation of rival York-rite lodges which attracted moderates and liberals. In a few months more than eighty York-rite lodges were organized.

Though he knew the proposal would not succeed, Poinsett later followed President Jackson's instructions and offered the Mexicans five million dollars for the territory of Texas. This gesture further discredited him in the eyes of Mexican politicians. Before Poinsett was recalled from Mexico, his life was threatened by insurgents, and he bravely protected liberal friends by sheltering them in his house. "He appeared before the insurgents, holding aloft the American flag, and by his personal bravery prevented their entrance into the courtyard," his biographer, J. Fred Rippy, would write.

Poinsett knew Mexico better than most Americans, but even he may not have understood how defensive Mexicans felt about the United States territorial greed. Brack writes, "Mexicans associated Americans with their tenacious defense of chattel slavery," and they feared Americans viewed their neighbors to the south as similar to Indians, Africans and mulattoes. Given the history of the treatment of Indians and blacks in the United States, "Mexicans were perceptive enough to recognize that a similar fate threatened them should they fall under American domination." It has also been pointed out that a newly independent country is especially fearful of losing the territory it has only recently won through costly revolution. In the words of Ramón Alcaraz and his fellow historians, Poinsett "left among us an unfortunate celebrity." At least one historian has observed that Poinsett failed in Mexico because he was more a "missionary" to spread democracy than a diplomat.

When Poinsett returned to the United States, he found himself involved in the bitter dispute over nullification. He was Jackson's most effective supporter in South Carolina, even raising a militia to defend the Union cause should that be necessary. His experience in Mexico had made him more devoted to the Union than ever, and he opposed secessionist rhetoric, then and later. According to J. Fred Rippy, Poinsett's "Mexican enemies referred to his 'highly polished and agreeable manners; his acquirements and the liveliness of his mind'; and 'the republicanism' which he uniformly displayed. In fact it was his talents that they feared."

In the view of José Fuentes Mares and other Mexican historians, Poinsett, a notorious and controversial figure in Mexican history to this day, set Mexico on the road to ruin and conquest. In his book *Poinsett: The Story of a Great Intrigue,* Mares quotes the historian Luis G. Cuevas: "[Poinsett] conceived the project, which was favored by contemptible types of Mexicans, of taking control of the popular [Masonic] lodges and organizing them so as to promote civil conflict."

The Mexican constitution adopted in 1824 had been virtually a translation of the U.S. Constitution, whose ideas "caused a festering because they were essentially alien to the Mexican reality." The American concept of federalism did not work well south of the border. One of the ideas for which Poinsett is especially blamed was the concept of "the two sovereignties." Nations such as the United States and Britain and France, in his view, had "absolute sovereignty" while developing countries such as Mexico had "relative sovereignty." According to Mares, Poinsett "proposed to establish on the part of the United States a virtual protectorate" over Mexico. Gene M. Brack points out that, "A new nation perhaps resents no insult so deeply as a slight to its sovereignty."

It made perfect sense to John Quincy Adams and Andrew Jackson and most Americans that Mexico, which showed so little interest in Texas, would be willing to sell the territory to the United States. It was considered mostly desert land, but some Americans were moving into eastern Texas and making the desert bloom. Americans "could make better use of their lands." Poinsett offered to buy Texas to get it off the hands of Mexico City. After all, Thomas Jefferson had claimed that Texas was actually a part of the Louisiana Purchase. Adams had conceded Texas to Spain in the Adams-Onís Treaty of 1819, but that agreement had been made with Spain, not Mexico. As Gene M. Brack explains, "Mexican independence had cancelled the treaty." And Adams, when he was president, had decided he had made a mistake about Texas. He was the kind of man who liked to admit and correct his mistakes.

For two decades John Quincy Adams, Poinsett, Andrew Jackson, James K. Polk, and many other Americans were baffled by the refusal of Mexico to give up any of the lands they were so ill prepared to populate, defend, or develop. To expansionist Americans, the Mexican refusal seemed arbitrary, if not downright perverse. Americans did not realize that their greed for the land inspired their southern neighbors to be all the more determined not to sell. As Brack says, "Yankeephobia was rampant in Mexico by the 1840s," and "Mexicans were as scornful of American Protestantism as Americans were of Mexican Catholicism." The Mexican leader Carlos María de Bustamante stated flatly that the United States was fated to be the "perpetual rival and enemy of Mexico." Belligerence toward the United States was necessary for any politician who hoped to win office.

The Mexican historian Carlos Bosch García has written extensively about how the United States perfected the technique of expansion: "provoke a situation of fact, and from there begin discussions which could provide a variety of solutions." In military terms the provocation could be sending Zachary Taylor and the U.S. Army to the disputed area between the Nueces River and the Rio Grande to invite an attack, but more often it was the sending of settlers into a region, so there was an American presence before and then a response before discussions even began. But García ignores the fact that American settlers often moved onto land independently, with little concern for United States policy. As the historian

Josefina Zoraida Vázquez puts it, "The North Americans kept up this continuous expansion, and the United States government followed their footsteps." García sees Americans' pragmatism and materialism as the sources of their villainy and power and their shallowness: "From this sense of the practical and of the economic came the very coloration of their being."

Other Mexican historians are equally critical of their own nation, and blame Mexican troubles on the internal dissension, the legacy of Spain and the Roman Catholic Church, and the corruption of the *criollo* leaders such as Santa Anna. A major weakness of Mexico was that military commanders such as "Santa Anna demanded of [the] army chiefs that they be first of all followers of . . . Santa Anna, although they might at the same time have been cowardly and inept." Most foot soldiers were Indians drafted by force into service. "Mexican recruitment consisted chiefly of capturing Indians, no more than one in ten of whom had ever *seen* a gun . . ." With untrained Indian soldiers and officers promoted more for political alliance than competence, the Mexican army hardly had a chance to repel a powerful invader as one corrupt regime succeeded another. Mexican generals were often political rivals and did not come to one another's aid. Both politicians and generals liked to brag of Mexican military superiority over the United States, dangerously overstating their relative strength. After Santa Anna was defeated at San Jacinto in April of 1836, a much larger Mexican army not far away chose to withdraw south rather than fight Houston's smaller force. As the historian and leader Carlos María de Bustamante says, "The army which remained under the command of General Filisola . . . could have destroyed the force which had attacked General Santa Anna." Whether Filisola's army could have destroyed Houston's smaller force we will never know, since Filisola promptly marched his men away toward the Rio Grande.

One of the best Mexican historians, the liberal leader Mariano Otero, was critical not only of the military and the instability of the governments of Mexico but of the pride of the nation, which he saw as false pride. "The *national honor* is one of those vain phrases in a country where the productive man has had to live isolated from the rest of society, without being able to quietly enjoy the fruits of his labor because of the maladministration of justice." Otero also blamed the Mexican defeat on Indian soldiers who were forced to fight for a country toward which they felt little loyalty. Summing up his view, Otero observed, "There is no national spirit because we are not a nation."

For their part, Mexican leaders and intellectuals of the period may not have understood the extent to which the United States felt threatened, especially by Great Britain in Canada to the north, in Oregon, in California, and even in Texas and Mexico. British influence was powerful even with the Mexican government, and Mexico had borrowed millions of pounds from British banks, which the British hoped to recover. As the historian Cecil Robinson says, "There was in Polk's aggressiveness a generous mix of defensiveness."

By opposing nullification and John C. Calhoun, Poinsett made himself unpopular with many other South Carolina leaders. And because of his "affectionate regard" for the Mexican people he would express deep regret when war was declared on Mexico. He urged the American armies to show compassion and understanding for a people who had lived under a "tyrannical military despotism." Poinsett was particularly afraid the war would turn the Mexican people away from their republican aspirations, and he deplored the prolongation of the conflict and the demand for Mexican territory. He believed the Mexican people were "so entirely republican" they would eventually establish a democratic government if left alone. Poinsett was appalled by the contempt Americans seemed to feel for Mexicans. "Why we are in the habit of abusing them now as a degraded race I do not understand," he wrote in the *National Intelligencer* in February of 1848.

———

ALMOST AS soon as Polk took office in March 1845 he dispatched Archibald Yell to Texas to urge that republic to accept the terms of annexation Tyler and the Congress had offered. The new president guaranteed that the United States would not only defend but would "not be satisfied with less than the whole of the territory claimed by Texas—namely to the Rio Grande." As it turned out, the insistence on the Texas boundary at the Rio Grande instead of the Nueces River at Corpus Christi was one of the most inflammatory issues between Mexico and the United States. The Mexicans seemed to feel that their honor required them to keep the border of Tejas at the Nueces. In the later negotiations with Mexico, only the ownership of the harbor at San Diego would be as controversial. Polk certainly did not understand that no Mexican leader could win or hold office who ceded territory to the northern neighbor. As T. R. Fehrenbach tells us, "It probably did not occur to Polk or his Democrats that the very offer would be taken as an insult by many Mexicans."

Tension between the United States and Mexico had been building throughout the 1830s and 1840s. American ships had been seized in Mexican ports, and at sea. On land "U.S. businessmen operating in the fledgling republic were abducted and impressed into servitude or thrown into jails without benefit of jurisprudence . . . Ships cargoes were stolen at gunpoint in Mexican waters." American citizens and the U.S. government had been petitioning Mexico for years for reparations, without success.

Polk infuriated senators such as Thomas Hart Benton by refusing to negotiate with Mexico on the border issue. Furthermore, Polk refused to share his orders to envoys such as Yell with the Senate. Not until Richard Nixon would another president be so concerned with secrecy, claiming both executive privilege and national security. Polk's penchant for secrecy and cunning would win him the title "Polk the Mendacious," and even Democrats would accuse him of being disingenuous, as Secretary of State Buchanan would make clear. But in his own mind his covert actions were prudent and practical, undertaken to serve the public good.

There was even some question of whether the Texas legislature would accept the terms of the annexation. But as it turned out, the Texas Senate, like Polk, decided to cut through the bureaucratic and diplomatic niceties and voted unanimously for annexation. On December 29, 1845, Polk signed the resolution of admission and Texas was officially one with and of the United States.

But Old Hickory did not live to see that part of his dream become a fact. He died at the Hermitage on June 8, 1845, two days after writing to Polk to congratulate him on the unity of his cabinet. Hardly strong enough to hold a pen, Old Hickory expressed his friendship and loyalty to Young Hickory. Sam Houston and his wife, Margaret, would arrive at the Hermitage for a visit in time to sit vigil with the body. The eulogy for Old Hickory in Washington was given by the New England historian

George Bancroft. Polk, like a son who has lost a powerful father, would see that it was now up to him to carry the republic forward to the West.

———

IT WAS the historian Bancroft, Polk's secretary of the navy, who visited the new president after his inauguration and later recorded his often-to-be-quoted words. After raising his hand and slapping his thigh, the normally quiet Polk "confided to Bancroft the 'four great measures of his administration.'" In Polk's mind "the Texas question had been settled."

Polk believed that he had greater leverage to accomplish these controversial goals because he did not plan to run for a second term. If it cost him popularity to do what had to be done, then so be it. He could afford to spend political capital. He would never be a hero to the masses, like his mentor, but he would achieve for the country what he understood she needed most. Polk had no hobbies, took no vacations. He did not hunt or fish or take any interests in sports such as horse racing. He seemed to have little interest in the arts or the sciences. He did not gamble or dance or attend any social functions he was not required to. More than almost any other president in history he was entirely focused on his work as chief executive of the nation.

It is astonishing to us in the twenty-first century to understand that in Polk's time the president had no staff. Polk hired as private secretary his nephew, Joseph Knox Walker, and paid him out of his own salary. With this one assistant he had to take care of all correspondence, business, signing land patents and army commissions, copying, and filing. When Walker had to be away Polk did the clerical work himself, while receiving countless visitors, most petitioning for jobs or other favors. Meticulous as ever, Polk tried to clear his desk every day before retiring to write in his diary.

Though his nephew was a loyal worker, he often failed to live up to his uncle's standards. Seeking diversion away his duties from time to time, the young man came in for censure in the president's diary. "In truth he is too fond of spending his time in fashionable & light society, and does not give that close & systematic attention to business which is necessary. This I have observed for some months with great regret." Polk scolded his cabinet members for any laxity he noted and warned them not to be absent from their duties even when Congress was not in session. In today's terms Polk was also a fanatical micro-manager, trying to oversee every detail of his administration himself. "I prefer to supervise the whole operations of the Government myself rather than entrust the public business to subordinates." The Polks would issue a directive that there was to be no dancing at the executive mansion. However, four mornings a week, and at other hours also, Polk would make himself available to any visitor who showed up, whether a social caller or a petitioner. He would record in his diary with some pride that he was "the hardest working man in this country."

Sarah, who was in charge of all social arrangements at the White House, and proved to be one of the most popular First Ladies in American history, saw that no spiritous liquors were served at social events. "But wine was available in abundance," Robert W. Merry writes. Sarah was able to charm even her husband's political rivals and enemies.

The new president made every member of his cabinet sign an acknowledgment that they would support the policies of the Democratic Party as stated in the platform of the 1844 convention. He promised that he would stay in Washington to get the job done and not travel either for recreation or political purposes. He instructed his cabinet that they must give full time to their duties, not running for higher office while serving him. But it was unlikely the canny Polk believed his ambitious secretary of state, James Buchanan, would refrain from putting himself forward for the presidential election of 1848. During the four years of his administration the secretary of state would frustrate and infuriate Polk again and again by disagreeing with him at awkward moments, but Polk would never get up the courage to fire Buchanan. And for all his determination, we know Polk almost always avoided face-to-face confrontations.

True to his strict constructionist views, Polk warned that he did not believe the Constitution authorized the federal government to fund "internal improvements," that is, the building of canals and roads, improving harbors, and other infrastructure projects. He feared that any such program would only exacerbate regional rivalries, creating "a disreputable scramble for the public money." He vetoed a bill that would fund such projects, certain it was a moral and not a political decision. Polk's confidence in the rightness of his decisions mirrored the new confidence of the nation, which saw itself as the finest expression in history of the democratic spirit, with a mandate to spread its Christian civilization and new hope for mankind throughout the hemisphere.

In 1845 the *New York Herald* proclaimed in an editorial that "a spirit has taken wing from the land of freedom which is destined to carry civil and religious liberty to the ends of the earth." No less a voice than the Sage of Concord, Ralph Waldo Emerson, would opine, "America is the country of the Future." The historian Sam W. Haynes has observed the connection between the country's romantic view of itself and the Romantic movement in Europe and Britain and North America. "American notions of cultural uniqueness were borrowed in large part from the Romantic movement then flourishing in western Europe, which held that special, innate characteristics stamped each people with an identity of its own . . . such ideas struck a particularly responsive chord among Americans, who had long sensed they were marked for greatness." The new German school of historical studies, led by Leopold von Ranke, which would influence so many American historians throughout the nineteenth century, was premised on just such a concept of national uniqueness and identity. Many in Polk's time, including the president himself, viewed westward expansion as a measure of the country's greatness. A great nation grew to make use of available space and resources, most of which lay to the west. In New York John L. O'Sullivan would describe expansion as "the fulfilment of our manifest destiny to overspread the continent allotted by Providence for the free development of our yearly multiplying millions."

To say the least, the Oregon question was complex. The British claims to the Northwest derived from Captain James Cook's and George Vancouver's sea voyages of the eighteenth century and the extensive overland explorations of Alexander Mackenzie in the 1790s. The American Robert Gray had claimed to discover the mouth of the Columbia River in 1792 and to have sailed a hundred miles up the river to the future site of Portland. American claims to the region had been reinforced by the 1804–6 Lewis and Clark expedition to the Pacific.

But ships of many nations traded with the natives on the Northwest coast and were engaged in the fur trade. The headquarters of the fur industry were at Nootka Sound on Vancouver Island. The British competed with the Russians in Alaska, and as far south as San Francisco, for dominance in the fur business in the region. British claims were strengthened by the considerable activities of the Hudson's Bay Company that stretched all the way across Canada from Hudson's Bay to Puget Sound and Sitka, Alaska, in the north. Chartered in 1670 by Charles II, the company was originally charged with finding the Northwest Passage. Absorbing other rival fur companies, the Hudson's Bay monopoly came to include most of Canada.

In 1811 John Jacob Astor had sent the American Fur Company to the mouth of the Columbia to reap some of the bounty of the Northwest fur trade. As the region was explored, it became obvious that Oregon was a treasure, a promised land of mild climate, rich soil, abundance far beyond the fur trade. With seemingly unlimited timber, its rivers and salmon fishing, blessed with a bounty waiting to be taken, there was an opulence beyond description. Leaders on both sides of the Atlantic saw what Jefferson had seemed to understand from the beginning: the Northwest was a land to be claimed and annexed.

In 1818 John Quincy Adams had negotiated a treaty with Great Britain establishing the boundary with Canada at the forty-ninth parallel as far west as the Rocky Mountains. Beyond the western Continental Divide the two nations agreed to a vaguely defined joint occupation, at least for the time being. But in the almost thirty years since the Adams Treaty, events on the ground had changed the region dramatically. While the mountain men such as Jim Bridger and Jedediah Smith, the Hudson's Bay Company, and American Fur Company had cleaned the beaver and otter out of the streams of the Rockies and Cascades, American missionaries and settlers had begun trickling into the Northwest.

Oddly enough, James K. Polk, as a young congressman from Tennessee in 1829, had voted to oppose a bill proposed by John Floyd of Virginia, calling for construction of American forts to support American interests in the Oregon country. Obviously Polk's vision of the future of the nation had changed over the intervening sixteen years as he witnessed the progress of westward expansion and began to hope for a republic that included the great harbors on the Pacific. Or perhaps he was mostly interested, even then, in expanding into the Southwest.

American missionaries began arriving in Oregon in the 1830s. Jason Lee and Daniel Lee sought to establish a mission among the Nez Perce nation in 1834, joining the trappers and fur traders in the region. The local official of the Hudson's Bay Company, Dr. John McLoughlin, encouraged them to settle south of Fort Vancouver on the Columbia River, about forty miles up the Willamette River. The Lees found the area a place of rich soil, temperate climate, and fine timber. Soon other missionaries would join them, near future Salem, creating a community more devoted to farming than to saving the souls of Indians.

Even more missionaries, including Marcus and Narcissa Whitman and Henry and Elizabeth Spaulding, crossed the Rockies with fur traders and mountain men to establish missions in the wilderness. Once women arrived, the settling of the region by whites was inevitable, because it was the presence of women that made settlement a reality. The Oregon Trail had been found and marked, and its fame spread as more and more followed its formidable distances and negotiated its obstacles to reach the green lands of Oregon.

As Cumberland Gap had been the key to the settlement of Kentucky and the lands of the Ohio Valley in the eighteenth century, South Pass in Wyoming was the dip in the Continental Divide through which the hopeful settlers poured into the Oregon country and California. South of the Wind River Range, the divide is only seventy-five hundred feet above sea level. The grade is gentle and the slopes covered, even today, with grass and sagebrush. There is ample water on both sides of the divide. Known to the Indians for thousands of years, South Pass was found in 1812 by Robert Stuart of the Astor Company, and later by Jedediah Smith in 1824. And later still Smith would guide the missionaries and settlers through the gap's welcoming contours. Those passing there still had a thousand miles of forbidding terrain to cross, but already they were drinking from streams that moved toward the Pacific or the Gulf of California. What is called the Great Migration came in 1843.

Family after family, wagon train after wagon train, left for the West. Newspapers were filled with stories of the westward trek. Landmarks along the Oregon Trail, such as Chimney Rock above the North Platte in Nebraska and Independence Rock in central Wyoming, became household words. The preferred vehicle for the overland journey was the prairie schooner, a lighter vehicle than the Conestoga wagon, pulled by oxen, and one that could float across rivers.

The renowned Henry Clay, "Harry of the West," probably denied himself the presidency once again when he opposed the settling and annexation of California. "I think our true policy is to settle and populate our immense territory on the east of those [Rocky] mountains and within the United States, before we proceed to colonize the shores of the Pacific; or at all events postpone the occupation of Oregon some thirty or forty years," Clay pronounced, showing again his lack of rapport with the deeper passions of his time.

In 1844 twice as many people as the year before launched out along the trail to Oregon, and in 1845 another five thousand began the overland march. While at the official level it may seem that Oregon was acquired by the firm diplomacy of Polk and Buchanan, the real claiming was done by those who made the long journey on foot across the plains and Rockies, land-hungry men and women, avid for adventure, willing to risk all for the promise of a better future. The graves along the trail are the record of the price many paid for that dream.

It was James Buchanan, the new secretary of state, who presented Polk's proposal on the Oregon question to the British ambassador, Richard Pakenham, on July 12, 1845. Buchanan explained that the United States was willing to accept a compromise on the Oregon issue, with a boundary at the forty-ninth parallel all the way to Puget Sound, giving Britain access to the ports on Vancouver Island. Though essentially the same offer that had been made before, it was a compromise, as so many Democrats in the United States were demanding "54°40' or Fight."

To Polk's surprise the British ambassador rejected the proposal without even consulting his government in London. He warned Buchanan that next time he should make an offer "more consistent with fairness and equity, and with the reasonable expectations of the British government." Since the British had not made a counterproposal, the ball was in their court. Polk would wait for them to make the next move. To clarify his thoughts and make a record for posterity, Polk began to keep his diary; as far as we know he had not done so before. His meticulous record keeping, his calm in the face of seemingly insurmountable difficulties, his patience and poker-playing coolness and daring, set him apart from most presidents in American history. But also on display in the diary, more than he realized, would be his icy defensiveness, his poisoning distrust of anyone who was not a Democrat, and a predilection for secret initiatives.

"We shall do our duty towards both Mexico and Great Britain," Polk told Buchanan. If need be Polk could keep his eye on the balls in several courts at once. After all, Texas, California, and Oregon were just parts of the same overall policy. A metaphor often used at the time was that Oregon and California and western lands were like ripening fruit, ready to fall. It was paramount that the United States be there ready to catch them before they fell into foreign hands. A transcontinental nation was not merely desirable, it was inevitable. Some have pointed out that Polk was heir to the "Jeffersonian paradox," desiring to expand the country westward while cherishing an agrarian vision of a small nation not entangled in imperial alliances and foreign wars. If Polk was aware of the paradox, he did not let it give him pause. In fact, Polk had decided that expansion was a way of preserving democracy, creating an extensive nation of farmers that the monied eastern elite could not easily control.

Polk knew what he wanted, and he could wait. Conferring with his cabinet in what was traditionally vacation time, Polk waited until August 30, 1845, to send another message to Ambassador Pakenham. By then the "54°40' or Fight" cry had swept the nation; John L. O'Sullivan's phrase *Manifest Destiny* began to be repeated and celebrated also. The whole country seemed intoxicated with the dynamic expansion to the West and to the North and South. To many Americans it seemed logical that the boundary of the United States should stretch north to the borders of Russian Alaska.

In the meantime Pakenham had been reprimanded by British foreign minister Lord Aberdeen for his precipitant rejection of Buchanan's offer. Aberdeen pointed out that Polk had used the rejection to place the burden of a proposal on the British. Pakenham was forced to call on Buchanan at his home and express his regret that the proposal of the forty-ninth parallel boundary had been withdrawn by the Americans.

Polk and Buchanan played hardball with Pakenham, refusing to make the forty-ninth parallel proposal again. They left the British wondering where the U.S. government now stood while the newspapers and the population were shouting "54°40' or Fight!" While he kept the British waiting, Polk had a lengthy conference at the White House with his friend and rival Thomas Hart Benton. The two expansionists agreed on the acquisition of Oregon and much of California. It was important to prevent Great Britain or any other foreign power from getting a foothold in California. "In reasserting Mr. Monroe's doctrine, I had California & the fine bay of San Francisco as much in view as Oregon," Polk would record in his diary. A new fear of Britain's designs on the West swept through the country. In the words of Sam W. Haynes, "As much as any single factor, it was this fear of British encirclement which converted many supporters of gradual expansion into apostles of the new imperialism."

In his annual report to Congress, Polk recommended terminating the earlier agreement with Britain over the joint supervision of the Oregon Territory. Polk not only resurrected the Monroe Doctrine but expanded it with reference to the West Coast. As the president would tell Congressman James A. Black of South Carolina on Sunday, January 4, 1846, "The only way to treat John Bull was to look him straight in the eye . . . A bold and firm course on our part [is] the pacific one."

It could be argued, and it was argued, that the United States had no claim whatsoever to California. It had always been Spanish territory since it was taken from the Indians. But Jefferson had had his eye on the harbors of San Diego, Monterey, and San Francisco and had cherished a vision of a United States that touched the Pacific. In the Adams-Onís Treaty of 1819 Spain had recognized U.S. claims to the territory north of the forty-second parallel. In the words of Robert W. Merry, "For America, it was that vision of a transcontinental power facing both east and west across two oceans, unmatched in naval and commercial prowess. For Britain its was the geopolitical imperative of thwarting that vision and becoming itself the dominant North American power."

In 1811 the Russians, hoping to expand their influence southward from Alaska, had attempted to buy at least part of California from Spain. Failing that, they established a base anyway at Fort Ross, north of San Francisco. In 1841 the Russians sold that fort to John Sutter, a Swiss immigrant who also bought land from the Mexican government. By then Americans were already arriving in California. On October 18, 1842, Commodore Thomas ap Catesby Jones of the U.S. Navy had taken over

Monterey, the provincial capital, in the name of the American government, only to have to withdraw when it was pointed out that the United States was not at war with Mexico as he had heard. (Jones had seen a clipping from a Mexican newspaper that stated war between Mexico and the United States had broken out.) The British were patrolling the same area with warships, and he may have been attempting to preempt any British move to seize the initiative. The Stars and Stripes flew over California for only thirty-six hours, but to many it seemed a sign of things to come.

Everyone knew that because it was so far from the government in Mexico City, and affairs in Mexico were so unstable, the Mexicans had never been able to establish a firm control of Alta California. Their presence there was so weak the territory seemed up for grabs. In *Huckleberry Finn* Pap Finn tells Huck that it's all right to steal a hen, and Huck finds one "that warn't roosting comfortable." To Americans California was just such a prize hen, restless on the roost. It would be a shame not to rescue it, and a double shame to let someone else such as Britain snatch the prize from under the American nose. And besides, the United States had a duty to extend the felicities of democracy to these western lands. Secretary of State James Buchanan stated that Americans had "a great and glorious mission to perform . . . extending the blessings of Christianity and of civil and religious liberty over the whole of the North American continent." However the mission was defined and celebrated, the reality was aggressive acquisition of new and valuable lands to be added to the republic.

A leading citizen of Monterey was Thomas O. Larkin, an American who had arrived in California in 1832. Larkin's half brother John Cooper also lived in Monterey and had married a sister of General Mariano Vallejo. Larkin married the widow of a sea captain and his business flourished. His home became a kind of embassy for Americans arriving in California, and he was appointed American consul in California in 1844. The first wagon train of settlers had arrived, after crossing the continent, in 1841, and it was soon followed by others. Larkin was charged with protecting American interests in the area. People began to ask when Americans in California would be "sufficiently numerous to play the Texas game," that is, to claim California as their fellow Yankees had claimed Texas in the decade before.

Misunderstanding the trauma Mexico had suffered, Polk and others guessed Mexico would never go to war to defend its borders against the powerful United States. The Mexican presence in California seemed even more tenuous than it had in Texas. For years the garrisons there had been manned by skeletal forces, undersupplied and with little motivation to defend the territorial claims.

By June of 1845 the Democratic Washington *Union* would shout in print, "Who can arrest the torrent that will pour onward to the West? The road to California will be open to us. Who will stay the march of our western people?" It became clear to Polk that compromising with Great Britain on Oregon at the forty-ninth parallel would leave the United States in a strong position to claim the whole West Coast southward to wherever the border with Mexico might prove to be. American ships had reached China as early as 1783, and it was imperative that the United States have ports on the Pacific from which to conduct trade with the Orient.

Robert Armstrong, American consul at Liverpool, reported the rumor that Mexico had given California to Great Britain as security for its foreign debt. And it was also speculated that in return for not recognizing the American annexation of Texas, Britain might be given free rein in California. The best plan for preventing such an outcome was to fight a war with Mexico and settle both the issues of Texas and California in one treaty that would end such a conflict. To achieve his ends, Polk *needed* a war.

Added to the rumor was the fact that the Hudson's Bay Company had for years furnished money and arms to the residents of California to keep their good will and lessen their loyalty to Mexico City. Now, with so many Americans arriving in northern California, it was rumored that Britain was urging Mexico to reassert its control over the region of upper California. And both the British and the French had established consulates at Monterey, though there seemed little business for them to conduct. Warships from both European nations made stops at the provincial capital.

Secretary of State Buchanan sent word to consul Larkin that the United States would never agree for a European power to assume control over California, and the government stood ready to aid any movement there toward independence from Mexico. However, if the people of California wished to be independent of Mexico and join the United States, that was another matter. "If the people should desire to unite their destiny with ours, they would be received as brethren, whenever this can be done without affording Mexico just cause of complaint."

Buchanan's message to Larkin was sent with Commodore Robert F. Stockton. Stockton was a particularly colorful and aggressive officer. Among his other adventures, he would try to provoke a war with Mexico at the mouth of the Rio Grande. Stockton sailed on the frigate USS *Congress* for California by way of Cape Horn. Secretary of the Navy George Bancroft had given Stockton sealed orders that were not to be opened until he was at sea. The orders: "Do all in your power to conciliate the good feeling of the people of that place towards the United States." As a backup plan, Stockton, who was to succeed to the command of the Pacific fleet of five warships, was to seize San Francisco and blockade Monterey in the event that war broke out with Mexico. In addition, Stockton was to land his forces and take control of as much territory as possible.

Since the sea voyage around the tip of South America would take at least six months, Polk used a second plan to get a message to Larkin and those on the ground in California. On October 30, 1845, Lieutenant Archibald H. Gillespie was commissioned to carry Buchanan's message to Larkin by sea to the isthmus of Tehuantepec, cross to the Pacific, and proceed to Monterey. Gillespie's cover story was that he was traveling for his health. Since Gillespie had a private meeting with the president himself before leaving, it has seemed to most historians he must have been more than a mere courier. In his diary for October 30, 1845, Polk simply wrote he had had "a confidential conversation . . . on the subject of a secret mission for which he [Gillespie] was about to go to California." It seems almost certain Gillespie carried with him other messages to be delivered verbally to Larkin, Stockton, or any other American officer (such as John Charles Frémont) who happened to be in California.

———

JOHN CHARLES FRÉMONT is one of the most controversial figures in American history. It would be hard to find anyone of the period about whom opinions were so extreme. To his wife, Jessie, and his many fans he would become the hero of the West, the "Pathfinder" and mapmaker of the Rockies, the Great Basin, and the High Sierras, not to mention the man who would claim California for the United States. To his many detractors Frémont has always appeared to be little more than a strutting buffoon, exaggerating or lying about his exploits, saved from his folly by scouts such as Kit Carson and Thomas "Broken Hand" Fitzpatrick and the public relations and political connections of his wife and father-in-law, Senator Thomas Hart Benton. Frémont saw himself as someone making history, but the role he assigned himself was often not the one history recorded. On one point virtually everyone seems to agree: he was an excellent topographical engineer and surveyor.

Frémont was born John Charles Frémon in Savannah, Georgia, on January 21, 1813. His mother, Anne Pryor, was married to a landowner more than forty years older than she. Charles Frémon, who taught Anne French, became her lover and fathered John Charles. Anne left her elderly husband without a divorce, and bore Frémon two more children. The family happened to be in the Nashville Inn when Andrew Jackson fought the gun and knife battle with the Benton brothers on September 4, 1813.

John Charles Frémont was a gifted and appealing child. In spite of the scandal of his birth, he made many friends growing up in Charleston, South Carolina, including Joel R. Poinsett. Skilled at mathematics and surveying, John Charles, who changed his name to Frémont, took part in surveys for railroads across the Appalachians to Cincinnati and then served with Joseph Nicollet in his surveys of Minnesota and the Dakotas.

Frémont seemed to be always adept at connecting himself with important people. Stationed with the Corps of Engineers in Washington, D.C., he became friends with Thomas Hart Benton and met Benton's sixteen-year-old daughter, Jessie, who fell in love with the twenty-eight-year-old lieutenant. To get rid of Frémont, Senator Benton arranged for him to join a survey team on the Des Moines River. But Jessie Benton was as strong-willed as her father, and when Frémont returned from the West the couple was secretly married on October 19, 1841.

The mighty senator was furious, but in the end, like most parents, he had to accept the inevitable. In fact he dedicated himself to promoting his new son-in-law's career. In 1842 Frémont was sent to follow the trace that was to become the Oregon Trail, all the way to South Pass and across the Continental Divide. He explored the mountains in the region, including the Wind River Range, and when he returned to Washington in the fall, he and Jessie collaborated on a book about his travels. The subject was one many thousands wanted to know about, and the account, colorfully written, became a hit, an exciting, exotic adventure story, as well as a guide for those interested in taking the Oregon Trail to the Far West.

When he was commissioned to explore the Rockies in 1843, to look for a gateway south of South Pass into the region that would become known as the Great Basin of Utah and Nevada, Frémont requested that Colonel Stephen Watts Kearny in St. Louis provide him with a short-barreled cannon called a howitzer and ample artillery ammunition. It was hard to explain why a surveying party in the Rockies would need such a weapon, but because of Frémont's new fame and connections to Senator Benton, Kearny granted the request.

Though he first headed west across Kansas to Bent's Fort, Frémont ignored his orders and turned northwest to South Pass. There was no easy passageway through the Colorado Rockies. Continuing on toward the Oregon Country, to the Whitman mission, Frémont descended the Columbia River and then turned southward. By midwinter the expedition had reached Pyramid Lake at the edge of the Great Basin, and the party ascended the Truckee River to Lake Tahoe. Incredibly, Frémont decided to cross the Sierras through what would later be known as Donner Pass in the deep snows of January and February. The heavy howitzer had to be abandoned somewhere in the rugged, snowy high country. Only the resourcefulness of his guide, Kit Carson, saved the party from a cold death. In March they arrived half starved and half dead at Sutter's Fort near the Sacramento River.

Continuing to make his survey, Frémont led the party in a sweep down California's great Central Valley and back across the mountains at Cajon Pass. With Carson's extraordinary skill as guide, they made it back to St. Louis in August of 1844 to a worried Jessie, just as Polk was running for president. Back in Washington, Jessie and John Charles wrote up a report of the so-called Second Expedition in such a colorful account that Senator Benton ordered five thousand additional copies printed. Jessie became good friends with the new First Lady, Sarah Polk, and

Frémont explained to the president-elect that the San Buenaventura and other rivers thought to drain the Great Salt Lake were fictions.

Frémont was used to charming older, powerful men as well as ladies. But he did not charm James K. Polk who appears to have thought the explorer "young" and having the "impulsiveness of young men." Frémont was sent by the army to the West again on his third expedition, this time to map the central Rockies and the headwaters of the Arkansas River, and return before the end of the year 1845. On October 24, 1845, Polk noted in his diary that he had a discussion with Senator Benton "concerning Capt. Fremont's expedition, and his intention to visit California before his return." It is hard to know exactly what instructions Frémont received from the president before his departure. Clearly a discussion of California had taken place.

When Frémont and his party reached John Sutter's Fort that winter, the Swiss trader informed both Mariano Vallejo and Thomas Larkin in Monterey of their presence. Frémont and a few of his men went on to Monterey and were entertained by Thomas and Rachel Larkin. Larkin loaned Frémont eighteen hundred dollars to resupply his expedition. It was understood that Frémont and his men were only passing through before heading for the Oregon country.

While camping near San Jose, Frémont was joined by a group that had separated from his expedition in the Great Basin, led by the scout Joseph Walker. There were now about sixty Americans with Frémont, and Mexican officials began to feel nervous. Their own forces were minimal, to say the least. Frémont was not at all conciliatory to the Mexican protests and moved his men to a fortified camp on Gabilan Peak (Hawk's Peak) and flew an American flag. When Mexican general José Castro raised a militia of two hundred men and marched toward Gabilan Peak, Frémont and his men abandoned the camp on March 9, 1846, and began moving north toward Oregon. As he worked his way slowly up the Sacramento Valley, Americans living in the region joined the little army. According to John Sutter, this force of American invaders made everyone uneasy.

On April 17, 1846, Lieutenant Archibald H. Gillespie arrived in Monterey and presented Buchanan's letter of the previous October to consul Larkin. The diplomatic Larkin, who hoped to keep things quiet, saw events were accelerating beyond his control. Gillespie hurried north with

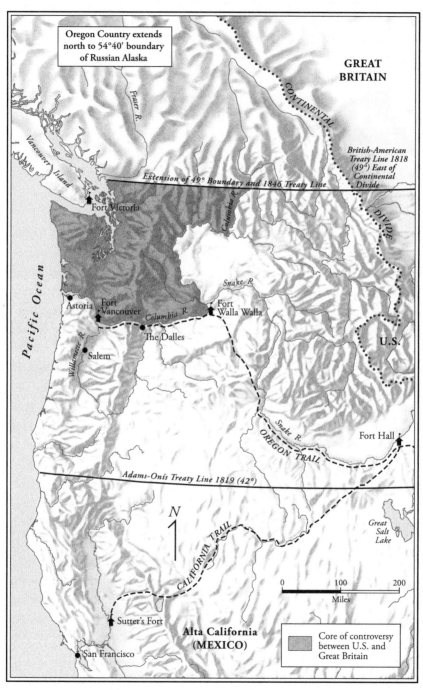

Oregon County, 1846

letters for Frémont from family and Buchanan. When the lieutenant reached Frémont on Upper Klamath Lake we can only guess that they discussed their personal orders from Buchanan and Polk.

Frémont had always seen himself as a man of destiny. And it seemed to him the time had come to act. In his later account he would write, "I saw the way opening clear before me. War with Mexico was inevitable; and a grand opportunity now presented itself to realize in their fullest extent the far-sighted views of Senator Benton, and make the Pacific Ocean the western boundary of the United States."

———

So FAR Mexico had refused to recognize the independence of Texas, and even if it did accept the fact that Texas was now one of the United States, there was still the issue of the border. When Polk ordered Brigadier General Zachary Taylor to move into Texas, he was precise as usual. "The Rio Grande is claimed to be the boundary between the two countries," he wrote, directing the general "to approach as near the boundary line, the Rio Grande, as prudence will dictate."

It seems likely Polk did not think there would be war with Mexico. After all, the Mexican army had been defeated by Sam Houston at San Jacinto in April of 1836. But whether there would be war or not, Polk meant to have the boundary at the Rio Grande. And he meant to have California as well, and Oregon too. Polk advised Zachary Taylor that if the Mexican army crossed the Rio Grande it was to be considered an act of war. He should retaliate, even if his own forces were not attacked. Once hostilities began, Taylor should not advance deeply into Mexico, but he should occupy Matamoros at the mouth of the Rio Grande and any other Mexican position along the river.

The president was still hoping to make a peaceful settlement with Mexico, which had broken off diplomatic relations with the United States in March of 1845 when the annexation of Texas became official. But when it came to diplomacy with Mexico, Polk exhibited blindness and ineptness from beginning to end. To open negotiations in Mexico City, Polk and Buchanan sent William S. Parrott, a failed dentist and somewhat shady figure who had traded with the Mexicans for years. Apparently Polk didn't realize that the Mexican government viewed Parrott as an exploiter and crook and detested him. To make Parrott's mission even more challenging, the Mexican government was again in disarray. Santa Anna had returned to power in 1841, but his corruption had made him even more enemies, and he was banished to Cuba in 1844.

José Joaquín Herrera had taken over the government in Mexico City but governed in a tense relationship with General Mariano Paredes y Arrillaga, who commanded the army in the north, near Texas. Herrera appeared willing to work out a deal with the United States over the issue of Texas, but General Paredes was a hardliner, a leader of the *puros* who were determined to resist American imperialism. Paredes has also been described by historians as "a drunken incompetent."

Mexico was a land of glorious volcanoes, peaks that reached so high they seemed to float in the firmament, shining with snow and smoking, erupting from time to time in magnificent displays of ash and fireworks. And Mexico was itself a kind of volcano, strangely beautiful but restless, given to rumblings and uneasy tremors, bursting out in coup after coup as one regime toppled another. T. R. Fehrenbach tells us that when Santa Anna had assumed power again, "He spent huge sums on parades, fiestas, and cannonades to cheer the populace." To pay for such extravagant entertainments he levied new taxes on everything, including windows.

The shifty William Parrott wrote back to Washington that he thought some sort of deal might be made but almost secretly because of the volatile political conditions in Mexico. His words raised hopes that a peaceful solution could be found. Polk proposed to his cabinet that the permanent boundary with Mexico be established at the Rio Grande and along the thirty-second parallel west from El Paso. He was willing to pay up to forty million dollars for the territory, if that much was required.

To carry this proposal to Mexico City, Polk selected John Slidell, a congressman from Louisiana, to undertake a secret mission. After Slidell left, Polk and Buchanan learned that the Mexican foreign minister Manuel de la Peña y Peña was indeed willing to talk but only if a commissioner without diplomatic rank were sent to Mexico to negotiate. After Parrott, the appointment of Slidell was an additional insult in the eyes of the weak Mexican government. Since diplomatic relations with the United States had been broken off when Congress voted to annex Texas, the only official the Mexicans would claim they could negotiate with was a special commissioner, not a ministerial diplomat. According to Ramón Alcaraz and his team, Mexico "would only admit him as a Commissioner *ad hoc* for the question of Texas." The Mexicans would argue that this fine point of diplomatic protocol was not negotiable. By ignoring the withdrawal of their ambassador from Washington, the president was acting as if Mexican actions and point of view were beneath his notice. In fact, in the correspondence leading up to Slidell's mission, the Mexicans state no such restriction. Merry points out there was "no suggestion that Mexico would reject an envoy with full diplomatic powers." We know that Polk cared little about the Mexican point of view, but in this case the Mexicans appear to have changed the rules after the envoy was on his way to Mexico.

It is also clear in hindsight that throughout his administration Polk's penchant for secrecy undermined many of his diplomatic efforts. He was adept at the backroom politics of Nashville and Washington but usually stumbled when attempting to bring those methods to international negotiations. Much of his political life had been conducted in private meetings with Old Hickory and other prominent Democrats. Throughout his administration, Polk kept looking for some equivalent method for dealing with Mexico and other foreign powers and never found it. And when he blundered he blamed those he had unwisely chosen, never himself.

Polk wrote to Slidell, "I am exceedingly desirous to acquire *California,* and am ready to take the whole responsibility, if it cannot be had for less, of paying the whole amount authorized by your instructions. If you can acquire both *New Mexico* and *California,* for the sum authorized, the nation I have no doubt will approve the act." But when Slidell arrived in Mexico, Peña y Peña refused to meet with him. The Mexican government had grown even weaker, under attack from General Paredes and much of the Mexican press. Slidell could only wait, hoping for a change of government. On January 2, 1846, the Herrera administration collapsed and General Paredes took charge. Paredes also refused to see Slidell and on March 12, 1846, the American envoy was officially informed that he would not be recognized. As Slidell prepared to leave Mexico, he wrote to Buchanan that "nothing is to be done with these people, until they shall have been chastised."

About this time Colonel Alexander J. Atocha, a citizen of Texas who had claims against the Mexican government, presented himself at the White House professing to be a close friend of Santa Anna, now in exile in Cuba. Atocha suggested that if Santa Anna could be brought back to power in Mexico, he might be willing to cede the northern lands of Mexico in return for cash, including the personal reimbursement Atocha hoped to secure. Atocha also advised that the only effective way to deal with Mexico was through a show of force. Atocha explained that all Santa Anna "wanted was to return to his homeland as a solider. He had no higher ambitions."

In his diary Polk reported his conversation with Atocha and the suggestion he had taken to heart that a show of force must be made with Mexico. It was the same assertion that Slidell had made: "We can never get along well with [the Mexicans] until we have given them a good drubbing." There is no reason to think Polk sought a war with Mexico if his ends could have been achieved diplomatically. What he was determined to have was Texas to the Rio Grande, New Mexico, and California from San Diego north. If war was the only way to accomplish these acquisitions, so be it. He might prefer a negotiated purchase, but if that failed he was ready to pursue other means. What he probably did not understand or even care about was that Mexican leaders felt the mounting hostility of their people toward the United States, and the prospect of war with their neighbor to the north gave them their best hope yet for unifying their own deeply divided nation. As Gene M. Brack states it, "Left with the choice of war or territorial concessions, the former course, however dim the prospects of success, could be the only one."

By the time Slidell returned to Washington in the spring of 1846, Polk was persuaded that the only effective means of dealing with Mexico were military. But whatever he had decided, events were already unfolding in the West following orders he had given earlier. General Zachary Taylor, called Old Zach by his men and later Old Rough and Ready because of his demonstrated willingness to share with them whatever hardships they encountered, was poised along the Rio Grande waiting for the Mexicans to make their move. He had constructed Fort Texas across the river from Matamoros.

On April 12, 1846, Mexican general Pedro de Ampudia, who has been described by Robert W. Merry as "famously sadistic and self-important," sent Taylor a note demanding the Americans withdraw to the Nueces River. In response Taylor called in the U.S. Navy to blockade the mouth of the Rio Grande. Mexican general Mariano Arista arrived and informed Taylor that war had begun and he meant to bring his forces against the Americans to drive them north to the Nueces. Taylor stiffened his patrols along the river, and on April 25, 1846, a company of American soldiers, twenty-five miles up the river, on the north bank of the Rio Grande, encountered several hundred Mexican cavalry. Eleven Americans were killed and twenty-six captured. As far as Taylor was concerned, the Mexicans had brought the war to American soil. "Hostilities may now be considered as commenced," he reported to Washington on April 26. The conflict Americans would call the Mexican War had begun. Mexicans would name the war "the North American Intervention."

Ramón Alcaraz and his fellow Mexican historians would describe the war between the United States and Mexico in April 1846 as a continuation of a conflict between the English and the Spanish that had gone on for centuries. "These sons of two distinct races, [were] now . . . destroying each other in the new continent as they had destroyed in the old. The one assumed the work of usurpation and treachery; the other defended a sacred cause in which it was true glory to die as a sacrifice." However the Mexicans saw themselves, as martyrs or aggressors, the old frontier fighter Zachary Taylor was determined to do his duty.

Zachary Taylor was born in Virginia on November 24, 1784, but his family soon moved to Louisville, Kentucky. Taylor was both a farmer and a soldier and had served in the War of 1812, defending Fort Harrison on the Wabash River. He owned several plantations in Kentucky and many slaves. Later he served in the Black Hawk War in the upper Midwest, and the Seminole War in Florida. He had been commissioned brevet brigadier general in Florida.

One of Taylor's daughters, Sarah Knox Taylor, fell in love with one of his junior officers, Jefferson Davis of Mississippi, and when her father opposed the marriage, she eloped with Davis. Sadly, Sarah Taylor died within months of her marriage. In Texas young Davis was serving once again under his former father-in-law as colonel of the Mississippi Rifles.

It took between two and three weeks for letters to reach Washington from Texas, but even before Polk received word of the fighting on the Rio

Grande, he was positioning his cabinet for a declaration of war against Mexico. On May 3, 1846, Thomas Hart Benton recommended that he wait until the Oregon question was resolved. On May 8 Slidell arrived in Washington and reiterated his opinion that war was the only effective means of dealing with Mexico at this point. The treatment Slidell had received in Mexico City was seen as an insult to the United States.

When Polk presented this opinion to his cabinet only Secretary of State Buchanan and Secretary of the Navy Bancroft demurred, stating that they would prefer to wait until Mexico had taken some hostile action. Polk decided to ask for a declaration of war anyway. But as it turned out, events overtook his decision. News of the fight on the Rio Grande arrived in Washington near sundown on May 9, 1846. American blood had been shed, and twenty-six men had been captured, including Captain Seth Thornton. As far as Polk was concerned, he must act as Old Hickory would have acted. The invasion of American soil and the taking of American life must be avenged. It could be put aside that he had been prepared to go to war over commercial interests in Texas and greed for western lands. Now the very honor of the United States was at stake in the chaparral along the Rio Grande. In his message to Congress, Polk used the phrase "American blood upon American soil." The House of Representatives voted 174 to 14 for the declaration of war. John Quincy Adams was one of the few opposed. In the Senate Thomas Hart Benton spoke against the declaration, then voted with the majority for it, 40 to 2. On May 13, 1846, Polk signed the declaration of war against Mexico.

Secretary of State Buchanan expressed his fear that Britain or France might intervene on behalf of Mexico, but Polk angrily assured the secretary that if it came to that he would fight Britain too and presumably France as well. Buchanan compromised finally and wrote to American diplomats, "We go to war with Mexico solely for the purpose of conquering an honorable and permanent peace."

By maneuvering Congress into such an overwhelming declaration of war against the opinions of many powerful politicians such as Benton, Adams, and Calhoun, Polk brought new power to the executive office, setting a precedent that would be followed by presidents over the next 165 years. On the other hand, one might argue, it is hard to see what else Polk could have done that would not have made the United States look weak and indecisive. The gauntlet had been thrown down. The Mexicans were determined to avenge themselves for the loss of Texas, and once the Lone Star Republic was admitted to the union, war was probably inevitable. Texas had been annexed by Tyler and Congress, and Texas claimed its border at the Rio Grande. To have retreated to the Nueces at that point might have invited further attacks from Mexican generals such as Arista and Santa Anna, who derived their popular support from saber rattling at the United States. Much has been made, correctly, of Polk's provoking the fight with Mexico, but it can be argued that most other presidents would also have declared war in May of 1846. As it turned out, Polk would not only change the shape and size of the United States by his declaration of war, he would change the powers and responsibilities of the executive branch forever. To describe this increased power of the executive branch historians have used "the hourglass metaphor," showing the president as the top half, Congress as the slim middle, and the populace as the large lower half of the hourglass.

Historians have never tired of belittling Zachary Taylor's generalship in Mexico. Most accounts of his victories in the Mexican War ascribe his successes to the valor and intelligence of the men serving under him and the superiority of American artillery. In his army were young officers such as Braxton Bragg and Ulysses S. Grant beginning their distinguished careers. It should also be pointed out that the Polk administration appointed as many Democratic officers as they could to serve under Taylor. While there is much evidence of Taylor's indecisiveness and bumbling, it cannot be denied that his forces won every major battle with Mexican forces, often against much larger armies than his own. Taylor had a common touch that endeared him to his men and officers serving under him performed brilliantly and heroically. He also had plenty of new and effective artillery. When a general is victorious in virtually every engagement against superior forces, he must be doing something right. Taylor would become a hero to the American people of the time, much to Polk's and the Democrats' distress.

Writing in 1943, the historian Bernard DeVoto could only see in Zachary Taylor "total ignorance of the art of war. And an instinct, if not for command, at least for leadership. He had been hardened in years of petty frontier duty, he had no nerves and nothing recognizable as intelligence, he was afraid of nothing, and he was too unimaginative to know when he was being licked, which was fortunate since he did not know how to maneuver troops. Add to this a dislike of military forms and procedures and a taste for old clothes and you have a predestinate candidate for the Presidency. The army and even some of the West Pointers worshiped him."

In spite of the derision of historians such as DeVoto, one must conclude that Taylor at least had the ability to choose the right men at the right time and assent to their wiser decisions some of the time. Otherwise his chain of victories in Mexico must be viewed as a series of accidents, or the Mexicans must be viewed as completely incompetent, which they were not. We can laugh at Old Rough and Ready if we want, but the fact is that when the time came he delivered what the president and Congress asked him to do. How he did it is a complex story.

Taylor planned to fight the Mexicans with bayonets, but the considerable enemy artillery at Palo Alto on May 8, 1846, soon tested and proved the value of American artillery. The Mexicans had only lead or bronze cannon balls, while the Americans had exploding shells. Mexican cannons fired at such slow velocities the Americans could see the rounds coming and dodge them. Even the larger Mexican cavalry led by Anastacio Torrejón could not prevail against the massed artillery. While the battle of Palo Alto raged Taylor calmly sat on his horse named Old Whitey, one leg hooked around the pommel of his saddle. Soon the exploding shells set the brush on fire and no one could see to fight in the dense smoke. The battle stalled out. The Mexicans still held their position, but ninety-two of their men had been killed and 116 wounded. American casualties were nine killed and 44 wounded. The American use of "flying artillery," small units of four mobile six-pounders, designed by General Winfield Scott and perfected by Captain Sam Ringgold, had proven effective.

During the night General Arista pulled his army back up the road about five miles to a place of bluffs and gullies called Resaca de la Palma. (A *resaca* is a slough.) Taylor could have waited for reinforcements before he advanced, but instead he chose to attack the Mexicans where they blocked the road. In the tall brush it was hard to locate Mexican artillery batteries. The Americans fired several rounds, and when those shots were answered it was clear where the Mexican cannon were located. Facing cannon fire in front and enemy cavalry converging from the side, Captain Charles May and his cavalry company charged the Mexican artillery position and seized the guns. But as Mexican infantry closed in, May was forced to withdraw.

Next, the American infantry under Colonel William G. Belknap attacked the cannon positions and prevailed, capturing General Rómulo Diaz de la Vega. The Mexicans began to withdraw, and later Arista acknowledged that 154 of his men had been killed and 206 wounded, with 156 missing. A number of Mexican soldiers drowned as they tried to swim across the Rio Grande. The Americans had lost 49 dead and 83 wounded. Young Ulysses Grant later wrote to his fiancée, "I think you will find that history will count the victory just achieved one of the greatest on record."

According to the historian Jack K. Bauer, one of Taylor's greatest weaknesses as a commanding general was his failure to follow up battles and destroy the enemy, thereby dragging out the war for almost two years. In all four of the major battles he fought in the Mexican War he permitted the Mexican army to withdraw. Bauer asserts Taylor lacked "the killer instinct" that great generals must have. Ramón Alcaraz and his fellow Mexican historians acknowledged that after the battle of Resaca de la Palma the Mexican army's "salvation was owing to General Taylor not having made use of his victory. If he had pursued our troops, and followed them across the river, it is undoubted that he should have completely destroyed them and taken Matamoros without opposition." But it should be pointed out that Taylor's instructions were to bring the Mexicans to agree to negotiations. It was assumed that this should be done with as little bloodshed as possible. Taylor and many others mistakenly believed that the Mexicans, once they confronted American will and might, would agree to settle the border dispute at the Rio Grande and sell their western territories. Pursuing and destroying a retreating army did not seem to support that policy and that assumption.

Arista and his army retreated past Fort Texas, renamed Fort Brown for Major Jacob Brown who had been killed, and the Americans followed, crossing the Rio Grande on May 18, 1846, and occupying Matamoros on Mexican soil. When news of the successes at Palo Alto and Resaca de la Palma reached Washington it sparked a euphoria of celebration.

Many assumed the war would soon be over and that the United States was victorious.

On May 11, 1846, Taylor rode to Point Isabel to confer with Commodore David E. Conner of the U.S. Navy. It was essential that the two branches of the service coordinate their efforts. Knowing that Conner was a spit-and-polish man Taylor put on his finest uniform for the meeting. Conner, understanding that Taylor rarely wore a uniform, put on civilian clothes. Both men were taken aback when they met and presumably had a good laugh before they got down to the serious business of their mission.

———

MEANWHILE POLK still had to resolve the Oregon question. Using the cries of "54°40' or Fight" and "All of Oregon or None" that swept the country, repeated in newspapers and speeches and on banners, to put pressure on the British, Polk waited for London to make the next move. Polk had the patience and toughness we associate with the pious, with those who are certain they are always right. Thomas Hart Benton might warn of the danger of war with John Bull over "54°40' or Fight," but Polk waited as the wagon trains of immigrants into Oregon and California swelled. It is estimated that by 1845 there were about five thousand immigrants in the Oregon Territory. The president told Benton he would consider a settlement at the forty-ninth parallel boundary, but Britain must make the first move. Like his mentor, Andrew Jackson, he thoroughly distrusted the British.

On April 11, 1846, the Senate finally passed a resolution giving Great Britain a one year termination notice of the joint agreement to oversee Oregon. The resolution, couched in diplomatic, conciliatory language, elicited a quick response from the British government, offering to settle at the forty-ninth parallel if the United States would cede to London Vancouver Island. With a war with Mexico looming, Polk decided to accept the proposal and submit it to the Senate, even as Buchanan reversed himself yet again and became an advocate of "54°40' or Fight." When Polk sent the final draft of the proposal to the Senate, the vote was 41 to 14 to accept. Polk had gotten what he had wanted all along. And now he was free to concentrate on the question of the southern border. It was unlikely he could settle things so easily with Mexico. An editorial in the *New York Herald* crowed, "We can now thrash Mexico into decency at our leisure."

By settling for only part of the Oregon Territory and declaring war on Mexico, Polk proved to many northern expansionists that he was more interested in expanding southern power and slavery than anything else. As James M. McPherson tells us, "When Polk . . . compromised with Britain on the 49th parallel but went to war with Mexico over the southern boundary of Texas many northern Democrats felt they had been sold out." Polk was more interested in promoting "Southern valves and interests than [they had] recognized." The sectional bitterness that would lead to civil war was already evident and growing.

Polk won another victory when the House of Representatives passed the Tariff Act of 1846 on July 3 by vote of 114 to 95. The next day the Senate approved the Independent Treasury Bill by a vote of 28 to 25. Three of Polk's four main goals had been accomplished in less than two years of his administration. The fourth, settlement of the boundary of Texas with Mexico and the acquisition of California and the land in between would take a little longer and lot more effort.

Now Polk took up Colonel Atocha's proposal of helping Santa Anna to return to Mexico from exile, on the understanding that once in power again the butcher of the Alamo and Goliad would negotiate a peace with the United States. Polk ordered Commander Alexander Slidell Mackenzie to meet Santa Anna in Cuba and offer him safe passage to the blockaded port of Veracruz and sufficient cash to aid his reassumption of power.

Why Polk imagined he could trust Santa Anna is unclear. Perhaps he thought the scheme unlikely to work but still worth the risk. He was willing to forget that Santa Anna was a demagogue and dictator who had gone back on all his promises to Sam Houston and Andrew Jackson in 1836. One source of Santa Anna's popularity had always been his militant anti-American stance. Congress voted two million dollars to cover the cost of the venture and on August 8, 1846, Santa Anna, accompanied by Alexander Atocha, sailed from Havana for Veracruz. In the words of Robert W. Merry, "The wily general and his unctuous agent, Alejandro Atocha, had snookered the president of the United States."

That very week the work of Congress got stalled over the issue of slavery in the new territories of the Southwest. David Wilmot, a Democrat of Pennsylvania, introduced an amendment that came to be called the Wilmot Proviso, outlawing slavery in the new territories. The debate was so furious and long that the bill was never voted on. As Walter LaFeber points out, though the Wilmot Proviso was not passed, "everyone involved understood that a political monster had appeared, one that could not be easily killed." It is often forgotten that the ostensible intention of Wilmot's proposal was "to maintain the new territories for the benefit of the white population of the United States and to protect areas where 'farmers and laborers' who were 'of my own race and color' would settle." Polk described the Proviso as "not only unwise, but wicked." The issue of slavery threatened to interfere with Polk's plan for both Texas and California. "What connection slavery had with making peace with Mexico is difficult to conceive," Polk wrote in his diary. Like many others, Polk found it hard to believe that the subject of slavery could not be pushed aside and ignored, especially when great issues such as territorial expansion were at stake. The president also believed that because the soils of northern Mexico were so dry and sandy slavery couldn't prosper there, and "Congress was raising the issue simply to embarrass him."

Whatever might be said in praise or rebuke of Polk, no one can deny that he was thorough. Deliberately, patiently, he set in motion all his extraordinary plans. In some ways he surpassed even Old Hickory in the reach of his vision and ambition. On May 13, 1846, he had sent a directive to Colonel Stephen Watts Kearny (pronounced "Karny") and his dragoons at Fort Leavenworth on the Missouri to move west to Santa Fe in the Mexican territory of Nuevo Mexico. Kearny was to take with him a thousand volunteers from Missouri. One goal of the expedition was to protect the traffic of American traders along the Santa Fe Trail. But Kearny was also ordered to occupy Santa Fe, the territorial capital, and then take most of his men west all the way to California. With Stockton and the U.S. Navy on the coast of California, and Frémont and his men somewhere in the north of California, Kearny was to see to the American interests in the south of Alta California.

The choice of Kearny for the expedition was wise. A veteran who had served since the War of 1812, he was married to Mary Radford, stepdaughter of William Clark of the Lewis and Clark expedition. At Leavenworth, Kearny had responsibility for patrolling both the Oregon and Santa Fe trails. A reporter was once astonished to see a private slap Kearny on the back at Fort Leavenworth and offer him a drink. The colonel did not seem in the least offended. At least one historian has described Kearny as "probably the army's finest high-ranking officer." Now he was told by Secretary of War William Marcy, "Take the earliest possession of Upper California. An expedition with that view is hereby ordered, and you are designated to command it." After taking control of Santa Fe he was to hurry west and place California under American control. Coordinating his actions with those of Captain Stockton on the coast, Kearny was authorized to draft Mormon emigrants and other Americans into his forces.

The secretary of war and Polk seemed to have forgotten about the Frémont expedition. Or perhaps it never occurred to them there could be a conflict of command in California once a brigadier general arrived with specific orders from the president and his cabinet. Kearny was given the brevet promotion effective as soon as he started west. The newly designated general sent two companies of dragoons, and two companies of Missouri Mounted Volunteers under the command of Colonel Alexander W. Doniphan, ahead to Bent's Fort. Before he left Fort Leavenworth on June 30, 1846, Kearny learned that New Mexico governor Manuel Armijo was expecting the arrival of three thousand to four thousand Mexican troops to defend Santa Fe.

Kearny was an effective commander and popular with his men. Included among his officers was Lieutenant William H. Emory, a topographical engineer charged with making maps of the country they passed through. A trader named James W. Magoffin, fresh from Washington, joined Kearny's party, bringing additional letters from Marcy and Polk, again urging Kearny on to California to "take military possession of that country as soon as it can be safely done."

Kearny sent Magoffin, accompanied by Captain Philip St. George Cooke, ahead to Santa Fe with a message for the Mexican governor Armijo. Kearny was coming to claim for Texas all the land east of the Rio Grande, including Santa Fe and Taos. Texans had long argued that the river was the true western boundary of their territory. Armijo acted outraged and called out a militia to resist the American invaders at the

Raton Pass. But when Kearny and his army reached the beautiful piñon-forested pass, they found no one to stop them and marched on to Santa Fe. Armijo fled to Albuquerque, and on August 18, 1846, Stephen Watts Kearny and the Army of the West rode into Santa Fe, seat of Spanish rule for more than two hundred years.

Some citizens made a show of welcoming the Americans and the Stars and Stripes soon flew over the Palace of Governors. The residents offered the American conquerors wine and brandy, turning the occasion into a celebration. Soon Kearny claimed that all of Nuevo Mexico, including the land west of the Rio Grande, was now part of the United States. When Polk learned of Kearny's success a few weeks later, he scribbled in his diary a rare note of approval. "General Kearny has thus far performed his duty well."

Alexander Doniphan and several other lawyers in the army drafted temporary laws for the territory that would be called the "Kearny Code." Later Whigs in Congress would accuse Kearny (and Polk) of far over-reaching their authority. While Polk and Buchanan back in Washington argued about the correctness of his conduct, Kearny appointed Charles Bent governor of the New Mexico Territory and set out for California on September 25, 1846.

ON OCTOBER 6, as Kearny prepared to leave the west bank of the Rio Grande at Socorro and head directly west, Kit Carson appeared with a party of sixteen men headed to Washington with letters from Frémont, Stockton, and Larkin for Polk and Marcy. Carson had an astonishing story to tell Kearny.

After Lieutenant Gillespie had caught up with Frémont at Upper Klamath Lake the previous spring, the American captain gathered up his force of soldiers and surveyors and headed back south. It was rumored the Mexicans were making plans to drive the American settlers out of the Sacramento Valley. On June 14, 1846, thirty-two Americans, led by Ezekiel Merritt, rode into Sonoma, north of San Francisco Bay, and took Mariano Vallejo prisoner, though Vallejo was neither on military duty at the time nor hostile to the Americans. One of the group, William L. Todd, stitched a flag, it's said, out of ladies' undergarments with a grizzly bear on its top half and "California Republic" written in the middle. The idea seemed to be to imitate the Texas rebellion that led to the Lone Star Republic. On July 4, 1846, Frémont and his men celebrated the new short-lived entity, "the Bear Flag Republic."

Meanwhile Commodore John L. Sloat of the U.S. Navy, arriving in Monterey with four ships, heard about the "Bear Flaggers" and ordered Mexican general Castro to abandon the capital. When Frémont and Gillespie rode into Monterey with 160 men Sloat designated them the California Battalion. Soon after that Robert Stockton arrived to replace Sloat and take command of the Pacific fleet.

Stockton quickly made plans for conquering all of California and sailed south with Frémont and his men to take San Diego and Los Angeles as the Mexicans retreated south to Sonora. Getting official word of the declaration of war against Mexico, Stockton proclaimed California a territory of the United States and dispatched Kit Carson with letters to Washington. After encountering Kearny and his men at Socorro, Carson turned back to California with Kearny and about a hundred men. On November 23, 1847, Kearny's soldiers captured a Mexican courier near the Colorado River and learned that the Mexicans had retaken southern California. On December 2, 1846, Kearny and his men reached Warner's Ranch sixty miles east of San Diego. Kearny sent a message to Stockton requesting reinforcements. In return they got (now) Captain Gillespie and thirty-nine men.

On December 6 Kearny and his men attacked the Mexicans at San Pasqual and suffered overwhelming casualties: twenty-one killed, twenty wounded. Kearny himself received nearly fatal wounds. Eventually they were rescued by two hundred sailors sent by Stockton, and Kearny marched his remaining force into San Diego.

As a brigadier general, Kearny outranked Stockton, but nursing the ugly wounds on his back and groin, Kearny let Stockton take over much of the reconquest of Los Angles in early January 1847. Kearny sent a message to Frémont, somewhere in the north, to warn him of the fighting in the south. In return he got a message from Frémont announcing that he, Frémont, had concluded a treaty with the Mexicans. Frémont soon rode into Los Angeles as a conquering hero.

Considering himself the commander in California, Frémont refused

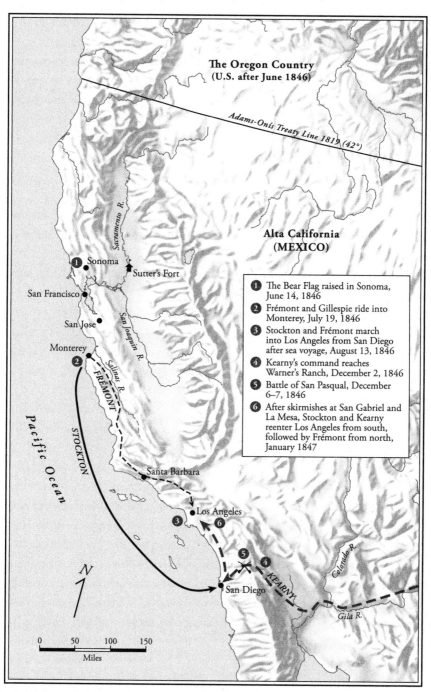

The Oregon Country
(U.S. after June 1846)

Adams-Onis Treaty Line 1819 (42°)

Alta California
(MEXICO)

1 Sonoma

Sacramento R.

Sutter's Fort

San Francisco

San Jose

San Joaquin R.

Monterey

2

Salinas R.

FRÉMONT

STOCKTON

Pacific Ocean

1 The Bear Flag raised in Sonoma,
June 14, 1846

2 Frémont and Gillespie ride into
Monterey, July 19, 1846

3 Stockton and Frémont march
into Los Angeles from San Diego
after sea voyage, August 13, 1846

4 Kearny's command reaches
Warner's Ranch, December 2, 1846

5 Battle of San Pasqual, December
6–7, 1846

6 After skirmishes at San Gabriel and
La Mesa, Stockton and Kearny
reenter Los Angeles from south,
followed by Frémont from north,
January 1847

Santa Barbara

Los Angeles

3 **6**

5 **4**

KEARNY

Colorado R.

San Diego

Gila R.

N

0   50   100   150
Miles

California Campaigns, 1846–1847

to submit to orders from Kearny and soon found himself under arrest and headed to Washington under escort for a sensational court martial that would divide the nation. When Polk refused to intervene on Frémont's behalf, he ended the friendship and cooperation with the powerful Senator Benton. In the end Frémont was found guilty by the court martial, but allowed by Polk to remain in the army. Angry that he had not been exonerated, Frémont resigned his commission and headed back to California.

———

POLK WAS ATTACKED in the press and in Congress, even by fellow Democrats. Some of the most telling and wounding arguments came from a young congressman from Illinois named Abraham Lincoln. As a lawyer familiar with the Constitution, Lincoln was appalled that the president had seemed to make war at his discretion. "Allow the President to invade a neighboring nation, whenever *he* shall deem it necessary to repel an invasion," young Lincoln said, "and you allow him to do so, *whenever he may choose to say* he deems it necessary for such a purpose—and you allow him to make war at pleasure." Yet fifteen years later the same Lincoln, when he was sitting in the Oval Office, would exercise executive powers far greater than any Polk had claimed or imagined. However critical of Polk's policies, the Whigs in Congress continued to vote funds for the armies fighting in Mexico.

Meanwhile Polk feared that the Whig General Zachary Taylor's victories on the Rio Grande would carry Taylor to a presidential nomination in 1848, and to the White House. Seeing Taylor as a threat to the Democratic Party, Polk could find no virtues in Taylor's actions or his victories. "General Taylor, I fear, is not the man for the command of the army," Polk wrote. "He is brave but he does not seem to have resources or grasp of mind enough to conduct such a campaign." Polk's jealousy of Zachary Taylor and Winfield Scott is usually explained as a political animosity. He was afraid one or both would gather military glory and win the White House. But Polk seems to have felt a general resentment toward professional military men. Never having worn a uniform himself, often sickly, he distrusted men of military experience who might question his decisions, even his authority. During his administration he again and again commissioned civilians with little or no military record as generals to undercut the authority of the professional soldiers. The truth is Polk had limited experience outside the world of politics. Men of wider experience such as Scott and Taylor probably threatened his sense of control and his own infallibility.

While camped around the town of Matamoros, Taylor tried to keep order and discipline among his men. Both soldiers and volunteers tended to ignore his decree not to loot or harass the civilians. An American volunteer shot a woman washing on the bank of the river merely to test his rifle. Mexican cattle were stolen and butchered, providing fresh meat for the men. The local cantinas and bordellos did a brisk business. A touring theatrical company, which included one Joe Jefferson, arrived in town and performed for the troops.

Taylor did not believe it practical to attempt to march from the Rio Grande across the mountains several hundred miles to Mexico City. He thought the best strategy was to secure the northern provinces of Mexico, Nuevo León, Coahuila, Chihuahua, to make the border with the United States safe. To accomplish this, the provincial capital of Monterrey had to be taken. Taylor ordered his men to pay for all supplies they took from the Mexicans. But he could not control the unruly volunteers serving under him who looted and assaulted local citizens. The Texas Rangers in particular seemed bent on revenge for the many raids into Texas over the past decade. And volunteers from Arkansas massacred between twenty and thirty Mexican civilians after one of their own was murdered. When Louisiana sent him three thousand untrained men, Taylor decided not to accept them into his army, which was already running out of supplies. His greatest shortage was not of men but of horses to pull the hundreds of supply wagons. The Americans ended up settling for lumbering oxen and pack mules to move their baggage. In August 1846 Taylor advanced his army, first to Camargo, which was extremely hot and humid. Many more soldiers were stricken with dysentery and fevers, and one in eight of the American soldiers died of disease there. The place was infested with "frogs, along with scorpions, tarantulas, mosquitos, centipedes, flies, fleas, biting ants, chiggers, rattlesnakes." Then they moved on ninety miles south of the Rio Grande, reaching the orchards and green farmlands of Cerralvo on August 25. After the humid Rio Grande valley the highlands seemed a paradise. There was plenty of clean water, and large groves of lemon, orange, peach, fig, and pecan trees. Lush cornfields covered the valleys while sheep and cattle grazed in the hills. Spies informed Taylor that general Ampudia was again in charge of the Mexican army to the south near Marín, on the road to Monterrey. The American army moved out at intervals, each man carrying rations and supplies for eight days. The ammunition provided for their muskets was "buck and ball," one ball and two buckshot for every shot. The percussion cap, introduced in 1841, was a distinct improvement over the old flintlock firing mechanism.

Meeting no resistance at Marín they continued on toward Monterrey and found the provincial capital heavily defended. Many of Taylor's men—perhaps as much as one-third of his army of three thousand regulars and four thousand volunteers—were still sick with dysentery and tropical fever. The general assembled his men in a peach orchard northeast of the city. They called the place Walnut Springs because of the many nut trees as well as fruit trees. Inspecting his artillery, Taylor saw he had four squadrons of field guns, two twenty-four pound howitzers and a ten-inch mortar.

Historians have generally thought Ampudia made a mistake in taking his stand at Monterrey. He had only 7,303 men to defend a large town and outlying positions. Santa Anna had ordered him to withdraw to Saltillo, but he defied the order. Ampudia may have decided to fight at Monterrey because it was a heavily fortified city, with a nearby ridge from which artillery could command the western approaches to the city. Or he may have thought it essential for psychological reasons to defend the regional capital.

Monterrey was located on the north bank of the Santa Caterina River, in the foothills of the Sierra Madre Oriental. Its cathedral had been turned into a fortress, called by Taylor's soldiers the Black Fort. There was another fort on a nearby hill called Independencia. The eastern end of the city was protected by two large forts named Diablo and Tenería. In the words of Ramón Alcaraz and his team of historians, "Monterrey, the capital of the frontier, is one of the most beautiful cities of the republic, being situated in a fertile valley in the midst of the most lofty and picturesque mountains . . . The buildings of the city are sufficiently handsome. Houses of hewn stone, streets regularly intersecting, spacious plazas, and

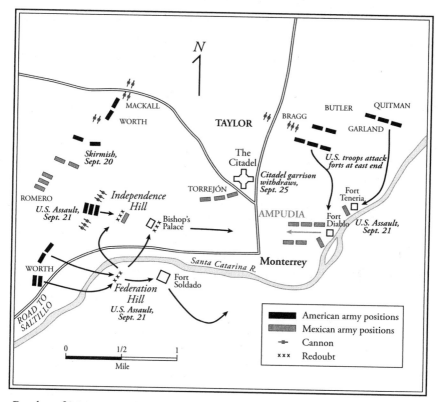

Battles of Monterrey, September 20–24, 1846

a cathedral church of magnificent architecture." On September 20, 1846, American forces under Brigadier General William J. Worth circled to the west and cut off Ampudia's line of communication with Saltillo. On September 22 Worth captured the gun emplacement at Independencia. Meanwhile Taylor had entered the eastern edge of the city and Lieutenant George C. Meade made a map of the city's fortifications. For some reason Taylor did not bombard the fortresses Diablo and Tenería and gun emplacements in the city's fortifications. Jack K. Bauer and others have suggested that Taylor was always reluctant to use artillery, believing the war in Mexico would be won by infantry bayonets and cavalry. As an old frontier fighter, he understood better the use of riflemen with bayonets who had proven so effective in Indian fighting. Taylor sent separate units to secure different parts of the city, fighting house to house and street to street. One unit of Mississippi volunteers was commanded by Jefferson Davis. Taylor lost 394 men killed or wounded in that action. Around three in the afternoon, Taylor withdrew his men from the city, expecting to renew the brutal fighting the next morning. Two Mexican heroes the Americans had confronted had been women: "Dos Amades," who led a devastating cavalry charge, and Doña María Josefa Zozaya, who fought with the men in the city.

But that evening Ampudia asked to be allowed to evacuate the city, and the next day the Mexican commander and Taylor actually met face-to-face. Robert W. Merry tells us that Ampudia "reported, falsely, that the United States and Mexico had entered into peace negotiations." It was also reported that the Mexicans had stored their ammunition in the cathedral, and fearing Americans would shell the sanctuary and blow it up, Ampudia thought it best to give up the city. After further negotiations Taylor agreed to an eight-week armistice, as the Mexican army retired to the south, in part to allow Taylor's own men time to reorganize and regain their health. The armistice seemed to be in the diplomatic spirit that Polk had espoused earlier, when still hoping for a treaty resolution to the dispute with Mexico and a purchase of the western territories. Mexican historians, recalling the city of Monterrey after Ampudia evacuated it, remembered it as "converted into a vast cemetery. The unburied bodies, the dead and putrid mules, the silence of the streets, all gave a fearful aspect to this city."

But in the meantime Polk had been stung by the whole Atocha–Santa Anna affair. Almost as soon as the Americans returned Santa Anna to Mexico the cunning general wangled his way back into power, rebuilt his army, and began marching north, bragging he would drive Taylor out of Mexico. Polk had chosen to forget that one of Santa Anna's surest sources of power had always been his militant anti-American stance and rhetoric.

Double-crossed by Santa Anna, Polk was furious when he heard about Taylor's armistice. Taylor had let the Mexican army escape again to regroup and reinforce itself. Polk sent Old Rough and Ready a reprimand with no thanks for his victory at Monterrey and an order to direct some of his troops on an expedition to subdue the province of Tamaulipas south of Matamoros. Taylor had done essentially what he had been ordered to do. But in the meantime Polk had changed his plans, and his deep resentment of generals had come into play. Taylor felt insulted and demeaned, which was probably what Polk wanted the Whig general to feel.

Polk liked to act quickly and expected to be obeyed quickly. But it took almost eight weeks for a message from Washington to reach Taylor's army south of the border. Because of the delay in communication, it often appeared to Polk that the general was not carrying out his orders. The lag-time in communication caused much of Polk's problems with Zachary Taylor, and later with Winfield Scott and also with the diplomat Nicholas P. Trist. In Robert W. Merry's words, "When news travels slowly and arrives in fragments, it breeds suspense." Even so, a less defensive executive might have handled the delayed communications much more wisely. In a hurry to conclude the unpopular war, and always suspicious of Whigs and generals, Polk thought the worst of any misunderstanding, lost message, or failure in communication. Polk appeared always ready to believe that the men he sent into the field were committed to defying his orders and undercutting his policies and authority. This suspicious irritability was probably Polk's greatest weakness as president. A man of outstanding vision and sense of political purpose, he almost canceled out some of his most important efforts by his affinity for secret maneuvers and his distrust of his subordinates.

Taylor received a sympathetic letter from Winfield Scott wishing that Taylor "will (as heretofore) defeat your enemies, both in *front* and *rear*." Ordered to proceed no farther south than Monterrey, Taylor hesitated to lead a planned assault on the port of Tampico as part of a campaign to subdue the Tamaulipas province. But before the Americans could land at that port city on November 12, 1846, Santa Anna intercepted a message to Taylor describing the plans of the attack, and the generalissimo quickly withdrew his forces from the area. When the Americans came ashore, there was no one there to fight, and Mexico City was still hundreds of miles away across deserts and nearly impassable mountain terrain. The folly of directing a war from a desk in Washington was proven once again, but the lesson was lost on Polk. Taylor then moved his army into Victoria, capital of Tamaulipas, but it was clear to all that the Tamaulipas campaign was a failure.

In his diary Polk wrote of Zachary Taylor, "He is evidently a weak man and has been made giddy with the idea of the Presidency. He is most ungrateful, for I have promoted him . . . beyond his deserts, and without reference to his politics. I am now satisfied he is a narrow minded, bigoted partisan, without resource and wholly unqualified for the command he holds." Reading Polk's words one would never guess that Taylor had won every single battle his army had fought in Mexico.

One of Polk's weaknesses as a leader was that when he was angry he saw in others his own obsession with power, partisanship, and the presidency. None of us when angry can take a balanced view. Taylor's victories in Mexico only made Polk more scornful of the Whig general. Every won battle seemed a calamity to Polk. Polk could not have been more critical of him if Taylor had *lost* those battles. Polk's anger at the general seemed to know no limits after the disappointment of the Tampico expedition.

It must be said that Taylor was equally scornful of Polk, but why would he not be? Not only did the president issue belittling and confusing orders from the comfort of the White House, he now commanded Taylor to advance no farther than Monterrey and to furnish most of his troops for the planned attack on Veracruz. Stopped in his tracks far from Mexico City and the new theater of war, Taylor chose to occupy Saltillo fifty miles away, following his original orders to maintain a defensive zone along the mountain chain south of the Rio Grande. Taylor and Worth led their troops south through the Pass of Rinconada onto the plain around Saltillo. Fields of wheat and oats stretched across the land, interrupted by large orchards of apple and cherry trees.

Taylor was now short of troops, but suddenly he was joined by Brigadier General John Ellis Wool and three thousand soldiers on their way from El Paso to Chihuahua. Among Wool's officers was a gifted topographical engineer, Captain Robert E. Lee. Deciding that if he continued to Chihuahua "all that we shall find to conquer is distance," Wool joined Taylor's depleted forces.

Assembling an Army of the North of 19,525 men from Ampudia's still intact forces, the garrisons at Tampico, and San Luis Potosí, Santa Anna planned to march north across the desert, drive Taylor from Saltillo, retake Monterrey, and push the Americans back across the Rio Grande. When the north was clear of Americans, Santa Anna would hurry back south to defend Veracruz against an American invasion. Santa Anna

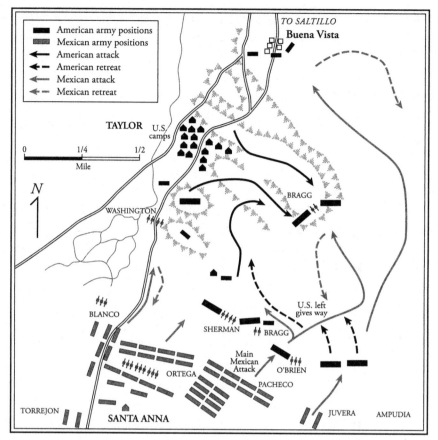

Battle of Buena Vista, February 23, 1847

seemed to care little about California; it was too far away to defend anyway. But driving the Americans back across the Rio Grande and out of
Veracruz must be accomplished before *any* negotiations over the western
territories could begin. Unfortunately the Mexicans had destroyed all
water tanks between San Luis Potosí and Saltillo to prevent Americans
from using them.

Wool's army joined up with Taylor's on December 21, 1846, at Agua
Nueva, between Saltillo and San Luis Potosí. Wool spotted an excellent
defensive position for the Americans at Angostura Pass, near the Haci-
enda of Buena Vista. Taylor doubted the Mexican general would bring
his large army across the desert in the middle of winter, but suddenly on

February 21, 1847, Santa Anna and his massive corps appeared from the south. General Wool persuaded Taylor to withdraw from the exposed plain to Angostura Pass just south of the ranch of Buena Vista.

The pass was only an excellent defensive position if Santa Anna did not choose to swing around the area to attack Saltillo and cut Taylor's supply lines. Luckily for Taylor, Santa Anna chose to attack directly, after marching his army across two hundred miles of forbidding desert. During that forced march the Mexicans lost three thousand men to death or desertion, weeding out the weak and unfit. Five mules had carried Santa Anna's gamecocks. Santa Anna first sent an ultimatum to Taylor, demanding that he surrender and promising fair treatment "with the consideration belonging to the Mexican character." Santa Anna's bravado is all the more remarkable when we consider that his men had exhausted their rations on the march north. They would have to fight on empty stomachs. Though Taylor let fly a stream of profanity when he read the note, he dictated a cool answer to Santa Anna. "In reply to your note of this date, summoning me to surrender my forces at your direction, I beg leave to say that I decline acceding to your request."

The Mexicans attacked on February 22, 1847, but had to fall back. The next day Taylor left the Indiana and Illinois volunteer regiments on the plateau near the pass and rode himself the six miles back to Saltillo to check on the safety of his supply base. While some historians have questioned Taylor's constant concern about his supplies, it should be remembered that far from home and any port city, Taylor could have been defeated by loss of rations, clothing, tents, and ammunition more easily than on the battlefield.

Since Santa Anna had lost about a quarter of his men to sickness and desertion on the brutal march across the desert, this left him with around sixteen thousand men to face the five thousand fit Americans. The Mexicans broke through the American position at one point and General Wool shouted to Taylor, "General, we are whipped." "That is for me to determine," Old Rough and Ready shot back. For hours the Mexican and American forces drove each other back and forth. Twice Jefferson Davis and the Mississippi Rifles gave a good account of themselves. A battery of Mexican artillery, manned by the San Patricio battalion, which included many Irish Catholic deserters from the American army, wreaked heavy damage on the First Illinois. The battle was probably Santa Anna's finest hour as a commander in the field. In the heat of the battle Taylor is rumored to have said calmly, "A little more grape, Captain Bragg."

As William Borneman writes, "Whatever his political or administrative sins, Zachary Taylor was a cool head once under enemy fire." However much later historians might disparage Old Rough and Ready, they would all agree on the importance of artillery in the Mexican War, especially at the Battle of Buena Vista. Serving with Braxton Bragg that day was a young lieutenant named George H. Thomas, who would later confront his former captain in September 1863 and become known as "the Rock of Chickamauga." Later historians would say that Taylor's worst mistake that day was ordering an unnecessary attack on the plateau. Facing overwhelming numbers, the American infantry suffered heavy casualties. "With the Mexican advantage in strength, [Taylor] could ill afford a battle of attrition," John Eisenhower would write. Fortunately an artillery barrage forced the Mexicans back and let the Americans rescue their wounded.

As mentioned earlier, Taylor had believed in the importance of the bayonet and the cavalry, but the Mexican War, especially at Buena Vista, proved him wrong. It was artillery that was the weapon of the future. At the end of the day Colonel Archibald Yell was dead, as was Lieutenant Colonel Henry Clay Jr. They had helped pay the price for Old Rough and Ready's victory. Taylor's luck had held, and next morning it was discovered that Santa Anna had withdrawn his diminished army back toward San Luis Potosí. Campfires had been left burning all night to make the Americans think the Mexicans were still there. The Mexicans had sustained about 3,500 casualties, with 594 killed, 1,039 wounded, and 1,854 missing. The Americans had lost only 272 killed, 387 wounded, and 6 missing. Santa Anna claimed victory in the encounter, asserting that he had stopped the American advance toward the Mexican capital and exacted a terrible price for the American invasion of Mexico. According to the historian Cecil Robinson, "Several military analysts have concluded that Santa Anna won the day but did not realize it. Taylor won by default. This combination of brilliant organization and tactics crowned by a miscalculation seemed characteristic of Santa Anna." The historian Daniel

Walker Howe argues that "the Battle of Buena Vista constituted a tactical draw, but in its true significance a major U.S. victory, since Santa Anna had not succeeded . . . in destroying Taylor's vulnerable force." Some historians argued that the real American hero at Buena Vista was General John E. Wool, who directed much of the most effective fighting.

Ramón Alcaraz and his team of historians would write in 1848 of the Battle of Buena Vista, "The truth is, our arms routed the Americans in all the encounters, and so far the issue of the battle was favorable to us. There had been three partial triumphs, but not a complete victory." But these same historians concede that whatever his successes at Angostura (Buena Vista) Santa Anna's army was virtually destroyed by the long, forced march back to San Luis Potosí. "The loss sustained from the Angostura to San Luis exceeded 10,500 men."

When news of the battle of Buena Vista reached Polk a few weeks later, he was not impressed. He refused to permit a fire of salute in honor of Taylor's victory, complaining that no such salute had been made to honor Jackson after the victory at New Orleans. About the general who had won all his battles in Mexico and held the defensive zone in the north, protecting the boundary at the Rio Grande, Polk wrote in his diary, "The truth is the indomitable bravery of our army saved Gen'l Taylor, and not his good Generalship, at the battle of Buena Vista. Had that battle been lost, he would have been condemned by the whole country for this rashness in violation of his orders in taking the advanced position he did." It meant nothing to Polk that Taylor had led his men to drive back an army three to four times the size of his own. Robert W. Merry tells us that at Buena Vista "Taylor once more had demonstrated his nimble tactical brilliance."

Polk's comments on Taylor's victory do not reflect credit on the president. Polk's spitefulness toward Taylor would set the tone for comments on Old Rough and Ready for future historians. For some reason, historians would want to hold Taylor's victories against him, giving all credit to the soldiers serving under him. Even when he won, he could do no right. One exception was Ulysses S. Grant, who served with Taylor and had enthusiastic praise for the general. And the electorate of the United States would find much to admire about Zachary Taylor and would send him to the White House in 1848.

— *Seven* —

WINFIELD SCOTT

OLD FUSS AND FEATHERS

GOES TO THE MOUNTAIN

THOUGH CONGRESS had voted to go to war with Mexico when the president asked for its assent, the Mexican conflict grew increasingly unpopular as time dragged on. Opposition was, as noted, especially strong in New England, where it was feared that expansion into the Southwest would tip the balance of power toward the South as slavery was extended into the new territories and that Jacksonian populism would dominate national politics forever. Intellectuals such as Henry David Thoreau vehemently denounced "Mr. Polk's War" as immoral and foolish. Thoreau saw the Mexican War as a power grab by Polk and his henchmen. "Witness the present Mexican War, the work of comparatively a few individuals using the standing government as their tool; for, in the outset, the people would not have consented to this measure." In *The Biglow Papers,* James Russell Lowell wrote, "They jest want this Californy, so's to lug new slave states in." Young Abe Lincoln of Illinois described Polk as "a bewildered, confounded, and miserably-perplexed man."

Polk always responded vigorously to challenges and in his second annual message to Congress he defended his policies and reasserted, "The War has not been waged with a view to conquest." By the late fall of 1846 Polk and his cabinet had realized that until it was defeated in its capital, Mexico City, Mexico would never concede and give up the territories the United States was determined to possess. Because the city of Mexico was protected by hundreds of miles of mountainous terrain far south of the

Rio Grande and sat high on a plateau surrounded by lakes and marshes and lofty mountains, the Mexican government felt invulnerable. The political life of Mexico had been chaotic, violent, and unstable since independence was won from Spain in 1821. But far from the ocean, in the fortress of formidable mountains, the Mexican government might feel its borders threatened but not its heart and seat of power. It had taken Cortés months of bloody fighting to conquer Tenochtitlán, capital of the Aztec Empire, in 1521. There was little reason to think the Americans would make such an extraordinary effort just to establish the Texas border at the Rio Grande. As for California, that was so far away it had never been of much use to Mexico anyway.

Because it was important to deprive Zachary Taylor of any further military glory that might put him in the White House in 1848, Polk ordered Old Rough and Ready to stay where he was in the north of Mexico. To actually win the war, an American army would have to land far to the south at the port of Veracruz, take that heavily fortified port city, and then march more than two hundred miles to attack an almost impregnable Ciudad de México. No one was available to lead such an expedition except General in Chief Winfield Scott, called Old Fuss and Feathers by his men because of his love of fine uniforms and ceremony and his belief in an elite, professional army. Scott's vanity was legendary. Ulysses S. Grant, who served with him in Mexico, later recalled that Scott referred to himself in the third person: "He could bestow praise upon the person he was talking about without the least embarrassment." Theodore Roosevelt, writing about Scott decades later, described the general as "a wholly absurd and flatulent personage." It irritated Polk that Scott was a Whig, an old rival of Andrew Jackson and someone who aspired to greater glory, namely the presidency. But, as Robert W. Merry observes, "The only viable candidate was the cantankerous and prickly Winfield Scott."

SCOTT HAD had a career of alternating failures and successes and could behave by turns with utmost arrogance or humility, depending on circumstances and his moods. In almost every way, some good and some bad, Winfield Scott was larger than life. He was born June 13, 1786, on a small farm outside Petersburg, Virginia. His grandfather, James Scott,

had fled Scotland after the failure of the "Bonnie Prince Charlie" uprising of 1745. His father, William, a farmer and lawyer, died when he was
six, and he, like Washington, like Jackson, like Houston, was raised by
his mother. "A strong-willed, quick-witted woman of independent spirit,"
Ann Scott was credited by her son as his inspiration in later life. "If I have
achieved . . . anything that my countrymen are likely to honor . . . it is
from the lessons of that admirable parent that I derived the inspiration."
As a boy, Winfield learned to make ingenious and labored arguments
to save himself from censure or punishment, a habit he carried into
later life.

In 1805 he entered the College of William and Mary and was drawn to
the study of French and law. His fluency in French would stand him in
good stead later as he studied and translated French military manuals for
training and tactics. Like George Patton after him, he was proud of his
command of the language of Napoleon and European military science.
Hoping to advance faster, he dropped out of college to read law in the office of David Robertson in Petersburg. Proving an able student, Scott was
admitted to the Virginia bar in 1806 and was employed in Robertson's
office. That year Scott attended Aaron Burr's trial for treason in Richmond, where he met Washington Irving, who became a lifelong friend.
The main witness against Burr was the overweight, treacherous General
James Wilkinson, who covered up his own collusion with the Spanish
government by accusing Burr. Wilkinson would figure unpleasantly in
Scott's life in the years to come.

Allan Peskin tells us Winfield Scott had an "oval face, wide eyes, aq-
uiline nose, and dark hair brushed stiffly back from his forehead." When
young he was very slim, but later grew corpulent, thanks in part to his
love of French cuisine. Burr later remembered him as "the most magnificent youth in Virginia."

The practice of law lacked the glamor Scott hankered for, and when
President Jefferson called for Americans to help patrol the coastline during the embargo on British shipping, Scott purchased a fine uniform and
joined a company, using his family connections to apply to President
Jefferson directly for a commission in the regular army. In May 1808 he
was made captain of an artillery company. Pompous even as a young
man, Scott pledged "my life, my liberty, my sacred honor" and paid a

tailor to fashion another splendid uniform. In his memoirs, written a half century later, Scott confessed that he admired himself in the mirror for two hours, unable to tear himself away from his own heroic image. This odd combination of vanity and confessional candor characterized Scott throughout his long life.

Sent to New Orleans in 1809 to serve under General Wilkinson, Scott soon found himself at loggerheads with the general. Camped in a swampy pasture called Terre aux Boeufs four miles down the Mississippi from New Orleans, he discovered army life to be a horror of "mud, snakes, filth and vermin. Their meat was rancid, their bread crawled with unwelcome visitors, and their drinking water was fouled with camp waste." Soldiers succumbed to dysentery, malaria, exhaustion, and, worst of all, yellow fever, or *el vómito,* as the Spanish called it. Half the soldiers of the brigade were lost to disease or desertion by the time they moved up the river to Natchez a few months later.

On the Mississippi, Scott acquired a lifelong fear of tropical diseases. For his complaining, Wilkinson would call Scott a "vainglorious coxcomb," but the general allowed Scott to ask for a furlough and return to Washington. Unsure he wanted to remain in the army, Scott asked to be sent to Europe to study military methods and training there. He wanted to learn engineering, artillery, tactics—the knowledge and skills that make a professional soldier. It would be his lifelong passion to create a professional army on the model of those in Britain, France, and Prussia. He saw military science as an intellectual discipline and he meant to be a scholar of war.

Scott's military education was only beginning. Peacetime armies are snake nests of rivalry and intrigue. With no war to fight, soldiers tend to create conflicts among themselves. Because Scott had personally advanced money to his men and then deducted the loans from their pay, he found himself charged with embezzlement. The charge may well have come from the scheming Wilkinson who often took revenge on his critics with such methods. Scott was charged not only with misappropriation of funds but with slandering his commanding officer and mutiny.

After a trial that began January 6, 1810, and dragged on for a month, Scott was declared innocent of embezzlement and mutiny but guilty of making derogatory statements about Wilkinson. The court suspended

Thomas Jefferson.
Painting by Charles Wilson Peale. Ca. 1791.
(Courtesy Independence National Historical Park,
Philadelphia, Pennsylvania)

Andrew Jackson.
Painting by Thomas Sully. 1824.
(Courtesy Wikimedia Commons)

Johnny Appleseed.
Engraving. *Harper's
New Monthly Magazine,*
November, 1871.
*(Courtesy Cornell
University Library)*

David Crockett.
Engraving by Chiles
and Lehman of
portrait by Samuel
Stillman Osgood. 1834.
*(Courtesy Tennessee State
Library and Archives)*

Sam Houston.
Miniature by unknown artist.
1837–38.
*(Courtesy Tennessee State
Library and Archives)*

General Antonio Lopez de Santa Anna.
Engraving. Ca. 1835.
(Courtesy Wikimedia Commons)

Joel R. Poinsett.
Painting by unknown artist. Ca. 1830s.
(Courtesy Department of the Army)

James K. Polk.
Painting by G.P.A. Healy.
Ca. 1846.
*(Courtesy James K. Polk
Memorial Association,
Columbia, Tennessee)*

General Zachary Taylor.
Photograph. Ca. 1848.
*(Courtesy Department
of the Army)*

General Winfield Scott.
Oil on canvas by
Minor K. Kellogg. 1851.
Accession # 1933.5.
(Collection of the New-
York Historical Society)

Manuel de la Peña y Peña.
Mexican president and statesman.
Engraving. Date Unknown.
(Courtesy Wikimedia Commons)

General Stephen Watts Kearny.
Photograph. Date unknown. *(Courtesy
Department of the Army)*

Kit Carson and John C. Frémont. Photograph. Ca. 1848. *(Courtesy Wikimedia Commons)*

Andres Pico, Mexican Commander at San Pasqual, December 6–7. Photograph. 1846. *(Courtesy Wikimedia Commons)*

Nicholas P. Trist. Photograph by Mathew B. Brady. Ca. 1860. *(Courtesy Wikimedia Commons)*

John Quincy Adams.
Painting after John Singleton Copley. 1795.
(Courtesy Adams National Historical Park, Quincy, Massachusetts)

him from all duties and pay for a year. In his year of leisure Scott fought a duel (in which he received a minor wound on the top of his head), then set himself to study British military manuals. Pursuing a military education few in America had acquired, he studied drill, fortification, maneuver, entrenchment, how to meet a flanking action, and how "to form a hollow square in the face of a cavalry charge." Scott committed himself to the scientific study of war, but he also saw war as an art—an aristocratic art.

As war with Britain loomed, he reasoned, "Should war come at last, my enthusiasm will be rekindled; *and then, who knows . . . I may yet write my history with a sword?*" When the War of 1812 began, Scott returned from a posting in Louisiana in time to run the British blockade of the Chesapeake and find himself promoted two ranks to lieutenant colonel at the age of twenty-six. Perhaps because of his height, his manner, his bearing, as well as his real gifts for leadership, Scott, like Washington before him, had a way of turning near defeats and partial victories into glory for himself. It was as though people wanted to remember him as a hero. It was as though he was able to project his image of himself onto those around him. In the War of 1812 Lieutenant Colonel Scott was sent to the Niagara Frontier between Lake Erie and Lake Ontario. His first assignment was to guard the shipyard at Black Rock where ships were being built by both the British and the Americans to patrol the Great Lakes to the west.

One of Scott's first successes was capturing two British ships, the *Caledonia* and the *Detroit,* in the dead of night and freeing thirty American prisoners on the ships who had been taken when William Hull surrendered Fort Detroit without a fight. After a string of humiliating American defeats, this success made Scott a hero. Even though in the next few months Scott would bungle several opportunities to defeat the British on the Niagara Frontier, what would be remembered was his bold attack on the British positions in the dark.

At Queenston on the Canadian side below Niagara Falls, Scott and his men took an artillery placement on top of a hill, but they were soon surrounded by the British infantry. Later folklore had Scott shouting, "In a moment the shock must come, and there is no retreat . . . Let us then die . . . arms in hand . . . Those who follow will avenge our fall." The

New York militia watched from the other side of the river in Lewiston but refused, or were not allowed, to risk a crossing to come to the aid of Scott's regulars. Throughout much of his career, Scott would be skeptical of the value of "citizen soldiers," who lacked training and discipline. Lieutenant Colonel Scott had no choice but to surrender. Though taken prisoner at Queenston Heights, Scott was remembered for his boldness there.

While a prisoner, Scott was attacked by two Indians but saved by a British officer. He was well treated and soon released on parole, agreeing not to fight again until a British officer held by the Americans was released in his place. Scott returned to Washington, where he lobbied for more support for his men on the frontier, and he found himself a celebrity, the Hero of Queenston Heights, and a full colonel. He was ordered to return to Niagara, to command the Second Artillery under Major General Henry Dearborn.

Becoming Dearborn's chief of staff, Scott reorganized the division. Planning an attack on the British across the Niagara River, he sought to take advantage of the element of surprise. It was also important to coordinate army actions with the navy boats commanded by young Oliver Hazard Perry. Scott made sure that adequate ammunition and equipment were brought forward, and he planned the precise movements of all his units. He already carried with him everywhere a portable library of military history and tactical manuals, and biographies, and strongly believed that the most effective fighting methods were offensive, rarely defensive.

The surprise attack forced the British to abandon Fort George. Scott pursued the fleeing redcoats, but he was ordered by Brigadier General John P. Boyd to break off the chase, and the British retreated safely to Burlington Heights on Lake Ontario. Dearborn praised Scott's victory, but Scott himself complained that had he been allowed to pursue the British, he could have destroyed the remnants of their army.

By the time General Dearborn decided to attack the British at Burlington Heights, they had regrouped and were ready for him. The Americans suffered one humiliating defeat after another. Scott led some minor attacks and sailed across Lake Ontario to burn York (later Toronto). In retaliation, the British would later set fire to Washington, D.C. While many of the small raids were successful, they were not the glorious battles Scott hoped for. He later wrote of himself, "It was his ambition to conduct sieges and command in open fields, serried lines and columns."

To Scott's astonishment, his old enemy James Wilkinson was sent to take command of the Niagara Frontier. Wilkinson planned a foolish assault on Montréal but excluded Scott from the invading force, leaving him behind to hold and reinforce Fort George. When, however, the British withdrew from the area after William Henry Harrison's victory at the Battle of the Thames on October 5, 1813, Scott believed it his duty to join Wilkinson's expedition with the eight hundred men who served under him. Thus, on November 7, 1813, Scott led a battalion to attack the British forces guarding a bridge at Hoople's Creek, near Utica, New York. In this engagement Scott positioned a few of his men in front of the enemy to draw their fire, while he sent the majority of his force to cross the stream at a ford a mile away to attack the British from behind. It was a tactic he would use again and again in his long career, especially in the Mexican War at Cerro Gordo and Contreras. The maneuver was not completely successful at Hoople's Creek, but it served as a good practice run for the future tactician.

Scott was saved from the failure to take Montréal by being summoned to Washington by President Madison himself to report on the disasters along the northern frontier. While he was conferring with the president and John Armstrong, secretary of war, news arrived that the Niagara Frontier had collapsed. Everyone seemed to forget that Scott had abandoned Fort George, which was now in British hands. As the hero of Queenston Heights, he was sent back to take command in the region as a brigadier general, at the age of twenty-seven. The stars had begun to fall on Winfield Scott.

Arriving in Buffalo on April 7, 1814, he established one of the first training camps in the American army at Flint Hill, a little west of the burned-out Buffalo. There he drilled his sixteen hundred men for ten hours every day for two months. He instructed them, Allan Peskin tells us, in "the service of outposts, night patrols, guards, and sentinels organized; a system of sanitary police, including kitchens, etc . . . rules of civility, etiquette, courtesy—the indispensable outworks of subordination . . . and the tactical instruction of each arm." Scott hoped to teach discipline through professional pride more than punishment. He required the men to salute. He organized a network of spies in the region. He was especially concerned about the health of his men and ordered supplies of wholesome bread and clean kitchens far from latrines. Efforts were made to supply clean drinking water, and the men were ordered to bathe three times each week. Sickness and death from disease decreased. Everybody could see that strict discipline paid off. And the drilling was relentless. A captain later reported, "General Scott drills and damns, drills and damns, and drills again." While it is well known that drill teaches recruits to follow orders without question, it is also a fact that extensive drill gives would-be soldiers a sense of pride in themselves and, more important, a sense of pride in themselves as a unit.

Compared with the British, the American armies were undisciplined, badly trained, and undersupplied. Scott saw that the army of the United States desperately needed an instruction manual. He had no time to prepare such a guidebook at Flint Hill, but he knew what he would write in such a book when the opportunity came. He first trained his officers and then trained his men so relentlessly they began to look forward to actual battle, both to prove themselves and to escape the rigors of drilling.

With his brigade at a pitch of readiness, Scott waited for orders to move. Finally he was given permission to proceed under General Brown to take Fort Erie on the Canadian side of the river and push on to Chippewa. The fort was taken July 3, 1814, without much resistance, but Scott allowed himself to accept an invitation to a fine breakfast at a local home and was almost captured by alerted British soldiers. He was later unable to believe his wealthy hostess had betrayed him.

Deploying his men on a plain near the Niagara River and the mouth of the Chippewa River on July 5, 1814, Scott found the months of training paid off as his troops fought the enemy with cool precision. The British were astonished to confront real soldiers, not scruffy militiamen. Forming his men into a V shape Scott drew the British in until they were effectively caught in a crossfire. The British fell like grass before a scythe. The survivors broke rank and ran.

The Battle of Chippewa was won, but it was not a rout. British reserves on the flanks prevented the Americans from pursuing the fleeing infantry as it crossed the Chippewa River. Artillery on the far bank kept

Scott and his men from crossing the stream. But the Americans held the field. The British had lost 148 dead and 320 wounded. American rifles and muskets had picked off many redcoat officers. The Americans losses were sixty killed, 248 wounded, and nineteen missing. It was an expensive battle for both sides, but the victory inspired the American army with new confidence, and inspired the nation with new hope after the many defeats suffered in the war.

In the context of the series of blunders that we call the War of 1812, Scott's victory on the Chippewa appeared momentous. Victory celebrations broke out across the United States, and Scott's fame soared. General Brown reported, "Brig.-gen. Scott is entitled to the highest praise our country can bestow—to him more than any other man am I indebted for the victory of the 5th of July. His brigade covered itself with glory."

On the Niagara Frontier some of Scott's mistakes were made because he failed to send scouts to reconnoiter and probe the area. At Niagara he more than once stumbled on a British army he should have known was practically under his nose. One of the best examples of Scott's scouting blindness at this time (in combination with his extraordinary commanding leadership) is the Battle of Lundy's Lane, near Chippewa, on July 25, 1814, where he blundered into a large British army just as it was about to be joined by even more reinforcements. Scott should have known that both units were in the area. Rather than withdraw to safety, Scott ordered his men into battle formation. British artillery occupied a hill overlooking the wide field between the two armies. Scott's instinct was always to advance, not to pull back. He reasoned that an aggressive attack might convince General Phineas Riall, the British commander, that Scott's forces were backed up by the larger American army under Brown.

Pinned down by heavy artillery fire from the hill, Scott could not advance, and he refused to retreat. Luckily Major Thomas S. Jesup arrived near dark and attacked the British left flank in a surprise advance from the cover of a grove of trees. General Riall himself was taken prisoner. And then General Brown, having heard the firing of the British cannons, arrived with his reinforcements and took the place of Scott's brigade, which had sustained appalling losses. Both the British and the Americans claimed victory after the slaughter at Lundy's Lane, but most historians see it as a "tactical draw." The British lost 878 and the Americans 860.

But the battle gave a much-needed boost to American morale and made Winfield Scott even more of a national hero. He was given a brevet promotion to major general.

Awarded a gold medal by Congress and commemorative swords by Virginia and New York, Scott was now the outstanding hero of the war. Boys were named in his honor, as well as counties and townships across the nation. Scott's mistakes were forgotten by all except his enemies. He was awarded an honorary degree by Princeton and treated in Philadelphia for his wounds by the famous doctor, actually named, Dr. Physick. Before he could return to the field a peace treaty was signed at Ghent in Belgium on December 24, 1814.

And then Andrew Jackson defeated the British at New Orleans on January 8, 1815, and became a hero surpassing in fame, in his own day, even Winfield Scott.

———

IN PEACETIME the young major general had set about to create a professional army for the United States, something the country had never had. Scott has been described as the first military technocrat. The historian Daniel Walker Howe praises in particular Scott's "recognition of the importance of logistics, training, and staff work, his meticulous attention to detail." Scott saw the military as "a calling, not an occupation." With a drastically reduced postwar army, suffering the intrigues and backstabbing of any peacetime force, he compiled the manual for the infantry he had been planning. The resulting *Tactics* became the guidebook for the army for decades to come. In his *General Regulations for the Army,* Scott urged better treatment for enlisted men. For all his love of pomp and strict organization, there was a kindness and generosity, even a sentimental side, to Scott, especially toward subordinates. He defined discipline as "a gradual and universal subordination . . . in the strictest observance of duty. It requires that enlisted soldiers shall be treated with particular kindness and humanity, that punishments, sometimes unavoidable, shall be strictly conformable to martial law."

Scott understood the army was both the promoter and main client of the new industrial culture. The army was a corporation and needed the structure and planning of a corporation. It was the biggest single business in the country and Winfield Scott seemed to understand the crucial role the military would play in the economic future of the nation. The young general was sent to France to observe military practice and organization there, and his knowledge of French proved a distinct advantage. In France he met a number of European leaders, acquired a passion for French cooking, and visited the aged Lafayette. Scott himself would become an expert cook and enjoyed demonstrating his culinary skills for guests.

When he returned home Scott continued courting the heiress Maria Mayo of Richmond, finally overcoming her resistance and marrying her in 1816. Considered one of the belles of her time, Maria was a friend of First Lady Dolley Madison. Opinion has been divided about how happy a marriage theirs was. What is certain is that they had seven children, several of whom died young. Maria and the children spent long vacations in Europe without Winfield, sometimes of several years duration.

As the greatest American hero after Andrew Jackson, married to a rich and attractive woman, one would expect Scott to be happy in the years after the War of 1812. But in fact it was a period of anxiety and uncertainty. Maria's family did not support the general's household as he had expected, and on his general's salary he found it hard to maintain Maria's lavish lifestyle. For all his high connections with the leaders of the day, Scott seemed lost and searching for a new direction in his life. Like many great soldiers, he was out of his element in peacetime. He considered returning to the practice of law, or running for public office. He seemed to pick quarrels without intending to and angered Andrew Jackson by lecturing him in a condescending way about military protocol. Jackson had a fearsome will and pride and a long memory. While Scott was a man who got over his piques and acted generously toward former foes, men like Jackson and Polk had less forgiving natures and could wait years to take revenge for a snub. Where other leaders acted with cool cunning and false friendliness, Scott would express his irritation and then put it all behind him. One cannot help but admire this straightforwardness and candor, as did most of the men who served under him. Old Fuss and Feathers could be silly, as indeed most of us can, but there was far more to him than the silliness. Among the Henry Clays and John C. Calhouns and James K. Polks of the day, the general was out of his political depth. And he seems a breath of fresh air in a foul atmosphere.

One of Scott's weaknesses was that when angered he took his pen and wrote page after page of argument and rebuttal and self-defense. He did not know when to stop. It was a trait he shared with a similarly arrogant, opinionated, and honest Virginian, Nicholas P. Trist. It was a trait that would make the two of them enemies at a very important time, before they became the most devoted of friends.

One of Scott's substantial virtues was his ability to profit from his mistakes. This willingness to learn may be one of the most essential features of greatness. Since we all repeatedly make mistakes, it is only those who can go forward and try not to make them again who achieve the most. When lectured by Lafayette on obedience to superiors, Scott judiciously retreated from his confrontation with the administration of Andrew Jackson and survived in his rank to fight another day.

In the 1830s, Scott was most effective as a diplomat, settling disputes with the British along the Canadian border at Niagara and in Maine. It was as though he had acquired a new patience and wisdom. In the negotiations over the boundary at Niagara, Scott demonstrated an extraordinary ability to find common ground in a dispute. As Daniel Walker Howe tells us, "By sheer energy and willpower Scott calmed the public and persuaded [Stephen] Van Rensselaer to evacuate his island bastion, though at one point the general had to face down an angry American crowd by drawing a line and telling them they would cross it only over his dead body." Scott discovered in himself a special ability to apologize and soothe tempers, not inflame them. More sympathetic with the North in the debate over the Tariff of 1832, he sided with the Unionists in the debate over nullification. His diplomatic talents surfaced when dealing with the most explosive issues. Because he favored a strong federal government he became a Whig.

As mentioned before, Scott was never an effective Indian fighter. Sent to Florida in the Seminole War of 1836 he did not disgrace himself, but he did not distinguish himself either. Elusive native warriors scattered throughout the swamps and hammock country of central Florida, in a climate of malaria and yellow fever, were not his kind of foe. In the Black

Hawk War, because of an outbreak of cholera, Scott managed to miss the most significant action. But he was effective in negotiating the peace.

Nothing in Scott's makeup or education helped him in wilderness fighting. He appeared tone-deaf and a little lost when sent to confront native forces. In fighting the rebellious Creeks, he ended up quarreling mostly with rival generals. Perhaps the least pleasant of all Scott's assignments in the 1830s was the rounding up of the Cherokees in the removal that led to the Trail of Tears. Cherokees had been removing to land grants in the West for two decades, with the help of the government. But the Jackson administration had made a treaty with some native leaders who did not represent the majority to send the remaining members of the Cherokee Nation to the Arkansas Territory. Whites were greedy for the Cherokee lands, houses, and cattle and other livestock.

It was the Reverend J. F. Schermerhorn who first made a treaty with a few of the Cherokees to take their lands in the East in exchange for land in Indian Territory. But that treaty was so obviously shunned by most of the Cherokee leaders that even Andrew Jackson rejected it. "The treaty, if concluded at all, must be procured on fair and open terms . . . without sacrificing the interest of the whole to the cupidity of a few," Old Hickory said. When the treaty was revised and brought to the floor of the House many, including David Crockett, opposed it. John Ridge and Elias Boudinot, the two Cherokee chiefs who represented mostly mixed bloods and slave owners, and had in December 1835 signed the Treaty of New Echota, agreeing to removal, were later assassinated in the West.

In the words of Horace Kephart, "The Cherokees were the mountaineers of the South. Like all highlanders, of whatever race, they were passionately attached to the rugged but healthful and picturesque land that gave them birth. The promise of a far away wilderness, encompassed and disputed by savages, in exchange for their ancient villages and cultivated fields, held no allurements for a people that was prosperous in the arts of peace and asked nothing better than to be let alone." The Cherokees had in mind a very different future for themselves than the one planned by the U.S. government.

In the period when they were being rounded up for removal, the Cherokees had been forced to give up their arms by the U.S. Army and were therefore vulnerable to attacks by hostile whites who wanted their land and cattle. A group of these Indians, led by Chief Yonaguska, slipped away into the high mountains. They were allowed to stay in the Smokies after one of the band, named Tsali (Charley), who had killed a soldier, turned himself in to be executed on the condition that the rest of the band be left alone. Those Indians hiding out in the high gaps and ridges lived on nuts and acorns when they could find them and on "toads, snakes, insects, berries, and the inner bark of trees," when they could not. Scott made every effort to carry out his unwelcome duties in a humane, gentle way. He threatened severe punishment for any soldier who mistreated a Cherokee. Beyond Scott's control, Georgia militiamen and local citizens harassed the Cherokees brutally, seizing their property as the Cherokees were driven into camps. Scott chose to ignore the civilian atrocities and go ahead with his duties. One Georgia officer would later say, "I fought through the civil war and have seen men shot to pieces and slaughtered by the thousands, but the Cherokee removal was the cruelest work I ever knew."

A sad fact of the Cherokee removal was that many of the more prosperous and ambitious of that nation had already gone to the Arkansas Territory between 1817 and 1836 and taken up large land grants there. Most had gone by steamboat down the Tennessee River, down the Ohio, down the Mississippi, then up the powerful Arkansas River to Little Rock, or as far as the boat could struggle against the formidable current. The twelve thousand Cherokees left were obviously those most reluctant to give up their traditional lands and way of life. These remaining Cherokees refused to budge until forced by the U.S. Army. Andrew Jackson was already out of office by then, but the policy he had set in motion was carried through to its brutal conclusion. It was a sorry episode in American history and probably the sorriest commission Scott was ever given.

Scott attempted to put the arrangements into the hands of the Cherokee leaders themselves, but Jackson and the Democrats saw that as a Whig plot, probably instigated by Henry Clay to embarrass Van Buren's administration. On the journey west, which the Cherokees called the Trail of Tears, as many as four thousand of their nation would die. Those in the final removal were among the poorest and most isolated of the Cherokee Nation, therefore the most vulnerable to disease and exposure and bad weather that helped turn the trek into a horror story. The dislocation broke the spirit as well as the health of many. Luckily for Scott, he was called away to another assignment just as the sad journey to the West began. That was bad luck for the Cherokees because Scott, with his tested organizational ability and kindness toward those in his charge, would no doubt have prevented some of the atrocities and suffering along the way.

Trouble had again broken out along the border with Canada in the Aroostook Valley between Maine and New Brunswick. Traveling for days in stage coaches and in sleighs, without sleeping, Scott negotiated with British officials and put on civilian clothes to wine and dine Maine legislators until they were persuaded to back away from their angry stance on the border dispute. Scott knew well the power of good food and drink and friendly chat to soothe tempers. Again a piece of incredible luck dropped into Scott's lap. The governor of New Brunswick, Major General Sir John Harvey, was the officer whose personal property Scott had saved from fire and returned after the Americans burned York in 1813. The two men had exchanged friendly letters ever since.

Working as an intermediary between Governor John Fairfield of Maine and Governor Harvey, Scott brought the Maine–New Brunswick boundary quarrel to a peaceful resolution. Diplomacy is not a talent we usually associate with generalship, but Scott was one of the most successful negotiators of his time. Even his penchant for elevated and sometimes pompous language served him well on those occasions. After all, it was the language of international diplomacy. "I see no reason to apprehend another cause of serious misunderstanding between the two portions of the great Anglo-Saxon race," Scott wrote to Harvey. "The ties of common blood, language, civil liberty, laws, customs, manners, interests must, in a reasonable period . . . work out a strong compact of reciprocal feelings."

Scott came to be called the Great Pacificator. It is hard to think of a finer title for a decorated soldier and war hero. Scott genuinely hated bloodshed in war and loved to negotiate peace. He was persuaded to run for the Whig nomination, for president in 1840 but was apparently simply used as a stalking horse for William Henry Harrison, hero of the war with the Shawnees and Tecumseh at the Battle of Tippecanoe River in

1811. Harrison won the nomination and "Tippecanoe and Tyler Too" became the slogan in the campaign that catapulted Harrison to the White House. When the old general died within a few weeks of his inauguration, the relatively unknown John Tyler served out the rest of his term.

While he did not win the White House, Scott was made a full major general and general in chief of the army on July 5, 1841. As he set about to organize the peacetime army for efficiency and effectiveness, he stepped on many toes and acquired even more of a reputation for vanity, ambition, pomposity, and arrogance. But those who knew him best knew that was only part of the story, and those who served under Scott, while conceding his flaws, usually spoke of him with true affection. An aide would recall, "But I did see a man, not free from defects of temper, but trying to be just—a man absolutely intolerant of wrong when the wrong was clearly to be seen—as free from personal vanity as any man of the world I have ever met, but so singularly frank and confiding to those whom he trusted that the absence of that reticence of suspicion—which we so generally see—gave occasion to charges of vanity and conceit."

Of Scott's vanity there is no doubt. Towering over virtually everyone around him, he liked to insist that he was six feet four and one-quarter inch, not a mere six feet four. And he liked to be described as "erect as an Indian chief." Grant as a young officer thought Scott "the finest specimen of manhood my eyes had ever beheld, and the most to be envied." Scott liked to repeat the stories of his feats in battle as a young man so often that those around him would wink and nudge each other behind his back. But then most old soldiers do repeat such stories and in Scott's case they were true. And Scott would even concede to his aides from time to time, "I sometimes say silly things."

Yet Scott could have a tantrum if a fellow officer spoke or wrote an ungrammatical sentence or misspelled a word. He adhered to British spelling and he demanded that soldiers on duty always be dressed in proper attire, including coats. He ordered for himself splendid uniforms from the best tailors and expected other officers to do the same. He was inordinately fond of whist and chess. When he drank a glass of water he liked it inspired with a teaspoon of gin, and his chewing tobacco had to be preserved "at a certain moisture." An Episcopalian, Scott was not overly devout, but he tried to read some of the Bible every day. And

Scott opposed slavery and believed the institution could be phased out gradually.

———

SCOTT PROFESSED to admire Thomas Jefferson more than any other leader. He tried to occupy a middle ground in the growing debate between the North and the South, though he found, like many others, that increasingly there really was no middle ground. He shared with Andrew Jackson a passionate loyalty to the Union and remained loyal to Jackson even after Old Hickory humiliated him by recommending that Scott be court-martialed for insubordination in the Seminole War in 1836. He and almost everyone else felt blindsided when James K. Polk became the Democratic candidate and then president in the election of 1844. Scott described Polk as a man whose "little strength lay in the most odious elements of human character—*cunning and hypocrisy.*" But whatever he thought of Polk, the new president was a man he would have to reckon with.

The courtly, outgoing, generous Whig Winfield Scott, was anathema to Polk from first to last. Scott opposed going to war with Mexico, but after the clash with Mexican troops on the Rio Grande, he believed the United States had no choice but to defend its claimed territory. It would have been logical to send Scott, a proven diplomat as well as soldier, to deal with the stubborn neighbor to the south. Such an effort might well have prevented the Mexican War and achieved most of Polk's desired results. But fearing a success by Old Fuss and Feathers might land the general in the White House in the next election, Polk chose Zachary Taylor as the lesser evil. Taylor was the opposite of Scott in most ways, often not even wearing a uniform while on duty, familiar with his men. Taylor was a backwoods fighter like Jackson, informal, improvising his strategy on the spot. Grant, who served under both generals in Mexico, admired them both. "Both were pleasant to serve under—Taylor was pleasant to serve with," Grant later wrote.

In theory Mexico was better prepared for war than the United States. With an army of about thirty-two thousand men, the Mexicans were experienced fighters, both from their revolution with Spain a quarter century earlier and their many internal conflicts. In fact, many European observers assumed the unproven U.S. forces had little chance to prevail in a war with Mexico. Since the humiliations of the War of 1812 the Americans had mostly fought Indians.

The logic of sending Scott to deal with the Mexicans was so overwhelming that Polk called him to the White House and offered him the command. Then Democrats persuaded the president to withdraw the offer and appoint Zachary Taylor instead. Scott infuriated Polk and his cabinet by writing to Secretary of War William Marcy in his face-saving letter, "My explicit meaning is—that I do not desire to place myself in the most perilous of all positions—*a fire upon my rear from Washington, and the fire, in front, from the Mexicans.*" It was nothing less than the truth but a truth he might well have kept to himself and not stated for the eyes of the spiteful Polk.

Angry as he was when he saw Scott's letter, Polk could do little to retaliate. Scott was the general in chief of the army in a desperate time and could not easily be fired for comments (all too true) made in a letter the president was not intended to see. But he did have Marcy send a letter of stiff reprimand to Scott, informing him again that he would not be sent to Mexico. In return, Scott wrote one of his long letters explaining his earlier words, but it did no good. Scott would stay at his desk in Washington while Taylor won victories in Mexico.

But the Scott of 1846 was not the Scott of 1836 or 1816. "Drawing upon reserves of patience and humility, which his younger self would not have been able to muster, he soldiered on at his desk while awaiting a fresh turn of fortune's wheel," Scott's biographer Allan Peskin explains. Scott had lived long enough to know that even humiliations can turn into opportunities and that talent, dedication, and persistence may win out in the end. Staying at his desk almost around the clock, Scott worked harder even than Polk, studying the challenges and possibilities of the conflict with Mexico. Methodically Scott drew up a proposal to win the conflict with Mexico by taking Veracruz on the Gulf coast and following Cortés's path over the mountains toward the city of Mexico. William H. Prescott's *History of the Conquest of Mexico* had been published to much acclaim in 1843 and many Americans were now familiar with Cortés's colorful, dramatic, bloody and victorious campaign against Montezuma. It is quite possible that Prescott's classic romantic best seller actually inspired some in government as well as the public at large to think of conquering the Halls of Montezuma.

Scott hoped that Mexico would surrender without the Americans having to occupy Montezuma's city. A show of force in the south should bring them to the negotiating table. Because yellow fever was so common along the coast of Mexico in summer, any campaign had to be timed to reach the mountains inland by early spring or risk losing hundreds of men to the fever. Veracruz was guarded by the fortress of San Juan de Ulúa, thought by many experts to be impregnable. Scott proposed attacking the city early in 1847 and, as soon as the port was secured, marching west along the ancient National Highway, skirting north of the great snowcapped volcano Orizaba.

In his diary Polk wrote, "The truth is, neither Taylor nor Scott are fit for the command of the army." Polk was passing judgment, in the case of Scott, on one of the outstanding soldiers in American history. But even Polk recognized that of the two generals Scott was the more accomplished and intelligent leader. When Scott was called to the White House and the president suggested the two men put aside their differences and proceed with Scott's plan with Scott himself commanding in Mexico, the general was so moved tears came into his eyes. Polk recorded in his diary that Scott was "the most delighted man I have seen in a long time."

Scott now had the chance he had been preparing himself for all his life. For this moment he had endured wounds and insults, studied the methods of classical and modern armies, drilled thousands of raw soldiers, taken tongue lashings and dressings down from superiors. He was willing to believe that Polk's expressions of confidence and goodwill were genuine and to tell Secretary of War Marcy that he had put aside his Whig sympathies. "I have felt very like a Polk-man." Scott would soon find out Polk had not changed his opinion of him, and the president for his part was amused by Scott's credulous, wholehearted sentiment.

Scott had no sooner departed for Mexico than Polk was hoping to get Congress to make Thomas Hart Benton a three-star general who would assume overall command in Mexico. Benton's military experience was limited at best. Marcy would later tell an interviewer that Polk had only gone "through the motions to flatter Benton and retain his political support." But whatever the president's intentions, the machinations were painful and offensive to Scott as he prepared his campaign. Polk could think only politically, not militarily. That he would even consider taking command out of the hands of one of the ablest generals in modern history, for fear he might run for president, and hand it over to a politician with little if any military experience suggests a small man, frightened by the truth and dedicated to politics and not to his country. More than anything he ever did, Polk's conduct toward Winfield Scott in Mexico tarnishes his legacy as a leader and as a man. Perhaps we should just say Polk was blinded by political ambition and leave it at that.

While Polk and his cabinet lamented that Scott might win glory for himself in Mexico, Marcy reassured them, "Before the war is ended we can easily take the wind out of his sails—he is sure to give us the opportunity."

On his way to Veracruz, Scott requisitioned many of Taylor's forces in the north of Mexico, leaving Taylor just enough men to hold his position there. Scott treated Taylor with respect and pronounced diplomacy, writing to him that he understood that the reassignment of his men "will be infinitely painful to you, and for that reason, distressing to me. But I rely upon your patriotism to submit to the temporary sacrifices with cheerfulness." Taylor was indeed furious to be passed over for the campaign in the south, but with his growing fame back home he already had his eye on Pennsylvania Avenue and there was little Polk and the Democrats could do to stop him.

Taylor refused to meet Scott face-to-face at Camargo on January 3, 1847. Scott then headed south for Veracruz, but his letter to Taylor describing his plans for the campaign somehow went astray and ended up in Santa Anna's hands. Now the enemy knew where he was going and what he planned to do when he got there. To make matters worse, several hundred American soldiers, of which many were Irish Catholic immigrants, deserted in Mexico and joined the Mexican army.

Even before he reached Veracruz, Scott knew Polk and his cabinet were undercutting his efforts. The president refused to let Scott convene a court martial to try the officers who had let the letter to Taylor fall into Mexican hands. And less than half of the ships, men, and equipment promised to Scott were actually sent to him.

One of Scott's most important decisions in the Mexican campaign was General Order No. 20, which on February 19, 1847, imposed martial law to protect both his soldiers and the citizens of Mexico. Timothy D. Johnson has described how Scott knew that looting and the brutality of soldiers toward civilians had ensured Napoleon's defeat in the Peninsula Campaign. By declaring martial law and punishing any soldiers who looted or assaulted civilians, Scott saved his army from extensive guerilla fighting and enabled his men to help sustain themselves on supplies bought in the towns they passed through. He believed a firm but diplomatic policy could end the war without unnecessary killing.

Remembering his experience on the Great Lakes in the War of 1812, Scott knew the importance of coordinating his own forces with the navy, and took special pains to cooperate with Commodore David Conner and his staff to plan the landing at Veracruz. With Lieutenant George M. Totten, Scott designed a landing craft to carry men and ordnance to the beach. The flat-bottom "surf boats" came in three sizes that fit one inside the other for easier transport. Built by a firm near Philadelphia, the boats cost $795 each, but of the 141 ordered only 67 were ever delivered.

Scott's flotilla assembled at the island of Lobos, more than a hundred miles from Veracruz. It was several weeks before all the regiments of regulars and volunteers arrived. While Scott had always been skeptical of the value of volunteers, he would discover in Mexico that those units could perform, once seasoned, about as well as the regulars.

Scott's senior officers included Major General William Jackson Worth, an old friend who had become increasingly jealous of Scott and was suffering from emotional instability. Worth had served, as we have seen, with Taylor in northern Mexico. Brigadier General David S. Twiggs was not obsessed with personal ambition, but he was a rough bear of a man, known for the verve of his profanity. Fellow officers joked that Twiggs knew only one maneuver, and that was to attack. Major General Robert Patterson, because of illness, would soon be replaced by Polk's former law partner from Nashville, Gideon Pillow. Pillow had little military experience or talent, but he was a spy for Polk and would libel Scott and most of the other effective officers in Mexico in his letters to the president. The historian David A. Clary has written, "Pillow thought the United States faced two enemies, the lesser one Mexico, the greater the Whig Party."

Pillow seems to have had a special gift for intrigue and lying, though Scott, oddly, found in him no "malignity." William Tecumseh Sherman, who served as a lieutenant in Mexico, would later describe Pillow as "a mass of vanity, conceit, ignorance, ambition and want of truth." John A. Quitman and James Shields commanded brigades of volunteers and against Scott's expectations they would prove to be able men and worthy soldiers. One of Scott's finest marks of character was his willingness to change his opinion of those he served with and to see the best in his men.

Leaving Lobos on March 2, 1847, Scott's armada set sail, more than a hundred vessels whose sails appeared to one witness like "a great white cloud." Four days later they reached the island of Anton Lizardo, only two miles south of Veracruz. Because of the imposing fortress in the harbor, Veracruz was often called "the Gibraltar of Mexico." Scott did not plan to attack the fort directly. While inspecting the defenses of the city from a steamer, Scott and his staff were fired on. On the boat, which quickly withdrew out of range, were the general's staff as well as young Robert E. Lee, Joseph E. Johnston, P. G. T. Beauregard, and George Meade.

The fortress on the island in the harbor, called San Juan de Ulúa, was the bastion that had been taken by the French in the so-called Pastry War of 1838. France had attacked Mexico to claim a six hundred thousand peso debt owed to French merchants, including a pastry company. It was in the confrontation with the French that Santa Anna lost a leg, the leg that was later buried with great ceremony at the cathedral in Mexico City. Though the Mexicans claimed victory in that conflict, they paid up the six hundred thousand pesos and the French sailed away. During that disturbance, riots had broken out in Mexico City as crowds shouted, "Death to the Anglo-Saxons and Jews!"

Using the tactics he had studied all his life, Scott chose Collado Beach three miles south of Veracruz for his landing site. Scott's approach was to avoid the place of the enemy's strength and attack where he was weaker. As the historian Timothy D. Johnson explains, Scott almost always chose turning movements rather than frontal assaults. "A turning movement occurs when a commander succeeds in positioning a part of his force such that it threatens the otherwise secure rear area of an opposing army.

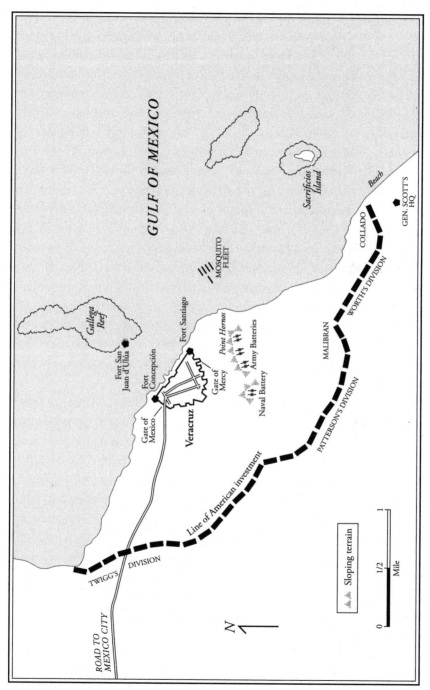

Battle of Veracruz, April–May 1847

Throughout the campaign, Scott took the path of least resistance, preferring to out-think and out-maneuver his opponent instead of trying to
pound him into submission on the battlefield." The "surf boats" were
loaded on the beach twelve miles farther south and given numbers to
match the platoons they would carry. Scott organized the landing to go
like clockwork, each segment falling into place. The landing craft were
towed forward into position in the assigned order, and the bands played
as troops and supplies were rowed ashore on March 9, 1847.

General Worth, who expected Santa Anna to be waiting for them
behind the dunes—after all the Mexicans knew their plans—led his
brigade with bayonets fixed through deep sand to the top of a dune, but
found nobody there. Instead of confronting Scott at Vera Cruz, Santa
Anna had moved north to defeat Taylor's diminished forces at Monterrey, only to be turned back himself at Buena Vista. For all his charm,
duplicity and resiliency, Santa Anna was perhaps his own worst enemy, as
he seemed determined to prove repeatedly. As T. R. Fehrenbach tells us,
Santa Anna "had the quality of being able to convince Mexicans again
and again of his genius and to make them weep at his pronouncements,
while at the same time he could convince foreigners of his honesty in
betraying his country."

General Juan Morales, the Mexican commander at Veracruz, chose
not to confront the Americans on the beach but to keep his men inside
the fortified town. According to Ramón Alcaraz and his team, the Mexican garrison at Veracruz had 3,360 men and the fortress of San Juan de
Ulúa in the harbor 1,030 men. By midnight on March 9, 10,000 American soldiers were camping on the shore in sight of the fortress, and not a
life had been lost. The Americans had executed one of the most successful landings in history, up to that time.

Working in deep, shifting sand among dunes as high as two hundred
feet, Scott's men dug trenches and established outposts in a five-mile
crescent around the city. Veracruz was sealed off by both land and sea.
General Robert Patterson and William Worth urged an immediate assault on the city, but Scott knew that siege was "a slow, scientific process."
A precipitant attack would cost many lives and might still fail. Better to
let isolation and starvation work on the Mexican defenders. Again, Scott
chose to use "brain over brawn."

One aspect of Scott's military ability was his understanding of psychology, as applied to his opponents. Again and again he would be criticized for moving slowly, going the long way around to attack from the least predictable position. Yet most of his delays and feints had the effect of throwing Santa Anna and the Mexicans off balance. Scott was fighting not just with gunpowder and steel and human flesh but by anticipating the plans of his opponents. Scott's junior officers were studying his methods in Mexico and his favorite junior officer, Robert E. Lee, seems to have taken Scott's psychological tactics and strategy to heart and used them later to legendary effect with the Army of Northern Virginia.

Lee was a lieutenant (later a captain and then a major) in the Corps of Engineers and the most promising young officer Scott encountered in Mexico. Scott told Lee and his circle of advisers that he wanted to take Veracruz with as little bloodshed as possible. The methods of siege had been perfected over the centuries. The attackers surrounded the fort and then offered the commander inside a bloodless surrender. When the offer was refused trenches were dug and artillery moved into place. As the bombardment began to have its effect on those inside, the trenches were dug closer, zigzagging toward the walls, leading either to a surrender or the scaling of the walls.

General Morales was expecting relief from Santa Anna, but no such reinforcements came. After the battle of Buena Vista, the generalissimo had returned to Mexico City to quell an insurrection there. Playing faction against faction, Santa Anna proved himself once again Mexico's strong man. But he did not go to the relief of Veracruz.

Scouting out artillery positions with Lieutenant Beauregard, Lee barely escaped an American sentry's bullet that brushed his jacket. By March 22 the guns were in place. After Morales was given another chance to surrender and refused, the bombardment began. The cannon fire throughout the night provided quite a fireworks display but did little damage to the stone fortifications. The walls of Veracruz were fifteen feet high, made of stone, shell, coral, and cement, and there were several fortresses and gun batteries along the walls. Scott had not been given the heavy artillery he had requested so he ordered the big guns on the warships brought ashore and allowed the naval gun crews to continue the bombardment on land. Once again, Scott's habit of cooperating with the navy paid off handsomely, as did his ability to improvise and compromise by letting the sailors fire their own guns on shore.

On March 24, the big naval guns began throwing thirty-two-pound balls and eight-inch exploding shells into Veracruz. A soldier watching the fireworks described it as a "sublime spectacle." By day's end a thirty-six-foot gap had been blasted in the city's wall and the buildings were pocked with hits by cannon balls. Altogether the American guns fired sixty-seven hundred projectiles into Veracruz. The next day European consuls in the city asked for a truce to allow women and children and neutrals to leave, but Scott refused the request saying they had been given ample warning before the attack began. He knew a surrender was much more likely if the noncombatants and foreigners were still in the city. And he demanded complete surrender guessing that the Mexicans did not know he was running low on ammunition.

The Mexicans agreed to negotiate a surrender, but when officers Worth, Totten, and Pillow went to parley in the middle of a sandstorm, they decided the Mexicans were temporizing, possibly still hoping for a rescue by Santa Anna. Knowing little of Mexican manners and little Spanish, the generals did not realize the document the Mexicans presented to them was in fact a surrender couched in face-saving rhetoric. When Scott translated the document, he was so pleased he agreed to let the Mexicans retain their arms and guaranteed the safety of the citizens and property in the city. The Castle of San Juan de Ulúa in the harbor was to be surrendered also.

Scott's generosity was part of his strategy. He still hoped that the conflict could be resolved with a treaty and transfer of land in the north to the United States without more bloodshed. He had taken the impregnable fortress with overwhelming firepower and little loss of American life—thirteen Americans killed and fifty-five wounded. Because so few soldiers were killed, Polk, and indeed the American people, were not so impressed with his extraordinary accomplishment. It is said the best art conceals the artistry. Scott was a commander who often made what he did look easy because he did it with relatively little loss of life and because he gave generous credit to those serving under him.

To the Mexicans, however, the bombardment of Veracruz did not seem so bloodless. The Mexican historian and leader Carlos María de

Bustamante, in *The New Bernal Diaz del Castillo*, would write, "More than five hundred innocents, children, women, and old people, perished under the enemy cannonade." In the telling of history, so much depends on the point of view, and the loser's story—what Robert Graves calls the "Persian Version"—is often quite different from the Greek, or victor's, version. According to Ramón Alcaraz and his fellow historians, the city was virtually rubble. "Not a single house was uninjured. The greater part of them were destroyed." Their account would list six hundred Mexican soldiers wounded and four hundred killed. In the words of the historian David A. Clary, Veracruz after the bombardment "was 'a multitude of horrors, desolation, and sorrow,' the wrecked houses hiding unburied corpses, the city walls collapsing."

The American military had never before occupied a foreign country. Scott was determined to make the campaign a model of correct behavior, with no looting or mistreatment of civilians. In the early days of the campaign, a thief was flogged and a rapist hanged. Also, Scott insisted that his soldiers pay for any goods taken from the Mexicans, though such a rule was hard to enforce. Polk had advised that soldiers seize supplies to support the army, but Scott rejected that suggestion as self-defeating in the long run. Threatened with such seizure, Mexicans could hide or destroy the needed rations. From the time he arrived in Mexico, Scott had in mind pacification, "presenting at once the olive branch & the sword" and winning the cooperation of the people. His policy was aimed at encouraging that cooperation. Scott and his officers attended mass, and the Mexican population, who had feared the Protestant barbarians from the north, were reassured by the display of piety. The respect Scott showed to Mexican culture won a grudging respect for the general from the people of Mexico. Even so, the Mexican resentment of the invasion and destruction of Veracruz inspired some guerilla action against the Americans, and sometimes locals sold the invaders buzzard eggs, claiming they were turkey eggs.

When two deaths from yellow fever occurred on April 9, 1847, Scott knew it was time to march inland to higher ground. The obvious route to Mexico City was the Camino Nacional across the mountains to the west, roughly following the route Cortés had taken to Tenochtitlán. Crossing the steaming *tierra caliente*, the highway skirted north of the volcano

Orizaba, through the cities of Jalapa, Perote, and Puebla in the central plateau, then crossed the high mountains into the Valley of Mexico, ancient stronghold of the Aztecs. Mexico City itself sat surrounded by its lakes and swamps at an elevation of about seventy-four hundred feet above sea level.

Exactly a month after landing on the beach at Collado, Scott's army began marching toward the interior. Twiggs led with his division, followed by Patterson and his volunteers, with Worth bringing up the rear. Worth felt insulted by his placement in the rearguard and never forgave Scott for the perceived slight. Scott's men encountered little resistance as they crossed the sandy plain, though the National Bridge at the Rio Antigua would have been a likely place for Santa Anna to confront them. Meeting so little resistance, Scott wrote Secretary of War Marcy that the war might be over by the summer.

Santa Anna had decided to make his stand near the village of Cerro Gordo, at the Cerro Gordo (Wide Ridge) Pass. He deployed a force of about thirteen thousand along the ridge near the National Highway, with artillery in place on two hills. At first glance the Mexican positions seemed impossible to dislodge. Any Americans who escaped the artillery barrage would then confront the large army lining and commanding the road.

Twiggs and his men walked into this ambush on April 13 and, persuaded by Patterson not to advance further, held the ground until Scott arrived the next day. It was said later Scott's presence "calmed the rising storm, and brought order out of chaos." Mexican historians would later comment on the irony of their apparent initial success at Cerro Gordo: "It is very remarkable that our resistance was greater when they only attempted to try our strength, than when they proposed decidedly to conquer us." For three days Scott studied the terrain and the positions of the Mexican artillery and infantry. He sent out scouting parties led by Beauregard and Robert E. Lee. In the supposedly impenetrable jungle and tangled chaparral on Santa Anna's left flank Lee found a trail that with some clearing and widening could be used to move men and artillery and supplies, with great effort, to attack the Mexicans from behind. Lee's work as a scout was not without its dangers. At one point in his

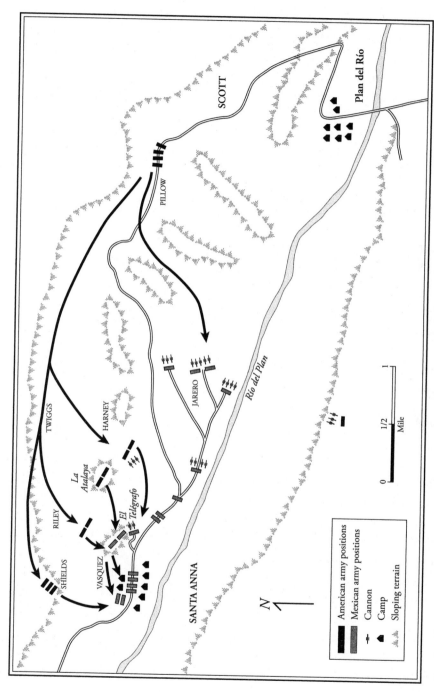

Battle of Cerro Gordo, April 17–18, 1847

spying he had to lie behind a log absolutely still "while Mexican soldiers sat on it and chatted only inches away."

Scott was willing to make the great effort, for once they were west of Santa Anna's army they could prevent its escape to the capital on the National Highway. After the initial charge led by Twiggs had been stopped, Santa Anna proclaimed victory for his forces, unaware that the Americans were planning simultaneous attacks from his front and his rear. This plan showed Scott's new willingness to violate the rules of classical warfare he had described in his handbooks.

Though the plan did not work quite as Scott had hoped, it did work overall. Mexicans in the rear, when surprised by the Americans, ran away and Santa Anna himself mounted a mule and fled, leaving his artificial cork leg behind. Pillow bungled his part of the plan and was slightly wounded. Other American officers scurried about shouting at each other. But because the battle was won in about three hours, Scott was later generous in his reports toward all his officers and men. Over a thousand Mexicans were killed and three thousand taken prisoner. Americans lost sixty-three men killed, 368 wounded. Scott released the prisoners on parole since he could not spare men to guard them or rations to feed them. With shame Ramón Alcaraz and his associates would write of Cerro Gordo, "The entire mass of men, panic-struck, without morale, without discipline, moved about in that small piece of road, in the most frightful state of confusion." The flight from Cerro Gordo was even more embarrassing than the battle itself. "All classes being confounded, all military distinction and respect were lost, the badges of rank became marks for sarcasms, that were only meted out according to their grade and humiliation. The enemy, now masters of our camp, turned their guns upon the fugitives." Santa Anna himself was "a lively picture of the fall of our country, of the debasement of our name, of the anathema pronounced against our race." Santa Anna's behavior at Cerro Gordo would embarrass the Mexican nation for years to come.

Scott marched his men into the town of Jalapa, and Worth advanced further to Perote, which surrendered without a shot being fired on April 22. Santa Anna had seized so much property from the population that many welcomed what they hoped were less greedy Americans. It was

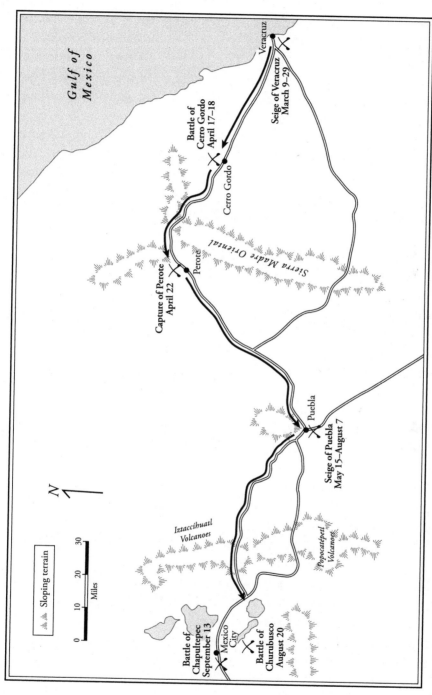

Mexican Campaign, March 7–September 14, 1847

expected by many, including President Polk, that Scott would march directly to the capital. Certainly Santa Anna expected such an early advance. But as he looked west along the National Highway, Old Fuss and Feathers had other ideas. It should be remembered that Scott's military campaign was always designed for political ends, chiefly to make peace with Mexico.

Scott had good reason to pause and consider his options for an attack on the city of Mexico. He was still a hundred miles from that prize and the mountains in his way were forbidding. Many volunteers in his forces had enlisted for only a year and, as their terms expired, four thousand chose to go home. Generals Patterson and Pillow returned to Washington, Patterson because of illness and Pillow to show off his small battle wound and receive a promotion to major general from the president. Promised reinforcements and supplies had not arrived in Mexico and when many of the volunteers returned home Scott was left with only about four thousand effective fighting men. As the historian T. R. Fehrenbach explains, "Scott was fighting . . . with less than a modern division, supported by a difficult and tenuous supply line, surrounded in hostile territory." Scott much preferred regular soldiers to volunteers, but now he had to make do with what he had. As noted, volunteers, once they acquired a little experience in the field, performed about as well as the regular soldiers. And a smaller percentage of volunteers deserted in Mexico than the regulars, 6.6 percent as opposed to 9.2 percent for regular regiments. Mexicans were surprised by the dirty motley uniforms the Americans wore.

Scott was astonished when he learned that Nicholas P. Trist had arrived in Mexico to negotiate a treaty with the Mexicans. Trist might have been picked by Polk and Buchanan because he was an obscure clerk in the State Department with no hope of running for president, but that was not the way Trist saw himself. As a former law student and protégé of Thomas Jefferson, private secretary to Madison and Jackson, consul in Havana, and married to Virginia Randolph, Jefferson's granddaughter, Trist understood he would be in charge of negotiations with the Mexican government and he was more than willing to assume that responsibility.

Trist quickly showed his lack of experience and respect for Scott by not meeting him in person, explaining his mission, and showing Scott the documents and peace proposal he carried to the Mexican government. He offended Scott by announcing his arrival in Veracruz with a brusque note, tersely stating that he was there to take over negotiations with Mexico.

Trist had no military experience, except for his cadet years at West Point and he had little appreciation of the pressures on Scott, as Polk and Marcy undermined his campaign yet demanded that he march immediately on Mexico City. It was insulting to the general that a peace envoy would be sent to treat with the Mexican government while he was still fighting to win the war—and it was intended to be insulting. Scott was so angry that he wrote to Marcy, "I beg to be recalled from this army," words that would later be used to punish him. And to Trist, Old Fuss and Feathers wrote, "The Secretary of War proposes to degrade me by requiring that I, the commander of the army, shall defer to you, the chief clerk of the department of state."

Trist and Scott exchanged bitter letters, complained to their respective bosses back in Washington, and did not meet face-to-face for almost two months, even though both were at army headquarters in Puebla. Then Scott thought better of his actions, as he usually did when he cooled off. As he waited in Puebla for reinforcements, he sent the ill Trist a gift of guava jelly. Quickly the two proud Virginians became friends and then firm allies. By complaining to their superiors in Washington, both men had made fatal mistakes, and they probably both soon realized their errors, as they attempted to move forward, hoping for a victory or a negotiated end to the war. And, because of the delay in communications, their angry accusations of one another were just being read in Washington as they were becoming fast friends and partners in the campaign in Mexico.

Instead of commending Scott for his impressive victories at Veracruz and Cerro Gordo, Polk complained of his slowness and instructed him on the proper route to the capital of Mexico. Scott studied his options and fumed and tried to help Trist initiate contact with the Mexican officials he was still at war with. It was British diplomats who suggested that a bribe might be necessary to open the way for negotiations. That was the custom of the country. Scott, after consulting his generals, including Gideon Pillow, now back in Mexico, and gaining their approval, agreed to provide ten thousand dollars, and up to a million out of his contingency funds, if that would lead to peace talks. Santa Anna apparently pocketed the money and kept rebuilding his army, but the attempt to open negotiations with bribe money would create trouble later on when Pillow tattled to Polk.

It has been said that "a dishonest politician . . . [is] one who will not stay bought." If that is the case, then Santa Anna is the perfect example. Santa Anna seemed to have an endless capacity for deceit and recovery. He had as many political lives as a cat, and then some. He even sent secret messages to Scott advising him on when to pause on the way to Mexico City and when to attack the capital. Apparently he hoped to stay in power even after an American victory.

As more reinforcements finally arrived at Puebla with the politician-turned-general Franklin Pierce, Scott had upward of fourteen thousand men, but three thousand were too ill for duty and one thousand were needed to guard the route from the sea. Santa Anna had now assembled a force of about thirty thousand men around the capital city.

An ancient military maxim holds that an invader needs 50 percent more troops than the invaded to be successful. Because of the difficult terrain and the distance to Mexico City, Scott knew he could not count on his supply lines from Veracruz. Once again he decided to imitate his ancient predecessor in the conquest of Mexico. In his *Memoirs,* Scott would explain, "Like Cortez, finding myself isolated and abandoned; and again like him, always afraid that the next ship or messenger might recall or further cripple me—I resolved no longer to depend on Vera Cruz or home, but to render my little army *'a self-sustaining machine.'*" It was a decision William T. Sherman would remember when he marched from Atlanta to the sea eighteen years later.

It was possible for Scott to sustain his army on the land in Mexico because he had been so careful not to alienate the Mexican people. Guerilla attacks on his forces were relatively few. For the most part Mexican farmers and merchants were willing to sell produce and supplies to the invaders, at inflated prices. While Polk and many Americans criticized Scott for his lenient policies toward the Mexicans, some Mexican people described the general as "noble and kind."

Scott was violating the very rules he had set forth in his *Manual.* But he had little interest in the rules now. He was interested only in winning this particular campaign, which was the culmination of his life's work. Pillow and Polk would call his decision foolhardy. Even the Duke of Wellington, following the campaign from London, would weigh in with condemnation: "Scott is lost . . . He can't take the city, and he can't fall back upon his base." The mighty victor of Waterloo would live to eat his words, but in the meantime Scott was on his own, with miles of impossible terrain between him and his goal, not to mention an enemy army about three times the size of his own, fighting on its own soil. He ordered his army forward and never looked back until they reached the summit of the Rio Frio range on August 10, 1847, and looked down into the Valley of Mexico from the Pass of Cortés. Mexico City spread at the bottom of a great valley "forty-six miles north to south and thirty-two miles wide." The thin mountain air at 10,600 feet worked like a telescope, making even the distant city seem within his grasp.

While in Puebla, Scott had sent Captain Robert E. Lee and Major William Turnbull, chief topographical engineer, to scout out the approaches and defenses of Mexico City. They had done their work well and reported in detail about the causeways approaching the city walls across the lakes and swamps. Scott had also employed a Mexican bandit named Manuel Dominguez and his two hundred highwaymen to provide information about activities in and around the city and to guide his forces as they moved forward.

Cortés had built the city of Mexico on the ruins of Tenochtitlán, "the Aztec city of lakes." In the baroque era, 1600–1750, so many grand buildings had been added to the capital of New Spain it became known as "the City of Palaces." With its lakes and canals and causeways, the city was sometimes called "another Venice."

Santa Anna had fortified the ancient city and had now gathered thirty-five thousand men to defend the Halls of Montezuma. Church bells had been melted down to make cannon to protect the city against the Yankee invaders. Foundries had worked round the clock forging new artillery and damaged arms had been repaired. On its high plateau the city was surrounded by lakes and swamps, as it had been when Cortés arrived there more than three hundred years earlier. Everyone, including Santa Anna, expected Scott to attack the capital from the east, along the causeway of the National Highway. Santa Anna decided to confront the Americans at the eminence called El Peñon, a few miles east of the city. Many people from the city came out to watch the preparations and morale soared as a victory seemed certain. The defense of the city became a kind of carnival. Fiestas, band music, carriages, beautiful women, and ornate uniforms were on display. "General Santa Anna came to El Peñon, accompanied with a brilliant escort and a numerous staff. They saluted him with the musical beats of honor and with enthusiastic vivas." To Ramón Alcaraz and his fellow historians this was a moment when Mexico displayed itself in its finest splendor. "Eastward from this is seen Texcoco, diminutive and lost in the spray of the lake, beautiful as the swan of fable, hazy, and far distant like our illusions of infancy . . . to the East, with their splendid pageantry, crowned in perpetual clouds, suspended in the heavens, the Popocatepetl, and the Ixtacihuatl, decorate this magnificent picture."

To Santa Anna's great surprise, Scott chose to swing around thirty-five miles to the south, through swamps and unfriendly terrain, while bluffing with a small force that demonstrated east of the city. General Worth's men had to clear an abandoned road around to the south, but with great effort the feat was accomplished. Worth would later claim it was his idea to attack from the south and west, though Scott had been planning the maneuver for weeks.

Scott set up his new headquarters at San Augustin on August 18, 1847, about ten miles south of Mexico City. Santa Anna, in response, moved his substantial forces from the east to San Antonio, blocking the route to the capital, and assigned General Gabriel Valencia to hold the position. Since he was moving shorter distances inside the circle, Santa Anna could shift his men faster than Scott could move his army on the outer perimeter through swamps and mud. In the manual Scott had written, as Allan Peskin points out, this advantage was called "the value of interior lines."

The only easy route from San Augustin to San Antonio was a causeway between deep ditches, a bog on one side and a brutal lava badlands called the Pedregal on the other. The lava stretched all the way to Padierna, near Contreras, where General Valencia was stationed. The Mexicans believed the city was unreachable except by the causeways.

Scott probed the Mexican positions and found them well defended.

A mule path across the southwest corner of the Pedregal was explored by Lee, Beauregard, and Zealous Tower. They reported that with a little widening, artillery could be hauled that way. On August 19 Pillow's division started work on the mule road with Twigg's division standing guard. When the Mexicans opened fire Twiggs ordered a response that was beaten back.

Santa Anna with about eight thousand men marched out to observe the battle but did not attack. The generalissimo stopped so close to American soldiers they could hear the Mexican bands playing. Though wounded slightly in the leg, Scott took charge of the battlefield and ordered Generals James Shields and Persifor Smith to join Lieutenant Colonel Bennet Riley's men at San Geronimo. Smith, though a latecomer to the soldier's trade, proved to be an effective general, cool under fire, generous and tolerant toward his officers. On the afternoon of August 19, 1847, he and his men helped prevent a potential disaster.

Discovering a deep ravine close to Valencia's rear, Smith moved his men under the cover of darkness to be ready to attack at dawn. He intended that a diversionary attack would be made in front of Valencia's forces, while the real assault would come from the opposite direction. In the middle of a violent thunderstorm Robert E. Lee volunteered to go to Scott and inform him of the plan. Feeling his way through the rough lava beds in the dark, relying on his capacious memory for detail and the frequent lightning flashes, Lee reached Scott's headquarters. Scott later described Lee's journey as "the greatest feat of physical and moral courage" of the campaign.

As soon as he delivered his message Lee turned and made his way back through the rain to Smith's camp. On his side, Valencia was celebrating his "great victory" over the Americans. Seeing Valencia's vulnerability at Contreras, Santa Anna ordered him at two in the morning to withdraw to a safer position, but Valencia refused.

At three in the morning, in the fury of the storm, Smith's division with Riley's brigade in front entered the ravine and waded through waist-deep water to reach the rear of Valencia's camp. At dawn Twiggs attacked Valencia's front and Smith gave the order to charge from the rear. As the shouting Americans rushed into Valencia's camp from the back, Mexican artillerymen tried to turn their cannons to meet the attack. As men ran to find and load their weapons, some were trampled by their own bewildered cavalry. The battle of Contreras lasted only seventeen minutes. Riding onto the battlefield, Scott encountered Lieutenant Beauregard. "Young man, if I were not on horseback I would embrace you," Old Fuss and Feathers shouted. The Americans lost sixty dead and wounded, but seven hundred Mexicans had been killed and many more were about to die at Churubusco.

Scott credited Lee, Beauregard, and Tower of the Corps of Engineers for the victory. "I doubt whether a more brilliant or decisive victory . . . without cavalry or artillery on our side—is to be found on record," he later wrote. But General Persifor Smith deserved a lot of credit also, for he was the leader of the attack on Valencia's rearguard.

Santa Anna ordered a retreat from San Antonio, leaving a smaller force to guard the river crossing at Churubusco, where roads from San Augustin and San Antonio converged. A stone church, convent, and walled garden, as well as a fort at the bridge, provided protection for the Mexican defenders. Scholars studying the battle later would say Churubusco could have been bypassed. But in the heat of the moment it seemed to Scott that the bridge must be taken.

The force holding Churubusco included the San Patricio Battalion, U.S. deserters who knew they would be hanged if captured, so they defended Churubusco with a superhuman tenacity. When the Mexican commandant attempted to surrender, the San Patricio soldiers tore down the white flag. As the Mexicans ran low on ammunition, some American forces slipped across the river and attacked from behind. But by the time the Battle of Churubusco was over, Scott had lost precious men and enough time to let Santa Anna regain the walls of the city. According to the Alcaraz account, the Mexican commander, pursued by the American forces, "mixed himself with the cavalry and desperate, gave the whip to some of the officers who fled."

With his men exhausted, Scott called a halt to the fighting. Worth's division was only a mile and a half from the city gate. Four thousand Mexicans had been killed or wounded and three thousand captured, including eight generals. Some reports put Mexican losses at about ten thousand for that day. Santa Anna had lost between a fourth and a third of his army in one day.

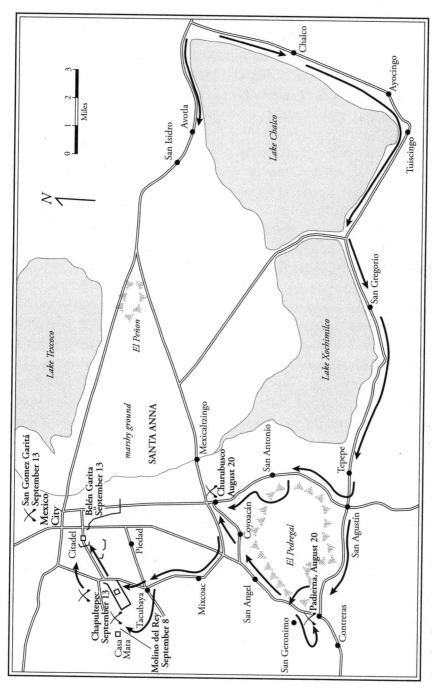

Battles for Mexico City, August–September 1847

Some of Scott's men and many civilians back in the United States would question Scott's decision not to attack the city immediately. But others see Scott's choice to halt after the brutal fighting at Churubusco as an example of his mature wisdom. An assault on the fortified city on the same day as Contreras and Churubusco might have led to victory, but his exhausted men might have been beaten back in the attack. If they had breached the walls and made it inside the city, the little army would have been trapped among a hostile population of two hundred thousand citizens and an unknown number of enemy soldiers, militia, and guerilla fighters. Besides, Scott still hoped for a Mexican surrender, without a final assault on the capital itself, with as little killing as possible. Unfortunately, many Mexicans would interpret Scott's benevolence as weakness.

While his hesitation just south of Mexico City was probably the wise choice, Scott's granting of an armistice to Santa Anna may not have been. When the Mexicans asked for a truce so they could bury their dead, Scott answered, "Too much blood has already been shed in this unnatural war" and declared he waited for the Mexican response. Taking advantage of Scott's generosity, Santa Anna, accustomed to braggadocio, treated Scott's agreement to an armistice as if it were a plea by a defeated foe. The differences between the two generals could not have been more dramatically illustrated. In his memoirs, written years later, Scott would explain that he had granted the armistice because an immediate attack would "scatter the elements of peace . . . excite a spirit of national desperation and thus indefinitely postpone the hope of accommodation."

The Mexican peace commission sent to meet with Nicholas Trist made ridiculous demands as if the United States were defeated and suing for peace. Americans attempting to buy supplies in Mexico City were stoned by mobs shouting, "Here come the friends of Santa Anna!" showing perhaps how much the citizens detested the dictator and wanted him overthrown. On September 7, 1847, Scott canceled the truce and prepared to attack. When news of the armistice reached Washington, Polk was enraged that Scott had let himself be duped by the scoundrel Santa Anna.

There are good arguments that granting the armistice was a mistake, but Scott's motives were admirable. He still hoped to end the war without a final assault on the capital. And like many others, including Polk, he was taken in by Santa Anna's scheming. There was also the influence of his new friend Nicholas Trist, ready to negotiate a treaty now that he was in contact with Mexican officials.

The Mexican historians working with Ramón Alcaraz would accuse Scott of cruelty because some of the San Patricio deserters captured at Churubusco were hanged, overlooking the fact that the Mexicans themselves executed many deserters from their army. In defense of Scott, the translator Albert S. Ramsey, who served in Mexico with the American army, would write, "The American general is one of the last men in the world against whom the charge of cruelty with any justice can be brought... In fact, the very generosity and excellence of his heart led him sometimes too far, and he has since reaped in ingratitude the good seed sown in the fulness of his noble sensibilities."

In their anger, the Mexican historians of 1848 were in no mood to recognize Scott's generosity. They saw Mexico as the republic taking the high moral course when they demanded that slavery be banned in any new territories the United States acquired. They chose to forget that almost every part of Mexico had enslaved Indians, and "nearly every Indian band had its slaves, either Mexicans or members of other tribes." They also believed that Scott used the armistice to rest and strengthen his army. They summarized the battle for Mexico City thus: "As one sun succeeds another sun, thus succeeded the scenes of blood and extermination, until the horses of the north arrived to trample the smiling, fertile, level fields of the beautiful valley of Mexico, and the degenerate descendants of William Penn came to insult the sepulchres of our fathers."

Determined to end the conflict once and for all, Scott moved his army to within two and a half miles of the city. The only roads were causeways through the marshes and a mile to the north rose Chapultepec, a hill that commanded the southwestern roads into the city. At the western foot of the hill stood a group of stone buildings that included a powder magazine, Casa Mata, and a number of mills and, supposedly, a cannon factory called Molino del Rey (Mill of the King).

It was rumored that the Mexicans were building cannons there and Scott ordered Worth to attack the complex on September 8. It is quite possible the rumors of the cannon factory had been spread by Santa

Anna, for he had stationed thousands of soldiers in the Molino area. If we can believe Ramón Alcaraz and his associates, Santa Anna established the majority of his forces around the mill and removed a number of them on the same night, then "withdrew to sleep in the Palace, and at daybreak marched to the garita of the Candelaria, a point which he believed would be attacked." The same historians say Santa Anna had somehow acquired a copy of Scott's battle plans for Molino del Rey, though they do not state their source for that information.

Not suspecting the trap, Worth attacked prematurely with only thirty-five hundred men, not waiting for an initial artillery barrage. They did not even have ladders for scaling the walls. One battalion, "the Forlorn Hope," was almost wiped out. Many were lost in a charge across an open field to take Casa Mata.

Americans won the battle of Molino del Rey in about two hours of desperate and heroic fighting, but 799 men were killed or wounded, including 58 officers. Worth lost 20 percent of his division. But the Mexicans had lost 3,000 men and another 2,000 deserted into the night. Molino del Rey was the most costly battle the Americans fought in Mexico and it turned out there were no cannons being made in the mill. One soldier said, "nothing was gained except glory," and another described the battle as "evidence of utter imbecility." Though he had not been present at the battle, Santa Anna proclaimed a victory for himself asserting that "a victory had been gained over the enemy, and that he had in person led the troops of the Republic."

But Scott knew the first responsibility for the costly battle lay with himself. He was visibly moved and irritable, distracted. There was noting left to do but attack the city of Mexico itself. On September 11 he convened a council of war at Padierna and announced he would not rise from his chair until a decision was reached. Most of the senior officers, including Pillow, argued for a southern approach to the fortified city. After all, the western gate was commanded by the Chapultepec eminence, which was too well fortified to be stormed.

It was Lieutenant Beauregard who argued for an attack on Chapultepec itself, since the Mexicans would expect an attack from the south. After a long moment of silence officers Pierce and Riley announced they agreed with young Beauregard. Scott was persuaded by the logic also and announced, "We will attack by the Western gates!" Expecting an attack from the south, Santa Anna had moved most of his forces to the entrances to that side of the city. In the words of Robert W. Merry, "Santa Anna . . . was no match for the resourceful and deft Scott, whose insistence on the western approach proved brilliant."

Twiggs was directed to make a dramatic maneuver toward the southern gate as a diversion while Pillow and Quitman shifted their divisions under cover of night to the west. Early on September 12, Scott ordered the bombardment of the fortifications on Chapultepec. The name Chapultepec means "Grasshopper Hill." With sheer cliffs on the north and east and marshes and deep ditches at its foot, the hill appeared unapproachable. Land mines had been placed in the ground around it. The castle on the summit appeared formidable. Constructed as a summer home for the Spanish viceroy, the building now housed a military academy, the Colégio Militar. In the words of Ramón Alcaraz and his associates, "Chapultepec [was] the key of Mexico, as then was commonly said." As the Americans began the assault, they didn't know that fewer than nine hundred men defended the heights above them. All along, Santa Anna assumed the attack on Chapultepec was a feint.

Pillow and Quitman led the charge from the southeast. As they crossed the muddy fields under intense fire, the land mines failed to explode, but the roar of the battle reminded one soldier of a hurricane, "a tempest at sea with the wind howling, hissing and whizzing." Pillow was wounded in the ankle and rested against a tree while his men rushed to the top, carrying ladders which they leaned against the castle walls. Later a legend grew that six cadets, who wrapped themselves in Mexican flags, jumped to their deaths rather than surrender. They became martyrs in Mexican history. Pillow's men climbed inside the castle just before Quitman's men. One Mexican officer exclaimed "God is a Yankee!" At first they began looting, killing the Mexican soldiers, now beaten and willing to surrender. But by 9:30 a.m. order was restored and the prisoners were placed under guard. The American flag was raised high above the castle for those in the city below to see. Whether he had planned it or not, Scott could not have found a more effective way of announcing to the citizens of the great city that the Americans had won.

In 1521 it took Cortés eighty-five days of siege to take the city of the

Aztecs. Scott was ready to enter the city only five days after he ended the armistice. Ulysses S. Grant would later describe Scott's strategy and tactics around Mexico City as "faultless." Outnumbered three to one by the Mexican army, the American forces had prevailed and inflicted four to five times as many casualties on their opponents as they themselves suffered. While the U.S. turncoats captured at Churubusco were tried and some hanged, Quitman was sent to advance toward the city along the Belen causeway and Worth approached toward the San Cosme *garita*, or sentry building. It took a day of fighting to get inside the gates themselves. Once inside the Americans had no choice but to stop, for it was dark and they were out of reach of their supplies and baggage. They hunkered down as the night grew extremely cold, unusually so for September, even for Mexico City.

In the middle of the cold night a delegation of Mexicans with a white flag appeared. Escorted to Scott's headquarters around 4:00 a.m., they said Santa Anna and his army had withdrawn from the city. With no one to defend it the capital was helpless, and they were willing to surrender to the Americans. Scott and his men had triumphed.

The Americans had landed on the beach south of Veracruz six months and five days earlier, marched hundreds of miles from the coast, fought seven battles against larger armies than their own, without losing a single battle. Depleted to a force of seven thousand, they now occupied a city of two hundred thousand. One American soldier there proclaimed, "The American army has enacted miracles." In the words of James I. Robertson Jr., "Never had an American general accomplished more, with fewer men, and with less support from his government."

Many American soldiers would attribute the victory to their own fighting spirit. When looked at battle by battle and maneuver by maneuver, it is clear the Americans, regular army and volunteer alike, had a tenacity, a staying power in battle that the Mexicans often lacked. This difference is especially notable because the Americans were the foreign invaders and the Mexicans were defending their own soil.

Several opinions have been put forward to explain the unlikely American victories in Mexico. One is that Mexican equipment was inferior or old and their artillery antiquated. This was true in some cases but not in others. Another is that the leadership of the Mexican forces was poor, especially at the top where Santa Anna missed opportunity after opportunity to hurl back the Americans, first at Veracruz, later at Cerro Gordo. Ramón Alcaraz and his fellow historians place much of the blame on the Mexican leadership. "For the grand conflicts, and for the great transactions of life, a creative, a well-balanced and directing head is requisite. All our operations in the war had felt this want, and in turn it flowed back exclusively upon the unhappy soldiers and the good meritorious officers." A further explanation has been that political instability in Mexico contributed significantly to the defeat. With so much intrigue and infighting among the leaders, an effective defense had been impossible. All of these are likely contributing factors to the American victory.

But it is also quite possible that the men on the ground, the Mexicans actually doing the fighting, who were mostly Indians, did not much believe in their cause, and when the fighting got really tough they were willing to back away. Ruled all their lives by the hidalgos, the upper classes, the corrupt generals, the imperious Santa Anna and others somewhat like him, they did not feel loyalty to their officers, to their units, or to the army. Many Mexicans of all classes hoped to be annexed by the United States as a solution to the chaos and corruption that had reigned since the 1821 revolution. Anything seemed better than what they had endured. Faced with an invader that seemed determined never to give up, they decided again and again in the heat of battle to surrender or back away and run for it. Whatever they were fighting for, it was not worth dying for the likes of Santa Anna. Impressed by his leadership and humanity, a delegation of Mexican leaders would offer the presidency of the country to Winfield Scott, but he would refuse.

When he got the news from Mexico City, Polk was willing to give credit for the victory to the American fighting men and to his friend Gideon Pillow. But not to Scott. That Scott had done exactly what he had been ordered to do, with fewer men and supplies than he had been promised, counted for nothing with Polk. As far as Polk was concerned, the Whig general could do no right. Whoever was responsible for the conquest of the Halls of Montezuma, it was not Winfield Scott.

More disinterested observers disagreed with the president. The Duke of Wellington, who had predicted disaster for Scott in the mountains of Mexico, followed the news avidly and pronounced Scott "the greatest living soldier . . . unsurpassed in military annals." Considering that the duke himself was still living, this was high praise indeed. Ulysses S. Grant, who participated in the campaign, would later write, "Credit is due to the troops engaged, it is true, but the plans and the strategy were the general's." Grant stated that he knew of no military campaign better executed than Scott's in Mexico. "General Scott's successes are an answer to all criticism," Grant concluded. The historian John Eisenhower observes that Scott "may well have been the most capable soldier this country has ever produced."

Polk and others might dwell on the bribery scheme, the truce outside Mexico City, the excessive casualties at Churubusco and Molino del Rey, but no one could dispute the victory of September 14, 1847, as Scott and his little army marched into the great city of Montezumas, with crowds cheering Old Fuss and Feathers as he neared the central square and the cathedral. On his magnificent horse Scott looked like a Roman leader. The crowds went wild with applause as the general dismounted and strode into the Halls of the Montezumas. Sitting down at Santa Anna's desk, he wrote to Secretary of War William Marcy, "This glorious army hoisted in the morning of the 14th, the colours of the United States on the walls of this palace." There would be some serious street to street fighting in the city and extended guerilla activity in the countryside, but the battle was over. Tens of thousands evacuated the city. "The roads were covered with families, a sight that gave an inexplicable pain, like birds who finding their nests destroyed by the storm, send forth the most plaintive notes . . . and fly to strange lands to seek skies more serene." Ramón Alcaraz and his associates would lament that "the sun which years before had seen Mexico liberated by her heroic youth, illumined now a people in slavery and resigned to their disgrace." To many Mexican people all seemed ruin and confusion.

One of the toughest critics of the Jacksonian policies that led to the Mexican War is the historian Daniel Walker Howe. But in his prizewinning volume *What Hath God Wrought*, Howe writes, "The conquest of that large republic [Mexico] by the small armed forces of the United States, despite formidable geographical difficulties and in the face of a hostile population, constituted one of the most amazing military achievements of the nineteenth century." Howe speculates that Americans have paid little attention to the extraordinary accomplishments of the Mexican campaign because they believe the annexation of the West was somehow a natural, inevitable process. To recognize the glory of Kearny's, Taylor's, and Scott's actions would lessen the sense of ordained, unfolding destiny.

———

THE CONQUEST of Mexico would turn out to be easier for Scott than the aftermath. Santa Anna had let the prisoners out of the jails to make trouble for the gringos, and there was some looting and sniping, quickly quelled. After three days the city was quiet and functioning again. The general now had to become an administrator. Polk had ordered Scott to make the Mexicans pay for the war, and while about $230,000 was collected to cover expenses for supplies and care for the sick and wounded, more than that was hard to come by immediately. Scott took $6,400 for his personal expenses and would later be accused of corruption by his enemies. Polk suggested the army levy $100 million from the Mexicans to pay for the war, but Mexico was broke and yielded only $4 million altogether.

Armies in the aftermath of a war tend to fall into disarray. Scott's was no exception. Armies that have conquered begin to lose discipline and in the peace old rivalries resurface. About the occupation Robert W. Merry has written, "In Mexico, Scott's war machine was sputtering in the wake of its victories. His command was a mess of petty jealousies, personality clashes, and competing ambitions." The additional troops promised by Washington finally arrived and now had to be housed and fed, though they were no longer needed. While Trist was struggling to make a treaty with the Mexicans, Scott worked to bring order to the country with a stable government that would agree to a lasting peace.

Scott's greatest trouble came not from Mexicans but from within his own staff and from Washington. Both Worth and Pillow started letter writing campaigns to newspapers to make themselves look like the true victors in Mexico. Though the letters used pseudonyms, the contents pointed to the sources. Every letter belittled or ignored Scott's contributions toward the victory.

One letter in a Pittsburgh paper accused Scott of denying Worth credit to prevent him from becoming a rival for the presidency. Worth, the letter claimed, had chosen the successful route south of Mexico City. The letter also lavished praise on Gideon Pillow and was followed by several more in other newspapers. A letter in the *New Orleans Daily Delta,* written by one "Leonidas," gave Pillow credit as the genius responsible for the victories at Contreras and Churubusco. Scott was not even present when the fighting occurred, the letter said. All credit belonged to Pillow.

Writing such letters to newspapers was strictly forbidden by the army code, but when Scott sent a stiff warning to his men about publishing such opinions, Worth, who was acting increasingly erratic, demanded that Scott explain himself. Worth wrote an angry, accusing letter to the Secretary of War, so insulting to his commander that Scott ordered him arrested. When Worth's friend, Colonel James Duncan, came forward and confessed that he had written the letters, he was put under house arrest also.

While professing to be Scott's friend, Pillow had written a series of poison letters to his old law partner Polk, but Scott had ignored those calumnies. Now that the "Leonidas" letters were printed and public, Scott reluctantly charged Pillow also. Pillow had been found with two Mexican howitzers in his baggage wagon. Taking such souvenirs was also forbidden. Though a court of enquiry found Pillow innocent of the charge of wrongdoing, it was clear most of the men thought he was lying about the howitzers. Blaming Scott for his troubles, Pillow wrote to Polk, calling Scott "a most malignant man." After conferring with his fellow Democrats, Polk announced he was recalling Scott from Mexico, and replacing him with a Democrat, Major General William O. Butler. Using as their excuse Scott's old offer to give up his command in the heat of the initial quarrel with Trist, Polk and Marcy fired the conqueror of Mexico, less than two months after Trist was also relieved of his diplomatic mission. Scott and Trist had achieved the two things that Polk would ultimately be remembered for and both were humiliated by the vindictive politician. One of the most eloquent comments on the recall of Scott would come from his junior officer, Robert E. Lee. "To suspend a successful general in command of an army in the heart of an enemy's country, [and] to try the judge in place of the accused, is to upset all discipline."

The proceedings against Worth, Duncan, and Pillow would drag on in Mexico City and then back in Frederick, Maryland, but Polk would make sure his friend suffered neither penalty nor censure. Old Fuss and Feathers would hang on, out of favor, while his Whig rival, Zachary Taylor, Old Rough and Ready, rode on his military fame to the steps of the White House in 1848.

It is always useful to look at events from different points of view and it is worthwhile to quote the Mexican historian José María Roa Bárcena on the conduct of the Americans who attacked Mexico in 1846–47. In his careful analysis of the conflict and the Mexican defeat, Bárcena concludes, "One word more about the campaign in order to do proper justice to the enemy: his grave and phlegmatic temperament, his lack of hatred in an adventure embarked upon with the simple intention of extending territory, his discipline, vigorous and severe among the corps of the line, which even extended to the volunteers, with the exception of some of the detached forces that were a veritable scourge, and above all, the noble and kind characters of Scott and Taylor lessened to the extent possible the evils of warfare. And the second [to arrive] of those chiefs cited, who commanded the first [largest] of the invading armies, was, once the campaign of the Valley [Mexico City and environs] was ended, the most sincere and powerful of the friends of peace."

— Eight —

KIT CARSON

Taking Boone's Trace to the Pacific

$\mathcal{T}$HE TRACE Daniel Boone and his men chopped through Cumberland Gap in 1775 acted as a sluice gate and irrigation ditch through which a swelling flood of settlers, speculators, and adventurers poured into the Trans-Allegheny west. One of those settlers was Lindsey Carson who brought his large family from North Carolina along Boone's Trace in 1793 and settled in Madison County, Kentucky, about four miles north of present day Richmond, Kentucky, and just a few miles south of Boonesborough. There on December 24, 1809, Lindsey's second wife, Rebecca Robinson, gave birth to Christopher, who would always be known as Kit. Lindsey Carson, who had fought in the Revolutionary War with General Wade Hampton, had five children by his first wife and ten by his second. Of Scots Irish descent, the Carsons were as restless as the Boones, and as prolific.

The year 1809 turned out to be a propitious one in which to be born. Edgar Allan Poe was born in Boston on January 19 to itinerant actors. Abe Lincoln first saw the light of day in Hodgenville, Kentucky, on February 12 of that year. In Shrewsbury, Shropshire, Charles Darwin was born on the very same day as Lincoln. In very different ways all four would radically affect the world they were born into in ways none of them might have foreseen.

When Kit Carson was about a year old his family followed Daniel Boone again, all the way to Missouri. Boone's sons Nathan and Daniel Morgan Boone had developed a saltworks 150 miles up the Missouri River at a place called Boone's Lick, and the trail to the saltworks became known as Boone's Trace. Because of the attraction of the famous Boone name, thousands of settlers poured into the area after the War of 1812, driving away the Osages and other local Indians. It was near the little town of Franklin that Kit Carson grew up among frontiersmen, Indians and trappers and traders heading farther west.

In 1810 Kit's much older half brother William married Daniel Boone's grandniece Millie Boone, who died giving birth to a daughter named Adaline. Adaline was only two years younger than Kit, and she became his favorite playmate. Later he would give his first daughter her name. William returned to Kentucky and married Millie's sister Cassandra Boone and brought her to live near the Carsons. The Boones and Carsons worked together, hunted together, and intermarried. The greatest scout of the nineteenth-century West was related by marriage to the greatest woodsman of the eighteenth-century frontier.

Used more and more, Boone's Trace would become the launching point of the two great roads to the Far West—the Santa Fe Trail and the Oregon Trail. Those on the way to the Rocky Mountains and the Spanish southwest of Nuevo Mexico would begin their trek there where the Boone Trail ended.

In a family of large Carson men, Kit was the runt of the litter. He grew slowly and even as an adult would never be over five feet six or seven inches tall. He was a quiet boy, stubborn and dependable, with blond hair and shining blue eyes. His brothers were hunters and woodsmen and his first toy was a wooden rifle carved by one of his brothers. Because he seemed unusually intelligent, his father hoped he would become a lawyer. The Boone's Lick country was still vulnerable to Indian attacks and children were often kidnapped by Potawatomis, Osages, and Winnebagos. Kit's sister Mary Carson Rubey later remembered that even as a boy Kit was a light sleeper, alert to the slightest noise. "I always felt completely safe when Kit was on guard duty," she recalled.

As a child, Kit played with Fox and Sac Indian children, and like Boone before him, Kit learned that all Indians were different. Not only were the nations different, but each Indian was an individual and had to be dealt with individually, just as white men and women were. That knowledge would stand him in good stead in his long career among native peoples.

In 1818 Lindsey Carson was killed by a falling limb while he was clearing new land. Kit was only nine years old, and instead of attending school he now had to help support his family, mostly by hunting and trapping. "I jumped to my rifle and threw down my spelling book—and there it lies," he would later say to Jessie Frémont.

When his mother remarried in 1822, the independent, stubborn Kit often found himself at odds with his stepfather. The next year he was apprenticed to David Workman, a saddle maker in nearby Franklin, Missouri. According to all reports Workman treated Kit well, but the boy hated the task of sitting at a bench day after day slicing and stitching leather. Many of the clients were hunters and traders on their way to the plains and mountains to the west and Kit drank in their stories.

After the Mexican Revolution of 1821, Mexican officials permitted Americans to trade in the provincial capital of Santa Fe. The Spanish government had always excluded Anglos from the territory, but now the way was open for a lucrative trade in the City of the Holy Faith, if one could make the long trek across the plains and up the Arkansas River, through territories of many Indian nations, some friendly and some hostile. As Kit listened to the tales of the vast land out there and the profits to be made in the West from trapping and trading beaver pelts, he determined to leave the saddler's shop. More than anything, he probably wanted to be a mountain man, trapping fur and exploring the Rockies and the land beyond, where Lewis and Clark and others had already gone.

Kit quietly applied for a job with a trader on the way west with his caravan. When asked what he could do Kit replied, "Nothing, except I can shoot straight." He was hired as a "cavvy boy" to look after the herd of mules, horses, and oxen. Kit was thrilled to get away from Franklin and possibly rode away in one of the saddles he himself had fashioned. David Workman seems to have been both a good boss and a man with a sense of humor. He was obliged by the law to advertise for his fugitive apprentice, and so he dutifully placed an ad in the *Missouri Intelligencer* a month later asking for help in locating his ward. The notice ended: "All persons are notified not to harbor, support, or assist said boy under the penalty of the law. One cent reward will be given to any person who will bring back the boy."

It is thought by some that Workman actually encouraged Kit to run away with the Santa Fe–bound caravan. Seeing how unhappy his apprentice was in the saddle shop, he made the best of the situation and helped Kit escape to the West he yearned for. Likely Workman knew Kit would leave sooner or later; it might as well be sooner so he could take on a more successful apprentice. The next year Workman himself would take the trail to Santa Fe with a trading caravan.

Years later, when he dictated his autobiography, Carson related only one incident from his first journey to the West. A hand named Andrew Broadus accidentally shot himself when a wolf was spotted. The wound grew infected and gangrene set in on his right arm. Broadus screamed with pain but would let no one amputate. Finally other men in the party grabbed the delirious Broadus and held him while one cut through the inflamed flesh with a razor and hacked through the bone with a saw, then cauterized the arteries with a red-hot king bolt from a wagon heated in the campfire. According to some accounts it was Kit himself who did the cutting. Whoever performed the operation, Broadus was completely recovered by the time the party reached Santa Fe.

Once there, Kit did not linger in Santa Fe long before making his way seventy miles north to Taos. Taos was a small town where Pueblo Indians, Mexicans, and mountain men returned from the Rockies, mingled, traded, fought, and sold and consumed a wheat-based moonshine called Taos Lightning. We can guess that Carson was attracted to Taos mostly because it was the starting place for the Rockies and for the fur trade. It would be his home, in so far as he had a home, for much of the rest of his life. Kit began to learn Spanish and the regional Indian tongues as well. Though he never learned to read or write more than his own name, he had a knack for picking up languages and soon knew Spanish well enough to sell his services as a translator for a trading expedition. He would master at least a half-dozen Indian languages as well as the universal sign language of the West. Part of his great value as a guide and scout was his knowledge of native tongues and his fabled memory for land and trails.

That winter Carson found work as an assistant and cook to a trader named Matthew Kinkead, who had known Lindsey Carson back in Missouri. Working with Kinkead, who ran a distillery, among other concerns, Carson apprenticed himself to the West with real commitment. Using his earlier experience with saddle leather, he learned to sew his own buckskin clothes. He acquired the rudiments of cooking, combining Indian, Mexican and American ingredients and methods. He began to turn himself into the kind of man who could do whatever was needed, hunt buffalo, cook up a stew, tan leather, parley with Indians.

In 1828 Carson joined a trading caravan going all the way down the Rio Grande to El Paso. Next he signed on as a cook with a mountain man named Ewing Young, who ran a store in Taos that outfitted trappers bound for the beaver country of the high mountains. The mountain men were accustomed to eating whatever meat was available, whether dog, mule, or panther, and the joke was they ate so much grease they "shed rain like an otter, and [could] stand cold like a polar bear."

Carson was hired as a translator for a commercial caravan bound for Chihuahua City, and traveled on the Camino Real to that beautiful metropolis with its baroque cathedral and memorable colonial architecture. Built from the wealth of the local silver mines, Chihuahua City was the most dazzling town Carson had ever seen. When he returned from the south he worked as a teamster at the Santa Rita silver mines in western New Mexico. But his dream was still to become a trapper, a mountain man who penetrated the Rockies and brought back a fortune in furs to trade at Taos. His chance came in 1829 when the same Ewing Young employed him to join forty men to explore the Gila River country looking for beaver. That region was largely unexploited by trappers. It was the opportunity Carson had been waiting for.

Part of the attraction of the life of a Rocky mountain man may have been its very difficulty. The trapping had to be done in cold weather in late fall and early spring when the beaver fur was at its thickest and sleekest, but usually not in the very depths of winter when the beavers stayed in their frozen lodges under thick ice. Trappers fought with the elements, with frostbite, rheumatism caused by wading in icy streams, infections from cuts or wounds. If a leg was broken far back on a beaver stream, you ran a good chance of dying of exposure or starvation.

And then there was the ever-present threat of Indians. Some might be helpful, some might steal your traps or your mules or your furs. Some might ambush you and take your scalp to hang in their lodge. Another might just want to trade for lead and powder. Some were furious that you were trespassing on tribal land or on land considered sacred and off limits to strangers.

A mountain man lived on any kind of meat he could get or on cottonwood bark or harness leather when there was nothing else. It is clear that Carson and other mountain men thrived on these dangers and challenges. The idea was to return to Taos or Bent's Fort on the Arkansas River with a fortune in furs. And year after year many of the mountain men did just that. Because of the fashion in Europe for beaver fur hats, one skin could bring as much as six dollars. A mule could carry several hundred pelts, called plews by the mountain men. Hundreds and even thousands of dollars could be made in one winter and quickly spent on Taos Lightning, Mexican or Indian women, and maybe a new Hawken rifle or new traps. By the time they were ready to return to the wilderness, the trappers would be broke and would need to buy supplies and equipment for the next season on credit from one of the many traders in the area. The traders got rich, and the mountain men remained poor.

Reading the accounts of Carson and Jim Bridger, Jedediah Smith, and other mountain men, one has the impression they could hardly wait to leave the safety and comfort of the trading post for the dangers of the desert and mountains. Ostensibly they were seeking furs and a fortune, but they were also seeking adventure, the breathtaking vistas of the lavender, orange, and pink buttes at sunset, the luminous snowcapped peaks at dawn, the alpine valleys no white man had ever seen before, and stars that whispered in the cold clear sky above their camp. They lusted for discovery, for the land, for the furs, and for the Indian girls that were the land's personification. Some probably looked for danger as well. Life in the East and in the settlements seemed an endless tedium compared with the dangers and fortune that waited across the next ridge or beyond the alkali desert mirage.

One special danger for the Rocky Mountain fur trapper was the grizzly bears. These big animals prowled the high valleys and aspen groves and trout-rich streams. In the East the men had known only black bears, usually timid and harmless. But grizzlies were the kings of the mountains and feared no one. And they were entirely unpredictable. Grizzlies might lumber away or rush at you, or they might first lumber away and then rush at you. They could rip a man to shreds with their claws and teeth. They could ambush you in thick timber. Even shot in the heart or head, a grizzly might keep plunging at you.

Carson's first extended trapping expedition into the Gila River country was especially dangerous. Not only were there the usual threats of starvation, Apaches, grizzly bears, and rattlesnakes, but in addition, the Mexican government forbade Americans to trap in the territory without a special license. Such a license, when granted, was costly, usually including a hefty bribe. To avoid suspicion Young, who had not obtained a license, led his men north from Taos for fifty miles before swinging to the southwest. Because few trappers had gone there, the Gila watershed was teeming with beaver.

Carson began to master the delicate art of beaver trapping, as Boone had seventy years before him. Chained to a stob or rock, a trap had to be set near a slide where beavers entered or left the stream, in water deep enough so the caught beaver would drown but shallow enough so the animal would not swim over it. A stick scented with castoreum from a beaver's sex gland helped draw the beaver to the right spot.

Though he already knew Spanish, Carson now learned the dialect of the mountain men, a combination of English, French, Spanish, and Indian words. For survival it was important to know the universal sign language of the West also. Perhaps most important of all was to know about Indians, many different kinds of Indians, from Apaches and Zunis to Arapaho and Cheyenne, Blackfeet, Crow, Ute, and Shoshone. Indians might be encountered anywhere, and it was essential to know when to bluff or withdraw, smoke a peace pipe, trade, or skedaddle. Indians could be allies or enemies, traders, lovers, guides, thieves, kidnappers, torturers, trusted friends. In manners, in clothes, in outlook, the mountain men came to resemble the Indians as much as they did white men. Many took up with Indian women and were called squaw men. On this first expedition to the Gila country Young's party was surrounded by Indians and Carson killed his first Native American and may have taken his first scalp. And he tapped a brass tack into the stock of his rifle as a way of recording his kill.

In the summer of 1835, when he was twenty-five years old, Carson attended the annual meeting of trappers and traders on the Green River in southwestern Wyoming. Trappers met there to swap their winter hoards of furs for new supplies, to drink and dance and gamble and take Indian lovers, wrestle and compete in shooting matches and other contests of strength and skill. The French Canadians gave the gathering the name the Rendezvous. Carson had been seriously wounded in the shoulder in a fight with the notorious Blackfeet Indians and he was healing slowly, and maybe looking for a wife.

An Arapaho girl named Waa-ni-beh, Singing Grass, caught his eye. Singing Grass was the belle of the Rendezvous, and a French Canadian bully named Joseph Chouinard set his cap for her also. Carson would later describe Chouinard as "a large Frenchman . . . an overbearing kind of man, and very strong." When Singing Grass chose Carson as her partner for the ceremonial "soup dance," Chouinard spoke insultingly to the beauty and took indecent liberties with her person. Drinking heavily, Chouinard threatened anyone in his way and marched into Carson's campsite later yelling he could whip any American there, saying, "Mewling schoolboys! I could take a switch and switch you."

Carson faced the bully and told him that he, Carson, "was the worst American in the camp." And with a smile he added, "Stop now or I'll rip your guts." Chouinard was so astonished to be challenged by the smaller Carson that he agreed to a duel. The two rivals arranged to meet as a crowd gathered. Grabbing firearms Carson and Chouinard mounted horses or mules and rushed at each other, then stopped so close their mounts were nose to nose and fired point blank at the same instant. Luckily for Carson, Chouinard's mount jerked to the side and his bullet only scratched Carson's face, burning his hair and leaving a small scar. Carson's bullet crushed the Frenchman's hand and blew away the thumb. In some accounts the bully later died of gangrene from the wound; in others Carson finished him off with a second shot. All Carson says in his autobiography is that the Rendezvous "had no more bother with this French bully." Since the code of the trappers was to fight to the death it is likely Carson killed Chouinard. It was the beginning of his reputation as a fearless and deadly opponent.

All accounts agree that the fight was out of character for Carson, who was usually adept at avoiding such confrontations. Knowing when to back away from a drunken brawl was a part of his plain practicality. After defending Singing Grass's honor, and his own, Carson offered her father, named Running Around, a bride price of three mules and a new rifle. For the new couple the Arapahos erected a fine teepee. But according to Arapaho custom the groom was not allowed to consummate the marriage for a trial period of several weeks, though the couple slept side by side. The bride was bound by ropes around her waist and crotch, a sign of her chastity. This probation period allowed the young bride to know her husband as a companion before he became a sexual partner. Presumably if she did not find him congenial, the marriage was off before it was ever consummated. To divorce him, all she had to do was set his weapons and gear outside the door of the lodge and the marriage was over.

According to accounts given by the Arapahos to the biographer Stanley Vestal in the 1920s, the marriage between Carson and Singing Grass was happy. Carson conformed to all the customs of the Arapahos. Vestal was told by relatives of Singing Grass that she was remembered as "a good girl, a good housewife, and good to look at." Arapahos were known for their pleasing language and their memorable songs. Their songs were learned and sung by other tribes as well. They also did impressive beadwork and Carson's clothes were adorned with colorful, intricate patterns.

Singing Grass accompanied Carson as he trapped for two winters with the Hudson's Bay Company. And then he joined Jim Bridger's outfit to trap on the Yellowstone and Big Horn and Powder Rivers. The beaver were still plentiful and he later described this period as "the happiest days of my life." It was a life of danger and hardship but also a life of freedom, adventure, romance, and domestic happiness. Carson would later say of Singing Grass, "She was a good wife to me." Often he came back to the teepee wet and cold from trapping. "I never came in from hunting that she did not have warm water for my feet."

Their first child, named Adaline for the niece in Missouri, was born in 1837. Some accounts say her Arapaho name meant Prairie Flower, though Carson himself seems never to have used that name. In 1837 a panic back in the United States threatened the fur trade. It was also the year that smallpox swept through the native population of the high plains and mountains, killing whole villages, especially among the feared Blackfeet. One mountain man remembered a Blackfeet camp where "Teepees stood smokeless. Wolves ran about the village, fat and impudent. The Indian dead hung in swarms in the trees and brown buzzards sat in rows along the bluffs, gorged on human flesh, drunk with ptomaines."

When concerned whites warned that those infected with smallpox should be isolated, most Indians were outraged. It was their custom to surround the sick and dying in a vigil of relatives and friends, to show affection and respect. They believed the disease was caused by an evil spirit, brought by the whites, and affectionate support might drive the demon away. As a result the epidemic spread quickly from teepee to teepee and village to village, from one nation to another.

After the smallpox worked its way through the valleys of the high plains and mountains, things began to change rapidly for the fur trade. Believing (rightly) the white man had brought the pandemic death to them, the natives who were left tended to be more suspicious of the white trappers, traders, explorers, and missionaries who kept arriving in ever greater numbers from the east. At the same time the economic downturn reduced the demand for beaver and other western furs.

But the economic slowdown was only the beginning of the threat to the mountain man's way of life. A change of fashion in Europe shifted the style from beaver fur hats to silk top hats, and suddenly there was little demand for the main commodity of the western fur trade. Compounding the problem was the fact that all the trappers and fur companies combined had mostly stripped the Rockies, and even the Cascades, of the beaver population. Relentless trapping had left the beaver colonies thriving in only the most remote and inaccessible places. In Oregon the Hudson's Bay Company had largely cleaned out the fur-bearing fauna: otter, beaver, muskrat, marten and fisher. Suddenly a way of life, of romance and danger, that had thrived for decades, came to an end. Rendezvous was held in 1840, but it was a smaller, anticlimactic affair compared with what had gone before. In his autobiography Carson would simply say, "Beaver was getting scarce. It became necessary to try our hand at something else."

In 1839 Singing Grass had given birth to another daughter, but the mother contracted a fever and died soon afterward. It was the Arapaho custom to place the bodies of the dead high in trees, wrapped with favorite belongings, tools, or ornaments, and then the tree was set on fire. Birds and animals picked over the charred remains. As the Arapaho relatives tore their clothes and hair and keened with mourning, Carson remained calm. When asked why he did not weep with grief, he answered that it was the custom of whites to weep in their hearts.

Carson was left with two daughters to raise and the necessity of finding a new livelihood. The Rendezous of 1840 was more a wake than a celebration. The fact that Carson was there showed how reluctant he was to give up his chosen calling. The largest trading post in the region was Bent's Fort on the Arkansas River, in what would become southeastern Colorado. The fort was built on the northern side of the river since Mexico claimed the land to the south. Trappers, traders, adventurers, and Indians hung around the fort with its thick adobe walls. The Bent brothers hired Carson to hunt for them, and while friends looked after his daughters Carson brought in a steady supply of antelope, buffalo, and deer, valuable both for the meat and the hides.

Carson married a second time in 1841, to a Cheyenne woman named Making-Out-Road. She was known as a beauty but headstrong and bad-tempered. This wife did not want to take care of Carson's two little girls, and the marriage lasted only a short while. After driving Carson out of her teepee, Making-Out-Road would marry a series of other men, some Indian, some white. Carson in turn would be involved for a while with a Spanish woman named Antonia Luna.

Most accounts of this period say Carson was already in love with the beautiful Josepha Jaramilla, teenage daughter of a leading Taos family. Carson became formally engaged to Josepha and decided to take his older daughter Adaline back east to be raised by relatives in Missouri, where she would be educated. He left his younger daughter with the Bent family, only to find when he returned that while he was gone she had fallen into a cauldron of boiling soap tallow and died.

In Missouri Carson learned that his mother had also died and the whole town of Franklin had washed away in a flood. Nearby was the town of New Franklin. Carson bought Adaline the finest clothes that could be had to replace her buckskin dress and left her with a sister and a niece who lived out in the country, with the understanding that the little girl would be sent to school. Then he headed back to the West and his new love, going some of the way by steamboat up the Missouri River.

For the rest of his life Carson would dream of establishing a home and stable business and raising a family as other men did. But his repu-tation as a scout and his willingness to do what was asked of him meant that though he did establish a family in Taos he was able to spend little time there. Because he could not read or write, and only later learned to sign his name "C. Carson" with difficulty, he, for most of his life, was willing to defer to better educated and more sophisticated men. Though he became famous and had few rivals as a guide and leader in the mountains and desert, he was always willing to follow orders and do what he understood to be his duty. The contradictions of Carson's life mostly revolve around this combination of extraordinary integrity and independence and a willingness to do what he was told was neces-sary. As a result he could commit acts against his conscience, things he would later regret, in the good faith he was performing his duty, as men of superior rank and education directed him. Carson was about to meet just such a man.

The next major turning point of Carson's life occurred on the steam-boat on the first leg of his return to Bent's Fort and Taos where Josepha waited. On the boat he would encounter none other than John Charles Frémont. Like Sam Houston before him, Carson seemed to be every-where and to meet everyone of his era. Frémont had just the kind of manner of confidence and authority Carson was willing to follow. And Carson had just the kind of knowledge and skill as a guide Frémont needed for his mapping expedition along the Oregon Trail. The meeting of Frémont and Carson changed the lives of both men, and, it is fair to say, changed the history of the United States as well.

———

HAMPTON SIDES has described Frémont as "a man of striking good looks, with a full black beard, hawkish features, and the manic expres-sion of a prophet." He was "fiercely intelligent, but of questionable eth-ics." Frémont had a passion for botany and geography, a strong sense of his destiny, "and a penchant for melodrama that could be insufferable." But as the son-in-law of Senator Thomas Hart Benton he had been com-missioned to map and write a description of the Oregon Trail all the way to South Pass. The Oregon Trail was already being used by traders, ad-venturers, missionaries, and hunters bound for the Columbia Valley, but

Benton and others wanted maps and guides that would both aid those traveling to the territory and tempt many more to consider journeying there. It seemed inevitable that the Pacific Northwest must become part of the United States if enough Americans settled there. What was needed was a map and a description that showed the location of streams and water holes, hard-to-recognize detours and mountain passes, the positions of Indian tribes, and the easiest routes to encourage more to make the great migration.

Frémont would later describe meeting Kit Carson: "He was broad-shouldered and deep-chested, with a clear steady blue eye." When Frémont said he was looking for a guide to take him to South Pass, Carson quickly replied, "I've been some time in the mountains; I could guide you to any point you wish to go." Frémont inquired among other hunters and trappers about Carson's reputation, and found he was held in high esteem. One of the great partnerships of western exploration was born.

In June 1842 Frémont and Carson set out with twenty-five men on a successful expedition to South Pass. Frémont even made a special effort to place an American flag on a peak in the Wind River Range, imagining it was the highest summit in the Rockies. Frémont impressed Carson with his toughness and resourcefulness as well as his air of authority. And when Frémont and his wife, Jessie Benton Frémont, wrote up his report and published it as *A Report on an Exploration of the Country Lying between the Missouri River and the Rocky Mountains on the Line of the Kansas and Great Platte Rivers* to great acclaim, Carson was featured prominently as scout and consummate mountain man. Boone had created the icon of the man of the wilderness. Now his kinsman Carson would take it further, all the way to blood-and-thunder dime novels of the Victorian era and to the Pacific shores.

The next summer Frémont, the darling of Washington society, was commissioned to map and write a detailed account of the Oregon Trail from South Pass to the Willamette Valley. He hired Carson to guide him on this second expedition. This time Frémont and his party would swing south in the late summer of 1843 and into the Great Basin after reaching Fort Vancouver in Oregon. On the way they saw Mount Hood, whose grandeur would figure in his later report. There had always been rumors that some great river, sometimes called the San Buenaventura, drained the interior and crossed the mountains to the Pacific. Frémont and his men found no such river.

California was Mexican territory and Frémont had no authorization to survey or map that region, but he took his men south anyway. His excuse was that he must prove whether the fabled Buenaventura River existed and ran through the Sierras to the ocean. As Frémont explored and mapped the West, his ambition grew. He wanted to make a name for himself as an important explorer and cartographer. Like Benton, and like Thomas Jefferson long before him, Frémont sensed that the future of the United States was connected with the future of Alta California. It was important to know firsthand what was there.

Only Kit Carson's wisdom and long experience in the mountain wilderness saved Frémont's party from disaster as they crossed the Sierras through deep snow and lost or abandoned the howitzer Frémont had demanded from Kearny in St. Louis and dragged for thousands of miles. They stumbled into Sutter's Fort at future Sacramento half starved and half dead from exhaustion. But after a short rest Frémont led his party south almost the length of the Central Valley of California, avoiding Mexican officials, then swung across the Mojave Desert and back into the Great Basin. It was Frémont who named the landlocked desert region the Great Basin.

Carson led Frémont across the Nevada desert, attacking Indians who stole their horses and showed the men that when all else failed water could be found in the pulp of the barrel cactus. The surveying party reached Bent's Fort on the Arkansas River in time for a July 4 celebration. When Frémont returned to Washington in August 1844 he and Jessie set about writing up the report of the Second Expedition. Printed and bound with the report of the First Expedition in a single volume, Frémont's narrative became a best seller and made him even more of a hero and celebrity. The army and the U.S. government were willing to overlook the fact that he had far exceeded his authority and trespassed deep into Mexican territory. In the year James K. Polk was elected president, most members of the legislature and the population seemed thrilled by what Frémont had done. Frémont would become known as the Pathfinder.

Kit Carson, the actual pathfinder of the expeditions, became almost as famous as the mapmaker. Given a prominent place in the narrative, described as fearless, patriotic, resourceful, Carson entered the collective imagination of the country. Like Boone before him in John Filson's account, Carson was presented as the consummate man of the wilderness. Soft-spoken and modest, he always knew what to do. Hampton Sides summarizes the portrait of Carson this way:

> *He was a fine hunter, an adroit horseman, an excellent shot. He was shrewd as a negotiator. He knew how to select a good campsite and could set it up or strike it in minutes, taking to the trail at lightning speed . . . He knew what to do when a horse foundered. He could dress and cure meat, and he was a fair cook. Out of necessity, he was a passable gunsmith, blacksmith, liveryman, angler, forager, farrier, wheelwright, mountain climber, and a decent paddler by raft or canoe. As a tracker, he was unequaled. He knew from experience how to read the watersheds, where to find grazing grass, what to do when encountering a grizzly. He could locate water in the driest arroyo and strain it into potability. In a crisis he knew little tricks for staving off thirst—such as . . . clipping a mule's ears and drinking its blood.*

The catalog of Carson's skills went on and on, for there seemed nothing on the trail that he couldn't do successfully. And beyond all his gifts and achievements Carson was agreeable, cheerful when others were glum or fearful, deeply principled, with a store of jokes and humorous tales, once he got started talking. The image of Carson, the character of Carson, fulfilled a need Americans had for viewing themselves as unpretentious and undaunted. He became such a hero because he seemed the composite of the virtues the society wanted to believe it represented. Readers and leaders wanted to see something of themselves in this portrait of a modest but endlessly accomplished man. As a result he entered the American consciousness as an ideal and has never left it. Frémont was extremely lucky to have met Carson, and Carson was perhaps no less lucky to have connected his destiny with Frémont's. To make it even more perfect, Carson seemed to care very little about, indeed he seemed to ignore, his reputation, to the end of his life. At least that was the impression he gave.

Frémont's accounts of his explorations had an impact far beyond the fame and legend of Kit Carson. Frémont's maps and his descriptions set off one of the most important migrations of U.S. history. As we have seen before, the great movements of history are made not only by heroes and notorious leaders, but by the people, thousands of people. Inspired by Frémont's account and celebrations of Carson and the West, tens of thousands began to think of crossing the continent to Oregon and California. Where before the land between the Missouri River and the Pacific had been a frightening mystery, now it was known, with maps and detailed accounts of crossings, with landmarks described, rivers surveyed. Excerpts from Frémont's account were reprinted in newspapers and magazines, and copies of the report were bought and passed hand to hand. Within two years the trail to South Pass would be lined with families, horses, mules, oxen and wagons, and graves of those who perished along the way from disease, exhaustion, or Indian attacks. In 1845 three thousand Americans would make the trek to Oregon, doubling the white population there. It would be Frémont's description of the Great Basin and the Great Salt Lake that would start Brigham Young thinking about taking his flock of Latter-day Saints to a new Zion in that region where they would be safe.

Historians have pointed out that one feature of the extraordinary bond between Frémont and Carson was the way they complemented each other. Frémont was eloquent, aggressive, proud, fond of fancy dress and sure of his destiny, his place in history. We know he was also something of a womanizer. Carson was practical, humble, rarely distracted from the business at hand, and he cared little about his reputation back east. Publicity seemed to seek out Carson, not he it. He would risk his life to recover horses stolen from a poor Mexican family. He would kill Indian thieves without a second thought. Like the Indians themselves, Carson believed he was in competition with all comers for control of the territory and his business there and, like the Indians, he was willing to do what was necessary to protect his interests. That was why the Indians both respected and feared him. His code was their code.

In hindsight we may see Carson as an aggressor, a trespasser on Indian territory. That is not the way he saw things at all. In the brutal world of the western wilderness he saw himself as much entitled to the fruits of the soil and the streams, the mountains and meadows, as the next man, be he white or Indian, and he was willing to do what was necessary to secure those fruits. Frémont had every intention of writing himself into history. Carson simply wanted to enjoy the freedom and grandeur of the West, and to survive for another hunt, another voyage of exploration, while dreaming of settling down in Taos with Josepha and raising a family.

Carson would always feel both gratitude to and admiration for his boss, John Charles Frémont. While others would ridicule Frémont's overweening ambition and claims for himself, Carson kept any reservation he might have about the Pathfinder to himself. Carson was the kind of man who never forgot someone who had befriended him, and his loyalty to Frémont was lasting. After the Third Expedition, he would not serve with Frémont again, but if that was because he became disillusioned with his former commanding officer he never said so. When he dictated his autobiography in 1856, Carson would say it was "impossible to describe the hardships through which we passed, nor am I capable of doing justice to the credit which [Frémont] deserves . . . I can never forget his treatment of me while I was in his employ and how cheerfully he suffered with his men."

When Frémont set out on his Third Expedition to the West in 1845, he made sure that Carson was his guide again. With Polk in the White House and Benton cheering him on, Frémont had great things on his mind, continental things, hemispheric things. We will never know exactly what the wily Polk told Frémont before he left Washington, but we do know it concerned California and Polk's interest, his passion, for extending the nation to the Pacific before the British or even the French might seize Alta California. While the Mexicans were mostly settled along the Pacific coast around twenty-one missions established by the Franciscans in the previous sixty years, Americans and others were moving into the great Central Valley along the Sacramento in the north and the San Joaquin River farther south. Richard Henry Dana Jr. had published the travel memoir *Two Years Before the Mast* in 1840 and encouraged thousands of Americans to think of California as a romantic, shining land of opportunity. The trickle of Americans entering California was swelling week by week.

Dana was a Harvard undergraduate who, suffering from eyestrain brought on by his studies, dropped out of school in 1834 and signed on the brig *Pilgrim* as a sailor. The *Pilgrim* was bound for California around

Cape Horn to trade a variety of goods ranging from shoes to silk scarves for cowhides at the towns along the Pacific coast. Dana would be gone from Boston for two years, and while away he kept a detailed diary that he later expanded into *Two Years Before the Mast*. Published in 1840, the book became a classic of American literature. One of the most detailed accounts of a sailor's life at the time, the memoir may have influenced Herman Melville to go to the Pacific in a whaler. Dana also presented one of the most authentic accounts of the Mexican state of Alta California at that period.

The compelling story of a sailor's life in Dana's narrative has made it a favorite in all the years since. The vivid descriptions of weather, work on the deck and yardarms, diet and floggings, make the memoir hard to put down or forget. But it is Dana's depiction of geography, climate, and people of California that may have had the greatest impact. Published at a time when all kinds of Americans were turning their attention toward the Mexican Southwest and the Pacific coast, and what would later be called Manifest Destiny was already on the minds of many, Dana's book would seem a virtual invitation to explore and take over California.

Dana described the fine and sheltered harbors of San Diego, San Francisco, and Monterey, the provincial capital. After the long voyage around the tip of South America any land would have looked inviting, and the California coast was especially beautiful. Every foreign vessel had to register at Monterey, which lay at the focal point of its wide bay. "The shores are extremely well wooded . . . and as it was now the rainy season, everything was green as nature could make it . . . The birds were singing in the woods, and great numbers of wild fowl were flying over our heads."

Much of Dana's description of the coast, the vegetation, and the Coast Range, makes California sound like a golden paradise. But the Mexican and Indian populations were another matter altogether. He gives great attention to the clothes of both the men and women. Men of the ruling class "have no suspenders but always wear a sash round the waist, which is generally red and varying in quality with the means of the wearer. Add to this the never-failing poncho, or serapa, and you have the dress of the Californian . . . the middle classes wearing a poncho, something like a large square cloth, with a hole in the middle for the head to go through."

Dana was much impressed by the emphasis the Mexican ruling class placed on fine attire, on velvet and lace, as well as silver ornaments and fine saddles. Dress seemed the most important sign of station. "I have often seen a man with a fine figure and courteous manners, dressed in broadcloth and velvet, with a noble horse completely covered with trappings, without a *real* in his pockets, and absolutely suffering for something to eat."

The Mexican women of California were just as concerned about dress as the men. They spent every real they had on cloth and shoes, jewelry and fancy scarves brought by the Boston trading ships. "The fondness for dress among the women is excessive, and is sometimes their ruin. A present of a fine mantle or of a necklace or pair of earrings, gains the favor of the greater part." Dana was struck by the great beauty of the women, not just of their persons but of their voices. "It was a pleasure simply to listen to the sound of the language, before I could attach any meaning to it . . . It is varied by an occasional extreme rapidity of utterance, in which they seem to skip from consonant to consonant, until, lighting upon a broad open vowel, they rest upon that to restore the balance of sound. The women carry this peculiarity of speaking to a much greater extreme than the men." Eloquence seemed to be a part of the culture in general, or at least the pretension to eloquence. As Dana comments, "A common bullock-driver, on horseback, delivering a message, seemed to speak like an ambassador at a royal audience."

Dana questioned the industriousness of the Californians, whom he saw as "an idle, thriftless people," recording that "the country abounds in grapes, yet they buy, at a great price, bad wine made in Boston." He was also struck by the rigidity of the Mexican caste system. The ruling class with their fine clothes and horses had lighter skin. "From this upper class they go down by regular shades, growing more and more dark and muddy, until you come to the pure Indian, who runs about with nothing upon him but a small piece of cloth, kept up by a wide leather strap drawn round his waist."

Everywhere he looked Dana saw unrepaired buildings, decaying missions. "They sometimes appeared to me to be a people on whom a curse had fallen, and stripped them of everything but their pride, their manners, and their voices." The California presidio and mission towns abounded in cowhides and silver to trade for goods. In fact the hides had become a dominant medium of exchange, often called "California bank-notes." A trading ship hoped to return to Boston with thirty or forty thousand hides to be made into shoes or other products that could be taken back and sold in California.

There were already a number of Americans living in the towns such as Monterey, Santa Barbara, and San Luis Obispo. Most had married into leading Mexican families and become Roman Catholics. "No Protestant has any political rights, nor can he hold property or, indeed, remain more than a few weeks on shore, unless he belong to a foreign vessel."

Besides sailing up and down the coast from San Diego to San Francisco, trading goods for hides, Dana sometimes worked on shore at the "hide houses," preparing hides to be cured and pressed into "books" for the voyage back to Boston. Living on the beach he got to know much of the life of the California towns. Most of the English and Americans who had settled there had prospered. "Having more industry, frugality, and enterprise than the natives, they soon get nearly all the trade into their hands." Many had risen to positions of leadership. "The chief alcaldes in Monterey and Santa Barbara were Yankees by birth."

At the San Diego mission the Indians tended a herd of cattle and worked in the large garden of several acres, "filled, it is said, with the best fruits of the climate." There was a great deal of gambling and cockfighting in the coastal towns. Many Hawaiians, called Kanakas, worked as sailors along the coast and some lived along the beach. Dana got to know them all as he mastered the art of hide curing and gathered wood in the hills, chasing both coyotes and rattlesnakes.

The missions along the coast of California had been built about a day's ride apart along the Camino Real, or Royal Highway. The priests of the missions in California had been stripped of their power by the Mexican government and most of the missions were in a state of decay. The administrators and officers from Mexico City appeared to be a sorry lot. Most "are strangers sent from Mexico, having no interest in the country . . . for the most part men of desperate fortunes . . . whose only object is to retrieve their condition in as short a time as possible . . . The venerable missions were going rapidly to decay."

Dana would later return to Harvard and study for the law. Observing the four presidios of Alta California—San Francisco, Monterey,

Santa Barbara (which included San Luis Obispo, Los Angeles, and San Gabriel), and San Diego—he found "nothing that we should call a judiciary." As was the case with Texas, "there is little communication between the capital and this distant province." The local government had experienced one revolution after another, as rebel leaders "seizing upon the presidio and custom-house, divide the spoils, and declare a new dynasty."

California was "a country embracing four or five hundred miles of seacoast, with several good harbors; with fine forests in the north; the waters filled with fish, and the plains covered with thousands of herds of cattle, blessed with a climate than which there can be no better in the world; free from all manner of diseases . . . and with a soil in which corn yields from seventy or eighty fold. In the hands of an enterprising people, what a country this might be!"

Many saw *Two Years Before the Mast* as an invitation to go to California and make the golden land fulfill its destiny. By 1845 James Gordon Bennet would write in the *New York Herald,* "Those who do not become part of this movement [across the continent] will be crushed into more impalpable powder than ever was attributed to the car of Juggernaut."

During his stay in California, Dana had transferred to the ship *Alert,* owned by the same Boston firm as the *Pilgrim.* As they set sail for home the ship contained forty thousand hides, thirty thousand horns, several barrels of otter and beaver skins, and a certain quantity of gold dust, "which Mexicans or Indians had brought down to us from the interior." Trading ships in California commonly acquired a little gold dust, but no one had an inkling of the significance gold would have in California's destiny.

———

WHILE HISTORIANS have speculated and debated for more than a century about any secret orders or understanding Frémont may have carried from his conversation with President Polk, Senator Benton, or his commanding officer, we can be certain that Young Hickory shared with the Pathfinder his belief that California, like Texas, must inevitably become part of the United States. Without giving him more specific orders, it's obvious the president encouraged Frémont to do all he reasonably could to bring about independence and then annexation, if the "people [of California] should desire to unite their destiny with ours."

Frémont's official orders in 1845 directed him to survey a route through the Rockies south of South Pass. But as soon as he and his men reached the Arkansas River in the late summer they turned north toward South Pass. No doubt Carson told his boss there was no easy route across the Colorado Rockies. From South Pass Frémont headed down into the Great Basin, exploring the Great Salt Lake and ordering his men to cross the most dangerous desert. Carson saved the expedition by riding sixty miles ahead, finding water and grazing, and building a huge bonfire to make smoke signals that guided the Pathfinder and his company to safety.

Before hard winter set in the party crossed the Sierras into the Sacramento Valley. Frémont began making contact with the Americans settled there, studying the uneasy political climate of northern California. There were reports that Mexican general José Castro had "induced the area's Indian tribes to attack American settlers." If a rebellion against Mexican rule broke out, he was ready to make the most of it. Frémont told the Americans he was there to protect their interests, and extended his reconnaissance to Yerba Buena (future San Francisco) and named the entrance to the bay the Golden Gate.

One of the most passionately anti-American of all Mexican historians, José Vasconcelos (1881–1959), describes Alta California when the Americans arrived there as a prosperous and peaceful state. The Spanish colony had seen "the rise of the missions and the baroque churches, the groves of olive trees, and the haciendas in which the pressing of the grape is still practiced. There were no mercenaries, and perhaps for that reason California was the one territory that defended itself against the Yankee conquest with positive gallantry." Vasconcelos especially celebrates a figure named Joaquín Murrieta, "the Robin Hood of El Dorado," who became an outlaw and fought the Yankee invaders even after gold was discovered and California became a state.

Finding the political climate volatile, Frémont moved his men to the vicinity of Monterey and set up camp near the provincial capital. Mexican authorities were not pleased to have around sixty American soldiers camped at their doorstep, and on March 5, 1846, General José Castro, commander of forces at Monterey, ordered Frémont to leave California. In response Frémont moved his men to Gabilan Peak in the Coast Range northeast of Monterey and built a rough fort. An American flag was hoisted on a tall pole.

Perhaps with the Alamo in mind, Frémont wrote to Consul Larkin in Monterey, "We have in no wise done wrong to the people or the authorities of the country, and if we are hemmed in and assaulted, we will die every man of us, under the Flag of our country." It would seem Frémont expected an attack that would provoke the Americans in the region to join in a fight for independence from Mexico, on the model of the Texas Revolution of ten years before.

When General Castro issued an order for the Californios to gather and drive the American trespassers from their fair land, Frémont decided the time was not quite right for the rebellion he'd hoped to spark. It is thought by some that Carson persuaded Frémont to back down and when the American flag fell of its own accord from the long pole, Frémont took it as an omen and marched his men back north of the Bay to await more propitious conditions.

Following the Sacramento River, Frémont and his party proceeded north all the way to Upper Klamath Lake in southern Oregon. Continuing his survey of the region, Frémont waited. Great events were in the offing and he wanted to be ready when opportunity presented itself. Whatever his faults and overriding ambitions, Frémont had a peculiar patience for waiting until things turned his way. He was buying time, because he was confident events would cooperate with him in the end.

It was near the shore of Upper Klamath Lake where Lieutenant Archibald Gillespie finally caught up with Frémont. Gillespie was as driven and almost as ambitious as Frémont. While sailing to Mexico to cross to the Pacific, he had committed to memory the dispatches he carried, in case they were lost or taken from him. He had disguised himself while crossing Mexico to the port of Mazatlan and only reached Monterey by way of a long detour to Hawaii. His dispatches were indeed lost; he recopied them and consulted with Consul Larkin when he arrived, then slipped away to the north to find Frémont.

Though we will never know the exact content of the messages, written and oral, Gillespie transmitted to Frémont, we have a good idea of their gist. In the event war broke out between the United States and Mexico, Frémont was to defend American interests in California and, if possible, make Alta California independent from Mexico City and a territory of the United States. Since the directions had been given the autumn before, three thousand miles away, they would have been general and somewhat vague, but their overall intentions were clear. How Frémont would carry them out was left to his discretion and the opportunities that presented themselves.

The American government, and especially Polk, feared British warships that were prowling the Pacific coast, monitoring the events as they unfolded and waiting for an excuse to move in. Perhaps the Mexicans had already promised California to John Bull in return for forgiveness of their substantial debts. While much has been made of the mystery of Frémont's precise orders from Washington, we know essentially what he was authorized to do. Whether his timing and judgment and methods were sound is another matter.

Perhaps unknown to Frémont or to Polk, a Roman Catholic priest named Eugene McNamara had gained permission from the Mexican government to establish a colony of Irish Catholics in a utopian community in southern California. It would please the British government to get rid of as many Catholics from Ireland as they could. The plan never came to anything, but is an example of British interest in Alta California. After reading Gillespie's dispatches, Frémont had no doubt that it was his duty to make sure California became a territory of the United States, and he as well as Polk and Senator Benton "regarded the California coast as the boundary fixed by nature to round off our national domain." Daniel Walker Howe has pointed out that there is no record in the papers of the Foreign Office in London of British intention to take California in the 1840s.

Frémont was so intent on the conquest of California that he forgot to post guards at the camp on Upper Klamath Lake. Carson was awakened in the night by a thud, and found his friend Basil Lajeunesse had had his head split open by an ax. As he gave the alarm Indians rushed into the camp, swinging axes and shooting arrows. When the Indian leader was killed the others retreated into the forest.

As Carson inspected the Indian dead he decided they were Klamaths, a band Frémont's party had befriended. The Indians' weapons were British, from the Hudson's Bay Company. It was possible the British had encouraged the Klamaths to attack the Americans, to discourage the settlement of the Oregon country. Angered that he had not been able to prevent the attack that killed three of his friends and by supposed British perfidy, Carson grabbed the fallen leader's British-made ax and chopped the dead Indian leader's head to pieces.

In retaliation for the raid, Frémont and his men decided the Klamath village must be destroyed. Because he had lost those three friends, including two trusted Delaware scouts, Carson moved with cold determination. Following the lake shore they came to the fishing village named Dokdokwas. As soon as their approach was spotted Carson ordered a charge. As the villagers ran into the woods or swam out into the lake, Carson and his men killed twenty-one of them. "We gave them something to remember," Carson later said. Though Carson said women and children were not harmed, the Klamaths would later claim otherwise. The village was burned and Carson described the conflagration as "a beautiful sight."

It is thought by the historian David Roberts that Frémont's camp had been attacked by Modocs, not Klamaths. In their fury Frémont and Carson blamed the wrong Indians and left an enduring impression among the Klamaths that Americans were ruthless killers, motivated by hate and cruelty beyond logic or cause.

In the aftermath of the destruction on the lake, a Klamath warrior who had returned to the village aimed a poison arrow at Carson but was ridden down by Frémont. Carson never forgot that the captain, whose life he had saved so many times, now saved his life. There is a peculiar dimension to the relationship between Carson and Frémont. When they were together they exhibited a brutality that exceeded anything either had shown on his own. It was as though they sanctioned the worst cruelty in each other. Frémont could order Carson to do the killing that he eschewed, absolving himself of the crime. Carson would do the killing because he was only following orders and was not himself responsible for what he had to do. It was a deadly partnership, and the episode at Upper Klamath Lake was perhaps the ugliest action in the life of either man.

On June 25, 1846, Frémont and his company of 160 soldiers and volunteers rode south into the village of Sonoma, just north of San Francisco Bay, where a celebration was under way, because on June 14 the group of Americans who called themselves Bears, or "Osos," had taken over the town, placed the leaders in prison, commandeered the weapons in the armory and all available horses and declared the region an independent republic, "the Bear Flag Republic." They had been celebrating their bravado ever since, with liquor and speeches. One of their leaders, a Dr. Semple, called their acts "high and holy" and added, "the world has not hitherto manifested so high a degree of civilization." Frémont's men joined in the festivities, but one would recall later his impression that the rebels of Sonoma were mostly "moved by nothing but the chance of plunder without the slightest principle of honor." The flag that flew over the town had been fashioned from scraps of ladies' undergarments, stained with a rough image of a grizzly bear made from berry juice. It was the model of the California flag of the future.

Frémont's presence in California had helped inspire this revolt, and he was happy to join the Bear Flaggers for Fourth of July celebrations. But such a rebellion was probably as inevitable in California in 1846 as it had been in Texas a decade earlier. The number of Americans streaming into the region guaranteed the takeover sooner or later. Frémont's earlier stand at Gabilan Peak may have been the catalyst that made it happen sooner. Frémont waited for the Mexicans to make the next move. The fact that General Castro in the north had been quarreling with Governor Pio Pico in the south gave further encouragement to the Americans.

Already General José Castro had ordered all Americans out of California and he had sent Captain Joaquín de la Torre north with a company to drive the Bear Flaggers out of their stronghold at Sonoma. Frémont had assembled his army of soldiers, farmers, trappers, adventurers, Indians, and immigrants of ten different nationalities to defend the rebels. But by the time they arrived at Sonoma, the Bear Flaggers had already driven the captain and his men away and resumed their celebrations. In the "conquest" of California, Frémont himself would fight only a few small skirmishes.

Taking command of the situation, Frémont signed his letters "Commandant of United States Forces in California." He wore a colorful uniform and assembled all available men into a California battalion. Frémont issued imperious orders, and when John Sutter questioned his judgment and authority he told the hospitable Swiss immigrant, "If you don't like what I'm doing, then you can go and join the Mexicans." Frémont trailed Joaquín de la Torre and his men to San Francisco, but the Mexicans managed to escape on a schooner into the fog.

Two Bear Flaggers who left Sonoma to procure gun powder for the camp were caught by Mexicans, tied to trees, and tortured to death. On June 28 Frémont's men apprehended three Californios, twins Ramon and Francisco de Haro and their uncle José de los Berreyesa. Carson demanded that they hand over any messages they might be carrying, but they denied they had any dispatches. Carson asked Frémont if they should take them prisoner. Frémont answered, "No, I have no use for prisoners." He paused, then added, "Do your duty."

Consulting with the men around him, Carson realized the captain meant for him to execute the three in retaliation for the lynching of the two Sonoma men. Still Carson hesitated and Frémont shouted, "Mr. Carson, *your duty*!" Carson and the men with him shot the Californios on the spot. Frémont later denied that he had intended for the three to be killed. Carson searched the bodies and found the dispatches he had guessed they were carrying.

The killing of the Californios is another example of Carson's willingness to follow orders from a superior. On his own he probably would have searched the men and let them go. He had no hatred of Mexicans; in fact he was married into a Mexican family. But he could not refuse an order from Frémont, the educated, confident leader. The fact that Carson does not mention the incident of the executions in his memoirs suggests he was indeed later ashamed of what he had done, even though one of the three men was, as it turned out, a courier for the enemy.

Frémont waited two weeks before marching his battalion south to the provincial capital of Monterey. By then the town had already surrendered to Commodore Robert Field Stockton of the U.S. Pacific Fleet. Stockton was as grandiose and ambitious as Frémont. With the Stars and Stripes flying over Monterey again, the commodore wrote to President Polk, "My word at present is the law of the land." He and Frémont became allies and partners in the conquest of Alta California.

Stockton designated Frémont's forces the Naval Battalion of Mounted Riflemen and commissioned Frémont a major, Gillespie a captain, and Carson a lieutenant. Their next move was to sail south and secure San Diego, Los Angeles, and Santa Barbara for the American cause. The British warship *Collingwood* kept watch in Monterey harbor but made no move to prevent the American actions. Unknown to Frémont and Stockton, the Mexican government had offered Britain both Baja and Alta California in exchange for forgiveness of their debt, but the British foreign minister, Lord Palmerston, had refused. John Bull had no stomach to interfere with an American campaign so far advanced, with so many settlers already occupying the territory. Palmerston believed the Mexicans had been foolish to take such a militant stand against the United States.

Though Carson and his mountain men suffered dreadfully from sea sickness on the four-day cruise to San Diego, they took the southern town with almost no resistance. But Carson vowed never to set foot on a boat again. "I'd rather ride on a grizzly," he swore. On August 13, 1846, Stockton and Frémont marched their combined forces of sailors, marines, mountain men, Indians, farmers, and adventurers into the Pueblo de los Angeles, as General Castro and the Mexican army escaped over the San Bernardino Mountains toward Sonora in Mexico. While they celebrated the easy victories, the two American commanders were unaware that General Castro and Governor Pico were setting about to reorganize their forces to the south and planning a campaign to retake Alta California. In the words of Robert W. Merry, "So intent was Stockton on indulging his characteristic self-absorption that he overlooked a budding resistance movement."

Anxious to get news of the victories to Washington, Frémont nominated Carson to carry letters across the continent to President Polk, Senator Benton, and Secretary of War Marcy. Such an assignment would be "a reward for his brave and valuable service on many occasions." With fifteen handpicked men and a string of spare mules, Carson promised to reach the nation's capital in sixty days. While the popular imagination tends to see scouts like Carson on horseback, the fact is they mostly relied on mules in the wide expanses of the mountains and deserts of the West. Mules could travel farther on less water, could eat almost anything, could smell water five miles away, sense an approaching storm, or approaching Indians. The West was won more by mules than by horses. With his mules, six Delaware Indians, and nine other men, Carson set out for the east coast on September 5, 1846.

When Carson met General Stephen Watts Kearny and his army near Socorro on the Rio Grande on October 6, he astonished the general by describing the events that had occurred in California. Kearny was disappointed that the object of his mission had already been accomplished. Historians have sometimes argued that Kearny was angry that he had been denied the glory of the conquest, but it is just as likely he was somewhat relieved. After all, the real fighting was to the south, where Zachary Taylor was confronting large Mexican armies. As soon as Kearny could establish a stable government in California surely he would be allowed to join the more significant theater of the war.

When Kearny ordered Carson to turn about face and guide him to California, the scout hesitated. He had orders to go to Washington, and he had promised Frémont to take his letters to the nation's capital. Carson was not sure where his duty lay. But talking the issue over with his men, Carson saw that as a lieutenant in the U.S. Army he had no choice but to obey the orders from a general. Reluctantly he handed the saddlebags filled with letters over to his old friend Thomas "Broken Hand" Fitzpatrick for the journey to the Potomac and turned his mule back toward the West with Kearny.

We have the testimony of a medical doctor traveling with Kearny, Dr. John S. Griffin, that the men heading west were taken aback that their mission in California had already been accomplished. "The feeling was one of disappointment and regret," the doctor wrote. "Most of us hoped on leaving Santa Fe that we might have a little kick-up with the good people of California but this blasted all our hopes."

Perhaps because he was irritated that he would not be the liberator of California, but had been preceded by the strutting Frémont, Kearny overreacted to the news. Since his forces were not needed on the West Coast and there was almost a thousand miles of desert to cross before he reached San Diego, Kearny sent two thirds of his men back to Santa Fe and continued west with a mere hundred men. It was the worst mistake of the campaign. But Dr. Griffin recorded in his diary that having

Carson as guide gave a new confidence to the dragoons who continued toward the Gila River. "We put out, with merry hearts & light packs on our long march—every man feeling renewed confidence in consequence of having such a guide."

Passing through Apache country, Kearny's party entered the territory of small desert tribes, known by such names as "Wolf Eaters, the Dirty Fellows, the Club Indians, the Pine Forest Dwellers, the Tremblers, the Albinos, the Fools." The Indians they encountered seemed as strange as the land itself. Many of them had never seen an American before. The buttes sparkled orange and pink and lavender in the sunset and gold at sunrise. The stars shivered brilliant and close at night in the cold desert sky.

Though he tried to keep up a front of cheer and good humor, as was his habit, it is thought Carson was bitterly disappointed not to have traveled to the East, which he had never seen, and to have missed meeting important people there, including the president himself, and Senator Benton. He had planned to stop for one night in Taos to see Josepha. He had set out to cross the continent in two months, and he had failed, and had failed in his promise to Frémont.

What Kearny didn't know was that the people of California had revolted against Stockton and Frémont and retaken all the towns in the south including San Diego. General Castro and Governor Pico had organized and marshaled the local resentment against the Americans into an effective force and succeeded. As Kearny and his men crossed the mysterious, fantastic deserts of Arizona and eastern California, their horses died, and even the general was forced to ride a humble mule.

Luckily the Americans encountered the Pima Indians who were not only friendly but were accomplished farmers with irrigation dams and ditches, and large crops of corn, beans, squash, tobacco, and cotton. They offered the Americans their hospitality and would take no pay in return. They likely felt pity for the dusty, half-starved, bedraggled white men who seemed lost and wandering in the desert. Of the Pimas, the topographer Lieutenant William Emory recorded, "It was a rare sight to be thrown in the midst of a large nation of what is often termed 'wild Indians,' who surpass many of the Christian nations in agriculture, are little behind them in the useful arts, and are immeasurably before them in honesty and virtue." It was an observation made many times on the frontier, that some Indian nations seemed more Christian in their charity than the whites who claimed to bring Christian love and charity to the savages.

On November 23, 1846, where the Gila empties into the Colorado River, Lieutenant Emory and his staff encountered a Mexican who tried to evade them. The man was arrested and brought into camp. He was found to be carrying letters in Spanish describing the victorious rebellion against the Americans in California. The letters were filled with bravado and all said the same thing: the Yankees had been defeated.

As soon as he absorbed the news, Kearny saw the mistake he had made at Socorro, sending two-thirds of his men back to Santa Fe. Carson's news had been dangerously outdated. But Kearny also saw he could not turn back. He must push on with his minimal forces and see what could be done. The conquest of California was still to be accomplished. Perhaps he could achieve that glory after all.

Suddenly Carson too saw the expedition in a new light. His friends and associates, including Frémont, might be in danger, might have been killed. It seemed providential that instead of going on to Washington he had turned back to California to help them at this hour of peril. Carson was not sentimental, but he had a deep regard for duty and loyalty and responsibility. He and Kearny's men crossed the Colorado River on November 25 and headed west with a new excitement and determination, and not a little apprehension.

Stumbling through miles of bleak desert country, they finally met a rancher named Edward Stokes about fifty miles east of San Diego. Stokes agreed to take a letter to Stockton, informing the commodore of Kearny's approach and asking to be brought up to date on recent events. On December 5, Captain Gillespie and thirty-nine marines showed up at Kearny's camp, bringing with them a four-pound cannon.

Kearny's men were delighted to have Gillespie's reinforcements, but the news they brought was chilling. Stockton had retaken part of San Diego, but most of southern California was indeed occupied by Mexican forces. Captain Andrés Pico and a large force of Californios were camped nearby at the village of San Pasqual, blocking the road to San Diego. The eager Gillespie suggested that with their combined forces Kearny might mount a surprise attack on Pico's men and "beat up their camp."

Carson supported the idea of a surprise attack. He argued that while Californios were individually brave they were poorly organized and untrained. "All you have to do is yell, make a rush, and the Californians will run away," he said. Carson's experience with Californios had been in the north, months ago. It would have been wiser to press on to San Diego, but neither he nor Kearny nor Gillespie knew what they were up against at San Pasqual. And Kearny saw a chance to win some of the glory he had thought had been denied him.

Unknown to Kearny or Carson, Pico had organized a force of expert horsemen. Neither Mexican soldiers nor militia, they looked with contempt on the government in Mexico City and its feeble army. But the arrogant intrusion of the Americans had moved them to resist the takeover. Wrapped in colorful serapes, these ranchmen rode fine horses that were quick and responsive. Though they had firearms, their weapon of choice was a long lance with a razor-sharp blade mounted at the end. With the lance they could slice into an enemy out of reach of sword or saber. These horsemen were far different from the Californios Carson had encountered around Sonoma. They did not consider themselves really Mexican, but Hispanic, with some Indian blood, a breed apart.

Almost everything about Kearny's planned attack at San Pasqual went wrong. A small force sent out to reconnoiter in the dark made so much noise Pico's men heard them and sounded the alarm. Fleeing into the dark the Americans dropped a jacket that had U.S. printed on it. Pico knew the American army was close by.

Still hoping to keep some element of surprise, Kearny ordered his men to mount up in the middle of the night and ride toward the Californio camp. A cold drizzle fell in the darkness as Kearny directed his dragoons to take prisoners and kill as few as possible. "Remember one point of the saber is far more effective than any number of thrusts," the general admonished.

It was December 6, 1846, as the dragoons began riding toward the San Pasqual encampment. Carson rode at the front with Kearny and Lieutenant Emory as they picked their way through the steep, rocky terrain. Three-quarters of a mile from the village Kearny gave the order to "trot," as the dragoons deployed in a long line, officers in front. But Captain Abraham Johnston misunderstood the order and thought he had heard

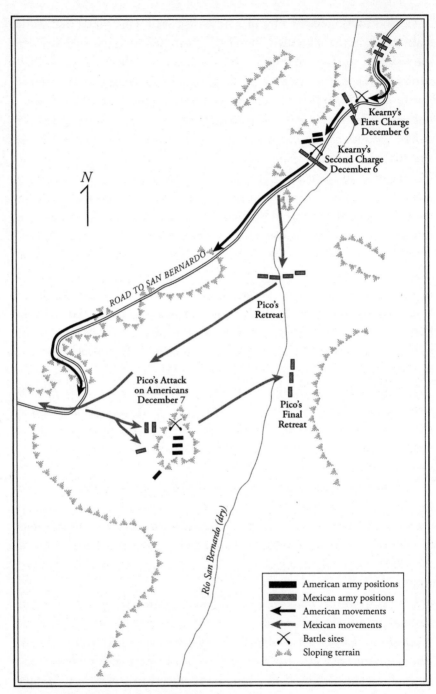

N

Kearny's
First Charge
December 6

Kearny's
Second Charge
December 6

ROAD TO SAN BERNARDO

Pico's
Retreat

Pico's Attack
on Americans
December 7

Pico's
Final
Retreat

Río San Bernardo (dry)

	American army positions
	Mexican army positions
←	American movements
←	Mexican movements
✗	Battle sites
	Sloping terrain

Battle of San Pasqual, December 6–7, 1846

"Charge!" The mistake was passed down the long line and the dragoons rushed forward at a gallop. The general saw the error, but it was too late to correct it. To compound the problem, the officers on horses ran far ahead of the enlisted men on mules, dangerously dividing the force. Carson urged his mount out ahead of all but Captain Johnston.

As they descended the hill toward the line of Pico's men, who had quickly mounted and assembled in formation, Johnston was killed by a musket ball. Carson's horse stumbled on the rocks and threw him to the ground, breaking his rifle stock. He was almost trampled by the dragoons following him but crawled away and seized the rifle of a dead dragoon. To make matters worse the powder in the dragoons' weapons had been ruined by the dampness.

The Americans were no match for the Californios who parried with their lances, slicing the dragoons, wheeled and regrouped, then charged again. They rode with assurance and ease and their unusual weapons took a terrible toll on the Americans. They literally rode circles around Kearny's men, jabbing and breaking away, coming forward again. As the Mexican historian José Vasconcelos describes their tactics, "They would allow themselves to be pursued, feigning flight, by the Yankee forces. Then suddenly, when the number of pursuers had diminished, they would turn around with fury and in a sweep eliminate whole bodies of the Yankee troops." Kearny himself received painful cuts on the arm, back, and buttocks. Almost every American who attacked the Californios was wounded or dead.

Hiding himself among the boulders, Carson shot and reloaded in the dawn light, picking off the horsemen one by one. With deadly efficiency from the side of the affray, he probably killed more of the enemy than all the dragoons rushing back and forth swinging sabers. Kearny fell to the ground and Lieutenant Emory came to his aid. Captain Gillespie was also knocked to the ground with a cut on the back of his neck and another lance thrust that ripped his lip and broke a tooth. And then he was stabbed in the lungs.

Gillespie limped to Kearny's side as the dragoons wheeled a cannon into place and fired a shot or two. But the Californios were expert ropers and they lassoed the artillery piece and dragged it away. The horsemen withdrew from the battlefield to confer, as the Americans tried to tend their wounded. Captain Pico was euphoric with his victory, though in a literal sense the Americans, though slashed to pieces, still held the field. Dr. Griffin rushed to treat Kearny's wounds, but the general ordered him to attend the other wounded first.

As the sun rose Kearny pushed himself up to survey the carnage. Twenty-one Americans were dead and as many more were critically injured. The rocky ground was covered with blood. As the general studied the scene he fainted from loss of his own blood. His men gathered close to him, expecting another attack from the agile lancers. But Pico and his men were waiting for reinforcements from General Castro in Los Angeles. As it turned out, Castro could send no one to San Pasqual because of an uprising of the prisoners of war in Los Angeles.

All day on December 6, 1846, the Americans waited with arms ready as the doctor treated the wounded. They could see Pico's horsemen stirring in the hills around them out of rifle range. An hour passed, and another hour and still there was no attack. Many of the wounded died on the wet, rocky ground. Dr. Griffin treated Kearny's multiple wounds and the general regained consciousness, though he had lost so much blood it was thought he would surely die. Command was passed to Captain Henry Turner.

The Americans cleaned their weapons and waited. Some men sharpened their swords on rocks. They could not bury their dead until dark for fear the graves would be desecrated by the Californios who kept riding around them. Pinned down on the rocky ground, they waited until dark, then dug a pit beneath a willow tree and placed the dead in it. Bodies of dead Californios, killed by Carson's rifle, were buried with the twenty-plus Americans. Attracted by the smell of blood, wolves circled the camp and howled in the night.

Instead of dying, Kearny actually revived a little overnight and reassumed command by daybreak. Struggling to get on his horse, in spite of the deep buttock wound, he ordered his men to move. The wounded were placed on crude litters pulled by mules. With cannon in front and unwounded dragoons on either side, packhorses and wounded in the center, the little army moved out as hurt men moaned and cried out on bouncing travois poles.

The Californios followed them in the rocky scrub country, apparently waiting for the right moment to attack again. It is a fact that civilians and untrained soldiers find it hard to attack people who are not attacking them. As they looked on at the pitiful American force, the ranchers waited for the spirit of attack to move them. Expecting a charge from the rear, the American were surprised when a group of concealed riflemen fired on them from a nearby hill. Lieutenant Emory was ordered to lead a cavalry charge against the position, and five Californios were killed and the hill taken. No Americans were lost in the action.

Kearny decided his forces were too exhausted to continue on to San Diego thirty miles to the southwest. The many wounded were simply unable to go farther. With the Californios on swift horses still riding around them at a distance, the Americans made camp on the hill Lieutenant Emory had taken. The men who were still fit carried rocks to build a kind of fortress on the hill. There was no water on the high ground. For rations they slaughtered the weakest mules and cooked them. The place has been known ever since as Mule Hill and the stone breastworks can still be seen there. As the Americans hunkered down on the hill they realized that the enemy forces were growing as more local citizens joined Pico to repel the Yankees. It was thought the Californios had outnumbered the Americans two to one before. Now the ratio was closer to four to one. The Americans assumed Pico could attack them whenever he chose.

Their only hope was to get a message to Stockton in San Diego asking for reinforcements. Otherwise Kearny's situation was hopeless. The Californios encircled them with three rings of sentries, and Gillespie knew that the road to San Diego was heavily guarded by Mexican soldiers. Even if somebody slipped out of the camp it would be a considerable challenge to reach the Americans at the harbor.

To no one's surprise Carson volunteered with Lieutenant Edward Beale of the navy to take the message to Stockton. Impossible missions were his specialty and while he could not read letters he again and again volunteered to deliver them for those who could. With Beale and an Indian named Chemuctah, Carson planned to slip through Pico's three lines of encirclement. He knew Pico was expecting him to attempt a breakout, for the captain was heard to admonish his men, "Se escapara el lobo" (the wolf will escape). The wolf he meant was Kit Carson. In the dark Carson and his two companion crawled off the hill. Because their boots made noise on the gravel and loose rocks they took them off and tucked them under their belts. Chemuctah kept his moccasins on. Because their canteens clanked on the rocks, they had to be abandoned. Gripping their weapons, the three inched forward on their elbows through rocks and brush.

As they approached the first line of sentries, Carson could see a long lance held upright against the star-lit sky. A mounted Californio struck a flint and lit a cigarillo so close Carson could almost touch his horse's hoof. Lieutenant Beale was so frightened Carson later said he could hear the navy man's heart knocking against his chest. The lieutenant came close to panic and hissed, "We're gone; let's jump up and fight it out!"

The cool, level-headed Carson whispered back, "Been in worse places before." Finally the sentry finished his smoke and moved on in the dark. As Beale and Carson crawled forward they discovered they had lost their boots. There was no way to find their footwear in the dark. They would have to make their way to San Diego through prickly pear and other cacti, sharp rocks and thistle, barefoot. Slipping into arroyos, draws and dry washes, they finally made it beyond the third line of sentries by dawn. Stumbling on their tender feet, they covered more than fifteen miles by the afternoon. All the roads into San Diego were guarded by Mexican soldiers. It was decided that each of the three would take a different route in hopes that at least one would get through to Stockton. Carson took the more difficult and indirect path, thinking that the more likely way to succeed. It took him another twelve hours to reach the American camp. Beale and Chemuctah were already there, as exhausted and footsore as Carson.

Stockton had already sent almost two hundred men to rescue Kearny and the dragoons at Mule Hill. Lieutenant Beale was so worn out and traumatized by his ordeal he was "out of his head." Put on board the USS *Congress,* it took him months to recover. According to one report, Chemuctah was in bed for a week, then vanished.

It took Carson several days to recover, his feet cut and blistered, pierced by prickly pear spines. The crawl from Mule Hill through three lines of guards would seal his reputation as a great hero of the West. Bernard DeVoto would call him "the master mountain man." A soldier who served at Mule Hill would write to his family in Connecticut, "Never has there been a man like Kit Carson. All that has been said about him, and more, is true. He is fearless as the lion, as stealthy as the panther, as strong as the oxen." The historian David A. Clary would observe that if any single person deserved credit for the American conquest of California, "it was the talented mountain man."

But his heroic mission at Mule Hill did not seem to loom especially large in Carson's memory. In his memoirs he merely said that they "finally got through, but . . . had the misfortune to lose our shoes . . . had to travel barefoot over country covered with prickly pear and rocks. We reached San Diego the next night."

While Carson and the two others made their way to San Diego and Stockton marched his two hundred sailors and marines to the northeast, Kearny and the dragoons were desperately holding out on Mule Hill. The Californios continued to circle and harass the trapped Americans and once stampeded a herd of wild horses toward the hill to drive the dragoons off. Pico assumed it was only a matter of time until the Americans surrendered. They had no water and no grass to feed their mules. The soldiers with deep lance wounds began to suffer from infection.

One of Carson's men, named Robideaux, had lost so much blood everyone assumed he would die. In his delirium, he began to call out that he smelled coffee. Since the battalion had no coffee, it seemed obvious he was hallucinating. "A cup of coffee would save my life," Robideaux begged. But then others smelled coffee too, and when they investigated they found someone, probably one of Gillespie's marines, boiling coffee over a small sagebrush fire. Lieutenant Emory took the coffee to the supposedly dying Robideaux. The French trapper drank the coffee and recovered.

With men dying, no water and no forage for their mules, Kearny decided they would have to break out, whatever the cost. It was likely Carson had never reached Stockton and no relief was coming. On the night of December 10, the general ordered all baggage except the absolute minimum to be burned. They could carry little except their weapons and the wounded for the thirty mile dash to San Diego, and whatever they left behind would be claimed by Pico's men. A great bonfire lit up the night as men tossed their belongings into the flames and the Californios watched from the surrounding hills. At dawn the Americans would try to make their getaway.

In the early hours of December 11, sentries heard the sound of marching feet. "Who goes there?" a guard shouted. The marching army came on and it seemed the Californios must have assembled an infantry for an attack.

"Hold fire!" someone shouted in the dark at the bottom of the hill. "We're Americans." The 120 sailors and 80 marines Stockton had sent marched into the light of the campfires. They brought a supply of hardtack and tobacco, fresh clothes, and full canteens. A bullet out of the dark hissed through the camp but no one was hit. Kearny's men laughed and shouted with surprise and glee.

The next morning Pico and the Californios seemed to have evaporated. What was left of Kearny's Army of the West began its journey to San Diego. It took them until the afternoon of December 12 to reach the harbor town in a cold driving rain. Lieutenant Emory later wrote, "The Pacific opened for the first time to our view, the sight producing strange but agreeable emotions. One of the men . . . exclaimed, 'Lord! There is a great prairie without a tree.'"

Stockton and Kearny planned the reconquest of Pueblo de los Angeles and waited for Frémont and his battalion to arrive from the north. Heavy rains had delayed his progress, but no Mexican army had confronted his forces. Frémont sent no word to Stockton of his whereabouts, and the retaking of Los Angeles was left to Stockton and Kearny and the dragoons, sailors, marines, and mountain men, including a few Delaware Indians. On January 10, 1847, they marched into the town with the navy band playing.

But one mountain man had found Frémont and rejoined his battalion — Kit Carson. Recovered from his devastating crawl and walk from Mule Hill to San Diego, Carson left Kearny and made his way north with a few of his men to find the Pathfinder whom he had served so faithfully.

It is obvious that Frémont was taking his time both responding to Kearny's letters and approaching Los Angeles. It was what he had done months before in the north as he waited for events to turn in his favor. It had worked then and Stockton had appointed him commandant of

U.S. Forces in California. But now a brigadier general, of all things, had shown up, a seasoned veteran of many battles, going all the way back to Queenston Heights in the War of 1812. Kearny was a hero when Frémont was one year old. And Kearny was the officer Frémont had coerced into giving him an artillery piece in 1843, the howitzer he had never fired but lost in the snows of the High Sierras.

Much has been made of the mystery of Frémont's personality. Scholars prefer to view him as a puzzling figure, brilliant at times, foolish at others. But some things are pretty clear about the Pathfinder. One is that he liked to assume roles he had not earned. It is important to remember that Frémont had little military training or experience outside of surveying. In the conquest of California this conqueror never fought a real battle, and he may never have fired a shot at a Mexican. He arrived at Sonoma after the Bear Flaggers had driven off the Mexicans under Joaquín de la Torre. He marched into Monterey and San Diego and Los Angeles against no resistance. Frémont's men had fought a skirmish with Mexican soldiers at La Natividad, a few miles north of Monterey on November 16, 1846, but it seems Frémont had not been present.

Having been commandant of U.S. Forces in California and calling himself the conqueror of California, Frémont was in a vulnerable position. Kearny and his men had just fought (and lost) a major battle in the Mexican War in California. Kearny himself had been critically wounded. Frémont's training was as a topographical engineer and his orders were to make maps of the West, yet he believed he had become a kind of Napoleon. He had the charisma of a Napoleon and he commanded the loyalty of brave men such as Carson and the scout Dick Owens. But suddenly the rough old soldier Kearny had shown up to usurp his command. In the mountains north of Los Angeles, Frémont temporized and pondered, sorting and resorting the pieces of the puzzle. Waiting might cause the prize to drop into his lap as it had before: maybe his luck would hold one more time.

The breakthrough came when Captain Andrés Pico, driven by Stockton and Kearny's forces from Los Angeles on January 8–9, 1847, sent Frémont a message that no more resistance would be offered to the Americans if he was allowed to withdraw. Pico also turned over to Frémont the American cannon seized at San Pasqual. Likely Pico expected

Frémont to pass his message up the chain of command or perhaps he feared Kearny would want to take revenge for the killings at San Pasqual and thought he might get better terms from Frémont. But Frémont acted as though Pico had surrendered all Mexican forces and all of California to him, the victor. Frémont met with Pico and granted him very generous terms, then rode with Carson at his side into Los Angeles as a conquering hero. One biographer would say that he came down out of the mountains into Pueblo de los Angeles like a Greek hero returning from Troy. And he did that apparently without firing a shot at the enemy.

As he recovered from his embarrassing wounds, Kearny simmered, watching Frémont strut and preen, signing his letters "Commandant of United States Forces of California." Had he been in better shape himself, Kearny would have shown Frémont his orders from Washington, which explicitly made Kearny commander in the West. As it was, Kearny bit his tongue in astonishment as the lieutenant colonel of the topographical engineers ignored the orders of a brigadier general of the line. Kearny behaved with the patience of a statesman. Frémont and his men returned to Monterey, as if Kearny had never appeared in California, and Carson was dispatched once again to cross the continent with letters for the nation's capital. The next year Frémont would be court-martialed for insubordination and found guilty of mutiny.

Carson had witnessed almost every phase of one of the most significant chains of events in American history. When he set out with Frémont in 1845, the United States stopped at the western Continental Divide. As he made his way toward Washington in the late winter of 1847, American claims would soon include Oregon and California and all the land he knew so well west of the Missouri River. Carson had witnessed more history than he could have imagined. And he had carried the messages of that history in his saddlebags.

———

IT MAY SEEM a little far-fetched to compare Kit Carson to Thomas Jefferson. At first glance it would be hard to think of a greater contrast than that between the Sage of Monticello, scientist, architect, philosopher, politician, and writer, and the illiterate scout and Indian killer of the Rockies and Far West. And even where they do share interests,

Jefferson would be the theorist and Carson the practitioner, Jefferson with his aristocratic polish talking of "buffalo bones" and the religious practices of Indians, Carson with his expertise at survival among those Indians, knowing how to drink the blood of a mule to keep from perishing in the blazing desert, how to avoid an Apache ambush.

But oddly enough it is in the area of science that these two unlikely fellow Americans have the most in common, especially if we include geography and ethnography as disciplines of science. In his *Notes on the State of Virginia* and in his letters and inquiries throughout his life, Jefferson studied the soils, minerals, climate, rivers, people, maps, harbors, animals, plants, and navigational and commercial potential of the continent. He corresponded with scientists and geographers, and he subsidized explorers. Carson devoted his life from about the age of seventeen to learning about those very subjects. Everyone who has left an account of Carson mentions his great knowledge as a pathfinder. He learned and remembered exactly what Jefferson had wanted to find out. It is unlikely any white man of his time knew the geography of the West and the native peoples there as well as Carson. He carried in his mind and memory and in the wisdom of his hands and eyes and ears the knowledge Jefferson had sought in charts, navigational logs, and written descriptions by explorers. Carson was also fluent in Navajo, Apache, Comanche, Cheyenne, Arapaho, Crow, and Blackfeet, as well as Shoshone, Paiute, sign language, Spanish, and Canadian French.

Rather than writing down his experience and wisdom, Carson remembered and acted. He knew Indian languages the way Jefferson knew classical and modern European languages. Carson could usually tell at a glance whether an Indian was a Digger, or Apache, or Cheyenne. As a young man Carson became fluent in Spanish and adapted himself to Hispanic culture and the Roman Catholic religion. As a young mountain man he learned to kill Indians on sight if they were Blackfeet or showed signs of hostility. If white men were killed by Indians, then Indians, almost any Indians, must die as retribution. In 1846 Carson helped destroy a California Indian village on the way to Upper Klamath Lake and then destroyed a Klamath village on the lake. Yet within a few years he became a most reluctant Indian fighter as he understood more and more about the different native peoples and their struggle to survive. By then he knew that many natives of the Southwest were driven to raid white settlements and other tribes because the game they had depended on for centuries was gone. When ordered by General James Carleton in 1862 to kill all male Indians, he ignored the order. He was a sympathetic Indian agent and a tireless spokesman for Indian rights. One of the major ironies of Carson's life was that he brutally rounded up the Navajos to force them onto the Bosque Redondo reservation in Texas and then became a forceful advocate for the return of the same Dine people to their traditional homeland. Like Jefferson before him, he kept learning and evolving in his thought and actions.

There has been a good deal of discussion about how Carson actually spoke. Since his letters and dispatches and memoirs were dictated and written down by others and no doubt polished and smoothed out in the process, it is not easy to hear his actual voice from those documents. We know he was an effective storyteller once he got started in the right company, cheerful and entertaining even in the midst of hardships. And we know the mountain men loved colorful speech, referring to themselves in third person in conversation as "this child," or "this soul," or "this nigger," or "this old coon."

From the spelling in the journals of Lewis and Clark and the spelling in some of Jefferson's letters to his relatives, we can construe how words were spoken by them, especially in informal contexts. What we hear is heavy Midlands dialect, with hard *r*s, where wheelbarrow becomes "wheelbarr" and fire becomes "farr," and path is pronounced "parth." It would be surprising if Carson did not speak in a similar way.

But unlike most of his contemporary speakers of that Blue Ridge Mountain dialect that made its way to Kentucky and then to Missouri and farther west, Carson was fluent in native languages as well. Harvey Carter, one of Carson's most important biographers, was certain Kit "said 'thar' and 'whar' and 'hyar' and 'fit' for fought and 'done' for did."

One old acquaintance recalled, "Kit never swore more'n was necessary," which fits our image of the quiet understatement of the man. Another corroborated this detail, saying, "He talked but little, was very quiet, and seldom used immoral or profane language." According to a report from 1864, Carson was riled by a suggestion that Indian women and children be killed and burst out, "I loathe and hate the man that would. 'Taint natural for brave men to kill little women and little children."

The Englishman George Frederick Ruxton, in an article for *Blackwood's Edinburgh Magazine* in June–November 1848, wrote down speech he had heard in 1846–47 while traveling with mountain men. One passage reads: "Do'ee hyar now? This nigger sees sign ahead—he does; he'll be afoot afore long, if he don't keep his eye skinned—*he* will. *Injuns* is all about, they ar': Blackfoot at that. Can't come round this child—they can't, wagh!"

"Wagh!" was apparently an interjection used frequently in the speech of the mountain men. It may have been akin to the "what" some Englishmen put at the end of their sentences or the "why" used by Midlands speakers for emphasis, as in "Why, I wouldn't give a nickel for his chances." Commenting on Carson's use of language, the historian David Roberts writes, "To imagine Kit Carson immersed in the world Ruxton celebrates is to hear him narrate his adventures with an almost Shakespearean indulgence in far-fetched conceit and homespun hyperbole."

In good ways and in bad ways, Kit Carson shared Thomas Jefferson's romantic vision of the West, of a republic washed by the waters of two oceans. Like Jefferson, Carson was willing to make extreme sacrifices for the service of his country. We may approve or disapprove of such pronounced dedication, but it was a part of who he was. When President Polk promised Carson a commission as lieutenant in the regular army in 1847 in recognition of his services and sent him back to California with messages, Carson discovered on his return at Santa Fe that the Senate had refused to approve the commission or his pay for two years work. Though disappointed, Carson decided to continue on his mission with letters from the capital.

My friends advised me to deliver the despatches to the commanding officer and not take them through. I considered the matter, reaching the conclusion that as I had been chosen as the most competent person to take the despatches through safely, I would fulfill the duty; if the service I was performing was beneficial to the public, it did not matter to me whether I was enjoying the rank of lieutenant or only the credit of being an experienced mountaineer. I had gained both honor and credit by performing every duty entrusted to my charge, and on no account did I wish to forfeit the good opinion of a majority of my countrymen merely because the Senate of the United States had not deemed it proper to confirm my appointment to an office I had never sought, and one which, if confirmed, I would have to resign at the close of the war.

The phrasing is probably that of the amanuensis, but the sentiment doubtless Carson's own. The words might be another's, but the word, his word, when he gave it, was his own, and he kept it forever.

— Nine —

NICHOLAS TRIST

The Search for a Father Voice

In 1818, when Nicholas Trist fell in love with Thomas Jefferson's granddaughter Virginia Randolph, he desperately wanted to declare himself to her before leaving Monticello to become a cadet at West Point. And though he saw the girl every day and they were devoted friends, he chose not to speak to Virginia directly but instead wrote to her mother, Martha Jefferson Randolph, who was the hostess and manager of Monticello and whom Nicholas also saw every day. It was a pattern Nicholas would follow throughout his life. When something important or difficult needed to be discussed, he always chose to write long formal letters in his perfect penmanship. If he was criticized, he wrote even longer letters, explaining and defending himself and often accusing his critics in sarcastic terms, launching into long essays like a teacher lecturing an obstinate pupil.

Later in his life Trist would negotiate one of the most important treaties in American history, acquiring almost a third of the land of the contiguous United States. He would serve as private secretary to Thomas Jefferson, James Madison, and Andrew Jackson and become the trusted friend of many more prominent figures, including Winfield Scott, James Buchanan, and Alexis de Tocqueville. Yet few Americans have ever heard of Nicholas P. Trist. Born June 2, 1800, in Charlottesville, Virginia, he lived until 1874 and spent the last twenty-five years of his life in obscurity.

Trist has remained something of a mystery to historians. Trained as a lawyer by Jefferson himself, confidant of the great men of his time, Trist failed at many of the things he attempted. Most who knew him considered him unusually intelligent and well educated. He was fluent in several languages, including Spanish and French. It cannot have been easy to impress Jefferson, as Trist certainly did. He was the main executor of Jefferson's estate and it was Trist who had to sell off most of his property after the great man's death to pay his debts.

Given Trist's high connections, his noted intelligence and education, his hard work and dedication, it's difficult to explain the downward curve of his career. Given his advantages and ambition, it would seem almost inevitable that he would have become a statesman, a secretary of state, an important author or scholar. A biographer must look for the key to an elusive personality, and several historians have noted Trist's inability to compromise and his arrogant defensiveness as flaws that cost him again and again the advancement and support he expected. But no historian or biographer seems to have noticed that one definitive fact of his personality was his fear of face-to-face meetings when crucial issues were at stake—that and an apparent terror of public speaking.

For all Trist's education and energy with his pen, it appears impossible to find an instance when he stood up in front of a group of people and addressed them. There is a report that he once gave a toast at a celebration of Jefferson's birthday, but no confirmation of that report has been found. Oddly enough, Jefferson himself was reluctant to speak in public and, as we have seen, never addressed the Continental Congress at all. As president, the Sage of Monticello may have presented only two speeches, his inaugural addresses. As if in compensation for this timidity or reticence, Trist could be pompous and superior in the long letters he wrote in his defense. When he was accused by the British foreign minister, Lord Palmerston, of aiding the slave trade in his position as American consul in Havana in 1839, Trist wrote a 140-page letter in his defense. In the course of the long epistle the consul discussed everything from the history of slavery to the faults and vices of the British Empire. He was declared innocent of wrongdoing by a congressional committee, but his career as a consul was soon over. With so many friends and allies in Washington, Trist could have easily gone to the capital to present his case to the committee investigating his conduct, but he chose instead to rest his defense behind his tireless pen.

When Trist was sent to Mexico to negotiate an end to the Mexican

War and acquire southwestern territory for the United States, it would have been logical for him to present himself to General in Chief Winfield Scott, explain his mission, ask for his help, and show the general the proposed treaty he carried. Instead, Trist sent a brusque note with a sealed draft of the treaty, telling the general to forward it on to the Mexican government, as though he, Trist, were now in charge of affairs in Mexico. Trist's actions were all the more insulting considering Winfield Scott had a notable history as a diplomat as well as a soldier. One courteous face-to-face meeting could have prevented two months of standoff and angry accusations between the two men.

Whatever his failures, there is no doubt Nicholas P. Trist had a gift for friendship. Many people he met became friends for life. His relationships with Jefferson, Madison, Jackson, Buchanan, prove he could be charming, useful, loyal. No one ever accused him of betraying a trust and in later years he served as informant to historians and biographers of the great leaders he had known. It was expected that he himself would write an account of the momentous events he had participated in and witnessed and of the great leaders he had known so well. Trist expected it of himself, but that book never got written. As far as we can tell it never even got started. He could write long letters defending himself or advising others on their books, and he could write anonymous articles for newspapers. But under his own name he apparently could not publish a paragraph of a memoir or study that would have been a valuable addition to the history of his era. The writer's block and his tongue-tied affliction at the most important occasions stayed with him to the end. He blamed overwork in his underpaid jobs and his responsibilities as a family man, his poverty, and the evil times in which he lived. He seemed to react to events rather than expressing his ideas. But whatever the reason, he could not bring himself to face his countrymen. He could not speak from the heart, in his own voice, or say what needed to be said, for his time and for the future.

Even so, Trist maintained a high opinion of his other abilities. In his own mind and in his writing, he was assertive, assured, even superior. That sense of authority came in part from his long association with the leaders of his time, especially Thomas Jefferson. Jefferson had a long-standing friendship with the Trist family. While attending the

Continental Congress in Philadelphia, Jefferson had lodged in the home of Mrs. Mary House. After Jefferson's wife died, he took his daughter Martha with him to Philadelphia and Mrs. House's daughter, Mrs. Elizabeth Trist, looked after the little girl and became a second mother to her. Mrs. Trist's husband had been a British army officer at the time of the American Revolution, but he became an American citizen and then died soon afterward. Jefferson helped the widow and her son Hore Browse Trist secure their inheritance in England, and he encouraged them to settle in Charlottesville near Monticello in 1800.

Elizabeth Trist remained a close friend of Jefferson and was a frequent correspondent with the statesman. And when Jefferson became president he appointed Hore Browse Trist to the post of collector of customs at the port of Natchez on the Mississippi in 1802. After the Louisiana Purchase, Trist was moved on to the port of New Orleans. His wife and two sons, Nicholas and Hore Browse Jr., joined him there. Sadly, he died of yellow fever a few months later.

A short time after his father's death, Nicholas's mother married a prominent New Orleans lawyer named Philip Livingston Jones. According to all reports, Jones treated his stepsons well, sending them to a classical school run by a Mr. Debecour and to dancing classes with a Mr. Digrain. He even took the boys on an exciting trip to New York. Trist's earliest preserved letter dates from this trip.

At school young Nicholas studied French and Spanish as well as classical languages, and he showed a special aptitude for American history. In 1812 he and his brother were enrolled in the College of New Orleans where they also studied mathematics, science, and literature. The Trist brothers were apt students and excelled at all their subjects. Around 1810 the stepfather Jones had died and Nicholas's mother had married a wealthy cotton and sugar planter named Tournillon. Because Nicholas and Hore Browse were away at boarding school, they did not become close to Tournillon. Some biographers have seen Trist's lack of an enduring father figure as a key to his personality. In compensation he would make much of his upper class English heritage from his grandfather Trist and his relationships with great men.

As a boy in New Orleans, Nicholas got to know the father of one of his closest friends, the lawyer Edward Livingston, who served as aide to

Andrew Jackson at the Battle of New Orleans in January 1815. Livingston would be a mentor to Trist in New Orleans and later at the State Department in Washington. After graduating from the College of New Orleans in 1817, Trist considered returning to his native Virginia to study at the College of William and Mary, but he lacked the money for tuition. It was at this time that Thomas Jefferson invited the two Trist boys to come to Monticello for an extended visit. Jefferson had impoverished himself by extending hospitality to so many friends and acquaintances over the years, but he knew the visit would please the boys' grandmother, and the Sage of Monticello enjoyed having young people around to join his grandchildren in picnics, games, parties, and dances.

A stream of national and international visitors was constantly arriving and staying at Monticello, and Jefferson turned nobody away, going deeper and deeper in debt to entertain his many guests. The estate was a magic place for eighteen-year-old Nicholas. In the mornings he had long conversations with Jefferson himself and they sometimes took horseback rides, chatting as they inspected fields and gardens and shops on the estate. Trist kept notes from his conversations with Jefferson, and some scholars have speculated that Jefferson's views encouraged Trist to become a lifelong critic of organized religion. Certainly Jefferson's political ideals influenced Trist and he would always be a staunch Jeffersonian.

The household at Monticello was managed by Jefferson's only surviving child, Martha Jefferson Randolph. Though her husband, Thomas Mann Randolph, became the governor of Virginia, Martha and her nine children did not move to Richmond but remained at Monticello. Martha was a remarkable woman, at least six feet tall, selfless in her dedication to her father and to her children. She became very fond of Nicholas and treated him like an adopted son.

The young people at Monticello had frequent dances on the lawn. A black fiddler and flute player provided music, and sometimes Jefferson himself would bring out his fiddle and accompany the dancers. Nicholas was an accomplished dancer, and his favorite partner became Martha's daughter Virginia. Within six months of his arrival at Monticello, Nicholas wrote to his mother he was in love with the granddaughter of the third president. His mother answered that of course at eighteen he was too young to even think of marriage.

According to the scholar Robert A. Brent, Virginia "was not a raving beauty." At a later date Nicholas's brother Browse stated that Virginia is "one of the most *amiable* and *sensible* girls in existence." Ellen Randolph (her sister), in a letter to Nicholas, said that Virginia was "a tall grown woman, and more beautiful than ever, but this opinion may understandably be biased."

Perhaps seeing the drift of things—there was little that Jefferson didn't notice—Virginia's grandfather suggested an appointment to West Point and a military career for Nicholas. Nicholas agreed, and before he left for the academy on the Hudson he wrote a lovesick confession to Virginia's mother, never declaring his affection to the girl herself. Martha answered with a gentle note, reminding him of his youth and expressing her sympathy.

Historians have speculated about Jefferson's choice of West Point for Trist. It is well known that Jefferson cared little about military things and as president had given minimal support to the fledgling military academy. Instead of a professional army, he preferred a citizen's army of local militias. A professional army smacked too much of aristocracy, privilege, and corruption. It is possible Jefferson had begun to change his mind about the academy, or perhaps he just wanted to get Nicholas out of the way as his granddaughter appeared to return the poor youth's affection. Or maybe Jefferson just thought military discipline was what Nicholas needed at that point in his life.

The West Point that Nicholas entered in 1818 was rocked by turmoil following the appointment of Major Sylvanus Thayer as superintendent in 1817. Thayer was strict and ambitious and he angered many cadets who had been accustomed to a more relaxed regime. Five leading cadets had petitioned Congress to have Thayer removed and found themselves dismissed from the academy. Trist sympathized with the rebels but did not take part in the protest. He did become a lifelong friend of Andrew Jackson's nephew, Andrew Jackson Donelson, a connection that would serve him well later.

As a physical specimen, Trist was not a promising cadet. He was six feet tall but frail, weighing only 120 pounds. All his life he suffered from various illnesses. But he proved to be an able student in the classroom where his preparation in languages and mathematics stood him in good stead. He even became an assistant to the French instructor.

In the early nineteenth century, the army was considered a career primarily for young men who were well off. Many of the cadets came from affluent families who subsidized their sons on the way to becoming gentleman officers. At West Point Nicholas depended on small sums his younger brother Browse sent to him with letters lecturing Nicholas on economy and practicality. All his life Trist would have trouble managing his finances and "handling money." Still pining for Virginia at Monticello and resentful of military discipline, he began to think of another profession, namely the law. His father had been a lawyer. And his special hero at Monticello, among his many other outstanding achievements, was a lawyer and legal scholar. His mentor in New Orleans, Livingston, was also a lawyer. After his third year at West Point, Trist was given a furlough in the summer of 1821. He hurried to Monticello and never returned to the military academy.

It would seem that Trist's courtship of Virginia was conducted by letter even when the two were living under the same roof at Monticello. From West Point he had written to Virginia's father, "I have long been convinced that happiness was to be enjoyed by one, if at all, as a married man and have cherished every feeling with which I set off for this place three years ago." With her mother's permission, he wrote to Virginia herself, now that he was back at Monticello, in an uncharacteristically nervous script, "Will Virginia Randolph favor me with a few minutes private conversation this evening or as soon as an opportunity affords if she finds that impossible?"

Perhaps the stiffness of the note put Virginia off, or perhaps she herself was nervous, wondering what awful news Nicholas might have to tell her. In any case, she declined to meet him and he had to screw up his courage to write to her again, this time being more explicit about his intentions. "The interview I yesterday requested . . . was for the purpose of making a declaration of a passion which unless my eye is not what the eye generally is, the 'index of the soul,' you must have often read in it. Since my return I have been in a state of suspense, which, if I have the smallest corner of your heart, you will be anxious to remove, and which, if I have been doomed to adore a woman without return of love, it is your *duty* to remove."

When they finally met and talked, Trist proposed, but Virginia answered that before they could wed he must complete his legal studies in New Orleans and return to Monticello to practice law. Trist had no choice but to agree and he returned to Louisiana to begin his legal education with his earlier mentor, Edward Livingston.

Livingston was a strict master to his students, but he was away from New Orleans on business so much his students were mostly left to pursue their studies on their own. The lovesick Trist wrote daily to Virginia. It was in this period of separation that he began to criticize his fiancée for her Christian faith. He seemed to resent any mention of the divine or the sacred, and he espoused a kind of secular stoicism that he may have associated with Jefferson's classical tastes and the wisdom of the Greeks and Romans. He wrote to Virginia, "Without going beyond our own earthly crust, we can discover the necessity of this resignation, to our happiness. For my part I believe that a man who had never even determined . . . to himself the existence or non-existence of a divine providence may be as perfect in this virtue as the most devout Christian."

It was a quarrel that would go on between them for much of the rest of their lives. It would become heated, at least in Trist's letters, when the question of their children's upbringing was at issue. One has the impression Virginia quietly went on with her own beliefs.

Rejecting any kind of spiritual faith, Trist took great pride in his own discipline and fortitude. He thought and wrote constantly about his health and took long walks in the cold. He lived at times on graham crackers and a few boiled potatoes, acting as though he dared nature to attack him. While we have no right to criticize Trist for what he believed or disbelieved, there is something unappealing about his tireless efforts to undermine Virginia's traditional faith. His comments make him sound intolerant and dogmatic.

Always forgiving and concerned for her fiancé's health in steaming, fever-prone New Orleans, Virginia persuaded her grandfather to invite Nicholas back to Monticello to study law with *him*. Trist jumped at the chance, and when he arrived on the mountain the great man set a course of study that was in effect a university education. "It required fourteen hours of reading a day for several years. His [Jefferson's] students read physical science, ethics, religion, and natural law before eight o'clock each morning; law (in at least three languages) from eight to noon; politics and history in the afternoon; and poetry, criticism, rhetoric and oratory from dusk to bedtime. His students' assigned goal was little less than a practical omniscience in human knowledge."

While Trist excelled at his studies, he also acquired an exaggerated formality in his expression, "elaborate metaphors and other verbal contrivances," legalistic abstraction, arrogance of tone. Much of the style he picked up and exaggerated as a law student was from the eighteenth century, and in the nineteenth century it often made him seem pompous and pretentious. But it was a style and tone of voice he could never resist, especially when challenged, when defending himself.

Even as Trist devoted himself to this ambitious curriculum, and daily discussions with Jefferson about his reading, he told Virginia he had little inclination to practice law. He loved the law in the abstract, as an intellectual discipline, but had little taste for the practical compromises a lawyer must make. He even told Virginia's father, in a rare moment of candor, that he could not practice law because of "the conviction that I could never make a speaker." This is one of the best clues to the puzzle of Trist's personality and his strange career. While making a heroic effort to study the law with one of the greatest legal thinkers in our history, he was already conceding that he would never practice, and the reason was that he could not speak in public.

But knowing Trist's weaknesses, we should not underestimate his gifts. He had an unusual talent for developing extended arguments, was tireless in applying logic, precedent, the unexpected reference. Men of the caliber of Jefferson, Madison, Jackson, and Tocqueville, sought his conversation and advice. But it was not just Trist's knowledge and mental ability they admired. It was equally his character, his idealism, his honesty. When challenged Trist could be arrogant and stuffy, but when conversing with an older leader who respected him his best talents and learning poured out for others to use.

Nicholas and Virginia were married at Monticello on September 11, 1824, and their first child, Martha Randolph Trist, was born in May of 1826, the only (white) great-grandchild Jefferson ever saw.

While devoting himself to the Herculean tasks of his legal studies, Trist also served as Jefferson's private secretary, answering floods of mail that arrived daily at Monticello from all over the world. When he revised his will in 1826 Jefferson made Trist one of his three executors. As Jefferson's health declined rapidly, Trist sat up with him night after night. On July 3, 1826, the old man refused laudanum and kept his eyes on the clock. "He whispered inquiringly, 'This is the Fourth?'"

Trist did not have the heart to tell Jefferson it was still the third. Jefferson was desperate to live until the fiftieth anniversary of the Declaration of Independence he had written. Trist only nodded assent. "'Ah', he [Jefferson] murmured as an expression came over his countenance which said, 'just as I wished.'"

Jefferson died at one o'clock in the afternoon on July 4, 1826, half a century after his great deed in Philadelphia. And far away in Quincy, Massachusetts, his old rival and friend, John Adams, four hours later whispered to his family, "Thomas Jefferson survives," and passed away. Oddly enough, couriers carrying the news of Adams's death from Massachusetts and Jefferson's passing from Virginia met in Philadelphia where the Declaration had been signed. It was truly the end of an era.

Among Trist's sad duties was the selling of Jefferson's many pieces of land, including Poplar Forest, the summer retreat near Lexington, Virginia. Saddest of all was the disposition of the slaves, including Sally Hemings. Several of her children had already been freed, and she could have had her freedom also. But freed blacks were required to leave Virginia within a year, and Sally preferred to stay in the state with the Randolphs, among the people and surroundings she knew. When Jefferson died he had in his bank account less than five thousand dollars.

Trist sold Jefferson's considerable library by auction, bidding himself on expensive volumes to push up the price. The debts of the estate were so considerable he had to depend on his brother Browse in Louisiana for living expenses. In this difficult period, when Trist was sorting out the chaos of Jefferson's affairs and settling the estate, he worked closely with James Madison at nearby Montpelier. Madison was now rector of the new University of Virginia, and because he was advanced in years, the fourth president and "Master Builder of the Constitution" came to depend on Trist as adviser, assistant, and author of annual reports for the university. In his many conversations with Madison Trist discussed the issue of states' rights and the nullification controversy beginning to loom so ugly and inevitable. Because Jefferson and Madison had been the authors of the Kentucky and Virginia Resolutions of 1798, which argued for states' rights in the response to the Federalists' Alien and Sedition Acts, many southern politicians looked back to Jefferson and those documents for a precedent in their assertion of independence for each state when federal law affected the interests of a state adversely. The southerners argued that such laws could and should be "nullified." From his conversations with Madison, it was clear to Trist that Jefferson (and Madison) would have opposed the nullification proposals. Using the ideas he discussed with Madison, Trist wrote a series of unsigned newspaper articles for the *Richmond Enquirer* on nullification that attracted a good deal of attention. Later, as the Civil War loomed on the horizon, Trist would be a strict Unionist as he was certain Jefferson and Madison would have been.

After Jefferson's death, Trist continued his legal studies and passed the Virginia bar exam in November of 1826. But as far as we can tell he never made an effort to practice. Rather, he decided to become a journalist. Since he had access to Jefferson's papers, he published some of the Sage's letters in newspapers, and, perhaps with money borrowed from Browse, bought a half interest in the *Charlottesville Advocate*. He hoped the paper would make him financially independent, and he wrote vigorous editorials supporting Andrew Jackson's campaign for the presidency, espousing the positions and policies he thought Jefferson would have chosen. But in spite of the energy he gave to the paper, it did not prosper and he ended up selling his share at a loss.

Casting about for some means of livelihood, Trist wrote to a relative of Virginia's, Burwell S. Randolph, who happened to be the navy commissioner in the John Quincy Adams administration. Randolph petitioned Henry Clay, secretary of state, to find something for Trist. Ignoring Trist's editorials in favor of Andrew Jackson, Clay offered Trist a post as clerk at a salary of fourteen hundred dollars per annum and explained that he did so because "it may contribute to the personal comfort of Mrs. Randolph, your mother-in-law." Word had gotten around in Washington that Jefferson's only surviving daughter, now a widow, was left with nothing when the estate was settled and that she depended on

Trist for support. True to his idealistic, honest nature, Trist wondered if he was qualified for work in the State Department, but he was assured by Burwell Randolph that Clay himself took care of all important tasks in the department. Clerks did only what Clay told them.

Washington, D.C., was still under construction in the 1820s. The streets were unpaved, sending up clouds of dust in dry weather, becoming rivers of mud in wet spells. Pierre Charles L'Enfant's plans were only beginning to be realized. Except for the Capitol and the executive mansion, most of the government buildings were temporary. Cholera and other diseases threatened the low-lying city in the hot months. Affordable houses were scarce and it took Trist months to find a suitable dwelling in Georgetown that rented for four hundred dollars a year. Martha Jefferson Randolph came to live with the Trists and her presence made Trist a minor celebrity. Dignitaries came to call or sent invitations to the daughter of Thomas Jefferson. James Madison loyally wrote letters of introduction to important people to further advance Trist's career in Washington.

When Andrew Jackson took office in March of 1829, many of the old government employees were swept out and replaced by Democrats. Because of his editorials in support of Jackson and because of his Jefferson connections, Trist was kept on at the State Department. Old Hickory himself came to Trist's house to call on Martha Jefferson Randolph, accompanied by Secretary of State Martin Van Buren. As it turned out, Trist's close friend from West Point days, Andrew Jackson Donelson, was by then private secretary to his uncle, the president. The Trists were invited to dine with the president and a friendship developed between the State Department clerk and the chief executive. Trist enjoyed talking about Jefferson and relating the many conversations he'd had with the aged statesman at Monticello. Jackson seemed to hang on every word Trist said about his legendary grandfather-in-law. The backwoods soldier and self-made politician wanted to know everything about the great thinker and was especially eager to know Jefferson's opinion of him, Old Hickory. Jackson knew that Jefferson had considered him a barbarian when he came to Washington as a senator from Tennessee in 1797, but he hoped Jefferson had changed his opinion over the years. According to all reports, Trist was diplomatic and pleased by the attention. He was himself a great admirer of the hero of the Battle of New Orleans, but he remained discreet about Jefferson's private comments on Jackson. Jackson was also anxious to learn more of Jefferson's ideas about emancipation of slaves and the issues of religious freedom. Trist was more than happy to relate Jefferson's comments on those subjects.

Jackson soon came to rely on Trist's conversation and advice. Trist was smart and well informed, trustworthy and generous. Jackson called on him whenever he needed advice. In the words of Robert Brent, "Trist was much more than a government worker to Jackson. He was a friend and companion to the lonely president. Trist was exactly the right man to fit a position like this. His polished air, his previous connections, his general intelligence, and his up-to-date analysis of the latest happenings in the political world, all combined to make him a constant source of relaxation to the aging Jackson."

When Mrs. Andrew Jackson Donelson, who served as hostess for Jackson, returned to Nashville, her husband soon followed her and Jackson asked Trist to become his acting private secretary. Trist served with notable success in that position until the Donelsons chose to return to Washington. Few people in Washington were as close to Jackson as Trist, though his salary, with raises, was still only seventeen hundred dollars a year. Jackson occasionally handed Trist checks for three hundred dollars to supplement his salary and gave him quarters at the executive mansion. Jackson's first major biographer, James Parton, writing in 1864, would say, "Among the young men who surrounded General Jackson during the early years of his Presidency, there was none who enjoyed more of his affection, and none who was more worthy of it, than Mr. Nicholas Philip Trist of Virginia."

As the controversy over nullification heated up, Trist came to the aid of the administration in trenchant polemical articles published anonymously in various newspapers. In fact some historians think it was Trist's pieces about the Union that inspired Jackson to oppose nullification so vigorously. Many of these articles were printed in the *Richmond Enquirer* and they got quite a bit of attention. Trist also helped Jackson draft his speeches and wrote many of his letters. Trist fulfilled the role that would later be called speech writer and ghost writer for the president.

Having apprenticed himself to both Jefferson and Madison, and being more idealist than politician, Trist was appalled by the pettiness, greed, and dishonesty he witnessed around him in Washington. Never one to hold back his criticism, he was admired by some and distrusted by others for the severity of his views. The French political writer Alexis de Tocqueville was touring America at this time and he and Trist struck up a friendship. Trist was probably one of the best informed Americans Tocqueville had met. The two intellectuals were about the same age and shared so many interests that Trist unburdened himself to Tocqueville on some of his misgivings about the course of American culture and politics. Trist agreed to gather material for the French scholar and to help him with his research on American penal systems and democracy. "Virginia was now only a shadow of her former self," Trist explained to Tocqueville. "The great men, even the noteworthy men, had disappeared . . . One no longer saw men of that kind rising to take their place."

Among the many factors contributing to Trist's growing disillusionment with the country was the dominance of commerce. The whole nation seemed bent mostly on making money. The neoclassical, agrarian world of reason, dignity, and liberty that Jefferson and Madison had envisioned had not come about. Instead, schemers, con men, salesmen, and revival preachers seemed to have overrun the new society. By 1813 Jefferson himself had spoken with contempt about the "world of speculation, banks, paper money, and evangelical Christianity." He felt the only hope for the future lay in the agricultural South and in the West. In Philadelphia, Charles Willson Peale's museum of paintings and scientific curiosities had been sold to P. T. Barnum. Ignorance, greed, labor, and profit seemed the order of the day. Ironically, it had been Trist's mentor, Jefferson himself, who had done the most to put power in the hands of the common people.

Tocqueville was not the only intellectual Trist knew at this time. Still arguing with Virginia about the kind of modern, nonreligious education their children should have, he sought advice from Robert Dale Owen, son of the founder of the utopian community of New Harmony in Indiana. Owen was connected to the radical activist Frances Wright, whom Trist had met when she visited Monticello. Owen and Trist became devoted correspondents over many years, discussing science, education, government, religion. Owen was only one of many such correspondents.

As a clerk and translator in the State Department, Trist also kept up a correspondence with diplomats around the world, including James Buchanan, minister to Russia.

Because Jackson had promised to improve Trist's financial situation, when the consulship in Havana became vacant the president appointed Trist to the post. It was a position that could be handsomely remunerative since the consul received a fee for all the American business that came through the busy port as well as a salary of two thousand dollars a year. The consul could easily earn between four thousand and six thousand dollars a year. In fact, the consulship was such a plum that at least one candidate for the job, John Hefferman of New York, tried to buy the post from Trist.

Though he had misgivings about the posting, Trist had little choice but to accept the appointment. He was supporting a large family, including his mother-in-law and two of his sisters-in-law and his son Jeff needed to attend an expensive school for the deaf in Philadelphia. But Trist believed he was vulnerable to diseases in tropical climates, and he especially feared yellow fever, which had killed his father in New Orleans many years before. And Virginia and the children would have to stay in Washington until he could find suitable accommodations in Havana.

It is also possible that by this time in his life Trist knew himself well enough to understand that he functioned best in collaboration with a mentor. When working with a Livingston, Jefferson, Madison, or Jackson, he performed confidently and brilliantly. When acting on his own, he became defensive, arrogant, and strident if faced with any challenge, disagreement, or criticism.

Trist was orphaned when four and grew up with two stepfathers, neither of whom he was very close to. It could be said he spent much of his life searching for a true father, for a voice of authority. Luckily he found such a father figure in Thomas Jefferson, in Andrew Jackson, and for a time in Secretary of State James Buchanan. And at the most important time of his life he found General Winfield Scott to guide and inspire him to achievements rarely surpassed in American diplomatic history.

In his prolix, rhetorical, antiquated style, he sought to capture that authority for himself which he associated with greatness. But it was when he was writing down or polishing the words of a mentor that his real talent flowered. Some of this Trist must have understood, for he put off going to Havana as long as he could. A retiring deputy consul in Havana had agreed to stay on and President Jackson wanted Trist to travel with him on an extended tour of the northeastern states. It was the better part of a year before Trist actually set foot in Cuba on March 26, 1834.

At first Trist showed some enthusiasm for the new assignment. The spring was beautiful and he loved the many kinds of fruit that flourished there, believing fruit to be good for his delicate health. He especially loved guava and he preferred above all else the marmalade made from guava. As American consul, he had a station, even a distinction, among the international community in Havana.

The duties of the consul were fairly light. According to the Consular Regulations he was charged with "(1) endeavoring to create a situation favorable to the importation and sale of American goods, (2) submitting frequent reports on commercial and other economic subjects, (3) replying to private inquiries of American citizens touching commercial and industrial matters, and (4) lending aid and service to American citizens doing or contemplating doing business within his jurisdiction." In addition the consul was supposed to protect the interests of American seamen and shipping in the port of Havana and sometimes serve as a banker for American travelers and businesses. Money deposited with the consul could be invested in whatever way he saw fit. It was also important to keep friendly relations with the host country (Spain in this case) as well as the international community.

Trist apparently got off to a good start. Though tall and thin, he cut a handsome figure with his courteous, even courtly manners. It helped a great deal that he was fluent in Spanish and French and he seemed knowledgeable about virtually everything. But his conduct began to spiral away from the early promise rather quickly.

After he rented a house outside the city, with a beautiful view of the sea, Virginia and the children arrived in Cuba, and Trist might have been expected to be happier. He was making more money than he ever had and his duties were relatively light. One would have expected him to take up his pen and write the kind of literary, philosophical, or political works he felt called to produce. Instead, he antagonized so many businessmen and sea captains that he ended up having to defend himself to a congressional committee investigating the charges against him.

Among the many complaints lodged against Trist, the more serious included: (1) the imprisonment of Captain Kendall of the brig *Kremlin* without cause; (2) the imprisonment of Captain Straw of the brig *Sarah Ann Alley* on a completely groundless charge; (3) the severe punishment of the seamen of the ship *William Engs,* without sufficient cause; (4) the justification of an outrageous assault upon Mr. Southall, the purser of the USS *Boston,* by a Spanish sentinel. The congressional committee also looked into many other charges of corruption, insolence, and failure to perform his duties.

And to top it all off the British foreign minister, Lord Palmerston, accused Trist of aiding and abetting the outlawed slave trade. Apparently that accusation arose from the report that slave traders often hoisted American flags to disguise themselves. Trist pointed out that if a ship came into Havana harbor flying American colors, how was he to know what its actual nationality or cargo might be? But true to his well-established habit, Trist went on to write the famous 140 pages of rebuttal to the British government, which included a strident attack on the British Empire, as though he were still fighting the Revolution or the War of 1812. The British were probably bemused as well as outraged by the document. Luckily for Trist, there was little sympathy for the British either in Congress or in the Van Buren administration. No one seemed anxious to find Trist guilty or to punish him. After all, he had been a favorite of Old Hickory and near the end of Jackson's administration had returned from Havana for five months to serve once again as the president's private secretary from August to December 1836.

Robert W. Merry has characterized Trist by referring to "his inordinate fear of illness, his conviction that Virginians were superior to other Americans, and a pugnacity of manner when challenged." While all these charges are true enough, Trist's most serious weakness as an official was his "lack of ability to distinguish the important from the trivial" when he was angry.

The congressional committee found Trist had broken no laws just as the Van Buren administration ended and William Henry Harrison and

John Tyler were taking office in March 1841. Trist had made a mess of his assignment in Havana, but strangely enough, he elected to stay in Cuba after he lost the consulship with the change of administrations. The Panic of 1839, brought on partly by Jackson's destruction of the Bank of the United States, leaving the economy "without a lender of last resort," offered few opportunities for starting over again. He bought a thirty-seven-acre farm near Havana and planned to sell vegetables in the city. He translated an obscure work on dairy farming from the French, *A Treatise on Milch Cows,* instead of writing the law books and philosophical articles he had planned. The farm did not prosper and Virginia took in boarders to make ends meet as Trist peddled vegetables in Havana. From being adviser and secretary to Andrew Jackson, Trist had fallen to penury and real want. He attempted some business ventures in Havana, but none succeeded. It was not the last time he and Virginia would feel the pinch of poverty.

Andrew Jackson himself would rescue Trist from this dead end. Though weak and ailing back at the Hermitage, Jackson kept an interest in things and in the careers of his favorites. Not only did the old lion work to get his protégé, James K. Polk, nominated and elected to the presidency, but when he learned of Trist's poverty he arranged for his former secretary to return to Washington as the chief clerk of the State Department in Young Hickory's new administration. After almost a decade in exile, Trist was coming home.

Though James K. Polk knew Trist, he never warmed to Andrew Jackson's favorite adviser. But then Polk warmed to very few and it mattered little to him that Trist had known Jefferson and was married to Jefferson's granddaughter. Polk did not have Jackson's big heart and infinite curiosity and enthusiastic sense of legacy. Trist's idealism probably put off the intriguing Polk as much as it had fascinated and stirred the admiration of Jackson. Polk likely thought Trist a little stupid or, at best, naive and harmless.

But if Trist did not find a mentor in Polk, he certainly did in Secretary of State James Buchanan. Born in Pennsylvania in 1791, Buchanan was known both for his oratory and his learning. He had served in the House of Representatives from 1821 to 1831, as ambassador to Russia from 1832 to 1833, and as senator from Pennsylvania from 1834 to 1845. It was while he was minister to Russia that Buchanan had gotten to know the able clerk in the State Department who had much impressed the ambassador with his knowledge and commitment to his duties.

Soon after Trist assumed the post of chief clerk of the State Department, he and Buchanan became close friends. Buchanan, like Jackson before him, came to depend on Trist for advice, for his efficiency, and for his wide knowledge of languages and world affairs. Buchanan was often a guest at the Trist home and he became friends with Virginia as well. Because he relied on Trist and because they shared so many interests and opinions, Buchanan could relax with the chief clerk. It was the kind of happy relationship Trist had had before with Jefferson, Madison, and Jackson. It was the kind of relationship in which Trist thrived.

As chief clerk of the State Department, Trist held the position and responsibilities that would later be called undersecretary of state. When Buchanan had to be out of town he left Trist in charge as acting secretary of state. As far as is known, Trist performed his duties in an exemplary manner: he was working under the direction of another congenial father figure.

As a Democrat, Buchanan shared Polk's distrust of Whig generals Zachary Taylor and Winfield Scott. Scott was particularly annoying because it was well known he had political ambitions; namely, he wanted to be president. But having started the war with Mexico, Polk and Buchanan had limited options. They had to use the army that existed, not having time to create a strictly Democratic officer corps. And while they could try gambles such as getting Thomas Hart Benton appointed commander in chief and making the oily lawyer Gideon Pillow a major general and slanderer of Scott, they finally had to depend on seasoned soldiers to fight the war they had created. It is not clear which Polk wanted more, to prevent a Whig from becoming president or to win the war with Mexico.

As chief clerk of the State Department, Trist did not have to be much concerned about such intrigues for the first two years of his tenure. He was quite familiar with John Slidell's mission to Mexico that failed in part because of the chaos of Mexican politics at the time. And he certainly knew about the negotiations with Britain over the Oregon boundary and the resolution of 1846. The controversy over Frémont's behavior in California was the talk of Washington with most citizens taking sides as the Frémont court-martial proceeded.

Polk's campaign slogan had been "All of Texas and all of Oregon," and though he declared war on Mexico in May of 1846, his ambition all along was to acquire land, not punish the Mexicans. Yet diplomatic bungling as well as the instability and pride of the Mexican government had made the war seem inevitable. Even so, a peace might be made with Mexico without the cost and bloodshed of further war. If a peace treaty could be negotiated with Mexico by a member of the Polk administration, Scott would at least be deprived of that glory. As General Scott and his army made their way to Veracruz to mount the invasion and march to Mexico City, Polk and Buchanan pondered the political dilemma of how to win the war yet prevent Scott from becoming a hero.

The only option that came to mind was to send someone else to make a separate peace, so no matter what Scott accomplished on the battlefield he would be deprived of the glory of the peace settlement. Absent the political consideration, Scott himself would be the obvious choice to make the peace, since he had a distinguished career of negotiating treaties, as well as being the outstanding living military hero of the United States. Given their political logic, Buchanan himself would be the obvious choice to negotiate peace with the Mexicans. But Buchanan also had his eye on the 1848 presidential election, little more than a year away, and he did not want to risk being absent from Washington.

It was Buchanan who proposed Trist for the secret mission to Mexico. Trist was fluent in Spanish and familiar with the failed Slidell mission. He had experience in Hispanic Cuba, was a loyal Democrat, extremely well informed and educated. Since he was not a politician per se, he was ideal for a covert mission as "executive agent of the president," not needing congressional approval. If he succeeded, he would not be a political rival; if he failed, he would not be much of an embarrassment.

Polk and Buchanan called Trist to the White House to present their proposal. To their surprise the chief clerk did not show the enthusiasm they expected. Most historians have ascribed Trist's hesitation to his reluctance to be away from his family and his fear for his health in a tropical climate. Likely these were factors that made him pause before answering. But by 1847, Trist had probably begun to know himself a little, knew that if sent off on his own on such a difficult task he was likely to stumble and fail. For all his manner of confidence, even arrogance, he must have recognized something of his own weakness, why he had failed to practice law, why he had failed to write the books he'd promised himself to write, why he had failed in his business ventures.

Waiting for Trist to respond, Polk said, "Mr. Trist, if you can but succeed in restoring peace, you will render a great service to your country and acquire great distinction for yourself."

Polk appealed to Trist's dedication to the nation, and the chief clerk had no choice but to reply, "The service shall be rendered, sir, if it be possible for me to do it. But as for the distinction, I care nothing for that."

Sensing Trist's lack of confidence, Polk and Buchanan made every effort to flatter and build him up. The president probably did not believe him when Trist said that rather than fame as a peacemaker he would prefer a quiet job as a storekeeper for the army, which would give him more free time. Buchanan put the first chill on the friendship with Trist when he privately told him that if he succeeded in Mexico, they might have to nominate him for president the next year. The comment was so obviously insincere and patronizing that the idealistic Trist began to have second thoughts about his boss and friend Buchanan.

In hindsight, the strangest part of Polk and Buchanan's instructions to Trist was the direction to work separately from Scott. How they expected Trist to make peace with Mexico in the middle of a war without coordinating his efforts with the commander in chief is baffling. Trist was told that if he needed to work in conjunction with the army he should contact the lawyer — now general — Gideon Pillow, who would tell him what to do.

The fact is Polk and Buchanan set up Trist's mission for failure from the very beginning. By proceeding as he was instructed, it's unlikely that he could ever have made a treaty. In the middle of a war, how would he even have made contact with the Mexican government? The Mexican countryside was overrun by guerillas, outlaws, bandits, and warring armies. The absurdity of the plan shows that even clever men can be made stupid by jealousy, fear, and political ambition. Polk came close to sabotaging almost every aspect of the fighting and peace negotiations with Mexico. The fact that both Scott and Trist succeeded there in spite of Polk and gave him his lasting glory, is a testament to their strong characters and to the astonishing quirks of history.

Taking the secret mission solemnly and seriously, Nicholas P. Trist set out for New Orleans, telling acquaintances he was traveling on family business. For all the care at concealing his mission, the news leaked out, and though Trist did not know it, northern newspapers were reporting he was being sent to Mexico as a peace commissioner. Polk furiously tried to find the culprit in his cabinet or in the State Department who had leaked the news, forgetting that he himself had told the editor of the *Daily Union*, Thomas Ritchie, supposedly in confidence. Modern historians have speculated that Buchanan himself leaked news of the secret mission, hoping to win favor with the press for his bid for the presidency in 1848.

Determined to keep the assignment secret, Trist pretended to be a French businessman named Dr. Tarro. In New Orleans he arranged for the collector of customs, Denis Prieur, to secure passage for him to Veracruz in a revenue cutter called *Ewing*. Before embarking, he bought a set of pistols and hired a Catalan servant named Juan Gilpin. There is something comic about Trist's efforts to maintain his cover while editorials in the Northeast were discussing his mission to Mexico.

Trist arrived in Veracruz on May 6, 1847, and stepped ashore at the American garrison a mile south of the city. Far in the distance the snow-covered peak of the volcano Mount Orizaba, or Citlaltépetl, shown in the sky like a ghostly tent, 18,700 feet above sea level, seeming to float many miles away. His greatest fear was of the yellow fever, *el vómito*, so common in the swampy steaming region along the coast.

Trist found that General Scott and the American army were at Jalapa, seventy-four miles inland on the National Highway, where they were resting after the great victory at Cerro Gordo. He was informed that the countryside between the coast and Jalapa was infested with guerillas and roving bands of outlaws. In a few days a thousand Tennessee Dragoons were due to arrive as reinforcements for Scott's forces and Trist could travel with them to Jalapa.

In the heat and perhaps in the fatigue of his journey, Trist did what he always did: he wrote, first a letter to Virginia, telling her his health was good. And then he made his first blunder. Learning that a courier was about to depart for Jalapa, Trist penned a hasty note to the commanding general informing him of his mission to make a peace treaty. He sent along a sealed copy of the *projet,* or treaty proposal, directing Scott to forward it to the Mexican government.

It is obvious Trist was not thinking clearly. If it was not safe for him to travel with the courier, why would he entrust the official *projet* to the courier? Trist's hasty note seemed to say that he, Trist, had arrived in Mexico in the middle of the war, to take charge of the peace process, with the authority to call an end to the fighting whenever that might seem necessary. That may not be precisely what Trist meant to communicate, but that is what he thoughtlessly implied. He had an unsealed copy of the *projet* with him which he could have shared with Scott, but he did not send that along. Buchanan had put the official *projet* under seal, thinking that would impress the Mexicans.

Old Fuss and Feathers was not one to suffer fools gladly, and he answered Trist in high dudgeon and acid sarcasm. The idea that Trist could decide when to suspend military action was both ridiculous and insulting. The greater error belonged to Polk and Buchanan in the way they directed Trist to Mexico, suggesting that he work separately from Scott. But even those who admire and respect Trist concede that he bungled the introduction to Scott. A little patience and tact would have saved him two months of bitter feuding with the general that did nothing to further the peace process. Both men would come to see that they had to complete their work in Mexico in spite of Polk's machinations and ignorant meddling and delayed communications. And that they had to work together.

As luck would have it, Winfield Scott tended to write long defensive letters just as Trist did. Without waiting to meet Trist and hear him out, he blasted the commissioner with invective and sarcasm and pointed out that there was hardly a Mexican government to negotiate with. The only real power lay with Santa Anna, who was commanding the army in the field while Pedro Maria Anaya served as caretaker of the weak administration in Mexico City. Written in angry haste, Scott's letter was filled with scorn and hyperbole, but at the end he offered Trist the best hospitality he could arrange when he arrived in camp.

Trist received Scott's letter at a stop on the way to Jalapa. He was outraged and stunned, seeing Scott's words as pompous, arrogant and the epitome of gratuitous insult. For once Trist had met his equal in writing long scornful letters. Trist sat down and wrote an eighteen-page screed of invective and accusation and self-defense. He lectured the old general as if he were a delinquent schoolboy. At the end, in a note of humility, or fake humility, he admitted he might not have been the best choice for a commissioner to negotiate with the Mexican government, but the president had sent him and he meant to do his duty.

Whether Trist knew it or not, Scott was an outstanding diplomat, as he had proven several times in the service of his country. When he was on the defensive, Trist liked to think of himself as the heir to the wisdom of Jefferson, Madison, and Jackson. He had been told to think badly of Scott and he wrote to Virginia that Scott was "utterly incompetent . . . decidedly the greatest imbecile I have ever met." Of course he had not met Scott and he decided he would avoid meeting the general. Now he had an excuse never to encounter Winfield Scott face to face.

However unpleasant the exchange with Scott might be, Trist had the good fortune to escape the coastal lowlands without contracting yellow fever. The historian Wallace Ohrt describes "the saffron haze" that hangs over the region in the summer fever season, when the natives claim "King Death in his yellow robe" has returned. As Trist and the Tennessee Dragoons passed through Cerro Gordo, decaying bodies from the recent battle still lined the road, as well as equipment abandoned by overheated, exhausted, and sick American soldiers. As they climbed into the hills they entered a more pleasant world of flowers, hedges, songbirds, little farms, and cornfields.

On May 14, eight days after landing on the coast, Trist arrived at Jalapa and was given comfortable quarters with Brigadier General Persifor Smith. The town of Jalapa was attractive, the climate mild, and the local people were not unfriendly to the Yankees. But there was nothing mild about the long letter Trist continued scribbling to Scott. As Wallace Ohrt tells us, "Piling insult on insult, he observed that he had not come to Mexico to exchange correspondence with the commander . . . [and] concluded with a warning against any interference with his mission, a warning he explained was intended to bring Scott to his senses." At the end of the angry missive Trist said sarcastically that of course the best choice for peace commissioner would have been "the gallant commander of our land forces in Mexico."

Scott answered in kind, "My first impulse was to return the farrago in insolence, conceit and arrogance to the author; but, on reflection, I have determined to preserve the letter as a choice specimen of diplomatic literature and manners." Unfortunately, both Scott and Trist sent the exchange of letters to their superiors in Washington, a mistake they would deeply regret later on. When Secretaries Marcy and Buchanan read the denunciations and fulminations of Trist and Scott against each other and showed the correspondence to Polk, the president ordered stiff reprimands sent to each man. Buchanan mailed two letters to Trist, one the official rebuke and the other a gentler personal note reassuring Trist of his support but chiding him for his intemperate words.

In the meantime Trist had taken the initiative and written to the head of the British legation in Mexico City, Charles Bankhead, asking for his help in contacting the Mexican government. Bankhead, who had friendly relations with the Mexican officials, delegated Edward Thornton to get in touch with Trist. Thornton then personally called on Generalissimo Santa Anna and delivered Trist's documents from Washington to Minister of Foreign Relations Domingo Ibarra. Santa Anna sent word that he thought an attack on the capital would make it more difficult to achieve peace, and Ibarra promised a response to Secretary of State Buchanan. It was a small opening in what had seemed an impenetrable wall.

There is some disagreement between American historians and Mexican historians about the role of Santa Anna in the defeat of Mexico. Americans tend to see the dictator as opportunistic and ruthless in manipulating both his people and the Americans for his own ends. But some Mexicans see him as virtually an ally of the Americans, who arranged the defeat of Mexico. The deputy named Ramón Gamboa again and again accused Santa Anna in the Mexican Congress "of treason during this war." According to Richard Griswold del Castillo most of Scott's decisions as the Americans approached Mexico City were made at the recommendation of Santa Anna, first to hold off an attack while negotiations were in progress, then to attack to bring the Mexican government to serious negotiations, then to desist again outside the gates of Mexico

City. In this view Scott followed "Santa Anna's script" almost from the beginning to the end of the campaign. "Later most Mexican historians held that Santa Anna was a traitor who orchestrated the final American conquest of Mexico." At the very least we know there were many instances of back-channeling, secret communications, between the Americans and Santa Anna, right up to the final days of the war.

At about the same time both Trist and Scott began to see they had acted foolishly and their haste, pride, and anger had been detrimental to their missions in Mexico. The first thawing of the relationship, or cooling of the tempers, came when Trist, in a letter in a new civil tone, passed along the information he had from Thornton. Suddenly Scott had to see that Trist was a man of some ability and as committed as he was to making peace with Mexico.

As had happened many times before in his life, Trist suddenly became very ill. We don't know exactly what he suffered from, but a good guess is the dysentery common among the soldiers in Mexico. The commissioner was confined to his bed for several days while General Smith looked after his comforts. Trist was weak and uncommunicative. Hearing of his illness, Scott sent Trist a box of guava marmalade, probably not knowing it was one of Trist's favorite delicacies. He enclosed a note to General Smith that Trist kept for the rest of his life. "My Dear Sir—Looking over my stores I find a box of guava marmalade which perhaps the physician may not consider improper to make part of the diet of your sick companion."

The unexpected gift of jelly seemed to work a miracle. Suddenly Trist rose from his bed and was talking again. He composed a note of warm thanks to Scott. To Buchanan he wrote, "With General Scott's reply to my letter I received a message from him evincing so much good feeling that it afforded me the sincerest pleasure to meet it, as I did, in a way which should at once preclude all restraint and embarrassment between us."

Trist asked Buchanan to withdraw his earlier letters about the general from the State Department files and Scott made a similar request to Secretary of War Marcy. But it was too late; the damage in Washington had already been done. And strangely—or perhaps not so strangely—the new friendship between Trist and Scott would irritate Polk even more than their quarrel, as the president feared his peace commissioner had sold out to the Whig devil. In his diary Polk would write, "[Trist] seems to have entered into all of Scott's hatred of the administration, and to be lending himself to all Scott's evil purposes." And he would add, "He has become the perfect tool of Scott."

Scott came in person to call on the convalescent Trist and finally they met face-to-face. The two men discovered that they liked each other. The old-fashioned Scott may have found a like mind in the old-fashioned Nicholas P. Trist. The earlier bitter contempt turned into mutual admiration and respect. They enjoyed each other's company, each other's conversation. Scott and Trist were both Virginians, far from home and their families, and deeply committed to serving their country. Both were idealistic to the point of seeming naive to a politician such as Polk. Both were classically educated and knew modern languages as well, both were esthetes, both were lawyers who had chosen not to practice, both were fond of formality, and both were generous and honest with a melodramatic self-image and sense of purpose. After the treatment Scott had received from Polk, it must have been a comfort to have in his camp a representative of the administration he could respect and trust. Scott had felt a terrible isolation in Mexico with Pillow and others spying on him and sending critical letters back to Washington.

For Trist, it is obvious he had found a new mentor. Scott was a great soldier and a great diplomat. He had been a national hero since 1813. He was the father figure Trist had always needed and the kind of leader who brought out the best in Trist. The commissioner's defensiveness and bad temper vanished. He began to act with confidence, patience, and deliberation, as he had with his former father figures.

As Scott had foreseen back in Washington, he was fighting the Mexicans at his front and the Polk administration to his rear. The general's every action was criticized by Pillow in his missives to the president. Whatever Scott did, or did not do, was portrayed in the worst light by the jealous, poison pen of Pillow. As the historian Wallace Ohrt puts it, "Although Pillow's military accomplishments were modest, his ego was not. The enlisted men detested him and the officers barely tolerated him." Some who served with Pillow in Mexico would not be surprised years later when they learned he was disgraced and relieved of command as a brigadier general in the Confederate army after he slipped away to safety and left his men to be killed or surrender to Grant at Fort Donelson in 1862.

One of the things Pillow took pleasure in passing on to Polk was the news that Scott and Trist had paid a bribe to the Mexicans, probably to Santa Anna, as a "lubricant" to get peace talks started. The British diplomat Thornton had made the suggestion to Trist and the generals on Scott's staff, including Pillow, had expressed agreement with the measure. There was a sense that anything was worth trying to achieve peace—when in Rome one must follow Roman customs. But Pillow in his letters to the president made it look as though Trist and Scott, instead of treating honestly with the Mexican government or fighting the war to a successful conclusion, were trying to bribe their way into favor with Mexican officials in a way that would embarrass the United States. Every item of gossip he received from Pillow enraged Polk further against Scott, and now against Trist also.

Encouraged by Pillow, the able but emotionally unstable General William Worth became an enemy of Scott. They had been friends ever since the War of 1812. Worth had named a son Winfield Scott in honor of his friend and fellow soldier, but now he had the name legally changed. It must have hurt Scott deeply to have his old friend turn on him. But he pushed on, attempting to end the war with Mexico with a minimum loss of life on either side. As he rode forward from Puebla, Trist often rode at his side. The two men discussed their options and plans as they crossed the spectacular mountain range through the Pass of Cortés and descended into the Valley of Mexico. The twin volcanic peaks Popocatépetl and Ixtacihuatl rose high into the hard blue sky. The snow on their summits was darkened by volcanic ash that fumed from the tops and blew into the faces of the marching Americans. Some soldiers sang as they marched. As they stepped through the pass where Cortés and his men had crossed centuries before, they saw three thousand feet below them the same great valley walled by the sharp mountains the conquistador had viewed. Six lakes sparkled on the valley floor, scattered among woods and fields. Church bells rang throughout the grand city of Montezuma, warning inhabitants of the approaching Yankees.

From his scouts and from the outlaw leader named Manuel Domínguez, captured by the Americans, Scott had learned a good deal about the defenses of Mexico City. As they descended from the pass and approached the capital, Scott had to decide on the tactics he would use. Patience and subtlety were two of Scott's greatest strengths as a general. Because his every move was being watched by Mexican spies, Scott chose to disguise his actions. Few of his senior officers knew what his real plans were.

To confuse Santa Anna, who expected an assault from the east and gathered his forces at a butte called El Peñon, Scott, as mentioned before, launched the feint attack on El Peñon, but directed most of his forces to march south around the muddy edge of Lake Chalco and Lake Xochimilco, to San Augustin ten miles south of the city. No one expected such an extreme maneuver, and after an exhausting slog through swamp and tangled brush the American army finally rested at San Augustin. As Scott and his staff planned the assault on the capital, Scott and Trist hoped to negotiate a peace rather than fight their way into the city of two hundred thousand.

As we have seen, Scott agreed to an armistice after the victories at Contreras on August 19–20 and Churubusco on August 20, 1847. Hoping some progress could be achieved at last, Trist prepared to meet the Mexican commissioners. The historian Wallace Ohrt points out the almost insurmountable difficulties that Trist faced at this point. The social as well as political history of Mexico made his work complex beyond description. For centuries the Spanish colonial powers had maintained a strict social, political and military structure in New Spain, and this stratification was strictly maintained. "Only the aristocracy could hold office, vote, own weapons, ride horses, or educate their children . . . Penalties for infractions of the caste laws were sufficiently severe to discourage even the boldest from taking liberties."

Trist met with a Mexican commission consisting of ex-president José Joaquín de Herrera, J. B. Couto, General Ignacio Mora y Villamil and a lawyer named Miguel Atristaín. To Trist's surprise, the issue they were most insistent on was the southern boundary of Texas. The pride of the Mexican nation appeared to depend on establishing and maintaining the Nueces River instead of the Rio Grande as the border with the United States. Trist made one of his greatest mistakes when he agreed to refer the boundary issue back to Washington, knowing full well Polk and

Buchanan had instructed him that the Rio Grande boundary was not negotiable. Apparently it did not occur to Trist that if the Texas boundary was not the Rio Grande then the ostensible reason for going to war, the Mexican invasion of United States soil, was false.

It is thought that Trist agreed to refer the question of the boundary back to his superiors in Washington as a way to buy time and keep the negotiations going forward until a more favorable government was in place in Mexico. If the talks broke off at this stage a treaty might never be made, given the instability of the Mexican government. But if Trist was buying time, it did him no good and did a great deal of harm with Polk and Buchanan. The Mexicans remained firm, making more exorbitant demands than Trist expected. They acted as if Mexico, not the gringos, had won the battles. Polk never forgave Trist for wavering on the question of the Rio Grande boundary for Polk realized, as Trist apparently did not, that even a discussion of the issue undercut the American claims in declaring war.

As it turned out, no one was happy with the armistice. Polk would accuse Scott of dithering just when he should be completing the conquest of Mexico. Santa Anna would accuse Scott of using the halt to rebuild his forces (partly true) and, urged by the hawkish *puros* to never negotiate with the Yankees, *el Presidente* claimed he had never intended to make any sort of treaty with the invaders.

Historians have generally been critical of Scott for agreeing to the armistice. Wallace Ohrt says, "From a strictly military viewpoint, the armistice was indeed antithetical to American objectives, for it was offered out of compassion, and compassion has no place in war." But it is not at all certain that Scott would have done better to attack the city immediately after the Battles of Contreras and Churubusco. His men were tired; many were wounded or sick. An assault on the large fortified city needed to be planned. We will never know for sure, but a rushed attack on the city might have been a disaster for both sides, with thousands killed, including thousands of civilians. What no one can gainsay is Scott's final victory: whatever our discussion of his methods and his timing, that victory is a fact.

It is possible that Scott proposed the armistice to give Trist a chance to meet with the Mexicans and begin negotiations and prevent more bloodshed. When it was clear the Mexicans were not negotiating in good faith but temporizing, Scott ended the armistice on September 6, 1847, and resumed his military campaign.

We do not know the exact degree of consulting and cooperation between Trist and Scott in Mexico. Since they saw each other daily there are no more letters between them. But it is likely Trist consulted the general often on his moves in response to both the Mexicans and Washington. With Scott's support, Trist displayed a new patience and perspicacity in his dealings with the Mexicans. He also had the help and advice of experienced British diplomats such as Bankhead and Thornton. No one would suggest that Scott was the author or coauthor of the treaty Trist would finally make with the Mexicans, but a lot of the diplomatic tact, firmness, patience, and skill Trist exhibited in Mexico must have been inspired by his constant contact with Old Fuss and Feathers. One of the historians who has understood the importance of the collaboration between Scott and Trist in the treaty-making process is T. R. Fehrenbach who, in a sweeping overstatement, writes, "Scott and Trist, his State Department aide, made rapid progress hammering out a treaty."

After the fortress at Chapultepec was taken on September 12 and Scott marched his army into Mexico City on September 14, Trist was faced with the prospect of negotiating with a government that had virtually disappeared. Street fighting, sniping, and prisoners released by Santa Anna before he fled threatened the city for three days. But after that the capital was quiet. The remnants of the Mexican army were scattered over the countryside. There was no one to treat with. Back in Washington, Daniel Webster would describe the strange impasse: "Mexico is an ugly enemy. She will not fight—and will not treat."

With Santa Anna gone, the elderly Manuel de la Peña y Peña was called upon to accept the Mexican presidency until an election could be held. Peña y Peña very much desired peace and in November the Mexican congress, now meeting in Querétaro a hundred miles north of Mexico City, rejected a proposal to make it illegal to even discuss ceding territory to the United States. Trist already knew Peña y Peña and many members of the Moderado Party who had come to trust and respect him. Trist wrote to the Minister of Foreign Relations Luis de la Rosa that the people of Texas had already made their independence a fact, with the

Rio Grande their explicit boundary. Trist kept his letter brief and to the point, as though he wrote with a new confidence, and Rosa's answer showed a new willingness to move forward with the negotiations.

While Trist and the Mexicans were planning on meeting as soon as the necessary documents could be assembled, there were signs of a new spirit of flexibility on the Mexican side. And then on November 16, 1847, Trist got the letter recalling him to Washington. If he had a treaty in hand, he was to bring it with him. Otherwise he was to break off all negotiations with the Mexicans, making no further offers. Because of his extraordinary secrecy and ability to play all sides against the middle, we will never know the full story of Polk's treatment of Trist. Howe points out that Polk waited twelve days after receiving "Trist's defiance before sending an order off to Mexico to abort whatever negotiations he might have underway." Apparently Polk wanted a treaty but took care to make sure that no blame could be attached to him if things turned out badly. Like Richard Nixon many years later, he made every effort to preserve "deniability."

Surprised and disappointed as he was, Trist saw no alternative but to pack his bags and return as soon as a safe escort could be arranged to Veracruz. He duly informed the British and the Mexicans of his recall. Just as the peace process was finally about to go forward he had to drop everything and leave. President Peña y Peña is supposed to have said when he got the news, "All is lost," and wept openly.

In the precarious state of Mexican politics, Peña y Peña and others who sought peace knew it was quite possible the *puros* and other hawks might overtake the government. They also knew that many factions, especially among the rich, favored the complete annexation of Mexico by the United States as a way of establishing stability. The leaders of the Roman Catholic Church in Mexico, tired of upheavals and heavy taxes imposed to pay for the war, were among those preferring complete annexation. Back in Washington, Polk himself had decided more Mexican territory should be acquired than that described in the original proposal Trist had taken to Mexico. By this time Polk's hatred of Trist brought him to write, "Mr. Trist has managed the negotiation very bunglingly . . . He has done more. He has departed from his instructions so far as to invite proposals from the Mexican commissioners to be submitted to his government." Apparently Polk's idea of negotiation was that the Mexicans would be told what they were going to do. Anything else was insulting to him personally.

As Trist waited for a military escort back to the port of Veracruz, a number of those around him asked him to stay and complete negotiations for a treaty. Among them were the Mexican peace commissioners, the British legate Thornton, and General Scott himself. Scott urged his friend to stay and negotiate, arguing that no treaty that followed the president's instructions would be rejected by either the administration or Congress. Unsure what to do, and what his status might be, Trist wrote Buchanan urging him to send another commissioner to replace him, now that the peace process was finally going forward.

Since Trist explained his actions in detail, we know a good deal about what he was thinking. Though he might feel "abandoned, abused, and resentful," he knew his government wanted peace and new territory. He was finally in a position to treat for both those goals. Given the political instability of Mexico, it might be years before such an opportunity came again. The Mexicans feared that whoever replaced Trist would be much more demanding in terms of territory. And since no one else had been sent to relieve him, Trist thought he might as well soldier on. Trist also knew that Polk and Buchanan and those in Washington had little idea of the actual situation in Mexico. Though Trist could not know that Polk's mind was poisoned by Pillow, he could see it was his duty to stay on and make the treaty, whatever it would cost him personally. Yet if he succeeded in negotiating a treaty, he would be doing so as a private citizen without portfolio, trusting that such a treaty would be accepted by the administration and by Congress when it was sent to Washington.

As Trist pondered the pros and cons and waited for his replacement to arrive, he received a visit from the journalist James Freaner on December 4, 1847. Freaner, a correspondent for the *New Orleans Delta,* had become a close friend of Trist. When Trist described his dilemma to the younger man, Freaner exclaimed, "Mr. Trist, make the Treaty. Make the Treaty, Sir! It is now in your power to do your country a greater service than any living man can render her . . . Your country, Sir, is entitled to this service from you." Freaner agreed that when a treaty was made he would rush it to Washington himself.

Trist later said that was when he decided to stay and conclude the treaty. There is no reason to doubt him. But it is likely that the suggestion from Scott that he stay and complete his work was equally influential. Embroiled with the intrigues of Polk and Pillow and Worth, Scott had shown a steady dedication to duty. Scott also asked Trist to stay on to testify in the court of inquiry of Pillow, Worth and Duncan and the letters written to newspapers about the war in Mexico. Trist would show that he was no less dedicated to his duty than Scott, whatever the consequences.

Amazingly, the British diplomats and the Mexican commissioners acted as if Trist's recall had never happened. Trist himself wrote a sixty-page letter to Buchanan defending his decision to stay on. Few diplomats in American history have demonstrated such independence and arrogance. As Robert W. Merry writes, the long letter revealed "every one of his many character flaws — the obsession with self, the quickness to querulous defensiveness, the unnecessary resort to insult . . . Nicholas Trist was treating with a foreign power illegally while poking his president in the eye." Trist decided he would act for the benefit of the United States whatever the petty, spiteful Polk might say or do. It was a dangerous course to choose, and Trist already knew that his career in government was almost certainly over.

When the long letter reached Washington, Polk's response was predictable. In his diary he recorded his outrage: "His dispatch is arrogant, impudent and very insulting to his Government, and even personally insulting to the president . . . I have never in my life felt so indignant . . . He has acted worse than any man in the public employ whom I have ever known." From Polk's acid words, one would never guess that Trist was about to sign the treaty that would be one of the glories of Polk's presidency, his career, and his era.

In his anger Polk officially relieved Scott of his command in Mexico on January 13, 1848, and replaced him with General William O. Butler, a good Democrat with an undistinguished military record. For almost a year Polk had waited to get rid of Scott, or at least undercut his efforts so he could not become a viable candidate for the presidency. Now that Mexico was conquered, Polk was free to act on his malice.

From his diary and letters, it is clear Polk had only a remote idea of conditions in Mexico. He had no knowledge of the *santanistas* who clamored to bring Santa Anna back as dictator, or the *puros* who only wanted to continue the war. Polk knew relatively little about Mexico, its history or culture. An intellectual like Trist, who understood the complexity and delicacy of the task at hand, was offensive and anathema to the politician Polk who saw most things in the context of political opportunity for the Democratic Party. Given Polk's personal limitations, it seems almost miraculous that he actually accomplished—in a mere four years—his vision of a republic that reached the Pacific.

True to his decision, Trist resumed meeting with the Mexican commissioners and they drafted and compared versions of a possible treaty. For the meetings the Mexicans chose the suburb of Guadalupe Hidalgo, north of Mexico City, site of the most sacred shrine in Mexico. It had once been the site of the temple of Tonantzin, "Aztec Mother of Gods." The Virgin of Guadalupe, who appeared there in 1531, was a Mexican, with dark skin and Indian features. A treaty concluded at Guadalupe Hidalgo might carry some of the mystical authority of the place. The Mexicans presented twenty-three articles, some just face-saving gestures they hoped would help ratification in the Mexican Congress. Historians have pointed out that Trist himself was the complete American delegation at these crucial meetings. He had no assistants, secretaries, translators, or rapporteurs, no one to assist with protocol. He had to serve as his own secretary and stenographer. He had to keep minutes of the discussions even while participating. And the often frail Trist seemed to grow healthier and more robust the harder he worked.

The mood of the Mexicans was different from what he had seen in the earlier negotiations. They clearly wanted a treaty and they wanted to make the treaty with Nicholas Trist before someone less agreeable arrived to take his place. Trist argued that the Rio Grande boundary had been established by force of arms and the negotiators now accepted the Rio Grande as the boundary of Texas. The ceding of New Mexico and California, Alta California, was implicit in the discussions. Trist established a courteous, businesslike rapport with the Mexicans. In the words of the historian Wallace Ohrt, "The Mexicans found his candor and honesty reassuring. They trusted and liked him, and with growing trust came the speedy resolution of issues for which many good men on both sides had given their lives."

One of the more difficult issues to resolve was the southern boundary of California. By then Trist had given up on the idea of acquiring Baja California. In any case, Polk and Buchanan had told him that was not essential. The Mexicans claimed the harbor of San Diego was within the boundary of Baja California. Luckily for Trist, Robert E. Lee and Persifor Smith found old Spanish maps showing San Diego was not only within Alta California but at one time had been the capital of the northern province. The line Trist drew for a southern boundary ran from the mouth of the Gila River on the Colorado River to a place seven miles south of San Diego. The present boundary of Arizona and California with Mexico would be established in 1853 with the Gadsden Purchase.

In return for so much territory, the Mexican commissioners had been told to demand thirty million dollars. In theory, Trist could have met that price given his original instructions from Washington, but Trist offered only fifteen million dollars, pointing out that by not negotiating earlier the Mexicans had prolonged and increased the cost of the war. Trist agreed that the United States would assume the claims of American citizens against the Mexican government, up to the sum of three million dollars. When the Mexicans objected to that limit, Trist raised the amount to three and a quarter million and pointed out it was unlikely the claims would amount to so much. It was agreed that Mexican citizens living in the ceded territories would become American citizens if they chose. If they preferred to leave, they would not be taxed for the removal of their property. Churches and church property would not be taken over by the American government. The United States would assume responsibility for raids by hostile Indians into Mexican territory. Of all the concessions Trist agreed to, the last would be the hardest for the United States to enforce in the years to come. The United States would be able to exercise little control over Apache and other Indian raids into Mexican territory.

As the end of January 1848 approached, both sides were anxious to get the treaty completed. The Mexicans feared that General Scott's replacement might be far more demanding, and it was understood that Trist's return to Washington was imminent. The treaty draft was sent back to the Mexican government in Querétaro, and Trist and the commissioners in Guadalupe Hidalgo waited for a response. Trist sent the Mexicans

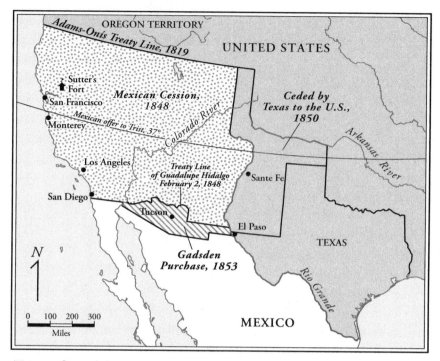

Treaty of Guadalupe Hidalgo Boundaries, 1848

a letter stating that if the treaty was not accepted immediately he would break off the negotiations and return to the United States. The new British minister Peter Doyle persuaded Trist to wait a few more days.

And then, like a miracle, it all worked. The Peña y Peña government accepted the treaty draft and on February 2, 1848, the treaty was signed at Guadalupe Hidalgo, near the shrine of the Virgin of Guadalupe. The document was called the "Treaty of Peace, Friendship, Limits and Settlement." Commissioner José Bernardo Couto, before he signed the document, turned to Trist and said, "This must be a proud moment for you; no less proud for you than it is humiliating for us."

"We are making *peace*," Trist answered. "Let that be our only thought."

One of the most vehement opponents of the treaty had been Manuel Crescencio Rejón (1799–1849), who denounced the negotiations from beginning to end. He wrote, "Gentlemen, what is proposed to us in this fatal treaty amounts to a sentence of death, and I wonder that there could have been Mexicans who would have negotiated it and subscribed to it, thinking all the while that it would be a boon to our unfortunate country. This circumstance alone dismays me and makes me despair of the life of the republic."

But others were just as passionate in defending the work of the treaty negotiators. The venerable Manuel de la Peña y Peña, distinguished lawyer and judge, said to represent "the conservative wing of the moderate liberals," eloquently defended the treaty in an address to the Mexican Congress on May 7, 1848. "The negotiators have accomplished all that can be expected from these types of transactions," he said. "Let us do the right thing, gentlemen; let us strip off the veil that has prevented us from seeing the reality of things, and let us hope for peace . . . opposing a resistance that drives blindly toward disorder and anarchy." Peña y Peña warned dramatically of the calamity further fighting would bring. "Contemplate . . . the confusion and anarchy into which we would see our country sink . . . social disorganization, insecurity among our people, danger along the highways, paralyzation of all branches of public welfare, and general misery."

The Mexican historian Carlos Bosch García would later view the Treaty of Guadalupe Hidalgo not only as a tragic turning point in Mexican and Latin American history but as a significant precedent in modern history. "The treaty that ended the Mexican-American War . . . had worldwide repercussions. . . . It established precedents that set in motion a march of events that would establish the United States as a world power."

Trist's friend James Freaner, as agreed, took the treaty to Washington in an incredible seventeen days. One can imagine the surprise of Buchanan and then Polk as they scanned the document. Polk was hardly on speaking terms with his secretary of state, and because of his anger at Trist, Polk's first inclination was probably to burn the document or use it as evidence for censuring the commissioner. By then Polk had decided he wanted to annex far more of Mexico than he had specified in the directions to Trist almost a year before. Many voices were clamoring to annex all of Mexico. According to Walter LaFeber, the All Mexico movement "had its most feverish supporters among northern Democrats, both among the sensationalistic press in cities such as New York and the agrarian-Manifest Destiny expansionists of the Midwest." But as he studied the instrument from the hand of the hated Trist, Polk saw it included all he had insisted Trist accomplish. As mentioned earlier, after consulting with his cabinet, he sent the treaty on to the Senate where it was eventually ratified by a vote of 38 to 14. The wit Philip Hone would describe the treaty as "negotiated by an unauthorized agent, with an unacknowledged government, submitted by an accidental president to a dissatisfied Senate."

With the treaty negotiations successfully completed, it would have been logical for Trist to return home immediately. With his work done he might have been expected to return to Washington to explain himself to the administration and to Congress and maybe take credit for his triumph. Many people at the time realized the significance of what he had done. He knew many important people and with a little care and diplomacy he might well have saved his government career.

But Trist did not return home to explain, defend, or take credit for the treaty. He stayed on in Mexico. His explanation to his wife was that he had to remain to testify in the hearings about Pillow, Worth, and Duncan and to help Scott in the difficult proceedings. The truth is that once his work was done Trist's behavior became bizarre. While negotiating the treaty, Trist showed intelligence, patience, and wisdom. With that work complete he seemed to go into yet another of his peculiar tailspins. Though repeatedly urged and even ordered to leave Mexico, he refused to budge. When Polk directed General Butler to arrest Trist if he didn't leave, Trist answered that as an American citizen he had a right to remain in Mexico and the president had no power to remove him. Trist was arrested and escorted humiliatingly to Veracruz and put on a ship to New Orleans.

Historians have puzzled over the strange veerings and reversals in Trist's behavior. How could he perform the Herculean tasks of the treaty negotiations and then act so foolishly and self-destructively a few weeks later? Was he suffering from exhaustion or the aftereffects of some illness?

Why did he not return to Washington and answer the charges against him? We know that Trist had always avoided meetings where he would have to speak to his critics face-to-face. Though he could be courageous and unbending in his letters, he seemed paralyzed by the prospect of confronting his detractors in person. Instead, he retreated into his pride and would not even ask Polk for the money due him. The unforgiving Polk would not volunteer to reimburse his commissioner, even after the great treaty was ratified, for the time spent in Mexico after the recall reached him on November 16, 1847.

Rather than face his critics and explain himself, Trist, on his own, was willing to accept a life of obscurity and poverty for his family. Moving to West Chester, Pennsylvania, he would spend much of the rest of his life working as a clerk and paymaster for the Philadelphia, Wilmington, and Baltimore Railroad. Virginia would run a school for young girls to augment their meager income. And instead of writing his own books, Trist would write long answers to questions from biographers of Jefferson and Jackson. Only as a frail old man in his seventies would he be awarded the back pay for his work in Mexico, thanks to the efforts of Senator Charles Sumner of Massachusetts, and he was also given a postmastership in Alexandria, Virginia.

Almost all historians who have written about Trist have made much of comments he uttered many years later about his efforts in Mexico. Rather than look back with pride on what he had accomplished at Guadalupe Hidalgo, he asserted that he had felt shame, which he kept to himself, even as he signed the momentous treaty. "Could those Mexicans have seen into my heart at that moment," Trist wrote, "they would have known that *my* feeling of shame as an American was far stronger than theirs could be . . . that was a thing for every right-minded American to be ashamed of, and I *was* ashamed."

We do not know if Trist really felt that ashamed when he signed the treaty of Guadalupe Hidalgo in 1848 or if that was only the way a bitter old man would look back on his greatest accomplishment. What we do know is that he said nothing of the sort at the time, when he proved to be a responsible and courteous, but a curiously firm and frugal negotiator. What he did is what we have lived with ever since.

When the Treaty of Guadalupe Hidalgo was ratified by the Mexican Congress in May of 1848 one of the commissioners who had worked with

Trist read a statement to the legislature: "Your Excellency will permit us to state before concluding that the favorable conception which in the first negotiations was formed of the noble character and high endowments of Mr. Trist has been completely confirmed in the second. Happy has it been for both countries that the choice of the American Government should have been fixed upon a person of such worth, upon a friend of peace so loyal and sincere: of him there remains in Mexico none but grateful and honoring recollections."

— *Epilogue* —

JOHN QUINCY ADAMS
OLD MAN ELOQUENT

To UNDERSTAND almost any controversial issue, it is necessary to study the opposing points of view. The most vocal and eloquent opponent of expansion into the Southwest, the annexation of Texas, and the Mexican-American War, was the venerable John Quincy Adams. To conclude a narrative of the westward expansion it is appropriate to consider briefly the career and opinions of this most passionate, sustained, and effective critic of Jacksonian politics. Adams's story is one of the most complex and significant of the era.

Adams realized early on that the westward expansion was, among other things, a diversion from the ugly argument about slavery, and he never let his countrymen forget it. In most accounts of John Quincy, he is seen as the nemesis of Andrew Jackson, Thomas Hart Benton, James K. Polk, and other lions of the westward expansion. Adams even refused to support a vote of thanks in Congress to the generals who had triumphed in the Halls of Montezuma. But the truth is that in his younger days John Quincy had been one of the most enthusiastic proponents of westward expansion, and he had been expelled from the Federalist Party for his support of Jefferson's Louisiana Purchase and Embargo Act of 1807.

John Quincy Adams was born to Founding Father John Adams and Abigail Adams in Braintree, Massachusetts, south of Boston, on July 11, 1767, the same year as Andrew Jackson's birth. Because his father was away from home much of the time serving in the Continental Congress in Philadelphia, the younger Adams assumed from an early age much of the labor and responsibility for looking after the family farm. He was taught to read when very young and showed a remarkable aptitude for learning, including classical languages and French. By the time he was ten in 1777, he was reading newspapers, Tobias Smollett's *Complete History of England, The Arabian Nights,* and Shakespeare.

No future president of the United States would ever have the kind of extracurricular education John Quincy Adams received. In 1778 he accompanied his father on his mission to France and witnessed both storms and naval battles while crossing the Atlantic. He made himself fluent in French and was enrolled at the Académie de Passy near Paris. When John Adams was directed on a further diplomatic mission to the Netherlands, young John Quincy accompanied him and was admitted to the University of Leyden in 1781. But instead of attending classes, the fourteen-year-old traveled to Russia with Francis Dana as assistant and translator on a mission to win recognition for the American cause from Catherine II. The language of the Russian court was French. While in St. Petersburg, he began to study the Russian language, a skill he would put to good use as a diplomat in later years. In the words of Walter LaFeber, Adams ultimately "utilized six languages." In France he had spent much time in the company of Thomas Jefferson and it is fair to say that Jefferson's conversation and vision had a deep influence on the gifted young man. He also knew Lafayette.

When John Quincy returned to the United States he enrolled at Harvard, and though he would graduate second in his class in 1787, he would be sharply critical of the education he received there. Compared to the scholars he had met in Europe, most of the faculty at Harvard seemed ignorant and provincial. While at the university John Quincy wrote a good bit of poetry and thought of himself as a literary man, even though he also had an abiding interest in science and the natural world.

But John Adams insisted that his oldest and most gifted son follow in his footsteps and study law. John Quincy read for the legal profession with the distinguished lawyer Theophilus Parsons of Newburyport, Massachusetts. While the young man performed his duties in the law office, he continued to write for local publications and to read widely. He was most impressed with Jefferson's *Notes on the State of Virginia,* which had been published in 1785. Among the many interests he shared with

the Sage of Monticello was the love of natural history and a special interest in horticulture, geography, and the commercial potential of North
America. And he was deeply inspired by Rousseau's *Confessions*. Contrary
to the popular image of John Quincy, he enjoyed attending parties and
was a recognized authority on wines.

All his life John Quincy was plagued by insomnia and periods of
depression. To combat these weaknesses he kept himself to a rigorous
regime of exercise, reading, and writing. He wrote many poems, passed
the bar examination on July 15, 1790, and set himself up to practice in
Boston where there was already a surplus of lawyers. While he waited for
clients to appear, he read Cicero, Tacitus, Clarendon, and Hume, and he
courted Mary Frazier.

Because they had great ambitions for John Quincy, who was just starting out in his professional life, his parents ordered him to break off his
connection with Mary Frazier. They feared an early marriage would
cripple his career. Though he acceded to their wishes, most biographers
think he never quite got over his intense attachment to the lively and
beautiful Miss Frazier. But ever a diplomat and dedicated worker, he
concealed his wound and spent much time hunting small game in the
countryside around Quincy. He would later say that year, 1792, was one
of the most dismal periods of his life. He rose before six every morning
and spent hours in concentrated reading. He wrote pamphlets under the
name Publicola, refuting much that Thomas Paine had said in *The Rights
of Man*. The verve of his warning against entanglements in foreign wars
was noticed by many, including President Washington. Arguments and
phrasing from one of John Quincy's eloquent essays would find their way
into Washington's renowned Farewell Address of 1796.

In fact, Washington had been so impressed with young Adams that
he appointed him minister to The Hague in 1795, kicking off what is
perhaps the most distinguished diplomatic career in American history.
Walter LaFeber would later write that the story of John Quincy "is the
story of many of American diplomacy's finest hours." On March 1, 1795,
John Quincy began writing his diary, which would grow to nineteen volumes of about five hundred pages each before he broke it off after 1845.
Thanks to his detailed account, we know a good deal about the events of
his life and the evolution of his thought over the course of his long career.

It is said that Washington came "to regard Adams as the ablest officer in the foreign service." Though he would be involved in government as a legislator and even as chief executive, John Quincy's greatest talent was for diplomacy. His fluency in European languages, his meticulous thoroughness in work, his great knowledge of history and geography and culture, made him the ideal negotiator, as he was to prove again both as minister and as secretary of state. Where his father had demonstrated impatience and awkwardness and ignorance of foreign languages and customs, John Quincy was a model of polish, fluency, and firmness. While his opinions and thoughts would evolve over the course of his long career, he was from first to last committed to "the continuance and preservation of the union." It has been said that only Washington, and perhaps Lincoln, were "as well prepared to understand the Union they served."

It was while serving at The Hague that John Quincy met Louisa Catherine Johnson, who, though from a Maryland family, had been born and raised in London. Her father headed a shipping company and was also American consul in London. Louisa suffered from ill health and lack of confidence in herself, but after many delays the couple were married July 26, 1797. It would prove a lasting but often troubled union. The overall impression is that the workaholic John Quincy may have given the vulnerable Louisa less attention than she needed or desired. Her grandson, the historian Henry Adams, would remember Louisa as the warmest and most endearing of all the Adams clan.

John Quincy never had anything but praise for Washington, and in this period he came to admire Napoleon also. His father was now president of the United States and John Quincy was sent to Berlin to represent his country in the Prussian court, where he served until 1801. But just before John Adams left the presidency he recalled his son, and John Quincy again opened a law office in Boston.

When John Quincy was chosen for the state senate of Massachusetts by the Federalists in 1802, he argued that the Democratic Republican minority should be given representation also. For the rest of his life he would attempt to rise above party politics, aspiring to represent "the whole Union." Believing government service should be a meritocracy in which only the most worthy and accomplished would hold office, John Quincy often offended politicians of all parties. His permanent ambition was to work for the common good. In 1803 the Massachusetts legislature elected him U.S. senator, and he arrived at the muddy construction site of the nation's capital where he outraged the Federalists by supporting Jefferson's Louisiana Purchase, which he described as "one of the happiest events which had occurred since the adoption of the Constitution."

At this time John Quincy was becoming, as Marie B. Hecht tells us, a "convinced continentalist and expansionist." And though he had been sent to Washington by the Federalists of Boston, Adams saw himself as a "representative not of a single state, but of the whole Union." Needless to say, such a stance would make him less than popular at times. "I am made a leader without followers," he would later write. During his summers, he was an equally dedicated gardener back at the farm in Quincy. John Quincy was much more of an outdoorsman and athlete than his popular image would suggest.

For the Federalists the last straw was John Quincy's support for Jefferson's Embargo Act of 1807. Reviled by his own party, he resigned from the Senate and returned to Boston where he had in 1806 been elected Boyleston Professor of Rhetoric and Oratory at Harvard, a chair he would hold until 1810. In 1809 President Madison appointed him minister to Russia and he moved with his family to St. Petersburg. While his salary was inadequate for the luxurious lifestyle of the splendid capital, and Louisa was much too shy to enjoy the glittering social whirl, John Quincy once again demonstrated his great skill as a diplomat. He became friends with Tsar Alexander I, who showed special favor to the American minister and the United States during the Napoleonic Wars and the invasion of Russia. And friendly relations with Russia proved important during the War of 1812 with Britain.

President Madison appointed John Quincy to the Supreme Court in 1813, but the diplomat refused the honor. The president then appointed him as one of the peace negotiators with Great Britain to end the War of 1812, and in June of 1814 he arrived in Ghent, Belgium, to serve with Albert Gallatin, James A. Beard, Henry Clay, and Jonathan Russell on the peace commission. Throughout the several months of talks and interruptions, Adams proved his diplomatic intelligence and firmness, bringing the conflict to an end with as much dignity as could be expected, just weeks before Andrew Jackson's victory in New Orleans on

January 8, 1815. It has been said that in the negotiations John Quincy the New Englander gave much of his attention to the issue of American fishing rights off Newfoundland and Labrador. From Ghent, John Quincy traveled to Paris, where he witnessed Napoleon's return from Elba and then continued on to London where President Madison had sent him as minister to Great Britain. Working again with Gallatin and Clay, he negotiated a treaty of commerce with the British Empire.

James Monroe assumed the office of the president in March of 1817, and on April 16 of that year John Quincy in London received a letter notifying him that he had been nominated and confirmed as secretary of state. His great work was about to begin. Many historians agree that John Quincy Adams was the most successful secretary of state in American history. The period 1814 to 1828 has been called "the Golden Age of American diplomacy."

ACCORDING TO the biographer Mary B. Hecht, John Quincy was "short, bald, and stout, with a small mouth . . . which gave him a slightly peevish look. His eyes, whose tendency to water had started in his youth, were now permanently afflicted. He had a cold, bristly, introspective personality coupled with an independent integrity that dazzled an opponent. He related poorly to people but his intellect and scholarship gained him respect. Like his father he had a deeply ingrained mistrust of Great Britain." John Quincy was known to be careless with his dress, and enemies once accused him (wrongly) of attending church barefoot and without a tie.

The American team at Ghent had surprised the British, indeed all of Europe, by its ability and strength. And no one had surprised them more than John Quincy Adams. To the negotiations he had brought his long experience as a diplomat in Europe, his considerable knowledge of history and culture, and the zeal for service to his country he shared with his father. Biographer Hecht observes that "what passed for rigidity in his personality was possibly an intense, almost romantic desire to see the world as he wished it to be." Some aspects of John Quincy's character have been explained by the religious heritage of New England. As Daniel Walker Howe puts it, comparing Adams to Nathaniel Hawthorne,

"While a Unitarian in his own religion [Adams] retained much of his Puritan ancestors' Calvinist sense of sin." Howe also points out that John Quincy was a dedicated reformer, like the famous evangelists of his time such as Lyman Beecher and Charles Grandison Finney. He was deeply influenced "by Enlightenment concepts of human rights and freedom."

Something biographers seem not to have noticed is that John Quincy was most effective when he was representing another leader, such as Madison or Monroe. Speaking for someone else he rose to diplomatic brilliance and statesmanship. When he became president himself things did not go so well. It's true that his administration would be plagued by party dissension, economic setbacks, and the uproar over the election of 1824 fueled by Jackson and his supporters. But the fact is that when sitting in the executive office himself John Quincy was not as effective as he was when working for another president. True, he was always independent, but he was best as an independent servant. As Walter LaFeber explains, John Quincy "lacked the personal warmth that wins the hearts of voters, and his adherence to principle alienated many of his professional political supporters as well." And later, as a legislator, he would be dramatically independent but independent as a representative of the people at large.

While trenchantly critical of those around him, John Quincy Adams was harshest with and most demanding of himself. He always sought to improve himself as well as his country. An admirer of Cicero and the moral philosophers of the eighteenth century, John Quincy saw the United States as the final stage of the struggle for freedom over the centuries of European history.

Adams also had a lifelong enthusiasm for science and technology and he shared with Jefferson a commitment to develop the resources, infrastructure, and commerce on the North American continent. His career would stretch from the building of the first important canals to the popular travel by steamboat and steamship, to the laying of railroads and the introduction of the telegraph. "The spirit of improvement is abroad upon the earth," he would write. He was deeply committed to what was called in those days "internal improvements" and would fight with the Democrats who wanted less federal support for canals and railroads, not more.

When he returned to the United States in 1817 to become secretary of state in the Monroe administration, John Quincy found not only a nation struggling to recover from the failures and embarrassments of the War of 1812 but a country still literally attempting to define itself. Its border in the south with Spanish Florida was a sore spot. Encouraged by the Spanish, Indians attacked American settlers in that region. Andrew Jackson had defeated the Red Stick Creeks in 1814, but many of the Red Stick rebels had joined their cousins, the militant Seminoles in Florida, and still considered themselves at war with the United States.

In the West the borders with New Spain (Mexico) were in dispute. Jefferson had argued that the Louisiana Purchase had included Texas, but the Spanish vehemently disagreed. At best the boundaries were vague. Zebulon Pike, attempting to explore the boundary region near the headwaters of the Arkansas River in 1806–7, had been captured by Spanish soldiers and returned to the United States in humiliation.

In the Northwest Lewis and Clark had established some claim to the Pacific coast at the mouth of the Columbia River and the Astor fur company had built the small port of Astoria there. But the British presence in the region was older and stronger, thanks to both the trading vessels competing with the Russians from the port of Nootka on Vancouver Island and the Hudson's Bay Company, which had built its forts and trading posts all the way across Canada. Even in the Northeast there was a dispute about the actual boundary between Maine and the Canadian provinces.

As secretary of state, John Quincy Adams demonstrated an unusual ability to work simultaneously on several fronts. Some historians have described his foreign policy as an early version of what came to be called "containment" during the cold war, that is keeping Britain in the north and west and Spain in the south and west from pushing into United States territory. But the fact is that Adams was more interested in expansion than containment in his early years. "The United States and North America are identical," he would proclaim. When Andrew Jackson invaded Florida in 1818, killing a number of Indians and executing two British citizens as spies, the Spanish howled with indignation as their empire in the New World continued to crumble. Many in Washington were also furious that Old Hickory had exceeded his authority, invading Florida without authorization from the secretary of war. Many assumed

Jackson would be court-martialed and relieved of his command. John Quincy was the only member of Monroe's cabinet to defend Jackson's actions. He saw Old Hickory's campaign in Florida as an opportunity that must be seized rather than apologized for. Adams asserted, "If the question is dubious, it is better to err on the side of vigor than of weakness— on the side of our officer [Jackson], who has rendered the most eminent services to the nation, than on the side of our bitterest enemies, and against him." He also said that if Spain could not control what happened in the Floridas, "she should sell them to the United States." John Quincy defended Jackson's actions because he saw "the raid as a lever to force Spain to sell Florida."

John Quincy wrote in his diary that a reprimand to Jackson "must give offense to all his friends, encounter the shock of his popularity, and have the appearance of truckling to Spain." Adams told the Spanish government that President Monroe had no intention of censuring Andrew Jackson for his actions in Florida, "the motives for which were founded in the purist patriotism."

John Quincy was willing to be firm with Spain in defense of Jackson's invasion of Florida because he had much more on his mind than the territory south of Georgia and Alabama. The historian Richard Kluger has called John Quincy at this period "a driven visionary as well as a calculating tactician." As much as Jefferson before him, Adams dreamed of a continental, hemispheric United States. He could be stubborn about acquiring and holding Florida because he was willing to drop Jefferson's claim to Texas in exchange for Spanish recognition of American claims to the Pacific coast. Let the Spanish give up all their territories east of the Mississippi, and he would concede to them the large, mostly empty region called Tejas. But in return the Spanish must acknowledge the American right to a presence all the way across the Rockies to the shores of the Pacific. The United States could never realize its full potential as a world power without harbors on the Pacific Ocean. For years Adams had hoped to acquire ports on the Pacific to aid in the American trade with China. While the British saw China as the Far East, Americans viewed it as the Far West.

But while the southern border in the West had to be negotiated with Spain, the northern border had to be negotiated with Great Britain and maybe also Russia. For John Quincy and many others, expansion into the Northwest was not only desirable because of the fur industry, the fishing, the timber, the land and the ports there. It was a necessity. As the southern states spread slavery into the new territories of the Southwest, as they were almost certain to do, it was crucial that non–slave states be added in the Northwest to offset the growing power of the South. As secretary of state, John Quincy began negotiations with the British and in 1818 signed a treaty establishing the boundary between the United States and Canada at the forty-ninth parallel as far west as the Rocky Mountains. The territory west of that was to be administered jointly by the two nations in a vague arrangement. Either side could end the agreement with one year's notice. Adams believed that in a few years the arrangement, as Walter LaFeber tells us, "would allow the American population explosion to seize Oregon peacefully."

Now Adams could put on hold the resolution of the Oregon question while he dealt with the more volatile issue of the border with Spain. Spain had lost many of its colonies in South America, and in 1821 it would be driven out of Mexico in that country's revolution. John Quincy was able to use his agreement with the British about Oregon in his negotiations with the Spanish, as he would use his treaty with Spain to reinforce his position with the British about the American claims to the Pacific coast. The ultimate claim to the western regions would be made by settlers arriving and establishing themselves there, and it is quite likely that John Quincy already understood this. Final negotiations for Oregon could be put on hold until enough Americans had arrived there.

Defining his foreign policy, Adams stated, "But she [the United States] goes not abroad in search of monsters to destroy. She is the well-wisher to the freedom and independence of all. She is the champion and vindicator only of her own." It is a statement repeated by diplomats, historians, and secretaries of state ever since. But beginning with the Truman Doctrine of 1947 its principles would be violated, and the stalemates of the cold war, and the quagmires of Vietnam, Iraq, and Afghanistan, among others, would result.

After a long series of meetings, starting and halting, drafting agreements and drawing maps, Adams, with the help of Albert Gallatin, was able to conclude the Adams-Onís Treaty of February 22, 1819. The

Spanish gave up their claims to all of Florida, retained Texas west from the Sabine River and granted American claims in the West and to the Pacific coast north of the forty-second parallel. In his diary John Quincy wrote, "The acknowledgment of a definite line of boundary to the south Sea forms a great epocha in our history." It was a triumph of firm diplomacy by any standard, and it was accomplished by statesmanship, not military force. "The gap between relative power and relative accomplishment is the true measure of statesmanship," the historian William Earl Weeks has written. The Adams-Onís Treaty would provide leverage for future negotiations with Mexico and like most treaties about the American West, it would be broken by tens of thousands of settlers flooding into Texas and then California and Oregon, settlers who would simply ignore the agreements. Within two years of becoming secretary of state, Adams had established official recognition by both the British and the Spanish of American claims to a considerable chunk of the Pacific coast.

THERE WAS a wonderful stubbornness about John Quincy Adams. His grandson, the great historian, in *The Education of Henry Adams*, would pay a tribute to the old man's quiet willpower. The young grandson was rebelling against going to school.

> *Henry showed a certain tactical ability by refusing to start, and he met all efforts at compulsion by successful, though too vehement protest. He was in [a] fair way to win, and was holding his own, with sufficient energy, at the bottom of the long staircase which led up to the door of the President's library, when the door opened, and the old man slowly came down. Putting on his hat, he took the boy's hand without a word, and walked with him paralyzed by awe, up the road to the town. After the first moments of consternation at this interference in a domestic dispute, the boy reflected that an old gentleman close on eighty would never trouble himself to walk near a mile on a hot summer morning over a shadeless road to take a boy to school, and that it would be strange if a lad imbued with the passion of freedom could not find a corner to dodge around, somewhere before reaching the school-door. Then and always, the boy insisted that this reasoning justified his apparent submission;*

but the old man did not stop, and the boy saw all his strategical points
turned, one after another, until he found himself seated inside the
school, and obviously the centre of curious, if not malevolent criticism.
Not till then did the President release his hand and depart.

If John Quincy, with his fierce determination, supported westward expansion with such effective energy when he was a senator and secretary of state, how did he come to play the role of nemesis to Jackson and Polk, to Texas annexation and the Mexican War? Did his ideas change as he grew older? This was the man who had defended Jackson when the general invaded and seized Florida in 1818. Yet by the presidential election of 1824 they were passionate opponents. Certainly they were polar opposites in many ways. Adams was scholarly; in 1821 he had written for Congress and President Monroe a technical study, *Report on Weights and Measures,* that is considered by many historians a forgotten masterpiece, too detailed, precise, and technical for most of his contemporaries to understand. He wrote the *Report,* in his busiest days as secretary of state, "by arising an hour or two earlier each morning—that is, 3:00 A.M." His youth and young manhood in Europe and at Harvard could not have been more different from Jackson's apprenticeship on the frontier.

When they became political rivals, John Quincy liked to snap that all Jackson and his supporters had to brag about was "the 8th of January and battle of New Orleans." And he would refer to Old Hickory as "a barbarian who could not write a sentence of grammar and hardly could spell his own name." Adams was known to be slovenly in his dress while Jackson spent enormous sums on the finest uniforms and most fashionable suits.

But the key to John Quincy's shift away from Jackson and the expansion issue is not to be found just in the great differences in their personalities and backgrounds, or even in their political rivalry, though those are important factors. As he grew older and more experienced at politics in Washington, John Quincy's ideas did not change so much as his perception of the country and of the South in particular. In his youth and middle years he shared with his associates, Henry Clay, Winfield Scott, and many others, the assumption that the institution of slavery would wither away in a natural process as the country grew and the economy grew. Technical and commercial progress would make slavery obsolete, a thing of the past. Therefore, the issue of slavery need not be uppermost, to be addressed aggressively and immediately, since time would solve the problem anyway.

As he served in Washington year after year and observed southern leaders such as John C. Calhoun, John Quincy slowly came to see that slavery was not going to fade away. It was the bitter debate that ended in the Missouri Compromise of 1820 that began to change John Quincy's mind. In the words of Walter LaFeber, it was then that "he first fully glimpsed the menace which the slavery debate held for the American empire." Since the Revolutionary period, southerners had become much more deeply committed to slavery. Threatened by northern pressure to change, southern planters would fight with tenacity to preserve their way of life. One of the ways slavery was going to grow and root itself ever deeper was to expand into the new territories such as Texas. According to the Missouri Compromise of 1820, slavery was prohibited north of the 36°30' latitude. But as slave states were added to the Union, that legislation might well be repealed. Rather than wither away, slavery would spread into the West in new states as yet unnamed and uninhabited. John Quincy came to see that "the greatest danger of this Union was the overgrown extent of its territory, combining with the slavery question." Near the end of his long career, John Quincy would view his whole life as a failure because he had been unable to resolve the issue of slavery.

Even enlightened southern leaders such as Jefferson, who deplored the institution of slavery, did nothing to end it. In the words of Gordon S. Wood, Jefferson had always sensed that "his 'empire of liberty' had a cancer at its core that was eating away at the message of liberty and equality and threatening the very existence of the nation," but he was unable to act on that knowledge. Slavery was " 'a Serpent creeping with his deadly wiles' " in their Arcadian "Paradise." The failure of the Founding Fathers to end slavery at the very beginning of the Republic had proved to be their greatest failure.

In the bitter election of 1824, John Quincy, with the help of Henry Clay, managed to win, even though Jackson had received the most votes on the first ballot. When Adams quickly made Clay his secretary of state, the Jacksonians cried foul, and for the rest of his career Adams would be accused of making a "corrupt bargain" with Clay to obtain the presidency. In retaliation, John Quincy's supporters would dig up and advertise the dirt about Jackson's courtship and marriage to Rachel Donelson Robards.

After serving as the extraordinarily successful secretary of state, he seemed to stall as chief executive. The Jacksonians united to criticize and block his every initiative, and Congress again and again failed to support his proposed legislation. One of his most original and important ideas was that the federal government should oversee "internal improvement," building roads, bridges, canals, harbors. Only the federal government had the funds and power to execute such projects. "Let not foreign nations with less liberty exceed us in 'public improvement,'" the president exhorted his countrymen. "To do so would 'cast away the bounties of Providence' and doom what should become the world's most powerful nation 'to perpetual inferiority.'" Because of the damage done by the outcry about the "corrupt bargain," John Quincy was unable to push through Congress most of his plans for "internal improvements."

The so-called Monroe Doctrine had been formulated by Monroe and Adams when he was Monroe's secretary of state and announced on December 2, 1823. The British had offered to make a joint declaration, warning European states against further colonization in the Americas. But Adams refused, knowing the United States would like to spread into Texas and maybe annex Cuba. For him, the Monroe Doctrine was a warning to Britain also to stay out of the way of the American expansion. There was nothing modest about his vision of the future of the United States and its position in the world. For all his brooding seriousness, John Quincy could proclaim with great enthusiasm his "plans for exploration, science, and education, which included a national university in Washington, D.C., and at least one astronomical observatory." His opponents mocked his grand ambitions for the nation. Austere and dour as he might seem in person, John Quincy was a progressive visionary in outlook, using the rhetoric of popular Millennialism to argue that "Liberty is power" and celebrating "the spirit of improvement." As Daniel Walker Howe tells us, "Adams stood for a vision of coherent economic progress, of improvement both personal and national, directed by deliberate planning. Instead of pursuing improvements, Jacksonians accepted America the way it was, including its institution of slavery."

It has often been pointed out that John Quincy came to the office of president with the best preparation of anyone who has occupied the executive mansion. Yet his presidency is usually considered a failure. Most historians agree that John Quincy Adams was one of the least effective presidents in our history.

But if John Quincy accomplished less as president than would be expected, it was not for lack of trying. As chief executive he kept to an even more rigorous schedule than usual. Rising in the morning before 5:00 a.m., he would exercise for two hours, taking long walks in winter and swimming nude in the Potomac in milder weather, wearing only goggles and skullcap. In winter he walked every day from the executive mansion to the Capitol and back. After his workout he read and wrote until breakfast, then spent the day from nine to five receiving visitors with complaints, petitions, and requests for jobs or favors. His staff consisted of one secretary. When warned that someone might try to kill him, Adams ignored the warning, and after an attempt on his life failed, he appointed the would-be assassin as surgeon on a navy ship, hoping to set an example of forgiveness. He appointed opponents to positions in his administration, believing the only qualification for office was merit. He attended church twice each Sunday and read the Bible through in one language or another each year. In 1826 he joined the Unitarian Church.

Most days John Quincy wrote in his diary, sometimes for as much as six hours. In the diary he recorded his responses to events and explored ideas, drafting opinions that would later be incorporated in letters, speeches, and legislative proposals.

As president, John Quincy came to believe he had made a mistake in accepting the Sabine River as the boundary with Texas in the Adams-Onís Treaty of 1819. In 1827 he directed the minister to Mexico, Joel R. Poinsett of Charleston, to negotiate a new boundary, offering a million dollars to Mexico for all of Texas. But, as we have seen, the Mexicans refused the offer outright.

Believing that government should be a meritocracy, above distracting party politics, Adams had made John C. Calhoun his vice president, only to find that Calhoun, presiding in the Senate, undermined much of Adams's proposed legislation. And though Adams would later oppose Andrew Jackson's Indian removal policy, he himself as president supported just such removals of native people from their eastern lands. On December 28, 1825, he quoted and agreed with Henry Clay, "[Indians] are not an improvable breed, and their disappearance from the human family will be no great loss to the world." Even when John Quincy thought an injustice had been done to Indians and ordered a new treaty negotiated, the revised document of January 1826 was little different from the first.

As early as November 29, 1820, John Quincy, writing in his diary, considered that slavery might only be ended by a cataclysmic war between the opposed sections of the country. He wrote: "A dissolution of the Union for the cause of slavery would be followed by a servile war in the slave-holding States, combined with a war between the two severed portions of the Union . . . Calamitous and desolating as this course of events in its progress must be, so glorious would be its final issue, that, as God shall judge me, I dare not say that it is not to be desired."

By August 11, 1835, we can see the continued hardening of John Quincy's thoughts about slavery and the future of the Union. He knew now the South was never going to let the institution die. "There is a great fermentation upon this subject of slavery at this time in all parts of the Union," he wrote. "Rouse in the heart of the slave-holder the terror of his slave, and it will be a motive with him paramount to all others never to vote for any man not a slave-holder like himself." A deadly war began to loom on the horizon. By April 2, 1837, he would record in his diary, "This subject of slavery, to my great sorrow and mortification, is absorbing all my faculties."

By 1837 Adams had probably seen, as Jackson had not, that though the country could be distracted from the slavery issue by the euphoria of westward expansion, such a diversion only postponed the inevitable collision. The issue would always be there, widening and deepening, as more and more territories were annexed. And eventually when the Pacific was reached and there was no further territory to expand into, the issue would explode, on a devastating scale. Expansion had not been a solution but a postponement and an aggravation.

John Quincy Adams is the only president in United States history who after his tenure as chief executive returned to Washington as a congressman. When Jackson was inaugurated in March 1829, John Quincy and Louisa were already on their way to Quincy, Massachusetts. Adams had been defeated by a Jackson landslide, and everyone assumed his political career was over. Jackson had been so angered by the smear attacks on Mrs. Jackson's character that he refused to pay a courtesy call on John Quincy when he arrived in the capital. In retaliation, Adams refused to accompany Old Hickory to the inauguration.

In September 1830 a friend proposed that John Quincy run for Congress from the Plymouth district of Massachusetts. He was sixty-three years old and had been serving in government in one capacity or another since the age of fourteen. To almost everyone's surprise the ex-president agreed and won by an overwhelming majority, becoming at least nominally a Whig, or National Republican, but actually an independent. Most historians agree that Adams's service in the House would be second in importance only to his work as a diplomat and secretary of state. He was made chair of the Committee on Manufactures and resolutely supported Jackson in the debate over nullification.

But in the years ahead John Quincy became the most notable and the most eloquent of Jackson's critics. He supported Henry Clay in the presidential election of 1832, and his candidate suffered a humiliating defeat, even in Massachusetts. In 1833 Adams, as a member of the Harvard Board of Overseers, tried to prevent the award of an honorary degree to Old Hickory, but he was overruled. Yet it was John Quincy who was chosen to deliver the oration in tribute to Lafayette before the joint houses and the president and cabinet on December 31, 1834. It was in this period that he acquired the nickname "Old Man Eloquent." When he spoke in his shrill voice and waved his arms with passion, his bald head flushed a bright red.

During his presidency, the Erie Canal had been completed, as well as the Ohio, Dismal Swamp, Chesapeake and Delaware, and Miami canals. The National Road had been extended from Wheeling to Zanesville, Ohio. The number of steamboats on American rivers had doubled. While serving in Congress, he continued his enthusiastic support of "internal improvements," against the objections of Democrats and even members of the Whig party who wanted to leave such responsibilities for infrastructure to the states. Though often depressed, prickly, and defensive to the point of paranoia, Adams never relaxed in his demands upon the nation and upon himself. Once he described the government of the United States as "the steamboat of moral and political being."

While he would vote against the declaration of war against Mexico in May of 1846 and vote for the Wilmot Proviso to outlaw slavery in newly acquired territories, John Quincy was vehement in his support for annexing nonslave Oregon, even to the 54°40' boundary with Russian Alaska. In 1824 he had concluded an agreement with the Russians that established the southern border of Alaska at exactly that point. In 1846 he would throw support behind Polk's agreement with Britain to annex all of Oregon between the Columbia River and the forty-ninth parallel.

To prevent divisive debate over slavery, southern legislators had passed a "gag law" on May 18, 1836, effectively preventing discussion of the issue. As a skilled lawyer, Adams explored ingenious ways to get around the gag law, introducing petitions at the start of each session, asking "the Speaker whether a certain petition was permissible" and then reading from it. Using his superb gifts as a parliamentary debater, John Quincy worked tirelessly to overturn the rule, and eventually succeeded on December 3, 1844. More than once he presented petitions to abolish slavery in the House, only to be defeated. He and other opponents of slavery, Joel Silbey tells us, "began to pick up allies in unexpected places, from among the disaffected 54°40' men, as well as from other angry dissidents determined to challenge what they deemed to be unacceptable." In 1841 he argued before the Supreme Court that the passengers on the *Amistad* should be free and was successful. In April of 1842 he delivered a speech in the House that foreshadowed Lincoln's Emancipation Proclamation of twenty years later.

While John Quincy had served in the executive mansion, the first commercial train service had begun in the United States, while he served in Congress, the sleeping car was introduced in 1836 on the line between Philadelphia and Harrisburg, Pennsylvania. While he was a congressman the first telegraph was strung between Baltimore and Washington, D.C., and the news of James K. Polk's nomination was tapped to waiting legislators. In 1838 the steamship *George Washington* had crossed the Atlantic to New York in fifteen days. All over the United States steamboats were plying the rivers, stimulating travel, growth, commerce. On November 9, 1843,

John Quincy realized a long-cherished dream when he laid the cornerstone in Cincinnati of the first astronomical observatory in the United States.

While the continued improvements in communication and travel strengthened the connections between the East and the West, there was no comparable growth in the ties between the North and the South. The bitter issue of slavery drove the sections divided by latitude further and further apart. "I want the country for our western pioneers," John Quincy said in the House of Representatives. But he, like many Whigs, favored a more diverse economy where trade and manufacturing and finance were as important as agriculture.

On November 19, 1846, John Quincy suffered a paralytic stroke in Boston, but he recovered enough to return to his duties in Washington. He was sitting in the House of Representatives writing on February 21, 1848, when he was hit by another stroke. He died two days later in a room of the Capitol Building. His last vote in the House had been a resounding no to a proposal to thank the generals who had conquered Mexico. In 1842 John Quincy had energetically defended his friend Winfield Scott against those who opposed his elevation to the rank of general in chief of the army. But in 1848 he was in no mood to honor those who had illegally (in his mind) invaded and humbled Mexico.

With the death of John Quincy Adams, the last living connection to the world of the Founding Fathers was gone. The Mexican War had been won and the expansion to the West was complete. The Pacific coast from San Diego to the forty-ninth parallel was now part of the United States, fulfilling Jefferson's dream of a continental nation. But the other challenge, which the Sage of Monticello had not been able solve, even in his most ambitious dreams, still hung ominously over the expanded nation. The division over slavery was wider and more bitter than ever. The United States had avoided confronting that division for decades, with the Missouri Compromise of 1820 and by turning its attention and energy to the West. Now there was nowhere farther west to expand, but there would be one final distraction from the accelerating forces on their way to inevitable collision.

In *Notes on the State of Virginia* Jefferson had written that he knew of only one instance when gold was found in the region, "interspersed in small specks through a lump of ore." Even he could not have foreseen how golden the West would prove to be, first in North Carolina and Georgia and then California. On January 24, 1848, as Nicholas Trist was waiting for the Mexican government to agree to the Treaty of Guadalupe Hidalgo, James Marshall, foreman of a crew constructing a sawmill for John Sutter on the Rio de los Americanos, the American River, at the site of future Sacramento, while inspecting a millrace, "noticed some distinctive particles amidst the watery sand. He carried them in his hat to the breakfasting workers and said, 'Boys, I believe I have found a gold mine!'"

The great gold rush occurred in 1849 as word slowly spread along the East Coast and to Britain, Europe, and around the world. More than half of those who arrived to search for gold took the overland route, turning the Oregon Trail to South Pass, and other trails, into beaten highways lined with abandoned equipment, animal bones and graves often marked by chair backs or boards from wagon beds. The routes explored by Jedediah Smith, Kit Carson, Thomas "Broken Hand" Fitzpatrick and others were now as familiar to the nation as the Boston Pike. So much gold was added to the U.S. Treasury that Jackson's opposition to paper money seemed justified.

But the intoxication and fever over gold were only a diversion. When California was quickly admitted as a state in 1850, partly to tax the new wealth there, it was admitted as a free state. For angry southerners and resolute abolitionists, the greater battle had only begun.

ACKNOWLEDGMENTS

———

$\mathscr{I}$ AM grateful to many individuals and institutions for their help in bringing this study to completion. First, I want to thank Michael Kammen and Walter LaFeber for their expert advice and priceless encouragement, for reading the text and saving me from dozens of mistakes. Of course, any remaining errors of fact and judgment are entirely my own responsibility.

I am most grateful to my editor of many years and many books, Shannon Ravenel, for her editorial wisdom and passion for good writing. I also owe a considerable debt to my agent, Liz Darhansoff, for encouraging this project from the beginning, and to Peter Workman and Elisabeth Scharlatt of Algonquin Books of Chapel Hill for giving me this opportunity to learn about and explore the westward expansion through a series of biographies. The staff at Algonquin Books has been unstinting in their efforts to make sure this book reaches the public, especially managing editor Brunson Hoole, art director Anne Winslow, Ina Stern, Michael Taeckens, and Craig Popelars. Once again, Jude Grant has done an exemplary job of copy editing. I am also grateful to Barbara Williams for her superb work as a designer.

I owe a debt of gratitude to many others for their help along the way, including my son Benjamin Morgan who scanned a number of illustrations, to Ted Arnold and John Niederbuhl of the Cornell Store for finding the books I needed, including a copy of the translation of *The Other Side: or Notes for the History of the War between Mexico and the United States* by Ramón Alcaraz et al. Chan Gordon of the Captain's Bookself in Asheville provided me with a copy of the Mexican original.

A number of librarians gave essential help in locating books and documents. The Olin Library staff at Cornell University, at the reference desk, interlibrary loan office, and photocopying department, gave valuable aid when I needed it most. Librarian Janet McCue directed me to a work by Horace Kephart I would not have found otherwise. The University of Virginia Library gave me access to an unpublished dissertation that proved a goldmine of relevant scholarship. The Southern Historical Collection at the University of North Carolina at Chapel Hill provided crucial letters in the Trist Family Papers.

I want to thank Sue Walker and Pat Covey of the University of South Alabama for making it possible to visit several historical sites in the region and also Ron Walker for driving me to the site of the Fort Mims massacre. The staff at Horseshoe Bend National Military Park offered generous hospitality and advice, as did the staff at the Hermitage; Carol Roberts at the Tennessee State Library and Archives in Nashville; Thomas Price at the James K. Polk Memorial Association, Columbia, Tennessee; the Adams National Historical Park, Quincy, Massachusetts; Karen D. Stevens of the Independence National Historical Park, Philadelphia; Kathleen Mylen-Coulombe of the Yale University Art Gallery; Nicole Contaxis of the New-York Historical Society; and Professor Timothy D. Johnson of Lipscomb University. I am grateful to the staffs at the David Crockett Birthplace State Park, Limestone, Tennessee; and the David Crockett Cabin & Museum, Lawrenceburg, Tennessee. The Department of the Army graciously provided several important illustrations.

Sincere thanks to Mary Lynn Bell of the Sam Houston Schoolhouse Memorial Site, Maryville, Tennessee; and to the staff of the James K. Polk Birthplace, Pineville, North Carolina. In Colorado the staff at Bent's Old Fort shared their considerable knowledge of the fur trade and Kit Carson's years there. I want to thank the staff at the Kit Carson Home & Museum in Taos, New Mexico; the staff of the Alamo Museum in San Antonio; and the San Jacinto Museum of History, La Porte, Texas. The staff at the Thomas Jefferson Memorial Foundation, Inc., in Charlottesville made available a rare portrait of Nicholas Trist. I am grateful to Dr. Joe Besecker of The Johnny Appleseed Society Educational Center and Museum at Urbana University in Urbana, Ohio, for sharing his expertise on the life and legend of John Chapman.

The support of a number of friends aided in the research and writing of this book. They are too numerous to name, but I would like to acknowledge in particular Jonathan Greene, Dobree Adams, Loyal Jones,

George Brosi, Richard Taylor, and Neal O. Hammon in Kentucky; Jessee Graves and Jeff Daniel Marion in Tennessee; John Lang, Robert Denham, and Martha Eads in Virginia; Robert West in Mississippi; Jeff Biggers in Illinois; and Michael Mcfee, Joseph Flora, Fred Chappell, Ron Rash, Cecelia Conway, Susan Weinberg, Sandy Ballard, Jeanne Dubino, Margaret Bauer, Rebecca Godwin, Michael Chitwood, and Tom Rash in North Carolina. Paul Sawyer, Laura Brown, Molly Hite, Ellis Hanson, Roger Gilbert, Ken McClane, Winthrop P. Wetherbee, and Helena Maria Viramontes gave me generous support at Cornell University.

Finally, I owe a great debt to my wife, Nancy, for her advice, for tolerating my long absences for research, and for her loving support of this project.

— NOTES —

EPIGRAPHS

vii   *"There is more of the material"*   Timothy Flint. *Recollections of the Last Ten Years* (1826, repr. New York: Da Capo Press, 1968), 240–42.

vii   *"The proud Anglo-Saxon race"*   Cecil Robinson, ed., *The View from Chapultepec: Mexican Writers on the Mexican American War* (Tucson: University of Arizona Press, 1989), xliv.

vii   *"There is properly no history"*   Ralph Waldo Emerson, *Essays and Lectures,* ed. Joel Porte (New York: Library of America, 1980), 240.

PROLOGUE—*The Empire for Liberty*

xvii   *"I can jump higher"*   James Kirke Paulding, *The Lion of the West,* (Stanford, CA: Stanford University Press, 1954), 27.

xviii   *"the Empire for Liberty"*   *Writings of Thomas Jefferson,* vol. 12, ed. Andrew A. Lipscomb (Washington, DC: Thomas Jefferson Memorial Association, 1903), 277.

xviii   *"There is properly no history"*   Ralph Waldo Emerson, *Essays and Lectures,* ed. Joel Porte (New York: Library of America, 1980), 240.

xviii   *"The real war will never"*   Walt Whitman, *Whitman: Poetry and Prose,* ed. Justin Kaplan (New York: Library of America, 1982), 778.

xviii   *"that many-threaded drama"*   Whitman, 779.

xviii   *"the untold and unwritten history"*   Ibid.

xix   *"the greatest folk movement"*   John Buchanan, "West in Their Eyes" (unpublished paper delivered at Burnsville, North Carolina, September 13, 2008), 1. In author's possession.

xix   *"The North Americans kept up this"*   Cecil Robinson, ed., *The View from Chapultepec: Mexican Writers on the Mexican American War* (Tucson: University of Arizona Press, 1989), 200–1.

xix   *the American Multiplication Table*   Walter LaFeber, *The American Age* (New York: W. W. Norton, 1994), 12.

xix   *Birthrates in North America*   Ibid., 14.

xx   *but "in the bedchamber"*   Ibid., 71.

xx   *"What is history"*   Emerson, 240.

xx   *"history by synecdoche"*   Wallace Stegner, *The Uneasy Chair: A Biography of Bernard DeVoto* (Lincoln: University of Nebraska Press, 2001), 72.

xx   *"We've been plowing"*   Nicholas Thompson, *The Hawk and the Dove* (New York: Henry Holt, 2009), 161–62.

xx   *"The actions of so-called makers"*   *Encyclopaedia Britannica*, 200th anniversary ed., vol. 5 (Chicago: Encyclopaedia Britannica, 1968), 64.

xxi   *"the force that decides the fate"*   Leo Tolstoy, *War and Peace* (New York: Milestone Editions, n.d.), 945.

xxi   *"look into the movements"*   Ibid., 984.

xxi   *"The forest does not change"*   Boris Pasternak, *Doctor Zhivago*, trans. Max Hayward and Manya Harari (New York: Pantheon, 1958), 453.

xxi   *"No single man makes history"*   Ibid., 454.

xxi   *"Every revolution was first"*   Emerson, 238.

xxi   *"A dynamic law requires"*   Henry Adams, *The Education of Henry Adams* (Charlottesville: University of Virginia Press, 2007), 375.

xxiii   *"a certain moralistic and legalistic"*   George F. Kennan, *American Diplomacy* (Chicago: University of Chicago Press, 1984), 169.

xxiii   *"a curious but deeply-rooted"*   Ibid., 158.

xxiii   *ourselves as the innocent party*   Reinhold Niebuhr, *The Irony of American History* (New York: Charles Scribner's Sons, 1952), 19, 133.

xxiii   *"a plea for . . . a greater humility"*   Kennan, 178.

xxiii   *a preoccupation with the future*   Daniel Walker Howe, *What Hath God Wrought* (New York: Oxford University Press, 2007), 853.

CHAPTER ONE—*Thomas Jefferson: Seeing the Elephant*

2   *"had a passion for science"*   Edward L. Bond, *Spreading the Gospel in Colonial Virginia* (New York: Lexington Books, 2004), 131.

2   *"to possess & enjoy every Thing"*   Ibid., 140.

2   *"to communicate Part of his own"*   Ibid., 142.

2   *"That no Religion ever appeared"*   Ibid., 155.

2   *Maury had a collection of fossils*   Lee Alan Dugatkin, *Mr. Jefferson and the Giant Moose* (Chicago: University of Chicago Press, 2009), 53.

2   *"master of [the] Ohio"*   Bernard DeVoto, *The Course of Empire* (Boston: Houghton Mifflin Company, 1952), 412.

3   *"instilled in his son a passion"*   Dugatkin, 53.

3   *He read John Ogilvy's*   Kevin Hayes, Jr., *The Road to Monticello* (New York: Oxford University Press 2008), 26.

3 *"walks in which Small"*   Dugatkin, 54.

4 *"a compulsion to collect"*   Ibid., 54.

4 *"canine appetite"*   Ibid., 63.

4 *But young Jefferson was not*   Hayes, 12.

4 *"It is impossible for"*   Thomas Jefferson, *Notes on the State of Virginia,* in *The Portable Thomas Jefferson,* ed. Merrill D. Peterson (New York: Penguin, 1977), 54.

5 *As a student at the College*   Hayes, 50.

5 *He studied calculus*   Ibid., 53, 10.

5 *He became fascinated by*   Ibid., 56.

5 *It was while Jefferson was studying*   Ibid., 82.

5 *He read Pufendorf's*   Ibid., 84.

5 *All his life he would be*   Ibid., 89.

5 *One of his first tutors*   Ibid., 20.

5 *After a fire destroyed*   Ibid., 3.

6 *"through his involvement with Peale's"*   Peter S. Onuf, Douglas Seefeldt, and Jeffrey Hantman, eds. *Across the Continent: Jefferson, Lewis and Clark, and the Making of America* (Charlottesville: University of Virginia Press, 2005), 106.

6 *"seven elephants"*   Lyman Copeland Draper, *The Life of Daniel Boone,* ed. Ted Franklin Belue (Mechanicsburg, PA: Stackpole Books, 1998), 248, n. 17.

6 *"Having an opportunity"*   Thomas Jefferson, *The Papers of Thomas Jefferson,* vol. 6, *21 May 1781 to 1 March 1784,* ed. Julian P. Boyd (Princeton, NJ: Princeton University Press, 1952), 139.

6 *"I Received your favor"*   Ibid., 6: 159.

7 *"It represents the South sea"*   Ibid., 6: 169.

7 *"The Spanish concealed"*   Onuf, Seefeldt, and Hantman, 18.

7 *"Permit me to present"*   Ibid., 6: 201.

7 *"I should be unfaithful"*   Ibid., 6: 204.

8 *"You were so kind"*   Ibid., 6: 219.

8 *"I received here about"*   Ibid., 6: 371.

9 *"I find they have subscribed"*   Ibid.

9 *"our rapid multiplication will expand itself"*   Walter LaFeber, *The New American Age* (New York: W. W. Norton, 1994), 53.

9 *"Jefferson regarded Spanish ownership"*   Joseph J. Ellis, *American Sphinx* (New York: Alfred A. Knopf, 1996), 205.

9 *"the various pieces of the empire"*   Gordon S. Wood, *Empire of Liberty* (New York: Oxford University Press, 2009), 366.

9   *"till we have planted such"*   Ellis, 206–7.

10   *"The territory would spread to the Pacific"*   Onuf, Seefeldt, and Hantman, 149.

10   *"the classical style"*   Wood, 558.

10   *In addition, Jefferson worked*   Hayes, 465.

10   *No Virginia planter before*   Dumas Malone, *Jefferson the Virginian* (Boston: Little, Brown, 1948), 144.

11   *On the slopes of Monticello*   Ibid., 151, quoting *Garden Book*, p.15, May 15, 1769.

11   *He valued simplicity*   Ibid., 148.

11   *"the discovery and imitation of Nature"*   Wood, 551.

11   *"His eye, like his mind"*   Malone, 144.

11   *"We are never tired"*   Ralph Waldo Emerson, *Emerson's Prose and Poetry*, ed. Joel Porte and Saundra Morris (New York: W. W. Norton, 2001), 31.

11   *"had his head in the clouds"*   Hugh Howard, *Thomas Jefferson Architect* (New York: Rizzoli, 2003), 25.

12   *It was Madison, for example*   LaFeber, 35.

12   *"Madison knew his friend"*   Wood, 150.

12   *"The mutual influence"*   Ibid., 147.

12   *"delighted in the notion"*   Howard, 19.

12   *From the height of Monticello*   Malone, xvii.

12   *"Mr. Jefferson [was] always singing"*   Hayes, 606.

13   *never a "great dog fancier"*   Ibid., 384.

13   *"older and wiser people"*   Ibid., 609.

14   *"The opinion advanced by"*   Jefferson, *Portable*, 78.

14   *"(1) the skeleton of the mammoth"*   Ibid., 75.

15   *"The truth is, that a Pygmy"*   Ibid., 78.

15   *Buffon, who never did field work*   Dugatkin, 18.

15   *"covered by an immense swamp"*   Ibid., 32.

15   *"It is by the assistance of"*   Jefferson, *Portable*, 79.

15   *And he adds that no naturalist*   Ibid., 85.

16   *In fact, when the English*   Hayes, 238.

17   *"In some future state of"*   Jefferson, *Portable*, 33.

17   *"From the mouth of this river"*   Ibid., 35.

17   *"remarkably cold, muddy"*   Ibid., 36.

17   *"the most beautiful river"*   Ibid., 37.

18   *"vessels may pass through"*   Ibid., 45.

18 *Before Jefferson's* Notes *was printed* Onuf, Seefeldt, and Hantman, 49.

18 *"If the United States could not control"* Ibid., 52–53.

18 *"The veins are at sometimes most flattering"* Jefferson, *Portable*, 56.

18 *"syphon fountains"* Ibid., 67.

19 *"The savage is feeble"* Ibid., 93.

19 *"the most precious spark"* Ibid., 93–94.

19 *"These I believe to be"* Ibid., 94.

20 *Indians "are known under these"* Ibid., 98.

20 *And traders who had married* Ibid., 98.

20 *Jefferson also notes that* Ibid., 95–96.

20 *"[H]e meets death with more"* Ibid., 96.

20 *"The women are submitted to"* Ibid., 96.

21 *"not in a difference of nature"* Ibid., 97.

21 *"Negroes have notoriously less"* Ibid., 98.

21 *"we shall probably find that they"* Ibid., 98–99.

22 *" 'I am convinced,' Jefferson wrote"* Ellis, 101; Jefferson, *Papers*, 11, 48–50, 92–93.

22 *"Jefferson's sentimentality"* Onuf, Seefeldt, and Hantman, 126.

22 *"Jefferson was not so much explaining"* Ibid., 72.

22 *"they will in time either incorporate"* Ellis, 201.

22 *In Jefferson's compartmentalized mind* Ibid., 202.

23 *"To promote this disposition"* Robert M. Owens, *Mr. Jefferson's Hammer* (Norman: University of Oklahoma Press, 2007), 76.

23 *"Deep rooted prejudices entertained"* Jefferson, *Portable*, 186.

23 *"it appears to me, that"* Ibid., 188.

23 *"They secrete less by the kidnies"* Ibid., 187.

23 *"They are more ardent after"* Ibid., 187.

24 *"the most important apostle for liberty"* Wood, 278.

24 *"the abolition of domestic slavery"* Ibid., 514, 518.

24 *Jefferson had no doubt* Ibid., 515.

24 *"tried to get slavery banned"* Richard Hofstadter, *The American Political Tradition and the Men Who Made It* (New York: Alfred A. Knopf, 1951), 21.

24 *"An accommodation was somehow made"* Bernard Bailyn, *The Peopling of British North America* (New York: Alfred A. Knopf, 1986), 118.

24 *It has been pointed out* Wood, 527.

24 *"Throughout his political career"* Dugatkin, 77–78.

24 *Jefferson speculated that if slavery* Daniel Walker Howe, *What Hath God Wrought* (New York: Oxford University Press, 2007), 149.

25 *"I regret that I am now"* Ibid., 157.

25 *"it was sixteen centuries after"* Jefferson, *Portable,* 101.

25 *And while America may not* Ibid., 102.

25 *"The sun of her glory is fast"* Ibid., 103.

25 *"stands at the crossroads of"* Hayes, 243.

25 *"a transitional work connecting"* Ibid., 244.

26 *"one of the classics of early"* Ibid., 246.

26 *reached France with its hair falling out* Dugatkin, 99.

26 *promised to revise Chapter 14* Ibid., 29, 100.

26 *Frederick the Great encouraged* Ibid., 36, 60.

26 *"American impotence"* Ibid., 107–8.

26 *"great unerring Nature"* Ibid., xii.

26 *The drain of population* Ibid., x.

26 *Humbolt expressed enthusiasm* Ibid., 114.

26 *the backlash against Buffon* Ibid., 117.

27 *"The eyes of the man are set"* Ibid., 127.

27 *"Can we never extract this"* Ralph Waldo Emerson, *Essays and Lectures,* ed. Joel Porte (New York: Library of America, 1980), 1022.

27 *"He is a person of ingenuity"* DeVoto, 416.

28 *"how he could determine latitude"* Hayes, 299–300.

28 *Jefferson gave Ledyard some* Ibid., 299.

29 *Altogether Jefferson raised $1,569* Thomas Jefferson, *The Papers of Thomas Jefferson,* vol. 25, *1 January 1793 to 10 May 1793,* ed. John Catanzariti (Princeton, NJ: Princeton University Press, 1992), 78.

29 *"on his return to communicate"* Ibid., 25: 81.

29 *"When, pursuing these streams"* Ibid., 25: 624–25.

30 *"Consider this not merely"* Ibid., 25: 626.

30 *began "fitting out French privateers"* LaFeber, 47.

30 *Genet also brought Benjamin Logan* Wood, 186.

31 *"'I told him,' Jefferson wrote"* DeVoto, 346.

31 *But Genet's plans* Ibid.

32 *"the bastard brat"* LaFeber, 51.

32 *Hamilton, in secret communication* Ibid., 46.

33 *"his delivery was so subdued"* Ellis, 169.

33 *"textual presidency"* Ibid., 193.

34 *"The day that France"* DeVoto, 392.

34 *Jefferson planned, if necessary* LaFeber, 55–56.

34 *With Mackenzie's exploration* Wood, 377, Onuf, Seefeldt, and Hantman, 53–54.

36 *"demographic imperialism"* Wood, 357.

36 *"Your situation as Secretary,"* Jefferson, *Portable*, 308.

36 *"embraces years of study and wonder"* Onuf, Seefeldt, and Hantman, 100–1.

36 *"Instruments for ascertaining by"* Jefferson, *Portable*, 308.

37 *"will entitle you to"* Ibid., 309.

37 *"Jefferson's design for the expedition"* Onuf, Seefeldt, and Hantman, 10.

37 *"The object of your mission"* Jefferson, *Portable,* 309.

38 *"Beginning at the mouth of"* Ibid., 309.

38 *"Your observations are to be"* Ibid., 310.

39 *"renders a knoledge of those people"* Ibid.

39 *"civilize & instruct them."* Ibid., 311.

40 *"treat them in the most friendly"* Ibid., 312.

40 *"you must decline it's farther* Ibid., 313.

40 *"the soil & face of the country"* Ibid., 311.

41 *"anything certain"* Ibid., 312.

42 *Since he would be without money* Ibid., 314.

42 *"as may serve to supply, correct"* Ibid.

42 *"Repair yourself with your papers"* Ibid.

42 *"to name the person among"* Ibid., 315.

43 *We know that the Declaration* Ibid., 1–21.

43 *"Securing a huge swatch"* Ellis, 212.

44 *"Those of the western confederacy"* Ibid., 213; Thomas Jefferson, *The Papers of Thomas Jefferson*, vol. 8, *25 February 1785 to 31 October 1785*, ed. Julian P. Boyd (Princeton, NJ: Princeton University Press, 1953), 295.

CHAPTER 2—*Andrew Jackson: Old Hickory at the Bend*

46 *identified themselves by clan name* Robbie Ethridge, *Creek Country: The Creek Indians in Their World* (Chapel Hill: University of North Carolina Press, 2003), 93.

46 *War leaders were drawn* Ibid.

46 *Their spirited ball games* *Encyclopaedia Britannica,* 200th anniversary ed., vol. 6, (Chicago: Encylcopaedia Britannica, 1968), 720.

47   *A delicacy they served to visitors*   Ethridge, 62.

47   *"coalescent societies"*   Ethridge, 23.

47   *"Creeks lived and dressed much like"*   Ibid., 1.

47   *Their houses were made*   Bernard Bailyn, *The Peopling of British North America* (New York: Alfred A. Knopf, 1986,) 107.

47   *"Purification by emetics was"*   Encyclopaedia Britannica 6: 720.

47   acee, *the "black drink"*   Ethridge, 105.

47   possau, *made from button snakeroot*   Benjamin Hawkins, *The Collected Works of Benjamin Hawkins, 1796–1810,* ed. Howard Thomas Foster (Tuscaloosa: University of Alabama Press, 2003), 79s.

47   *"Upper Creeks lived on"*   Ethridge, 31.

47   *they sold both Indian and black*   Ibid., 23–24.

47   *were called "mustees"*   Bailyn, 110.

48   *"principal agent for Indian affairs"*   Hawkins, 6s.

48   isti atcagagi, *"beloved man"*   Ethridge, 18.

48   *"a solemn symphony of the steady"*   Ibid., 44.

48   *rituals of gift giving*   Ibid., 198.

48   *At best, the boundary lines*   Ibid., 215, 222.

48   *"Master of Breath"*   Ibid., 239.

48   *McGillivray would become known*   John Buchanan, *Jackson's Way* (New York: John Wiley and Sons, 2001), 79.

49   *Abigail Adams would later write*   Ibid., 103.

49   *The treaty ceremony was accompanied*   Gordon S. Wood, *Empire of Liberty* (New York: Oxford University Press, 2009), 128.

50   *There is evidence that some*   Daniel Walker Howe, *What Hath God Wrought* (New York: Oxford University Press, 2007), 417.

50   *"Sell a country! Why not"*   Walter LaFeber, *The American Age* (New York: W. W. Norton, 1994), 61.

51   *In the euphoria, they felt*   James W. Holland, *Victory at the Horseshoe* (Fort Washington, PA: Eastern National and University of Alabama Press, 2007), 7.

52   *"Let the white race perish"*   Robert V. Remini, *Andrew Jackson,* 3 vols. (Baltimore: Johns Hopkins University Press, 1998), 1:188.

52   *"Your blood is white"*   Ibid.

52   *The British had never evacuated*   Wood, 112.

52   *"To mock the Americans' hunger"*   Ibid., 129.

53   *Red Sticks killed nine*   Holland, 7

53   *On August 30, 1813, there were*   Remini, 1:189.

53 *Since no hostile Indians had*   Holland, 9.

54 *Instead of directing a patrol*   H. W. Brands, *Andrew Jackson* (New York: Anchor Books, 2006), 194.

54 *According to some reports*   Buchanan, 222.

54 *"With few exceptions they were naked"*   Brands, 194.

55 *The Red Sticks had threatened to kill*   Buchanan, 220.

55 *Reports of the number present*   Brands, 195.

55 *"Indians, negroes, white men, women"*   Ibid.

56 *"Even by frontier standards"*   Howe, 329.

58 *Jackson's mother had thought*   Brands, 17.

58 *At an early age Jackson*   Ibid., 18

58 *"The memory of my mother"*   Ibid., 32.

59 *"three hundred or four hundred pounds"*   Ibid., 33.

59 *"In the 1780s the law"*   Ibid., 35.

60 *Jackson was sued for disorderly*   Ibid., 39.

60 *Lister was unable to collect*   Ibid., 39–40.

60 *"He always dressed neat"*   Ibid., 40–41.

60 *Benjamin Franklin had said*   Ibid., 49.

60 *"could . . . travel thousands of miles"*   Buchanan, 65.

61 *Luckily the savvy Avery*   Brands, 54.

61 *"beautifully molded form, lustrous"*   Ibid., 57.

61 *When Jackson learned of Robards's*   Buchanan, 110.

62 *Mrs. Donelson accompanied*   Brands, 63.

62 *The divorce was not actually granted*   Buchanan, 117–18.

62 *"The union, however irregularly"*   Brands, 64–65.

62 *With little American money*   Ibid., 67.

63 *When Blount was expelled*   Ibid., 82.

63 *"He is one of the most"*   Ibid., 97.

63 *"I recall with pleasure"*   Buchanan, 162.

64 *Years later Jefferson would*   Brands, 97.

64 *more effective as an executive*   Ibid.

64 *He had become a Royal Arch Mason*   Howe, 241.

64 *"Surrender, you infernal villain"*   Brands, 101.

64 *He was her main source*   Buchanan, 160.

65 *Jackson also had special admiration*   Brands, 94.

66 *"Agent 13 of the Spanish government"*   Wood, 114.

66 *the struggle for popular rights*   Brands, x.

67   *He went out of his way*   Ibid., 150.

67   *"There was more of the woman"*   Jon Meacham, *American Lion: Andrew Jackson in the White House* (New York: Random House, 2008), xxii.

68   *"Americans were more dependent on"*   LaFeber, 59.

68   *the British sold Americans*   Ibid., 47.

68   *"this authorized system of kidnapping"*   Bernard Bailyn et al., *The Great Republic: A History of the American People* (Boston: Little, Brown, 1977), 379.

68   *"the British look upon us"*   Wood, 668.

69   *"War hawks wore black armbands"*   LaFeber, 61.

69   *"The British . . . had three fighting ships"*   Ibid., 63.

69   *"We have met the enemy"*   Bailyn et al., 384.

69   *they "gave the loudest yells"*   Wood, 686.

69   *Flames from the conflagration*   Ibid., 691.

70   *"the best American naval officer"*   Ibid., 690.

70   *"Popular mythology soon converted"*   *Encyclopaedia Britannica*, 200th anniversary ed., vol. 23 (Chicago: Encyclopaedia Britannica, 1968), 224.

70   *maintaining the status quo*   Wood, 695.

70   *"Notwithstand[ing] a thousand"*   Ibid., 699.

71   *A new governor of Tennessee*   Buchanan, 199.

71   *"In the day of danger"*   Brands, 170.

71   *Before the War of 1812*   Buchanan, 196.

71   *to form an even closer alliance*   Wood, 676.

72   *"The disaster of the northwestern"*   Brands, 179.

72   *"It is my duty"*   Buchanan, 203.

73   *"in a savage, unequal, unfair"*   Brands, 189.

73   *Among the witnesses*   Ibid., 190.

73   *Some in Nashville were inclined*   Ibid., 192.

73   *"Old Hickory's own image"*   Howe, 437.

74   *"martial manhood"*   Ibid., 707.

74   *"Brave Tennesseeans!" he proclaimed*   Brands, 196.

74   *"My health is good"*   Ibid.

74   *"wear white plumes in their hair"*   Ibid.

74   *Marching south in three columns*   Buchanan, 239.

75   *In at least one case the raiders*   Brands, 197.

75   *"He has executed this order"*   Ibid., 198.

75   *Jackson's plan was to hew*   Buchanan, 193.

76 *"I am determined to push forward"* Remini, 1:192.

76 *When Red Eagle surrounded* Ibid., 1:196.

76 *Jackson organized his forces* Ibid.

77 *Jackson lost fifteen dead* Ibid., 1:197.

77 *"I will most cheerfully divide"* Ibid.

77 *A great many were barefoot* Brands, 205.

77 *Colonel William Martin, commander* Ibid., 206.

77 *When he could, Crockett* Ibid., 211.

78 *No more troops could be provided* Remini, 1:203.

79 *"Jackson seemed to gain"* Ibid.

79 *"I have long since determined"* Ibid., 1:204.

80 *"In the midst of a shower"* Ibid., 1:208.

80 *Though he received a frantic* Ibid., 1:209–210.

81 *"essential to the preservation"* Ibid., 1:212.

83 *"It is impossible to conceive"* Ibid., 1:214.

83 *A bullet hit his head* Ibid., 1:215.

84 *Some warriors dashed toward* Buchanan, 289.

85 *"Heaven designed to chastize"* Holland, 26.

85 *Their figures suggest that* Ibid., 27.

85 *The Thirty-ninth Infantry Regiment* Ibid.

86 *Spies reported that remaining* Ibid., 29.

86 *As Jackson's force approached* Ibid.

86 *"I am in your power"* Remini, 1:218.

86 *"I have not surrendered myself"* Ibid.

87 *"When the War of 1812 ended"* Ibid., 1:219.

87 *It is said Weatherford trained* Buchanan, 295.

87 *"Your general is pleased with you"* Remini, 1:221.

88 *"We have conquered"* Ibid.

88 *By his reckoning, the Creek* Ibid., 1:226.

88 *It was at this point* Ibid., 1:227.

89 *"Until this is done"* Ibid., 1:229.

89 *"What Jackson had done"* Ibid., 1:231.

CHAPTER 3 — *John Chapman: Apples and Angels*

90 *"The greatest service"* *Times Literary Supplement,* May 30, 2008, 9; Richard Hofstadter, *The American Political Tradition and the Men Who Made It* (New York: Alfred A. Knopf, 1951), 23.

90 *The Romans recognized* *Encyclopaedia Britannica,* 200th anniversary ed., vol. 2 (Chicago: Encyclopaedia Britannica, 1968), 138.

90 *"the Apples of Knowledge"* Ralph Waldo Emerson, *Emerson: Collected Essays and Poems,* ed. Joel Porte (New York: Library of America, 1983), 255.

93 *John Chapman was born in Leominster* Robert Price, *Johnny Appleseed: Man & Myth* (Urbana, OH: Urbana University Press, 2001), 10.

93 *"ten good bearing fruit trees"* Ibid.

93 *Nathaniel is believed to have fought* Ibid., 12.

93 *"Remember, I beseech you, that"* Ibid., 14.

94 *The name came from the tall grass* Ibid., 23.

95 *Chapman's name appears* Ibid., 26–27.

95 *"He was a singular character"* Ibid., 30.

95 *"He seemed to be as much"* Ibid.

95 *"He could chop as much wood"* Ibid., 31.

95 *He is reported to have lived* Ibid., 32.

96 *"The bees work without wages"* Ibid., 44.

96 *in the region called the Seven Ranges* Ibid., 49.

96 *"Franklin. February 4, 1804, for value"* Ibid., 36.

97 *"wash out the pomace at cider mills"* Ibid., 36–37.

97 *The French had long ago* Ibid., 38.

98 *"When orchards had been established"* Ibid., 40.

98 *"pasteboard with an immense peak"* W. D. Haley, "Johnny Appleseed– A Pioneer Hero," *Harpers Monthly Magazine,* vol. 43 (November 1871): 832.

98 *And he was a gifted storyteller* Ibid.

99 *Over the years since the 1794* Price, 83.

99 *One of his largest nurseries* Ibid., 84.

100 *"Flee for your lives—the Canadians"* Ibid., 88.

100 *they moved on to Fredericktown* Ibid., 89.

100 *an elderly Wyandotte Indian* Ibid., 91–92.

100 *According to an early historian* A. Bannon Norton, *A History of Knox County, Ohio, from 1779 to 1862 Inclusive* (Columbus, OH: 1862), 50.

100 *"The British and Indians are coming"* Price, 94.

100 *"The spirit of the Lord is upon"* Ibid.

101 *But those accounts are later additions* Ibid., 101.

102 *it was Maria Barclay's husband* Robert Price, *Epilog* (Urbana, OH: Urbana University Press, 2006), 36.

102 *At the core of Swedenborg's teaching* F. L. Cross and E. A. Livingstone, *The Oxford Dictionary of the Christian Church* (Oxford, England: Oxford University Press, 1997), 1563.

103 *He was the colporteur of the New* Price, *Johnny Appleseed,* 113.

103 *"he changed the conversation"* Ibid.

103 *"I could not enjoy myself better"* Ibid., 115–16.

103 *When he was younger* Ibid., 116–17.

103 *"There is in the western country"* Ibid., 120.

104 *It was William Schlatter* Ibid., 125.

104 *"I have sent some books"* Ibid.

104 *"finding him to be intelligent"* Ibid., 126.

105 *"The land that he offers"* Ibid., 129.

106 *"One very extraordinary missionary"* Ibid., 132–33.

106 *"It was his custom, when"* Haley, 834.

107 *"His main bump seemed to be"* Price, 133.

107 *He returned the favor by arguing* Ibid., 116.

107 *That work would influence* Gordon S. Wood, *Empire of Liberty* (New Oxford University Press, 2009), 616–17.

107 *The new republic would become* Ibid., 618–19.

108 *Resurrection was merely a continuation* Price, 138–39.

108 *"Here's your primitive Christian"* Haley, 385.

109 *"a coarse coffee-sack, with a hole"* Price, 235.

109 *The body was buried* Ibid., 236.

109 *"It is remarkable how closely"* Henry David Thoreau, *Excursions,* ed. Sophia Thoreau (1863; repr. facsimile ed. New York: Corinth Books, 1962), 266.

109 *"As the apple-tree among the trees"* Thoreau, 267.

109 *"Our Western emigrant is still"* Ibid., 269.

110 *"The flowers of the apple"* Ibid., 271.

110 *"I love better to go through"* Ibid., 277.

110 *"have a kind of bow-arrow tang"* Ibid., 290.

110 *The most "spirited and racy"* Ibid., 292.

110 *"when the pomace-heap was the only"* Ibid., 305.

CHAPTER 4 — *David Crockett: Comedian and Martyr, His Life and Death*

114 *"Performance in blackface"* Daniel Walker Howe, *What Hath God Wrought* (New York: Oxford University Press, 2007), 639.

114 *"Butternuts"* Ibid., 139.

115   *His great-great-great-grandfather*   James Atkins Shackford, *David Crockett: The Man and the Legend* (Chapel Hill: University of North Carolina Press, 1956), 293.

116   *Crockett's aunt Sarah Hawkins*   Ibid.

116   *It has been recorded that*   Constance Rourke, *David Crockett* (New York: Harcourt, Brace, 1934), 5.

116   *His famous son would record*   David Crockett, *A Narrative of the Life of David Crockett of the State of Tennessee,* ed. James A. Shackford and Stanley J. Folmsbee (Knoxville: University of Tennessee Press, 1973), 17.

116   *"Panthers crouched in tall sycamores"*   Rourke, 6.

117   *It is said that David's father*   Ibid., 10.

117   *Worn out and disillusioned*   Shackford, 9.

117   *After reaching Front Royal*   Ibid., 10.

118   *Before they parted, Henry took*   Ibid.

118   *It was time for David*   Ibid., 11.

118   *"to cypher some"*   Crockett, 49.

118   *"whose name is nobody's business"*   Ibid., 50.

119   *"I continued in this down-spirited"*   Ibid., 57.

119   *"Nobody can dance longer"*   Rourke, 24.

119   *"footed it gayly"*   Ibid., 25.

119   *"I thought I was completely made up"*   Crockett, 67.

119   *"I found I was better"*   Ibid., 68.

119   *"It was here that I began"*   Ibid., 69.

120   *"Crockett can outsmart most any coon"*   Rourke, 37.

120   *"to throw his voice . . ."*   Ibid.

120   *"The moon was about the full"*   Crockett, 78.

120   *"We now shot them like dogs"*   Ibid., 88.

120   *"the oil of the Indians"*   Ibid., 90.

120   *"Be always sure you're right"*   Shackford, 26–27.

121   *But Crockett did return*   Ibid., 27.

121   *Indian skulls scattered about*   Crockett, 122.

121   *"Death, that cruel leveller"*   Ibid., 125.

121   *"was a large woman,"*   Shackford, 34.

121   *"Old hook, from now on"*   Ibid., 35.

122   *Thousands of settlers were pouring in*   Howe, 125.

122   *"I know'd this was a whapper"*   Crockett, 132.

122   *Crockett was the right man*   Shackford, 40.

122   *As a hunter and scout*   Ibid., 42.

122 *Because he had helped build* Ibid., 42–43.

123 *"Well, colonel, I suppose we"* Crockett, 143.

123 *"It was wild and strange"* Rourke, 86.

124 *"Bears is witty"* Ibid., 111.

124 *"She's a mighty rough old piece"* Ibid., 115.

124 *"could grin most any varmint"* Ibid., 45–46.

124 *"the great bear hunter of the West"* Ibid., 116.

124 *"I improved my handwriting"* Crockett, 135.

124 *His fame grew and many people* Rourke, 83.

125 *"This matter of west Tennessee lands"* Shackford, 48.

125 *"fit for cultivation"* Ibid., 49.

125 *From the first, Crockett focused* Ibid.

125 *It was one of the issues that* Ibid., 51.

125 *"the gentleman from the cane"* Ibid., 52.

127 *As Jon Meacham points out* Jon Meacham, *American Lion: Andrew Jackson in the White House* (New York: Random House, 1998), 339.

127 *The biographer Mark Derr* Mark Derr, *The Frontiersman: The Real Life and the Many Legends of Davy Crockett* (New York: William Morrow, 1993), 80.

127 *But their first child was born* William Groneman III, *David Crockett: Hero of the Common Man* (New York: Forge, 2005), 62.

128 *"When I got home"* Crockett, 160.

128 *One measure of the respect* Derr, 186.

129 *"Well, Bet, I am beat"* Manley F. Cobia, Jr., *Journey into the Land of Trials: The Story of Davy Crockett's Expedition to the Alamo* (Franklin, TN: Hillsboro Press, 2003), 15.

129 *"Crockett himself could be profligate"* Derr, 87.

129 *"better to keep a good conscience"* Crockett, 145.

129 *David and Elizabeth's four children* Buddy Levy, *American Legend: The Real-life Adventures of David Crockett* (New York: G. P. Putnam's Sons, 2005), 83.

130 *As with many women* Derr, 158.

130 *"She had grown accustomed"* Levy, 177.

130 *"I . . . have not tasted one drop"* Ibid., 155.

130 *There is no real evidence* Derr, 81, 109.

131 *While Crockett's claims of ignorance* Shackford, 45.

132 *The first afternoon they killed three* Ibid., 75.

132 *At the end of the hunt* Ibid.

132   *When the dogs set off*   Ibid., 75–76.

132   *"So I got down, and my dogs"*   Crockett, 190.

133   *When daylight came he hung*   Ibid., 191.

134   *"literally skin'd like a rabbit"*   Ibid., 198.

134   *"Here I met with a friend"*   Ibid., 199.

135   *"Crockett and his men hit"*   Levy, 132.

135   *"As he thought I needed"*   Crockett, 201–2.

136   *"Most authors seek fame"*   Ibid., 3.

136   *"I have endeavored"*   Ibid., 6.

136   *At the beginning of his memoir*   Ibid., 5.

136   *"I can't tell why it is"*   Ibid., 7.

136   *only a fifth son, not*   Ibid., 16.

136   *He describes how his father's*   Ibid., 21.

136   *"My heart was bruised"*   Ibid., 54.

136   *"When I made the report"*   Ibid., 82.

137   *"rough sort of a backwoodsman"*   Ibid., 123.

137   *"It was the doing of the Almighty"*   Ibid., 125–26.

137   *"The thought of having to make"*   Ibid., 143.

137   *Crockett dramatizes at length*   Ibid., 156.

137   *"I want the world"*   Ibid., 172.

137   *"This was considered"*   Ibid., 206–7.

137   *"What is more agreeable to my"*   Ibid., 210.

137   *"You will find me standing up"*   Ibid., 211.

138   *"towar for his health"*   Shackford, 155.

138   *In Philadelphia he spoke*   Ibid., 157.

138   *In Lowell, Massachusetts, Crockett*   Ibid., 159.

139   *He was blamed for being*   Ibid., 164.

139   *"leave the united States, for"*   Ibid., 173–74.

139   *"Since you have chosen"*   Ibid., 212.

140   *"By 1834, a widely used"*   Walter LaFeber, *The American Age* (New York: W. W. Norton, 1994), 72.

140   *"With his open frankness"*   Shackford, 214.

140   *"taken the oath of government"*   Ibid., 216.

140   *most Americans simply ignored*   LaFeber, 104.

141   *"I am rejoiced at my fate"*   Shackford, 216.

141   *"If Houston represented Andrew Jackson"*   Ibid., 221.

142   *"I am induced to believe"*   Ibid., 225.

143 *"Travis, Fannin, Crockett"* Ibid., 226.

144 *Travis was courting a beauty* Randell Jones, *In the Footsteps of David Crockett* (Winston-Salem, NC: John F. Blair, 2006), 226.

144 *Crockett and twelve men* Ibid., 229.

145 *It was said that Crockett killed* Ibid., 229–30.

145 *"The Hon. David Crockett"* Ibid., 230.

145 *Señor Crockett seemed everywhere* Ibid.

145 *Though he set out on the mission* Ibid., 231.

146 *"I am determined to perish"* Ibid., 232–33.

146 *"Crockett and a few of his friends"* Ibid., 235.

146 *"David Crockett (now rendered immortal"* Ibid., 235–36.

146 *Many newspapers across the United States* Ibid., 237.

146 *"His presence at the Alamo"* Ibid., 239.

147 *"he advanced from the Church"* Shackford, 231.

148 *In his own account* Jones, 235.

148 *"The Mexican officers ran"* Ibid., 238.

148 *And in fact the authenticity* Bill Groneman, *Defense of a Legend* (Plano: Republic of Texas Press, 1994), 132.

149 *"His life was one of wholehearted"* Shackford, 238–39.

CHAPTER 5 — *Sam Houston: The President Who Loved to Dance*

152 *He married a wealthy Scots Irish beauty* Marshall De Bruhl, *Sword of San Jacinto* (New York: Random House, 1993), 16.

152 *Elizabeth Houston has been described* Ibid.

152 *She gave birth to six sons* Marquis James, *The Raven* (1929; repr. Austin: University of Texas Press, 2008), 7.

152 *Major Houston disapproved* De Bruhl, 18.

153 *"One sword, $15"* James, 11.

153 *Elizabeth, who had been born to* Ibid., 13.

153 *"gifted with intellectual and moral"* Ibid., 14.

153 *He fell in love with the heroic* De Bruhl, 26.

154 *Sam quit school* C. Edwards Lester, *Sam Houston: Hero and Statesman* (New York: John B. Alden Publisher, 1883), 16.

154 *It was the whites who gave them* De Bruhl, 28.

154 *In his 1791 Travels* Ibid., 29.

154 *"a Franklin amongst his countrymen"* Ibid., 31.

155 *he preferred "measuring deer tracks"* Ibid., 31; Lester, 17.

155 *The boys hunted, trapped, fished* Ibid., 32–33.

156 *For the rest of his life Houston*   Ibid., 34.

156 *He charged eight dollars*   James, 26.

156 *His mother gave him*   De Bruhl, 38.

156 *After the Cherokees crossed*   James, 32.

158 *Elizabeth Houston did not recognize*   De Bruhl, 44.

158 *Initiated April 19, 1817*   Ibid., 55.

158 *Washington in his Masonic apron*   Gordon S. Wood, *Empire of Liberty* (New York: Oxford University Press, 2009), 477.

159 *"the Darkening land, abode of"*   James, 42.

159 *He would always view Calhoun*   De Bruhl, 60–61.

160 *"the largest if not"*   Ibid., 63.

160 *After practicing law for only*   Ibid., 64.

160 *Thomas Jefferson had referred to*   Ibid., 67.

161 *"Jacksonianism was for the ages"*   Ibid., 89.

162 *And it is thought she was still*   Ibid., 96.

162 *Some have suggested the marriage*   Mary Lynn Bell, manager of the Sam Houston Schoolhouse Memorial Site, interview, Maryville, TN, April 10, 2009.

162 *"I wish they would kill him"*   De Bruhl, 98–99.

164 *"She was cold to me"*   Ibid., 101.

164 *the shame of Nebuchadnezzar*   Daniel 4:33.

165 *And then Houston asked to be baptized*   James, 82.

165 *"In reviewing the past, I can only"*   De Bruhl, 103.

165 *They must have discussed*   Ibid.

165 *But an eagle swooped*   Ibid., 104.

165 *"I knew then," he said*   James, 85.

166 *The old chief had adopted*   Ibid., 102.

166 *"Like Jackson he also believed"*   De Bruhl, 114.

166 *In such a state he could*   James, 115.

166 *"Our Federal Union"*   H. W. Brands, *Andrew Jackson* (New York: Anchor Books, 2006), 446.

167 *"Give my compliments to my friends"*   De Bruhl, 116.

167 *(The famous Will Rogers*   James, 151.

167 *When he fell desperately ill*   Ibid., 118.

167 *Perhaps he felt his case*   De Bruhl, 121.

168 *He had, as well, taken part*   James, 157.

168 *Marquis James suggests that*   Ibid., 140.

169 *"unpleasant consequences of popular"*   De Bruhl, 127.

170 *Houston described the dour*   Ibid., 131.

170 *No such right was provided*   Ibid., 132.

171 *"But, sir, so long as that flag"*   Ibid., 132–33.

171 *"Houston, take my laurels!"*   Ibid., 133.

171 *"He had found the Caucasian's"*   James, 147.

171 *described as "the New Estremadura"*   Ibid., 174.

172 *It has been said that as Houston*   Ibid., 186.

172 *He bought enough land for himself*   De Bruhl, 145.

172 *becoming "a Muldoon Catholic"*   James, 203.

172 *And he negotiated with*   De Bruhl, 146.

172 *"has already beaten and repelled"*   James, 190.

173 *at least fifty changes in the presidency*   David A. Clary, *Eagles and Empire: The United States, Mexico, and the Struggle for a Continent* (New York: Bantam, 2009), 24.

173 *"crossed the international boundary"*   Daniel Walker Howe, *What Hath God Wrought* (New York: Oxford University Press, 2007), 658.

173 *By the mid-1830s*   Ibid., 660.

173 *"The disadvantage of her [Mexico's]"*   Ramón Alcaraz et al., *The Other Side: Or, Notes for the History of War between Mexico and the United States,* trans. Albert Ramsey (1850; repr., New York: Burt Franklin, 1970), 2.

173 *"The first settlers of the United"*   Ibid., 4.

173 *"In their choice of expedients"*   Ibid.

173 *There were already more than*   James, 175.

173 *"Mexican leadership, liberal or conservative"*   T. R. Fehrenbach, *Fire and Blood: A History of Mexico* (New York: Da Capo Press, 1995), 376–77.

173 *"The Hispanic contempt was rooted in"*   Ibid., 379.

174 *"The resolving of the question"*   Ibid., 376.

174 *"Mexico—or more precisely"*   Enrique Krauze, *Mexico: Biography of Power: A History of Modern Mexico, 1810–1996,* trans. Hank Heifetz (New York: HarperCollins, 1997), xiv.

174 *Krauze also points out*   Ibid.

174 *The patron saint*   Ibid., 72.

174 *"the Children of Cuauhtemoc"*   Ibid., 25.

174 *"latecomers, invading and conquering"*   Clary, 451.

174 *still a medieval society, without a class*   Ibid., 13.

174 *"a theatrical performance, or a dream"*   Ibid., 19.

174 *"the country of inequality"* Robert W. Merry, *A Country of Vast Designs* (New York: Simon and Schuster, 2009), 180.

175 *"Mexico, despite its pretense"* Ibid., 184.

175 *"The constitution of 1824 deprived"* Cecil Robinson, ed., *The View from Chapultepec: Mexican Writers on the Mexican American War* (Tucson: University of Arizona Press, 1989), 123–24.

175 *"The state of Coahuila fulfilled"* Ibid., 124.

175 *"This law peremptorily forbade"* Ibid., 125.

175 *He was a moderate, hoping* James, 205.

176 *He became friends with James Bowie* Ibid., 191–92.

176 *And like many others he* Ibid., 197.

176 *"Austin . . . knew that the Hispanic mind"* Fehrenbach, 379.

176 *"I am made to revel"* James, 206.

176 *When he attended the theater* Ibid., 184–85.

177 *When a close friend asked him* Ibid., 202.

177 *Mexican political history* Ibid., 197.

177 *"WAR is our only recourse"* De Bruhl, 168.

177 *By some accounts, this is considered* Howe, 661.

177 *The rebels hoped that moderates* Ibid.

177 *"The morning of glory is dawning"* De Bruhl, 168.

177 *Houston sold four thousand acres* James, 209.

178 *President Jackson would indeed* De Bruhl, 198.

178 *In June of 1836 Gaines* Robert V. Remini, *Andrew Jackson*, 3 vols. (Baltimore: Johns Hopkins University Press, 1998), 3:357.

179 *Opposing the dictator Santa Anna* James, 214.

179 *President Henry Smith referred* De Bruhl, 173.

179 *Their hurried taking of San Antonio* James, 218.

179 *"Permit me, through you"* De Bruhl, 173.

180 *The treaty was crucial to the future* Ibid., 180.

181 *"endowed with all the rights"* Ibid., 183.

181 *But the ground was silent* James, 228.

181 *"You will, as soon as practicable"* De Bruhl, 184.

181 *"from injuries that could have been"* Howe, 665.

181 *Instead of submitting to his forces* De Bruhl, 185.

182 *It was he who brought* James, 229.

182 *The casual whittling masked* Ibid., 231.

183 *Houston provided the music* Ibid., 235.

183   *"the slaughter of some four hundred North Americans"*   Fehrenbach, 383.

183   *"Houses were standing open"*   De Bruhl, 192–93.

184   *No doubt the Texans prayed*   James, 237.

185   *Their withdrawal has been described*   De Bruhl, 193.

185   *"For Heaven's sake, do not drop back"*   Ibid.

185   *His silence has been compared to*   James, 239–40.

185   *"a conjunction of good and bad"*   Robinson, xiv.

185   *"He had once been a good"*   Ibid., xv.

186   *"a showman's flair, a gambler's"*   Merry, 181.

186   *"a creole caricature of Bonaparte"*   Krauze, 135.

186   *"the barometer of national upheavals"*   Ibid., 142.

186   *"always playing a role"*   Clary, 39.

186   *The* Yellow Stone *had a distinguished*   De Bruhl, 196–97.

186   *"Sir, The enemy are laughing"*   Ibid., 201.

187   *As Jackson had done*   Ibid., 202.

187   *"Houston saw that his moment"*   Howe, 667.

188   *"It is wisdom growing out of"*   De Bruhl, 203.

188   *"It is vain to look for present"*   Ibid., 204.

188   *They were camped among oak trees*   James, 246.

188   *The ground there has been called*   Ibid., 248.

188   *"march to their duty and not fly"*   De Bruhl, 206.

188   *But according to Marquis James*   James, 248.

188   *"The sun of Austerlitz . . ."*   Ibid.

189   *Houston asked the veteran scout*   Ibid., 249.

189   *"two bites of one cherry"*   Ibid.

189   *Most historians agree*   Ibid.

189   *"I never thought that a moment"*   Clary, 44.

189   *He had not even placed*   De Bruhl, 208.

190   *Suddenly "orange dots"*   James, 251.

190   *As his boot filled with blood*   De Bruhl, 210.

190   *"Me no Alamo! Me no Alamo!"*   James, 252.

190   *He was laid on a blanket*   De Bruhl, 211.

192   *"My God, all is lost"*   Ibid.

192   *"To the right and to the left"*   Ibid.

192   *It was a trophy*   Ibid., 212.

192   *According to some*   Bell, April 10, 2009.

193   *"A unified nation"*   Fehrenbach, 385.

193   *"San Jacinto corn"*   James, 256.

193   *"I never saw a man"*   Ibid., 261.

194   *The dictator told the diplomat*   Krauze, 142–43.

194   *His portrait was painted*   James, 285–86.

CHAPTER 6—*James K. Polk: Young Hickory Keeps a Diary*

195   *"Mr. Trist set out on his mission"*   James K. Polk, *The Diary of James K. Polk*. 3 vols., ed. Milo Milton Quaife (Chicago: A. C. McClurg, 1910), 2:478, April 16, 1847.

196   *"small of stature and drab"*   Robert W. Merry, *A Country of Vast Designs* (New York: Simon and Schuster, 2009), 2.

196   *"in many ways a smaller-than-life"*   Ibid., 131.

196   *"He possessed a trait of sly"*   Ibid., 238.

196   *Polk was the last major president*   Sam W. Haynes, *James K. Polk and the Expansionist Impulse* (New York: Longman, 1997), ix.

196   *"as one of the half-dozen"*   Walter LaFeber, *The American Age* (New York: W. W. Norton, 1994), 106.

197   *"made an incision"*   Walter Borneman, *Polk: The Man Who Transformed the Presidency* (New York: Random House, 2008), 8.

197   *"As James matured"*   Haynes, 9.

198   *admitted to the bar*   Borneman, 11.

198   *"A new era"*   Haynes, 12.

199   *"had large brown eyes"*   Borneman, 13.

199   *Besides beauty, Sarah*   Haynes, 14.

199   *"viewed the young republic"*   Ibid., 14–15.

200   *"considered slavery a side issue"*   Merry, 130.

200   *"Napoleon of the stump"*   LaFeber, 107.

200   *who referred to Old Hickory as*   Borneman, 25.

200   *"city of magnificent distances"*   Haynes, 20.

200   *"has no wit"*   Ibid., 18.

200   *"In the end, he had manufactured"*   Ibid., 19.

200   *Jackson distrusted paper money*   Ibid., 26.

201   *Methodism inspired him*   Ibid., 30.

201   *In return, Spain agreed*   Borneman, 31.

201   *"carried the water for Old Hickory"*   Ibid., 32.

202   *"sustained himself as well as any"*   Haynes, 41.

202   *"Log Cabin and Hard Cider" campaign*   Ibid., 47.

203 *considering talks with Britain* Borneman, 74.

203 *"The British Empire had never made a secret"* Joel Silbey, *Storm Over Texas* (New York: Oxford University Press, 2005), 37–38.

203 *"The essence of Calhoun's mistake"* Richard Hofstadter, *The American Political Tradition* (New York: Alfred A. Knopf, 1951), 88.

203 *"You might as well . . . attempt"* Silbey, 66.

203 *On December 29, 1845* LaFeber, 108.

203 *"Texas must be ours!"* Borneman, 88.

204 *seemed to many little more* Haynes, 60.

204 *But when Polk won the election* Daniel Walker Howe, *What Hath God Wrought* (New York: Oxford University Press, 2007), 688.

204 *"I intend to be myself"* Haynes, 65.

204 *"the house that Jackson built"* Ibid., 68.

204 *the new immigrant vote* Silbey, 79.

205 *"The glorious result"* Borneman, 134–35.

205 *"Foreign governments do not seem"* Ibid., 142–43.

206 *There were about ten times* Merry, 162, 164.

206 *"Expand or die"* LaFeber, 95.

206 *"only that they had neighbors"* Gene M. Brack, *Mexico Views Manifest Destiny, 1821–1846* (Albuquerque: University of New Mexico Press, 1975), 17.

206 *Better informed liberals* Ibid., 20.

206 *envy of American prosperity* Ibid., 16.

207 *"[The United States] desired"* Ramón Alcaraz et al., *The Other Side: Or, Notes for the History of the War between Mexico and the United States,* trans. and ed. Albert C. Ramsey (1850; repr., New York: Bart Franklin, 1970), 3.

207 *real power was in the hands* David A. Clary, *Eagles and Empire: The United States, Mexico, and the Struggle for a Continent* (New York: Bantam, 2009), 7.

207 *"In late 1788 the viceroy of New Spain"* Peter S. Onuf, Douglas Seefeldt, and Jeffrey L. Hantman, eds., *Across the Continent: Jefferson, Lewis and Clark, and the Making of America* (Charlottesville: University of Virginia Press, 2005), 27.

207 *"to occupy the best harbors"* Ibid., 23.

208 *"John Quincy Adams, who was never"* J. Fred Rippy, *Joel R. Poinsett, Versatile American* (1935; repr., New York: Greenwood Press, 1968), 32.

208 *"one of the most versatile"* *Encyclopaedia Britannica,* 200th anniversary ed., vol. 18 (Chicago: Encyclopaedia Britannica, 1968), 97.

208 *In Santiago he established*   Rippy, 56.

208 *"was designed not only to serve local"*   Ibid., 73–74.

209 *"the best account"*   Ibid., 90.

209 *From Mexico he brought a plant*   T. R. Fehrenbach, *Fire and Blood: A History of Mexico* (New York: Da Capo Press, 1995), 380.

209 *In a few months*   Rippy, 122.

209 *"He appeared before the insurgents"*   Ibid., 128.

209 *"Mexicans associated Americans with"*   Brack, 29.

210 *"Mexicans were perceptive"*   Ibid., 181.

210 *It has also been pointed out*   Ibid., 28.

210 *In the words of Ramón Alcaraz*   Alcaraz et al., 14.

210 *because he was more "missionary"*   Clary, 32.

210 *"Mexican enemies referred"*   Rippy, 131.

210 *"[Poinsett] conceived the project"*   Cecil Robinson, ed., *The View from Chapultepec: Mexican Writers on the Mexican-American War* (Tucson: University of Arizona Press, 1989), 166.

210 *"caused a festering because they were"*   Ibid., 156.

210 *The American concept of federalism*   Ibid., 162.

210 *"the two sovereignties"*   Ibid., 158.

210 *Poinsett "proposed to establish"*   Ibid., 168.

210 *"A new nation perhaps resents"*   Brack, 28.

211 *"could make better use"*   Ibid., 170.

211 *"Mexican independence had cancelled"*   Ibid., 22.

211 *"Yankeephobia was rampant in Mexico"*   Ibid., 11.

211 *"Mexicans were as scornful of"*   Ibid., 170.

211 *"perpetual rival and enemy"*   Ibid., 32.

211 *Belligerence toward the United States*   Ibid., 173.

211 *"provoke a situation of fact"*   Robinson, 186.

212 *"The North Americans kept up"*   Ibid., 200–1.

212 *"From this sense"*   Ibid., 185.

212 *"Santa Anna demanded"*   Ibid., 122.

212 *"Mexican recruitment consisted chiefly"*   Brack, 172.

212 *Both politicians and generals*   Ibid., 9.

212 *"The army which remained"*   Robinson, 62.

212 *"the national honor is one of those"*   Ibid., 16.

212 *Otero also blamed the Mexican*   Ibid., 20.

213 *"There is no national spirit"*   Fehrenbach, 402.

213   *"There was in Polk's aggressiveness"* Robinson, xxxii.

213   *"Why we are in the habit"* Robert W. Johannsen, *The Halls of the Montezumas: The Mexican War in the American Imagination* (New York: Oxford University Press, 1985), 294.

213   *"not be satisfied"* Borneman, 145.

214   *Polk certainly did not understand* Brack, 179.

214   *"It probably did not occur to Polk"* Fehrenbach, 393.

214   *"U.S. businessmen operating in the fledgling"* Merry, 184–85.

214   *"Polk the Mendacious"* Haynes, 71.

214   *On December 29, 1845* Borneman, 148.

214   *The eulogy for Old Hickory* Howe, 689.

215   *After raising his hand* Borneman, 150.

215   *"the Texas question had been settled"* Clary, 64.

215   *More than almost any other president* Haynes, 72.

215   *Meticulous as ever* Ibid., 73.

215   *"In truth he is too fond"* Ibid., 74.

215   *Polk scolded his cabinet* Ibid.

216   *"I prefer to supervise the whole"* Ibid., 74–75.

216   *Polk would make himself available* Ibid., 76.

216   *He would record in his diary* Ibid., 78.

216   *"But wine was available in abundance"* Merry, 270.

216   *avoided face-to-face confrontations* Ibid., 221, 440.

216   *"a disreputable scramble"* Haynes, 84.

217   *"A spirit has taken wing"* Ibid., 87–88.

217   *"America is the country of the Future"* Ibid.

217   *The historian Sam W. Haynes* Ibid., 88.

217   *A great nation grew* Ibid., 89.

217   *"the fulfilment of our manifest destiny"* LaFeber, 95.

219   *Those passing there* Borneman, 158.

220   *"I think our true policy"* Ibid., 159.

220   *"more consistent with fairness"* Ibid., 162.

221   *"We shall do our duty"* Ibid., 163.

221   *A metaphor often used* Haynes, 90.

221   *Some have pointed out that Polk* Ibid., 91.

221   *If Polk was aware* Ibid., 92.

222   *"In reasserting Mr. Monroe's doctrine"* Polk, 1:71.

222   *"As much as any single factor"* Haynes, 95.

222 *"The only way to treat John Bull"*   Borneman, 169.

222 *"For America, it was that vision"*   Merry, 169.

223 *(Jones had seen a clipping . . .)*   Clary, 41.

223 *In* Huckleberry Finn   Mark Twain, *The Adventures of Huckleberry Finn* (Berkeley: American Heritage Press with University of California Press, 1985), 90.

223 *"a great and glorious mission"*   Haynes, 98.

223 *"sufficiently numerous to play"*   Borneman, 175.

224 *For years the garrisons there*   Haynes, 111.

224 *"Who can arrest the torrent"*   Borneman, 177.

224 *American ships had reached China*   Gordon S. Wood, *Empire of Liberty* (New York: Oxford University Press, 2009), 202.

224 *And it was also speculated*   Borneman, 178.

224 *To achieve his ends, Polk*   Merry, 240.

224 *Warships from both European nations*   Borneman, 180.

225 *"If the people should desire to"*   Ibid., 181.

225 *Among his other adventures*   Merry, 153, 160.

225 *"Do all in your power to conciliate"*   Borneman, 181.

225 *"a confidential conversation"*   Ibid., 182; Polk, 1:83–84.

228 *But he did not charm*   Borneman, 186.

228 *"concerning Capt. Fremont's expedition"*   Polk, 1:71–72, October 24, 1845.

228 *Larkin loaned Frémont*   Borneman, 187.

228 *According to John Sutter*   Ibid., 188.

230 *"I saw the way opening"*   John C. Frémont, *Memoirs of My Life* (1887; repr. New York: Cooper Square Press, 2001), 490.

230 *"The Rio Grande is claimed"*   Borneman, 191.

230 *Once hostilities began*   Ibid.

230 *William S. Parrott, a failed dentist*   Clary, 67.

231 *Herrera appeared willing*   Borneman, 193–94.

231 *"a drunken incompetent"*   Fehrenbach, 391.

231 *"He spent huge sums"*   Fehrenbach, 390.

232 *"would only admit him"*   Alcaraz et al., 28.

232 *By ignoring the withdrawal*   Haynes, 115.

232 *"no suggestion that Mexico"*   Merry, 210.

232 *"I am exceedingly desirous"*   Borneman, 196.

232 *"nothing is to be done"*   Ibid., 197.

233 *"wanted was to return"*   Clary, 80.

233 *"We can never get along"* Haynes, 127.

233 *What he probably did not understand* Ibid., 129.

233 *"Left with the choice"* Brack, 179.

233 *"famously sadistic and self-important"* Merry, 241.

234 *"Hostilities may now be considered"* Borneman, 201.

234 *"the North American Intervention"* Fehrenbach, 394.

234 *"These sons of distinct races"* Alcaraz et al., 46.

235 *the only effective means* Borneman, 203–4.

235 *The treatment Slidell received* John S. D. Eisenhower, *Zachary Taylor* (New York: Times Books and Henry Holt, 2008), 44.

235 *"We go to war with Mexico solely"* Borneman, 208.

236 *"the hourglass metaphor"* LaFeber, 98.

236 *"total ignorance of the art"* Bernard DeVoto, *Year of Decision 1846* (Boston: Little, Brown, 1943), 189–90.

237 *The Mexicans had only lead* Borneman, 212.

237 *Mexican cannons fired* Jack K. Bauer, *Zachary Taylor* (Baton Rouge: Louisiana State University Press, 1985), 155.

237 *While the battle of Palo Alto* Bauer, 155.

237 *The American use of "flying artillery"* Borneman, 213; Eisenhower, 48.

237 *(A recasa is a slough.)* Clary, 111.

237 *Facing cannon fire* Borneman, 213–14.

238 *A number of Mexican soldiers drowned* Eisenhower, 50.

238 *"I think you will find"* Borneman, 214.

238 *According to the historian Jack K. Bauer* Bauer, 157.

238 *"the killer instinct" that great generals* Ibid., 162–63.

238 *"salvation was owing to General Taylor"* Alcaraz et al., 56.

239 *Both men were taken aback* Bauer, 163.

239 *It is estimated that by 1845* Haynes, 117.

239 *And now he was free* Borneman, 223–24.

240 *"We can now thrash Mexico"* Howe, 720.

240 *As James M. McPherson tells us* Silbey, xii.

240 *Polk was more interested* Ibid., 103.

240 *"The wily general"* Merry, 310.

241 *"everyone involved understood"* LaFeber, 120.

241 *"to maintain the new territories"* Silbey, 125.

241 *"not only unwise, but wicked"* Ibid., 128.

241 *"What connection slavery"* Haynes, 148.

241 *"Congress was raising the issue"* LaFeber, 120.

242 *see a private slap Kearny* Clary, 150.

242 *"probably the army's finest"* Merry, 297.

242 *"Take the earliest possession of"* Borneman, 235.

243 *"General Kearny has thus far performed"* Ibid., 239.

244 *Kearny sent a message to Stockton* Ibid., 275.

246 *"Allow the President to invade"* Borneman, 288.

246 *the Whigs in Congress continued* Howe, 763.

246 *"General Taylor, I fear"* Polk, 2:119, September 5, 1846.

246 *Never having worn a uniform* Eisenhower, 52–53.

247 *shot a woman washing on the bank* Clary, 119.

247 *A touring theatrical company* Bauer, 170.

247 *And volunteers from Arkansas massacred* Howe, 771.

247 *one in eight* Ibid.

247 *"frogs, along with scorpions, tarantulas"* Clary, 163.

248 *The ammunition provided* Bauer, 176, n. 38.

248 *The percussion cap* Clary, 137.

248 *Or he may have thought* Bauer, 178.

248 *"Monterrey, the capital of the frontier"* Alcaraz et al., 65.

249 *Taylor was always reluctant* Bauer, 179.

250 *Taylor lost 394 men killed or* Ibid., 181.

250 *Two Mexican heroes the Americans* Clary, 195, 199.

250 *"reported, falsely, that the United States"* Merry, 312.

250 *fearing Americans would shell the sanctuary* Howe, 773.

250 *"converted into a vast cemetery"* Alcaraz et al., 80.

251 *"When news travels slowly"* Merry, 351.

251 *"will (as heretofore) defeat your enemies"* Bauer, 186.

251 *"He is evidently"* Polk, 2:249–50, November 21, 1846.

252 *"all that we shall find"* Borneman, 248.

253 *Mexicans had destroyed all water tanks* Clary, 223.

254 *Five mules had carried* Ibid., 272.

254 *"In reply to your note"* Eisenhower, 69.

254 *"General, we are whipped"* Howe, 777.

255 *"A little more grape"* Eisenhower, 70.

255 *"Whatever his political"* Borneman, 251.

255 *"the Rock of Chicamauga"* Ibid., 252.

255 *"With the Mexican advantage"* Eisenhower, 71.

255 *Campfires had been left burning* Howe, 777.

255 *The Mexicans had sustained* Bauer, 206.

255 *Santa Anna claimed victory* Eisenhower, 72.

255 *"Several military analysts"* Robinson, xviii.

256 *"the Battle of Buena Vista"* Howe, 778.

256 *the real American hero at Buena Vista* Clary, 280.

256 *"The truth is, our arms"* Alcaraz et al., 128.

256 *"The loss sustained from the Angostura"* Ibid., 140.

256 *"The truth is the indomitable bravery"* Polk, 2:462, April 7, 1847.

256 *"Taylor once more demonstrated"* Merry, 354.

CHAPTER 7 — *Winfield Scott: Old Fuss and Feathers Goes to the Mountain*

257 *"Witness the present Mexican War"* Henry David Thoreau, *Thoreau: Collected Essays and Poems,* ed. Elizabeth Hall Witherell (New York: Library of America, 2001), 203.

257 *"They jest want this Californy"* Quoted in Walter R. Borneman, *Polk: The Man Who Transformed the Presidency and America* (New York: Random House, 2008), 253.

257 *"a bewildered, confounded"* Joel Silbey, *Storm over Texas* (New York: Oxford University Press, 2005), 129.

257 *"The War has not been waged"* Borneman, 254.

258 *"He could bestow praise"* Timothy Johnson, *Winfield Scott: The Quest for Military Glory* (Lawrence: University of Kansas Press, 1998), 2.

258 *"a wholly absurd and flatulent personage"* Ibid., 3.

258 *"The only viable candidate"* Robert W. Merry, *A Country of Vast Designs* (New York: Simon and Schuster, 2009), 319.

259 *"A strong-willed, quick-witted woman"* Allan Peskin, *Winfield Scott and the Profession of Arms* (Kent, OH: Kent State University Press, 2003), 2.

259 *"If I have achieved"* Ibid.

259 *His fluency in French* Johnson, 9.

259 *"oval face, wide eyes"* Peskin, 4.

259 *"the most magnificent youth"* Ibid.

259 *"my life, my liberty"* Johnson, 12.

260 *"mud, snakes, filth and vermin"* Peskin, 10.

260 *"vainglorious coxcomb"* Ibid.

260 *he meant to be a scholar* Johnson, 19.

261 *"to form a hollow square"* Peskin, 14.

261   *Scott committed himself*   Johnson, 19.

261   *"Should war come at last"*   Peskin, 14.

261   *"In a moment the shock"*   Ibid., 24.

262   *Throughout much of his career*   Johnson, 27.

262   *He already carried with him*   Ibid., 28.

263   *"It was his ambition"*   Peskin, 33.

263   *The stars had begun to fall*   Ibid., 36.

263   *"the service of outposts"*   Ibid., 37.

264   *He organized a network*   Johnson, 45.

264   *"General Scott drills and damns"*   Peskin, 39.

264   *He was later unable*   Peskin, 42–43.

265   *The Americans losses were sixty killed*   Peskin, 45.

265   *It was an expensive battle*   Johnson, 52.

265   *"Brig.-gen. Scott is entitled"*   Peskin, 47.

265   *but most historians see it*   Johnson, 59.

266   *"recognition of the importance"*   Daniel Walker Howe, *What Hath God Wrought* (New York: Oxford University Press, 2007), 779.

266   *"a calling, not an occupation"*   Peskin, 58.

266   *"a gradual and universal subordination"*   Peskin, 67.

266   *It was the biggest single business*   Ibid.

267   *Scott himself would become*   Johnson, 71.

268   *"By sheer energy"*   Howe, 519.

268   *Scott discovered in himself*   Peskin, 85.

269   *In fighting the rebellious Creeks*   Ibid., 97.

269   *"The treaty, if concluded at all"*   Horace Kephart, *Cherokees of the Smoky Mountains* (Ithaca, NY: privately printed, 1936), 17.

269   *the two Cherokee chiefs*   Howe, 415–16.

269   *"The Cherokees were the mountaineers"*   Kephart, 25–26.

269   *The Cherokees had in mind*   Howe, 345.

269   *the Cherokees had been forced*   Kephart, 27.

270   *"toads, snakes, insects,"*   Ibid., 32.

270   *"I fought through the civil war"*   Peskin, 107.

271   *The two men had exchanged*   Ibid., 110.

271   *"I see no reason to apprehend"*   Ibid., 111.

272   *"But I did see a man"*   Ibid., 127.

272   *And he liked to be described*   Ibid., 124.

272   *"the finest specimen of manhood"*   Ibid.

272   *"I sometimes say silly things"*   Ibid., 125.

272   *"at a certain moisture"*   Johnson, 139.

273   *Scott opposed slavery*   Ibid., 145.

273   *Scott professed to admire*   Peskin, 129.

273   *"little strength lay"*   Ibid., 131.

273   *Scott opposed going to war*   Johnson, 151.

273   *"Both were pleasant to serve under"*   Peskin, 135.

274   *"My explicit meaning is"*   Ibid., 140.

274   *"Drawing upon reserves of patience"*   Ibid., 141.

274   *Scott worked harder even than Polk*   David A. Clary, *Eagles and Empire: The United States, Mexico, and the Struggle for a Continent* (New York: Bantam, 2009), 146.

275   *A show of force in the south*   Johnson, 157.

275   *"The truth is, neither Scott nor Taylor"*   James Knox Polk, *The Diary of James K. Polk, 1845–1849*, 3 vols., ed. Milo Milton Quaife (Chicago: A. C. McClurg, 1910), 2:328, January 14, 1847.

275   *"the most delighted man"*   Ibid., 2:245.

275   *"I have felt"*   Peskin, 143.

275   *"through the motions to flatter"*   Howe, 774.

276   *"Before the war is ended"*   Peskin, 144.

276   *"will be infinitely painful"*   Ibid., 146.

277   *Timothy D. Johnson has described*   Johnson, 166–68.

277   *Built by a firm near Philadelphia*   Ibid., 160.

277   *Fellow officers joked*   Clary, 311.

277   *"Pillow thought the United States"*   Ibid., 191.

278   *Pillow seems to have had*   Peskin, 149.

278   *"a mass of vanity"*   Merry, 389.

278   *"a great white cloud"*   Peskin, 150.

278   *"the Gibraltar of Mexico"*   Johnson, 172.

278   *"Death to the Anglo-Saxons"*   T. R. Fehrenbach, *Fire and Blood: A History of Mexico* (New York: Da Capo Press, 1995), 387–88.

278   *Using the tactics*   Johnson, 174.

278   *"A turning movement occurs"*   Ibid., 175.

280   *"had the quality"*   Fehrenbach, 396.

280   *According to Ramón Alcaraz*   Ramón Alcaraz et al., *The Other Side: Or, Notes for the History of the War between Mexico and the United States,* trans. and ed. Albert C. Ramsey (1850; repr., New York: Bart Franklin, 1970), 183.

280   *The Americans had executed*   Peskin, 152.

280   *Scott chose to use*   Johnson, 176.

281   *The walls of Veracruz*   Ibid., 175.

282   *A soldier watching the fireworks*   Ibid., 177.

282   *American guns fired*   Howe, 781.

282   *And he demanded complete surrender*   Peskin, 158.

282   *He had taken the impregnable*   Johnson, 178.

283   *"More than five hundred innocents"*   Cecil Robinson, ed., *The View from Chapultepec: Mexican Writers on the Mexican-American War* (Tucson: University of Arizona Press, 1989), 68.

283   *what Robert Graves calls the "Persian Version"*   Richard Ellmann and Robert O'Clair, eds., *The Norton Anthology of Modern Verse*, 2nd ed. (New York: W. W. Norton, 1988), 575.

283   *"Not a single house was uninjured"*   Alcaraz et al., 189.

283   *Their account would list*   Ibid., 195.

283   *"a multitude of horrors"*   Clary, 301.

283   *"presenting at once the olive branch"*   Johnson, 180.

283   *The respect Scott showed to Mexican*   Peskin, 160.

283   *sold the invaders buzzard eggs*   Clary, 303.

284   *Meeting so little resistance*   Peskin, 163.

284   *"calmed the rising storm"*   Ibid., 164.

284   *"It is very remarkable"*   Alcaraz et al., 207.

286   *"while Mexican soldiers sat on it"*   Howe, 783.

286   *"The entire mass of men"*   Alcaraz et al., 212.

286   *"All classes being confounded"*   Ibid., 214.

286   *"a lively picture of the fall"*   Ibid., 215.

286   *Santa Anna's behavior*   Merry, 382.

286   *Santa Anna had seized*   Peskin, 168.

288   *Promised reinforcements and supplies*   Peskin, 169.

288   *"Scott was fighting"*   Fehrenbach, 400.

288   *And a smaller percentage*   Peskin, 170.

288   *Mexicans were surprised*   Clary, 319.

289   *"I beg to be recalled"*   Peskin, 172.

290   *"a dishonest politician"*   Ibid., 174.

290   *Santa Anna had now assembled*   Ibid.

290   *"Like Cortez, finding myself isolated"*   Ibid.

290   *"noble and kind"*   Johnson, 193.

291 *"Scott is lost"*   Peskin, 175.

291 *"forty-six miles north to south"*   Clary, 346.

291 *The thin mountain air*   Johnson, 197.

291 *Scott had also employed*   Johnson, 195.

291 *"the Aztec City of lakes"*   Enrique Krauze, *Mexico: Biography of a Power; A History of Modern Mexico, 1810–1996,* trans. Hank Heifetz (New York: HarperCollins, 1997), 3.

291 *"the City of Palaces"*   Ibid., 61.

291 *"another Venice"*   Ibid., 35.

291 *Foundries had worked*   Alcaraz et al., 239.

292 *became a kind of carnival*   Clary, 345.

292 *"General Santa Anna came"*   Alcaraz et al., 250.

292 *"Eastward from this"*   Ibid., 252.

292 *Scott chose to swing around*   Peskin, 178; Johnson, 199.

292 *Worth would later claim*   Johnson, 197.

292 *In the manual Scott had written*   Peskin, 178.

293 *Scott later described Lee's journey*   Ibid., 180.

293 *Seeing Valencia's vulnerability*   Alcaraz et al., 279.

293 *At dawn Twiggs attacked*   Peskin, 181.

294 *The battle of Contreras*   Ibid.

294 *"Young man, if I were not"*   Ibid.

294 *"I doubt whether a more brilliant"*   Ibid.

294 *pursued by the American forces*   Alcaraz et al., 286.

294 *Some reports put Mexican losses*   Johnson, 200.

296 *Unfortunately, many Mexicans would interpret*   Ibid., 201.

296 *"Too much blood"*   Peskin, 183.

296 *"scatter the elements of peace"*   Merry, 384.

296 *"Here come the friends"*   Peskin, 184.

297 *"The American general"*   Alcaraz, 295n.

297 *They saw Mexico as the republic*   Alcaraz et al., 308.

297 *"nearly every Indian band"*   Clary, 187.

297 *"As one sun succeeds another sun"*   Alcaraz et al., 300.

298 *"withdrew to sleep in the Palace"*   Ibid., 344.

298 *The same historians say Santa Anna*   Ibid., 347.

298 *Not suspecting a trap*   Peskin, 185–86.

298 *Americans won the battle*   Ibid., 186.

298 *"nothing was gained except glory"*   Ibid.

298 *Santa Anna proclaimed a victory* Alcaraz et al., 351.

299 *"We will attack"* Peskin, 187.

299 *"Santa Anna . . . was no match"* Merry, 388.

299 *Chapultepec means "Grasshopper Hill"* Clary, 368.

299 *"Chapultepec [was] the key"* Alcaraz et al., 355.

299 *All along, Santa Anna assumed* Clary, 370.

299 *"a tempest at sea"* Peskin, 188.

299 *six cadets, who wrapped themselves* Clary, 371–72.

299 *"God is a Yankee!"* Ibid., 372.

300 *Ulysses S. Grant would later describe* Johnson, 206.

300 *Outnumbered three to one* Ibid.

300 *It took a day of fighting* Peskin, 190.

300 *"The American army"* Ibid., 191.

300 *"Never had an American general"* Johnson, 207.

301 *"For the grand conflicts"* Alcaraz et al., 359.

301 *Impressed by his leadership* Johnson, 209.

301 *"the greatest living soldier"* Peskin, 191.

302 *"Credit is due to the troops"* Ibid.

302 *"General Scott's successes"* Ibid.

302 *"may well have been"* Howe, 790–91.

302 *"This glorious army"* Peskin, 193.

302 *"The roads were covered with families"* Alcaraz et al., 381.

302 *"the sun which years"* Ibid., 382.

302 *To many Mexican people* Ibid., 383.

302 *"The conquest of that large republic"* Howe, 2.

303 *"In Mexico, Scott's war machine"* Merry, 401.

304 *"Leonidas," gave Pillow credit* Peskin, 198.

304 *"a most malignant man"* Ibid., 199.

304 *"To suspend a successful general"* Howe, 791.

305 *"One word more about the campaign"* Robinson, 49.

CHAPTER 8—*Kit Carson: Taking Boone's Trace to the Pacific*

307 *In 1810 Kit's much older* Thelma Guild and Harry L. Carter, *Kit Carson: A Pattern for Heroes* (Lincoln: University of Nebraska Press, 1984), 4, 9.

307 *"I always felt completely safe"* Hampton Sides, *Blood and Thunder* (New York: Doubleday, 2006), 9.

308 *"I jumped to my rifle"* Ibid., 10.

308 *"Nothing, except I can shoot"* Ibid., 11.

308 *"All persons are notified"* Ibid.

310 *"shed rain like an otter"* Ibid., 13.

313 *"a large Frenchman"* Ibid., 30; Kit Carson, *Kit Carson's Autobiography* (Chicago: Lakeside Press, 1935), 42–43.

313 *"Mewling schoolboys!"* Sides, 30.

313 *"had no more bother"* Carson, 44.

314 *"a good girl"* Sides, 32.

314 *"the happiest days of my life"* Ibid.

314 *"She was a good wife"* Ibid.

314 *"Teepees stood smokeless"* Ibid., 33.

315 *"Beaver was getting scarce"* Ibid.

316 *When asked why* Ibid.

317 *"a man of striking good looks"* Ibid., 51.

318 *"He was broad-shouldered"* Ibid., 52.

318 *"I've been some time"* Ibid.

320 *"He was a fine hunter"* Ibid., 61–62.

321 *In 1845 three thousand Americans* Walter LaFeber, *The American Age* (New York: W. W. Norton, 1994), 112.

322 *"impossible to describe the hardships"* Carson, 126–27.

323 *the memoir may have influenced* Hershel Parker, *Herman Melville: A Biography,* vol. 1, *1819–1851* (Baltimore: Johns Hopkins University Press, 1996), 181.

323 *Dana described the fine and sheltered* Richard Henry Dana Jr., *Two Years Before the Mast* (1868; repr., Mineola, NY: Dover, 2007), 42.

323 *"The shores are extremely well wooded"* Ibid., 53.

323 *"have no suspenders"* Ibid., 57.

324 *"I have often seen a man"* Ibid.

324 *"The fondness for dress"* Ibid., 60.

324 *"It was a pleasure"* Ibid.

324 *"A common bullock-driver"* Ibid.

324 *"an idle, thriftless people"* Ibid., 58.

324 *"From this upper class"* Ibid., 60.

324 *"They sometimes appeared to me"* Ibid.

325 *"California bank-notes"* Ibid.

325 *"No Protestant has any political rights"* Ibid., 62.

325 *"Having more industry"* Ibid.

325 *"The chief alcaldes in Monterey"* Ibid.

325 *"filled, it is said,"* Ibid., 91.

325 *There was a good deal* Ibid., 112.

325 *Dana got to know them* Ibid., 119–21.

325 *The missions along the coast* Daniel Walker Howe, *What Hath God Wrought* (New York: Oxford University Press, 2007), 21.

325 *"are strangers sent from Mexico"* Dana, 130.

326 *"nothing that we should call"* Ibid., 131.

326 *"there is little communication"* Ibid.

326 *"seizing upon the presidio"* Ibid.

326 *"a country embracing four or five"* Ibid., 133.

326 *"Those who do not become part"* Howe, 698.

326 *"which Mexicans or Indians had brought"* Dana, 215.

327 *"people [of California]"* Walter R. Borneman, *Polk: The Man Who Transformed the Presidency and America* (New York: Random House, 2008), 181.

327 *"induced the area's Indian tribes"* Robert W. Merry, *A Country of Vast Designs* (New York: Simon and Schuster, 2009), 303.

327 *"the rise of the missions"* Cecil Robinson, ed., *The View from Chapultepec: Mexican Writers on the Mexican-American War* (Tucson: University of Arizona Press, 1989), 135.

327 *"the Robin Hood of El Dorado"* Ibid., 136–37.

328 *"We have in no wise"* Sides, 71.

329 *"regarded the California coast"* Ibid., 73.

329 *Daniel Walker Howe has pointed out* Howe, 736.

330 *Angered that he had not* Sides, 81.

330 *"We gave them something"* Ibid., 86.

330 *described the conflagration* Ibid., 87; Carson, 100.

330 *It is thought by the historian* David Roberts, *A Newer World* (New York: Simon and Schuster, 2000), 160.

331 *Dr. Semple, called their acts* Sides, 93.

331 *"moved by nothing but the chance"* Ibid.

331 *The fact that General Castro* Clary, 91.

332 *"If you don't like"* Sides, 95.

332 *"No, I have no use"* Ibid., 96.

332 *"My word at present"* Ibid., 97.

333 *Palmerston believed the Mexicans* Enrique Krauze, *Mexico: Biography of Power; A History of Modern Mexico, 1810–1996,* trans. Hank Heifetz (New York: HarperCollins, 1997), 144.

333 *"I'd rather ride on a grizzly"* Sides, 99.

333 *"So intent was Stockton"* Merry, 294.

333 *"a reward for his brave"* Sides, 100.

334 *"The feeling was one"* Ibid., 131.

335 *"We put out, with merry hearts"* Ibid., 133.

335 *"Wolf Eaters, the Dirty Fellows"* Ibid., 140.

335 *"It was a rare sight"* Ibid., 145.

336 *The eager Gillespie suggested* Ibid., 149.

337 *"All you have to do"* Ibid.

337 *"Remember one point"* Ibid., 151.

339 *the powder in the dragoons' weapons* Clary, 242.

339 *"They would allow themselves"* Robinson, 135.

340 *As it turned out* Alcaraz, et al., *The Other Side: or, Notes for the History of the War between Mexico and the United States,* trans. and ed. Albert C. Ramsey (1850; repr., New York: Bart Franklin, 1970), 412–13.

341 *Now the ratio was closer* Sides, 160.

341 *"Se escarpara el lobó"* Ibid., 161.

342 *A mounted* Californio Sides, 162.

342 *"We're gone; let's jump up"* Ibid.

342 *"Been in worse places before"* Ibid.

342 *"out of his head"* Ibid., 163.

342 *According to one report, Chemuctah* Clary, 244.

342 *"the master mountain man"* Berndard DeVoto, *The Year of Decision: 1846* (Boston: Little, Brown, 1943), 358.

343 *"Never has there been a man"* Sides, 163.

343 *"it was the talented mountain man"* Clary, 293.

343 *"finally got through, but"* Carson, 116.

343 *"A cup of coffee"* Sides, 164.

344 *"Hold fire!"* Ibid., 165.

344 *"The Pacific opened"* Ibid.

344 *On January 10, 1847* Clary, 256.

345 *Frémont's men had fought a skirmish* Alcaraz et al., 411; John Charles Frémont, *Memoirs of My Life* (1887; repr., New York: Cooper Square Press, 2001), 594–95.

346 *like a Greek hero* Roberts, 177.

346 *Kearny behaved with the patience* Clary, 258.

348 *"this child," or "this soul"* Roberts, 77.

348 *Harvey Carter, one of Carson's* Ibid., 75.

348 *"Kit never swore"* Ibid.

348 *"He talked but little . . ."* Ibid.

349 *"I loathe and hate the man . . ."* Ibid.

349 *"Do 'ee hyar now?"* Ibid., 77.

349 *"To imagine Kit Carson immersed"* Ibid., 78.

349 *"My friends advised me to deliver"* Carson, 125–26.

CHAPTER 9 — *Nicholas Trist: The Search for a Father Voice*

354 *Trist's earliest preserved letter* Robert W. Drexler, *Guilty of Making Peace: A Biography of Nicholas P. Trist* (Lanham, MD: University Press of America, 1991), 17–18.

354 *Some biographers have seen* Ibid., 18.

355 *Certainly Jefferson's political ideals* Ibid., 21.

356 *"was not a raving beauty"* Robert A. Brent, *Nicholas Philip Trist: Biography of a Disobedient Diplomat* (PhD diss., University of Virginia, 1950), 13.

356 *"one of the most amiable . . ."* Ibid.

357 *He even became an assistant* Wallace Ohrt, *Defiant Peacemaker: Nicholas Trist In the Mexican War* (College Station: Texas A&M University Press, 1997), 23.

357 *"I have long been convinced"* Drexler, 29.

357 *"Will Virginia Randolph favor me"* Ibid.

357 *"The interview I yesterday requested"* Ibid., 29–30.

358 *"Without going beyond"* Ibid., 31.

358 *"It required fourteen hours"* Ibid., 32–33.

359 *"elaborate metaphors and other verbal contrivances"* Ibid., 33.

359 *"the conviction that I could never"* Ibid.

359 *the only (white) great-grandchild* Brent, 33, 37.

360 *"He whispered inquiringly"* Drexler, 35.

360 *"Thomas Jefferson survives"* David McCullough, *John Adams* (New York: Simon and Schuster, 2001), 646.

360 *Oddly enough, couriers* Daniel Walker Howe, *What Hath God Wrought* (New York: Oxford University Press, 2007), 243.

360 *Sally preferred to stay* Drexler, 36.

360 *he had in his bank account* Brent, 39.

361 *Trist would be a strict Unionist* Drexler, 37.

361 *"it may contribute"* Ibid., 38.

362 *James Madison loyally wrote letters* Ibid., 43.

363 *Jackson was also anxious* Brent, 69.

363   *"Trist was much more"*   Ibid., 89.

363   *"Among the young men"*   Ibid., 80.

364   *"Virginia was now only a shadow"*   Drexler, 48.

364   *"world of speculation"*   Gordon S. Wood, *Empire of Liberty* (New York: Oxford University Press, 2009), 736.

364   *had been sold to P. T. Barnum*   Ibid., 725.

364   *Ironically, it had been Trist's mentor*   Ibid., 736.

365   *As a clerk and translator*   Brent, 74.

365   *In fact, the consulship*   Ibid., 90.

366   *"(1) endeavoring to create"*   Ohrt, 79.

367   *Among the many complaints*   Ibid., 92–93.

367   *"his inordinate fear of illness"*   Robert W. Merry, *A Country of Vast Designs* (New York: Simon and Schuster, 2009), 360.

368   *"without a lender of"*   Howe, 504–5.

368   *From being adviser and secretary*   Ohrt, 98.

370   *Most historians have ascribed*   Ibid., 103.

371   *"Mr. Trist, if you can"*   Ibid.

371   *"The service shall be rendered . . ."*   Ibid.

372   *Buchanan himself leaked news*   Howe, 801.

372   *Determined to keep the assignment*   Ohrt, 106–7.

372   *Before embarking, he bought*   Ibid., 107.

374   *"utterly incompetent"*   Ibid., 113.

374   *"King Death in his yellow robe"*   Ibid.

374   *"Piling insult on insult"*   Ibid., 114.

375   *"the gallant commander"*   Ibid., 112.

375   *"My first impulse"*   Ibid., 115.

375   *Thornton then personally called*   Ibid., 116.

375   *The deputy named Ramón Gamboa*   David Clary, *Eagles and Empire: The United States, Mexico, and the Struggle for a Continent* (New York: Bantam, 2009), 362.

376   *"Later most Mexican historians"*   Robert Griswold Del Castillo, *The Treaty of Guadalupe Hidalgo: A Legacy of Conflict* (Norman: Unversity of Oklahoma Press, 1990), 28–29.

376   *"My Dear Sir"*   Ohrt, 117.

376   *"With General Scott's reply"*   Ibid.

377   *"[Trist] seems to have entered"*   James K. Polk, *The Diary of James K. Polk, 1845–1849*, 3 vols., ed. Milo Milton Quaife (Chicago: A. C. McClurg, 1910), 3:283, January 4, 1848.

377   *"He has become the perfect tool"*   Polk, 3:283; Clary, 406.

377 *"Although Pillow's military accomplishments"*   Orht, 119.

378 *but now he had the name*   Ibid., 120.

379 *Patience and subtlety*   Ohrt, 124–25.

379 *The historian Wallace Orht*   Ibid., 128.

379 *"Only the aristocracy"*   Ibid., 129.

380 *"From a strictly military viewpoint"*   Ibid., 132.

381 *"Scott and Trist, his State Department"*   T. R. Fehrenbach, *Fire and Blood: A History of Mexico* (New York: Da Capo Press, 1995), 401.

381 *"Mexico is an ugly enemy"*   Ohrt, 132.

382 *Rosa's answer showed*   Ibid., 134.

382 *"Trist's defiance before sending an order"*   Howe, 808.

382 *"All is lost," and wept openly*   Ohrt, 134.

382 *"Mr. Trist has managed"*   Ibid., 136.

383 *Scott urged his friend*   Merry, 399.

383 *Though he might feel "abandoned, abused"*   Ohrt, 137.

383 *"Mr. Trist, make the Treaty"*   Ibid., 140.

384 *"every one of his character flaws"*   Merry, 410.

384 *"His dispatch is arrogant"*   Ohrt, 142.

385 *"Aztec Mother of Gods"*   Clary, 402.

385 *the often frail Trist*   Ohrt, 143.

385 *"The Mexicans found his candor"*   Ibid.

386 *The line Trist drew*   Ibid., 144.

387 *"This must be a proud moment"*   Ibid., 145.

387 *"Gentlemen, what is proposed"*   Cecil Robinson, ed., *The View from Chapultepec: Mexican Writers on the Mexican-American War* (Tucson: University of Arizona Press, 1989), 98.

388 *"the conservative wing"*   Ibid., 101.

388 *"Let us do the right thing"*   Ibid., 109–10.

388 *"Contemplate . . . the confusion"*   Ibid., 112.

388 *"The treaty that ended"*   Ibid., 178.

388 *"had its most feverish supporters"*   Walter LaFeber, *The American Age* (New York: W. W. Norton, 1994), 121.

389 *"negotiated by an unauthorized agent"*   George C. Herring, *From Colony to Superpower: U.S. Foreign Relations since 1776* (New York: Oxford University Press, 2008), 205.

390 *"Could those Mexicans"*   Ohrt, 145–46.

391 *"Your Excellency will permit"*   Ibid., 151.

Epilogue—*John Quincy Adams: Old Man Eloquent*

393 *By the time he was ten* Marie B. Hecht, *John Quincy Adams: A Personal History of an Independent Man* (New York: Macmillan, 1972), 17.

393 *While in St. Petersburg* Ibid., 34.

393 *"utilized six languages"* Walter LaFeber, *John Quincy Adams and American Continental Empire* (Chicago: Quadrangle, 1965), 15.

393 *In France he had spent* Hecht, 39.

394 *And he was deeply inspired* Ibid., 53.

394 *Contrary to the popular image* Walter LaFeber, *The American Age* (New York: W. W. Norton, 1994), 75; LaFeber, *Adams*, 15.

394 *But ever a diplomat* Hecht, 63.

394 *He would later say* Ibid., 71.

394 *He rose before six* Ibid., 105.

394 *The verve of his warning* Ibid., 76.

394 *Walter LaFeber would later* LaFeber, *Adams*, 13.

394 *On March 1, 1795* Hecht, 88.

395 *"to regard Adams"* *Encyclopaedia Britannica*, 200th anniversary ed., vol. 1 (Chicago: Encyclopaedia Britannica, 1968), 126.

395 *While his opinions and thoughts* Hecht, 104.

395 *only Washington, and perhaps Lincoln* LaFeber, *Adams*, 14.

395 *John Quincy never had anything* Hecht, 131–32.

395 *"the whole Union"* Ibid., 179.

396 *"one of the happiest events"* Ibid., 146.

396 *"a convinced continentalist"* Ibid., 149.

396 *"representative not of a single state"* Ibid., 162.

396 *"I am made a leader"* Ibid., 174.

396 *an equally dedicated gardener* Ibid., 170.

397 *the issue of American fishing rights* LaFeber, *Adams*, 17.

397 *"the Golden Age of American diplomacy"* Ibid., 13.

397 *"short, bald, and stout"* Hecht, 223.

397 *known to be careless* LaFeber, *American Age*, 88.

397 *"what passed for rigidity"* Hecht, 247.

397 *Some aspects of John Quincy's character* Daniel Walker Howe, *What Hath God Wrought* (New York: Oxford University Press, 2007), 634.

398 *"by Enlightenment concepts"* Ibid., 245.

398 *"lacked the personal warmth"* LaFeber, *Adams*, 24–25.

398 *While trenchantly critical* Howe, 245.

398 *John Quincy saw the United States*   Ibid.

398 *"The spirit of improvement"*   Ibid., 253.

398 *He was deeply committed*   Frederick Merck, *History of the Westward Movement* (New York: Alfred A. Knopf, 1978), 219.

399 *Some historians have described*   LaFeber, *American Age*, 76.

399 *"The United States and North America"*   Ibid.

400 *He saw Old Hickory's campaign*   Walter R. Borneman, *Polk: The Man Who Transformed the Presidency and America* (New York: Random House, 2008), 31.

400 *"If the question is dubious"*   John Buchanan, *Jackson's Way: Andrew Jackson and the People of the Western Waters* (New York: John Wiley and Sons, 2001), 367.

400 *"she should sell them"*   Howe, 103.

400 *"the raid as a lever"*   LaFeber, *Adams*, 20.

400 *"must give offense"*   Richard Kluger, *Seizing Destiny: The Relentless Expansion of American Territory* (New York: Vintage, 2007), 340.

400 *"the motives for which"*   Ibid., 345.

400 *"a driven visionary as well as a calculating"*   Ibid., 347.

400 *For years Adams had hoped*   Howe, 108.

400 *While the British saw China*   LaFeber, *American Age*, 101.

401 *"would allow the American"*   Ibid., 78.

401 *"But she [the United States] goes not abroad"*   Ibid., 82.

402 *"The acknowledgment of a definite"*   Howe, 109.

402 *"The gap between relative power"*   LaFeber, *American Age*, 88.

402 *"Henry showed a certain"*   Henry Adams, *The Education of Henry Adams,* ed. Edward Chalfant and Conrad Edick Wright (Charlottesville: University of Virginia Press, 2007), 10–11.

403 *"considered by many historians"*   LaFeber, *Adams*, 15.

403 *"by arising an hour or two"*   LaFeber, *American Age*, 76.

403 *"the 8th of January"*   David S. Reynolds, *Waking Giant: America in the Age of Jackson* (New York: HarperCollins, 2008), 39.

403 *"a barbarian who could not write"*   Ibid., 40.

404 *"he first fully glimpsed"*   LaFeber, *Adams*, 23.

404 *Since the revolutionary period Southerners*   Howe, 148.

404 *"the greatest danger"*   LaFeber, *American Age*, 81.

404 *Near the end*   LaFeber, *Adams*, 24.

404 *"his 'empire of liberty'"*   Gordon S. Wood, *Empire of Liberty* (New York: Oxford University Press, 2009), 737–38.

404 *"a Serpent creeping"* Ibid., 738.

404 *The failure of the Founding Fathers* Ibid., 508.

405 *"Let not foreign nations"* Howe, 253.

405 *John Quincy was unable* LaFeber, *Adams*, 25.

405 *For him, the Monroe Doctrine was* LaFeber, *American Age*, 85–86.

405 *"plans for exploration"* Howe, 252–53.

405 *popular Millennialism to argue that* Ibid., 253, 287.

405 *"Adams stood for a vision"* Ibid., 279.

406 *wearing only goggles and skullcap* LaFeber, *Adams*, 16.

406 *In 1826 he joined* Reynolds, 46.

407 *"[Indians] are not an improvable breed"* Merck, 186.

407 *Even when John Quincy* Ray Allen Billington, *Westward Expansion: A History of the American Frontier* (New York: Macmillan, 1974), 300.

407 *"A dissolution of the Union"* Allan Nevins, ed., *The Diary of John Quincy Adams, 1794–1845: American Political, Social, and Intellectual Life from Washington to Polk* (New York: Charles Scribner's Sons, 1951), 246–47.

407 *"There is a great fermentation"* Ibid., 462.

407 *"This subject of slavery"* Ibid., 477.

408 *"Old Man Eloquent"* Reynolds, 36.

408 *During his presidency* Ibid., 61.

409 *"the steamboat of moral"* Howe, 245.

409 *In 1824 he had concluded* Borneman, 155.

409 *In 1846 he would throw support* LaFeber, *Adams*, 22.

409 *asking "the Speaker"* Howe, 514.

409 *"began to pick up allies"* Joel Silbey, *Storm over Texas* (New York: Oxford University Press, 2005), 179.

410 *"I want the country"* Howe, 720.

410 *But he, like many Whigs* Ibid., 686.

410 *In 1842 John Quincy* John S. D. Eisenhower, *Agent of Destiny: The Life and Times of Winfield Scott* (New York: Free Press, 1997), 209–10.

410 *"interspersed in small specks"* Thomas Jefferson, *The Portable Thomas Jefferson*, ed. Merrill D. Peterson (New York: Penguin, 1977), 56.

411 *"Boys, I believe"* Howe, 813.

411 *So much gold was added* Ibid., 815.

— BIBLIOGRAPHY —

Adams, Henry. *The Education of Henry Adams.* Edited by Edward Chalfant and
　Conrad Edick Wright. Charlottesville: University of Virginia Press, 2007.
Aguilar-Moreno, Manuel. *Handbook to Life in the Aztec World.* New York: Oxford
　University Press, 2006.
Alcaraz, Ramón, et al. *La historia de la guerra entre Mexico y los Estados-Unidos.*
　Mexico City: Tipografia de Manuel Payno, 1848.
———. *The Other Side: Or, Notes for the History of the War between Mexico and
　the United States.* Translated and edited by Albert C. Ramsey. 1850. Reprint,
　New York: Bart Franklin, 1970.
Bailyn, Bernard. *The Peopling of British North America.* New York: Alfred A.
　Knopf, 1986.
Bauer, Jack K. *Zachary Taylor.* Baton Rouge: Louisiana State University Press,
　1985.
Billington, Ray Allen. *Westward Expansion: A History of the American Frontier.*
　New York: Macmillan, 1974.
Bond, Edward L. *Spreading the Gospel in Colonial Virginia.* Lanham, MD: Lex-
　ington Books, 2004.
Borneman, Walter R. *Polk: The Man Who Transformed the Presidency and America.*
　New York: Random House, 2008.
Boyd, Julian P. "Thomas Jefferson's 'Empire of Liberty.'" *Virginia Quarterly Re-
　view,* vol. 4, no. 4 (autumn 1948): 538–554.
Brack, Gene M. *Mexico Views Manifest Destiny, 1821–1848.* Albuquerque: Univer-
　sity of New Mexico Press, 1975.
Brands, H. W. *Andrew Jackson.* New York: Anchor Books, 2006.
Brent, Robert Arthur. *Nicholas Philip Trist: Biography of a Disobedient Diplomat.*
　PhD dissertation. University of Virginia, 1950.
Buchanan, John. *Jackson's Way: Andrew Jackson and the People of the Western Wa-
　ters.* New York: John Wiley and Sons, 2001.
Carson, Kit. *Kit Carson's Autobiography.* Chicago: Lakeside Press, 1935.
Carter, Harvey Lewis. *Dear Old Kit: The Historical Christopher Carson.* Norman:
　University of Oklahoma Press, 1968.

Clary, David A. *Eagles and Empire: The United States, Mexico, and the Struggle for a Continent*. New York: Bantam, 2009.

Cobia, Manley F., Jr. *Journey into the Land of Trials: David Crockett's Expedition to the Alamo*. Franklin, TN: Hillsboro Press, 2003.

Crockett, David. *A Narrative of the Life of David Crockett of the State of Tennessee*. Edited by James Shackford and Stanley J. Folmsbee. Knoxville: University of Tennessee Press, 1975.

Cross, F. L., and E. A. Livingstone, eds. *The Oxford Dictionary of the Christian Church*. New York: Oxford University Press, 1997.

Cutter, James M. *The Conquest of California and New Mexico*. Albuquerque: Horn and Wallace, 1965.

Dale, Harrison Clifford, ed. *The Ashley-Smith Explorations and the Discovery of the Central Route to the Pacific, 1822–1829*. Glendale, CA: Thomas H. Clark, 1941.

Dana, Richard Henry, Jr. *Two Years Before the Mast*. 1868. Reprint, Mineola, NY: Dover, 2007.

De Bruhl, Marshall. *Sword of San Jacinto*. New York: Random House, 1993.

Del Castillo, Bernal Diaz. *The Discovery and Conquest of Mexico*. New York: Noonday, 1956.

Del Castillo, Richard Griswold. *The Treaty of Guadalupe Hidalgo: A Legacy of Conflict*. Norman: University of Oklahoma Press, 1990.

Derr, Mark. *The Frontiersman: The Real Life and the Many Legends of Davy Crockett*. New York: William Morrow, 1993.

DeVoto, Bernard. *Across the Wide Missouri*. Boston: Houghton Mifflin, 1947.

———. *The Course of Empire*. Boston: Houghton Mifflin, 1952.

———. *The Year of Decision: 1846*. Boston: Little, Brown, 1943.

Drexler, Robert W. *Guilty of Making Peace: A Biography of Nicholas P. Trist*. Lanham, MD: University Press of America, 1991.

Drumm, Stella M. *Down the Santa Fe Trail and into Mexico: The Diary of Susan Shelby Magoffin, 1846–1847*. New Haven: Yale University Press. 1962.

Dugard, Martin. *The Training Ground: Grant, Lee, Sherman, and Davis in the Mexican War, 1846–1848*. New York: Little, Brown, 2008.

Dugatkin, Lee Alan. *Mr. Jefferson and the Giant Moose*. Chicago: University of Chicago Press, 2009.

Eisenhower, John S. D. *Agent of Destiny: The Life and Times of General Winfield Scott*. New York: Free Press, 1997.

———. *So Far from God*. New York: Random House, 1989.

———. *Zachary Taylor*. New York: Times Books and Henry Holt, 2008.

Ellis, Joseph J. *American Sphinx*. New York: Alfred A. Knopf, 1996.

Emerson, Ralph Waldo. *Emerson's Prose and Poetry*. Edited by Joel Porte and Saundra Morris. New York: W. W. Norton, 2001.

———. *Essays and Lectures*. Edited by Joel Porte. New York: Library of America, 1983.

Ellmann, Richard, and Robert O'Clair. *The Norton Anthology of Modern Poetry*. New York: W. W. Norton, 1988.

Ethridge, Robbie. *Creek Country: The Creek Indians and Their World*. Chapel Hill: University of North Carolina Press, 2003.

Fehrenbach, T. R. *Fire and Blood: A History of Mexico*. New York: Da Capo Press, 1995.

Frémont, John Charles. *Memoirs of My Life*. 1887. Reprint, New York: Cooper Square Press, 2001.

Gordon-Reed, Annette. *The Hemings of Monticello*. New York: W. W. Norton, 2008.

Graebner, Norman. *Empire on the Pacific*. New York: Ronald Press, 1955.

Groneman, Bill. *Defense of a Legend: Crockett and the de la Peña Diary*. Plano, TX: Republic of Texas Press, 1994.

Groneman, William III. *David Crockett: Hero of the Common Man*. New York: Forge, 2005.

Guild, Thelma, and Harvey L. Carter. *Kit Carson: A Pattern for Heroes*. Lincoln: University of Nebraska Press, 1984.

Haley, W. D. "Johnny Appleseed—A Pioneer Hero." *Harpers Monthly Magazine*, vol. 43 (November, 1871): 830–36.

Hart, Stephen Harding, and Archer Butler Hulbert. *The Southwestern Journals of Zebulon Pike, 1806–1807*. Albuquerque: University of New Mexico Press, 2006.

Hawkins, Benjamin. *The Collected Works of Benjamin Hawkins, 1796–1810*. Tuscaloosa: University of Alabama Press, 2003.

Hayes, Kevin J. *The Road to Monticello*. New York: Oxford University Press, 2008.

Haynes, Sam W. *James K. Polk and the Expansionist Impulse*. New York: Longman, 1997.

Hecht, Marie B. *John Quincy Adams: A Personal History of an Independent Man*. New York: Macmillan, 1972.

Herring, George C. *From Colony to Superpower: U.S. Foreign Relations since 1776*. New York: Oxford University Press, 2008.

Hofstadter, Richard. *The American Political Tradition*. New York: Alfred A. Knopf, 1951.

Holland, James W. *Victory at the Horseshoe: Andrew Jackson and the Creek War*. Fort Washington, PA: Eastern National and University of Alabama Press, 2007.

Horwitz, Tony. *A Voyage Long and Strange*. New York: Henry Holt, 2008.

Howard, Hugh. *Thomas Jefferson Architect*. New York: Rizzoli, 2003.

Howe, Daniel Walker. *What Hath God Wrought: The Transformation of America, 1815–1848*. New York: Oxford University Press, 2007.

Huff, Archie Vernon, Jr. *Greenville: The History of the City and County in the South Carolina Piedmont*. Columbia: University of South Carolina Press, 1995.

James, Marquis. *The Raven: A Biography of Sam Houston*. 1929. Reprint, Austin: University of Texas Press, 2008.

Jefferson, Thomas. *The Papers of Thomas Jefferson.* Vol. 6, *21 May 1781 to 1 March 1784.* Edited by Julian P. Boyd. Princeton, NJ: Princeton University Press, 1952.

———. *The Papers of Thomas Jefferson.* Vol. 8, *25 February 1785 to 31 October 1785.* Edited by Julian P. Boyd. Princeton, NJ: Princeton University Press, 1953.

———. *The Papers of Thomas Jefferson.* Vol. 25, *1 January 1793 to 10 May 1793.* Edited by John Catanzariti. Princeton, NJ: Princeton University Press, 1992.

———. *The Portable Thomas Jefferson.* Edited by Merrill D. Peterson. New York: Penguin, 1977.

———. *The Writings of Thomas Jefferson.* Edited by Andrew A. Lipscomb. Washington, DC: Thomas Jefferson Memorial Association, Vol. XII. 1903.

Johannsen, Robert W. *To the Halls of the Montezumas: The Mexican War in the American Imagination.* New York: Oxford University Press, 1985.

Johnson, Timothy D. *A Gallant Little Army: The Mexico City Campaign.* Lawrence: University of Kansas Press, 2007.

———. *Winfield Scott: The Quest for Military Glory.* Lawrence: University of Kansas Press, 1998.

Jones, Randell. *In the Footsteps of David Crockett.* Winston-Salem, NC: John F. Blair, 2006.

Kastner, Joseph. *A Species of Eternity.* New York: Alfred A. Knopf, 1977.

Kennan, George F. *American Diplomacy.* Expanded ed. Chicago: University of Chicago Press, 1984.

Kennedy, Billy. *Three Men of Destiny: Andrew Jackson, Sam Houston, and David Crockett.* Greenville, SC: Ambassador International, 2008.

Kephart, Horace. *The Cherokees of the Smoky Mountains.* Ithaca, NY: privately printed, 1936.

Kluger, Richard. *Seizing Destiny: The Relentless Expansion of American Territory.* New York: Vintage, 2007.

Krauze, Enrique. *Mexico: Biography of Power; A History of Modern Mexico, 1810–1996.* Translated by Hank Heifetz. New York: HarperCollins, 1997.

LaFeber, Walter. *The American Age.* New York: W. W. Norton, 1994.

———. *John Quincy Adams and American Continental Empire: Letters, Papers, and Speeches.* Chicago: Quadrangle, 1965.

Lavender, David. *Climax at Buena Vista.* New York: J. P. Lipincott, 1966.

Lester, C. Edwards. *Sam Houston: Hero and Statesman.* New York: John B. Alden, 1883.

Levy, Buddy. *American Legend: The Real-Life Adventures of David Crockett.* New York: G. P. Putnam's Sons, 2005.

Lofaro, Michael A., and Joe Cummings. *Crockett at Two Hundred: New Perspectives on the Man and the Myth.* Knoxville: University of Tennessee Press, 1989.

Malone, Dumas. *Jefferson the Virginian.* Boston: Little, Brown, 1948.

McCoy, Drew R. *The Elusive Republic: Political Economy in Jeffersonian America.* Chapel Hill: University of North Carolina Press, 1980.

McCullough, David. *John Adams.* New York: Simon and Schuster, 2001.

Meacham, Jon. *American Lion: Andrew Jackson in the White House.* New York: Random House, 2008.

Merck, Frederick. *History of the Westward Movement.* New York: Alfred A. Knopf, 1978.

Merry, Robert W. *A Country of Vast Designs.* New York: Simon and Schuster, 2009.

Moody, Ralph. *Kit Carson and the Wild Frontier.* 1955. Reprint, Lincoln: University of Nebraska Press, 2005.

Moore, Stephen L. *Eighteen Minutes: The Battle of San Jacinto and the Texas Independence Campaign.* Dallas: Republic of Texas Press, 2004.

Nevins, Allan, ed. *The Diary of John Quincy Adams, 1794–1845: American Political, Social, and Intellectual Life from Washington to Polk.* New York: Charles Scribner's Sons, 1951.

Nicolson, Harold. *Diplomacy.* London: Oxford University Press, 1963.

Niebuhr, Reinhold. *The Irony of American History.* New York: Charles Scribner's Sons, 1952.

Norton, A. Banning. *A History of Knox County, Ohio, from 1779 to 1862 Inclusive.* Columbus, OH, 1862.

Ohrt, Wallace. *Defiant Peacemaker: Nicholas Trist in the Mexican War.* College Station: Texas A&M University Press, 1997.

Onuf, Peter S. *Jefferson's Empire: The Language of American Nationhood.* Charlottesville: University of Virginia Press, 2000.

Onuf, Peter S., Douglas Seefeldt, and Jeffrey L. Hantman, eds. *Across the Continent: Jefferson, Lewis and Clark, and the Making of America.* Charlottesville: University of Virginia Press, 2005.

Owens, Robert M. *Mr. Jefferson's Hammer: William Henry Harrison and the Origins of American Indian Policy.* Norman: University of Oklahoma Press, 2007.

Parker, Hershel. *Herman Melville: A Biography.* Vol. 1 *1819–1851.* Baltimore: Johns Hopkins University Press, 1996.

Parkman, Francis. *The Oregon Trail.* 8th ed. 1883. Reprint, Mineola, NY: Dover, 2002.

Pasternak, Boris. *Doctor Zhivago.* Translated by Max Hayward and Manya Harari. New York: Pantheon, 1958.

Paulding, James Kirke. *The Lion of the West.* Stanford, CA: Stanford University Press, 1954.

Peskin, Allan. *Winfield Scott and the Profession of Arms.* Kent, OH: Kent State University Press, 2003.

Pletcher, David M. *The Diplomacy of Annexation: Texas, Oregon and the Mexican War.* Columbia: University of Missouri Press, 1973.

Polk, James Knox. *The Dairy of James K. Polk, 1845–1849*. 3 vols. Edited by Milo Milton Quaife. Chicago: A. C. McClurg, 1910.

Prescott, William H. *History of the Conquest of Mexico*. 1843. Reprint, New York: The Modern Library, 2001.

Price, Robert. *Johnny Appleseed: Man & Myth*. 1954. Reprint, Urbana, OH: Urbana University Press, 2001.

Reid, John, and John Henry Eaton. *The Life of Andrew Jackson*. 1817. Reprint, Tuscaloosa: University of Alabama Press, 2007.

Remini, Robert V. *Andrew Jackson*. 3 vols. Baltimore: Johns Hopkins University Press, 1998.

Reynolds, David S. *Waking Giant: America in the Age of Jackson*. New York: HarperCollins, 2008.

Rippy, J. Fred. *Joel R. Poinsett, Versatile American*. 1935. Reprint, New York: Greenwood Press, 1968.

Roberts, David. *A Newer World*. New York: Simon and Schuster, 2000.

Roberts, Sir Ivor. *Satow's Diplomatic Practice*. New York: Oxford University Press, 2009.

Robinson, Cecil, ed. *The View from Chapultepec: Mexican Writers on the Mexican-American War*. Tucson: University of Arizona Press, 1989.

Ronda, James P. *Revealing America: Image and Imagination in the Exploration of North America*. Lexington, MA: D. C. Heath, 1996.

———. *Thomas Jefferson and the Changing West*. St. Louis: Missouri Historical Society Press, 1997.

Rourke, Constance. *Davy Crockett*. New York: Harcourt, Brace, 1934.

Savage, Henry, Jr., and Elizabeth J. Savage. *André and François André Michaux*. Charlottesville: University Press of Virginia, 1986.

Shackford, James Atkins. *David Crockett: The Man and the Legend*. Chapel Hill: University of North Carolina Press, 1956.

Sides, Hampton. *Blood and Thunder: An Epic of the American West*. New York: Doubleday, 2006.

Silbey, Joel. *Storm over Texas: The Annexation Controversy*. New York: Oxford University Press, 2005.

Smith, Justin H. *The War with Mexico*. 2 vols. New York: Macmillan, 1919.

Stegner, Wallace. *Beyond the Hundreth Meridian: John Wesley Powell and the Second Opening of the West*. 1954. Reprint, New York: Penguin, 1992.

———. *The Uneasy Chair: A Biography of Bernard DeVoto*. Lincoln: University of Nebraska Press, 2001.

Stilgoe, John. *Common Landscape of America, 1580–1845*. New Haven: Yale University Press, 1982.

Thompson, Nicholas. *The Hawk and the Dove: Paul Nitze, George Kennan, and the History of the Cold War*. New York: Henry Holt, 2009.

Thoreau, Henry David. *Collected Essays and Poems*. Edited by Elizabeth Hall
   Witherell. New York: Library of America, 2001.
———. *Excursions*. Edited by Sophia Thoreau. 1863. Reprint facsimile edition.
   New York: Corinth Books, 1962.
———. *Walden*. Princeton, NJ: Princeton University Press, 1971.
Tolstoy, Leo. *War and Peace*. Translated by Constance Garnett. New York: Mile-
   stone, n.d.
Twain, Mark. *The Adventures of Huckleberry Finn*. Berkeley: American Heritage
   Press and University of California Press, 1985.
Vestal, Stanley. *Kit Carson: The Happy Warrior of the West*. Boston: Houghton
   Mifflin, 1928.
Williams, William Carlos. *In the American Grain*. 1925. Reprint, New York: New
   Directions, 1956.
Wills, Garry. *Henry Adams and the Making of America*. New York: Houghton Mif-
   flin, 2005.
Wood, Gordon S. *Empire of Liberty: A History of the Early Republic, 1789–1815*.
   New York: Oxford University Press, 2009.

— INDEX —